The United States and Mexico

THE AMERICAN FOREIGN POLICY LIBRARY

CRANE BRINTON, EDITOR

THE
UNITED STATES
AND
Mexico

By
Howard F. Cline

REVISED EDITION, ENLARGED

HARVARD UNIVERSITY PRESS
Cambridge, Massachusetts
1965

Distributed in Great Britain by

OXFORD UNIVERSITY PRESS

LONDON

MAPS PREPARED UNDER THE DIRECTION OF

ARTHUR H. ROBINSON

PRINTED IN THE UNITED STATES OF AMERICA

PREFACE

Howard F. Cline's *The United States and Mexico* was originally published in 1953 as a volume in the American Foreign Policy Library edited by the late Sumner Welles and the late Donald C. McKay. The editors, convinced by their experience during World War II that the United States could not deal effectively in the struggle against the Axis powers unless a larger proportion of American citizens took an informed and responsible position on many questions of foreign policy, planned their volumes as something more than popular journalism and something less than specialized monographs. They sought to have each volume written by a person thoroughly familiar with the past and present of the country or area he was writing about, directly acquainted with its language, its peoples, its folkways, its relations with the United States and the rest of the world, and possessed of a discriminating knowledge of the bibliography of his subject.

This volume has enjoyed the kind of success the founders of the American Foreign Policy Library had hoped for. Dr. Cline has from his undergraduate days built up through long travel and residence in Mexico that intimate and by now intuitive kind of knowledge for which no amount of specialized academic knowledge is by itself a substitute. He has also the necessary latter kind of knowledge, and the ability to write clearly and well. He likes Mexico and the Mexicans, for no volume in this series could be effectively written by a person fundamentally hostile to the people about whom he was writing. He has, however, a full measure of objectivity towards his subject; neither of those damning suffixes, "-phile" or "-phobe," applies to him.

From the beginning Messrs. Welles and McKay intended that each volume should be revised at suitable intervals, for one important function of each was to serve as a handbook of ready reference, and for that purpose each had to be kept as far as possible up-to-date. The years since 1953 have not brought in the development of domestic affairs in Mexico the kind of striking change that has come about in France, for example, since about 1950. But these ten years have wit-

Preface

nessed important changes in the international politics of the Americas, of which the Cuban revolution is the most dramatic, and the foundation of the O.A.S. perhaps the most significant. Even within Mexico itself the fascinating twentieth-century revolution begun so long ago with the fall of Diaz has in these ten years worked itself out in many ways and fields. All these changes Dr. Cline has experienced and studied, and has brought to bear as assimilated knowledge on this revision of the original book. It is a great pleasure for a new editor, who can claim none of the credit for the book, to welcome it in this new form to the Library.

CRANE BRINTON, EDITOR
American Foreign Policy Library

AUTHOR'S PREFACE

The reader should realize that the pages which follow were mostly written in 1950. The volume first appeared in 1953, some materials having been added through July 1952. A second edition, with only minor corrections of fact, was published in 1961. Except for this Preface, an Epilogue, and an attempt to bring the bibliography up to date, the present or third edition is the same text as that of 1961.

Several reasons underlay the personal decision to let the 1953 text re-appear without substantial revision. The original volume was the product of a particular moment in Mexico's development and a given point in the author's knowledge. It historically reflects a time when World War II had not long before ceased, when the Atomic Age had yet to be named, and when only inklings of the Cold War were clearly evident. Quite disparate voices were then assessing Mexico and forecasting its future. Many reviewers and critics of *The United States and Mexico* thought its tone and predictions overoptimistic.

Fortunately, events and developments in the ensuing decade generally supported the views recorded. There has been little or no reason subsequently to change a basic conclusion that closed the volume, written early in 1952: "A salient feature of recent developments in Mexico is a clear demonstration that beneficial social and economic change *can* be brought about in so-called 'underdeveloped areas' while preserving and increasing political and economic democracy as defined in the New World."

For those interested in a continuation of the Mexican story through the administration of Adolfo Ruiz Cortines (1952–1958) and part of the present one of Adolfo López Mateos (1958–   ), I have recently prepared for the Royal Institute of International Affairs in London a parallel survey. Nominally it covers the years 1940–1960, but the main emphasis is on the decade 1950–1960. Systematically it extends many of the same topics found in Part IV of the present work. The subtitle there expands in detail an early statement here (p. 6) that "Almost imperceptibly, evolution has replaced revolution

Author's Preface

as the historical dynamic of today's Mexico." * While by no means a summary of that volume, an Epilogue in this work provides highlights of the decade following 1952.

To aid the general reader, the teacher, or the student who may wish to explore further some aspects of Mexico's past and present, I have also added a supplement to the bibliographical essay originally appended. It contains most of those titles recorded in the 1962 volume mentioned above, as well as a few more recent ones.

To the Acknowledgments of 1953 need be added a few names. Gratitude and appreciation are expressed to the respective editors of the Harvard University Press and Atheneum for making *The United States and Mexico* more widely available in the present format. The general map preceding the text was carefully prepared by Lewis Buck to replace and bring up to date the four-color version that served as endpapers in the two previous editions. Again it must be repeated that although the author now is Director of the Hispanic Foundation in the Library of Congress, the original work and this present augmented one carry no "official" cachet. Sins of omission and commission are exclusively his own.

Howard F. Cline

Arlington, Virginia
February 18, 1963

* Howard F. Cline, *Mexico: Revolution to Evolution, 1940–1960* (London: 1962. Oxford University Press. 375 p.).

ACKNOWLEDGMENTS

Pleasant but difficult is the duty of attempting to particularize the many hands that helped shape the present work. The author's thanks first go to Messrs. Welles and McKay for the opportunity of contributing to the American Foreign Policy Library by a volume on which no restrictions were placed, and for their helpful aid along the way. I am especially indebted to the Graduate Research Committee of Northwestern University for substantial money grants which permitted collection of research materials, research help, and preparation of a manuscript. A grant from this source, plus a grant-in-aid from the Social Science Research Council, though made for archaeological research, permitted travel in Mexico during 1951; it was helpful in evaluation of recent matters, especially the Papaloapan Project.

Two scholars graciously made available to me unpublished materials, fruits of their independent research on Woodrow Wilson's handling of Mexico. Dr. Philip Lowry, whose excellent Yale Ph.D. thesis on the subject provided much new information, kindly authorized extensive use of his work; Professor Arthur S. Link, a colleague in the History Department at Northwestern, similarly opened his bulging files on Wilson, from which came data to corroborate and shade Lowry's findings. An unpublished Northwestern University M.A. thesis on the Bucareli Conferences by Mary Holt brought together a body of material on petroleum (from overt sources) that was quite useful. I am grateful to *Business Week* for their special permission to reproduce the railway map on p. 347. Department of State and other United States officials, as well as their counterparts in the Mexican system, have been unfailingly obliging. No restricted or classified materials, however, were utilized, and the views expressed in the following pages are often far from "official."

Special mention should be made of the tireless efforts which Mrs. R. S. Barnes gave to typing and editorial scrutiny of the manuscript in its early stages, when it was twice the present size. Much of the

Acknowledgments

final editorial credit must go to my wife, Mary W. Cline. She alone has had the fortitude to read the work again and again; her labors reduced tangled ideas and unruly sentences to coherence; she speared numerous solecisms in the verbal underbrush. Professor Arthur H. Robinson has added much to the utility of this synthesis by his careful craftsmanship and supervision of the maps.

I have freely borrowed statistical sources, which I have tried to acknowledge in the appropriate places; in most instances I have adapted the original data to my own needs and have worked out percentages to slide-rule accuracy. I have made no attempt to carry materials here beyond July 1952, except in a few isolated instances where last-minute items seemed worthy of insertion in printer's proof. None of the mentioned persons are, of course, responsible for errors and interpretations.

Howard F. Cline

July 15, 1952

CONTENTS

Contents

Contents

Contents

MAPS

MEXICO

PART I: CONSTANTS AND VARIABLES

1. Perspectives

Discussion of modern Mexico and its relations to the United States starts from a number of fundamental considerations. The first and foremost is that Mexico is not a crisis area. From the point of view of the United States, the hemisphere, or the world, Mexico is an asset, not a liability. Despite a century or more of somewhat checkered international developments that have produced alternating periods of strain and uneasy peace between them, Mexico and the United States are genuinely firm friends. The points of contention that might lead to serious friction have been largely eliminated in recent years. Mexico is not a major pawn in the struggle between Russia and the United States. In the sense that there is a China Problem, a German Problem, or a Spanish Problem, there is no Mexican Problem. Minor differences and clashes of interest occur; but rather than fumbling to outline a new policy toward Mexico, the present requirement of the United States is to strengthen and improve the policies already evolved by trial and error over many years. Tested since before World War II, recent United States dealings with Mexico have proved amazingly successful. In the international field we are discussing success, not failure.

Relations between Mexico and the United States have seldom been better than at the present time. The underlying factors which condition the position of the countries toward each other are fundamentally sound. The general atmosphere of harmony in the diplomatic realm is more than a superficial accord pressed on both in response to troubled world situations. It has solid roots both in peoples and their governments.

Secondly, Mexico has taken giant strides toward solving many of its long-standing domestic difficulties. Real inroads have been made on political, social, and economic problems. Five or ten years ago the popular and technical reports about Mexico were tinged with a pessimism then shared widely by Mexicans themselves. Most of the gloomy predictions of 1945 or thereabouts have now been revised and reversed because of recent accomplishments. These have created a salutary climate of optimism and high national morale that promises well for the future, even in face of the real barriers which remain to be hurdled. Again, the record of the past decade is one of significant achievements.

Thirdly, Mexico remains and will remain very Mexican. Modernization of agriculture, urbanization, industrialization, and other movements have begun substantially to change the face of the ancient area, but Mexico is still an underdeveloped foreign land. The tides of change have not made of it a Spanish-speaking facsimile of the United States. The future towards which Mexicans are now vigorously building reflects in an unmistakable fashion their own patterns of the past. One lesson learned from dealings with Mexico and Mexicans in recent years has been that the people there are irrevocably determined to define their own future and will seek it in their own way, no matter what the ultimate costs. Mexico is a friend and partner, not a satellite of the United States. Physically near, in its spirit, outlook, and heritages Mexico remains a faraway land. It takes some effort to understand.

Finally, the Mexican Revolution of 1910 continues to transform Mexico; it draws a line between the "old" and "new" ways of approaching problems. For Mexicans, their Revolution, always written with a capital "R" to dignify it and to distinguish it from mere barracks uprisings, is a set of historical and emotional experiences. It has provided the people with a set of Utopian goals toward which they firmly believe that the nation as a whole should constantly be moving. The revolutionary creed and *mystique* also prescribe the route. From the historian's perspective it is easily seen that the Revolution absorbed nearly all the earlier aspirations of the Mexican people and added to them still others which were gaining world-wide currency at the beginning of the twentieth century. Like so much else in Mexico, the Revolution is a complicated affair. Unmistakably ancient elements intermingle with the ultra-modern and form a unique, peculiarly Mexican amalgam.

An informed understanding of Mexican problems and their possible interest to the United States deserves more than the present cursory glance at the deep historical roots most of them have. Rates of change, as well as their directions and goals, are intimately bound up with regional and class interests that have been created by the historical processes operating in Mexico for centuries whose number is beyond the ken of the average North American. Though perhaps recent as a democracy, Mexico is an ancient land: Many of its customary habits were already fixed when Anglo-Saxons were still amazing Caesar's legionaries by painting themselves blue and dancing to the Druid's tunes.

One useful approach to the inescapable tangles and snarls that confront the newcomer to modern Mexico is the historical one. From the time that the contorted Mexican land was first trod by paleolithic men to the present covers a span of perhaps 15,000 or even 20,000 years. The human record is imperfect and hazy until less than a thousand years ago. One climax in Mexican cultural history came in the sixteenth century, when in 1519 Spaniards burst on the aboriginal scene and began the continuing attempts to shape it anew in accordance with the norms and uniformities of Western European cultures.

From the Stone Age, Mexico was suddenly projected into the "modern" world, the world of the Renaissance and then of the Reformation. The local Mexican Indian cultures lacked any awareness of what had shaped those external influences or why conformity to the new ways was deemed so essential. Before Conquest in the sixteenth century aboriginal Mexico was a melting pot of peoples and cultures, and afterwards it continued to be a laboratory of change, though the peoples and cultures then entering were different in kind from aboriginal emigrants, pioneers, and rulers.

Broadly conceived, Mexican history is the record of literally hundreds of little units and groups interacting with one another over a period that spans almost two hundred centuries. Anthropologists use the terms "assimilation" and "acculturation" in describing the mysterious ways in which traits from one social unit are transferred to others when they come into contact. Both these processes have been constantly occurring in Mexico for as long as we have even the sketchiest knowledge. Peoples, classes, tribes, regions, have developed, changed, interacted, and have sometimes disappeared almost without leaving more than a wisp to indicate their existence. But there has been a slow movement toward integration. Through the centuries larger and larger unities have emerged from the historical process, pointing Mexico toward nationhood.

Nationalism, an eighteenth-century idea, is the goal toward which recent Mexicans have been working: an attempt to form one coherent national unit from the galaxies of smaller ones that have preëxisted. As we shall see, the objective has not even yet been wholly achieved, so deeply rooted are localistic sentiments implanted earlier in the Mexican past.

The most recent period of Mexican history is called "The Revolution." It is an extension and intensification of historic Mexican trends, combined with explosive ideas that have come to dominate the twentieth century in protean guise.

The Revolutionary Process in Mexico. Still one of the most frequently heard words in Mexico is "Revolution." It is a word which normally mobilizes intense attitudes everywhere in the world. Psychological responses to it by individuals and governments indicate that it carries an emotionally freighted idea, one which gets violent approval or disapproval without much deliberate or rational consideration. In general, the very words "revolution" and "revolutionary" defy very precise definition in any language, but at least they carry with them the impression of change, often far-reaching, and usually of a violent and unpredictable nature. So it is in particular with the Mexican Revolution.

The situation which the Mexicans set out to change in 1910 is still typical of much of the world outside Europe and the United States. Grouped in a few cities was an "overworld"—a ruling élite with the trappings of modern civilization ostentatiously displayed to prove membership in the civilized portion of mankind. A small coterie of national landlords, bureaucrats, with a sprinkling of industrialists and foreign entrepreneurs, controlled the political power and manipulated the expanding, semicolonial economic system for their own benefit. When not an active partner, the Catholic Church seemed to acquiesce in the proceedings. Apart from this tiny overworld, and separated from it by wide gulfs, was a peasant "underworld," tied by various institutions to large landed estates or living in isolated clusters throughout the countrysides. At best, life was precarious and primitive for the majority. This was a pattern hallowed by time, and seemingly immutable. Its basic features had existed in Mexico almost from the dawn of history.

The late-nineteenth-century Mexican system against which the Revolution was launched had been largely constructed and run by Porfirio Díaz and his supporters. Continued operation of it depended on the myth of the politically irresponsible but indispensable man, one whose rooted bureaucracy maintained peace, order, and dispensed personal justice. The Mexican Revolution has sought to obliterate almost every vestige of that neatly contrived mechanism by thoroughly wrecking its instruments and stamping out its concepts.

In the vacuum thus created Mexicans since 1910 have been valiantly and stubbornly starting nearly everything from scratch. The task has proved to be enormous, and in many ways impossible. No nation can wholly free itself from its own past or from the inescapable obligations imposed on it as a member of the community of nations. Mexicans have now learned this.

Implications of the Revolution. The Mexican Revolution is a classic example of modern social change on a large scale. It serves as a prototype of much now going on in other parts of Latin America, the Near East, the whole of Asia, and just over the horizon in Africa. Mexicans decided in 1910 to overturn the *status quo* in quest of a better life. This search aroused bitter xenophobia, generated masses of local power that could find no suitable locus or direction, and utterly disrupted the normal procedures for carrying on relations among states.

By refusing even to honor the long-established rules of international intercourse and assumptions on which they are based, the Mexicans posed unprecedented problems. From its genesis to the present, the Mexican Revolution has affected the United States, its attitudes toward Mexico, and toward social changes in general. From William Howard Taft to Harry S. Truman every administration has had to wrestle with the problem of how to handle this neighboring country which is obviously bent on regrouping its social classes, reorienting its economy, and completely reshaping its political structures in the expressed hope of bettering the masses of its people, often to the detriment of vital American interests within the area. The interplay of domestic and external forces through the past half century has changed and molded the Mexican Revolution and has endowed it with special value as a case history. Violence, instability, and virulent and irrational nationalism that thrived on slogans against oppressors (real and presumed) have given way to tranquillity, stability, and a sense of accomplishment. Almost imperceptibly, evolution has replaced revolution as the historical dynamic of today's Mexico. Early and inchoate drives for social justice, betterment of underprivileged masses, and economic decolonization have, over the years, been successfully amalgamated with the main traditions of Western-style political democracy. The Mexican episodes have long since passed the sloganeering phases. Painfully and slowly the nation has developed a coherent pattern of attitudes and mechanisms that form a unique New World "Middle Way." Perhaps the main contribution that a survey of modern Mexico can make is to illustrate the cheering truth that from the bloody chaos of mass revolution a sturdy and respected democracy can emerge, solidly rooted at home and respected abroad.

Purposely the following pages stress the fact that the major goals which the Mexicans have set for themselves grow out of their own circumstances and experiences, and the future toward which they aspire is a Mexican one. It is now a matter of national pride for most Mexicans to point out that the chief ideals and characteristic institutions embraced by the Mexican Revolution predate the Russian Revolution by a substantial margin and that the New Deal in the United States came a quarter of a century after the outbreak of their epic Mexican Revolution.

The direct and indirect significance of the Mexican Revolution for the United States needs emphasis. Nearly half a century of dealing with it has added a vast body of unique experience. This aided the building of an effective Latin-American policy; more important, it is now capable of extension to even wider reaches of foreign relations. Implications of the interplay over fifty years between the United States and Mexico as a major member of Latin America were underscored in November 1952 by Arnold J. Toynbee, British historian and cautious prophet. For an audience at Edinburgh University he forecast the world fifty years hence. He predicted a major role for this country, one which found the "Big Stick" unworkable. "The states of Europe and Asia within the United States' sphere of influence are going to be as touchy as the Latin American states," he said, "and the United States is likely to handle them by a diplomatic technique that she has learned from her Latin American experience." That is a major motif in the pages that follow.

2. Space

Modern Mexico is easily placed by a glance at a map. It unrolls between seas for more than 2000 miles southward from the long slanting boundary which marks it off from the United States. Its southern extremities are fixed by its boundaries between British Honduras and the republic of Guatemala. At neither extremity of the modern Mexican area are there "natural frontiers" of major consequence. Political and historic influences have set these national limits. They have remained stable for a century and are likely to continue unchanged into the foreseeable future.

With its base at the United States, the republic of Mexico forms a somewhat uneven triangle whose apex comes near the narrow Isthmus of Tehuantepec. Beyond, the land widens slightly to include the thumb-like peninsula of Yucatan, part of whose territory is shared with the British colony. From Yucatan to Cuba is a short jump and the distance from the latter to the United States is small. At its front door Mexico has the Gulf of Mexico, an open portal to the main trade routes of the North Atlantic. In this connection it should be stressed that Mexico is also the largest of the Caribbean states and shares their strategic and economic importance. The opening of the Panama Canal at the beginning of the twentieth century inevitably brought Mexico within the enlarged security zone of the United States.

1. MEXICO AND LATIN AMERICA

When Mexico is statistically assessed relative to the United States it is overwhelmed, as are its individual companions in the Latin-American community. But when measured against other Latin-American countries and areas in the group as a whole, the outcome is quite different. It helps account for Mexican leadership there.

Though the United States has four times as much territory as Mexico, and six times as many people, Mexico itself is the largest of the Spanish-speaking republics of Latin America. About a sixth of the Latin-American population is Mexican. The Argentine Republic (at the southern tip of South America) has more territory.

The most striking characteristic of the Latin-American community, however, is the reduced size of each nation in comparison with the United States. It stands as a giant surrounded by pygmies in

POPULATION, AREA, DENSITIES, AND INCOMES OF AMERICAN REPUBLICS, 1950

Population Rank	Country	Population (thousands)	Area (thousands) Sq. Mile	Density Per Sq. Mile	Per Capita Income 1947 (dollars)
1	Brazil	50,000 [b]	3,288	14.7	112
2	Mexico	25,209 [b]	759	33.2	121
3	Argentina	16,318 [a]	1,079	15.0	346
4	Colombia	11,015 [a]	440	25.0	132
5	Peru	8,133 [a]	482	16.8	100
6	Chile	5,677 [a]	286	19.8	188
7	Cuba	5,195 [a]	44	117.8	296
8	Venezuela	4,545 [a]	352	12.8	322
9	Bolivia	3,990 [a]	413	9.7	55
10	Haiti	3,700 [a]	11	326.0	40
11	Ecuador	3,077 [b]	116	25.8	40
12	Guatemala	2,786 [b]	51	54.6	77
13	Uruguay	2,340 [a]	72	32.5	331
14	Dominican Rep.	2,116 [b]	19	111.0	75
15	El Salvador	1,858 [b]	13	143.0	92
16	Honduras	1,533 [b]	59	26.0	83
17	Paraguay	1,270 [a]	157	8.1	84
18	Nicaragua	1,053 [b]	57	18.4	89
19	Costa Rica	794 [b]	20	39.7	125
20	Panama	763 [a]	31	24.8	183
	Latin America	151,372	7,749	20.0	
	United States	150,697 [b]	3,022	50.0	

Sources:

Population:　[a] OAS (Organization of American States) estimates, January 1, 1950, *Annals of the Organization of American States*, II, No. 2 (1950), 181.
[b] Preliminary returns, 1950 Census.

Income:　U.N. Publications.

all but territory. The one country in Latin America given an outside chance to become a great power is Brazil. Territorially it is larger than the continental United States, which could be dropped within its bounds with space to spare. But aside from sheer area (much of which is useless land), even Brazil is dwarfed on almost every measurable score. It, in turn, towers over the nations of Spanish heritage; only Mexico is even half its size. As the accompanying tabulation indicates, the populations of the Dis-United States of Latin America are widely scattered in space, in size, and the degree to which they have solved pressing social and economic problems common to them all.

Rated on statistics alone, Mexico with its 25 millions is larger than the combined nine Caribbean republics (described for readers of this series by Dexter Perkins *). Mexico's population approaches the five "Bolivarian" republics of South America covered by Arthur P. Whitaker in a comparable volume.† To carry matters one step further, Mexico alone is about the size of the combined Platine republics—Argentina, Uruguay, Paraguay—plus Chile. Compared with its own southern neighbor, Guatemala, Mexico itself is a potential "Colossus of the North" with twelve times the area and nine times the population. Within the Latin-American context, then, Mexico is a power of first magnitude, second only to Brazil.

Because of its size, its proximity to the United States, and because of consistent leadership in hemispheric affairs, Mexico is often the main touchstone of Latin-American opinion about the United States and its actions. Mexican interpretation or response to statements and policies of the United States carry great weight below the Rio Grande, or, as Mexicans prefer it, the Rio Bravo del Norte. Mexican potentialities for mobilizing Latin-American opinion are an added item in its special significance to the United States and thus it happens that when the United States is apparently dealing directly only with Mexico, it is often dealing indirectly with nineteen other hemispheric colleagues who will be influenced by Mexico's stand. Thus the boundary between Mexico and the United States is not only a line between two countries of unlike heritage, it is the frontier between the United States and Latin America.

---

* Dexter Perkins, *The United States and the Caribbean* (Harvard University Press, 1947).

† Arthur P. Whitaker, *The United States and South America: The Northern Republics* (Harvard University Press, 1948).

MEXICO IN LATIN AMERICA, 1950

	Individual Nations Population	Area	Regional Total Population	Area
Mexico			25,209	759
The Caribbean				
Costa Rica	794	20		
Cuba	5,195	44		
Dominican Rep.	2,116	19		
El Salvador	1,858	13		
Guatemala	2,786	51	19,798	305
Haiti	3,700	11		
Honduras	1,533	59		
Nicaragua	1,053	57		
Panama	763	31		
The "Bolivarian" Republics of Northern South America				
Bolivia	3,990	413		
Colombia	11,015	440		
Ecuador	3,077	116	30,760	1,803
Peru	8,133	482		
Venezuela	4,545	352		
The Platine Republics and Chile (Nontropical Latin America)				
Argentina	16,318	1,079		
Chile	5,677	286	25,605	1,594
Paraguay	1,270	157		
Uruguay	2,340	72		
Brazil			50,000	3,288

(Population in thousands of persons; area in thousands of square miles)

2. PROBLEMS OF PROXIMITY

All other considerations apart, Mexico and the United States are constantly aware of each other's presence because they share an unfortified transcontinental boundary of 1500 miles which bisects the North American continent from the Atlantic to the Pacific. Mexico is the only republic in the world that has such a common frontier with the United States. It is a political line which symbolizes the fact that both geography and history have linked the two nations in an indissoluble fashion. In the broadest sense, international relations are constantly occurring. People, goods, and ideas flow back and forth from one nation to the other across this invisible line.

The location of the boundary itself is the result of controversial historical events of the nineteenth century. It does not represent a "natural frontier" of any sort, like the Pyrenees. Mexicans are less prone to forget than Americans that all the area now occupied by the United States was for centuries claimed by Spain under exclusive grants from the Vatican in 1493 and was ruled from Mexico City; John Smith, the Pilgrims, and other late-comers were considered interlopers. Even more significant are the historical memories of the nineteenth century. Much of the South and most of the West of the United States were formerly and indisputably Mexican territory, but were wrested from Mexico by one means or another and added to the rapidly expanding American union. Mexico was the chief victim of Manifest Destiny, as any map of the two areas easily demonstrates.

The nearly final outlines of modern Mexico were permanently stabilized between 1836 and 1853. A process of contraction that had been going on since 1803 then slowed to a stop. Between 1835 and 1855 Mexico lost nearly half its territorial domain. Successively revolution, annexation, conquest, and purchase clipped pieces off Mexico and added them to the United States, as the northern republic pushed its frontier south and west by additions of Texas, California, and the territory known as the Gadsden Purchase.

In passing, it may be noted that transfers involved real estate, not peoples. Before the Texas revolution of 1836 and after the Gadsden Purchase of 1853, the population of Mexico remained at about 8,000,000. Worth remembering, too, is the fact that Centralist Mexican leaders during the Mexican War with the United States had a standing army several times as large as that of the United States, and were sanguine enough in 1847 to expect that perhaps they would dictate a conqueror's peace from Washington.

The actual outcome of those historic troubles came as a profound shock to Mexican sensibilities, because of the major losses of territory and prestige which accompanied them. But the functioning of the Mexican nation was not seriously impaired, as no resources of critical worth at the time changed hands. Special conciliatory gestures in recent years have tended to cover with scar tissue those ancient wounds to pride. Orators of both nations find it increasingly convenient to stress the theme that bygones are bygones. It should be remembered, though, that memories of Manifest Destiny fade much more slowly south of the Rio Grande than north of it.

Mexico and the United States have developed side by side, and a major thread in the respective national histories has been their mutual influences over a long period. From aboriginal times onward this interplay is visible in cultural fields. It has been especially accelerated in the twentieth century, rising in crescendo from the nineteenth. In 1848 and 1853 (when the final lines between the nations stabilized) the contiguity of the United States and Mexico was actually more apparent than real. The international limit separating them passed through an underpopulated and almost uninhabitable strip of land stretching between the oceans. The arid border zone was then a thousand miles from the populated heart of either nation, from the Mexican Mesa or the humid areas of the United States. Contacts between these neighboring countries were sporadic, weak, and relatively unimportant.

Technology and transport, however, have increasingly changed that situation. Dry farming, irrigation, oil, burgeoning rail and highway nets, have been instrumental in filling the previously unattractive border zones. This change has occurred both on the United States and the Mexican sides; previous blanks on the map are now filled with growing numbers of people. And as each republic has become more integrated and self-conscious, the international problems along the boundary have increased in number and intensity.

As the cultures, economies, and populations on each side of the United States-Mexican boundary continue to grow like Jack's beanstalk, the problems of their mutual relations at points where they come most frequently into contact sprout even faster. Subsequent pages show that the Mexican economy is welded into that of the United States at most of its key points; roads, railroads, and airlines have obliterated space between the countries. The thousands of tourists pouring into Mexico from one side, the thousands of migrant laborers coming from the other are a constant socio-economic feature that has tied the neighbors together. If Mexico got no United States tourists, and the United States no Mexican labor, difficulties would hit large parts of the economy in each nation.

Some Boundary Problems. The boundary itself, the Rio Grande, is a disputed economic and social item. It carries water through an otherwise almost waterless land; to complicate matters, it is an unsteady river. In its weaving and bobbing from one channel to another it creates problems of sovereignty: south of the river is Mexico, north is the United States; but the river may place your land in one country for a while, then capriciously circle and leave it in the other a little later. A number of political and social difficulties arise from this moodiness of the Rio Grande. It comprises about 60 per cent of the international limit between the United States and Mexico. The stream itself is usually either a trickle or a torrent; in the flood season, until irrigation works recently curbed its wanderlust, the Rio Grande had the unfortunate habit of migrating out of its previous channels.

The characteristics of the river and the boundary in general were of small importance until the twentieth century. International incidents involving cattle rustlers, warring Indians, smugglers, fugitive slaves, only occasionally disturbed tranquillity along the line. For most of the late nineteenth century the boundary marked the limit to which either nation could exert effective political control from its main heart.

As people began to populate the arid and semi-arid border zone, it became clear from the number of problems that arose that the river was an unsatisfactory limit. The treaties of 1848 and 1853 which delimited one nation from the other set the line as "the middle of the stream, following its deepest channel." But the channel varied from season to season, with consequent shifts in nationality of people and property. The two republics in 1894–1895 agreed to redefine and resurvey the limit. These treaties also set up a unique body.

International Boundary Commission. The International Boundary Commission, established by the nineteenth-century Mexican-American water treaties, is a mixed Mexican-American quasi-investigative, quasi-judicial, and quasi-executive mechanism to quiet the tensions stemming from the erratic behavior of the river. Its main task was first to eliminate transfers of sovereignty due to stream changes by finding out where the original channel ran and to settle disputes over the nationality of lands. Most of its cases have dealt with farm lands of the lower Rio Grande. Its decisions cannot be appealed to either country's courts; it is a supreme and final authority. As riverine questions have come before it and have been settled, it places permanent markers along the old, original channel of 1848–1853. In 1933 it was empowered to carry on flood control and to try and finally settle the Chamizal question. The Rio Grande created that problem by changing its course.

Chamizal. The Spanish word *chamizal* means brush-patch, but internationally speaking "the Chamizal" means a headache. It is a six-hundred-acre tract in South El Paso claimed by both the United States and Mexico; each nation has nationals living in it. Besides tenements and brothels, it contains a United States Custom House and an expensive El Paso High School.

Mexicans claim that the original course of the Rio Grande left the patch in Mexico. Subsequent changes in channel seemingly placed it under the United States flag. The question now is whether Chamizal is a part of the Mexican town of Ciudad Juárez which extends into the United States or part of El Paso, Texas, which intrudes into Mexico. Litigation over the matter originally led to international arbitration. In 1911 a Canadian arbiter ruled that one-third of Chamizal belonged to the United States, and two-thirds to Mexico. The United States refused to accept the judgment; since it has been made, each side has poured more people into the disputed spot. Any arbitrary division is bound to cause serious dislocations.

In Mexico the Chamizal dispute represents a purported revival of United States land hunger; any discussion of it refreshes the memories of 1848 and 1853. The nation as a whole refuses to retreat a step, and demands that the United States honor the Canadian arbitral award of 1911. A number of Mexican presidents have negotiated the matter, and in 1933 President Rodríguez was willing to take a cash settlement for Mexico to erase its claims, but the matter was too hot politically to touch. Perhaps in the pleasant warmth of present relations some final settlement of this old matter can be arranged.

Irrigation and Flood Control. Tensions over impounding the water of the Rio Grande and the streams that feed it have also proved increasingly bothersome. Three areas have been centers of conflict: the delta of the Colorado River, bifurcated by the boundary; the delta of the Rio Grande, similarly divided; and a series of arable basins from El Paso to the point where the border begins to be a surveyed line running across country to the Pacific. These are the main points where agriculture, chiefly winter vegetables and cotton, is possible. Streams which water the Colorado Delta rise on American soil, while those making agriculture possible in the Rio Grande basins largely start in Mexico. The construction of Hoover Dam and irrigation works on the United States' side intensified the issues and kept them alive. Selfish water-grabbing by either nation inevitably leads to a shriveling of important economic interests on one or the other side of the boundary.

To get the potentially dangerous matters straightened out, a series of comprehensive water allocation treaties were signed in 1945. These divided the water available from the Rio Grande, the Colorado, and the Tiajuana rivers to assure Mexico some moisture; at the same time the agreements provided for further flood control. Opposition within the United States (mainly from California) and within Mexico was overcome, and the arrangements were ratified by both governments on November 8, 1945. These removed a chronic source of friction between the nations.

Falcón Dam. Under the Water Treaties, the 361,705 square kilometers of land capable of irrigation from Rio Grande waters are divided to give Mexico enough to irrigate 211,177 and the United States 150,528. On both sides, floods have proved a serious handicap to best utilization of land. Mexicans and Americans have each placed subsidiary networks of irrigation and flood works on their respective sides, but for mutually beneficial use of the scarce hydraulic resource, the two governments are jointly undertaking a hydraulic program. Their plans include a large series of dams across the Rio Grande that not only will provide more irrigated land for valuable crops, and end threats of floods, but also provide much needed electric power.

The first of these is Falcón Dam, now under construction. It is about twelve miles north of San Pedro, Tamaulipas. Its reservoir will hold 4070 million cubic meters of water, and will irrigate 220,000 hectares (545,000 acres) of Mexican croplands, as opposed to the 45,000 hectares (112,000 acres) now available. The electric power generated by the huge work will be 63,000 KW, divided equally between the United States and Mexico; after generating power, the water will be conducted by a network of aqueducts and canals to the thirsty lands. Falcón Dam will make northern Mexico bloom just as its American counterparts around Brownsville, Texas and the Lower Rio Grande Valley have made this one of the richest agricultural areas in the United States.

Labor. In preference to speaking of hired "hands," Mexicans call them "arms," *braceros.* The recent intertwining of the United States and Mexico along the boundary has intensified and brought to public and diplomatic attention a troublesome matter that becomes increasingly difficult to solve. For many years there were more Mexicans on the United States side of the boundary than on the Mexican; the Mexican side was unexploited, while the blossoming of agriculture along the northern banks required labor and offered cash wages. The strong pull of cash drew migrant labor from Mexico to the United States, even after various restrictions had been placed on entrance of Mexican workers, to safeguard the wage levels in the

United States. As *Time* magazine remarked, though, legislation on migrant labor is like "making international agreements about locusts."

Instead of stemming the tide, United States domestic legislation merely made it illegal. The Federal border patrols have always been inadequate in number and strength to keep Mexicans from swimming or wading the river to gain employment. Since they emerge dripping, the general name for these furtive migrant laborers is "wet-backs" (*mojados*). Once in the United States, they are forced to work for low wages according to American standards but the 20 to 30 cents an hour they get to pick perishable crops is far better than they could hope to receive in rural Mexico. They have been subject to exploitation and general discrimination in Texas and other areas which they have entered, as appears in detail later.

3. THE GEOGRAPHIC FRAMES

Within the somewhat abstract international limits at the north and south, and the more definite water boundaries on its east and west, lies Mexico. It is an ancient and contorted land whose physical beauties have been the wonder of travelers for centuries. European first-comers like Hernando Cortés and Bernal Díaz attempted to capture in prose Mexico's awe-inspiring vistas and vivid contrasts. Literary paths marked out by these sixteenth-century pioneers have been well traveled to the present. New ones have been opened up by successive waves of artists and photographers of varying merit. The diversity and variety of landscapes, peoples, and juxtaposed traditions which form the main theme of many such works are indeed a keynote of Mexico, ancient or modern.

The geographic unit of Mexico consists of a high highland in the center of its area, flanked by dependent regions of one sort and another which are connected in various ways to it. This heart of Mexico is a great central plateau, the Mesa Central. Ringed by mountains on three sides (leaving it open only to the north), the Mesa is divided internally by lesser ranges and spurs from these three principal chains. Rising close to the waters on the eastern and western edges of Mexico, two of the mountain walls parallel the Mesa. They run from near the American frontier southward to converge below Mexico City and there form a single third range which continues its southern thrust until it dies at the Isthmus of Tehuantepec. Here, too, at the Isthmus, join the coastal lowland areas which have paralleled these ranges and narrowly separated them from their adjoining seas. This slender and flat isthmus across southern Mexico provides one of the few east-west passages between the Gulf of Mexico and the Pacific Ocean not complicated by mountain barriers. Southward from Tehuantepec a new set of foothills rise to give way to other mountain chains which course irregularly through Central America to the Isthmus of Panama.

The central plateau of Mexico is further delimited and shut off from the more southern parts of the nation by one of the largest volcanic belts in the world. It cuts across Mexico in an east-west direction just south of the Valley of Mexico in which is found Mexico City, capital of the republic. Hundreds of volcanoes, inactive and active, thrust their regular cones above the southern portion of the Mesa and tower above the lesser peaks in the chains of mountains already mentioned. At least nine of the volcanoes have altitudes greater than 12,500 feet; three are perpetually snow-capped. These are famous in Mexican annals. Two, Popocatepetl with an altitude of 17,845 feet and Ixtacihuatl, 17,343 feet, stand guard over Mexico City itself. Mount Orizaba, reaching up to 18,548 feet, rises athwart and divides the critical trade and military routes from the capital to its major Atlantic outlet, the tropical port of Veracruz. Its gleaming peak is a landfall visible many miles to sea.

Quite literally much of Mexico lives atop a volcano. Volcanic ash, one of the best soil bases in the world, supports much of the agriculture of the Central Mesa, but frequent tremors, occasional earthquakes, and recurrent violent temblors serve to remind Mexicans that their land is not wholly a passive backdrop to the human drama. Activity in the western parts of this volcanic axis made headlines in 1943 when from the middle of an Indian's corn patch a new volcano, Paricutin, emerged in spectacular and destructive fashion. To its scarcely cooled and barren slopes Tarascan Indians are already returning to till the soil above their once prosperous and orderly Michoacan villages.

One of Mexico's major physical characteristics is its mountainous nature. Reportedly when a courtier was asked by Charles V what the land recently conquered by Cortés looked like, he replied by crumpling a piece of paper into a ball, and saying, "Like this." More prosaically, technical reports record that two-thirds of Mexico is classified as mountainous, and the remaining third "rolling" except for 8 per cent considered "level." Mountains act as a storehouse of vast mineral treasures, as barriers to communication, as defensive walls for the great plateau, but above all as the habitat of many Mexicans. Like the wrinkled hide of an ancient elephant the landscapes seen from the air are seamed and endlessly jumbled, occasionally interconnected by a careless filigree of footpaths, here and there ribbons of roads between the peaks to the valley floors beneath, themselves often thousands of feet above the level of the sea. Few Mexicans live or die far from the shadows of mountains.

Mexico's mountains are both an asset and a liability. The high altitude of most of Mexico makes habitation possible. Gradual drops in latitude as the Mexican land rolls toward the hot equator are in great part offset by the rising altitude of its area going in the same direction. A connection between these two things, latitudes and altitudes, is important.

Height rather than position is likely to control a given spot. This imparts to space in Mexico a three-dimensional quality. To the conventional spatial coördinates (length and breadth, longitude and latitude) one must add whether the place is up or down. Its characteristics will vary accordingly. To save themselves endless trouble, Mexicans normally take into account these up-and-down concepts by subdividing their area into three vertical zones and abbreviating conditions in each by calling them the *tierras*.

Lowest and hottest is *tierra caliente*, or hot land. It ranges between sea level and perhaps 3000 feet. As the name *tierra templada* indicates, it is temperate; this area is generally found somewhere between 3000 and 6000 feet, and life and conditions in *tierra templada* often approximate middle latitude conditions such as are found in the southern half of the Mississippi Valley. Above 6000 feet or so even the tropical land is called "cold": *tierra fría*. Population densities in *tierra templada* and *tierra fría* tend to be much greater than in the hot lands, where tropical diseases are added to uncomfortable temperatures and overabundant vegetation. *Tierra caliente* parallels both the Gulf and the Pacific coasts of Mexico and includes the level and low peninsula of Yucatan and that of Lower California; patches of *tierra caliente* occur elsewhere in the republic, especially in portions of the central south. Most of the high plateau of central Mexico is considered *tierra templada*, and obviously the heights around it, especially in the volcanic belt, move up into *tierra fría*.

The mountainous structure of Mexico has a direct bearing on another of its dominant physical features. Moisture-laden trade winds, warmed by the tropical sun in their journeys across the Caribbean and Gulf, drop large proportions of their watery loads on their contact with the cooler eastern mountain wall. As one result, some of the seaward slopes of this eastward barrier are drenched with as much as 120 inches of rain annually and are blanketed with almost impenetrable vegetation of all sorts. Short swift torrents eat away the mountain sides carrying with them rich deposits of black dirt. Where these are laid down in quantity, as in the state of Veracruz, rich agricultural islands in the generally poor lands of *tierra caliente* are produced. Less dramatic are the results on the lee sides of the range, where lesser rainfall produces slower streams that cut their way towards the central plateau. Passing westward across the country these prevailing winds absorb rather than drop moisture until they hit the tops of the western barriers. Again their moist load is dropped. Those which continue past the western mountains again begin to blot up moisture on the Pacific side, with the result that much of the Pacific slope is desert. In part the westerlies which blow across the Pacific accentuate the same process; cooled by Pacific currents, they expand on contact with warm western Mexican land and, spongelike, soak moisture from the surface. Mexicans claim that in areas where westerlies blow that it "rains upwards"—water goes from ground to sky rather than the usual direction.

With the mountains acting as condensers, rainfall in most of Mexico is insufficient, irregular, and often almost nonexistent. Coincidence of proper rainfall distribution with the proper temperature for growing crops is the exception rather than the rule in Mexico. Important to any consideration of Mexican problems is the fact that less than 7 per cent of Mexican territory can regularly produce food crops without some form of irrigation. The Ministry of Hydraulic Resources in Mexico has calculated this humid area at around 2,000,000 hectares.* By somewhat different criteria an American geographer, Thornwaite, arrived at around 13 per cent. But by any measure it is clear that most of Mexico lacks reliable and adequate water. It is a thirsty land.

This relatively small humid territory is badly located. Here rainfall is sufficient, sometimes overabundant every year. It consists chiefly of *tierra caliente*, patches on the tropical coasts of the Gulf and the Pacific. Somewhat similar and usually adjacent are areas

* One hectare is a metric measurement equivalent to 2.47 acres.

called "semi-humid," in which rainfall is generally adequate for agriculture but irregular; it usually fails perhaps every fourth or fifth year.

A little less than a third of Mexico is considered semi-arid, without much moisture. These semi-arid zones have highly irregular rainfall, which in the majority of years is insufficient for agricultural development. Where there is abundant rain, it is badly distributed through the seasons—either all at once or just a little over a long time. In such territories, success of agriculture is a matter of pure luck as to whether the clouds will mass and deliver the needed moisture in proper quantities at the appropriate times. The lower part of the Central Mesa, on which cluster the greatest number of people, is generally semi-arid.

More than half of Mexico, 52.1 per cent, is arid. Rainfall here is a miracle, not often seen. It is too insufficient to permit any agriculture without some form of irrigation. The whole northern half of Mexico, beyond 22° north latitude, as well as a small section of Yucatan, the coasts of Oaxaca and Guerrero, is arid. In favored tiny spots an occasional lucky patch gets some rain.

To support human life on a sure and stable basis, irrigation is a crying need which is now being met. Some parts of Mexico need only supplementary irrigation, just enough to regularize the somewhat whimsical cycle of rainfall; others demand large-scale, permanent hydraulic works to bring water to thirsty areas where rainfall is almost negligible. Some of the more enterprising communities in arid places have contracted with United States commercial firms to salt the clouds with dry ice or silver iodide to precipitate moisture. In one such experiment (tried in Coahuila in June 1949) local skeptics were confounded when rain really fell for ten hours. A native woman, who thought it might never cease, carried a crucifix around to stop it and was imprisoned by local authorities for sabotage. Mexicans themselves are experimenting with this new and somewhat controversial technique, but the bulk of effort must necessarily be placed in more orthodox lines, the laborious construction of irrigation works.

The grim irony of rainfall in Mexico is that the humid and semi-humid areas are in the tropical lowlands where public health situations are the worst. Where there is water, there is disease; where there is scanty water, there is little disease. Expensive and extensive public sanitation programs must precede settlement on the fertile and humid coastal strips of *tierra caliente*. Water, as much as ownership

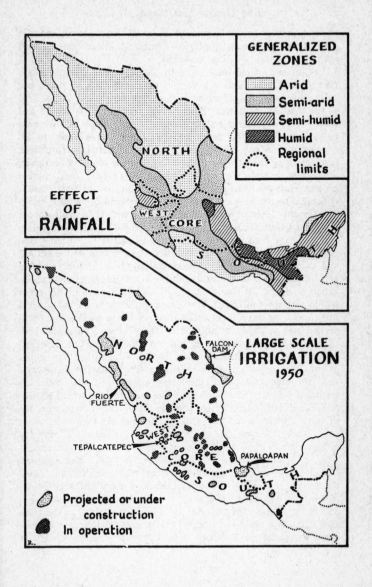

GENERALIZED
ZONES

Arid
Semi-arid
Semi-humid
Humid
Regional
limits

EFFECT
OF
RAINFALL

NORTH

WEST

CORE

S

O

T

H

LARGE SCALE
IRRIGATION
1950

NORTH

FALCON
DAM

RIO
FUERTE

TEPALCATEPEC

WEST

CORE

SOU

PAPALOAPAN

T

H

Projected or under
construction
In operation

R.

of land, is a powerful instrument of social control and economic production in nine-tenths of Mexico. Agrarian problems center around both of these scanty natural resources.

The amount of cultivable land in Mexico seems pitifully small. (See Appendix I, Table 6.) Various estimates differ in detail but concur in placing the figure somewhere between 9 and 12 per cent of the total Mexican area. Much of the arable land is eroded and otherwise in a precarious state. Generally only about half is under cultivation, though this figure is rising. These arable lands are not concentrated in one major clump but are scattered in patchwork fashion among the valleys of the plateau and the southern highlands, often with imperfect communications even to their local market centers. Plots are often so small that mechanization of agriculture is difficult. The remainder of Mexico is pasture land of variable carrying capacity, forested areas, and outright desert. It is small wonder that agrarian unrest and problems connected with land, its allocation and use, have been a continuing Mexican motif from earliest times.

Mexican geography spawns diversity. Atomization of the natural and cultural landscapes by the several dynamic influences makes generalizations about the land and people subject to infinite qualification in detail. Striking contrasts of view and ways of life occur within very short distances. The village on the lee of the mountain is often a strange and distinct entity from one of the same ethnic background and at the same altitude on the windward side, and both differ from similar groupings up and down their respective slopes.

Space on maps is often an optical illusion. Time rather than spatial extent is the common measure of distance. The characteristic distance unit in southern Mexico is the league (*legua*); despite official attempts to standardize a league and give it a widely accepted equivalent, it naturally changes from place to place, since it represents the distance a mule loaded with two hundred pounds can travel in an hour. Where the mule can go faster, leagues are longer. Though the airline distance separating them is small, two market centers in adjacent mountain basins are likely to be many such leagues apart. Usually they are precariously linked by trails and twisting roads rising from one valley floor over intervening passes between peaks. But in this trek the traveler may see coconut palms, bananas, rice, and cacao in the valley, wheat and cereals part way up the trail, then climb into apple and fragrant pine country before passing back down the range. In less than an hour one traverses a variety of products that in the United States would be equivalent to a journey from New England to Texas.

Many of the myths about Mexico explode in the face of stubborn geographic fact. Rather than basking in a languid tropical paradise, most of the Mexicans live in areas where frost is not uncommon, and even snow may be a constant feature. A view widely held from the time Europeans entered Mexico, that it was a cornucopia of plenty, persisted until the nineteenth century, when famous Mexican publicists like Justo Sierra and Francisco Bulnes tried to convince their compatriots that they were living in a difficult environment whose potentialities could be overcome only by thorough knowledge and hard work. It is quite true that Mexico has vast untapped natural resources, but in general these are badly placed and inadequately known. Current Mexican emphasis on hard work, productivity, and unremitting enterprise is a salutary indication that responsible officials are no longer under the delusions that sometimes befuddled their nineteenth-century counterparts.

A common tendency to oversimplify and attribute Mexico's social and economic evils to cultural legacies of its aboriginal and colonial past similarly has to be broadened by inclusion of geographic factors. North Americans brought up in institutional structures based on an economy of abundance and richness, in an environment lavishly supplied, are prone to underestimate the strains that inadequately endowed tropical and subtropical areas are likely to impose. The incubus of one particular system of philosophy, a form of religion, or a set of political doctrines have not been the only factors operating through Mexican history to keep the area poverty-stricken and on the margin of existence. Nor yet is the endemic difficulty the result of a "capitalist conspiracy." Changing the social mechanisms does not automatically alter the habitat. The complexities of the country are reflected in its institutional life, and in its turbulent history.

Forging a Mexican nationality has been a long, baffling, and seemingly insoluble chore. In space and in time there have been many Mexicos. Their national government is presumed to speak for the Mexican people, but the latter have never been a unit. Mexicans are still found scattered on mountainsides and in tropical jungles, isolated in deserts, and hived up in towns and cities. Which of these groups is the real Mexican people? Each of the successive political regimes from Spanish times onward has had a special answer and has sought to shape the whole society accordingly.

3. Ancient Legacies

The first Spaniards in Mexico were convinced that the Devil himself had been at work. They claimed he had preceded them to the area with the express and malignant purpose of thwarting the later Christians who found this pagan land. Spanish military men, priests, and administrators never ceased expressing amazement at the puzzling regions and peoples. They deplored the seemingly insuperable barriers they found to their attempts at civilizing and enlightening its varied inhabitants. Men of lesser conviction would have despaired, but stubbornly for three centuries Spaniards tried to make moderns out of the Stone Age groups they had found in Mexico.

1. ROOTS

When the Spaniards arrived they encountered the whole range of possible Indian cultural developments. Some native areas had flourished and were already far down the cultural gradient—in Yucatan, for instance. Others were approaching an apogee—the Central Mexican groups most notably, under the tutelage of centers of "high culture." Still others had long remained undisturbed, static at varying degrees of sophistication, reflecting a long intricate history. As the Spaniards learned, Indians emerged from the unreal "Indian."

The achievements of the outstanding cultures were many. Collectively the Indians had created physical monuments of extraordinary size and beauty, built and decorated by the patient rubbing of stone on stone and with untold expenditure of manpower. They had produced a monumental and unique architecture. Sculpture, crafts, learning of great merit and substantial content had also existed. But at the same time violence, disruption, cataclysm, had equally been embedded in traditions. Small areas formed the limits of thought. No broadly unifying concepts of religion, politics, or common destiny bound aboriginal Mexico together into any sort of unity. Rather the reverse was true.

New technical reports come flooding in so rapidly from investigators seeking to unravel the ancient past of Mexico that many, if not most, seemingly immutable suppositions about the tangled realm of aboriginal history are now as extinct as some of the animals and peoples that are coming to light. Until rather recently scientists generally believed that man was a late-comer to the Mexican scene, but the spectacular uncovering of an old human skeleton, together with remains of prehistoric animals and human artifacts, near Tepexpan (just outside Mexico City) in 1947 unequivocally pushed the chronological frontiers back to 10,000 B.C. and subsequent intensive search indicates that 20,000 B.C. is well within the range of probability for the undated appearance of these crude hunters.

It is still an open question whether these several groups of paleolithic peoples were the immediate ancestors of the later inhabitants for whom archaeology provides testimony. Although the working hypotheses currently used to explain the sudden masses of new and upsetting findings of the past five years or so are still in flux, they do embrace a number of broad sequences. The large gap (? 20,000 B.C.– 1000 B.C.) between the paleolithic hunters and the cultures for which archaeology provides some clue is now tagged "Basic." During this time nomadic tribes settled down to agricultural pursuits, tamed plants and animals, and acquired skills of pottery-making and weaving.

Slowly, around the years 1000 B.C. or perhaps 500 B.C., the "Basic" cultures gave way to a "Formative" stage. It is the first stage that actually yields enough consistent material on which to make intelligent guesses about how ancient Mexicans lived and died. From the thick rubbish heaps on their small habitation sites it is inferred that generation after generation lived as primitive agriculturists subsisting on maize, and that their uneventful lives were spent under simple theocratic governments uncomplicated by much ritual apparatus. For reasons beyond our present ken an unknown number of these little groups suddenly burst into bloom by at least A.D. 300.

The ensuing three or four centuries witnessed an almost unparalleled cultural and political florescence in which mammoth and extraordinary building activity, high intellectual and aesthetic achievements, and complicated religious beliefs and social structures were keynotes. Neither metal tools nor the wheel aided these astounding efforts. Both the Middle American highlands and the lowlands underwent transformation; peaceful interchange of ideas and goods between city-states is well attested by the innumerable physical remains constantly unearthed by investigators throughout the modern Mexican areas. Military motifs are lacking.

Pottery in Mexico from Basic days onward evolved without the use of a potter's wheel, which is still shunned by most native craftsmen there today. A variety of woven fabrics and techniques seemingly were tried out during Basic days, though no specimens have endured. Perhaps the salient lasting achievement of aboriginal Mexico was domestication of plants, for food and for other uses—dyes, medicines, and the like. Outstanding in this connection was the creation of a unique New World all-purpose cereal, corn (or maize), whose technical label is *Zea mays* L. It is now the world's second most important food crop.

For many years scientists believed that maize was first domesticated in Mexico. Recent probing not only has disproved that assumption but has changed other opinions about maize as well. A number of areas now have more valid claims than Mexico for primacy in its domestication, which is now widely thought to have followed the raising of gourds, legumes, and other tropical plants. Apparently for many years, perhaps centuries, a tapioca-like substance known as manioc was the staple of much of America (and especially southern Mexico) before the all-important maize plants appeared. There is scarcely a domesticable plant in America that was not known and used by American Indians during the Basic Period. Potatoes, tomatoes, peanuts, cacao, pineapples, pumpkins, cotton, are but a few of the contributions. But of all, maize was paramount.

As an economic item, maize is extremely important: it has relatively high food value, but more important, it can be grown in almost any climate and soil which will grow vegetation at all. In 1492 there were at least 700 varieties, some growing in areas of less than ten inches of rainfall, others where 200 inches fall. This all-purpose, all-weather food item is peculiarly American, and especially Mexican, though now it grows on all continents. In Mexico it has almost always been accompanied by its smaller companion, the lowly but important bean, and often by the useful gourd. Squash-maize-beans are the crop foundations on which aboriginal Mexican societies rested and on which half of modern Mexico still depends.

Maize now forms about 90 per cent of the diet of rural Mexico, and its symbolic significance is even more important than its economic. In Yucatan, for instance, on plantations where workers are given excellent and balanced modern diets, workmen still make a small *milpa*—corn patch—in which to carry on old rites and to link themselves with the forces of nature thus propitiated. Maize agriculture is a way of life as much as an agricultural technique, and many of these symbolic practices apparently date from Basic days.

Much in the rhythm of European history following the fall of the Roman Empire, a Dark Age crept slowly over some of these classic Indian societies, while others seemingly collapsed in cataclysmic fashion. By about the year 1000 the previously peaceful, seemingly stable and prosperous scene had given way to civil wars, migrations, and incursions of wild tribes. Like the European Goths and Visigoths, these new intruders themselves settled down and took on more advanced ways while altering the earlier patterns almost beyond recognition. By perhaps 1300 the initial chaos of the Dark Age of Mexican prehistory began to pass, unveiling a group of militaristically organized social units. It was the further unrolling of this phase of early Mexican development that the coming of the Spaniards interrupted. Its now common label is "post-Classic."

What the Spaniards Found. A dominant note of late pre-Conquest Mexico was institutionalized violence. The written record (for now we begin to have native codices, some manufactured before the Spaniards came, some after) and archaeological testimony reveal a multitude of flayings, decapitations, animal and human sacrifices. Some of the sacrificial victims were children, others were prisoners of war. To supply their bloody gods, main Indian groups on the Mesa Central arranged ritual wars in order that each could systematically replenish its stock of sacrificial prisoners. Frontiers marking off domains from one another were now fortified, and, as might be expected, warrior and warrior-merchant classes played a large part in society. A plutocracy was developing.

Characteristic organizations of post-Classic times were loose confederations of native states, unstable coalitions that have been misnamed "Empires." Of these the most famous is the Aztec. Centered at Tenochtitlán, a city on an island in the middle of Lake Texcoco (where modern Mexico City stands) to which the barbaric Tenocha-Mexica had been exiled for bad behavior during the aboriginal Mexican Dark Age, it was merely a loosely associated group of Indian tribute-paying towns and villages. Joined by a like-minded tribe called the Culhuas, they conquered their neighbors. The Aztecs drew a variety of goods and services from innumerable subjugated hamlets and larger centers around the lake and through southern Mexico. The Mexica-Culhuas ("Aztecs") did not develop an effective central administrative apparatus for their "empire." However, they did make a start toward keeping records in rebus-writing. From their tribute records R. H. Barlow recently (1949) reconstructed the extent and nature of the groupings over which they extracted levies. So complex was the situation in 1500 that he was forced to subdivide the "Aztec Empire" of that date into seven major provincial divisions and 38 sub-provinces, each of which included diverse speech and cultural groupings clustered in village combinations. It covered the east central part of modern Mexico.

To the south, the situation was equally complex, though without even the rudimentary organization represented by the Mexica-Culhua confederation of the Mesa Central. Some states, like Tlaxcala, were sturdily independent. In Oaxaca as many as four rulers would claim jurisdiction over a given village, which usually had to pay tribute to all four. The Maya of Yucatan were divided into seventeen or eighteen dynastic units. To the west of the Valley of Mexico the Tarascans and other neighboring peoples soundly defeated Aztec attempts to bring them within the central web, but did not themselves join together on even a semi-permanent basis. The north was still the land of barbarians—"Chichimecs"—whom no one bothered, but against whom frontier defenses were kept in readiness. On all sides war had joined religion as the localized organizing and integrating principles of group and individual life.

Perhaps the main feature of the whole Mexican area was its heterogeneity, within groups and between groups. While the leader of the Culhua-Mexica, the Moctezuma, was being served trout cooled by snows which his servants had fetched from Popocatepetl, people like the Huastecs, the Otomi, and the "Chichimecs" continued to live much as others had during the Basic or Formative Periods. In some cultural pockets the land had been continuously occupied since perhaps the time of Tepexpan Man. At least two hundred and perhaps as many as four hundred languages and dialects reflected the distinct usages and ways of thought of as many tribes.

The truncated record of aboriginal Mexico here so sketchily presented tends to place its own conclusions before the reader. Taproots of certain and important current Mexican practices are deeply embedded in a solid substratum of pre-Columbian experiences. Aboriginal days provided Mexico with some common usages and outlooks—agricultural methods, diet, social stratifications. But more impressive is the long sequence of major transformations, each ushered in on sharp breaks with previous tradition. Discontinuities outrank continuity and homogeneity in the aboriginal epochs.

2. THE HAPSBURG COLONIAL EXPERIMENT, 1521–1700

Contemporary Mexican culture is a cosmopolitan mixture of elements drawn from many sources, but its matrix is Romance, specifically Spanish. Iberian traditions provide the broad frameworks that still give order and meaning to all subsequent introductions. From the very outset, of course, extant Indian usages permeated this Hispanic stream and even now they peep through the Iberian overlay in surprising fashion. Very early the African Negro made an appearance and contribution. In later days other European modes, borrowed from England, France, and the rest of the continent, were Mexicanized. More recent influences come from the United States and even Russia. But notwithstanding these critical modifications, Mexico remains fundamentally Spanish-American.

On every hand magnificent Indian ruins inevitably recall Mexico's aboriginal glories, but often more compelling to the eye and the mind are monuments to the epoch when Imperial Spain dominated Mexico. For three hundred years, from 1521 to 1821, Europeans forced the passage of Mexican culture from the Stone Age toward modernity. As visible reminders of this feat they left material remains without number. Perhaps a main clue to the transformation which Mexico underwent during that long and critical span is that the known Indian ruins are points of interest for casual sightseers, while Spanish constructions are still used by the Mexican people in their daily lives.

The intangible legacies of the colonial past are even more impressive and widespread. The language that one hears everywhere is nearly always Spanish. In other overt ways, as well as in thousands of subtle and hidden ones, the Iberian culture placed an ineradicable stamp on the Mexican land. The deeper one delves into the Mexican colonial period the more apparent becomes the truth of E. G. Bourne's declaration that "What Rome did for Spain, Spain did for America."

To control its overseas holdings Spain evolved a bewildering and novel battery of organs and organizations that set models for later-comers in the imperial field—the French, the Dutch, the English. Unlike their Portuguese contemporaries the Spanish imperialists felt that they were carrying out a universal mission and that their duty was clear, to force conformity to regnant sixteenth-century norms. Though their lofty aspirations often outran their achievements and although the hazards of distance, communications, and discords at home hampered their efforts, they persisted in them. When all Spanish shortcomings are subtracted, the net accomplishment is stupendous and largely beneficial. Even to begin an enumeration quickly passes space limitations, since there is scarcely a phase of daily life in Mexico that escaped some tincture of Hispanic influence.

One of the great adventure stories of all times is the tale of Hernan Cortés and his handful of followers who in 1519–1521 conquered aboriginal Mexico. It has been given classic form by William Hickling Prescott, and many subsequent hands have set down the lesser narratives that describe how Mexico was secured and organized for Hapsburg Spain by its doughty pioneers. Once the first shock of conquest was past and the primary wave of romantic adventurers had washed southward to repeat their exploits in South America, Mexican institutional life adjusted itself on the new basis.

By at least 1580 Mexico had settled down to its main colonial occupations. As in earlier days, agriculture was the main concern of nearly all the population; now Spaniards had organized their own enterprises, plantations and farms, rather than attempting to live off the scanty surpluses that reluctant Indians could furnish, as in the first post-Conquest days. To existing use of the land, the Europeans added the raising of animals and the extraction of silver from the Mexican earth.

With changing conditions went altered economic institutions. After the realm was stabilized, for instance, free labor, forced servitude peonage, and outright slavery coexisted; land tenure became equally complicated. Institutional frameworks at all levels became increasingly intricate as the web of decree and law dropped over one activity after another. This highly articulated institutional context was one of the major legacies of colonial Mexico to the modern republic.

Local and regional diversity continued to exert its powerful pressures on Mexican developments, but these were enveloped in an all-embracing imperial system that was premised on unity of culture and religion, mediated through a centralized and absolute political system. In sharp contrast to the later English attitude toward its North American colonies, the Spanish Crown constantly exercised vigilance in large and small matters and piled agency on agency to execute directives through a chain of command that started with the Crown in Europe and reached to village squares all over the New World, Mexico included. The structure and superstructure evolved before the Reformation, with its justification for individual dissent from authority. Therefore they had as one integrating element the intertwining of Church and State into a single Catholic whole. Colonists and officials came to Mexico as loyal subjects of an absolute Crown, not as dissenters. A main policy was to make equally loyal vassals of newly converted Mexican Indians.

The coming of Europeans to Mexico raised the standards of living of the area and elevated the moral tone of many of its indigenous groups. Cannibalism disappeared. As European heirs of the Renaissance, Spaniards arrived with a new and revolutionary knowledge by which to transform aboriginal Mexico. Indians, individually and in groups, competed with one another to obtain and share these material benefits.

Spaniards brought them new food items, simple but essential techniques, as well as effective instruments and implements. Citrus fruits, wheat, numerous herbs and vegetables, sugar cane, rice, olives, added to chickens, beef, pork, mutton, milk, and the like suddenly expanded the preëxisting dietary. Blends of the two have produced a Mexican cuisine unlike either the original Spanish or Indian. From the backs of Indians a considerable weight was shifted onto the humble burro and his more esteemed cousins, the mule and the horse. Without them modern Mexico would seem unnatural.

Before the coming of the Spaniards, no one in Mexico could dig deeply enough to produce a really workable well, and a similar lack of cutting tools threatened the whole agricultural system. No scythes, nor even sickles, were available to combat weeds. Even to chop down a tree required many and painful strokes with a pointed stone—a poor substitute for a Toledo steel ax or a Seville-made saw. Houses and public buildings had been restricted to honeycombs of small rooms, dark and unwindowed for want of glass and from absence of ideas about constructing a true arch; even nails were a European novelty. For lack of knowledge of the wheel, no one could make a cart. Nor could anyone read a real book, much less write one. It shocked Spaniards to find so many native people sleeping on the ground. Among their very first chores they felt it necessary to teach Mexican Indians to weave hammocks (a trick which the Spaniards themselves had picked up from natives in the West Indies) and to build cheap but comfortable beds from cane. A popular Spanish innovation was distilling—native drinks as well as foods increased in number. The roster of material improvements could be amplified to incorporate medicine, clothing, weapons, and almost every other phase of everyday living, the main concern of most men. Even the wooden plow pulled by an ox was an improvement over a pointed digging stick.

Against these material and tangible items one must place intangible, human considerations. The social and personal losses, especially psychological ones, were great. They were the price of civilization. No one then or now has found how to impart revolutionary technical benefits without losses and changes. The central focus of Indian attention was ruthlessly twisted. The first psychological and physical strains of enforced acculturation took their toll of life, as did new diseases and unhealthy habits acquired from the Spaniards. The cherished native value systems were rudely and completely upset, with a consequent personal and group trauma, which hardened into a "psychological unemployment." The emotional bases for the Indian way of life were officially declared to be dangerous and inferior, and became the prime targets for extirpation. The Spaniards conquered minds as well as lands.

The final evaluation of the total colonial experiment is almost impossible to make. One difficulty is its sheer magnitude. Another is the highly emotional nature of all discussions about it, even by professional investigators. The larger answers they achieve visibly take on the colors of their individual and contemporary attitudes toward such controversial matters as Catholicism, the rights of labor, foreign penetration, the "welfare state" (of which the colonial government was an early and prime example), and similar fundamental and vital questions that enliven debates today. The colonial past lives on in current Mexican polemics.

In summing up the colonial period and its legacies to modern Mexico, perhaps the keynote is the slow and quiet change that occurred after the initial shocks. Peace and prosperity prevailed in New Spain at a time when in Old Spain a prolonged decadence had already begun to set in. Mexican population losses from the Conquest and its disturbed aftermath had been made up by at least 1650. By that time too, militarism had faded from the scene, though the tradition was not wholly dead. In the scattered colonial cities, local literary and aesthetic movements had already begun to voice a dim spirit of "Mexicanism," a creole nationalism that reached full bloom much later. So tranquil and undramatic are the middle years of the colonial period, from around 1600 to 1750, that few historians even bother to look at them. This void in our information robs the investigator of nearly all details on which any final judgment of the colonial period can be based.

Rising above considerations of the "goodness" or "badness" is the major significance: the Spanish colonial period of Mexican history really represents a vast experiment carried on in innumerable laboratories. The mingling and intermingling of diverse European, African, and variant Indian cultural traits was universally occurring in small hamlets, on large haciendas, at countless mineheads, and even more intensely in the blossoming urban centers of New Spain. The results of this mixing, blending, compounding, and interplay give to colonial "Mexicanism" a fascinating complexity, one which has been projected into the present. Much of the cultural impress of colonial times is indelible. In the Hispano-Indian culture that the colonial melting pot produced, the native Indian and the imported Negro emerged vastly more changed than did the intrusive Spaniard. These centuries and elements forged the modern Mexican template.

From the close of the fifteenth century, European Spaniards conducted over a period of ten generations a series of experiments in imperialism and acculturation. On a foundation created from existing native Mexican materials they built a lasting edifice. The collective Western European, Christian traditions provided its specifications. The preponderance and strength of these patterns, when stretched overseas, linked Mexico to the civilized world of the time. It has been part of the Western community ever since. As the first modern European nation to attempt the thankless task of transoceanic colonizing, Spain reaped the rewards but also suffered the penalties of such an innovation. In both the literal and the figurative sense Spaniards were pioneers in Mexico, as elsewhere in the Americas.

But though Spain had labored long and lovingly to alter Mexico, the home country had (for complicated reasons we need not enter into) itself lapsed into a decline in which much of its former power and glory were eclipsed by poverty and impotence. When the last Hapsburg king of Spain, Charles II, literally an idiot, could produce no direct heir, nearly every rival state in Europe waited tensely for him to die. Each hoped to establish some claim to the vacant Spanish throne or perhaps obtain a juicy portion of the rich and ancient Spanish Empire in America. Charles II died in 1700. The international sweepstakes then were officially started. The Spanish Empire, including Mexico, was the prize.

3. ENLIGHTENMENT AND REVOLT, 1700–1821

Initial impetus for innovating movements in eighteenth-century Mexico stemmed from a dynastic change in Spain following the death of the last Hapsburg, Charles II. In the scramble to succeed him, the grandson of Louis XIV of France, Philip V, was the successful candidate. With him, Bourbon ways superseded the long regnant Spanish Hapsburg policies. Under the Bourbon dynasty, France had risen to first magnitude; the family had decided that its Spanish branch should now apply the successful French formulas to the Iberian peninsula. For political reasons they wanted to rehabilitate an impoverished and decadent Spain, the junior partner of the new French-Spanish axis. Political renovation, however, waited on economic and social rejuvenation.

Eighteenth-century Spanish Bourbon Kings and their French-trained advisers tried their best to obliterate remnants of the Spanish Middle Ages at home and in the Empire. From 1700, they made continuous efforts to close the gap between the old sixteenth-century ideals and practices they had found and the modern and up-to-date eighteenth-century standards they brought to Spain. The homeland and its possessions overseas were in for a thorough housecleaning and basic remodeling. France, and especially seventeenth- and eighteenth-century France, served as the pattern. Old Spain, and New Spain as well, were to become "enlightened" and "modernized." The cumulative results are the "Bourbon Renaissance."

The Bourbon Renaissance Policies. The Bourbons believed devoutly in the Divine Right of kings to rule. Their concept of what they wanted to do as monarchs was considerably different from earlier Spanish Hapsburg notions. Divergences came in policies, methods, organizations, and emphasis. Hapsburgs had based their system on large landholders, large monopolistic merchants, and Iberian institutions hallowed by history. The new Spanish Bourbons, equally absolutist, took an opposite tack.

They preferred to foster a smaller-farm society (yeomen), new middle-class industrialists, and numerous and diverse small commercial groups to compete with one another. Outsiders themselves, they freely imported European technicians and scientists to appraise and change old usages (however "hallowed") which did not meet the eighteenth-century norms of reason, utility, and immediate economic advantage. This reversed Hapsburg suspicion and fear of foreigners. Where Hapsburgs, especially the later weak ones, had considered the Church as a coördinate and even dominant arm of government, interlocked with the sprawling secular bureaucracy at every level, the Bourbons frankly distrusted the Spanish Church and insisted on supremacy of the civil power over the spiritual. They went even further; they were markedly anticlerical.

The Hapsburgs had governed by an infinite delegation of power to councils and semiprivate organizations, each with its own law or *fuero*. Activities of such corporate groups were scrutinized by a Hapsburg bureaucracy chiefly constituted of the sons of landowners, merchants, and minor aristocrats. In most instances, even tax-collecting had been farmed out to semiprivate enterprise. Bourbons would have none of this.

They wanted a clearly organized, centralized system where the direct lines of command and responsibility were uniform and unmistakable. They preferred to staff their fewer, more powerful, agencies with sons of the middle class, each professionally trained as a secular administrator. Ministers at home and their able subordinates in colonial posts were given wide latitude of discretion. The colonial officials were broadly instructed to do all in their power to foster industry, spread useful knowledge, rejuvenate agriculture, and streamline administration. The Bourbons wanted results, but were willing to pay for them. In all this new program, there was not the slightest leaning toward democracy. In an age of "Enlightened Despots" the Bourbon kings of Spain, their counselors, and their subordinates all agreed that everything should be done *for* the people, nothing *by* the people. The prime drive was to increase the wealth of the realm, but now national wealth was measured in production of goods and services, not in the amounts of bullion that a state could hoard, as in the sixteenth century.

In the specific case of Mexico, Spanish Bourbons made numerous

changes aimed particularly at increasing local prosperity and productivity. After surveys in the 1750's and 1760's, Mexican colonial
officials were given large grants of authority to make needed changes.
Many of the duplicating and overlapping agencies which the Hapsburgs had created as a purposeful system of checks and balances were
scrapped or reduced almost to nullity. The land was divided into
intendancies, like France; these became the frames of the modern
states of Mexico. In the 1770's a train of able administrators and a
succession of great viceroys were sent off to Mexico City to see what
could and should be done about further improving the military, economic, and social conditions of the potentially rich area. Schools
were founded and institutes started. Local interests were encouraged
and foreign experts were hired to restore and multiply the mines,
classify the plants, draw modern maps, beautify the cities, create
roads, construct port works, and in short, remake the old place into a
modern country. The Bourbons lost little time in ousting the Mexican Jesuits (1767), an eighteenth-century symbol of superstition
and as a "state within a State," a threat to civil power. Insofar as
possible such "feudalism" was to be uprooted; only reasonable,
utilitarian, scientific institutions would do. But changes, even by
eager and zealous men, go slowly in Mexico. Bourbon programs always outran the actual results, substantial as some of these were.

Bourbon monarchs and their like-minded subordinates did not stop
with mere negative activities—eliminating barriers to progress (which
had become a watchword of the times). Officials in New Spain re-
drew administrative lines, knocked the shackles off commerce, and
encouraged all manner of invention and innovation. Under these
aggressive policies the total real wealth of Mexico increased, its population expanded, overseas commerce leaped, and royal revenues
mounted upward to unprecedented heights. Local savants were encouraged to form discussion groups which shared with one another
and the country the latest scientific knowledge of the world and blue-
printed improvements in their regional or local economy. Their
journals (for each such society felt almost duty-bound to disseminate
new knowledge) covered a vast range of topics, from proper measurement of the equator to the advantages of vaccines, steel plows, and
fertilizers. Benjamin Franklin was constantly hailed as a model for
Mexicans to follow.

In the international field, Spain's Mexican possessions were being
threatened by aggressive British Americans of North America, and

by Russians thrusting down the Pacific coast from Alaska. To meet these, and to tack down the northern approaches (borderlands of only strategic, not economic, value) which protected the significant parts of Mexico, Bourbon officials in Mexico City sponsored military and exploring expeditions. They extended the Mexican frontier by planting a line of mission-military outposts stretching from California (1769) eastward across what was then called the Great American Desert—the modern American Southwest. As part of the Bourbon military preparedness drive, militia companies were formed in nearly every town in the populated heartland a thousand miles further south. They were usually officered by local Mexican creoles,* proud to strut in their gaudy uniforms and willing to pay for commissions and even to finance the outfitting of their soldiers as well. Guns and eighteenth-century ideas, a truly explosive combination, entered Mexico about the same time. But with the rising levels of prosperity, able government, and continued peace, a rosy, quiet future seemed in store for Mexico under Bourbon guidance.

Struggles for Independence. If Mexico was faring so well under the Bourbon Renaissance, the query naturally arises why did the colony join in the general American movement for independence from Spain? The answers are, unfortunately, less simple than one could wish. The explanation breaks into three parts: confusion in Europe at the rise of Napoleon and a consequent reversal of Spanish efforts; the flaming examples of the American and the French Revolutions; and, finally, happenings in Mexico itself. The first two of these circumstances had universal results in Hispanic America, while the third gave to Mexico the peculiar and unusual stamp which its particular movements for independence display when compared to others of the Americas.

The revolutions for independence in Hispanic America were civil wars. Not until after Napoleon's fall could Spain dispatch many professional soldiery overseas to reinforce the efforts of its loyal colonial subjects, who tried to preserve Crown authority and its apparatus in the colonies. The colonial world thus became divided between loyalists and separatists, between royalists and republicans. In most places the two issues were fused into one: victory of the revolutionists commonly meant the establishment of an independent republic. Elements wedded to the old way—the local bureaucrats,

---

* Creole is a descriptive term applied to Spanish families and persons born in the American colonies rather than in the Spanish peninsula.

established merchants, landowners, and ruling Spaniards and upper clergy—normally opposed both separation and republicanism. The patterns of success of one side or the other varied in detail from country to country.

September 16, 1810 is Mexican Independence Day. On that memorable date Padre Miguel Hidalgo uttered the *Grito de Dolores*—"Independence and death to Spaniards!" His original force of four Indians swelled as they surged toward Mexico from Michoacan, spreading rapine behind and terror ahead. Whites, both creole and Spanish, linked arms to quash this primitive caste-war, and Hidalgo was defeated and then executed. José María Morelos nursed the embers of the Hidalgo movement and added republicanism to it before he too failed and died in 1813. By 1817 only sporadic bands carried on the new crusade lighted by Hidalgo.

Mexican movements formed a unique pattern. The twin issues of independence and the formation of a republic were separately resolved in such fashion that in place of destroying the traditional bases of royalist rule, it preserved them. Because of its responsibilities within the Spanish Empire, Mexico City and its immediately surrounding areas formed a stronghold of royalist strength, military and ideological. Separatist and republican military movements which neared the viceregal capital were crushed without much real difficulty. Not until the conservative elements of Mexico had belatedly decided that their main interests were more secure outside the Empire than in it, did the independence movement succeed. To protect their religion, social system, and position from a radical Spanish Cortes, moderates and conservatives joined an independence movement originally carried on by republicans. The price of such support was a Mexican monarchy, independent but dominated by the older colonial groups. These compromises soon failed.

Basically unchanged, the old Spanish viceroyalty of New Spain became the independent Mexican Empire in 1821, and then (in 1823) the Republic of Mexico. The changes in form did little to rearrange the traditional operation of power, and left society almost undisturbed. Paradoxically the elements which elsewhere in Latin America had been the main barriers to independence and chief targets of revolutionary activity were in Mexico the very ones which cut it adrift from Spain and controlled its national destinies for half a century thereafter.

4. Modern Heritages

1. SOVEREIGNTY AND NATIONALITY

After 1821, Mexico was a sovereign nation, in the political sense. Power to make decisions resided within the area, rather than in Spain. Despite the ups-and-downs, changes in form and actions of its national government, Mexico has not since lost her political sovereignty nor national identity. Achievement of these were the undeniable major consequences of the revolution for independence. Henceforth its international relations and its domestic problems were the sole responsibility of Mexico and the Mexicans. Foreign nations now dealt directly with Mexico rather than through Spain, and on Mexican shoulders alone rested the responsibility of the actions of their own government, whatever at the moment that might be.

The main outlines of Mexico remained much the same for a considerable period after it first started on its independent political life despite the heat lightning of partisan politics and the thunder of diplomatic exchanges. The severing of political lines that had bound it to Spain did not automatically transform society or even all ideas, much less institutions around which Mexican life had revolved for so long. Neo-Colonial Mexico in the social sense began to pass into Recent, or the most recently modern, Mexico, around 1867 when some of the old institutions and ideas were eliminated as the major determinants of the Mexican decisions. A long printed page can easily be filled with the names of those who headed early-nineteenth-century Mexican governments while the nation was experimenting politically.

Newly independent Mexico was socially much the same as it had been under the Bourbon viceroyalty. Economically, however, it was a buyer without funds and a seller without goods; seemingly as events unrolled, Mexico was doomed to increasing impoverishment.

This, in turn, bred political difficulties, both national and international. A vicious circle of deterioration was characteristic: forced to look abroad for capital and loans to rebuild a shattered economy and run their affairs, governments found their credit sinking lower and lower as default upon default made financial aid to them more and more risky; the ruinous rates of interest left smaller and smaller amounts of principal available. Even more serious, the future national revenues were increasingly pledged as collateral, so that eventually only foreigners benefited from any collection of customs dues, the main source of public funds. Politically, Mexico was sovereign and independent but the country was economically a fief. Poverty and misery only intensified the intestine factional struggles over power and policy.

The chief domestic political issues first centered around the form which the new nation should assume. Implicit was the major question of all politics: who should rule, and for what ends? The failure of a limited monarchy to satisfy the vast majority of creoles led to a temporary eclipse of the monarchical principle and its ultra-conservative supporters. By 1823 there was fairly general agreement in Mexico that a republic would be the only appropriate framework of the new nation. Beyond this, opinion was as varied as the individuals.

Political sentiments and platforms divided into two main streams. Names and labels changed but the general complexion of each remained much the same. One was a shifting coalition formed by Colonial and Neo-Colonial creoles who wished to preserve the earlier practices and institutions intact but narrow their application from an imperial to a national ideal. Their opponents, products of Independence, shared with them the idea that the Mexican nation should work out its own destinies and improve its economic base, but differed markedly as to the pace and direction, as well as by what instruments changes should proceed.

The first group looked mainly to Europe for inspiration and aid; the second, to the North American republic for guidance and models. Time and circumstance shifted their tag, but the former were usually called Centralists, and the latter, Federalists. Each was named after the type of republican government it proposed to operate if and when it came into power. Iturbide's flimsy Empire was overthrown by Federalists in 1823 but after a brief and unsuccessful flurry at organizing the republic which displaced it, their group (with one or two breaks) remained out of power for more than a generation. Federalists, from 1824 to 1855, were in almost constant opposition to the ruling Centralists.

2. EXPERIMENTS, 1824–1853

The Centralist Experiment. The Centralist group had ability, concentrated power, and a program that continued the ideals of the Bourbon Renaissance. Local circumstance stripped the anticlerical biases of the Bourbons from their program, and added the necessity of including militarism as an essential feature. The political theory and ideology of Centralists can be compared, without major distortions, to the Hamiltonian concepts that helped shape the early United States.

The essential goal of Centralists was to form a stable, powerful, central, national government responsive to the desires of the main economic groups, the established supporters of Colonial and Neo-Colonial Mexico. Most of the Centralist political strength derived from the economic province concentrated in a small, highly developed geographical area; it included the Spanish-founded mining centers just north of Mexico City, the grain-growing country of the hacendados adjacent to both, the urban industrialist centers of Puebla in the corridor to the outlet at Veracruz, and part of the port itself. Centralists were also strong in other urban centers of the nearby provinces, where like-minded creoles hoped to join and emulate developments guided from Mexico City. As in the past, they looked to Europe, especially France and England, for guidance, support, and models.

Basically the Centralist position was strongly nationalist, economically and politically conservative, and culturally European Catholic. Its power base was the capital and its attached economic auxiliaries. The inclinations of the Centralists inevitably led them toward strong executive rule, as in Bourbon days. They were a homogeneous body, most of whom had received good educations at home or abroad. Their coalition embraced the military, the Church, and the creole upper classes.

If successful, their program would make an agro-industrial unit of Mexico, supplemented by swelling foreign commerce and mining. In the historical arena of power, the chief instrument of the Centralists was a colorful and demagogic general from Veracruz, Antonio

López de Santa Anna; in the sphere of policy and foreign relations, their leader was Lucas Alamán. His death in 1853 weakened centralist power and allowed extremists to dominate. Party prestige was diminished by the chaos and discredit accruing from the disastrous American War, and the short-lived attempt of Santa Anna to reëstablish a personal empire. Rifts within the Centralist group, plus the growing strength of its opponents, the Federalists, equalized power between these two main Mexican political divisions. Parity of strength led to a protracted period of civil war for two decades after 1847.

The Federalist Experiment. At nearly every point (except nationalism and the hope for a rosy Mexican future) the Federalists were the antithesis of Centralists. They were scattered in space and outlook among the outlying margins and provinces of Mexico, united only in their determination to oust Centralists from rule and to substitute their own programs. Federalists represented the republican, revolutionary strands of the late eighteenth and early nineteenth centuries. They accepted Bourbon ideals of education, transportation, scientific agriculture, and the like. Similarly they retained Bourbon anticlerical biases and the Enlightenment insistence on reason and utility over tradition. Again without violence to either, their position was comparable to the Jeffersonian-Jacksonian outlook in the United States. Liberty, equality, fraternity seemed much more important to them than stability and economic welfare, when choices had to be made.

Collectively they viewed Mexico as a loose collection of little sovereignties. The sovereign states, bound together in a mutually beneficial national association, had as their agent a limited national government whose chief feature was a small, trained bureaucracy, controlled by Congress. Their political theory was based on innovation, a major break with the past: at no earlier time had sovereign Mexican states even existed, let alone exercised local power; Congress (the center of their system) was a far cry from the colonial Audiencia, responsive only to the monarch and his decrees. By and large, Federalists were rural-minded, distrustful of city ways, and unashamedly and almost lyrically provincial. They exploited and even created localistic loyalties which Centralists hoped to extirpate as barriers to "progress." In their devotion to lush diversity, Federalists were politically romantic, in contrast to the more disciplined, classic emotions of the Centralists.

The United States, as the only republic in the world successfully operating on federal principles, magnetized Mexican Federalist attention, and Federalists attributed the growing strength and prosperity of the northern country to its decentralized political system. Generally speaking, Federalists were notably short on economic analysis. The general admiration for the United States carried over into their other international views where a strong anti-European bias was notable. They considered Yankee aggressiveness attributable to Southern slavery factions not unlike their own Centralists. Federalists abolished slavery in Mexico in 1824. One of the reasons for the rapid United States success in the 1845–1847 war against Mexico was the widely diffused feeling in the provinces that it was a "Centralist's War." Political disagreements among Mexicans more than military divisions from the United States made possible the capture of Mexico City.

The credo of the Federalists had been formulated by many minds, but it was in the 1830's intellectualized by an obscure figure, Dr. Luis Mora. Strong in his attack against Centralist views, he was somewhat weak on a comprehensive positive program to replace them. In Mora's outline, Federalists stood for antimilitarism, on both theoretical and practical grounds: militarism was feudal, dangerous; large armies locked up manpower needed for utilitarian ends such as building roads and schools. Mora rejected the earlier easygoing optimism of the eighteenth century about the inevitability of Mexican progress—political or material—and stressed the affirmative need to rid Mexico of its feudalistic vestiges, especially *fueros*. These were ancient legal privileges given the military and clergy. His attack on the Church and the military men used economic, political, and cultural arguments: The Church was monopolistic, *ergo*, bad. Science, not religion, should be the common bond among Mexicans; it was rational and universal, modern and beneficial.

The first task of Federalist leaders, as Mora saw it, was to uproot the Church and the army and bring all the nation under one set of laws. Institutions stemming from these would promote equality, science, and material benefits. *Fueros* were the obvious and visible symbols of all that Mora and the Federalists opposed. Therefore, the first steps toward further "decolonizing" and "modernizing" of Mexico were aimed at judicial reform—exterminating the special privileges of corporate groups. This anti-corporative bent was later easily transferred to business, especially foreign corporations.

3. REFORM AND REVIVED EMPIRE, 1853–1872

The Reforma and the Constitution of 1857. Exiled in Paris, Mora scribbled away in sickness. But events in Mexico were shaping an opportunity for his theses to develop into political programs to be carried on by others. In the provinces a second generation of Mexicans was coming to maturity, younger men who had been born after Mexico had achieved political nationhood. They entered local politics. Soon many of them tasted the frustrations produced by Centralist rule from Mexico City over their areas. Centralist programs took no account of local aspirations that did not further their own interests. Two of these local leaders, Melchor Ocampo of Michoacan and Benito Juárez of Oaxaca, spearheaded a Federalist movement of protest which has come down in Mexican annals as "The Reform." One was the son of an hacendado, the other a full-blooded Zapotec Indian; each had served ably as governor of his state. Neither had shown much inclination for any kind of radicalism until clashes with Church authorities led Centralist officials in 1852 to exile them both to New Orleans.

There, with other Mexican political dreamers and schemers, they eked out a paltry living in the day and debated Mexico's future endlessly through the night. In the dreary circumstance of exile, they were hardened intellectually and morally. More important, as a group, these expatriates formulated a program to end Mexican miseries, if ever they could capture power in Mexico City. This seemed a hopeless prospect for middle-aged provincials without personal means or military support.

Dramatic episodes opened the future to them. In the provinces of Mexico a republican revolution headed by an old veteran of Independence Wars, Juan Alvárez, gained headway against the insufferable Santa Anna. This 1853 "Revolution of Ayutla" seemed at first to be merely one of the interminable local uprisings, except for one fact: it became a huge military success. Even Centralist elements (displeased with Santa Anna's fantastic airs and ways) joined it. Without really major difficulty the military leaders made themselves masters of Mexico and elected Juan Alvárez president. This tough but humble old Indian knew his limitations; he had power but no skill in government, so he turned over these matters to a coterie of Federalists which included the New Orleans exiles.

Backed by power, they were given a broad mandate, to put a real Federalist reform into effect. The results are known as *La Reforma*. It started in 1853 and continued for a troubled decade and a half.

The Reform Surges. The avowed objects of the Reform group (Federalists all, but divided into liberal and moderate wings) were to make Mexico a modern, middle-class state, based on a federal republican constitution, the supreme law. The first moves in that direction were to liquidate the special *fueros* of the military and clergy, and to subordinate these groups to secular, civil authority. Their economic reforms envisaged increasing the Mexican wealth by putting the monopolized assets of the Church into streams of commerce, and of building a nation of small landholders, each with his own farm purchased from the large ecclesiastical holdings now held in mortmain. If one likes such terms, the *Reforma* can be described as a bourgeois revolution, carried out by and for *mestizos;* it was equally antagonistic to the Europeanized creole Mexicans and to the seemingly brutish and superstition-soaked Indians controlled by the clergy.

Soon Mexico began to ring with legislative changes and the political responses to them. Chief initial Reform laws were the *Ley Juárez* (November 23, 1855) and the *Ley Lerdo* (June 1856). The former reorganized the system of Mexican justice and abolished *fueros* by suppressing the military and ecclesiastical courts' jurisdiction over civil matters. This, of course, rubbed across the sensitive nerve-ends of the two most powerful institutions in the country, and was the signal for uprisings, plots, and the reshuffling of political coalitions. But the Reformers plunged on.

The *Ley Lerdo* had even more far-reaching repercussions on the present and future of Mexico. Aimed at the Church, it ordered corporate bodies to divest themselves of their landholdings. The theory was that Church sales would stimulate commerce, that the national Treasury would tax the sales (and thus keep sums flowing in), and that peasant tenantry would become small private holders, as preference in sale was to be given to those occupying tracts. It turned out, however, that the law did not force the division of these ecclesiastical *latifundias* and that only existing large landholders were rich enough to pay the prices asked. Actually, at this time, few transfers of this sort were made.

An even more unexpected and far-reaching consequence of the *Ley Lerdo* was to strip native communities of their traditional possession of communal lands. To encourage small private property interests, the Reformers considered village governments to be corporate groups, equally required to rid themselves of lands. In the ensuing sales, outsiders rather than villagers snapped up the best bits, and even a belated amendment, allowing communal holdings to be divided into private plots among the heads of families in the community, was ineffective in keeping the ancient fields under local ownership and control. The whole Federalist economic theory was based on the idea of sanctity of private property and its dynamic incentives to the middle-class virtues of thrift, hard work, and morality. This attitude underlay both their reform of the upper-class system and that of the lower, the Indians.

Constitution of 1857. Culmination of the Reform program came in the Constitution of 1857, which guided the Mexican nation until 1917. It embedded the whole Federalist credo into the highest law of the land. It opened with a long Bill of Rights to guarantee individual liberties of all sorts. The basic theoretical precept throughout the document was equality of all persons and every group before the law. Conversely stated, all special privileges were rejected.

But even the Constitutionalists of 1857 decided not to go the full route and disestablish and disendow the Church. Confiscation ran counter to their whole theory of a limited government and the sanctity of property; disestablishment was still too explosive a concept to all but Radical Liberals. Consistently hostile to corporate groups, the Constitution stressed democracy, states' rights, the authority of Congress over the executive, and supremacy of national law over particular interests. It was an eclectic charter which borrowed from the Spanish Constitution of 1812, from documents of French and American Revolutions, and from practices used by Federalist state governments and those established in the United States. Indians, workers, military men, and clerics had been excluded from drafting its provisions, with the result that it was the product of provincial lawyers, small merchants, fiery (but until then unknown) journalists, and others of the same social stratum. The Constitution of 1857 aimed almost exclusively at solving political problems, with scant attention to social or economic ones.

Promulgation of the Reform Constitution, coming on the heels of the *Ley Juárez* and the *Ley Lerdo,* split Mexico again. Part of the Federalists thought the program too radical, others not radical enough. The vocal opposition of excluded Centralists turned into political and military pressure. One group—Centralists and disaffected moderate Federalists—repudiated the Constitution and drove its proponents from office. Thereupon the Centralist-Moderate coalition set up a new regime in Mexico City. Juárez and his Radical Liberal Federalists (usually shortened to Liberals or Constitutionalists) created another Mexican government at Veracruz, governed by the Constitution of 1857. For three years Mexico went through another blood-bath. The cruelest form of strife—civil war—ravaged the land as two governments disputed whether the Constitution of 1857 and the Radicals would rule all of Mexico. The civil war between the Constitutionalists of Veracruz and their opponents in Mexico City had international repercussions. The United States supported Juárez, while European powers—including England—backed the other group.

The split in Federalist ranks permitted the Juárez government to complete the *Reforma*. The Moderate factions had sided with the Centralists who repudiated the Constitution of 1857; the Church was furnishing them with funds to carry on war. Both principle and need coincided in Juárez' decrees which disestablished and disendowed the Church. Church property was made subject to nationalization, a confiscation which would provide the Radical Veracruz government with funds while denying resources to their opponents. Further, the State rather than the Church was made agent for performance of legal marriages and of supervising burials. Ecclesiastical fees for religious ceremonies (in addition to the civil) were placed under government control. These decrees became Constitutional amendments in the 1870's; at the time they were war measures, valid only if the Constitutionalists could oust their tenacious and powerful enemies from Mexico City. This they finally did in 1861. They reproclaimed the Constitution of 1857 as the sole organic law of the land and themselves the only government. Their triumph was short-lived.

Intervention and Revived Empire, 1861–1867. Defeated on the domestic field, the Centralists-Moderate Federalists sought aid abroad. The international situation was ripe for such action. Spain, France, and Great Britain had several reasons to intervene in Mexico, among them to collect their long overdue debts, on which Radicals had suspended payment. The American Civil War then raging made interposition by the United States improbable. To find England acting so European by agreeing to armed intervention came as a shock to many Mexicans, and Latin-Americans in general. But for diplomatic reasons (connected with wider affairs in Europe and the world) Great Britain was a full partner in the Mexican Intervention of 1861.

Troops of the three European countries landed at Veracruz. For humanitarian reasons Mexicans allowed them to move up into the highlands above the port to avoid the perils of yellow fever. Dissension among the allies revealed the scheme of debt collection to be a mere pretext on the part of France (under Napoleon III) to add Mexico economically and politically to her satellite holdings. Spain and Britain then withdrew from the adventure.

French troops, however, broke their promises to remain immobile and pushed on to capture Mexico City. The check of their march at Puebla, where on May 5, 1862 Mexicans beat them badly, turned the debt collection pretext into one of French Imperial honor. Reinforcements followed. Juárez' legal government left the ancient seat of power in 1863. Without real military forces at his disposal, President Juárez called on Mexicans to employ guerrilla tactics like those so successfully used in Spain during the campaigns against the first Napoleon. But despite these, Mexico fell to the French. Juárez' government was forced into the northern Mexican deserts and kept on a constant move until 1867.

A fantastic subplot had been spun by Mexican monarchists in Europe during the 1840's. It now bore fruit. The French ruler, Napoleon III, using Mexican intermediaries, persuaded Maximilian of Hapsburg to accept the throne which the monarchists and even the Centralists were now willing to support. Maximilian, egged on by an ambitious wife and his own romanticism, solemnly took the proffered crown. This critical decision was made only after French troops had rigged a plebiscite in Mexico which resulted as expected—the Mexican people demanded Maximilian as their ruler. Under terms of agreements signed in Europe, Maximilian was to have French military support until the new Mexican Empire became stable, and in return was to give French concessionaires special privileges; it was assumed (because of the Pope's approval of the scheme) that he would restore the Church properties taken under the Mexican Reform, and would proceed to shape a program acceptable to the French monarch and the old Centralist elements in Mexico. None of these things happened.

Maximilian alienated conservative domestic and Papal support by acting like a Liberal. But he didn't win Liberal backing, even though he had misjudged the temper of Mexican affairs so far as to invite Juárez to collaborate with him! European affairs and the hostility of an armed United States, newly freed from the Civil War, caused Napoleon III to withdraw his military support of Maximilian. The success of the guerrilla campaigns against the Mexican Emperor was an added feature which doomed the throne. Steadily Juárez and his followers surged south, and finally, in 1867, Republican forces (under Porfirio Díaz) recaptured Mexico City, isolated Maximilian's forces, and, after a summary trial, shot the Emperor and his two main Mexican military aides. His wife, Carlota, had embarked on a vain trip to Europe to secure support from Napoleon III and the Pope; she went mad, and lingered on as a tragic reminder of the phantom Empire until her death in 1927.

Liquidation of Neo-Colonialism. Once again that squat and somber figure, Benito Juárez, ruled Mexico as a symbol of Mexicanism. During the Intervention and Empire his moral stature had grown to gigantic heights; as the implacable foe of special privilege, professional militarism, and the political Church, and the inflexible champion of law and constitutionalism, he had brought the Mexicans through the most severe crises of their national history to date, largely by strength of character and belief in the Mexican people's abilities to shape their own fate. The liquidation of Intervention and Empire and the final triumph of *La Reforma* put an end to some of the main features of Neo-Colonial Mexico.

The Church and large landholders were henceforth doubly suspect as collaborators and instigators of the enterprise so costly in Mexican lives and honor. Both were on the social and political defensive. Their traditional and favored position at the elbow of government was no longer generally considered natural and desirable; they were now "colonial." Corporate interests had chosen the wrong side in this final showdown of force, and suspicion spread to cover all corporate entities. With loss of position, their outcries against the Constitution of 1857 were muted and, though constant, not very important. Moreover, for once and for all the idea of a Mexican monarchy had been seared out of the political realm. Mexico was a Federalist republic, governed by Mexicans under the precept of the Constitution of 1857. Technically that was what all the fighting had been about. Foreigners had disturbed that arrangement in 1861, and had been ejected.

Equally important for the Mexican future was the dim sense of Mexican national consciousness that had begun to pulse during the Intervention and Empire. Then one was either a *mocho,* roughly equivalent to a Quisling, or a *pelado,* a true Mexican willing to make any sacrifice to rid the land of meddling foreigners. Unlike the American War fifteen years earlier, Mexico's struggle against the French gave Mexicans a common goal and glimpses of a common future. The Mexican culture, so rich and so varied, was beginning to take on a political cast. Nationalism had at its base a stable territory, an established frame of government, and now a set of common emotional experiences to give it coherence, force, and direction. It was only a beginning, a foreshadowing.

Mexican culture had been further enriched by Intervention. France's political domination had been unequivocally rejected, but its culture, so forcibly intruded, had been thankfully retained. Maximilian had renovated Mexico City in the French mode; French goods had changed Mexican tastes; and French books and plays had made a deep impression in urban centers. Sophistication and French became almost synonymous. Odd vulgarizations, the typically Mexican filtering of foreign ideas, spread the Gallic leaven by imitation from the upper into the lower and less literate levels of society. In 1883 the French language was even taught in primary schools. For nearly half a century after France had ceased to be an active political factor in Mexican political affairs, French culture thrived. The whole *milieu* of the late nineteenth century in Mexico was Franco-Mexican.

When Juárez resumed his interrupted tenure in Mexico City in 1867 he faced a prospect both heartening and dismal. The liberal ideals so long disputed and so deeply cherished now seemed irrevocably established. Mexico was free of foreign commitments and liens, repudiated with Intervention. It could shape its own international future. But its flimsy political institutions had collapsed under continuous civil strife; its people were wretchedly poor and without means to better themselves; and violence had again become a way of life for the major part of the citizenry. Many of them had never been peacefully employed; their trade was guerrilla scrounging and plundering. Banditry and revolution had been a patriotic duty for so long that any attempt at discipline seemed to infringe upon an inalienable right.

The economic outlook was pessimistic. Long ago the mines had been abandoned even by foreigners. Each little Mexican state, trying desperately to make ends meet, had built a high tariff wall around its domain, so that the inconsequential amount of goods that could bump their way on the backs of mules from one valley to another were scarcely worth sending or receiving, so exorbitant was the price. Mexico had neither diplomatic nor trade ties with European nations; even individuals capable of supplying the credit, capital goods, and ideas necessary to a modern economy were justifiably skeptical of the Mexican future. Not a bank, nor less a railroad, functioned while Juárez was still alive. Indian revolts and bandit forays kept life insecure and precarious. Juárez, with heartfelt thanks but no pensions, rapidly dismantled the guerrilla-trained army and let its unpaid hordes loose on the countrysides.

Juárez died in 1872, shortly after Porfirio Díaz, a war hero, had narrowly missed defeating him at the polls for his third term as president. His passing closed an era. He immediately joined other Mexican immortals in the pantheon of national heroes. Under him and his Federalist-Liberal group Mexico had, between 1853 and 1872, made another of its critical passages toward the present.

4. MATERIALISM AND OPTIMISM, 1872–1910

After a troubled interregnum under President Lerdo de Tejada, Mexicans were ready to pay nearly any price for peace and order in 1876. From its inception the nation had oscillated between war, revolution, and shorter and shorter postwar periods in which to make some fundamental adjustments to changing times. Reforms had never had much chance to affect the old structures; reconstruction and rehabilitation always outranked improvement as the pressing need of the moment. Lack of economic and political stability had bred further poverty and increased misery; these in turn always set off another cycle of strife that scattered any productive forces. How to end it? That was the question in many minds. Typically, one Mexican wrote (in 1877) that Mexico was once again at a crossroads, "Between a past that horrifies, a future not clearly seen." It had always been thus.

It was at this point that Porfirio Díaz stepped onto the political stage and offered some attractive solutions. At first his programs were less important than the man; later the balance shifted. Personally he was the very model of Adam Smith's "frugal man." He neither drank nor smoked, and had built up a reputation for unshakable personal integrity. His patriotism had been proven by his war record against the French, and his Liberal Federalism was unquestioned. Though an army man, he was anti-militarist, and wherever he had been stationed as zone commander, schools had risen and prosperity had bloomed as his soldiery built roads and straightened trails.

Díaz came to power on a military coup and a program of no reelection. At the end of his first term he dutifully stepped down, as did all his patronage appointees. As a honeymoon for his second wife he made a triumphal tour of the United States. Things in Mexico went poorly while he was away. As the indispensable man, he was called back to the president's chair in 1884.* He did not leave it until 1911. This was the Porfirian Era, created by Díaz.

Unencumbered by political debts, in 1884 he set about solidifying his power and shaping Mexico to the models of the age, the age of Victoria and Grover Cleveland. His bureaucrats, few in number and high in skill, collected endless statistics to help him frame policies. Technical advisers, young men weary of strife, flocked to his side.

The whole apparatus of a modern economy was dropped into place within a generation: railroads, banks, heavy industry, stable currency and gilt-edged national credit abroad. Above all, there was peace, even though the army had dwindled to a clutch of mummified generals and the total protective force in the country was merely a handful of colorful *rurales*—a national constabulary created by his predecessor.

Díaz's rule was not pinned together by bayonets, but by ideas. Those ideas have been discredited with the passage of time and the success of the Revolution, aimed at overthrowing Díaz and all his works. Even in his day the doctrines conflicted with many earlier strands of the Mexican tradition, itself a skein of contradictions. Díaz and those who advised him were concerned primarily with two major issues: to preserve Mexico from further foreign aggressions and meddling (like the Intervention and Empire), and to make the nation great. The two were intertwined objectives in which international and domestic affairs were joined.

Porfirio Díaz and the men around him analyzed Mexico's problems in economic rather than in political or social terms. They sincerely believed that the salvation of Mexico, from the trauma of endemic

---

* He had prearranged his election.

civil war and foreign interventions, lay in making it solvent. This
was a necessary measure to break the vicious circle of degeneration.
Their views coincided with those of all the articulate Mexicans of
their time: Conciliation among factions, and peace, were essential.

For the first fifteen or twenty years of Porfirio Díaz' rule, his
regime was probably the most popular government that independent
Mexico had enjoyed to that time. Its strength was based on a conscious policy of reconciliation among divergent interests and factions.
By a sharp bit of political surgery (1876–1880) Díaz established his
supremacy. Thereafter he rarely resorted to what he called "spill-
ing a little bad blood to save all the good." Another version was "Join
us or die" (*Pan ó palo*). Francisco Bulnes, one of the Porfirian advisers, characterized the power system as one based on "the maximum of benevolence, a minimum of terror." Much of Díaz' power
was purely mythical.

Individual liberties, one of the Liberal legacies from the *Reforma,*
again were subordinated. These, as well as older vested interests, had
to be sacrificed to make Mexico a powerful and respected nation.
Liberty alone was not enough to preserve Mexico. Among the political advisers of Díaz the conviction grew that guarantees of a
political constitution had little meaning unless there was solid economic power to make them meaningful. Quite typical is one statement, "The day that we may say that the fundamental charter has
given us a million colonists, then we have encountered the constitution that really suits us; it will not be a phrase on the lips—it will
be a plow in the hands, a locomotive on the tracks, and money
everywhere." Liberty bred anarchism in Mexico, they said, so liberty was a luxury which Mexicans could not yet enjoy.

Emphasis, then, was to be economic, not political. The ideology of
the administration unconsciously combined many earlier strands of
Mexican political traditions. The limited nature of the state, whose
job was to provide peace and order, had been at the heart of the
Federalist credo. Díaz expressed it often. One of his slogans was
that under him there would be few politics, much administration
(*poca política, mucha administración*). Hapsburgs would have understood that formula, but Bourbons and Centralists too would have
applauded its motive—economic betterment of Mexico through private enterprise, protected but not aided by government.

Men around Díaz gave to the general Doctrine of Wealth, current in the United States and Europe, a local Mexican habitation

and a name: "scientificism." * Mexicans concocted a philosophy based on French Positivism to justify their actions. *Científicos* saw the future of Mexico dependent on the scientific allocation of scarce skills and scanty resources by an appointed élite, drawn exclusively from the "rational" (science-minded) and productive Mexicans. The middle class—between the rude Indian and the arrogant aristocrat—was to act as a trustee for the rest of the nation until the national economic plant, created by self-interested bourgeoisie, poured out goods and services. These, trickling downward, would make liberal democracy a possibility. To reach political democracy—never abandoned as an ultimate ideal—the active enterpriser was to be encouraged. On him the future rested.

In the *científico* scheme Mexico would go through a difficult transitional period. In it only a minority—"rational" and productive groups—could be favored. To squander slender fiscal resources on humanitarian and welfare programs among Indians and *mestizos*, who were characterized by Porfirians as being unscientific—fanatic and superstitious—seemed an obvious economic and political fallacy. They must wait.

Economic analyses convinced the *científicos* that within the Mexican nation there was little available liquid capital. It was insufficient to finance the rosy future they foresaw; obviously, therefore, most of the needed sums had to come from abroad. But in the 1880's, and later, Mexico was only one of several rival underdeveloped areas competing for such foreign investment. To attract capital and keep it from skittering off to more stable or financially more attractive areas (such as the Far East and Africa), Mexican returns on investment must be high. Further, the Mexican social situation had to remain relatively static; constant turmoil was no way to trap one elusive franc, pound sterling, or dollar. Their ultimate hope was that such foreign investment, pouring into Mexico, would mix with whatever small local capital there was available and create (by the multiplier principle) a constantly greater store of local funds. These in turn would then force out the more intrusive investment from abroad. After all, that was the way the United States rose to power. This general Mexican policy began to work out specifically in the railroad field, but in few others before the Revolution.

---

* Proponents of the doctrines were *científicos,* a name at first applied to a small group of young intellectuals who voiced the credo, then later applied widely to those who believed it.

One other main strand of Porfirian ideology is worth noting. Like all Mexican governments from the time of independence, the men around Díaz stressed Mexican nationalism. For economic and for social reasons, they proposed that all Mexicans be brought into the same psychological circle by indoctrinating them with the universal truths of science. Education was to be "neutral"—it should not impart religion or even controversial political doctrines. It was to be scientific and modern, utilitarian and civic. Under a limited national government, it became the duty of local units—towns and states—to provide schools modeled on the purposely few but advanced national ones of the capital. Federalism was still a potent word; it meant limited national government and states' rights.

As a social doctrine, the *científicos* resurrected both the Colonial and the Neo-Colonial traditions. The idea that "blood" somehow affected social capabilities (a basic premise of the sixteenth century) went through a world-revival at the end of the nineteenth; its Mexican adaptation was the theory that Indians and mixed breeds were a pretty hopeless and dangerous lot, doomed by biology to inferiority and wardship. Dictatorship of the creole, white bourgeoisie seemed destined to last until these unfortunate anachronisms could somehow be absorbed.

But money everywhere made up for lack of proper biological background. It was *prima facie* evidence of economic and social virility. The country that had millionaires was obviously endowed with virtues; Mexico wanted many. Fooled so long by intangible abstractions like liberty, justice, and the like—promised but never delivered—*científicos* claimed that the Mexican people needed roads, bridges, dams, buildings, and other such solid, visible achievements. Far from being out of step with their times, the Porfirian *científicos* were in the main streams of world opinion. Under Díaz the universal ethic of materialism, a common bond of the period everywhere in the western world, was a mixture of the Mexican past and new international viewpoints being developed in the late nineteenth century. The new dynamism of Positivism from France, and social Darwinism, basically English but widespread in the West, were engrafted on earlier Mexican traditions. Nearly all precluded government action in the social and economic spheres except to encourage the agents of Progress, the élite enterprisers. To indict the Porfirian Era on its manifest insensitivity to social woes is to reveal basic ignorance of contemporary trends throughout the world.

5. THE REVOLUTION, 1910–

As events soon showed, the shapers of the Porfirian traditions became victims of their own success. They also made a number of critical errors. Local Mexican capital did emerge as envisaged. But rather than pouring into productive activities, it tended to gravitate to the ancient symbol of prestige in any Iberian country—the land —where it was immobilized. The functioning economic system, financed by foreigners, was controlled from abroad. The presumably transitory system of strict control over lower-class populations of town and country hardened into a permanent feature. The "trickle theory" did not work out in practice. Great material benefits accrued to Mexico, but they did not soak downward to the masses. Rather, they were increasingly monopolized at the upper levels or drained off to alien shores.

When the early transitional phases of the Porfirian system began to pass their usefulness (around 1892) there was a rising pressure of criticism. As the middle class (that the *científicos* had hoped to evoke) actually began to appear, its members were closed off from most benefits they believed justly due them. An inflationary spiral complicated matters; rural and industrial wages were kept constant by custom and by force while prices moved steadily upward. Finally, in 1910, these contained pressures exploded in flamboyant fashion. That was the Mexican Revolution. It shook up society and regrouped the historically developed elements of the nation. The tremors thus initiated form the driving forces of Mexico since that time.

At the turn of the twentieth century, scattered bands of critics and analysts—collectively tagged as the Precursors—probed the Porfirian structure for these weaknesses and exposed them to the world. From this intellectual turmoil emerged a number of political programs whose aims were to reform and replace the going system. A small military revolt headed by Francisco I. Madero, an open critic of the domestic and foreign policies of the Díaz administration, succeeded in overthrowing Díaz in 1911, much to the surprise of nearly all concerned.

With the myth of the indispensable man temporarily exploded, Díaz was exiled to Europe and the Madero revolutionaries, joined by other factions, started a political house-cleaning. Before this had proceeded very far, however, the elements that had sustained the Díaz system rebounded to power by a counterrevolution, one that hoped to restore the *status quo ante*. In the episodes connected with this phase, Madero was murdered in 1912.

From that time until 1917, increasing chaos was the rule in Mexico. Autonomous guerrilla bands of revolutionaries joined to dislodge the usurpers of the Revolution of 1910 and ostensibly claimed to be restoring constitutional order to Mexico, while pushing various social reforms they believed to be essential. Combined efforts of these revolutionists, plus aid from Woodrow Wilson, eliminated the Neo-Porfirian clique. Revolutionary chieftains then split and fought each other for power and control of national destinies.

By 1917 one coalition, headed by Venustiano Carranza, managed to pacify the important central parts of the Republic around Mexico City permitting it to consolidate its political position. To justify and strengthen their military success, these political heirs of Madero rewrote Mexico's old Constitution of 1857, itself a product of dissent in mid-nineteenth century. The Mexican Constitution of 1917, which governs the country today, was thus a product of the Revolution. The epic or military phases of the Revolution, which started in 1910, drew to a slow close after 1917. President Carranza, nominal First Chief of the Revolution, was himself forced out in 1920 and his place taken by an oligarchy of successful military men, who formed a cartel to keep the peace.

From 1920 through 1933 the chief problems in Mexico were reconstruction and rehabilitation, especially of the political machinery. The old apparatus that had served Díaz not only was discredited, but had nearly been blotted out in the decade of civil wars. There was clear and apparent danger that Mexico might dissolve into its component regions, each of which displays many characteristics of a small nation. The hopes of social benefit and violent change for the common welfare were subordinated to the protection of a political unity against internal forces of dissolution.

The Revolution was still on the defensive. Men and institutions, around which further counterrevolutionary efforts could center, were by no means absent nor have they yet been wholly eliminated. During the epic phases, campaign promises had been made to agrarians, workmen, and other collective groups who had suffered under Díaz and had helped fight the Revolution. The fulfillment of them was deferred and postponed by Fabian political tactics, strong in words, weak in deeds. The contained and mounting pressures for real change burst forth anew in 1933, when a revolution within the

Revolution took command of policy. The promises came home to roost.

From 1933 through 1940, under President Lázaro Cárdenas, the Revolution of 1910 went through a renaissance, an aggressive epilogue. The resurgence shook structures of politics, economics, and social life to their very foundations. The military oligarchy that had ruled Mexico from 1920 was in its turn discredited and exiled, as Díaz and Carranza had been.

The coming of World War II and the problems of postwar readjustment have added still another chapter to the lengthening story of the Revolution, originally brewed by the Precursors under Díaz. Currently the Revolution has passed into another phase of stabilization, consolidation, and slow but orderly extension. There is a widely shared belief in Mexico that the earlier aggressive and combative phases provided the nation with appropriate revolutionary institutions. Now the problem is merely to operate them more effectively. This shift of emphasis and view is reflected in the name applied to the events since about 1940. Then the "Institutionalized Revolution" was ushered in; it was officially baptized as such in 1946.

A recent Mexican description of the Revolution sums up a great many current attitudes there. Even the overexaggerations are typical. The Revolution (writes Jesus Silva Herzog) is

a complex phenomenon, not a little mysterious, and above all, home-grown —that is the Mexican Revolution. Complex—because its roots reach into every field of sociology. Mysterious—because it constitutes a vital impulse toward the *future* which surges up spontaneously and almost intuitively despite the perils which have beset it, and it *continues*. Home-grown— because it came about without foreign influence of any kind, the result solely of the people's hunger—very American—hunger for justice, hunger for bread, hunger for land, and hunger for liberty.

This capsulizes the feelings of most Mexicans about their Revolution.

* * *

Thus Mexico has painfully inched its way over the centuries toward "modernity." Science, technology, democracy, nationalism— all the newer catchwords—have worked their way into the background and are now part of the Mexican tradition. Nearly any program or factional scheme finds historical justification in Mexico's past, so varied and so peculiarly Mexican has it been since Spaniards first joined it to the western world.

5. People

It is the people of Mexico as a whole who will determine its fate in the future. Their tastes, their mores, their health conditions, their levels of culture, their income, their capital, and their skills are all major determinants of what they can do with their natural resources to transform Mexico into the rich and happy nation towards which they are striving. The political and economic trends towards "decolonization" in Mexico have proceeded so far that the Mexicans are now determined to guide their own destinies and internal changes. Outsiders at best can do little more than suggest and aid, and, at worst, temporarily retard, movements towards goals which the Mexicans have set themselves. Who and what are the Mexicans?

Statistics are an admittedly poor substitute for meeting the Mexicans face to face and noting how delightfully they vary individually in size, shape, and personal talents. But figures do have some uses. They act as a lens through which we can examine hidden matters of some importance which even the most observant traveler cannot possibly see. The total size of the Mexican group, its rate of increase, and the numerical weights and movements of its component parts can scarcely be discovered without resort to quantitative materials, dull as they always are. These social trends vitally affect current and future developments, and they cannot be ignored. In a lighter vein, one can attempt the ancient game of summing up Mexican national traits on a subjective, impressionistic basis; unsatisfactory as that method is, it at least has the merit of emphasizing that Mexicans are people, not abstractions, and that however much they differ by class, race, and sectional habits there is an underlying unity to the way Mexicans behave in given situations.

The Mexican people never have formed and still do not constitute one homogeneous body. Historical influences shaping social and cultural landscapes have not had uniform results in all parts of the modern Republic, nor among the various strata of its society. The coming of the new has seldom if ever completely obliterated the old.

One of the perennially fascinating aspects of Mexican life is the coexistence of many traditions; they blend to produce a kaleidoscopic effect. Mexico City has most of the attributes of cosmopolitan and metropolitan centers like New York, Chicago, London, or Paris. But close by the technological laboratories where important work on atomic fission is being pushed forward by skilled Mexican scientists, one may still hear ancient Nahuatl—the speech of the Aztecs. Down the broad boulevards one may occasionally see an Indian carrier with an enormous burden on his back; he dogtrots through traffic sprinkled with Rolls-Royces, Buicks, and Fiats. The diversity of Mexican ways and peoples is an enormous asset to the nation and obviously an enormous challenge to those who hope to weave the multi-colored strands into a strong fabric of nationalism.

1. TRAITS

The important traits of Mexican character, as judged by themselves and by foreigners over the years, include a number of favorable sides, as well as some that evoke strong criticism. Both are "Mexican." Perhaps a noteworthy primary fact is that on a great number of matters Mexicans are ambivalent; they show two faces, and have at the same time two opposed views. Therefore, paradoxes are continuously appearing in their words and deeds. No one is certain *why* this occurs, but it is a basic and bewildering fact.

All courteous and well-intentioned foreigners find the Mexicans friendly and extremely responsive, ready to chat and strike up acquaintanceships—a far cry from the stiffness of the Chileans or the Argentines. At the same time there is a strong substratum of distrust and withdrawal from foreigners, which is likely to erupt into mass xenophobia. The Iberian tradition of attempted exclusiveness and the innumerable unfortunate historical experiences of the Mexicans perhaps help to account for this. However, Mexican defensive attitudes against foreigners and their criticisms mobilize quickly and often inhibit real discrimination between ignorant and self-seeking foreigners and others who with some understanding and sympathy offer requested critiques of Mexican ways. If asked, a foreigner is on safer ground to match the Mexican inquirer's politeness until he is sure the question is not a rhetorical one!

Despite poverty which has been endemic since the Stone Age the Mexicans have been a happy, though by no means carefree, people. In the face of harsh circumstances, geographical and historical, they have generally submitted and adjusted their lives accordingly. Broad currents of humor and a sense of the ridiculous permeate all strata of society. In the more intellectual circles these take the form of a mordant wit whose quick shafts are often devastating. The combination of a great tradition of graphic arts and this comic spirit have made Mexicans outstanding as cartoonists and caricaturists in Latin America.

Somewhat allied is a bent toward self-criticism, often in overexaggerated terms misunderstood by foreigners. The most vicious and overextended attacks on Mexicans and Mexican institutions come from local sources, not from abroad. On the one hand, then, Mexicans often take themselves and their doings overseriously; but rising like a bubbling spring is a refreshing tendency to treat everything as a huge cosmic joke, to be savored and then forgotten. For those who depend on literature to reflect local life, the double stream of reporting has proved baffling. On the one hand a great group of Mexican novelists have painted the Mexican people, especially the lower and disinherited classes, in somber terms. Another band of modern novelists—José Ruben Romero and Carlos Merino Fernández, for example—take an equally true but much lighter and happier view of the same situations. Fernández, in gently satirizing the foibles of life in a provincial area, states in a recent work, "I don't want to paint sad pictures nor ugly Indians who have suffered for centuries without hope of redemption. The town of Huehuetlan is happy; it takes as a joke all the ills done it by those who would try to make it a big place. . . . Tragedy is converted into a farce, and the romanticism of the actors, together with their tears, is turned into a grotesque buffoonery." *

Running in parallel channels to gaiety, humor, and wit is a deep morbid strain. This sadness or *tristeza* is attributable to both European and Indian backgrounds and manifests itself in innumerable facets of Mexican life. Melancholia underlies song and story. Death is not feared; it is a constant companion whose presence is taken as natural rather than shocking. The coexistence of melancholia and optimism seems unlikely, but one needs only to note as evidence the presence of crowds of *señoritas* dressed in mourning outfits of deep

* Carlos Merino Fernández, *Retablos de Huehuetlan* (Mexico, 1950).

black (believed to enhance beauty) at political rallies where politicians are cheered for optimistic statements about Mexico's future. Privately queried, the same speakers will often mutter direly.

Connected in obscure ways to pessimism and submission is a pattern of violence and relative indifference to personal suffering and cruelty to humans and animals. Callousness and violence are as much a part of the Mexican heritage as the strong Mexican emphasis on humanitarianism and an easy-going tolerance of individual and group diversity. Both the Spaniard and the Indian had in their background the necessity for recognizing that other people had different and perhaps equally good customs, and even today strange behavior, especially by an outsider, is shrugged off as "his custom." Cultural relativity does not have to be inculcated—it exists.

"Custom" is the sanction most often evoked in response to queries as to the origin and reason for particular practices in the Mexican countrysides. Memories of these things extend backward to unexpected distances which put the present in its true historical perspective. Lawsuits over land and village boundaries often hinge on establishing who occupied the disputed sites some 500 years ago; not infrequently pre-Columbian maps are hauled out of village archives to establish such a claim. In somewhat similar vein a group of Tlaxcalan Indians, whom the Spaniards resettled at Villa Alta in Oaxaca in the 1580's, recently announced that the government in Mexico City was not living up to promises made their ancestors and that therefore they were going "home"—back to their original village some 400 miles away. Time, it can be seen, seems an infinitely elastic commodity, in terms of centuries or even hours.

Contrary to the joke-makers, the Mexican assurances about immediacy are seldom couched in terms of *mañana*—tomorrow. More characteristic is the statement that anything desired will be done "less than right now" (*ahorita*). But that may turn out to be what the historian calls "the specious present"—an hour, a day, a month —depending on circumstances. In the Mexican view, time, like good wine, should be savored.

The insistence of Mexicans on legalism and tradition is another keynote of the national character. From Roman times in Spain and from the earliest recorded materials on Indian groups in Mexico, there was an emphasis, amounting almost to obsession, on law. Form rather than substance often was outstanding. During the colonial period insistence on legalizing every act has left so voluminous an array of written records that investigators are appalled at their very bulk. Indians were especially notable as litigants and were quick to exploit the possibilities of an infinitely ramified administrative-judicial system evolved by colonial Spaniards. The urge to bring every action into the framework of a universal law and the multiplicity of codes, to record, notarize, countersign, and annotate the growing packet of documents, has by no means disappeared. Mexicans call it *papeleo*—the mania for paper work. It, too, has ancient sanctification in age-long habit.

Both the colonial Spaniards and modern industrialists report the Mexicans eminently teachable and eager to learn. The area was and continues to be a vast reservoir of individual and group skills. There is also a powerful cultural sanction to change traditions and customs in the material phases of life. New techniques are adopted faster than new ideas. Though literacy is low, intelligence is high, and once utility can be demonstrated effectively, there is sometimes an overzealous shift to new ways of doing old tasks.

In the governmental sphere this tendency often has led to a distressing lack of continuity. In the popular realm the same proclivity stimulates "deculturation," a situation in which the old and reliable methods are given up and become extinguished before newer ones have been thoroughly tested. For instance, villages lose the knack of weaving by becoming dependent on machine-made cloth, only to find that the nearby mill goes bankrupt and can no longer supply them. This process is being accentuated under the impact of modern technology and industrialism, but again this is nothing new.

Perhaps part of the same complex is *proyectismo*. This is the drawing up of grand projects and then discussing and proclaiming their results before the ink is dry on the scheme. This tendency exists in nearly every modern society, but Mexicans have raised the substitution of blueprints for the finished edifice to a truly noble exercise in sleight of hand. But when this same imaginative flair is transferred to arts and letters, products without peer are likely to result, from the popular to the most sophisticated levels of creative activity.

One final paradox remains to be noted, though the list could be extended indefinitely. There are two equally strong, essentially antithetical strains in Mexican culture. One emphasizes individual efforts and the maximum development of each separate personality; the other lays its stress on collective effort and group responsibility. Mexican craftsmen or workmen usually attempt to endow their products with individual personalities of their own; often they rewire and otherwise change a machine to differentiate it from any other one and, as a final gesture, baptize it with a special name. They may also refuse to duplicate a piece already produced. Resistance to standardization, though, is but one facet of the total complex; in contrast, by A.D. 500 the ancient peoples of Teotihuacan were mass-producing votive figurines by clever molds. The real urge to maximize the potentialities of each individual and protect his rights is at constant war with equally strong pressures to follow group norms—family, locality, nation, or mass production.

Social Organizations. If one were to describe Mexican society in sociological and anthropological terms, one of the first features noted would be that it is strongly "male-oriented" and patriarchal. It is a man's world where virile qualities have highest prestige. To be *muy macho* is a requisite; it is a label of approval for outstanding achievements in the ancient provinces of love, war, and politics.* Generally reserved for the male is the important business of making a living, running politics, and dominating the cultural scene. Traditionally woman's place is in the home and in the Church. One of the reasons that Mexican politicians have been reluctant to extend suffrage to women is this general feeling that the sexes are created unequal, to which has been added the consideration that the female vote might be dominated by the Church. Since the Mexican Revolution some of these attitudes are slowly disappearing. Women now help to choose local officials and may hold minor elective and appointive offices, as well as have professional careers of their own.

The strong Mexican feeling of sex differentiation as a social force is reflected in a double standard of sexual morality. At lower levels of society this has been expressed in a somewhat casual attitude towards marriage. At the upper, there has been almost a cultural prerequisite that a man keep a mistress, as a sign of his manhood. Again the Iberian background and the Indian arrangements sanctioned these attitudes; sexual urges were considered a force to be recognized in overt fashion. Members of army units and their common-law wives and children make the headlines from time to time when a benevolent commander has mass marriages performed to convert existing consensual unions into legal ones. This general tolerance should not be viewed as license for orgies and promiscuity by stran-

---

* *Macho* is also applied to the male mule; *mula* is a euphemism for prostitute.

gers; in this explosive field of human relations local customs are numerous and rigidly enforced.

At least a quarter of the Mexican population is classified by census enumerators as living in "free union," while the remainder have been united by the Church, by the State, or by both. If one took seriously the constitutional prescription, that only couples united in civil ceremony are legally married, at least half the Mexican unions would be illegal, and their offspring illegitimate. The stability of family groups varies quite widely by region, by social class, as well as by place of residence. Mexican unions are rather prolific, but the high infant mortality keeps the average household group to less than seven persons. Most children are trained at home rather than by the more formal educational system which, though improving, is too small and frail to be considered a major socializng agency.

Attitudes underlying education in Mexico have always favored segregation of the sexes. Policy is based on the premise that "man and woman are profoundly different physically, intellectually, and morally . . . maternal education is desirable for both sexes up to the age of six years; but gradually, paternal education should predominate for boys. . . . It is urgent that at the proper time the father intervene to form the boy's character." Even at tender ages, males are given preference by society.

Girls are much more restricted in freedom than boys. With some justification, the Mexican father looks on any male outside the family group as a potential ravisher. The culture has adjusted accordingly. Contacts between the sexes come at fairly restricted intervals and places, the chief of which are at Church, in the movies, and at weekly promenades held in the village squares. In these latter colorful rites the girls promenade as a group around the village plaza in clockwise direction while the males as a group stroll by them on the outside in counter-clockwise fashion while the village band tootles vigorously for an hour or so. Conversation is held usually more with eyes than with lips; on a specially festive occasion older males may pepper their choices with confetti or flowers. Fiestas, too, are times when the rigid restrictions are lifted a shade or so.

The family is still a prime unit in Mexico. It includes more than the mother and father and minor children; in one family household three generations may be found living under the guidance and direction of the family head, often the grandfather. Although advice of the sons is sought, it is not necessarily heeded and in matters that touch the whole family's range of interests, the group of elders determine policy. With the double standard of morality in the background, marriages are often arranged for economic or political advantages. Generally these fall within the same social class. The Cinderella story of crossing class lines is not as often carried out in practice in Mexican society as it is in the United States, where the family unit is smaller and where the grown children become heads of their own families.

One important feature of Mexican family life which influences a number of larger groupings is the institution of *compadrazgo*. This is an extension of family bonds by choice rather than by biology. The *compadre* is a godparent; at baptism, at confirmation, and at other points in the life cycle, parents of a child select a new pair of godparents for it. The *compadres* are responsible for the child's upbringing if its natural parents die or become poverty-stricken; when they agree to sponsor a child before God they share a responsibility with its biological parents and become part of the family group. The "real" and the "fictitious" parents are now relatives—*compadres*—"co-parents." It is not unusual for close friends to stand as godparents for each other's children and thus doubly unite the families. In effect the adults choose the relatives they wish they might have had.

Compadres are often selected because of their higher social position and greater wealth; a powerful politician is likely to be godfather to hundreds of families in his area. That means they will cling to him and he to them as though they were united by bonds of blood. The relationship between *compadres* is often more stable and binding than that between blood brothers. The children are expected to obey their godparents with the same degree of veneration and respect as their own parents. This institution is found in most Catholic countries, but in Mexico the concept has received strength from pre-existing native practices.

The *compadre* system has been adapted to a variety of circumstances and local conditions, especially among Indian and semi-Indian groups. It helps to cement localisms. For instance, Zapotec Indians, who are great travelers and merchants, are likely to have their selected *compadres* scattered in the villages along their trade routes, to assure them of protection and of hospitality in their fixed rounds. *Compadrazgo* has accentuated nepotism in government. A successful political figure may be suddenly faced with requests from his *compadres* for their share of security in the form of jobs or favors. Obligations of this fundamental nature cannot be lightly brushed aside by appeals to abstract concepts of public morality.

The institution of *compadrazgo* reaches a high point in Mexico and there it is adapted to various social circumstances. In the face of recurrent natural and social disasters it has been a combined social security system and insurance policy. Many of the tasks that a "welfare state" is now expected to fulfill have for generations been carried on by these institutionalized family arrangements in Mexico. The closely linked group has stood ready to respond to all emergencies.

2. TRENDS

Population. Traditionally the growth of the Mexican nation has been slow, but a demographic revolution during the past fifty years is far-reaching in its implications. The size of the aboriginal population of 1519 which Cortés found would normally be a useful fixed base from which to compute the rise and fall of the historic populations, but to date no general agreement exists as to this figure. The choices have recently narrowed to the selection of a figure between 4,000,000 and 11,000,000 Indians. Investigators do agree, though, that the Mexican population in mid-sixteenth century, in 1565, was about 4,500,000 souls; nearly all these were Indians, with a handful of Spaniards, a sparse group of Negroes, plus a very few crossbreeds.

Demographically speaking, the colonial period was static and the net increases in total population were negligible. When eighteenth-century Mexican *savants* and Bourbon officials began to count heads in New Spain they found that in 1793 the number of people was still about 4,500,000, though the composition of the population had changed considerably. Under the stimulus of the Bourbon Renaissance (and more accurate tabulations) this scanty population had apparently increased to between 6,000,000 and 7,000,000 persons by the time Mexico had declared its independence of Spain in 1821. The turmoil of the nineteenth century slowed some of the Bourbon rhythms, so that in 1872, Juárez' Mexico, only about 8,000,000 to 9,000,000 inhabitants could be counted. Peace and prosperity under Díaz fostered upswings comparable to the late Bourbon days. In 1895, when the first official national census was taken, it enumerated

12,632,427 Mexicans; that of 1900 tabulated 13,607,272. During the nineteenth century the Mexican population had just about doubled, an average increase of about 70,000 per year.

The accelerated growth which had started under Díaz was stopped until the Revolution settled down in 1920. The population from 1900 through 1920 remained static. Then came the enormous increases which have concentrated in the past thirty years. They are continuing. From 1930 through 1940 Mexico's population increased 18.7 per cent (as compared with a 7.2 per cent gain in the United States); it grew from 16,500,000 to 19,600,000, or by 300,000 a year. Even more spectacular have been the jumps after 1940. The recently completed 1950 census set the present population at 25,-200,000; over the past decade it grew at the rate of 560,000 a year. In other words, more than the total population of the Hapsburg colonial realm has been added to the republic since the outbreak of World War II; there are some 5,600,000 new mouths to feed.

Most Mexicans are delighted with these babies. They have been the only real immigrants to Mexico. The blooming of the Mexican population has come about by natural increase, not by waves of migrating foreigners, like those who swelled the Argentine Republic and the United States. At no point in Mexican history (after the first rush of Spaniards in the sixteenth century) have Europeans or Asiatics entered Mexico in any significant numbers; their almost infinitesimal numerical weight has been counterbalanced by permanent emigration by Mexicans, also small.

The excess of births over deaths accounts almost completely for the demographic surges. Mexico's birthrate is among the highest in the world, with an average (1935–1940) of 43.8 births per thousand. To recent times the Mexican death rate has similarly been at the top of the world's list, with 23.6 deaths per thousand. But even so, this has given Mexico a plus margin. Much of the loss by death has come from infant mortality.* Welfare programs, health and agricultural improvements, and generally improved social conditions have begun to lower the death rate and to increase the birth rate. Since 1893, for instance, live births have increased by 50 per cent;

---

* Coefficients of infant mortality are calculated by a long formula. The Mexican coefficient is officially 122; more nearly true is 200. This can be compared with the United States (45); France (73); Holland (43); Chile (200); Spain (143); Italy (116); Ecuador (139). The lower the coefficient, the lower the infant mortality.

stillbirths have been decreasing. The general death rate has declined over the same span by about 3 per cent. Balancing all these demographic elements, it turns out that on a world scale Mexico again is very near the top in its rate of natural increase. Into the foreseeable future the nation will continue to grow at a phenomenal speed. More people are born, fewer die each year.

Mexican demographers are somewhat vague about the future. On a short-term basis they believe that in the second half of this century the Mexican population will again double, so that by the year 2000 there will be 50,000,000 Mexicans. Since, demographically speaking, the Republic is young and immature, a number also believe that rapid growth will continue to about the year 2050 before it will stabilize. No one is wholly certain what effects industrialization, urbanization, and education will have on birth rates; all these eventually seem to lower them.

Both the present and the future growth in the number of Mexicans poses serious and difficult problems. Infinite in number, they can be simplified to a single but twofold task: to bring up to par the present inadequate facilities for feeding, housing, and servicing the present population, while at the same time expanding institutions and services as fast as or faster than the new and larger generations appear. The Mexican people are much more fertile than the Mexican land. Governments can either try to decrease the population or increase the productivity of the soil, at present the most feasible course.

Ecologists, conservationists, and some social planners see a perilous situation shaping up in the expansion of the Mexican population. They argue that the people are already outrunning Mexican resources and that if growth is not curbed, Mexicans inevitably face a lowered standard of living and even worse disasters as their land gives out. The most widely known spokesman for this Neo-Malthusian hypothesis is William Vogt, whose *Road to Survival* is a generally compelling plea for conservation and whose widely read chapter on Mexico forecasts a gloomy prospect indeed.*

Nearly as persuasive are Mexican proponents of a much more optimistic counter-case. They view an expanded Mexican population as a constantly augmenting internal market for goods, a greater working force, and, in short, the requisite of a large and powerful Mexican nation. To divert the statistical attacks of the conservationists and ecologists, they point to the fact that now only half the arable

* Published by William Sloane Associates in 1948.

land is being used; they claim that with irrigation and other modern agricultural techniques—fertilizers, higher yield seeds, better planning—the land can support many more people, perhaps even greater numbers than the demographers now envisage.

In this clash of extreme views a glance at the following recent figures is illuminating. They indicate two things: Mexico is accelerating its food production and Mexicans are currently eating more and better than at any time for which we have figures. As a result of a tranquilized countryside, expanded credits, increased acreages, and the beginnings of technological improvement, food production, as well as its consumption, has outsprinted the phenomenal increases in population.

Statistics, for the moment, are on the side of the optimists rather than on the side of the Cassandras who have projected production figures representing the turbulent thirties and the war-cramped forties. In 1950 a Mexican family of five consumed at least 233 more pounds of staple food than in 1938. Further, it was nearly all grown in Mexico. The downward spiral that was correctly reflected in the pessimism so rampant in the mid-forties does not now exist. The trend has reversed. Only the barest start has been made toward mechanizing and otherwise improving Mexican agriculture, so that even these recent upward swings are but a foretaste of the future. No one at present can reliably predict the absolute future ceilings on Mexican agricultural output or its population.

The accompanying tabulation reveals the absolute increases in food production that have already occurred. It should give pause to those who proclaim Mexican agrarian programs an economic failure.

INCREASES IN SUBSISTENCE PRODUCTION
(Thousands of metric tons)

Items	1925–29 [a]	1940–44 [a]	1945 [b]	1950 [c]
Maize	1,960.7	2,067.1	2,186.2	3,122.0
Beans	169.6	167.0	161.7	251.0
Wheat	348.2	429.6	346.8	587.0
Rice	82.2	111.6	121.1	136.0
Totals	2,560.7	2,765.3	2,815.8	4,096.0

Sources: [a] Nathan L. Whetten, *Rural Mexico* (1948), Table 46; [b] *Anuario Estadístico, 1943–1945* (1950); [c] President Alemán, *V Informe, Sept. 1, 1951;* Report of Secretary of Agriculture, *Tiempo*, No. 456 (Jan. 26, 1951), pp. 36–38.

More important to the individual Mexican and his family than the global figures of national production is his share in it. Here, too, independently derived figures substantiate the statements above. The increased *per capita* shares and the augmented individual consumption go far to explain President Alemán's political success. In Mexico political turmoil seems to vary directly with the available amounts of these basic foodstuffs.

PER CAPITA PRODUCTION AND CONSUMPTION OF BASIC FOOD STUFFS, 1930–1950[a]

(In Kilograms per Person)[a]

	Production Share per Person[b]				Consumption[c]	
	1930	1940	1945	1950	1938	1948
Maize	118.7	110.5	93.2	124.0	89.9	117.9
Beans	10.3	8.2	6.9	9.3	5.5	8.7
Wheat	21.5	21.8	14.7	23.5	24.8	31.3
Rice	4.9	5.7	5.1	6.7	3.9	5.7
Potatoes					3.9	5.7
Totals	155.4	146.2	119.7	163.5	148.0	169.2

Sources: [a] Above table. One kilogram equals 2.2 lbs. Difference in maize probably represents animal consumption of grain. [b] Population from *Anuario Estadístico,* Census 1950, etc., as follows (in millions): 1930, 16.5; 1940, 19.6; 1945, 23.5; 1950, 25; [c] *Problemas agricolas e Industriales de Mexico,* II (No. 1, 1950), 43, Table 18.

As a final note on this critical controversy over Mexico's ability to support its expanding population, within the past decade Mexico has turned most of its deficits into surpluses. In a number of cases it is *exporting* items that it formerly *imported* to feed its people. Rice and beans are such items. Mexico has not quite reached the point of self-sufficiency in wheat, though it probably will in the 1952–1953 agricultural cycle. At the moment Mexicans feel it wiser to grow on their restricted lands crops of 30-cent cotton and purchase 12-cent wheat under special arrangements within the international wheat agreements.

Critics of modern Mexico discredit its achievements by overstressing Mexican import of its basic food, maize. Even during World War II these purchases were less than 5 per cent of needs. In 1949–1950, the nation met local demands for the commodity and divided the small surplus into exports and a locally held stockpile. Drought, hail, and grain speculation in 1950–1951 shortened the maize supply needed to feed Mexicans and led to the import of some 130,000 tons; this represented 4 per cent of Mexican maize consumption. Estimates for the 1951–1952 agricultural year foresee another surplus. Mother Mexico *is* feeding her children!

The increased food production of Mexico is even more remarkable than the above figures indicate for it has been achieved by a relatively dwindling number of producers. That is merely another way of saying that another demographic current, urbanization, has been adding to the number of mouths to be fed by those who remain behind on the land.

The Urban Revolution. A parallel movement to the increases of Mexican population has been the redistribution of the people by a sudden wave of urbanization. To 1900 there was hardly a modern city in the whole republic. Mexico City itself was small and sleepy; though the Federal District contained a shade over half a million souls the national capital still had the air of an overgrown village. Its nearest rival was provincial Guadalajara with about 100,000 people. These urban centers, as well as other regional capitals like Monterrey and Puebla, boomed with the increase in the number of Mexicans following 1920. The Federal District expanded from less than a million people in 1921 to a million and a quarter in 1930, then to nearly two millions in 1940; now (1950) it has an enumerated population of 3,053,588 in Mexico City and suburbs. Its size has tripled in a generation and has brought with it innumerable problems connected with rapid urbanization.

While Mexico City has been growing, it has been changing and modernizing. Its skyscrapers, modernistic architecture, and busy traffic seem to have small relation to its storied past or even to the rest of the republic. But at a less spectacular rate larger towns have blossomed into cities, and villages into towns. Such regional and local centers as Monterrey, Guadalajara, and Puebla, situated on main routes, have suddenly become metropolitan in their outlook and, to a great degree, in their appearance and influences.

Without major qualification it probably could be said that in 1900 Mexico was at least 90 per cent rural by almost any set of measures. In 1950 the picture is more complex. Lamentably, detailed figures exist only for 1940; from even that recent time much urbanization has been going on all over the republic. But even by 1940 the population had been significantly regrouped since the turn of the century. In 1940 about one-third (35.1 per cent) of the Mexicans lived in

URBANIZATION IN MEXICO, 1900–1950
(Thousands of people)

Year	Mexico City (excluding suburbs)	Guadalajara	Monterrey
1900	368.9	101.2	62.3
1910	471.1	119.5	78.5
1921	615.4	143.4	88.5
1930	1,029.1	179.6	132.6
1940	1,448.4	229.2	186.1
1950	2,233.7	378.4	331.8

Source: José E. Iturriaga, *La estructura social y cultural de México* (Mexico City, 1951), p. 89 (adapted).

towns and cities; a little better than half (54.7 per cent) dwelled in agriculturally inclined villages; the remainder, less than 10 per cent, were found in hamlets, isolated family-size farmsteads, and tiny Indian *ranchos*. Thus though the urban centers—cities and towns—accounted for less than 1 per cent of the total places inhabited, they contained a substantial proportion of the Mexican people. Nathan L. Whetten in his useful *Rural Mexico*, published in 1948, has provided refined data on rural-urban proportions in Mexico as of 1940. A brief excerpt from his findings is presented in tabular form in Appendix I, Table 5.

It emphasizes the salient fact that Mexico is still primarily and predominantly a land of small villages and the consideration that social problems in Mexico are fundamentally rural problems. But this work should also highlight the often overlooked fact that Mexico is not wholly rural. The urban group is ponderable in numbers, in influences, and in organized strength. Justifiably it demands a share in the running of the country. A sentimental agrarianism which would ruralize the whole of Mexico overlooks the existence of this group and the strong tides of urbanization which have been flowing and continue to run in the republic. Mexico is becoming less rural with each passing year.

These tides of demographic change—swelling of numbers and regrouping of people from farm to village to city—are silent revolutions of utmost significance. Already they have altered the culture and class structures, also one of the main targets of the historic social Revolution of 1910.

3. CULTURE, RACE, AND CLASS

Colonial Spaniards and Neo-Colonial Mexicans really believed that blood and ethnic background conditioned social traits. The modern popular mind has been reluctant to give up the neat but fallacious idea that Indians, mestizos, and whites are distinct, each group with its peculiar but recognizable physical and cultural "racial" characteristics. A vast accumulation of modern findings to the contrary have failed to dispel the old stereotypes. Glib generalizations, embellished with rhetorical flowers, still paint the Indian as dour, uncommunicative, resentful, and withdrawn. Mestizos—ethnic crosses between white and Indian—though usually pictured as shifty, unstable, opportunistic—are possibly a potential boon to the nation. Whites consistently appear as exploiters, the cultured but ruthless masters of Mexico. Not one of these characterizations is wholly true.

Race. As early as 1921 the Mexicans charged with taking the national census found that the shopworn categories of Indian, mestizo, and white were technically unsatisfactory. None could be defined with any amount of precision; further, they rested on dubious assumptions which made their practical validity for social planning extremely limited. Actual people didn't fit the presumed qualities attached to the terms.

More than a generation ago, anthropologists clearly demonstrated that Nature had preceded Man in democracy. Within the same general limits all human beings have about the same degree of learning capacity; the presumed superiority of one ethnic stock or breed is less a biological mandate to rule the rest than a greater opportunity to acquire the tastes and skills that modern culture has to offer. Further, the access to economic opportunities rather than skin color or ancestry helps determine how wide the door to cultural opportunities will swing. The dominance of white stocks and European values over so much of the earth was recognized to be a result of important but accidental cultural surges in that small European area rather than superior innate biological or intellectual potentialities; the reasons for early and widespread white control were summed up in a verse

> What ever happens, we have got
> The Maxim gun and they have not.

In short, scientific minds have moved steadily away from "racism" —the combined identification of social and ethnic traits. But almost simultaneously it was becoming the basis for mass social and political movements like those of Hitler and the Hispanicists of Latin America. The ethnic and biological classification of Mexicans into "Indian," "mestizo," and "white" is still of some interest to physical anthropologists, but for serious investigations of the Mexican social scene other terms must be used. The stratifications with which we are dealing are essentially cultural and social ones. Their correlation with racial ones are probably coincidental, if they exist at all.

The Two Worlds. Colonial Hapsburg social and political policies were based on the assumption that there were two distinct and separable worlds in Mexico, defined in terms of ancestry and culture, Indian and European. Passage from the one to the other was theoretically possible; even long before the end of the colonial period this simple dichotomy had in fact been broken down by the appearance of unexpected hybrids and new blood groups like the Negroes.

But the assumed basic division, undisturbed by these new elements, has carried down to the present. With the rather recent shift in ideas about race, cultural and economic status have not entirely replaced earlier racial ones; these linger. The "Indian" world is now generally equated to "rural and underprivileged," while the European or modern one is often implicitly defined as "urban, and probably overprivileged." Statistics do not entirely support this assumption, either.

Some major cultural and economic traits do seem to divide Mexico into these two great groups. Those with lower prestige, negligible cash incomes, and scanty material goods, are also those who cling to diets of maize, go barefoot or wear sandals (*huaraches*), sleep on the ground, in hammocks, or on cane beds; many speak native tongues and preserve their ancient costumes and village mores. This seems to be the Indian world of yesteryear.

The other group differs. It includes those with higher incomes and more material goods; they tend to prefer wheat breads, wear shoes, sleep in beds, and habitually and exclusively speak Spanish. Many of them are literate, and all use money. By most cultural and economic criteria they seem to be "modern," even to the point of having favorite television programs and movie idols.

Mexican and American sociologists who have examined these matters agree that the nation is thus divided almost evenly between those who have a standard of living about the same as that of the Indian in the colonial period and another half which is better endowed culturally and economically. This seems to bear out the contention that there are two worlds, now as then.

But one troublesome matter always comes to light. There is a group which does not fit into this broad scheme. It is composed of individuals and communities which are neither quite Indian nor wholly modern. They retain a strong impress of the Indian matrix, yet much of their life is carried on in modern contexts and is guided by a mixture of norms. Further, there is movement, both physical and social, from place to place and status to status. When an Indian learns Spanish, begins to wear shoes, dons modern dress, and goes to the movies every Saturday night, is he still an Indian?

The Third World. Mexico, after four centuries of interplay among groups is so mixed culturally, ethnically, and biologically that the old simple divisions no longer reflect the current social reality. Semantics lag behind the facts. Obviously now a large "transitional" population demands a sociological recognition not yet accorded it. The third world is a few cultural paces ahead of the true Indian world, and is still weakly and poorly connected with the "modern" one, into which it is merging. In speech, and, to a large degree, in dress and social outlook, it leans toward modernity, but in many daily habits and community usages it is strongly tinctured with Indianism.

The "transitional world" is a residual category. It is what is left when on the one side we isolate the recognizably Indian individuals, chiefly by speech, and on the other, the clearly "modern" people. Where the lines of division among Indian, transitional, and modern should fall is of course a highly subjective and controversial matter. But they exist. The "transitional world," then, is formed by Mexicans who are neither clearly "modern" but who can no longer really be tagged "Indian."

The accompanying tabulation is an imperfect effort to schematize some of the major cultural divisions among the present Mexican popu-

MAJOR MEXICAN GROUPS, 1940

Cultural Divisions	Persons (thousands)	Per Cent
The Indian World	2,945	15.0
The Transitional World	7,268	37.0
The Modern World	9,441	48.0
Total	19,654	100.0

Source: Appendix I, Table 8.

lation in very broad terms. Those who are interested in a numerical presentation of the subcategories of these three Mexican "worlds" to supplement the following discussion of them will find the data in Appendix I (Table 8).

Culturally speaking, there are three subsystems in Mexico which intermesh to form "the" system. Each has a pyramid shape, with numerous inner ramifications. If put on paper it might look something like the accompanying diagram:

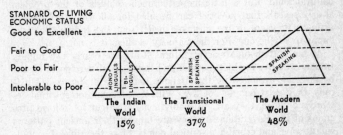

STANDARD OF LIVING
ECONOMIC STATUS
Good to Excellent
Fair to Good
Poor to Fair
Intolerable to Poor

MONO-LINGUALS
BI-LINGUALS
SPANISH SPEAKING
SPANISH SPEAKING

The Indian World 15%   The Transitional World 37%   The Modern World 48%

Generally speaking, the Indian world is small, shrinking, and impoverished. The "Transitional World" is twice as large, recruited from Indians rising in the scale of living, but it is constantly being drained off into the "Modern" sector. In both these living and social conditions runs a wide gamut of possibilities. Let us glance at each a moment.

The Indian World. The cultural and historical processes in Mexico since the Conquest have nearly liquidated the Indian, strictly and culturally defined. From the 100 per cent aboriginal groups found by Cortés, the number who speak only Indian languages and live much as did their forefathers represent a bare 7.5 per cent of the 1940 population; when to this scattered band is added another 1.5 million who use native languages, but share it with Spanish, we have the Indian world, 15 per cent of the Mexican people. There are no "pure" Indians left if we mean by that natives who live exactly as they did in 1500. Even the most primitive clusters use steel tools, guns, and other items which their original cultures lacked; all but an infinitesimal number are nominally Catholic and are often surprisingly conversant with ways of the modern universe. Even the pagan Lacandons (who number less than 200) will use aspirin, when they can get it, to supplement their ancient curing lore. At present no Indian group numbers even half a million. The largest of linguistic and cultural islands are those who speak various dialects of Nahuatl, the tongue of the Aztecs; only three Indian speech groups, apart from this one, contain more than 100,000.* From an administrator's point of view the assimilation of 1.5 million monolingual Indians into the national culture via language is not an insuperable task.

Many sincere and warm-hearted people raise objections to disturbing the Indian ways and attempting to force them into a new cultural mold. But a little more thorough analysis of the problem clearly reveals that no brief can be filed for allowing them to remain as they are in the mistaken belief that the Indian's lot is a happy or idyllic one. For the majority of them it is not.

At the bottom of Mexican cultural strata are nearly two million Indians who live in abject squalor and travel about barefoot. Plagued by diseases, exploited by their fellows and more modernized Mexicans, they exist but do not live. With no economic or spiritual resources or hope, they are justifiably a major target for reform programs of the Revolution. As they are taught, their ancient patterns will dissolve and crumble at critical points. Since they live at a mudsill level, cut off from the larger universe by a language barrier, nearly anything that is done for them is a net gain.

It would be an egregious error, however, to assume that all Indians live in such dire straits. More than a quarter of the monolingual Indians and half of those who retain their native languages and speak Spanish (bilinguals) range upward from a miserable but tolerable life to outright luxury. Just above the barefoot group are those who wear *huarches* but retain native costumes, in whole or part; numbering nearly half a million, they often have ranchos of their own or subsist in village communities that are generally inadequately supplied with elementary cultural equipment. More changed, and sometimes happier, are still another group of nearly equal size who have given up their native costumes for the characteristic peasant dress of rural workers—white pajama-like pants and blouses and straw hats; many now even wear overalls like the unskilled laborers of towns and cities. Except for their ignorance of Spanish they are Mexican; they are Indian only in language, and even that sometimes is shared.

Though they speak little or no Spanish, or at least habitually speak a native idiom, there are more than 100,000 Indians who live

* See Appendix I, Table 7.

better than the great majority of more culturally "modern" people. By clinging to their native costumes, but combining them with the use of shoes—a sign of affluence in Mexico—they really complicate the definition of an Indian. This advanced group, economically and socially speaking, own fertile lands, operate lucrative businesses, and often are the true chieftains of Indian areas. In many cases they exploit Indians and even Spanish-speaking peasants in worse fashion than any Mexican would dare; as a result of their political and economic importance, this Indian élite enjoys considerable influence in the towns and cities in or near their areas.

Much the same socially and economically are more than 150,000 individuals who speak Indian tongues habitually, but have a knowledge of Spanish and have forsaken native dress. Some are *rancheros* with good lands and hired labor, or holders of excellent nationalized land parcels, *ejidos*. They dress and often act like townsmen, and are Indian chiefly by speech alone. Their standard of living is far above the slum-bred Mexican urbanite who continues to condescend to these *indios*. The latter are near the top of their "world."

In a sense these interesting bilingual people are "immigrants." They or their fathers have recently come into a new cultural context and mastered most of its intricacies while still preserving some memories of the old way. Culturally still part Indian, socially they are lower middle class. They are on the threshold of a complete transition, accomplished when they and their children lose their native language. Perhaps now it can be seen why no one really familiar with Mexico likes to generalize very broadly about "the Indian." One of the persistent official myths, widely believed and still circulated by sentimentalists, is that Indians want to be left alone, that they resent attempts to alter their cultures. Usually it is the manner, not the matter, that they object to. In the realm of nonmaterial things change comes slower than in the material, demonstrable ones. Most Indian and semi-Indian groups are perfectly rational and are eager to borrow, even steal, techniques which are clearly better than their own. They object to the way in which non-Indians try to alter their lives; their feelings are comparable to the modern Mexican's attitudes toward similar efforts by the United States, but most Indian dialects lack a good word for "imperialism" to chasten the meddlers.

In general the experience of most professional workers in the field of Indian affairs is that natives want a greater rather than a lesser share in the benefits of modern living. Petitions filed at the regional Indian Congresses during 1937–1938, when concern for the Indian was in its heyday, are useful testimonials. When Indians were asked what they wanted they requested typewriters, electric lights, medicines, fountain pens, surveying instruments, sewing machines, pumps, and the allied technical gadgetry typical of modern life. One group, visited in 1943, wanted a helicopter and a juke box.

If the Indian is viewed as a man trying desperately to make a living for his family rather than as a symbol, programs for his improvement are likely to gain more ready acceptance among the people they are trying to help. In short, the "Indian Problem," because of its relatively small size and the scattered nature of the Indian groups, tends to merge easily and almost imperceptibly into the serious national problems of rural illiteracy, poverty, disease, and other social ills of the Mexican countrysides.

In fact, if one *must* generalize about Indians, the tendency of sentimentalists to lump them together and to plead for them as a special and heartrending case is perhaps more provocative of resentment than any other one factor. The Indian does not want to be a "special case," with its patronizing overtones of his presumed wardship and minority status. The oceans of rhetoric about "the Indian" create or intensify a division that at present really hardly exists. Professional Indianists often do more harm than good. Typical of the actual Indian attitudes toward his situation, as distinguished from what non-Indian urbanites think the Indian thinks, is a long letter published in May 1949 by the leaders of the Tarahumara Indians, a very small group in northern Mexico. In part they stated "we want more schools and more schoolmasters, native boarding schools which will accommodate not 200 but 1,000 children; a hygiene center which will guide us and aid us to combat illness; roads that will bring people honorably disposed to work, not parasites; . . . finally, we do not wish to be the objects of curiosity, but Mexicans useful to the nation."

The Transitional World. Language marks "Indians" off from the rest of the Mexicans. On this score, 92.5 per cent of the nation is "modern" and at a minimum 85 per cent of the Mexican population has no direct knowledge of the ancient tongues and dialects. This large segment habitually and exclusively speaks Spanish. But though many people have put some small distance—social or actual—between them and the native world where dialects clack, they have moved only a short way, measured in both cultural and material terms. Some have gained only the Spanish language; this they speak, but they still share many traits with their Indian colleagues of past and present and live at a roughly equivalent social and economic level. Unlike Indians (who are rural), transitional people are found both in towns and countrysides. Spanish now is the major language even in rural areas and there is no native group without someone who speaks it. It may be quaint but it is readily understandable by those with a fair command of rudimentary Spanish.

To give the transitional world a technical name, it is composed of "deculturated" Mexicans; they have lost numerous native ways but nothing has replaced them. The transitional group, by its nature, is disparate. It amounts to a little over 7 million people, 37 per cent of the 1940 population. Its common denominators are the use of the national language, and to some degree, underprivileged status. Strong influences both from the Indian backgrounds and from the modern one are visible. Some try to call it a "folk culture," a misleading label which emphasizes unity rather than its true heterogeneity. Even within one fairly sizable "folk community" in contemporary Mexico the degree of wealth, status, and extent of "modernization" has an extraordinarily large range among individuals and families.* In many cases the transitional world is the direct result of the Mexican Revolution, which cracked some of the older ways; in others various historical processes are responsible. In some areas and communities the mixture of old and new has resulted from the early Hispanicization by colonial authorities and subsequent isolation. All the transitional world speaks Spanish, is Roman Catholic, customarily eats maize rather than wheat, and looks to modern centers for many of its values and equipment, physical and cultural. It is the backbone of rural Mexico and is now flooding the cities.

Those who have put but small distance between themselves and the world where native dialects yet persist are many. Some 3.4 million of these transitional Mexicans still go barefoot, live in abject misery, and are distinguishable from the lower strata of the Indian world only by speech. When the bottom layers of the Indian and

---

* Oscar Lewis, *Life in a Mexican Village: Tepoztlán Restudied* (Urbana, Ill., 1952), summarizes and criticizes much recent material before presenting his own able findings on this community first investigated by Robert Redfield in 1926 (*Tepoztlán: A Mexican Village*, Chicago, 1930).

transitional spheres are summed, it is seen that almost six million Mexicans—from a quarter to a third of the population—hover just at the survival point. They are the "underdogs" whose economic and social redemption the Revolution has promised. In general they want food more than literacy. About half (47 per cent) of the transitional group is in this lamentable squalor.

A little over a million of these "transitional" Spanish-speakers still wear Indian costumes. They are relatively well off, though by no means rich. Some 1,051,000 combine their native dress with *huaraches,* while 83,000 use it with shoes. As a whole the subdivision of costumed, Spanish-speakers is composed of independent ranchers, merchants, political leaders, and a wide range of villagers whose originally Indian area was early brought into the Spanish colonial web and Europeanized. But for their language and slightly improved social and economic status they would still be Indians. To cover this group the term *Ladino*—"Latin"—has been borrowed or revived from the colonial past.

In some ways less psychologically and economically secure than those who prefer native costumes and often the life of their neighborhood and its *mores,* are a fairly mobile cluster of some three million transitional Mexicans who have given up Indian dress and who use *huaraches.* Most of them still eat maize tortillas and follow a highly secularized form of old customary behavior. This group includes the recently emigrated masses of unskilled labor in cities, and occasionally the small artisan or the marginal merchants, the lottery vendor or the man who has a tiny tray of cigarettes or candy on a slum street corner. In the rural areas the poorer *ejidatario,* the wage-worker or sharecropper on the few haciendas, the very small independent farmer, the traveling merchant, the mule driver, and a host of other picturesque types, can be lumped under this rubric. They are really not very class conscious, but as demographers say, their "social capillarity" is intense; they absorb new ways quickly. It doesn't take much to boost them into the "modern world." Despite their affinity, they resent the term "Indian" as a label.

The Modern World. Developments and stratifications in the sector of Mexican culture which habitually speaks Spanish, dresses in the modern fashion, and (however imperfectly) is aware of national and international trends, need not detain us long here. Most of this volume concerns them directly. They range in cultural equipment from the ignorant and squalid people pictured by Magdalena Mondragon's novel, *Some Day the Dream,** dwelling on the garbage dumps of Mexico City, to world figures like Jaime Torres Bodet, chairman and a spark plug of UNESCO. Estimates of the numbers falling into any one subcategory must be hazardous and subjective, since the fluid situation created by the Mexican Revolution has not yet taken final shape. Perhaps the single greatest bond among these disparate groups is their self-consciousness as "Mexicans" rather than their attachments to *patrias chicas,* local neighborhoods.

As part of the flux of modern Mexico, cultural and social lines are vague, and cultural mobility is the rule. This is in marked contrast to the rigid and static Hapsburg colonial social system, and to the less rigid but still immobile situation of Neo-Colonial days. Though it has not yet integrated and equalized all Mexicans, the Revolution has at least promoted movement and has succeeded in eliminating a number of the élite from the upper-class ranks, while slowly wiping out the various bottom strata by pushing them toward the "transitional" world. Combined with the demographic and urban revolutions has been an allied cultural revolution that has materially reshaped Mexican society in the past fifty years. It is reflected in revamped class structures. The two distinct ways of looking at Mexican society—by cultural groups and by social classes—are merely different aspects of the same thing: all Indians are not "lower class," nor are all "moderns" middle-class people.

The Classes. The doorman and the manager of your hotel in Mexico City are both "modern," culturally speaking. So too is the government official you see passing in a shiny Cadillac, as well as his wife's maid at home. By glancing at census figures which tabulate how many persons speak Spanish, wear shoes, sleep in regular beds, are literate, and eat wheat bread, probably all four of these Mexicans would qualify as modern; they would be thus statistically equal. But it is clear that socially, economically, and even politically, there are important differences among them. The sociological shorthand way of combining and noting the significant social and economic differences (as distinct from cultural ones) is to divide people into socio-economic classes.

The Mexican class system is simpler than its multitude of Mexican cultural strata. There is a tiny Mexican upper-class group, a small but growing middle class, and a huge mass of what Mexicans refer

* Magdalena Mondragon, *Some Day the Dream* (New York: The Dial Press, 1947).

to euphemistically as the "popular class." All the upper class and nearly all the middle class belong to the "modern world." It also contains a fair share of the "popular classes." Nearly all the "transitional" and the "Indian" worlds are made up solely of the "popular" class.

In Mexico, as elsewhere in the changing modern world, it is hard to define a class, and especially an upper class. It is now something that can be achieved; once upon a time the only way to get in was by birth. Status is based on possession of high prestige, but now derived from attainable position bestowed by political power, economic wealth, and sometimes intellectual talents. Abundant leisure, a high standard of living, and a general air of "refinement" are also usually present. Normally, pride in lineage and consciousness of who is "in" and who is "out" of the class are strong, but in Mexico the Revolution has damped down much talk of that, though some of the older families are still avid genealogists. Political conservatism, the tendency to look abroad for social and economic models, and incomes drawn from large investments, could be joined to these other items to complete a profile of the upper class. Recruits come from rising middle-class families; occasionally a successful Indian leader, like Juan Amaro, rises up into this stratosphere. It is a very small group, probably composed of no more than from 10,000 to 30,000 individuals in contemporary Mexico, though this is but a guess. No one has ever counted this group, which now includes a handful of large property owners, industrialists, large merchants, private bankers, successful national politicians, and large-scale entrepreneurs. In Mexico, as elsewhere, "upper class" is a shadowy matter.

Lines between the middle and the upper class are thin. Mainly the middle class is defined by its economic dependence on personal work which requires education, technical training, or administrative abilities, equipment the individual has developed for himself. Middle-class or "white-collar" standards of living ape the upper class on a little lower scale. A middle-class trait is the urge to keep up the appearances of gentility and to observe proper social forms, even at considerable economic sacrifice. Traditionally the components of the class have been bureaucrats, teachers, small businessmen, storekeepers, skilled laborers, small industrialists, intellectuals, and members of the professions. In Mexico, recruits to the middle class have come from above and below. Dispossessed *hacendados* and their sons, social victims of radical agrarianism, drop a notch or so, for instance, as do displaced politicians whose influence and income wane when their faction drops from official favor. The expanding business and government bureaucracy, the industrialization and the constant upgrading of labor, the agrarian programs building individual yeoman-size units, the urbanization, and the developing system of technical and higher education, all create routes by which the members of the "popular class" and their children can move up the scale.

Mexican social and political systems are now based on the "popular class," which in any other society would be called an outright "lower class." Like their counterparts all over the globe, these various Mexican groups fall below minimum standards in education, living quarters, furnishings, clothes, diets, even recreational pursuits. Most if not all are manual laborers, dependent on their hands and backs rather than their minds for livelihoods, sweated out in drudgery. Their low economic skills bring them small cash incomes, with the subsequent marginal standards of living. As one consequence, the group as a whole is subject to more disease, higher death rates (especially infant mortality), than the middle or upper classes. Illiteracy and poverty are closely allied conditions of the lower-class Mexican, whether in town or country, whether Indian, transitional, or "modern."

EVOLUTION OF CLASS STRUCTURE, 1895–1940

(Thousands of persons)

	1895		1940	
	Number	*Per Cent*	*Number*	*Per Cent*
Upper classes	183.0	1.44	205.6	1.05
Middle classes	989.8	7.78	3,119.0	15.87
Popular classes	11,525.5	90.78	16,329.0	83.08
Total	12,698.3	100.00	19,653.6	100.00

Source: José E. Iturriaga, *La estructura social y cultural de México*, Table 6, p. 28 (adapted).

Although "class struggle" and "classes" are some of the most frequently encountered words in Mexican social writing, not until 1951 had a Mexican seriously investigated the modern social structure of his country and tried to quantify his results.* José E. Iturriaga's pioneer synthesis concluded that the Revolution had altered Mexi-

* *José E. Iturriaga, La estructura social y cultural de México* (Fondo de Cultura Economica, Mexico, 1951).

co's class structure by reducing the number of upper-class people
and the "popular" classes as well, while expanding the middle class;
he predicts that when the Census of 1950 is published, it will be
found that from 20 per cent to 25 per cent of the Mexicans will be
found to be "middle class." In simplified form his major conclusions
were tabulated in the preceding table.

Before the appearance of Iturriaga's excellent work, the following
tabulation was independently compiled in an effort to answer the
same general questions. It joins the analysis of the cultural worlds
sketched above with a similar attempt to delimit the number of
people in the main Mexican classes. Supported in the main by Iturriaga's findings, it outlines the main elements of Mexican social life.
They are all being affected by the Revolution, a continued driving
force moving 25 million Mexicans.

CLASSES AND SUBCLASSES, 1940

(Thousands of persons)

| | Cultural Divisions | | | Total | |
Class Divisions	Indian	Transitional	Modern	Number	Per Cent Total Population
Popular Classes					
Survival level or below	1,868	3,365	750	5,983	30.0
Impoverished	810	3,820	4,754 *	9,384	48.0
Total	2,678	7,185	5,504	15,367	78.0
Middle-Upper Classes					
Marginal, mobile	159	...	2,377	2,536	13.0
Stable Middle Class	108	83	1,000 †	1,191	6.1
Semi-leisure Class	...	...	500	500	2.5
Leisure Class	...	...	60	60	0.4
Total	267	83	3,937	4,287	22.0
Totals	2,945	7,268	9,441	19,654	100.0

* Estimated ⅔ of "marginal."
† Estimated ⅔ of "comfortably equipped."
Source: Appendix I, Table 8, rearranged.

* * *

Mexican society contains a mass of contradictory attitudes and
social institutions which condition its development. There are urban
groups and rural groups whose ways differ considerably; there are

important sex differentiations, and class mores, and strong regional traditions to make generalizations about the Mexican people extremely hazardous. Moreover, currents of change since the late nineteenth century have been operating at an uneven tempo and intensity to reshape many of these. Broader trends can be understood and signalized in terms of statistics, but only in part. The Mexican is an elusive figure who escapes subjective description and the strait jacket of figures. Collectively he is the most important resource of Mexico.

6. Many Mexicos

The interplay of history, geography, economics, and cultures has carved Mexico into a congeries of units. Often they have no clear political delimitations but nonetheless they play a critical part in the life of the Republic as a whole. Of these several types of non-political units it is useful here to select the two in which a variety of Mexican developments have combined and characteristically expressed themselves. One is the *patria chica;* the other is Mexican regionalism.

1. LOCALISM AND REGIONALISM

To a Mexican his *patria chica* is the little area where he and his family feel psychologically at home and among friends. Outside it he is a stranger in a puzzling world. The Spanish words mean "little homeland." The allegiance to its ways has historically outweighed any such attachment that people might feel to the largest unit, the nation. Contrasted with the *patria chica,* the national unit is nearly always called "the Republic" (*La República*). One is near and concrete; the other is remote and abstract. Like the Republic, the *patria chica* is really an abstraction, but its physical boundaries are much less distinct. Its extent is set by emotion and local customs rather than by formal and agreed lines of political demarcation. The *patria chica,* one of the smallest meaningful territorial units to which Mexican loyalties attach themselves, can be compared in size and nature to the rural "neighborhood": one either "belongs" or is forever a "stranger," a "newcomer."

The *patria chica* almost defies definition. It is, in general, a group of individuals, families, or even villages who have unconsciously formed a territorial unit to which they feel bound sentimentally; within it they will coöperate among themselves in a great variety of matters, usually guided by a strong common local tradition. In all except formal political apparatus they form a little nation, which may be no larger than one mountain basin, a range of hills, or parts of a state. They often overlap state boundaries, even language provinces.

Strong loyalties to a state itself are sometimes considered evidence that it is a *patria chica*. Often that is true. Tlaxcala, for instance, is a Mexican state whose boundaries very closely approximate the pre-Columbian unit governed by Tlaxcalan Indians, preserved by the Spanish in the colonial period and given political recognition after Independence. Other states, like Oaxaca, have numerous *patrias chicas*. In the Republic as a whole there are literally hundreds of them. Localism, particularism, thus takes on a name, the *patria chica*. It preserves the old ways.

Another important grouping of sentiments and tradition within Mexican territorial bounds is the region. It is a larger unit than any *patria chica;* it contains many of them. In it the bonds among its members are less numerous, more tenuous, but in given circumstances most of them will respond characteristically; they feel a certain consciousness of kind, which approaches nationalism. Where the *patria chica* carves up political units like states into subdivisions, the region combines them into a larger unity that falls short of covering the whole Republic. Regional loyalties are powerful social and political forces.

In Mexico a fairly long range of criteria combine to delimit the main regions, but the principal one is psychological. The people within any one of these regions feel they are different from those living elsewhere in the Republic. Specifically they usually base this feeling on the distinct qualities of their habitat and their peculiar geographical problems. Then, too, the pre-Columbian usages and organizations act as dividing or integrating elements. To these are added the way the colonial governments administered the area for three hundred years; how Europeanized it became under their sway or later; how land tenure operates; how well it is endowed with modern economic apparatus.

Most important, though, is what a region's people propose or hope to do. The diverse combinations of geography and history have thus created for each region a distinct *ethos*—its spirit, its subconscious outlook, and its set of attitudes. These guide the regional decisions and help determine the role it will play in national development.

In Mexico, because of its geographical structure and its long and troubled history, there is still an important residue of sectionalism or regionalism, and its persistence makes the integration of Mexico a difficult task. The political problem as well as the cultural, economic, or any other, is to devise a formula which will link the various sections harmoniously together into a functional whole.

Each of the main regions in Mexico can be compared to a small Latin-American republic. The most important of these regions we can call the Core; except in area it is roughly comparable in structure and problems to the whole Argentine Republic. Divided from the Core by mountains and volcanoes lies the Mexican South; it is equal in area, outlook, and problems to the South American republic of Ecuador. Between the Core and the Pacific has developed the Mexican West; in many respects its arrangements parallel those of Uruguay. The vast reaches between the Core and the United States border form an ill-defined unit we call the North; its developments strongly resemble those of Venezuela, to which it is also quite similar in area and aspiration.

These analogies, of course, cannot be pushed too far. The four main Mexican regions are not independent; they must somehow work together as a unit. But the existence of such unlike areas, each with basic characteristics of an autonomous republic, highlights a recurring Mexican problem. It is comparable to the task which would be involved in trying to fuse Argentina, Ecuador, Uruguay, and Venezuela into one harmonious workable combination. In Latin America only Brazil has a regional difficulty whose magnitude and nature approach and surpass the Mexican one.

The regions of Mexico are the living reminder that varied and complex forces have been at work through centuries to set Mexicans off from one another. Only the torrential force of the Revolution has been able to sweep aside some of the physical and psychological barriers and endow the inhabitants of Mexico with "Mexicanism." The statistical indices on which the present regions have been determined appear in Appendix I, Tables 2, 3, and 4.

2. THE CORE REGION

Its lengthy tradition of hegemony is the chief characteristic of the Core. From the time of Tepexpan Man to the present it has contained half the people of Mexico; quantitative data from the sixteenth

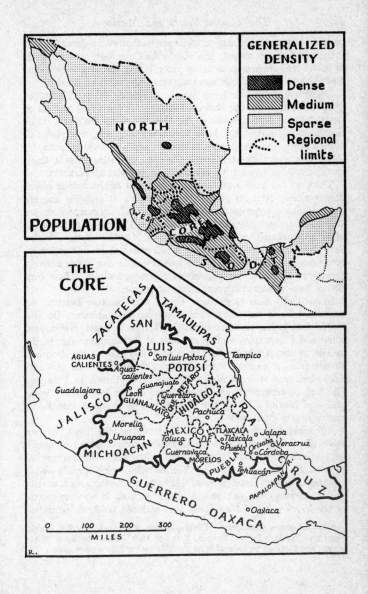

GENERALIZED
DENSITY

Dense
Medium
Sparse
Regional
limits

NORTH

POPULATION

WEST

CORE

SOUTH

THE
CORE

ZACATECAS
TAMAULIPAS
SAN
LUIS
POTOSI

AGUAS
CALIENTES
Aguas-
calientes

San Luis Potosi

Tampico

Guanajuato
Querétaro

VERA

Guadalajara

JALISCO

León
GUANAJUATO

Querétaro
HIDALGO
Pachuca

Morelia

MEXICO
Toluca
D.F.

TLAXCALA
Tlaxcala

Jalapa
Orizaba
Veracruz
Córdoba

Uruapan

MICHOACAN

Cuernavaca
MORELOS

Puebla

CRUZ

Tehuacán

PUEBLA

PAPALOAPAN R.

GUERRERO
OAXACA

Oaxaca

0   100   200   300
MILES

R.

century support archaeological evidence to that effect. Areas around it have waxed and waned, and within the Core itself various shifts of power and prestige have taken place, but in the long view it has traditionally been and continues to remain the heart of Mexico.

Definition of the area leans heavily on history. As used here, the Core region includes the Federal District (Mexico City) and all or parts of eleven central states on the Mesa.* Around the single major metropolis, Mexico City, have been integrated the chief colonial mining areas, an agricultural hinterland, and an industrial nucleus; these have been connected to the Gulf and the Atlantic by a single corridor split at Orizaba to join again at the port of Veracruz.

The Core has been made up of the series of linked *patrias chicas* arising mainly from its geographical structure. It occupies roughly the southeast quarter of the high Mesa Central. Its components are a series of inter-mountain basins and valleys, each of which tends to be a closed unit; with the exception of Morelos, all these basins have their floors above 5000 feet, which places them in *tierra templada* or *tierra fría*. Thus they are free of disease and have relatively propitious conditions for permanent tillage agriculture. These conditions have attracted concentrations of people.

In pre-Columbian times these basins were "culture hearths" on which developed the outstanding aboriginal high cultures. On this native foundation the Europeans built their colonial civilization. They added important mining interests at the northern edge in the middle of the sixteenth century. Under impulses of the Bourbon Renaissance, a nascent industrialism was sponsored in the corridor that runs from Mexico City to Puebla, thence to Veracruz. The web of commercial activity centered in Seville (Spain); Veracruz and Mexico City served to integrate the colonial core as an economic and social unit.

Administrative continuity also characterizes the Core, despite shifts of power from one group to another over a period of nearly six hundred years. The Spaniards built their administrative capital of Mexico City on the ruins of Tenochtitlán, which already had a continuous history from at least 1325. As a colonial administrative center, Mexico City performed a triple function: It was the capital of the Viceroyalty of New Spain that included far-flung dependen-

* Aguascalientes, Guanajuato, Hidalgo, Mexico, Michoacan, Morelos, Puebla, Queretaro, San Luis Potosí, Tlaxcala, Veracruz. Only part of the latter (port) counts, but it cannot be isolated from statistics gathered on a state basis.

cies in the Pacific and the Atlantic; it was also the coördinator of the two major realms and several minor units (including the area of the present United States and Central America) on the mainland and in the area which is now the Republic of Mexico; finally, it was the local regional capital of one of these realms, the Realm (*Reyno*) of Mexico.

The dividing line between the Realm of Mexico and other parts of what is now Mexico ran from around Tampico to San Luis Potosí thence southward through Michoacan to the Pacific. The southern boundary of the Reyno was the Isthmus of Tehuantepec. The Realm was geographically (but not administratively) bisected by the transverse line of volcanoes and mountains which set its capital apart from the southern portion of the single Realm of Mexico. The basins within easy access of Mexico City were the major colonial provinces: Mexico, Puebla, Michoacan, and Tlaxcala. Under the Bourbons, some of these older divisions were regrouped into smaller units, *intendencias,* which provided the outlines for the modern Mexican states. Mexico, Puebla, Tlaxcala, Guanajuato, San Luis Potosí, Veracruz, and Valladolid (Morelia) each became an *intendancy,* with its own government. During the nineteenth century the Federal District and the minor states surrounding it were carved from the old Intendancy of Mexico (with the metropolis as its capital).

The drama of Mexican history has always unrolled most vividly on the Core. This long sequence of peoples, cultures, and governments has left many legacies. On the one hand it has always been the most "modern"; on the other, vestiges of the past live on because of their deep roots. In touch with European and world trends, the novelties of the larger universe in terms of ideas and things have usually made their appearance in the Core first and then gradually diffused to other areas. Ripples of change work outward from the only real metropolis.

It is here that modernism is more than a veneer. It is an integral part of a substantial portion of the population. A glance at the statistical tables will indicate that in the matter of modern apparatus like telephones, railways, use of electric energy, and a host of other items not easily quantified, the Core stands preëminent. More than a quarter of its population live in urban areas where change is intense. Even those in rural sections are within relatively short distance of urban influences. The high density of its population is adequate evidence of this. People live in touch with one another.

The upper class and the ruling class (not always synonymous) customarily take up residence in one of the urban centers of the Core, the capital, if possible. Mexico City has always been great, but continues to grow. The general sensitivity of these urbanites to cultural, economic, and political currents outside Mexico has always been an active agency in changing the *mores* of the Core. To it also have flocked the foreigners, both as residents and more recently as waves of tourists. In short, most of the formulas for change and modernism, as well as the instruments by which they can be achieved, are concentrated in the Core, and especially in Mexico City. The net of communications linking the basin capitals with the metropolis provides the avenues and channels by which they reach a large number of the Mexican population rapidly and constantly.

Paradoxical as it may seem, the Core is also one of the major areas of ancient Indian tradition. In isolated groups on mountain tops, in hidden valleys, on haciendas, and even in the suburbs of the larger towns, these older ways obtrude themselves in the form of speech, dress, and a myriad daily habits. The largest groups of modern Indians who retain their language and customs are spread throughout the Core in fragmentary fashion. At the edges of the Core dwell vital, smaller, unlike Indian groups. In the border state of Michoacan, for instance, active and progressive Tarascans have reacted to modernism since 1550 in a fashion completely opposite to others nearer Mexico City. Though retaining many of their earlier ways, Tarascans often if not usually speak Spanish (in addition to their several subdialects) and are an economically active group. They are one of the ancient groups of Mexico, whose tongue has given us most of the old places names in Michoacan. At present there are probably not more than about 40,000 Tarascans.

The Core also has a large share of "transitional" people, those somewhere between "Indian" and "modern." Both as urban and rural proletariat they now generate challenging social problems. Caste, class, and social lines are relatively flexible so that social and geographical mobility of peoples in the Core is a common characteristic. Often this means that both the most active and intelligent villagers as well as the most inept of them are likely to drift to the nearby cities and ultimately to the capital. The one emigrates to improve economic and social status, the other merely swells the rootless dwellers of Mexico's slums, a feature of the city since the sixteenth century. The capital has been and is a great magnet for all strata of society.

Apart from its mushrooming metropolis, the Core has remained relatively static. Part of the explanation for its comparatively slow growth lies in the increasing importance of other booming regions, like the North, which has attracted internal Mexican immigration for half a century. Another and perhaps more important explanation is the small amount of cropland within the Core. It is a mature, crowded area. But despite the slow growth of the Core, the salient fact remains that better than half the population of Mexico is contained in it. Yet it represents only one-sixth of the total area of the Republic. It is rich in people, poor in land and space.

As might be expected, its land tenure systems are rooted in the dim past. By the late sixteenth century and early seventeenth century large colonial Spanish subsistence haciendas dotted the area. Interspersed among them were native and *mestizo* landholding villages and towns. This situation underwent no major change until the middle nineteenth century. During the *Reforma*, many of the landholding villages lost their possessions to *rancheros* and *hacendados* under the *Ley Lerdo*. An added strain on scant resources made its appearance in the late nineteenth century, when several parts of the Core were used to produce commercial export crops like sugar. This led to further land grabs from village units. Agrarian unrest, therefore, became explosive. Violent land reform, an ideal of the Revolution, was first identified with Emiliano Zapata from Morelos, on the edge of the Core.

The agrarian reforms of the Revolution have gone furthest in the Core. In the state of Morelos itself nearly 85 per cent of the cropland has passed into the revolutionary *ejido* programs (whose complexities will be touched on later). In the region as a whole, old *latifundia* holdings have been almost completely liquidated, both as an economic and a social force. Traditional strife and competition for land within the Core has been between the large hacienda and the landholding village. Foreign owners always formed a relatively minor proportion of the landholders in this area. Since before 1910 and continuing currently, agrarian reform has been one of the major needs and wishes of the Core.

It is not strange to find that the Core has a long history of industrialization. The region has dense populations, large urban groupings, and accessibility to water power. With a reservoir of capital and available markets, with craftsmen of the high native cultures near at hand, Puebla and Mexico City even in colonial times were minor industrial centers. Textile manufacturing and light industries, fostered by the Bourbons, tended to center especially around Puebla and Orizaba, where waterfalls and raw materials coincide. It was in this section that the French and other foreign entrepreneurs helped to establish industrialism in the nineteenth century. These industrial activities were aided by the unfolding of the rail net from Mexico southward, completed almost a generation before comparable development in other parts of Mexico. The industrial workers of the Core were among the first to chafe under political and social restrictions of the Díaz regime. It became a center for early revolutionary activity growing out of the series of bitter and bloody labor clashes.

Mexico City and its nearby dependencies form the single largest industrial aggregate in Mexico. It outranks the vaunted Northern industry by several fold. The prospects for continued and successful industrialization of the region probably could be rated good to excellent, although there are serious bottlenecks which will be discussed in detail later.

With these various elements focused in this one region it can be seen rather easily why it has always been the heart of the country. Its political influence has been paramount, and from the early colonial period onward military and political control of Mexico City has constituted effective domination over the whole. Capture of the capital is tantamount to capture of the whole country. Even if the connections with its dependencies should break down and the peripheral sections drop off or be captured, it has meant a crippling but not fatal excision so long as the city is intact.

Conversely, the breakdown or disappearance of the political apparatus centered in Mexico City has always brought confusion and created chaos throughout the Republic. The Core cannot be governed from afar, and it has no real rival. The crux of much of the historical political instability in Mexico as a whole is that Mexico City and its well-developed political mechanisms have been used for its own regional end rather than for national ends. It has tended to be a regional capital rather than a national capital. The long history of Mexico has already illustrated that.

To sum up, the Core has a peculiar *ethos*. With its mixture of modernism and primitivism, with its wider horizons, with its concentrations of wealth and power within fairly limited space, its inhabitants often confuse their own regional interests with the total national interest. Since historians reared in the Core have written most of the national histories, and its various other writers have explored major Mexican economic and social themes, the point of view of the Core has received widespread and permanent recognition. They usually tag regional aspirations of the sections far from it as "intrusive" or "disturbing." Whether Centralist or Federalist, dwellers on the Core have shared the supposition that what is best for Mexico City and the groups in its immediate hinterlands is automatically best for the whole nation. The result, of course, has been to build up anxiety and resentment in other regions, each fearful of the political, economic, and cultural "imperialism" of the Core.

Traditionally the Core and its people have been much more strongly linked to Europe and the United States than to its own marginal Mexican regions. The result has been that "foreign imperialism" has been aided and reinforced by groups in the Core who want to make changes in the rest of the Republic. The identification of "foreign" with "metropolitan" has been close. Other regions have some difficulty in distinguishing between home-grown imperialisms of the capital and those originating outside the country, but transmitted through this central apparatus.

In very broad terms it can be said that no political stability is possible in Mexico unless the governing system takes into account the divergences in interest between the metropolis—a hydrocephalic unit in which more than 10 per cent of the total population are concentrated—the Core region, and the remainder of the country. Fortunately the present administration, headed by President Miguel Alemán, is quite conscious of the explosive regional problem. Somewhat apologetically he told an enthusiastic audience in the south not long ago (1950), "We always speak a little lightly of the Mexican nationality. One must now comprehend that in many regions of the Republic, and particularly in its Center, we are a little selfish. We do not always give proper account to the isolation and problems of the regions apart." One of the main doctrines of recent regimes has been to adjust their programs to such regional needs rather than to clamp down a Core-centered view on the whole Republic.

3. MARGINAL MEXICOS

By a process of substituting a part for the whole, poets often achieve striking results. Speaking of a "sail" when they mean the whole vessel, their shorthand is usually intelligible. But in social investigations, this sort of metonymy is dangerous. Too often foreigners and Mexicans alike have identified the national scene and national interest with the Core area just described. But nearly half the people in Mexico live *outside* the Core.

They are divided, however, by distances and outlook into three distinct parts, each of which is broken into smaller subdivisions. On rare occasions they have all combined to control the destinies of Mexico, usually under the Federalist label. In power, they have often been as shortsighted as the groups which they have temporarily displaced. Historically they have been uniformly unsuccessful in their attempts to provincialize and ruralize the Core. More often, however, they fail to agree on any common program, so disparate are their interests and backgrounds.

* * *

The South. The area which we have here called the "South" is slightly larger in area and population than the Andean South American country of Ecuador, which it resembles in many ways. Southern Mexico is Indian Mexico. Unlike the Core, it has no one regional metropolis to focus its activities; its main centers are widely scattered. In fact, the South is really three or even four subregions whose common bonds are their indigenous base and their difficult problems.

One such subarea is formed by the state of Oaxaca and a part of the state of Veracruz. As a unit it lies just south of the Mesa Central, delimited at the north by mountains and at the other end by the Isthmus of Tehuantepec. Then beyond the Isthmus the Chiapas Highland and its fringes form another subunit. A third definable little cluster of *patrias chicas* lies on the Peninsula of Yucatan; it is separated from the mainland at the Chiapas and Veracruz areas by thick belts of impassable tropical vegetation. Conditions in the state of Guerrero very nearly approximate those in the other parts of the South, so it has been included here as a very minor subunit.*

The geographical base of the South influences its main problems. The Valley of Oaxaca, largest of the subregions, is in many respects similar to one of the several basin settlements in the Core. The chief

---

* The modern units included in the South are Campeche, Chiapas, Guerrero, Oaxaca, Quintana Roo, Tabasco, and Yucatan. Parts of Michoacan approximate conditions of the South.

difference is that Oaxaca is isolated from all nearby centers like it. It is separated alike from the main port at Veracruz and from its southern colleagues of Chiapas and Yucatan by mountains and by long stretches of barren and almost impenetrable territory. Chiapas has always been a marginal province, incompletely explored; sometimes it has been more closely connected to Guatemala than to Mexico, and occasionally parts of it have been in dispute between them. The peninsula of Yucatan forms a clear geographical unit, but politics and culture have subdivided it into several small entities. It is a low, level, limestone plain, which is capable of supporting a population of any size only on its extreme northern and western parts.

There has been no particular tradition of political unity to bind the South together. In pre-Columbian times the high cultures of Oaxaca—Zapoteco and Mixteco, for example—differed in many important respects from both the tribes of the Mesa Central and from the Maya groups further south. In colonial days the state of Oaxaca was nominally part of the Realm of Mexico, which centered in Mexico City. Its local regional center was Antequera, now Oaxaca City. This was the meeting point for several unlike indigenous cultures. Chiapas, for much of its colonial life, was directed by a subordinate to the viceroy, a captain-general at Guatemala City. Nearly autonomous was the province of Yucatan, whose governor and lesser captain-general was always given a wide measure of local administrative latitude. For the Hapsburg colonial world, the South produced very little of major economic importance to the Empire, and was usually considered a deficit area, necessary to hold but not very valuable. In the eighteenth century, cochineal for dyestuffs was perhaps the main export item from the South.

It was in the South, too, that the *encomienda* system took deep root. The small creole society depended to a great extent upon Indian tributes for their livelihood. Long after *encomiendas* disappeared elsewhere, a special dispensation prolonged their life in Yucatan until 1785. The loss of colonial markets after independence hit the South particularly hard, and it was not until after midcentury that other mainstays began to emerge. In Yucatan, henequen, a fiber important for binding twine, began to be exported in increasing quantities and became the leading nonmetallic export of Mexico in the late nineteenth century. Some mining and commercial activity kept Oaxaca alive, especially after railroads entered the area in the late nineteenth century. The local rail net of Yucatan was not connected into the national roads of the mainland until 1950. It can be said that the South has always been administratively and politically divided since aboriginal days, a culturally and economically heterogeneous area.

The Indian base of the South has been both a unifying and a dividing element. From the central administrative point of view, problems facing Indian areas are much alike, regardless of the particular tribes involved. The bewildering number of the latter persisting in the South is a constant source of amazement; they remain a tangle of ethnic mysteries which still baffle investigators. There are perhaps forty Indian dialects and subdialects spoken in Oaxaca alone, and in Chiapas almost every village in the highlands not only retains its native tongue, but also preserves its characteristic costume. The Maya of Yucatan and Chiapas remain a ponderable numerical group, split into subtribes.

Southern Mexico, with these pervasive indigenous ways, is also intensely rural. The urbanites are a conscious minority in the small cities of Oaxaca, San Cristobal Las Casas and Tuxtla Gutiérrez (capital of the state of Chiapas), Campeche, and Mérida. Only Mérida has significant contacts with the outside world. Due in part to the international nature of the henequen trade, for which it is the Mexican center, its cosmopolitanism has earlier backgrounds.

The pattern of settlement varies by these subregions, but in general it is somewhat similar for all of them. The landholding village has been the basic unit, and remains so. Local native tradition often prescribes that Indians and Indian-like *mestizos* hold their lands in common; equally often custom provides for private individual ownership. Haciendas have always been of relatively minor importance on the mainland part of the South, as opposed to the peninsula of Yucatan.

On the mainland there have been some few colonial subsistence haciendas centered at fertile places in occasional broad valleys, but by and large these have been small and somewhat unimportant localized phenomena. In the nineteenth century, under Díaz, several large grants were made to foreign concessionaires for production of tropical crops and tobacco in the state of Oaxaca; the scandals arising from exploitation of labor in the Valle Nacional were uncovered by muckrakers in the early years of the twentieth century and did much to shake the prestige of the Díaz regime, as did similar exposés of conditions in Yucatan. In parallel fashion there have been important commercial hacienda enterprises based on coffee-growing in parts of the state of Chiapas; these were often in German hands.

But the typical pattern for Southern settlement is a series of rather small Indian towns surrounding a main market center such as Oaxaca. In turn each of these smaller towns has its own still smaller satellite villages and ranchos. Milpa rather than tillage agriculture is usual. Since so much of the South is low, it falls heir to the difficulties of tropical life and agriculture at their worst.

Agrarian unrest, as it is understood in the Core, is relatively absent in the South. Disputes over land are much more likely to be intervillage squabbles than to involve haciendas. Village land feuds sometimes date from pre-Conquest times. Most villagers can obtain some land from neighbors by rental or by other peaceful means. The general tendency in the area is for each village to be as self-subsistent as possible; normally each will raise a small money crop to meet the purchases of few but essential manufactured goods such as axes and machetes.

Although overwhelmingly Indian and agricultural, the South has never fully endorsed the Revolution's *ejido* programs. Less than a third of the agriculturists of the whole South are included in them. This number is largely concentrated in the *ejido* programs of Guerrero and in the collectivized henequen fields of Yucatan. The markedly Indian and mezti-Indio states of Oaxaca and Chiapas are not particularly enthusiastic about agrarian reform as proclaimed from the Core.

Each of the subareas composing the South has a vigorous local culture. Within each of the states are numerous *patrias chicas* of varying size. Often these are portions of an ancient tribal unit. Characteristically, however, linguistic and ethnic bonds among Indians are less strong than might at first be suspected. Several neighboring villages of the same stock have engaged in bitter feuds that inhibit very effective coöperation. For example, when it was decided to make military battalions from the Indians of the Sierra de Juárez, a *patria chica* containing Zapotecs and Chinantecs, Army officials found it impossible to group tribal units together. Each of the two battalions finally formed was a mixture of Chinantec and Zapotec Indians from alternating villages along the range of hills.

It can be seen readily that with its widely scattered and unintegrated rural populations, with small urbanization, with lack of adequate transportation and market facilities, and with only a minor tradition of industrialization, the South does not especially look forward to rivaling Pittsburgh or even other parts of Mexico in the race toward industrialization. In the national market the South should probably be heavily discounted as an immediate large outlet for Mexican-produced consumer goods. They still make their own, by hand. As yet, neither the tastes for industrial products, the outlets for their distribution, nor plans for changing this situation, are very far advanced.*

The role of the South in modern Mexico is likely to remain locally agricultural. Here much can be and is being done. Another and important resource of the South is its archaeological treasures and its scenic and cultural panoramas. Now that trunk highways and railways are completed from the Core to the South, it can look forward to an increasing invasion by Mexican and foreign tourists. It should get a large and increasing share of tourism.

In summary it may be said that the Indian problem of Mexico centers in the South and is shared in some degree by the Core. Unlike the latter, where modernism is dominant and where it overshadows the Indian, the Indian ways in the South will perhaps continue to prevail for many generations. These may be altered in detail and a blend of the new with the old can, if properly handled, produce satisfactions for the Indians and the nation alike. The scattered and dispersed nature of these small and unlike populations makes their integration into the Mexican nationality (as it is being defined elsewhere) an expensive task in terms of patience, talents, money. Indians have survived many attempts to regenerate them and will continue to do so.

The West. Conditions in the West contrast strongly with those of the South. If South Mexico can be compared to Ecuador, the West turns out to be very similar to Uruguay. Their area, total population, density, and fundamental traditions are much alike. But the basic differences are profound: Uruguay is an important Atlantic South American republic; the West of Mexico is a national section which faces a barren Pacific across which flows little commerce.

The West of Mexico, however, only narrowly missed becoming a republic in its own right. It has the dubious distinction of being one of the two colonial Audiencia jurisdictions which did not serve later

* The exceedingly important Papaloapan River Project is here considered an extension of the Core, although it embraces part of Oaxaca; see below, pp. 382–386.

as the basis of a modern Latin-American republic.* The forces that elsewhere created republics around Audiencias have operated to give the West a local tradition that falls just short of true nationalism.

The Audiencia at Guadalajara was stabilized in 1560. To almost the end of colonial days its executive governor-general administered a separate Mexican division, the Realm of New Galicia, composed of administrative subdivisions: Jalisco, or Nueva Galicia proper; Zacatecas; and Colima. In the later sixteenth and seventeenth centuries, as the Spanish frontier moved northward, the newly acquired areas were placed under the Audiencia of Guadalajara rather than Mexico City. Nominally the colonial officials of Guadalajara controlled an area as far north as the present state of New Mexico in the United States. As an administrative, commercial, and cultural center, Guadalajara has remained the Metropolis of the West, rich in traditions and pretty señoritas.

One factor of extreme importance has conditioned the development of cultures in the western area. This was the absence of large-scale, concentrated, and deeply rooted Indian groups such as those found in the Core or the South. In 1565, according to the somewhat over-liberal calculations of two American investigators (Cook and Simpson in 1948), there were only about 200,000 Indians in the Realm of New Galicia as compared with the 4.2 millions in the Realm of Mexico (areas that we have called the Core and the South, exclusive of Yucatan). Archaeology confirms the fact that the West was settled rather late by pre-Columbian groups who remained few and scattered.

The absence of Indians in the West accounts for many differences between it and other regions. It is Un-Indian Mexico. The West has culturally been a "White Man's Country." Late-sixteenth-century Iberian traditions took direct hold there without being filtered and changed by a long contact with native ones. Even the Spanish spoken in the West reflects this; it contains many archaisms and only relatively few words borrowed from Indian tongues. The *encomienda* was never a prime issue there. The interests of the Church and the settlers were nearly always identical.

---

* The other was at Cuzco in southern Peru, established late (1787) to shield the natives against exploitation by their own Indian governors. It was merely a judicial tribunal and it had no great political significance. Here the West includes the states of Colima, Jalisco, Nayarit and Zacatecas. Again, the western part of Michoacan is more like the West than the Core, but statistically has been included in the latter.

The region has continued to cherish its Catholic faith and culture based on it. The physical stock of the West is also predominantly European, without native admixtures. Westerners resemble the northern Spanish people—tall, well-built, often with blue eyes. Apparently the basic physical type was not visibly affected by the remnants of small native groups and the occasional intermarriage with Negroes imported into the area during the late colonial period. The West was never really conscious of the Indian or much concerned with him, in contrast to the Core or the South where natives have posed continuous problems.

The geographical base of the West is a single wide basin around Guadalajara. It is similar to the other intermont basins of the Central Mesa except that it is lower and larger. On its eastern extremity lies part of the *Bajío*, known as Mexico's granary because of the fertility of the soil. Control over the *Bajío* is often a point of issue between political authorities of Guadalajara and rivals in Mexico City; it is one of the few areas in Mexico which can regularly produce surplus food for export to urban centers. There were parallel jurisdictional disputes between the Core and the West over Zacatecas and its mineral resources.

The hinterland of Guadalajara is limited on the west by deeply eroded areas (known as the *barranca* country) between the basin floor and the western mountain ranges. On the Pacific coast itself, Guadalajara's outlet to the sea is a choice between San Blas in Nayarit and Manzanillo in Colima, neither a first-rate port. Each port has resented rather than favored the western metropolis' attempt to dominate it, and has invoked aid from Mexico to check "imperialism" by merchants and officials of Guadalajara. Two of the burning political questions in Mexico throughout the nineteenth century were whether Colima should have greater autonomy and if Nayarit should become a separate state in its own right. The political leaders of the Core encouraged these local disputes to cut down the size of their rivals at Guadalajara. As a reward for its services to the Revolution, Nayarit achieved statehood in 1917.

Both the geography and the history of the first colonizations of the West combined to produce settlements and land tenure that differ sharply from those of the Core and the South. In general this pattern is represented by a group of small to medium-sized towns (a reflection of the Iberian urban tradition), a few large landholdings, and a multitude of smaller haciendas and farm-size plots run by *rancheros.* In this sense, the *ranchero* is a yeoman proprietor rather than an incipient *latifundista.** Again the agrarian strife in the West has seldom been between landholding villages and *hacendados,* but rather between individual *rancheros* and their fellows. On nearly all rural holdings the social differences between owner and worker groups were not comparable to the wide gaps between the Indian peon and his elevated *patrón* of the Core.

The usual land measure in the West was a 4428 acre *sitio.* Few colonial landowners owned or controlled more than two or three of them at best. Such ranges were used for pasturage of stock—principally sheep, cattle, and horses—and for a variety of small agricultural pursuits. Fixed early and still customary in the West is a tradition of land rental and private ownership of these small colonial holdings. Their size was reduced and their number increased during the nineteenth century by their division among several heirs. In 1879 the estimated number of proprietors in the rural population of the West was approximately 10 per cent; by 1928 it was 25 per cent. In 1909 there were 99,539 holdings worth less than 1000 pesos and 162,851 valued at from 1000 to 250,000 pesos. This means that there was a large rural middle class, with few large owners, and even fewer landless.

A sort of "natural agrarianism" has been characteristic of the area. Custom in the West has prescribed equal inheritances among the heirs. In large families this has meant fractioning originally small landholdings into lesser and lesser parcels. At the same time there has been no particular cultural inhibition against selling family land to erstwhile renters. These practices contrast sharply with the customary usages of the Core, where (during much of its history) primogeniture and entail kept large blocks of property in a single family; it passed intact in the same group from one generation to another, and sometimes was combined with other large holdings by cross-marriages. In the conservative West the mere threat of radical *agrarismo,* as expounded by the reformers of the Core, has often been sufficient to accelerate the long-established tendency to break up larger holdings and sell them to renters. With some of these elements in the background it is relatively easy to see why the Cárdenas col-

* *Latifundia* is a large landholding, part of which often lies idle; the land system of *latifundia* usually means that very few families monopolize land ownership. *Latifundista* is a large landowner, a member of the landlord group of large holders.

lective *ejido* programs made rather small appeal in the modern West. As *Cristeros,* many westerners sprang to arms in open resistance against "radicalism" from The Core.

Guadalajara, capital of the West, boasts almost a century of minor industrial tradition. It is now expanding into a major interest. As early as 1850 a local bank with half a million pesos' capital was established there to finance agriculture and industry; in the same year some signs of the changing ways of the area were the appearance of the first Socialist periodical in Mexico (*El Socialista*) and one of its first modern strikes. Local workmen in a *rebozo* factory had refused to take a cut in wages during the depression following the war with the United States and established a sort of primitive picket line to keep out scabs; some 400 workers were involved. Even then a few skilled hands were earning more than two pesos a day. But until the last decade industrialism in the West has been a small show.

With an agricultural hinterland capable of mechanization, a fairly mobile population, with no insurmountable barriers to weaving the whole together by a transportation net, there is no reason to think that the prospects for the industrialization of the West can be rated less than from fair to good. This is especially true of light industries producing for the national market. Since 1939 the West has been more firmly tied to the Core by the opening of highways. Under active construction are direct trunk lines from Guadalajara to Nogales and other connections in the United States. In November 1950 it was announced that the private Bank of America made a loan of $15,000,000 to Mexico, $9,000,000 of which will go to finish the Guadalajara-Nogales road.

The *ethos* of the West could probably be characterized as mildly conservative, Catholic, and nationalist. Emphasis falls on the historic Iberian elements of Mexico's heritage rather than looking to the Indian or even to Europe. The West is profoundly creole. Without major barriers to "modernization" it is being woven rather readily into modern Mexican nationalism based on the middle-of-the-road and tolerant approaches so studiously cultivated by national political administrations over the past decade.

The North. Many adjectives can be used to describe the North. It is large, thirsty, active, new, and above all, unique. If the South and the West of Mexico can be equated in structure and problems respectively to Ecuador and Uruguay, it may be said that the North of Mexico most closely resembles the republic of Venezuela. The North has about the same area, density, and similiar problems arising from seminomadic Indians, pastoral conditions, and then a great influx of foreign investments in the late nineteenth century, especially in extractive industries controlled from abroad. Though in both instances the areas were known and even occupied in colonial times, they became of greater importance only in the eighteenth century, under the Bourbons. One of the outstanding features of the North of Mexico is that it has always been a frontier area. Its traditions are strongly interwoven with those of the southwestern United States, which until a century ago formed part of the North of Mexico.

Speaking very generally, one may say that the North of Mexico is the area between 22° North latitude and the United States–Mexico Border. In terms of Mexican geography, that means the area above a line running from Tampico on the Gulf of Mexico to San Luis Potosí, Zacatecas, and thence to the Pacific Ocean. The region contains seven large states, the Peninsula of Lower California, and should also include the northern parts of the states of Zacatecas and San Luis Potosí.* Taken together these several political units occupy more area than all the other Mexican regions combined. As a whole, the population density of the area is very low, but this is misleading. Much of North Mexico is outright desert. People cluster in the valleys of the eastern and western mountain ranges where there is water, and more recently they have flocked along the Border.

There is historical justification for nearly any subdivision of the North. Its jurisdictions were ephemeral during the colonial period, since few people lived there. For most purposes all the North was within the jurisdiction of the Audiencia of Guadalajara.

When strategic and economic possibilities of the North drew eighteenth-century Spanish Bourbon attention to that area, they made an effort to give it some coherent administrative form and even a certain internal unity, primarily military. The whole North was a sort of proconsulate.

In 1776 these northern states were called the Internal Provinces

---

* For statistical purposes the North has been defined here to include Baja California N, Baja California S, Coahuila, Chihuahua, Durango, Nuevo Leon, Sinaloa, Sonora, and Tamaulipas. The statistical areas and the "real" regions do not always coincide.

and put under a commandant-general, responsible directly to the King of Spain, and independent of the Viceroy at Mexico City. The capital of the area was first in Sonora, but later it moved to Chihuahua. From that time until about 1812, the area was subdivided and redivided and its erstwhile autonomy was lost; vigorous protests by the Viceroy in Mexico City brought it back under the sway of the Core. One of the important regional aspirations of the Bourbon Renaissance period was to possess its own independent Audiencia, comparable to that of Guadalajara and Mexico. It consistently sought more control over its own destinies, although as a frontier zone it was economically a deficit area, dependent upon Mexico City for troops and funds, and Guadalajara for justice and directives. But consistently these urges were balked in Mexico City.

One of the conditioning factors throughout the history of the North, extending down even to the days of Díaz, was the warlike nature of its Indian populations. Comanches, Apaches, Mescaleros— these are but a few of the many roaming tribes that harassed white settlements from the early sixteenth century. Most of them were small roving bands of wild hunters. The Aztecs and the Spanish colonial period knew them as "Chichimecs," or just plain "Indios bárbaros"; their raids on small communities on both sides of the modern international boundary between Mexico and the United States long constituted an irritating international problem. They never formed a docile labor supply, nor yet a firm indigenous base on which to build modern cultures. The chief preoccupation of the colonial Core was (so far as the North was concerned) to keep the Chichimecs from raiding down to the important Hispano-creole mining and agricultural establishments of the Mesa. The Jesuit missionaries were dispatched to this forlorn area but they had indifferent success.

Cattle-raising and agriculture formed a large part of the northern tradition. Mining and manufacturing were added later, in the middle and late nineteenth century. In colonial times northern crops included some wheat and cotton for "export" to other parts of New Spain, especially to the textile areas of the Core and the mining regions on its northern edge. Literally thousands, perhaps even millions, of wild cattle roamed the area, ancestors of the famous Texas Longhorns. Their value lay in their hides. Northerners raised horses and it is here that the Mexican cowboy, the *charro*, was evolved as a type. His skills and vocabulary describing his work diffused north of the Rio Grande to become part of the heritage of the United States.

The North evolved as a frontier area. With land suitable only for scrubby cattle and without resident Indian populations, it is not surprising that the characteristic land tenure of the North has been the huge hacienda. Collateral has been the growth of a *ranchero* group. These *ranchos* of the North tend merely to be smaller haciendas. In the old days rather than count their landholdings in thousands of acres, they were often reckoned in hundreds of thousands. Most of these enormous grants were seemingly useless lands, unless irrigated. Water rather than land is the critical commodity in the North.

Many of the older haciendas (dating usually from the eighteenth century) were veritable fortresses, more functional and unadorned than the fancier holdings in the Core. Again, historic tensions over land have been less between the hacienda and the Indian village than among *hacendados* and *rancheros;* the classic conflicts between agriculturists and the pastoral groups have also made their appearance in the North of Mexico. The general tone of the area has been unremittingly middle-class and socially mobile, without great extremes of social class.

The nineteenth century witnessed important changes in the North. One was a series of unsuccessful local attempts to convert the North as a whole into a separate political republic. More lasting was the influx of foreign capital to exploit the enormous mineral riches of the mountain chains on each side of the Mesa. As part of a general movement of enterprise and the western expansion of railroads in the United States, northern Mexico after mid-century became the scene of American projects to endow it with rail transportation. At about the same time, a number of the older haciendas turned to raising commercial crops, such as cotton, on irrigated land; attempts were even under way to mechanize its regional agriculture. The great bulk of foreign capital in northern Mexico came from the United States; Great Britain, France, Spain, and Germany more or less confined their activities to the Core and the South.

Both as individual adventurers and promoters, and as the advance agents of large corporations, Americans swarmed through northern Mexico in the latter part of the nineteenth century. Around 1900 it was estimated that the Greene Consolidated Copper had a capital of $7,500,000 invested in Mexico; Phelps-Dodge had more than $2,000,-

000, and a number of other smaller firms had as much as $1,000,000 apiece. As a natural corollary to this mining activity, foreign-built metal foundries began to appear in the North, located principally in Monterrey. The sudden opening up of the North of Mexico to foreign and local capitalists in the late nineteenth century is comparable to the expansion of the American West during the same period.

On this expansionist wave, some of the older balances within the section were disturbed. Monterrey, rather than Saltillo, moved towards leadership of the regional economic and political interests. Its spokesman under the Díaz regime was Bernardo Reyes. As early as 1850 the city of Monterrey and the state of Nuevo Leon (currently attempting to be Mexico's center of industry) had taken impressive steps towards industrialization. There were, in 1850, about 5,000,000 pesos invested in industry, a fifth of which were located in this one city. A vigorous state government reorganized the local fiscal system and took steps towards alleviating debt peonage.

These modest beginnings of industrialism were continued during the nineteenth century, especially after railroads linked Monterrey to the Core. Highways have followed in the twentieth century. The North is the fastest-growing region of Mexico. The growth in northern Mexico has met a similar expansion southward from the United States. There have come into being in this area, long inhabited by wild Indians, new tensions and peculiar social problems.

Northernmost border towns of Mexico are much more Americanized than they are Mexicanized. Some of the more sordid features of both cultures are distressingly blatant. The peculiar Border mixture of lower-class Mexican and North American ways is sometimes called *pochismo*. Neither wholly Mexican and by no means American, the *pochos* are marginal men, representatives neither of Mexico nor of the United States.

North Mexico has always been something of a melting pot. Its early settlers came chiefly from northern Spain in the eighteenth century. New additions have been made to its ethnic stock as new labor supplies were needed. Orientals were imported during the nineteenth century to work in the mines and on the railroads. To its industrial centers, Mexican emigrants from all other sections of the Republic have come. With the exception of minor islands of Indians like the Yaqui and the Tarahumara, the scanty aboriginal biological stock has been absorbed or extirpated. In much the same way, a cultural group evolved in the North, made up of many diverse elements. Most of them are "recent" as history is measured in Mexico. In more than just a geographical sense, the North is a transitional zone between the technologically based society of the United States and the older Hispano-Indian culture of the Core of Mexico.

In short, the North of Mexico is peopled by true heirs of the Bourbon Renaissance. With regional stress on utility, knowledge, industry, and science, the North has little or no historical memory of the Hapsburg colonial period or its knotty problems. Church hierarchy, *encomiendas, corregidores,* and the other complex features of the colonial matrix of southern Mexico, had no real roots and no cultural meaning for this vast northern section. As a cattle, mining, and missionary frontier its traditions are of a different order, in kind and in degree. Among the first and most persistent of these is exploitation by the Core.

It is not strange to learn that one of the fathers of early Federalism in Mexico came from the North. He was Dr. Miguel Ramos de Arizpe, and he gave permanent form to many of the aspirations of the North. His 1812 report to the Cortes in Spain, entitled "On the Natural, Political and Civil Condition of the Provinces of Coahuila, etc.," presents a typical local view of the section. He set forth ideals to which most *norteños* would still subscribe when he claimed that these Northerners are

truly inflexible to intrigue, virtuously steadfast, haters of tyranny and disorder, justly devoted to true liberty, and naturally the most inclined toward all the moral and political virtues. They are very much devoted also to the liberal and mechanical arts. . . . With this combination of such excellent qualities, which result from the celestial climate and are cultivated by such honest occupations, each citizen becomes a worker, each worker a soldier, and each soldier a hero that is worth a hundred ordinary soldiers.

One of the punier offspring of North Mexican sentiments is known as "Texas brag."

*   *   *

Thus we have the peoples and regions of Mexico from which the Mexican nation is being formed. Heterogeneity is its keynote. Viewed as a national unit, the Mexican scene is a complicated one. Analysis of the problems by regions highlights the fact that there is no one single, simple, and obvious answer to Mexican difficulties.

PART II: EPIC REVOLUTION

7. The Birth of Modern Mexico

Current Mexican history takes the successful Madero revolt against Porfirio Díaz as its point of departure. Events that occurred forty years ago color the present. The ideas which emerged from a decade of struggle among Mexicans themselves and with the United States form the creeds which guide individual and national actions today. Mexico is the Revolution, and the Revolution is Mexico.

The epic phases of the Revolution followed an incubation period during which intellectual unrest and the development of explosive doctrines began to undermine the established order. From 1910 through 1920 the Porfirian world collapsed, never to be revived. The political system dissolved, the economy was swamped, and society lost its moorings in those years of violence and large-scale transformations. In the wrecking process, one that preceded the rebuilding of yet another modern Mexico, moral authority lost its sanction, and with it crashed law and order. In large measure the main task before Mexicans since 1920 has been to reconstruct the new Mexico by replacing the discredited past with a tolerable present and a brighter future. The following pages tell of this collapse and first attempts at renovation.

1. GENESIS: THE MADERO REVOLT

Francisco I. Madero and the Precursors. Madero's reputation, even his biography, have fallen into the hands of overardent friends and overcritical enemies. The hagiographers of the Revolution have, because of his importance, called him the "Apostle." That is the title he bears in the official pantheon of Revolutionary heroes. The myths which surround his activities are now legion, and can hardly be disentangled from truth, itself elusive.

Francisco I. Madero was born to a wealthy and large family which is said to have emigrated to northern Mexico in the eighteenth century. Some of the Apostle's ancestors were of Portuguese-Jewish stock who prospered in the state of Coahuila. Francisco's grandfather had been a political crony of Díaz and was, for one term (1876–1880), Federalist governor of the state. The Madero enterprises included ranching, agricultural, mining, and industrial activities. When Francisco I. Madero was born in 1873 his family was considered a powerful, well-to-do clan. At the age of twelve Francisco was enrolled in a Jesuit seminary in Saltillo; thence he transferred to a Catholic secondary school in Baltimore, Maryland. To complete his studies, he was shipped off to Paris, where he received an excellent rounding in commercial studies and political economy. Chiefly to perfect his English and to top his career, Francisco finished up his schooling at the University of California, in Berkeley. While there, he met a Mexican upper-class girl whom he subsequently married; the ceremony was performed by the Archbishop of Mexico. This was hardly the expected training for a revolutionary.

On his return to the family estates, Francisco peacefully settled down to the quiet life of a well-bred *científico*. He set out to become a practical business success as a model *hacendado*. He introduced new agricultural techniques on his well-run hacienda and even wrote pamphlets about irrigation which won the favorable attention of Díaz and Jose Y. Limantour, his powerful Secretary of Treasury. The peons on the Madero estates and others in the vicinity later remembered Francisco as a jolly, happy little person (he only stood about five feet, four inches) who was able to win their affection and esteem. One told John Reed in 1913 that Madero "used to come to the great haciendas and make speeches. When he began, the peons hated him; when he ended, they were crying."

Two important things happened to young Madero which indirectly have shaped the whole course of recent Mexican history. The first was his revived interest in spiritualism, and growing out of that, his determination to enter political life. As a lonesome student in France, Madero had dabbled briefly in spiritualism but had paid little attention to it after he assumed family responsibilities in Mexico. Among his other talents, Francisco was a homeopathic physician. One evening while attending a patient, he was sitting quietly in a darkened room, doodling on a pad of paper; later Madero said he felt psychic forces begin to move the pencil, which inscribed in firm letters, "Love God above all things and thy neighbor as thyself." Somewhat skeptical, Madero set about experimenting with spirit writing under more controlled conditions. The same message recurred, and others soon followed.

Madero turned from his business concerns, which had already netted him a fortune of about half a million dollars, to a sort of personal social mysticism. During his sessions with the occult, he was moved to pen essays on moral and political themes which surprised his family and friends by their excellence; normally he was only an indifferent writer. Madero was gradually convinced that he was in touch with great minds of the past, and that he was a chosen instrument to regenerate Mexico, Latin America, perhaps the world. By June 1904, at the age of 31, he was certain that his destiny was clear.

His analyses of history and the essays he had written had persuaded him that the Latin nations did not evolve smoothly and evenly, but went ahead by leaps, each surge followed by a long quiescence. Madero believed that the time was now nearing for such a leap, this one toward humanitarianism and the amelioration of social ills. He felt that it was his lot to aid this coming movement and thus should prepare himself for national, then international, leadership, by first entering local politics.

His maiden political attempt was a fiasco. He gathered a group of friends around him and tried to unseat the local Díaz candidates for state offices by organizing Anti-Re-Election political clubs throughout Coahuila and by publishing a paper. The novices were overwhelmed by the Díaz machine in the local elections of 1905, but Madero decided to remedy the defects of his political education and try again, on a larger scale.

The Creelman Interview of 1908. The Creelman Interview marks a major turning point in the genesis of the Mexican Revolution. James Creelman was an obscure American journalist who, by some rather mysterious means, was chosen by Díaz to publish a long and eulogistic article in the United States. It came out in *Pearson's Magazine* for March 1908, entitled "Porfirio Díaz, Hero of the Americas." It was a high-flown appreciation of all that Díaz had accomplished and was doing for Mexico. The piece was based on a long personal interview Creelman had been granted. While querying Díaz on many matters, Creelman had asked the old Caudillo about the political future of the Mexican nation.

In reply, President Díaz stated that the whole purpose of his government was to prepare Mexicans for democracy and that he now believed they had reached a point in their evolution where a loyal opposition party should share in governing the country. Díaz said that if such a party appeared, he would protect it (and guide it!). No one now really knows whether these statements were sincere. They may have been only for export purposes, to counteract the rising criticisms from abroad, but there were immediate repercussions to the Creelman article in Mexico.

Mexicans inferred from it that Díaz would not be a candidate for the presidency in 1910, and that henceforth his repression of political activity would be lightened. The interview acted as a powerful stimulus to polarize incipient political groupings. Each hoped to qualify as the "loyal opposition" and share with Díaz the honor of running Mexico. The statements by Díaz permitted covert discontent to become open criticism. Thence was but a short step to action, though until 1910 nonrevolutionary discussions were the rule.

Political bodies fathered by the Creelman interview were numerous and alike in many respects. Nearly every one of them carefully refrained from criticizing Díaz himself. They urged improvements but contented themselves with accepting the capitalist system, the democratic ideal, and a concept of national unity based on old Federalist-Liberal principles of 1857. Díaz had mentioned in the Creelman interview that the rich were too busy getting richer and that the poor were as yet too ignorant to attempt to rule the country, so that the political burdens devolved upon the middle class. This indeed was the stamp of several groups who responded. The most significant middle-class parties were the Democratic Party and the Reyistas, as well as an ever-enlarged Madero Anti-Re-Electionist Party. Each contributed a share to the revolutionary ideology, though each was designedly nonviolent. Lower-class discontents were voiced in stronger terms by the "Regeneration" spokesmen.

The Regeneration group was more powerful in final ideological influence. It was a radical, proletarian movement, primarily headed by the Flores Magón brothers, Jesús and Ricardo. They were born in Oaxaca, but early in life had migrated to the Core, then to the

North. In their travels they had affiliated themselves with a newly organized, European-directed, revolutionary labor movement based on anarchism, the International World Workers. Ricardo and Jesús, aided by their followers, published a violent paper called *Regeneration;* it took the anarchist line that capitalist society was rotten and doomed, and that to hasten its collapse the Mexican proletariat should undermine it by every possible means. The Regeneration program was directed more toward class than national ends, though its particular targets were the Porfirian state and the economic system of Mexico whose destruction was a prerequisite to the regeneration of the masses. These radicals were hunted and exiled by Mexican authorities. Most of them fled to the United States, where they bombarded Mexico with propaganda calling for revolution.

The Mexican Liberal Party (Regeneration Group). In September 1905 the Regeneration group of expatriated, radical Mexican workers formed themselves into the Mexican Liberal Party. From its headquarters in St. Louis, Missouri, the executive committee hoped to coördinate, organize, and help revolutionary bands in Mexico to overthrow Díaz. Their avowed aim was to seize the government and turn Mexico into an anarchist workers' state. To this end they fomented strikes in Mexican industries and even sent a few, unsuccessful military expeditions against northern Mexico in the hope that the countryside would rise against the tyrant. Their main contribution to the Mexican Revolution, however, was the formulation of the first all-inclusive action program, a lengthy bill of indictment against Díaz.

The platform of the Mexican Liberal Party was drawn up in 1905 and published in St. Louis in 1906. It was circulated widely among the lower classes by local Regeneration cells in Mexico. The platform or program contained 52 specific points for the reorganization of Mexican political and economic life. Nearly all these eventually worked their way into the Mexican Constitution of 1917.

The program of 1906 covered constitutional reform, education, anti-foreignism, the Church, and other traditional Mexican issues. But because of their interest in economics, Party members wrote a series of significant planks touching on the relationships of capital and labor during the transitional period before anarchism triumphed. They demanded labor codes which would permit collective bargaining and regulate hours and wages, as well as working conditions. Specifically they opposed child-labor and other abuses, and claimed workmen's compensation, profit-sharing, and other seemingly Utopian privileges as the just rights of labor. Though industrial reforms were the longest and most important sections of the platform, it also contained demands for agrarian reform, rearrangement of the tax systems, and protection of native peoples.

The Party promised to confiscate the properties of Porfirian *cientificos* and apply the proceeds to the social betterment of the Mexican masses. It pledged itself to restore lands unjustly taken from communities and Indian groups. The Liberal Party platform was specific, concrete, and disturbing. Its influence on subsequent revolutionary ideas was powerful, as regional and class groups lifted parts for further elaboration. It offered something to everyone, especially to those outside the closing circle of *cientificos*. Its undertones of violence, however, repelled middle-class supporters. The latter favored evolution, not revolution.

But the Mexican Liberal Party, operating from the United States, and with international class struggles as its prime focus, never was more than a small and irritating practical element in the pre-Revolutionary decade. The open national opposition groups were equally or more important. The major one was the Madero Anti-Re-Electionist Party. To promote his schemes Madero got in touch with various dissident groups, among which were the Flores Magón anarchists. He sent them money to carry on labor activity and propaganda, and enclosed a note saying: "We all sympathize with your ideas, and we believe that your 'regeneration' must cause a rebirth of the country, inflaming all Mexicans against their tyrants."

With seeming clearance in the Creelman interview, Madero and his backers vigorously pushed forward their own program. It attracted much of the dissatisfied youth of the cities. The program itself was widely diffused in a volume which Madero wrote; its Spanish title can be translated as *The Presidential Succession of 1910*. Not many people seem aware of the fact that the views of the Anti-Re-Electionists in the three successive editions of the work varied with the shifting of Madero's aims. When Madero in early 1908 first penned the tract—now a classic political text of the Revolution— his family was divided as to whether it should be published or not, but with his father's and grandfather's permission, Francisco let it circulate.

The work is a prolix review of the history of Mexico and of despotism in general. It attacked militarism and absolute power as two defects which would cause the Mexican political edifice to crash unless immediately checked. Madero rehearsed the evils of the Porfirian system of rigged elections, irresponsible state governors, and made strong pleas for education. There was also a strong note of anti-foreignism; Madero accused the Díaz administration of being subservient to foreign interests, especially to the United States. In the first edition of the work (1908), Madero's program was based on the idea that Díaz would be reëlected president in 1910, but that a new vice-president plus a new set of representatives, senators, and state officials should replace the puppets now in office. The tactics of the Anti-Re-Electionists were based on the assumption that a man as old as Díaz would probably die between 1910 and 1916 (his eighth term as president) and that the transition to the new ways would be simplified by preventing any of his underlings from being reëlected.

A second edition of the work (1908) sharpened the criticism of the Díaz system, and called for the formation of an overt political party whose slogan would be "liberty of suffrage and no reëlection." It proposed that when the party developed strongly enough it should make a transaction with Díaz: he would remain as president, but to clean Mexico up gradually the Anti-Re-Electionists would be given the vice-presidency, a large share of Congress, and a number of state governorships.

Events in 1909 moved rapidly and caused important shifts in sentiments and political alignments. The Democratic Party began to see the futility of campaigning vigorously without any candidates, and considered supporting Madero, whose background and interests paralleled their own. Díaz apparently vetoed Reyes' political aspirations; the unannounced vice-presidential candidate informed his followers, the Reyistas, that he would not run. They had a machine of sorts built up, but now no purpose. They, too, looked toward Madero, a Northerner with progressive ideas. Finally, Madero had an interview with the old president. This secret attempt to arrange a political deal proved impossible. Díaz ridiculed Madero to his face by comparing him to a silk-hatted but otherwise shabby crackpot, Zúñiga, who as sort of a national joke always ran against Díaz for the presidency. On his part, Madero was amazed to find how senile the aloof "Hero of the Americas" had become; he reported to his followers, "Díaz no es gallo"—"He's no longer a fighting cock." He could be beaten.

The Anti-Re-Electionists therefore shifted their objectives and their strategy. Madero became a presidential rival rather than a vice-presidential possibility. A third edition of the *Presidential Succession* (1909) was issued, with the definite hope of wooing Democrats and Reyistas to support Madero. The controversial items that would split such a potential coalition were eliminated; the Anti-Re-Electionists stole the Democrats' slogan and campaigned on a platform of "Effective Suffrage, No Re-Election." The watered-down, somewhat vague quality of the final edition of Madero's book stems from an attempt to be ambiguous enough to win fringe support. This move was successful; it brought support, but also many contradictory views into the Anti-Re-Electionist camp.

Once these decisions had been made and the apparatus in order, Madero made three swings around the circuit in 1909 and 1910. He and his orators stressed three simple points: "The Principles of '57 and Tuxtepec" (anticlericalism, democracy, no reëlection), reform, and anti-despotism. Madero's reform program borrowed from all writings up to his time. He advocated judicial reform and attacked the Porfirian justice that was only for the rich; he promised a free and extensive educational system at state expense. He castigated wars against the Indian groups like the Yaquis, and, above all, the constant violations of Mexican integrity by Díaz' truckling to the United States. He promised agrarian and labor reforms—not quite so far-reaching as those demanded by the Regeneration band, but more than the Democrats had been willing to extend. The Madero campaign speeches thundered away at the absolutism of Díaz as a peril to the national future.

The Elections of 1910. Díaz did not seem to be much worried about the political agitation that preceded the general elections of July 1910. Taking the hundredth anniversary of the Grito de Dolores as a pretext, the government planned a mammoth centennial celebration, part of whose function was to impress foreign visitors with the culture and progress of the nation, and to dispel any incorrect notions that various muckrakers might have spread abroad. A few days before the elections, Madero was imprisoned on charges of inciting the nation to armed revolt. While preparations for the big celebration were in progress, the elections were held.

The stupendous centennial reached its peak on September 15–16, 1910, and shortly thereafter Díaz permitted Madero to "escape" from his confinement in San Luis Potosí and seek honorable exile in the United States. Then the election results were released. According to the official figures, Díaz had received the usual millions of votes, but his small opponent, Madero, had garnered a total of only 196; a last-minute Reyista candidate, Dr. Vasquez Gómez, was allotted 187. Plans were laid to inaugurate Díaz and his unpopular but reëlected vice-president, Ramon Corral, in November.

Once on Texas soil, Francisco I. Madero issued a manifesto, known as the "Plan of San Luis Potosí," which touched off the Mexican Revolution. Dated as if written from jail in Mexico on October 5, 1910, Madero called for a nullification of the July 1910 elections as patently fraudulent and a denial of the people's will. He called for the Mexican people to revolt against the tyrant Díaz, and set November 20 as the day for a mass uprising. He named himself provisional president and promised that new and honest elections would be held and that political, social, and economic reforms would follow. November 20, 1910, then, is the dividing line in recent Mexican history between "Old" and "New." The Revolution officially started on that day and it has been continuing ever since.

2. EXODUS, 1910–1911

The actual Madero Revolution of 1910 was scarcely the mass uprising of a downtrodden people. Nor was it the instrument of rapacious foreign capitalism. The few and feeble attempts that the Madero family made to obtain loans in the United States to carry on a revolt against Díaz were flatly turned down, on the basis that the whole scheme outlined in the Plan of San Luis Potosí seemed a poor business risk. The Madero Revolution was essentially a colossal bluff that succeeded. Many of the details about its critical episodes are still controversial; no thoroughgoing investigation has yet appeared. But the available published materials point unmistakably to the conclusion that less than 20,000 men, and less than 1.5 million dollars (raised in Mexico) killed an era. Even by Mexican standards it was a small affair, but its repercussions were great.

Tiny bands of devoted Maderistas rallied to the Plan of San Luis Potosí which denounced the election of Díaz as fraudulent. Premature outbreaks occurred on November 18, 1910 and sporadic local fighting sizzled thereafter at widely separated points in the Republic. The strength of the Madero forces, if such they could be called, lay in the Northwest. Venustiano Carranza, Pancho Villa, Pascual Orozco—all destined soon for wider recognition—here recruited ranchers, smugglers, drifters, and patriots to the Madero cause. Unable to operate effectively in his home state of Morelos, a peasant leader, Emiliano Zapata, and his more dreaded brother, terrorized Guerrero, while lesser chieftains in Sinaloa, Puebla, Zacatecas, and the isolated peninsula of Yucatan moved in narrower circles behind Díaz' main lines.

Gustavo Madero, main organizer for his brother, kept careful account of the effectives at the movement's disposal; his estimates reveal how small and regionalized was the affair, even at its apogee in May 1911. More than three-quarters (76.8 per cent) of the total fighting strength of the Madero revolution was concentrated in the western and northern states of Mexico. All told, the number of guerrillas was less than 17.5 thousand.*

But the Maderos had difficulty keeping even this small force supplied with arms and ammunition, almost the sole source of which lay in the United States. With no funds coming from the United States commercial circles, the Maderos were forced to raise all the loans they could on their own properties, to the point where they were reduced to having their laundry done on credit in Texas. Small sums came from captured villages. Bannerman and Company, suppliers of arms to revolutionists throughout the Latin-American world, were unsentimental enough to want cash on the barrelhead. Lack of cash and supplies set up a vicious circle: without ammunition there were no Madero victories, and without victories, morale and confidence among the irregulars dropped. Generals like Pascual Orozco were wont to expend a million rounds of rifle cartridges in one engagement; it cost $15,000 to replace them, and when, from shortage of funds, further supplies were not immediately forthcoming, the guerrillas suspected treachery and political transactions.

The inability of the Díaz government to quell these small revolutionary brush fires revealed the hollowness behind its impressive façade. For reasons best known to himself, Díaz had sent Bernardo Reyes and José Limantour to Europe into "honorable exile." Within the Mexican government all was disorder; Díaz, senile and drugged

---

* Gustavo noted the following, here rearranged to fit the regional frameworks discussed in Chapter 6 (in thousands of troops):

Core: Puebla, 1.5; Total, 1.5. (8.7 per cent.)
South: Guerrero, 1.5; Yucatan, 1.0; Total, 2.5. (14.5 per cent.)
West: Sinaloa, 2.0; Zacatecas, 0.8; Total, 2.8. (16.3 per cent.)
North: Chihuahua, 5.2; Coahuila, 1.0; Sonora, 4.0; Nuevo Leon, 0.2; Total, 10.4. (60.5 per cent.)
Total: 17.2. (100.0 per cent.)

for a jaw infection, could himself give no coherent direction to affairs. There was little with which to work. The army had proved to be mostly a myth—padded rosters showed 30,000 men, but half were fictitious; in a showdown Díaz had no power. By February 1911 the crisis had been prolonged for ten weeks but there was still hope for his survival in office. Though the government had not scattered the revolution, neither had the Maderistas gained significant victories.

At this point Díaz recalled Limantour. En route from Paris, the financial genius interviewed the Maderos and fellow revolutionists in New York. Despair had split their ranks; one clique, the Vasquez Gómez ex-Reyistas, were willing to settle on an amnesty basis, but the Maderos bluffed.* They talked grandly and ambiguously about large resources being placed at their disposal by sympathizers in the United States; privately Gustavo was writing to Francisco at revolutionary headquarters in Texas that for want of a few cartridges and a little money the whole revolution was in jeopardy. Without the victories envisaged, the revolutionists had a poor bargaining position.

Limantour returned to Mexico City, where he took charge of the government. He promised changes, and sent word to Reyes to hurry home. Both the revolution and the government were losing prestige daily. As insurrectionists converged on Ciudad Juárez, across the border from El Paso, a serious international incident that could lead to United States intervention seemed a growing possibility. Neither side wished that. They started to haggle.

The negotiations at Ciudad Juárez were a failure but they paved the way for Díaz' final removal. The Maderistas demanded the resignation of the president, recognition of Francisco as provisional president, expulsion of *científicos* from Congress, eighteen state governorships, and payment of the expenses of the revolution to date, late April 1911.† Limantour, whose agents were carrying on these talks,

* Most accounts, taken from Vasquez Gómez' memoirs, reverse this; the Gómez group consistently and unjustly disparaged the role of the Maderos, who wrote no memoirs beyond a small, unfinished autobiography by Francisco that goes only to 1907.

† American business now began to interest itself in the Maderistas. Allegedly Standard Oil offered aid; the U. S. State Department disapproved of the proposed contract. Independently Madero rejected it, and Standard later disavowed it. This seems to be the only basis for later claims by General Orozco (and Henry Lane Wilson) that the Madero Revolution received sums from American oil companies.

refused. The uneasy armistice between Federal forces and the revolutionary troops was broken after quarrels among the opposing forces led to sporadic shootings, then to a pitched battle. In it Orozco and Villa captured Ciudad Juárez for Madero by storm on May 10. Unconnected but important was Zapata's taking and sacking Cuautla on May 12; this town was a southern Federal stronghold. Success of this nature emboldened the lukewarm and wavering revolutionaries; at the very last moment, numerous small bands calling themselves Maderistas emerged to take over local and state governments.

The Díaz cause was lost. A treaty signed by the government (Limantour's agents) with the revolutionaries on May 21 ended the immediate fighting. In it both Díaz and Limantour agreed to resign. A somewhat colorless but powerful Catholic politician, Francisco de la Barra, was to assume the provisional presidency of Mexico until new elections (to replace the fraudulent ones of July 1910) were held.

Díaz was never fully aware of what Limantour's agents had done. When news of the treaty reached Mexico City on May 23 he attempted to disperse the mobs that formed to demand his immediate resignation. In the great square of Mexico loyal troops sprayed one demonstration with machine-gun fire; in a few moments two hundred Mexicans had been killed. Finally friends and relatives of the old Caudillo persuaded him that there was no alternative; early on the morning of May 25, 1911 Porfirio Díaz resigned. The Madero revolution was a military success.

Díaz left Mexico quietly, carried to exile in Paris on the steamer *Ypiranga*. Behind him he left a full treasury but a rapidly dissolving political situation. While Mexico was going through a blood bath, Díaz died in Paris, July 2, 1915, convinced to the end that he had served Mexico well.

3. MADERO'S MEXICO

Now that the stated object of the Madero uprising had been accomplished, Mexicans could and did stop to assess what had occurred. In the intoxicating atmosphere of "liberation" they paid the most concern to domestic aspects. The Iron Hand, so talked about in the propaganda of 1909 and 1910, had been lifted with the exile of Díaz. Freedom was a heady brew.

From every nook and cranny of the articulate Mexican overworld, cliques and individuals poured forth to reap the benefits of unexpected liberation. Each group believed the Madero revolution had been fought to remove some restriction that the Díaz system had placed on their particular economic or emotional interests and that they alone could rehabilitate the nation. For the first time Mexicans began to inquire about the real causes of the revolt and what should now be done to remedy the ills associated with the Porfirian system, but there was no agreement, no plan, no ideology.

Madero's government was necessarily a coalition among dissident forces. Each of them sought to undermine him politically and destroy his prestige. Congress was split between de la Barra's followers, radical intellectual revolutionaries, Vasquez Gómez henchmen, moderate Maderistas. The president's cabinet openly plotted against him, while a venal and irresponsible press unmercifully caricatured the little, distracted, and often undignified president and his family. It is doubtful that any individual, of whatever size and however gifted, could have controlled and guided the fluid situation facing Madero after his inauguration. He was determined to be democratic in a land where democracy had been more often praised than practiced.

Countercurrents, 1912–1913. The warming sun of liberty brought forth strange and exotic Mexican plants. In Mexico City a *Casa del Obrero Mundial*—House of the World's Workers—came into being as a center of I. W. W. propaganda similar to that which the Flores Magón groups had furtively circulated for years. Anarchists and socialists alike were anti-Maderista; their views were that to displace Díaz by another capitalist was small gain, and what Mexico needed was a real Revolution. For ex-*científicos,* Madero seemed too progressive and radical; for the proponents of direct action in town and country, he was too mild, too polite.

The Zapata agrarians, direct actionists, did not hesitate long in denouncing Madero as a Judas and a traitor. Less than a month after his inauguration they issued the Plan of Ayala; it demanded immediate partial confiscation of hacienda properties. Zapatistas always purported to be the real heirs of the Plan of San Luis Potosí, which they claimed Madero had scuttled. Theirs was a localized, by no means dangerous, agrarian uprising; probably involved were less than 500 persons. Ideologically the movement proved of great importance later, but at the time the Zapata demands represented an attempt to test the power of the new executive. That always occurs in Mexico.

As part of the same probing process came unsuccessful counterrevolutions. The first of these was headed by Bernardo Reyes. He had arrived from Europe too late to aid Díaz but now he hoped for a quick rise to the presidency via revolution. Reyes' plans were made in Texas, but United States officials friendly to Madero ousted him. The Reyes revolt in the North failed miserably; no one supported him and he was soon imprisoned in Mexico City.

The most serious of these military uprisings that tried to unseat Madero and reverse the revolution was headed by Pascual Orozco. Displeased with his share of the spoils and bribed by landed interests in Chihuahua, he withdrew his allegiance to Madero and tried to mobilize the North against him on a Plan that copied its demands from the Mexican Liberal Party; in the Plan, Orozco claimed that Madero had sold Mexico for "Washington gold."

Government forces at first made little headway against Orozco, who easily captured Ciudad Juárez, until Madero put Victoriano Huerta in charge of operations. His rapid success against Orozco brought him favorable notices. General Huerta was an ex-Porfirian officer who had performed excellently for Madero against Zapata. Tough, intelligent, and able, he has been compared to General U. S. Grant in his capacity for hard liquor, his military talent, and his unconcern about public moneys. When Huerta was unable to account for a million pesos of military funds, Madero dismissed him. But unlike Orozco, who faded into obscurity, Huerta was destined to play a major role in Mexican history.

Another principal whose subversive activities shaped the final course of the Revolution soon came onto the crowded stage. Félix Díaz, nephew of the deposed dictator, "pronounced" against Madero in Veracruz, but again negligible support came to his revolution early in October 1912. Within a few days government troops captured him. A drumhead court-martial sentenced Díaz to the firing squad. Madero intervened to save his life and commuted the death penalty to life imprisonment. From his comfortable cell in Mexico City Díaz immediately began to spin further intrigues.

Overthrow. After the unsuccessful revolts of Orozco and Díaz, Mexican Congressional elections had been held, which returned a majority of Maderistas to Congress. Once the superficial political consolidation of the regime had taken place Madero began moving toward an economic and social reform program; he thus mobilized the dormant opposition among vested interests. Manuel Calero, an ex-Porfirian opportunist whom Madero had been forced to dismiss as his Ambassador to the United States, came before the new Congress and announced that the president had instructed him to misrepresent conditions in Mexico to the American government. This started a campaign of vilification against Madero's presumed ineptness and hypocrisy. Obstructionist tactics of small Congressional groups kept Madero from negotiating needed loans in the United States and Europe, while rumors of interlocking conspiracies increased.

President Madero unwisely dismissed the insistent talk of plots as a normal condition of Mexican politics. In this instance, though, the rumors were founded on fact. Bernardo Reyes and Félix Díaz had suborned substantial parts of the army and had set February 9, 1913 as the date for a military *coup* that would reëstablish a system modeled on that of the early Díaz period.

On the appointed morning, bribed guards released Díaz and Reyes from their prisons. Reyes headed the troops who were to arrest Madero. The president's guard, under the persuasion of Gustavo Madero, proved loyal; in the exchange of shots, Reyes was killed. Díaz' contingents and the now leaderless *Felicistas* holed up in the military prison, the Ciudadela, a few blocks west of the National Palace in the heart of Mexico City. When President Madero arrived at the National Palace around nine in the morning, the abortive rebellion, like its earlier counterparts, seemed already to have fizzled. Now Madero made a fatal blunder. In the absence of more trustworthy military subordinates, he appointed General Huerta to command the government forces, with orders to capture the besieged rebels. But rather than protecting the government and Madero, Huerta eventually betrayed them.

For nine days, the "Tragic Ten" (February 9–17, 1913), Huerta and Díaz engaged in a continuous but destructive artillery duel across the heart of Mexico City. Though they failed to harm each other, they did manage to destroy the American consulate, damage scores of other buildings, and wound or kill uncounted innocent noncombatants, including some foreigners. The fallen bodies of bystanders, too numerous to be buried during the carnage, were soaked with kerosene and burned; the intolerable stench permeated the business district, chief scene of the duel. Normal activities of the metropolis ceased, and confused rumors clouded the provinces.

On February 17 Federal reinforcements sufficiently large to put a speedy end to the devastating stalemate arrived from Toluca, but were not used by Huerta. Later evidence indicated that some of the fighting had been deliberately planned to chew up units faithful to Madero. Huerta got in touch with Díaz to arrange an immediate end of hostilities. Huerta then made clear his intention of betraying Madero. Though this decision was in the classic or Santa Anna pattern of early-nineteenth-century Mexican *caudillismo,* its twentieth-century revival by Huerta has led H. B. Parkes in his *History of Mexico* to term Huerta "a villain on the Elizabethan scale." To the reflective, Huerta seems an anachronism.

On February 17 Díaz and Huerta arranged a secret agreement, the *Pacto de la Ciudadela.* By its terms Huerta was immediately to become provisional president of Mexico, and it was understood that Díaz might succeed him at the following election.

4. THE UNITED STATES AND MADERO

William Howard Taft was President as revolutionary events began to loom in Mexico. Within the executive power, Philander Knox, Taft's Secretary of State, played a minor role in formulating Mexican policy; that problem was delegated to an Assistant Secretary, Huntington Wilson. When major difficulties began to appear in the Mexican presidential campaigns of 1910, Henry Lane Wilson—no relation to the Assistant Secretary—was appointed Ambassador. He was a brother of the Republican boss in the state of Washington; as United States Minister to Chile, Wilson had made a reputation as an able man in the old framework of Dollar Diplomacy. Taft leaned heavily on H. L. Wilson's advice, and consulted him before making any important decision about Mexico. Taft, however, did not always follow the Ambassador's suggestion to the letter.

President Taft had made no overt and few covert attempts to influence the outcome of the Madero revolt, though his sympathies lay with Díaz. To patrol the border and prevent possible damage to the United States, at H. L. Wilson's suggestion Taft mobilized 16,000 troops. Great pains were taken to convince Díaz that the mobilization was not a hostile demonstration against him or Mexico. To add assurances, Taft forbade United States naval vessels to visit Mexico. But a sympathetic American border population kept the revolutionists supplied with material and moral aid. Díaz' imprisonment of Madero had swung popular sympathy to the underdog. When the dictator fell, most of the United States border troops were withdrawn. Taft was no crusader, and preferred to keep within the narrow bounds of correctness.

President Taft quickly recognized the duly inaugurated Madero government in November 1911, and aided it materially in its initial difficulties. When Orozco rebelled, Taft privately offered Madero American railroad facilities for transporting Mexican troops across Texas; Taft was somewhat disturbed at the little man's immediate "ingratitude"—circulating false rumors of imminent Yankee intervention when Taft, after explanation to Madero, merely stationed troops along the border to prevent rather than create international difficulties.

As the Orozco rebellion dragged on, Taft had Congress refurbish an old 1898 resolution that allowed the President to embargo arms to American countries where domestic violence existed. Woodrow Wilson later used this as a major instrument of diplomacy. On March 14, 1912 such an embargo was laid down to prevent arms from reaching either side in Mexico, in the hope that it would pinch off fighting. Two weeks later, however, shipments to Madero's government were exempted from the embargo; but Madero's opponents were deprived of such aid. To prevent possible untoward incidents and complications that would arouse interventionist talk in the United States, Taft warned all Americans in Mexico to take no part in Mexican politics and provided facilities to evacuate them.

Part of the Taft policy toward Madero was conditioned by the fact that 1912 was a presidential election year in the United States. Democrats had begun to make political capital of Taft's apparent inability to protect American interests and his seeming indifference to loss of American lives and property in Mexico. To neutralize Mexico as an American domestic campaign issue, Taft issued strongly worded statements to both Orozco and Madero in April and again in September 1912. Congressional opposition and popular talk of armed intervention died down when it seemed that Taft would act, if necessary. In the bitter "Bull Moose" campaign Theodore Roosevelt made a few vague references to Mexico; Woodrow Wilson voiced none at all.

From the outset Taft had determined not to use force against Mexico under almost any provocation. He reiterated this stand in notes and conversations; in one he said "I suppose it will do no harm to threaten them a little." Madero's several enemies in Mexico City made political use of the strong American threats, issued from time to time by Taft for domestic political reasons. No one in Washington had any doubt of the basic stability of the Madero government.

Ambassador Wilson's role in Mexico is a matter of bitter controversy. Every United States ambassador since his day has lived in the shadow of Wilson's actions during the first stages of the Revolution. As dean of the diplomatic corps and as a strong-minded, aggressive representative of American business, he sincerely felt that the inexperienced Madero government should respond directly to his slightest suggestion. He took a stronger line than did President Taft or the Department of State.

The hard-headed businessman, Wilson, had little but personal contempt for the tiny, shrill-voiced President of Mexico. This personal antipathy mounted almost to an obsession and unbalanced Wilson's judgments of the Mexican situation to a degree which so alarmed his superiors that they began to distrust his reports. Wilson decided that Madero should go; he took every legitimate means to harass and discredit him and his government. Carried away by his own feelings, Wilson apparently ventured into murkier corners of Mexican politics to achieve his end. It was a personal vendetta rather than a national policy that he was pursuing, as the documents reveal.

Despite Wilson's actions and local ferment, however, the Madero regime weathered one difficult year, 1911–1912. At the opening of 1913 it was in a no more precarious position than could be expected of a loosely organized coalition government of inexperienced men who could seldom agree about the particular course to be taken. Nine-tenths of the republic was peaceful and was already settling down to routine existence. Madero evoked enthusiasm from all but coffee-house politicians, disappointed fanatics, and the United States Ambassador, Henry Lane Wilson.

This general complacency accounts for the mystification of Taft and the Department of State when, in January 1913, their Ambassador began to bombard them with pessimistic reports which described Madero's position as "hopeless." They didn't even know it was threatened. As late as January 27, Knox told Taft that he could see no reason for Wilson's gloom. The Ambassador's perturbing reports were based on Mexican rumors and on Wilson's own dislike and contempt for Madero, plus a correct estimate of the military forces that would be arrayed against him.

The United States and the Huerta Coup. The Reyes-Díaz revolt of February 9 surprised Taft and the Department of State. For three days they did nothing. On February 12 Ambassador Wilson was specifically cautioned not to make the United States even indirectly responsible for the outcome of the military rebellion. On February 14 Taft sent four battleships to Veracruz, but rejected categorically Ambassador Wilson's request for "firm, drastic, perhaps menacing" instructions and control over this naval power. In Mexico City itself, the Ambassador was acting with vigor to rescue all foreigners caught in the line of artillery fire. He demanded that both sides guarantee to protect them and their interests, on threat of United States intervention; this threat was an unauthorized position taken by Wilson, in defiance of instructions.

On February 14, Madero's Minister of Foreign Affairs (who sold out to Huerta) told Wilson that the president ought to resign. Thereupon the Ambassador, on his own but with backing of the British and German Ministers, formally urged Madero to step down, with the result that a false report of Madero's resignation appeared in American newspapers. To counter this hurtful action Madero sent a public telegram to Taft, the text of which he gave to the press. In it Madero asked the President to withdraw his orders to land Marines at Veracruz. No such instructions had been given, but Taft wasn't really sure what Ambassador Wilson was doing or saying. In a flurry of cables both sides apologized. The United States regretted asking for the legal president's resignation; Madero apologized for the false report about the Marines. Denials are never as dramatic as the original charges and great injuries to both countries, as well as to Madero personally, had been done.

By February 16 Ambassador Wilson had successfully secured a temporary armistice between Huerta and Díaz to evacuate foreigners from the danger zones. The State Department—Secretary Knox— commended him so warmly on this that he thought it approved the whole strong line he was taking. Henceforth, though he had been specifically cautioned on February 12 not to implicate the American government, he pursued unofficial mediation attempts on his own. The outcome of his "mediation" was the Pact of the Embassy on February 18, a black day in Mexican revolutionary annals. In the Pact of the Ciudadela, Madero's fate was sealed by Huerta and Díaz, with the blessing of the American Ambassador, still acting without instructions.

To clear the way for Huerta, the president's brother, Gustavo Madero, was tricked by Huerta and captured on February 18. Huerta turned him over to the Reyista-Díaz rebels in the Ciudadela where he was tortured, mutilated, and then mercifully shot. In the meantime, one of Huerta's generals arrested Francisco Madero and Pino Suárez, his vice-president.

Huerta notified Ambassador Wilson of Madero's arrest, his own assumption of power, and formally asked Wilson to use his good offices as mediator between the government and the rebels. Huerta also notified Congress and all state officials that he had assumed charge of the government. At Ambassador Wilson's invitation, Generals Huerta and Díaz met in the American Embassy at eight P.M. on February 18 where openly and formally they concluded the secret pact already agreed upon during the previous day.

This open "Pact of the Embassy" provided that Huerta would govern Mexico as the republic's provisional president, and that his administration would be guided by a cabinet made up of Reyistas and headed by de la Barra of the Catholic bloc; in the next election Felix Díaz could be a candidate.* When this document had been signed, Ambassador Wilson presented the two generals to the assembled foreign diplomatic corps; Wilson applauded Huerta as the savior of Mexico, and urged that all foreign governments recognize him as the new head of Mexico.

On February 18, 1913 Huerta appeared on the balcony of the National Palace, where he received the homage of the City of Mexico as the man who had brought peace to the capital and the country. The counterrevolution was successful, and seemingly only details remained to be cleared up.

The urge to legalize his position led Huerta through a farce. By promises of immunity for themselves and families, he persuaded Madero and Pino Suárez to resign their offices; thus the traitorous Minister of Foreign Affairs momentarily became Mexico's acting president. During his brief term of an hour, he appointed Huerta *his* Minister of Foreign Affairs. Then the ephemeral acting president stepped out, which left Huerta legally the provisional president of Mexico. Congress approved these complicated and meaningless moves. The Huerta *coup d'état* was thus by a political sleight-of-hand wrapped in a thin cloak of Mexican constitutionalism.

But Huerta's pledges of safe and honorable exile for Madero and Pino Suárez were not kept. National and international pressures were

---

* Woodrow Wilson always mistakenly believed that the Spanish *próxima* (next) election meant "early," and that Huerta had agreed not to be a candidate; neither was true.

put on him to guarantee their lives. Mrs. Madero asked Ambassador Wilson to use his influence with the new government to safeguard their existence. The Ambassador replied that he could not meddle with the internal affairs of the Huerta regime.

Under mysterious circumstances Madero and Pino Suárez were both killed while being transferred from one prison to another. Huerta always disclaimed any responsibility for his predecessor's demise, but the finger of suspicion points directly at him. Henry Lane Wilson accepted the official Huertista explanation that hotheaded Maderistas had tried to rescue the two men and that in the excitement they were inadvertently slain.

The murder of Madero shocked the world. Up to this time international opinion had considered the Huerta *coup* an unfortunate but normal Latin-American *cuartelazo*—barracks uprising—neither the first nor probably the last of its kind in the hemisphere. But the rules of that game nearly always provide for safeguarding the deposed. Ambassador Wilson's insensitivity to humanitarian appeals dogged him forever.

In the rise and fall of Madero from 1910 to 1913, Henry Lane Wilson spoke for the whole United States in Mexico, but unfortunately much that he said represented nobody but Henry Lane Wilson. During his tenure as Ambassador there were two, sometimes three, United States Mexican policies: the State Department's, Taft's and the Ambassador's own. Taft consistently wanted to preserve constituted authority; the State Department chastised Wilson and warned him against meddling, but in 1913 they were willing to back him up if (on his own personal responsibility) he was successful; and, as seen, Wilson was determined to unseat his *bête noire* at almost any cost and by whatever instruments which came conveniently to hand. He succeeded, but the costs to him, the United States, and Mexico are incalculable.

Unaware or indifferent to the rising protests in the United States against Huerta, Wilson urged his superiors in the United States to recognize Huerta. But the powerful shock of the Madero murder made the waning Republican administration extremely circumspect about action in Mexico. Liberal opinion in the United States clamored for immediate intervention to redress the crime. Taft's last presidential statement on the Mexican situation was an appeal for patience and a rejection of imperialism. "I have no sympathy, none at all, and the charge of cowardice does not frighten me," he said, "with that [proposed policy] which prompts us for purposes of exploitation and gain to invade another country and involve ourselves in war, the extent of which we could not realize, and the sacrifice of thousands of lives and millions of treasure." Following established practice, Taft also withheld immediate recognition of Huerta until he could get specific pledges from him on a number of outstanding disputes between the United States and Mexico, chiefly fiscal. A new phase of the developing epic revolution was at hand.

8. New Crusades

It is interesting but fruitless to speculate about what might have happened to the Mexican Revolution had President Taft recognized Huerta, as Ambassador Wilson so vehemently urged. But he did not. Taft left the thorny situation to his successor, Woodrow Wilson, whose administration was to take office on March 4, 1913. For more than eighteen months thereafter relations with Mexico were the most serious international problem facing the United States. Mexico itself was again split into warring factions in the familiar nineteenth-century pattern. The Mexican Revolution of 1910, which seemed to have closed with Madero's successes, was in fact just beginning as his political heirs set about reversing the Huerta stroke. The Revolution was reborn.

1. REVIVED REVOLUTION

In widening ripples, the difficulties arising from Huerta's anachronistic *coup* spread as domestic and international forces formed and combined to support or oppose him. Nearly all semblance of order disappeared from Mexico as a result. The provisional president in February 1913 found an empty treasury and a demoralized bureaucracy, a riven society and a shattered political apparatus.

Huerta, therefore, promised to restore the Golden Age of Díaz. After two years of constant bloodshed and upheaval many now approved of his program. Like any well-trained Latin-American *caudillo*, Huerta began replacing elected state governors with his own trusted military men. At first the Church was distrustful, but gradually moved toward his support. The Huerta regime evolved toward the classic form of Latin-American dictatorship. But opposing forces, within Mexico itself and from the United States under Woodrow Wilson, thwarted the successful operation of Huerta's plans. The interaction of pressures in Mexico and around it forms one of the most complicated eras of domestic politics and an even more complex tale of its relations with the United States. There is still no general agreement about the success of Woodrow Wilson's Mexican policy during these turbulent months following the fall of Madero. Fortunately Wilson's reputation does not rest wholly on his generally poor handling of this thorny problem.

One of the first needs of the new Huerta government was money. To obtain it, internal peace was essential. The United States and Europe were the sole sources of funds, but until foreign governments officially recognized his government, their bankers would make no loans to Huerta. His diplomatic objective was at first very simple: to secure recognition of his government. Domestically his policy was to pacify the country and to consolidate his shaky hold on the National Palace. The two aims were intertwined.

Response at home came in the historical Mexican pattern. At centers where resentment to the domination by the Core was traditional, resistance against Huerta mobilized. Wrapping themselves in the mantle of Madero's idealism, new regional leaders took advantage of the Apostle's martyrdom to disavow allegiance to Huerta and the new Centralism. "Madero dead was a far more potent force than the living man," an informed student has written.

From the North came immediate revolt against Huerta's plans for a Neo-Porfirian regime. Venustiano Carranza, governor of Coahuila, and Abram González, governor of Chihuahua, immediately refused him the allegiance of their states. The North became inflamed over the murder of Madero and the renewed attempt to subjugate it to the Core. When Huertista henchmen captured González and then threw him under a moving train, this atrocity sparked a military uprising that continued for seven years. The Revolution again got under way as anti-Huerta Northerners rose in arms.

On March 26, 1913 Carranza published the Plan of Guadalupe. It was a short, simple political statement that constitutional government must be restored to Mexico in accordance with Madero's earlier (1910) Plan of San Luis Potosí. From his state troops and willing guerrillas Carranza organized a politico-military Constitutionalist Army of which he became "First Chief."

A stubborn, middle-aged, and gray-bearded figure, the First Chief evoked either fanatical loyalty or undying antipathy among those who dealt with him. A northern *hacendado*, Carranza had been a senator under Díaz but had early joined the original Madero movement. Reminiscent of the progressive *científicos,* he took a cautious, gradualist, and essentially political approach to the solution of social problems; his was a narrow and inflexible outlook. Touchy about personal and national honor, he and his later great opponent, Woodrow Wilson, were temperamentally akin in many ways.

To the Constitutionalist cause rallied a motley collection, all nominal subordinates of the First Chief. Together they formed an unstable coalition pledged to rid Mexico of Huerta. Nearly all were old Maderistas. In Sonora, Alvaro Obregón avowed his allegiance to Carranza and organized a formidable force. Obregón was an ex-school teacher who, as an industrial worker for a short while, had picked up the rudiments of socialism. He had a remarkable talent for the type of military improvisation and staff planning that won battles; he never lost one. His contingents were a little better disciplined and uniformed than those of fellow *caudillos.*

Pancho Villa and Emiliano Zapata were the two other main chieftains in the Constitutionalist coalition of regional forces. Though one was a northerner, the other a southerner, their characteristics were quite similar. Both were great natural leaders of men; both had the same feral and amoral instincts, qualities that made them lethal, almost natural, forces. Themselves from the exploited classes, they could attract and lead masses of underdogs. Their Indians, *peons,* and small *rancheros* made terrifying and effective guerrillas and light cavalry, admirably suited to the mobile and fluid tactics developed by the Revolution. But though they could concentrate and manipulate these bolts of human energy, both Zapata and Villa were politically naïve and socially insensitive.

Their concepts of Mexico as a nation were but enlarged and hazy projections of the way of life in their respective *patrias chicas.* Zapata expected to exterminate all Europeanized Mexicans in southern Mexico and make of the land a milpa-studded collection of *ranchos* in the Indian mode. Villa thought that the annihilation of national government would lead to a sort of primitive and idyllic Mexican anarchism in which good Northern military companions would tend their cattle, regale each other with stories, and join to extirpate anybody who thought this was not the best possible life.

Each had a revolutionary "brain-trust" of refugee intellectuals who concocted high-sounding programs. They were brushed aside when the serious business of killing was paramount. Though the later folklore of the Revolution has endowed them with a burning sense of social justice and historic mission, Zapata and Villa at the time were fundamentally symbols of naked and massive power—unpredictable in direction, overwhelming in strength. Their deeds stirred the imagination, not the mind. Actions spoke louder than words.

From hamlets and ranchos, from mines and milpas, small bunches of malcontents, adventurers and patriots were drawn into revolutionary ranks. A local guerrilla leader usually headed each of these small knots, which in turn attached itself to a larger grouping under a Constitutionalist "colonel" or "general" who kept his post only by personal bravery, success, and loot. Chiefs and subchiefs professed loyalty to one or another of the four main divisions of the Constitutionalists. Shifting from one to another was frequent. Whether a little band, a larger body, or one of the main hordes, each unit preserved a wide autonomy; the cement holding the Constitutionalists together was not ideology but personalities and success of guerrilla leaders, heretofore unknown persons.

The personal loyalties and reputations engendered during this phase of the Revolution have colored Mexican politics ever since. The epic marches, strikes, retreats, and stratagems of each band and region provide a mine of literary material whose exploitation has created a unique and boldly powerful modern Mexican art and literature. These are but later sophistications of the folk-epics originated during the Revolution by a people in arms. The emotional attitudes that gave birth to a literary and artistic renascence after the fighting had stopped have also enveloped the explanations and the formal historiography of the Revolution; it is largely folklore with footnotes. No scholarly evaluations have appeared from Mexico.

The epic of the Revolution is peopled with villains and heroes, each limned in bold line, without shadings. It goes without saying that the symbols of good are Madero, Villa, Zapata, Obregón, even Carranza, and a host of lesser *jefes* (chiefs) who weave through scenes of tragedy, suspense, humor, and earthy sensuality, in fascinating complexity. The roster of villains, equally stereotyped, is headed by Huerta and Henry Lane Wilson. Curiously enough Woodrow Wilson is on this list too. His verbal duel, first with Huerta, then with Carranza, has been simplified and fitted into the ballad-like framework typically employed even by erudite Mexicans to convey and interpret the Revolution for later generations.

Locally, and for various reasons, the Constitutionalist groups were determined to oust the Usurper (as they always termed Huerta) from the presidential position he had achieved by climbing on Madero's dead body. The international tensions of Europe, on the edge of war, affected the factional jockeying in classic fashion, and rubbed across vital United States security, property, and moral interests long embedded in Mexico. Local aspirations combined with international aims in a shifting pattern as strength of the several elements altered with circumstances. Mexico was in flux. It was strikingly similar to Asiatic and Near Eastern situations at mid-twentieth century.

2. WOODROW WILSON AND MEXICO

Some of the most crucial decisions that determined the ultimate fate of Mexico and its Revolution were not made within the area at all, but in Washington, London, Berlin, and Paris. Perhaps the single most critical constant element of the whole era was the varying attitudes and actions taken by Woodrow Wilson, President of the United States from 1913 to 1921. The position of the United States vis à vis Mexico and the European crises that led to the first World War affected all parties, and formed the context in which relations with Mexico were carried on for nearly a generation.

Through a split in Republican ranks, Woodrow Wilson was elected Democratic President of the United States in 1912 and was inaugurated March 4, 1913. In most respects he was the opposite of his predecessor, Taft. Wilson felt that the President should be a strong leader. As the only member of the government who did not represent a special or partial interest, the President should personally represent the whole people.

Neither avowedly a pacifist nor an imperialist, Wilson was an idealistic nationalist. His political creed drew heavily on the stern Christian morality his Presbyterian father had inculcated in him as a youth. He sought the truth, and once he believed he had found it, rarely did he change his mind. He seemed intolerant of criticism, and often considered opposition to his views the result of insufficient study by his opponents. If they persisted in criticism he immediately suspected personal, materialistic interests. Like Carranza, Wilson made many friends but eventually lost most of them; his political opponents inevitably became personal enemies. Wilson thoroughly enjoyed political fighting, perhaps feeling that he alone was overcoming the forces of evil that would otherwise undermine the world, the United States, and the Democratic Party.

More than most Presidents, Wilson was his own Secretary of State. The first nominal incumbent of that important office was William Jennings Bryan, too great a party power to be kept out of the cabinet. Bryan was a pacifist and was notoriously indiscreet. Distrustful both of Bryan and the Republican-riddled Department of State, Wilson by-passed the orthodox handling of Mexico by using his own special agents and by keeping the tangled threads of negotiations in his own supple but unskilled hands. He personally wrote, often on his famous portable typewriter, every major diplomatic dispatch; copies of some of the principal ones are not even on file in the Department of State.*

From the inauguration until Bryan resigned when European affairs grew too hot in June 1915, Mexico was the chief international problem of the United States; Woodrow Wilson was almost the only policy-maker. In this field even the influential Colonel E. M. House stayed aloof. The President was unprepared by experience or inclination to handle delicate international matters. His tendency was to project his domestic policy—where he could control the situation—into international affairs and try to control those elements in the same manner that he could force tariff bills through Congress.

For many months before and after March 1913 Woodrow Wilson believed that Mexicans were fully prepared for democracy in the American style. He assumed that the Mexican nation, though at a less advanced stage, was basically the same as the Anglo-Saxon ones; by some quirk of circumstance Mexicans spoke Spanish instead of English and lived outside the United States rather than in it, but their problems and outlook were parallel to the ones with which he was familiar through study or experience. Wilson acted as though the differences were superficial rather than fundamental. His early policies were predicated on the belief that if Mexicans would hold a free election and follow constitutional practices their troubles would evaporate. He learned that such was not the case.

* I am indebted to Dr. Philip H. Lowry for permission to use materials from his excellent but unpublished "The Mexican Policy of Woodrow Wilson" (Ph.D. Dissertation, Yale, 1949), which is based on a wide range of private and archival materials in the United States, hitherto unutilized. In addition, I have drawn on data furnished me by Professor Arthur S. Link, whose researches into Wilsonia are only partially published. Interpretations are mine.

In a program of moral imperialism President Wilson placed the weight of the United States behind a continuous, sometimes devious, effort to force the Mexican nation to meet his ill-conceived specifications. Though he oozed sympathy, good will, and idealism, his basic misunderstanding of the main elements of life in the southern republic brought disaster in its train. Unfortunately Woodrow Wilson in 1913 was a man with a single view of Mexico and that one was wrong. He learned from experiences in Mexico and these lessons stood him in good stead later on the world stage. A difficult man to appraise, Wilson was a great one. These first efforts in Mexico are a minor part of a significant career. The Mexican episodes here bulk large because of the restricted frames of time and space. In the larger perspective of Wilson's total national activity, they shrink to more modest proportions and are counterbalanced by qualities and achievements not evident in his first brushes with the ruder facts of international life.

Wilson was slow to voice a Latin-American, much less a Mexican, policy. He early issued a prepared statement, March 11, 1913, which assured the world that in Latin America the United States had no sympathy with those who "seek to seize the power of government to advance their own personal interests or ambition." The windy and unclear sentiments puzzled everyone. The pronouncement was widely interpreted to serve notice on Central American revolutionists that Wilson would not favor their attempts to overthrow existing governments and that he was displeased with Huerta. That was true.

The larger significance of the initial statement was that it heralded a new and deviant policy of recognition when changes in form and personnel broke continuity. When a government succeeds by overturn, recognition is required; since that has happened often, the United States had by mid-nineteenth century established a policy to guide its actions. Writing in 1848, Secretary of State Buchanan had summed up the historic policy by saying that the United States always recognized *de facto* governments—ones that really had come into control. "We do not go behind the existing Government to involve ourselves in the question of legitimacy. It is sufficient for us to know that a government exists, capable of maintaining itself; and then its recognition on our part inevitably follows." To this time-tested formula had been added the ability of governments formed by revolution to comply with international obligations, especially the protection of foreign interests. If it existed and was stable, recognition merely registered that fact; it carried no cachet of approval or of disapproval. It was almost a routine diplomatic operation. Wilson proposed to change that.

For the mere fact of existence—*de facto*—and occasionally a pledge that it would protect third parties, Wilson substituted a new doctrine to decide whether a new government should be recognized by the United States. He thus reversed the settled policy. His was the test of "constitutional legitimacy." It implied the right of the United States to inquire fully into whether the new government was complying with its own national constitution and even to go behind its existence to scrutinize whether it had come to power because its leaders were motivated by personal interests and ambition, or whether they were really trying to pry off despotism by the historic right of revolution. Scrutiny and inquiry seemed to most Latin-American nations the same as meddling in their internal affairs.

Thus there were "good" revolutions and "bad" revolutions in the Wilsonian view. The latter brought only venal, unidealistic people to power, while the former put the particular nation back on the constitutional track by overthrowing an unconstitutional tyrant. As events in Mexico and elsewhere ultimately showed, the test of "constitutional legitimacy" was unworkable, especially in Latin America. The United States once renounced it as a national policy in 1921, though its shades rise constantly to plague international affairs since Wilson's time. In the case of Mexico, Wilson had to decide whether Huerta's was a "good" revolution, worthy of recognition, or a "bad" one, unworthy. If the latter, some "good" revolution had to overthrow Huerta to win the coveted accolade which Wilson now had made of recognition.

Europeans followed the old rules; Wilson made up his own. That was a core issue in the subsequent Wilsonian conflicts with Huerta, with Huerta's domestic opponents, and with Europe. When Wilson formally announced the new departure on March 11, 1913 he did not foresee the snarls and entanglements that might ensue. He was against bad men and for constitutionalism, worthy attitudes but hard to fit to specific international situations.

Public opinion in the United States was somewhat divided and restive over the continued Mexican civil war and Wilson's subsequent long silence. Taft had told Americans in Mexico to get out, and the orders stood. Arms were still going to Huerta; the Constitutionalists were under an embargo. As in the days of Díaz, a sympathetic border population kept the revolutionists well supplied, both for immediate profits and from a genuine disgust with Huerta, who was already following Díaz' pro-European proclivities. The American border population, chiefly Democrats, were represented more fully in Congress, with the admission of Arizona and New Mexico to statehood in 1912. Though a Republican, Senator Albert Fall of New Mexico became a spokesman for the border zone, and as a colorful member of the Foreign Relations Committee kept himself and Mexico in public consciousness by picturesque, often unscrupulous, speeches and interviews. The days of discreet silence and inactivity, in which a Mexican policy could be formulated and carried out by an Assistant Secretary in the State Department, had closed. Extremists—some for Huerta, some for Carranza—talked of intervention by the United States to stabilize Mexico.

From the Mexican republic Ambassador Wilson was showering the President and the Department of State with requests to recognize Huerta, and pressing for instructions. He was completely uninformed about the national policy.* Perhaps there was none.

The President himself was none too certain of the situation. He distrusted the information sent through Embassy and State Department channels, as too apt to reflect special interests. He sent a friend, a minor author and journalist, William Bayard Hale, to Mexico as a presidential agent to provide him with presumably unbiased and firsthand accounts. Hale knew little of Mexico, but was loyal. At about the same time, Bryan authorized one Reginald del Valle to carry out the same job for him. When these two agents met in Mexico City, the regular Ambassador was confused and speechless. The United States was speaking with three tongues, all different.

Following hallowed practice, Great Britain provisionally but routinely recognized Huerta's government on March 31, 1913. The other European nations followed this lead. So did the other Latin-American nations, with the exception of Argentina, Brazil, and Chile, who agreed among themselves to await the decision of the United States. By April Huerta was thus in a position to get needed loans and ammunition from Europe. The American Ambassador was in an anomalous position and stepped up his requests for recognition, action, even guidance.

---

* To avoid confusion, Henry Lane Wilson will be referred to as the Ambassador, while Woodrow Wilson will be called President, until the former shortly drops from view.

On June 14, 1913 the President in his own hand answered one such note. The confidential dispatch told the Ambassador that the President did not think Huerta's government was moving toward conditions of "settled peace, authority, and justice." *Mexicans* lacked good faith that the provisional president would "safeguard constitutional rights and methods of action." Therefore, before the United States could recognize him, the President wanted satisfactory proof of Huerta's plans and purposes.

That meant, he continued, that General Huerta must hold an early election free from coercion, must guarantee an amnesty, and must "observe his original promise not to be a candidate." The President offered the good offices of the United States as mediator to bring peace between the Government and the Constitutionalists. To his original misconception that Huerta had promised to hold an early election the President wedded a second fallacy (which he took as a basis for his policy): that Huerta had promised in the "Pact of the Embassy" not to be a candidate.*

Apparently in June 1913 if Huerta had promised these things— whether he kept the promise or not—the President would have recognized his government. What then would have happened to the Mexican Revolution is anybody's guess. "Mediation" to Woodrow Wilson's mind meant getting Huerta to agree to hold an election in which he would not run.

Hale's reports (in July) to the President stated that there was no doubt that the controversial United States Ambassador had been implicated in the Huerta *coup*. Even then, July 15, the Ambassador was busily rounding up influences to urge recognition or intervention. In late July 1913 the Ambassador was recalled by the President, who then had to face the problem of whether to replace him—constituting recognition. President Wilson had to act.

By now the President had decided that he would never recognize Huerta, and he did not swerve from that view, no matter what obstacles loomed. Privately he stated, "I will not recognize a government of butchers." Since in Wilson's mind recognition was tantamount to approval, to bestow that favor on Huerta would be condoning murder, countenancing unconstitutional practices, encouraging other barracks-uprisings in Central America, but above all, be taking the advice of Henry Lane Wilson, who represented everything President Wilson deeply distrusted—unprincipled opportunism, Big Busi-

* See above, p. 132.

ness, Dollar Diplomacy, Republicans. In addition, recognition of Huerta would mean the defeat of the Constitutionalists, whose very name hypnotized President Wilson. In short, Huerta's revolt was "bad"; that of the Constitutionalists was "good."

He believed the Mexican problem to be a political one, to be solved by free elections which would put into power a government that would govern constitutionally. Since Huerta was both unscrupulous and unconstitutional—double damnation—he must go. Discreet hints by the British that perhaps a joint intervention was needed to bring peace to troubled Mexico made it clear to the President that he must abandon his "do nothing" attitudes on Mexico.

The Lind Mission. Wilson determined to "mediate," but in such a way that Huerta would be eliminated and so that the Constitutionalists, by default, would be favored. Wilson showed himself the veriest tyro in diplomacy by not first taking the elementary precaution of finding out whether the Constitutionalists were willing to have such "mediation." Wilson named John Lind as his special presidential agent to dicker directly only with Huerta.

Lind knew nothing of Mexico, Spanish, or diplomacy. He was a tall, gaunt Swede who was a Democratic party power in Minnesota, where as governor he had battled the trusts. His arrival in Mexico created confusion; in addition to the Embassy staff (under a Chargé d'Affaires), Hale was also voicing the President's presumed views. Now a third plenary United States representative was added. The Lind Mission was well-meaning, but doomed almost from the outset when newspapers in the United States and Mexico headlined a story that he was going to get Huerta's resignation.

His instructions were not quite that drastic. He was directed to tell Huerta that the United States was "acting on the behalf of the rest of the world" (whom Wilson had not let in on the secret) and to demand as the price of mediation, four things: an armistice between the government and the Constitutionalists, an early election, Huerta's promise not to be a candidate, and his assurance that he would accept the results.

Lind's orders closed with a novel plea, "Can Mexico give the civilized world a satisfactory reason for rejecting our good offices? If Mexico can suggest any better way in which to show our friendship, serve the people of Mexico, and meet our international obligations, we are more than willing to consider the suggestion." Huerta made such a suggestion: friendship and all these other matters could be unmistakably shown by recognizing his government, the traditional symbol of amity. Otherwise he refused to consider this unwarranted series of proposals to bring peace to the land. He viewed the Constitutionalists as troublesome bandits.

Lind wrote Wilson that Huerta needed money and suggested a loan. Wilson approved, and on his second attempt, Lind offered American presidential help in arranging such a New York loan if the General would call an armistice and hold early elections.* Huerta refused this bare-faced bribe. Lind, with permission, threatened that President Wilson would recognize the Constitutionalists or intervene directly in Mexico, but Huerta knew it was a bluff. The Constitutionalists had not even formed a provisional government, and in the United States Senate a resolution fathered by Republicans asking for armed intervention in Mexico had been snowed under by presidential orders to the Democratic faithful.

But in answering Lind's notes, Huerta's Secretary of Foreign Affairs wrote that the Mexican Constitution prevented the provisional president from standing for reëlection. Lind took this back-handed comment as agreement that Wilson's terms for mediation had been accepted, and wired the President on August 27, 1913 that the mission was a success. It was not. Huerta had agreed to nothing, let alone resignation or mediation.

Joining the Issues. Upon receiving Lind's overoptimistic news, Woodrow Wilson went before Congress to explain his Mexican policy, his first major public statement on the matter. Part of Wilson's motivation was to quiet persistent demands for action, part to put public opinion against Huerta and on Wilson's side. He explained that patience was necessary and claimed that with his mediation efforts the United States had done its international duty; the next move was up to Huerta, to accept them, that is, resign. If he did not, he was an ingrate. Fighting might continue in Mexico, said Wilson, and therefore United States citizens were urged to leave, though the executive promised to protect those who did not. In a burst of rhetoric that was more emotional than logical, Wilson

* Outlines of a scheme whereby Huerta would be recognized if he would hold early elections had been proposed by spokesmen for the Southern Pacific Railway (Mexico), Phelps Dodge, Greene Cannanea Copper Co., and Doheny oil interests; Bryan thought it "seemed to offer a way out" and Wilson approved at this stage. Bryan and Wilson encouraged Huerta to send a confidential agent to Washington to work out details. (Arthur S. Link information, from manuscript sources.)

claimed that the United States was going to be "neutral" by embargoing arms both to the rebels and to Huerta; this, he said, was following the "best practices of nations," an untrue statement.

For about a month there was a honeymoon period, when tension relaxed. In September Huerta announced "his ardent desire to turn government over to a constitutional successor" and when Catholics named his Secretary of State as candidate for the forthcoming elections, Bryan privately wrote to Wilson "I feel that we have nearly reached the end of our trouble." The State Department announced it would recognize Gamboa if he were elected, even though the rebellious states of northern Mexico did not take part in the elections. Entrance of a new element, the British, disturbed the tranquillity.

Wilson sat back to await the outcome of Mexican elections called for October 26. They might liquidate the whole matter. If Huerta lived up to his tacit acceptance of Wilson's terms of mediation, constitutional government would return to Mexico. But from the Embassy in Mexico reports flowed to Washington that Huerta was busily rigging the election. News of Constitutionalist victories raised the President's hopes that the "good" revolution would triumph. The Constitutionalists had captured the rail center at Torreón and had cut Huerta off from his northern outposts. Huerta support began to wane rapidly.

Then on October 12 Huerta reacted understandably to the crisis. He scattered Congress (which had been elected with Madero) and imprisoned 112 deputies, exempting only the Catholic bloc. This action was termed "lawless" by Wilson, who immediately dropped all thoughts of recognizing the results of any election held while Huerta was still in power. On election day Huerta announced that so few people had turned out to express the nation's will that, though a new (Huertista) Congress would be seated, he himself would remain as provisional president—which he did until April 1914.

Wilson now bent his whole effort to ridding Mexico of Huerta so that the Mexican people could hold a real plebiscite and form a constitutional government that the United States could recognize. Appeals to Huerta's patriotism and cupidity had failed, as had bluffing. Wilson began a long feud with Huerta, who proved an agile and resourceful opponent to the very end. Wilson's difficulties are an eloquent rebuttal to those who think it is a simple matter to dislodge even a small-time Strong Man, under optimum circumstances. Short of armed invasion, a last resort, nothing worked. Wilson tried nearly every other trick in the book before that. Even armed force proved no major success, but rather was a tragic accident.

3. THE ANTI-HUERTA CRUSADE

Wilson began in late October to sound out the United States Congress on the possibility of armed intervention in Mexico. At the same time he tried to isolate Huerta from Europe and to aid his domestic foes, the Constitutionalists.

Wilson and Europe. Huerta was being supplied with money and munitions from European sources, nations that had followed Britain's lead in recognizing his *de facto* regime in March. They were, Wilson found, following Britain's Mexican policy, so the diplomatic problem for Wilson boiled down to persuading the English Foreign Office to withdraw its recognition from the provisional government and join the United States in boycotting the obnoxious Mexican. A note to the British and other nations suggested this course; it drew noncommittal replies. Wilson wanted Great Britain, France, and Germany to follow his plans; when they proved recalcitrant it raised Wilson's temper and hardened his determination to bring them to heel, so that Huerta would disappear.

Especially irritating to Wilson were the British. On the very day after Huerta had imprisoned the Mexican deputies, the new British Ambassador, Sir Lionel Carden, had ostentatiously handed his credentials to the provisional president—reiterating unmistakable recognition of his regime. Huerta naturally publicized the ceremony as approval, which it may have been. Thus even before the Mexican elections Wilson was enraged at "perfidious Albion" and cynical Europe. He decided to bend them to the Wilsonian will.

On October 25 or 26, Wilson tapped out on his little typewriter a blistering memorandum. He turned the draft over to John Bassett Moore, Counselor of the State Department, to put into shape for circulation to all the major powers. Wilson expected to dispatch the finished note after results of the Mexican voting—which Wilson now knew would be fraudulent—were made public. The proposed circular note was timed by the fact that when Britain had provisionally recognized Huerta in March, it had announced that the matter would be reconsidered after the October 26 elections. Wilson expected to sway the British, and Europe, at this critical point.

He was convinced that British policy was being dominated by

English commercial interests, especially oil companies. The Foreign Office was now going to have to choose between supporting Huerta or the United States. The Memorandum is an extraordinary production, significant in its revelation of Wilson's ignorance of the rudiments of normal international intercourse. Never published, it contains a number of flat statements for Moore to put into "as strong and direct language as the courtesies and proprieties of pacific diplomacy permit." *

The note Moore was to write for Wilson was based on six propositions. The United States, as the nation of paramount influence in the Western Hemisphere, has the greatest responsibility toward Mexico. The political fortunes of all Central America are involved. The government of Huerta, based on usurpation and force, would long ago have broken down but for the financial aid derived from its recognition by other nations without regard to the wishes and purposes of the United States. The continuance of Huerta's rule is impossible without the consent of the United States. No joint intervention will be considered. Will other, that is, European, governments coöperate with the United States, or is it their policy "to antagonize and thwart us and make our task one of domination and force"? A good question, but irrelevant.

The Mobile Address. Wilson delayed dispatching his proposed note, but instead gave the gist of it in a famous public speech at Mobile, Alabama, on October 27, 1913. This was a day after the Mexican "elections," and though the speech purported to cover Wilson's general Latin-American policy, it was aimed specifically at Great Britain and Huerta. Its theme was that businessmen (meaning British) had handicapped the development of Latin America (Mexico); foreign policies of nations (Great Britain) there had been based on material ("sordid") interests that had retarded growth of political liberty. The United States was going to stop all that. Wilson foreswore any annexationist designs on Latin America (Mexico).

The President's self-denial of territorial aims was clever and purposeful. If Europe failed to coöperate, the only alternative to throwing Huerta out might be armed intervention. In advance the Mexicans were thus assured that such invasion would be for "idealistic" not "imperialistic" ends; the statement also anticipated and denied

---

* Dr. Lowry found this draft in the National Archives, State, 812.00/9625a, as did Dr. Link. I have followed their independent syntheses and gloss, but have reversed Propositions 5 and 6.

beforehand the growing Republican demands for annexation of all
or part of Mexico if such armed intervention actually got under way.
Wilson had decided Huerta must go, no matter how, short of declared
war.

When Wilson returned from Alabama, Moore read him an unfor-
gettable lesson on international manners, especially those concerning
recognition, and impugning the motives of friends. No European
power need ask permission of the United States to recognize governments, Latin-American or not. Moore pointed out that the "sordid
motives" attributed to the British foreign policy operated similarly
in the United States: the Congress had exempted American vessels
from paying tolls at the Panama Canal, in violation of the 1901
treaty with Britain. Moore mentioned other cases where fundamental
economic or strategic concerns were justified as mainsprings of
United States foreign policy. Economic and strategic stakes are often
as vital as idealistic ones, and in some cases are more so. Policy may
compound them all. Never again did Wilson speak publicly or diplo-
matically about the commercial exploitation of Latin America by the
British. Nor did he send his projected note asking if Europe was
trying to "antagonize and thwart us" by following the standard
international usages sanctioned by experience and time.

The month of November 1913 was a tense one in Mexico City.
After all Wilson's threats, bombast, scurryings, and alarms, a rupture
of relations and war between Mexico and the United States seemed
imminent. Mexicans rallied behind Huerta, who now became (to his
own surprise) a symbol of political independence in the face of Wilsonian pressures. Probably he was never so strong. He seemed im-
pregnable.

Wilson had so far violated every rule of good diplomacy. He had
opened negotiations without first obtaining support from groups and
countries who might be affected. His first notes were strong and
ominous, then they dribbled toward weakness. Time after time he
said all patience was exhausted, but he always reopened negotiations.
He had threatened, then failed to carry out his threats: Lind and
others had told Huerta that if he stood as a candidate in October,
Wilson would recognize the Constitutionalists or intervene. Neither
had happened.

Huerta correctly saw through all this as a colossal bluff. He could
count on the fact that two members of Wilson's cabinet (Bryan and
Josephus Daniels, Secretary of Navy) were well-known pacifists.

Republicans were demanding intervention, and it was doubtful if Wilson would let them direct his foreign policy. Congress was not fully behind Wilson. Further, parallel negotiations with Carranza to line him up with Wilson's Mexican policy were going as badly as those aimed at ousting Huerta.

4. THE CONSTITUTIONALIST CRUSADE

On October 17, 1913 Carranza had formed a provisional government and a cabinet, to which Wilson sent William Bayard Hale as his personal agent. Through him Carranza was told that Wilson was going to lift the arms embargo against him, and would never annex an inch of Mexican territory. Carranza was uninterested in these statements. He wanted immediate recognition, without conditions. He also refused to sign an armistice with Huerta and to participate in any elections held under a provisional president not chosen by himself, and so boycotted the October 26 farce. Hale reported that Carranza would never negotiate with Huerta. The First Chief loudly demanded total extinction of the Usurper and his supporters.

Carranza rejected out of hand any interference or mediation by Wilson or the United States. He warned Hale that such actions, if pushed, would "rekindle old animosities." He was as tough as Huerta. Carranza considered Wilson's offer of lifting the arms embargo merely diplomatic byplay to allow Wilson first to get rid of Huerta, then to select a government of his own choosing, a thing which Carranza would never permit, for patriotic and personal reasons. He was no pawn.

The obstinate Constitutionalist attitudes distressed Wilson. Whether or no, he wanted to aid their cause but they were making it difficult. He wrote to Hale on November 16 that "he would not be willing, even indirectly, to help them if they took so narrow and selfish a view. It would show that they do not understand constitutional processes." Wilson never did grasp the axiom that any Mexican leader, Huerta or Carranza, who was caught dealing secretly with the "Colossus of the North" was committing political suicide. A Revolution was in the making.

The anti-foreignism that had been a major element in the overthrow of Díaz had reached even greater heights under Madero. Mexicans attributed most of their ills—incorrectly, it may be said—to control from outside. Carranza's hold on his rowdy, jealous, and sus-

picious subordinate chieftains was at best precarious. Perhaps the
one thing that would strengthen it most was formal recognition of
his self-proclaimed provisional government.

But the American leader felt he was in no position to meet that
demand. The Constitutionalists controlled much territory, but only
a minor part of Mexico. If Huerta was ultimately successful in sub-
duing them, Wilson's recognition of Carranza's revolutionary *junta*
as the true government would wipe out all American claims against
Huerta; recognition would also lead to serious reprisals against Americans in Huerta's important bailiwick, the Core, the South, and the
West. Carranza publicly repudiated Wilson's offers of aid, which
complicated Wilson's diplomacy.

As November 1913 ended, the United States' Mexican policy as
outlined by Wilson was at an impasse. Huerta thrived under pressure
from Washington; his domestic foes were equally Mexican and
equally adamant. The alternatives were narrowing. Wilson could turn
again to Europe or to armed intervention. To abandon his attempts
to force Huerta out never occurred to the President. The best that
he could get from Europe was a promise not to interfere.

Europe, the United States, and Mexico. Old World statesmen
looked on Wilson's sincere but blundering efforts to bring constitutional government to Mexico as an unnecessary subterfuge for annexation. His moves were construed by them to be a purposeful
weakening both of Huerta and the Constitutionalists preparatory to
gobbling up the neighboring republic. The sincerity of his quixotic
quest was further open to serious question (from the European point
of view) when the British learned by inquiry that Wilson had no
plans or policy in the event Huerta did tumble. Short views seemed
incredible in so serious an effort. Europeans were not particularly
incensed but were a little amused. Had the United States been less
powerful or the European situation itself less dangerous, the chuckles
might have been louder.

But in the face of a menacing Germany, Britain and France were
willing to pay almost any price for friendship with the United States.
It was a difficult matter for the British to turn over the full control
of Mexican affairs to Wilson. Their navy had only recently been
converted from coal-burners to oil-burners and at that time the chief
source of this essential fuel was Mexico. To protect that vital strategic
stake, the Foreign Office had aided and encouraged British petroleum
companies and had given them especially vigilant diplomatic aid.

Wilson's blasts in the October 26 Memorandum and the Mobile address had been directed against these operations.

But the international stakes were now getting higher. Huerta, even oil, was not as important to Europe as Wilson. Lord Grey, British Foreign Secretary, sent his own emissary, William Tyrrell, to Washington to smooth matters over. Anglo-American friendship had to be cemented at all costs. The long conversations between Tyrrell and Wilson created an unwritten agreement. In return for British pledges not to interfere in Wilson's Mexican policy, the United States assumed the responsibility of protecting British interests in Mexico; Wilson would do his best to have the discriminatory Panamá Canal tolls rescinded by Congress.

Wilson's public statement of the arrangements appeared in his first annual message to Congress on December 2, 1913. All efforts would be made to protect American *and other foreign life and property* in Mexico; no exclusive advantages for the United States would be sought there. He called his general policy "watchful waiting." It was. Now that Europe was neutralized, Wilson was waiting for Huerta to commit an act that would justify intervention; waiting for the Constitutionalists to win.

The British side of the tacit bargain was kept. When the British Admiralty insisted on having an officer at Tampico who outranked all the Americans (and therefore by custom would command any joint foreign intervention), Wilson was assured by the Foreign Office that he would not take part as commander. Lind, still in Mexico, wrote Wilson that Ambassador Carden was vigorously pushing British interests to the detriment of American ones. At Wilson's demand (toned down by Walter Hines Page), Carden, after a decent interval, was transferred to Brazil.

When Wilson was expected to deliver on his side of the Anglo-American agreement, he could not. Pancho Villa shot and killed an Englishman, William Benton, in what he claimed was self-defense. When the British government did nothing about it, waiting for Wilson to move, the cabinet almost fell. Wilson ordered an American investigating committee to establish the facts, and to this Villa willingly agreed. But the "First Chief," Carranza, vetoed any such action. He told Wilson that the United States could look after its own nationals, but was not to represent all foreign powers in Mexico.

Both patriotism and strategy lay behind this position, which Wilson could never get Carranza to change. If European interests were adequately safeguarded by the United States, other nations would have no incentive for recognizing the provisional Constitutionalist government. Further, such assumption of responsibility by the United States would extend the Roosevelt Corollary (by which the United States policed public debts in Latin America for Europeans) to all diplomatic matters. Mexico would always be facing only the United States. Carranza did not intend that Mexico should be treated in the highhanded way in which Wilson was treating Nicaragua and Haiti. Part of Carranza's inflexibility arose from the fact that Constitutionalists in December 1913 were winning victories again.

But the fortunes of the campaign began to swing in the other direction during January 1914. Huerta had suspended payment on national bonds, and with the diverted money had enlarged his army and purchased quantities of arms which enabled him to recapture Torreón and split the revolutionaries. From their camps came rumors of dissension, passed on to Washington by Wilsonian presidential agents attached to each of the main Constitutionalist groups. With morale lowered as the result of these defeats, there was increased grumbling over Carranza's sluggish caution and stubbornness. Villa's butchery caused concern in Mexico and the United States.

To rehabilitate the Constitutionalist cause in Wilsonian eyes, Carranza sent Luis Cabrera to the United States. He explained to Wilson that idealism was the drive behind the Constitutionalists and outlined the difficult social problems of the nation. This broadened Wilson's narrow view of Mexico from a political to a socio-political problem; under Cabrera's tutelage Wilson was convinced that until Mexican land reform was accomplished, there would be unrest in the republic.

The test of "good" Mexican governments now depended on their being composed of agrarian reformers. So delighted was Wilson with his new knowledge that he wanted it passed on to the American public; he had the editors of the *Saturday Evening Post* send him an interviewer who published the new Wilsonian view in their May 23, 1914 issue. A more crucial result of Cabrera's influence was Wilson's note to the Secretary of Treasury to have customs agents blink shipments of arms to the Constitutionalists.*

Back and forth teetered the military balance in Mexico. Then

---

* The actual embargo was lifted February 3 when Carranza promised that his government would respect foreign property rights, including "just and equitable concessions." This mobilized much opinion behind Huerta, now posing as an anti-Wilson Mexican.

partial success of the Constitutionalists inadvertently set up Wilson's long-awaited opportunity to intervene. By a master stratagem, Pancho Villa recaptured the key rail center of Torreón; the victory opened the way to Mexico City. Revolutionaries began to mop up outlying Federalist strongholds, of which the oil refining center at the port of Tampico was crucial. The battle for Tampico was a turning point both in the long duel between President Wilson and Provisional President Huerta, and in the Revolution.

5. MORAL IMPERIALISM AND INTERVENTION

Strung along the Panuco River that empties into the Gulf at Tampico were foreign-owned oil installations—wells, storage tanks, and a little refining apparatus. The petroleum colony, chiefly British, were apprehensive that purposely or accidentally Mexicans might set these strategic properties afire in an engagement between Federalists or Constitutionalists. British, French, German, and even Spanish war vessels converged to protect the threatened interests of their nationals.

Since Taft's day, at least, the American Navy had been patrolling Gulf waters. One battleship was permanently at Tampico, while others hung off Veracruz. As Secretary Knox once said, the purpose of the battlewagons was to keep Mexicans "in a salutary equilibrium, between a dangerous and exaggerated apprehension and a proper degree of wholesome fear." Wilson's feelings about the danger of the Mexican situation could be gauged by the number of vessels hovering in Gulf waters. With a major battle for Tampico looming, he had the Navy outnumber and out-gun the combined European units there. Admiral Mayo commanded at Tampico, while Admiral Fletcher, with a smaller force, stayed at Veracruz.

Various national naval commanders warned both Constitutionalists and Federalists away from the oil installations. None had qualms about enforcing their warnings with action. With a critical battle going on, Tampico was tense. It was in this atmosphere that a German gasoline salesman rushed aboard Admiral Mayo's flagship and reported that seven American sailors and an officer had been arrested and jailed by Huerta's men.

From a dock that everyone had been forbidden by Huerta's Federalists to use, these Americans had been loading gasoline into a whaleboat flying the American flag. Ordered out of their boat by the government patrol, they had been marched off to the Tampico prison. Immediately Admiral Mayo sent his aide to the Huertista commander and demanded the release of the men. Apologetically General Zaragosa explained that his subordinate had made a mistake, and the Americans were released. The whole incident from beginning to end had not occupied an hour.

Admiral Mayo, however, decided that the Mexican explanation was an inadequate recompense for the indignity to the United States Navy. He sent his chief-of-staff (in full uniform) to the commander with an ultimatum: by six o'clock the following evening General Zaragosa was to "hoist the American flag on a prominent position on shore and salute it with twenty-one guns, which salute will be duly returned by this ship." Moreover, the Mexican officer responsible for the "humiliating arrest" of American personnel was to be court-martialed, and a written apology from General Zaragosa was to be sent to Admiral Mayo. Thus spake the Navy for the United States.

Almost simultaneously two other aggravating Mexican incidents occurred. In Veracruz one of Admiral Fletcher's mail orderlies had been arrested and taken to jail by an overzealous Mexican soldier; there had been a Navy reward posted for an AWOL sailor and the optimistic Mexican had hoped that this was the right one. Then, unaccountably, cable messages from Mexico City to the United States were held up for nearly twelve hours by the Mexican censor, just at a time when wires were buzzing to straighten out the Tampico and Veracruz incidents. These matters were lifted from local handling to the hands of the respective national leaders. Huerta faced Wilson.

Huerta was willing to apologize in written form to Mayo and to court-martial the unfortunate officer, but he would not salute the American flag with twenty-one guns, the main issue at stake. It would have been political suicide to do so, since he was buoyed up to a great extent by posing as the stalwart defender of Mexican nationalism; even if he did fire the salute, he was running the risk that the United States might not return it—disastrous to his prestige! With alarming incidents coming so close together, Wilson's mind linked them together as a plot to discredit the United States. He had no realization of the intense anti-foreign atmosphere and the normal minor peccadilloes of Mexican life.

On April 13 Wilson spent the whole day studying what he ought to do. He had convinced himself that Huerta was deliberately launching a campaign to lower the dignity of the United States. Wilson delayed his decision until John Lind returned on April 14. As Lind was a heated proponent of intervention his advice did little to weaken the President's determination. Here was an issue that warranted intervention, unsullied by dollars or issues over property. Nobody could vote against an insult to the flag.

Intervention. At his cabinet meeting on April 14 Wilson announced that he was going to make a strong naval demonstration against Huerta. The whole Atlantic fleet was then ordered to Tampico, an additional seven battleships and six smaller vessels to complement the units already there. The three at Veracruz were to remain. The Navy warned Wilson that such a concentration might lead to war. Apparently Wilson was aware of the risk he was running; when he left his cabinet he remarked "If there are any of you who still believe in prayer, I wish you would think seriously over this matter between now and our next meeting."

Huerta would be shown that Wilson's bluffing was over when firepower surrounded him. Yet Wilson did not want war. The United States naval commanders were told that the Administration wanted no hostilities. This, then, was an out-size bluff. Until Huerta fired the salute, the Navy would patrol Mexico and cut off needed supplies, which Huerta was purchasing in Germany.

Wilson and Bryan then wrote a soft note to Huerta. They appealed to his "military honor" to fire the salute. The agile Huerta suggested that the whole matter of the demands be submitted to the International Court of Arbitration at the Hague. Wilson remarked to visitors that this was "one of the humors of the situation." The Fleet would reach Tampico about April 22, and Wilson had to inform the country about the mounting crisis. He had decided that the salute must be fired, or else. Or else what? No detailed plans were made beyond that.

On Saturday, April 18, Wilson sent a last ultimatum to Huerta. The President gave him until noon Sunday to fire the salute or Wilson would lay the whole matter before Congress. At the very last minute, Huerta's Minister of Foreign Affairs—José López Portillo y Rojas—informed the American Chargé d'Affaires that Huerta would fire the salute if the United States would guarantee to return it immediately. The Chargé hurried this proposal off to Washington, where Wilson brushed it aside. The hour passed; no salute.

Bryan set about convening a joint session of Congress for Monday afternoon, April 20. The President was in West Virginia, writing his speech and a resolution giving him permission to use the armed forces against Huerta to secure his "recognition of the dignity of the United States." On his return, the President was jaunty, well-rested, and sanguine that his schemes were working well. He told reporters "I have no enthusiasm for war. I have an enthusiasm for justice and the dignity of the United States, but not for war."

The cabinet meeting on Monday morning modified Wilson's plan. Wilson learned that his projected naval blockade had two serious loopholes: the interdiction of Mexican ports could not, under law of nations, affect third parties—German or British vessels could load or unload their cargoes of munitions at will. Secondly, Huerta was even at that moment receiving a ponderable supply of stores which might tide him over. On Sunday the steamer *Mexico* had unloaded a thousand cases of ammunition. Due soon was the German vessel *Ypiranga* bringing 200 machine guns and 15 million rounds of cartridges. The blockade scheme had to be revised.

The seizure of Veracruz was therefore at this meeting substituted for a naval demonstration off Tampico. The object was capture of Huerta's incoming munitions. The timing of the new operation had to be nice. The only way the Americans could prevent ammunition on the *Ypiranga* from passing into the Mexican president's hands was to seize it on the dock after it had been unloaded, but before it could get transshipped toward Mexico City. Thus at the end of the cabinet meeting on Monday morning all knew that there was going to be a landing at Veracruz. The time of it would be set by the arrival of the *Ypiranga*.

Next on Wilson's tight schedule that crowded day was a conference with Congressional leaders. As a show of bipartisanship in national crisis, Wilson called together the Republicans and Democrats on the House and Senate Foreign Relations and Affairs Committees and read them his speech and resolution. Henry Cabot Lodge, a powerful Republican, objected to both, but with seeming arrogance Wilson silenced him.

In his Congressional message on April 20, 1914 President Wilson rehearsed the three Mexican incidents and asserted that they would lead to an unwanted war if allowed to continue. Even if conflict should come, he stated, it would be only against "General Huerta and those who adhere to him," not against the Mexican people.

After reaffirming his intentions to respect the sovereignty and territorial integrity of Mexico he requested that Congress approve his use of armed force. There was little or no jingoistic talk in Congress, as in 1846. But Wilson's earlier handling of Lodge now bobbed up to plague him. By accident, the Republicans had a temporary majority on the Senate Foreign Relations Committee, which they used to embarrass and harass Wilson.

Lodge refused to allow passage of the resolution as drawn by Wilson. He pointed out that it lacked any references to loss of American life and property, and that the United States could not threaten by name a foreign person, however obnoxious; governments, yes; individuals, no. He wanted all references to Huerta cut out and loss of property and life inserted as the causes of intervention. All Wilson's and Bryan's cloakroom buttonholing could not get the unamended resolution through in time to authorize a landing on April 21, the date the *Ypiranga* was to arrive. When the normal party balances were restored it was passed April 23. But without his resolution, Wilson went ahead with his altered plans, the details of which occupied his attention now.

After his Congressional speech Wilson called a private conference. To advise him, the senior admirals and generals were present, as were Lind, Bryan, and Daniels. Certain technical difficulties had appeared. Mayo's units could not get from Tampico to Veracruz in time to help Fletcher, and the bulk of the fleet, now deflected toward the southern harbor, would not arrive until even later. There might be inadequate forces to take the port. Everyone agreed that it was to be taken, and that Admiral Fletcher would have to do the best he could. The civilians, including Wilson, were convinced that the Mexicans would not fight. When the definite arrival time was known, Washington would flash orders to Veracruz to set Admiral Fletcher in motion. Everyone went to bed for a while.

Later in the evening Bryan got word about the *Ypiranga's* arrival. It would be 10:30 A.M., April 21. Wilson had Josephus Daniels (later Ambassador to Mexico) order the Navy to carry out the agreed scheme. About 8:30 A.M. on April 21 Admiral Fletcher, who had been alerted earlier, received the fateful orders: Take Veracruz. He immediately made arrangements with the Huertista commander to turn over to him unopposed the customhouse and docks. At 11:30 A.M. the United States Navy took the principal Mexican port.

An hour later the *Ypiranga* hove into port. All sorts of legal and international difficulties ensued about that ubiquitous Teutonic vessel. She was temporarily impounded and spent some time evacuating

Americans. Finally, with the once important original munitions still in her hold, she docked at Puerto Mexico on May 26 and calmly unloaded them. It turned out that months before and all through the American military occupation of Veracruz, munitions had been reaching Huerta through this secondary port.

The actual taking of Veracruz on April 21 seemed to be moving like clockwork. During the afternoon, however, the Mexican civilian population, led by 200 Mexican naval cadets of the Veracruz Academy, opened lively fire on the few American Marines and sailors. Admiral Mayo withdrew them to his two battlewagons for the night and awaited the arrival of the rest of the fleet. Next day the enlarged force pulverized the Naval Academy and put an end to fighting by naval gunfire. The casualties of the occupation were 19 American dead, and 71 wounded; the Mexicans lost over 300, including some naval cadets.

When Wilson got news that fighting had actually occurred, with unexpected deaths involved, he was appalled and unnerved. He had not wanted trouble; it could lead to even more serious conflict. Both Huerta and Carranza immediately issued strong statements condemning the occupation and demanding the withdrawal of American personnel. Pancho Villa came to the favorable attention of Americans by stating that the American military forces could remain as long as they liked, just so they did not enter Constitutionalist territory.

In the United States, recruiting offices were jammed, but nobody quite knew whether the United States was at war with Mexico or not. This was the chief end product of moral imperialism. A national sigh of relief went up on April 24, 1914 when the Ambassador of Brazil and the Ministers of Argentina and Chile in Washington jointly offered their good offices to mediate the difficulties between the United States and Mexico. Wilson recovered his nerve, swapped Army occupation for the Navy in Veracruz, and accepted the Latin-American mediation offer. Huerta was still in power in Mexico City, more than a year after the vendetta had gotten under way.

6. RELEASE

The Niagara Mediation Conference. The national rejoicing over the President's acceptance of the offer of mediation between the United States and Mexico was eloquent testimony that the United States as a whole had no real will to war with Mexico, nor aggressive designs on that republic. To Wilson the proposal came as a handy way to extricate himself from an unexpectedly complicated situation. It also permitted him to pursue the aim he had harbored all along: ousting Huerta. "Mediation" was still one-sided.

Wilson made it clear in a confidential memorandum to the Latin-American mediators that he expected to control the outcome of the projected conference. It was to carry on his contest with Huerta, while relieving Wilson himself of the charge of unilateral action. The note put the elimination of Huerta as a *sine qua non;* a single provisional Mexican government would form and immediately elect a permanent government in strict accordance with the Mexican Constitution. It would be committed to necessary domestic reforms.

The mediators demanded an armistice between the contending parties in Mexico, and a strict enforcement of the arms embargo against both sides by the United States. Huerta and Carranza both reluctantly accepted mediation. Then Carranza refused to send a delegation, and would not agree to an armistice. He was winning. But he was running short of ammunition. Wilson was caught in a transparent subterfuge that aided the Constitutionalists, a galling experience for the great idealist.* Wilson delayed calling the group together, hoping for a Constitutionalist sweep.

After considerable bickering the Mediation Conference formally opened on May 18, 1914, at Niagara Falls, Ontario. The American delegates had no power; they had to refer all questions to the White House. Wilson would not let a word be said about the original cause of intervention, Huerta's refusal to salute the flag. Wilson adroitly made the conference carry on his policy.

It only discussed a settlement of Mexico's internal problems. The single recommendation Wilson was willing to accept was the naming of a new provisional government to receive power from Huerta; the only provisional government he would approve must be made up of Constitutionalists. But Carranza would not hear of the Niagara Conference determining Mexico's fate. Those who glibly write about Wilson's fathering of the Pan-American movement at the Niagara Conference have not looked at the record. Finally, to save their own faces, by June 30, 1914 the mediators had patched up a protocol.

A provisional government pledged to general amnesty and free elections should be established in Mexico and recognized by the United States and the A.B.C. group.† The United States was to seek

* Carrying arms the schooner *Sunshine* came into Tampico "under stress of weather" en route from Galveston to Havana; the day was bright and clear.
† Argentina, Brazil, Chile.

no indemnity. Wilson would not allow his commissioners to sign even this innocuous document. It was never even sent to the Constitutionalists. The Conference was a successful propaganda device: it seemingly showed the world that Wilson was willing to listen to reason and to consult Latin America, but in fact he kept control and would not compromise. His policy had merits.

Success. While the Conference wrangled, the Constitutionalists advanced. The United States' hold on the Veracruz customhouse was visibly bankrupting Huerta. He had no revenues to feed his troops or to buy munitions. His paper money had become worthless. He was through. On July 14 he convened Congress, and resigned, after appointing the Chief Justice of the Supreme Court to negotiate with Carranza for the surrender of Mexico City. On the next day Huerta left for France. Again the *Ypiranga* played its role; it carried Huerta to exile as it had Porfirio Díaz, only three years earlier. The formal surrender of Mexico City to the Constitutionalists took place on August 20, 1914.

Over the storied cobbles of Mexico Obregón and Carranza rode in triumph. Wilson's policy had been successful, it seemed. Huerta was out. Wilson had at one time or another sent ten special agents; at times there were as many as six American diplomatic representatives in Mexico to carry on the feud between Wilson and Huerta. Carranza and Constitutionalism were the involuntary but main beneficiaries.

* * *

The lengthy record of discord during the years 1913 and 1914 carries its own lessons. One is that international problems are more complex than slogan-makers sometimes assume. A set of worthy attitudes is no substitute for coherent policy. Part of Wilson's difficulties were based on sheer ignorance and the naïve assumption that one man with a portable typewriter and self-righteousness could handle the innumerable details of foreign policy. Lack of technical ability was second only to lack of adequate staff-work and planning. Wilson stumbled from crisis to crisis in Mexico with neither clearly formulated objectives nor alternative plans to reach them, and brought the nation to the brink of war as a consequence. Above all, however, was his determination to control a nationalist revolution and bring it to a predetermined conclusion. He learned much, as the next round of interplay clearly revealed.

9. War and Revolution I

After the independent but quite discordant efforts of the United States and the Constitutionalists had forced Victoriano Huerta from Mexico, that unhappy land drifted further into anarchy. The Constitutionalist coalition dissolved into its component parts and the republic was ravaged with civil war that did not cease until one faction emerged as the dominant one. In this the Mexican Revolution differs from the Russian. No one clique with a clearly defined and rigidly enforced orthodox ideology was able to consolidate its power as the élite group of trustees for the future. The result of the civil wars from 1914 through 1917 was an uneven and uneasy balancing of military power among Constitutionalist groups and a failure to liquidate the various institutions and dissidents around which future counterrevolutions could cluster and perhaps come to power as Huerta had.

Continued chaos in Mexico persisted until an alliance between Alvaro Obregón and Venustiano Carranza brought uneasy peace to much of the area. It was sealed by redrafting the Constitution which embraced the old victories of Juárez in the nineteenth century and now included the newer social and economic demands generated by revolution.

As earlier, the United States and Mexico swung through a cycle of recrimination, short-lived bursts of coöperation, and unstable equilibrium. Woodrow Wilson, now immersed in the tasks posed by the outbreak of the first World War in Europe, let Mexico simmer and boil, but some of the widening ripples of the Revolution could not be ignored, and therefore the United States was occasionally but reluctantly moved to action, including a punitive expedition, in Mexico. International and domestic issues remained fused and continued as a football of partisan politics in each nation.

Hardly had the "Usurper" left when the Constitutionalist coalition smashed into pieces and turned to internal bickering. In May 1914 Pancho Villa and Venustiano Carranza, "First Chief of the Constitutionalist Army," had agreed that a convention should be called to select a provisional president. Villa had the power; Carranza had the plans. Carranza wanted the convention to select a civilian government to carry out a gradualist reform program and to reduce the military element in Mexican life. Villa and to a lesser degree, Zapata, would not agree. It is not clear whether their desires for direct, radical reform or ignorant jealousy were at the root of their position. No one was sure of Obregón's attitude. Through his efforts, however, the convention met on "neutral ground" at Aguascalientes in October 1914. Villa packed the town with followers and the military convention elected an honest, intellectual general without troops—Eulalio Gutiérrez—as its president, with Villa as his Secretary of War. Zapata and Villa drove Carranza out of Mexico City on November 14 and installed their puppet regime when he repudiated the Convention's scheme.

Much in the Juárez pattern, Carranza withdrew to Veracruz, still claiming to be the only legitimate government of Mexico. Obregón joined him there, and early in 1915 the Carranza-Obregón combination began to fish for wider support: Agrarian and labor decrees—the first social legislation of the Revolution—were published as *Additions to the Plan of Guadalupe.* Zapata and Villa tired of playing with Gutiérrez and drove him out of the capital but could agree on no political plan by which to govern the whole nation. They were *caudillos,* not statesmen.

In this utter factional confusion, Obregón began to win battles for Carranza. First he contained Zapata to his old bailiwick (of no particular military importance) in Morelos and Guerrero, then drove Villa from Mexico City. Carranza came back to that ancient seat of power in February 1915.

Obregón drove on. In a series of exciting and crucial engagements he trounced Villa and drove him back into the North. By late autumn 1915, Pancho Villa, who had once been at the head of 100,000 invincible *Dorados,* was reduced to the regional *jefe* of Chihuahua; he could irritate but not seriously threaten the Obregón-Carranza axis. It safely possessed Mexico City, most of the Core, the South and West, and a main corridor through the North to the United States border. In a military sense the Obregón-Carranza union controlled Mexico. Pockets of resistance and minor local areas under autonomous chiefs, as well as the larger Zapata realm and the Villa principality, defied even military domination.

1. THE CONSTITUTION OF 1917

The national panorama facing the Carranza coalition in 1915, still headed by the nominal "First Chief," was not unlike that viewed by Porfirio Díaz in 1876. Floods of paper money issued by competing bands had eaten away the fiscal base of the economy, and five years of vicious guerrilla wars had squandered the economic gains of the *científico* generation. Disease and hunger stalked the land; manpower had been in revolutionary motion and fields lays untilled. Any universally recognized national authority had evaporated; control was scattered into the hands of local military *caciques* of varying stature and power. Daily existence in every walk of life was disturbed and precarious.

Promises of social benefits, even food, were enough to recruit armed men to any leader potentially able to deliver on such pledges. Carranza and Obregón had capitalized on this seething discontent by outbidding other factions and stealing their issues. From conviction and from military necessity, *Additions to the Plan of Guadalupe* issued in December 1914 by their government-in-exile promised overdue changes. Like the final Laws of Reform, promulgated by Juárez in similar circumstances during the mid-nineteenth century, the *Additions* and the specific Carranza decrees filling in their generalities were campaign promises and war measures, good only if their side eventually won. Thus ideological factors crept into the military struggles.

The *Additions* were promises of social, economic, and political improvements, stated to be indispensable for the Mexican people's needs. Included in them were planks covering municipal liberty, agrarian reform, labor legislation, nullification of foreign contracts and monopolies, tariff realignments, credit for Mexicans, and a series of promises of political readjustment.

A Carranza decree of January 6, 1915, the "Law of Restoration and Donation of *Ejidos*," which implemented one of the *Additions*, is generally considered to mark the transition from the purely military and political phases of the Mexican Revolution to a broadened economic and social movement. It pledged Carranza's coalition to carry out an agrarian program like that of Zapata. Labor decrees, patterned on the early Flores Magon demands, soon won urban support to the Carranza group; everywhere that Obregón's armies succeeded in winning a town from Villa or Zapata, a "House of the World's Workers" was established by the Red Battalions which helped him gain his victories. When Carranza won, he had a long list of obligations.

The Constitution of 1917. Carranza attempted to give some shape and coherence to the Revolution once he was again in Mexico City. For tactical ends and from ideological conviction, he and his advisers believed it necessary to commemorate the reëstablishment of Carranza by a new national constitution. It would distinguish him from other leaders called "Constitutionalists," legalize his position, and by embedding the *Additions* into a permanent document, create a powerful magnet for drawing dissident elements to the support of the shaky *de facto* regime.

In Mexican intellectual circles the evolutionary hypothesis had permeated all strata. It was widely accepted that Mexico had evolved beyond the point where the Constitution of 1857 covered current needs; a "modern" charter should replace it. The constant late-nineteenth-century emphasis on "organic bodies"—municipalities, unions, classes—had led many to think that eighteenth-century concern with individuals and individual liberties should be modified to conform with the ideas that had gained currency since the Juárez Constitution had been adopted.

The Mexican constitution that emerged from the epic Revolution was thus a party platform, an eclectic summary of past and future Mexican hopes, and a factional product of the Carranza group. For purposes of political and military expediency it included nearly every reform demand that had been voiced seriously since 1900; it preserved all the gains made by the Reforma, of mid-nineteenth century. Self-contradictory and often imprecise, its stipulations could subsequently be tailored to give any desired solution a "revolutionary" patina. It turned out to be more explicit on the negative side—things that the Revolution will not tolerate—than in its affirmative prescriptions, where alternatives were more numerous.

Around Carranza had clustered an ever-enlarged "brain trust" of intellectuals, headed by Luis Cabrera. They now busied themselves preparing revisions of the old Constitution of 1857. The sources for their working draft were numerous and sometimes obscure: the Constitution of 1857 itself, the scattered writings of the Precursors, the several main revolutionary Plans, state constitutions, and their own convictions. Nearly all shades of revolutionary opinion were represented, but those of the middle-of-the-road gradualists (reflecting Carranza's outlook and temperament) were preponderant. They controlled the Carranza production, a preliminary revision or working draft.

On September 14, 1916 Carranza authorized the calling of a constituent convention at Queretaro in November. His convocatory decree stipulated that representatives to the convention should be loyal Carranza followers, selected by the people to reform the Constitution of 1857. On October 22 the election of these representatives, within territories controlled by Carranza and Obregón, was the nearest that the Constitution of 1917 has ever come to popular ratification. In some electoral districts a single candidate ran, in others none.

The constituent body convened in November and started to work on December 1, 1916. By taking the long and detailed Carranza draft prepared for them as a basis, special committees were able to finish their work in a short time. Unofficial lobbyists for particular revolutionary ideas managed to have them introduced into the convention, and on the floor itself some important modifications of the Carranza proposals were made in open debates. When the new document was completed on January 31, 1917 it was returned to the First Chief. He promulgated the Constitution of Queretaro by personal decree on February 5, 1917. It is the oldest operating constitution of the major Latin-American republics; it has been in effect, with important amendments, ever since.

The long new charter included some outstanding and important innovations, but more than two-thirds of the document copied the Juárez 1857 version verbatim. Some of the old practices were modified only slightly.

Tranquillity had to be achieved through Executive means; Carranza was First Chief and Obregón was his Secretary of War. The crisis-born charter curtailed the power of the Legislature, which by the 1857 document could impeach the president by a majority vote; in the 1917 version the only grounds for his impeachment were high treason and grave moral offenses of a criminal nature. No domestic political crime can bring Congressional reprisal. In 1857 the Reformers denied the president a veto, but in 1917 he was authorized to veto Congressional legislation in whole or in part; he was given the power to initiate legislation to which Congress must give first priority. If that were not enough, he was (and is) permitted broad scope in personal decrees—law by executive fiat, signed only by the appropriate Executive Cabinet minister. After the unsatisfactory Porfirian experiences with vice-presidents, the Constitution of 1917 abolished that office. Its absence further enhanced the distance that the chief executive towers above all others.

The contradictory nature of the Mexican Revolution was reflected in the Constitutional Convention and the document it produced. Within its body, one group, chiefly Carranza's followers drawn from civil and bureaucratic ranks, preferred to stress the gradualist, evolutionary approach to the solution of social problems, especially those connected with property and property rights. Placing more emphasis on radical departures, no matter what the cost, were others whose nominal allegiance was more directly paid to Obregón; many, if not all, were military men. In the jockeying for committee assignments, a representative of the latter faction, Francisco Múgica, was placed in the key post, Chairman of the Committee on Constitutional Reform.

As a result of the division in views among the delegates, the final Constitution of 1917 was neither as self-consistent as Carranza's original draft nor as radical as the majority of Obregonistas wished. It was a compromise between factions; neither Carranza nor Obregón had controlled the final outcome. There was actually a greater body of agreement than of disagreement between the proponents of the Carranza and the Obregón approaches to revolutionary problems.

But the split is reflected in the controversial articles of the charter. Articles 3, 27, and 123 (dealing respectively with education, agrarianism and foreign property rights, and labor) were subjects to considerable debate and change from Carranza's original proposals. Article 3, governing education, reflected both the strong anticlerical biases of the Revolution and the nationalizing tendencies of the Carranza regime by espousing as the national government's responsibility and duty the furnishing of free public elementary education, of a lay nature. It went much further than Carranza had expected, but fell short of a demand for "socialistic" teaching proposed by a Jacobin minority in the Convention.

Article 27 was a departure from earlier Mexican practices. It remains one of the most controversial features of the revolutionary charter; it wrote into this fundamental law of the land the accumulated but diverse agrarian programs of the Revolution stressing both small private holdings and collectivized communal systems, and reiterated the old Iberian doctrines of sovereign control over subsoil rights. It defined property in terms of "social function" rather than in accordance with common law precedents; it canceled various types of grants made by Díaz. In contradiction, Article 14 reasserted the sanctity of contracts and private property. The strong anti-foreign currents of earlier times and the Revolution were legalized in Article 33; it still gives the president sole and plenary power to deport, at his discretion, any foreigner "whose presence he judges inconvenient."

Perhaps the major contribution of the Convention and its main deviation from Carranza's specifications was the famous Article 123, often called the "Magna Carta of Mexican Labor." It grew out of numerous specific Convention proposals and attempted amendments; ultimately the delegates decided to package these in a separate title or chapter, entitled "Concerning Labor and Social Welfare." Long and detailed, Article 123 included propositions made much earlier by Flores Magón in 1905, borrowing from European legislation like the famous Waldeck-Rousseau Law (1884) in France, and advanced ideas on labor legislation and welfare from the world at large, from New Zealand to the United States.

Article 123 enjoined on the state the fostering of a strong Mexican labor movement and gave the state powers to regulate it. It recognized labor unions as "moral persons" with a long list of duties and responsibilities. It voiced the need for social security legislation and provided a set of Utopian norms for the conditions and remuneration of Mexican labor. The basic principle of Article 123 was that labor was a status, a way of life, for which the minimum essentials were now constitutionally guaranteed, rather than an economic commodity, subject to the market vagaries of supply and demand.

The idea that the Mexican Revolution had a special world mission to perform was mainly responsible for making a special chapter for this long array of new constitutional rights and privileges. One of the representatives expressed it by saying, "Just as France, after its Revolution, had the high honor of consecrating in the first of its constitution the immortal Rights of Man, so the Mexican Revolution will have the rightful pride of showing the world that it is the first to place in a constitution the sacred Rights of Labor."

This sense of historic mission is a special and noteworthy feature of the men who drew up the Constitution of 1917. They were, they felt, responsible for outlining a total Revolution for future generations to inherit. In debates one said,

Apart from the mere political reforms which the Revolution has already proclaimed . . . such as free municipalities, suppression of the vice-presidency, the principle of no re-election, and so forth, we, the renovators, come here to sustain in the Constituent Assembly the social reforms which Luis Cabrera has synthesized. . . . These may be thus condensed: fight against peonage, or the redemption of the rural workers; fight against exploitation of labor, or the legitimate revindication of laborers, as much in small shops as in the factories or the mines; fight against the hacienda, or the creation and formation, development and multiplication of small property; fight against monopolistic capitalism, against privileged and all-absorbing capitalism; fight against clericalism— let us fight against clericalism of all religions; let us fight against militarism, without confounding militarism with our citizen army. . . . We are liberals, undoubtedly, but progressive liberals, liberals under much socialist influence: We find ourselves located about equal distance between the passionate and sentimental school of [socialistic] demagoguery and the Old School liberals, of that old school which established as its corner-stone and basic fundamental the Manchester principle of "laissez faire." . . .

The years of seemingly inconclusive revolutionary turmoil had not been wholly in vain. Mexico's new nationalism had, at the cost of innumerable lives, been slowly defined and labeled "The Revolution." Its program henceforth was the Constitution of 1917. Its slogans could now be used to mobilize the new forces in society and politics necessary to implement its goals—social justice, exploitation and redistribution of national wealth and resources, extirpation of special privileges, especially corporate and foreign, and the extension of "modernism" to the polyglot and still heterogeneous Mexican people.

The problem now was to apply these doctrines, to create the instruments by which the Revolution could be brought from a plane of rhetoric, theory, and campaign oratory to operational reality. Given the complexity of Mexico, that would be no easy task. Cycle after cycle of renovation had failed to alter very materially the conditions and institutions in which generation after generation of Mexicans had spent their lives.

Even more important at the time was the fact that Mexico, disturbed as it was, was not living in an international vacuum and that important segments of the country did not subscribe to Carranza's leadership. Pressures from abroad continued to shape the slowly emerging Revolution. These influences came primarily from the United States.

2. RETREAT FROM MEDDLING, 1914–1916

Elements of the Mexican problem and its handling in Washington differed from the anti-Huerta crusade. Europe was now engaged in a great struggle of pressing concern to the United States and Wilson. Mexican affairs became secondary. Local winds were allowed to blow themselves out. In the United States the control over the Mexican policy returned gradually and quietly to the State Department, as Robert Lansing, first as its Counselor, then (after June 1915) as Secretary of State, brought the conduct of affairs back into normal diplomatic channels and followed more orthodox usages. Woodrow Wilson's urges to crusade shifted to the European stage, and (with but few exceptions) he personally took small notice of Mexico. With the outbreak of World War I, the scope of action of the United States was increased. Clearance with France, Germany, and Great Britain was unnecessary; their gunboats were not in the Gulf.

The Fuller Mission. Wilson was as bewildered as the Mexicans as to which of the Constitutionalist leaders would emerge as political victor from the melee of the dissolving military coalition. To inform himself, and in an attempt to preserve some order in Mexico, he dispatched one of the last of his personal agents, Paul Fuller, of Coudert Brothers. Wise, able, and Spanish-speaking, Fuller was to visit the major chieftains in the hope of getting them to settle their differences and agree on a constitutional president of Mexico. The plan was, if possible, to unite Zapata, Villa, Obregón, and Carranza. Fuller first met Villa, who impressed him very favorably; along with a glowing report on the virtues of the Centaur of the North, Fuller dispatched a signed agreement in which Villa promised in writing to hold early and free elections, establish a constitutional democracy, and safeguard American rights if he became president of Mexico; he also agreed, as did Obregón, to form a coalition government. In Mexico City Fuller soon learned that Zapata was intractable and Carranza was obdurate. The First Chief would not discuss in detail the political future of Mexico until Wilson withdrew armed forces from Veracruz, but professed himself friendly to the

United States. Apparently on the strength of Fuller's reports and his own feelings, Wilson felt that the future president of Mexico should be Pancho Villa, but he was not over-eager to enmesh himself in the developing Mexican imbroglio. Soon Lansing replaced Bryan as Secretary of State. More and more the Mexican policy was shaped by the Department rather than by the President. The Fuller mission drew to a close in September 1914, productive of much information but no real formula.

The United States and Mexico, 1914–1915. The nature of Mexican problems was now different. No clear-cut moral issue was at stake. The first problem was to liquidate American intervention. Troops were still in Veracruz, running it. Inhabitants of the port were worried that Carranza would take reprisals on them and refuse to honoi taxes they had paid to the occupation authorities. When Carranza finally agreed to an amnesty, he was no longer in Mexico City; the United States then had to convince Villa that withdrawal of Americans was not designed to aid Carranza. Finally Villa gave his consent. Before he could change his mind, Wilson ordered the troops out on November 23, 1914.

Mexico was drifting into unconstitutional anarchy, yet Wilson made no real move to influence a final solution. He had learned salutary lessons from his difficult apprenticeship. Though Americans were being pillaged and shot by various revolutionists, Wilson wrote in March 1915 that renewed intervention in Mexico by the United States was not more than "a remote possibility." But as the dismal toll of Mexican and American lives and property mounted, his resolve not to interfere cracked. On June 2, 1915 he again personally appealed to the leaders of all Constitutionalist factions to compose their differences and form a single government. He would give moral support to whatever ruling group *they* selected; nothing came of this. For a while the embargo on arms was lifted in the hope that the military stalemate would be settled by sheer local power; this too failed. Then it was clamped down on all bands.

To end disorders in the neighboring republic Wilson turned to collective or "Pan-American" intervention, moral rather than military. He agreed to Lansing's suggestions that the five ranking Latin-American envoys in Washington should confer, and help the State Department pick a Mexican faction to back as the single *de facto* government of that unhappy land. Everyone, from Zapata to Villa, was eligible for this new form of accolade.

When this news got around, every Mexican group secured for itself powerful American backers in the hope of winning the prize in this important lottery. All but one faction of the Constitutionalists was bound to be disappointed in the outcome. The State Department believed at first that Carranza was the main obstacle to peace and unity; Lansing suggested that all the lesser chiefs form a coalition which the United States could support. Wilson, though personally disgusted at Carranza (because he had just learned that the "First Chief" was selling Red Cross supplies supposed to succor the wounded and ill in Mexico City), did not support Lansing's suggestion. Wilson approved the idea of the Latin-American invitations, but he had learned much since 1913. He opposed, or at least did not underwrite, the necessity of immediate free Mexican elections. Social reform outranked that as a need, he felt, in echo of Fuller's recommendations. Further, he warned Lansing that to deal Carranza out—the man in Mexico City with the most troops and victories—would be "to ignore some very big facts."

The Five Power Conference. The Five Power Conference met on August 3, 1915. Argentina, Brazil, Chile, Guatemala, and Uruguay were called together to help Lansing pick a winner. They all agreed that an invitation should be sent to every Mexican leader, asking them all to meet at a neutral place and, under the auspices of the Conference, form a government, restore order, and then hold a free election. If they could agree on a provisional government, the States at the Conference would recognize it.

Invitations to the several Mexican leaders went out August 13, 1915; by August 30 all but Carranza had replied affirmatively. His chiefs had all cleared their replies through him. By this time Villa's military backbone was being snapped; his stock as the probable winner visibly dropped as Obregón penned him in the north. In the face of these "very big facts" Lansing shifted the United States' support to Carranza; as Obregón's nominal master, he was the man to be recognized. Wilson approved. Far astern was the early Wilsonian doctrine of "constitutional legitimacy," already unworkable.

Now Lansing had to overcome the Latin-American envoys' conviction that the United States was flouting their advice to ignore Carranza and was using them as a cover for unilateral dealing. They felt strongly about Carranza; he had just insulted Brazil. They would not recognize him until he promised a general amnesty. His neglect of their invitation had also hurt their pride. Carranza had from the outset taken the view that this Conference could not interfere in the domestic concerns of Mexico and he would promise it nothing; he contented himself with telling meddlers, American and Latin-American, to mind their own business.

But facts were facts. Carranza, through Obregón, controlled most, though not all, of Mexico. Zapata had a small enclave, and Villa a larger but less critical one. Lansing delayed recognition. He asked a pledge from Carranza that his government would scrupulously protect foreign lives and property and comply with its other duties and obligations under international law. With unusual promptness Carranza replied with the requested pledge. Lansing finally assuaged the wounded feelings of the Latin-Americans, and the Conference finally agreed that Carranza was the winner.

On October 19, 1915 the five Latin-American countries, followed by the United States, formally recognized Carranza as *de facto* president of Mexico. He was still stubborn and "unconstitutional" but he controlled. By presidential proclamation the United States declared an embargo on shipment of arms against all groups in Mexico but Carranza's.

A combination of elements had seemingly brought temporary tranquillity to Mexico and its relations with the United States. These factors included the military victories of Obregón and his continuing loyalty to Carranza, the eclipsing of Zapata and Villa, and, above all, Wilson's determination to follow a "hands off" policy in Mexican internal affairs.

3. LULL AND STORM, 1916–1917

After Carranza's *de facto* recognition there was a short-lived era of good feeling and coöperation. He was receptive to a State Department note in October 1915 asking the Mexican government to take action on eighteen outstanding problems between the nations; he asked and received permission to transport Mexican troops across Texas and Arizona to reach the rebellious Villa's domain in Sonora. Preparatory to resuming full-scale formal diplomatic relations with Mexico, broken since the withdrawal of Henry Lane Wilson, the American President proposed the name of Henry P. Fletcher as American Ambassador to Mexico. His departure was delayed, as the opening months of 1916 saw dissipated the small pool of coöperation between Mexico and the United States.

Controlling features in the mounting crises between the two countries through 1916 were threefold. Carranza's coalition was still a struggling one, plagued by shortage of funds and an abundance of military uprisings, the most dangerous of which were led by Pancho Villa. He had to convert a shaky hold into a strong one. Secondly, Wilson and the United States were slowly but inexorably becoming enmeshed in the European struggle; Mexico was no longer their number one foreign problem. Finally, in the United States 1916 was an election year. Wilson's handling of Mexican matters became a campaign issue. On both sides of the border the domestic situations visibly affected foreign policy; international issues fused readily with national questions in an emotionally overcharged atmosphere.

In the United States the Republican Party opened the Presidential political campaign of 1916 with an increasingly bitter indictment of Wilson's inept handling of Mexican affairs. Senator Fall, Theodore Roosevelt, and Henry Lane Wilson pounded away on the theme that Wilson had defaulted on his Democratic pledges of 1912, to protect American lives and property abroad. They presented his many expressions of concern for the Mexican people as proof that the Democratic president thought more of their welfare than that of his own countrymen.

Villa's Vengeance. A new factor was suddenly injected into this potentially explosive situation. Deflated and resentful, Pancho Villa purposely tried to embroil Mexico and the United States in war. Such a struggle, he believed, would make it possible for him to regain his lost power by posing as a national hero and by fighting the Americans while Carranza puttered in Mexico City. Villa could not forgive Wilson for scuttling him and recognizing Carranza, whom Villa regarded as a feeble old woman. Though the crude scheme of thus regaining power and perhaps the presidency failed, Villa's unsolicited and unaided effort did achieve one of its basic goals, that of inflicting personal revenge on both Carranza and Wilson by stirring up international trouble that embarrassed each of them at delicate points in their respective careers.

The first episode in Villa's vindictive campaign came January 10, 1916. Relying on Carranza's promises of protection for foreigners, a group of American engineers were unexpectedly attacked en route to reopening a mine in northern Mexico. Sixteen of them were killed at Santa Ysabel, Sonora. The inability of Wilson to provide adequate safeguards for American nationals in Mexico gave color and added glow to the heated charges the Republicans were making. Though Carranza promised to apprehend the culprits, he did nothing. He had neither the money nor the power to do so; his hands were more than full in just stabilizing his own position in Mexico City. The excitement over the Santa Ysabel massacre had calmed only a bit in the United States when a second and more serious incident perpetrated by Villa lit up public opinion in both nations and led to a real danger of war.

On March 9, 1916 about 400 Villa raiders crossed the border into Columbus, New Mexico. In broad daylight they shot down everyone in sight, had a brush with an Army cavalry patrol, and then disappeared into the Chihuahua hills. With nonpartisan unanimity the American press and public broke into an uproar; they demanded punishment. Wilson publicly said that troops would be sent into Mexico to capture Villa and disperse his bandits who were thus terrorizing the American border zone.* The President delayed sending an expedition of American troops into Mexico until he could get Carranza's consent. This permission seemed likely; in October 1915 Wilson had aided Carranza by allowing Mexican forces to cross Texas and Arizona to get at Villa.

Carranza was personally willing to accommodate Wilson, but he had to be politically circumspect. To an immediate American query for permission to dispatch troops, the Mexican responded with an oblique suggestion: to renew and broaden an old (1882) agreement between the countries that permitted either nation to pursue marauding Indians who tried to use the international line as a protective device by escaping across into their sanctuaries. The sensitivity of the situation was revealed by a strong note which Carranza sent when he heard that Wilson had publicly promised to send American troops into Mexico. Carranza warned Wilson that his men would fire on them; he issued a national call to arms, ostensibly to repel the projected violation of Mexican sovereignty.

Washington interpreted these moves as necessary domestic shuffling so that Carranza could remain a patriot in good standing. The State Department sent a second request; it again asked permission to dispatch an expedition, promised to keep Mexican sovereignty inviolate, but suggested that the old boundary agreement be discussed

---

* This was the first problem that Newton D. Baker, a reputed pacifist, found on his desk when he accepted the appointment on March 9 (day of the raid) as Wilson's new Secretary of War.

and broadened. Carranza's government found the note "acceptable" on March 13. Taking this for tacit approval by Carranza, President Wilson ordered General John J. Pershing to take regular United States Army units into Mexico.

The Pershing Punitive Expedition. Both national leaders were operating in an inflammable atmosphere. Neither wanted a war, though factions in their countries did. To prove his revolutionary virtue, Carranza was constantly pushed to taking as strong a verbal line as he could against the United States without actually precipitating a full crisis; he was convinced that Wilson would not dare to intervene in Mexico and thus be made a captive of his opposition party's criticism; Wilson's Presidential campaign was shaping up on the pacificist slogan "He kept us out of war."

On his part, President Wilson had to quiet the partisan criticism bent on making political capital of his inactivity as well as the subdued restlessness in his own party. Far more than all his critics realized though, the United States was teetering on a knife-edged balance between peace or war in Europe. Wilson knew it.

Perhaps each leader realized that the safest course at the time was verbal sparring and a minimum of action, a risky but necessary game that both had to play. Villa kept the situation inflamed as much as possible by extending his radius of terroristic raids into Texas; he had nothing to lose. But for the responsible men, Carranza and Wilson, any action might precipitate an inexcusable international conflict. Yet complete inaction was impossible in the face of rising feelings at home.

Only a week elapsed between Villa's Columbus raid and March 16, 1916, when General Pershing led 6000 troops onto Mexican soil. There was a discrepancy between the President's public statements about the object of the punitive expedition and the actual orders given to General Pershing. He was merely to scatter the Villistas and thus end the constant threat of raids. No mention was made in Pershing's orders about capturing that picturesque bandit leader. Wilson cautioned Pershing not to cross the border at all if Carranza's men put up any resistance. Congress approved the Presidential moves without hesitation. Momentarily the Republicans were taken aback at Wilson's decisiveness; his own and his party's prestige rose.

Starting on March 18, Carranza set out to make as good a diplomatic record as he could. His talent for vitriolic rhetoric against the United States was an asset in these circumstances. In a series of notes he complained of insults to Mexican sovereignty and tried to narrow reciprocal border crossing agreements to permit him to specify the numbers and sorts of troops as well as their disposal. From this he passed on to set up rigid conditions under which Pershing could operate; they were tight. The United States mildly agreed to most of these political demands. Wilson desired to minimize friction at the border and (within reason) to placate an increasingly bolder Mexican president. Larger issues were at stake at home and abroad in Europe.

The War Department directives, altered by each successive Wilsonian concession to Carranza, hampered the military effectiveness of Pershing's operations by hamstringing the way, and circumscribing the areas in which he could employ his command. He had been given a military task to perform, but for diplomatic and political reasons, not always apparent to him as field commander, he was prohibited from using the obvious means to complete it. Pershing disapproved personally of many of these restrictions, but as a good professional soldier he loyally did his best under all-but-impossible conditions.

The seeming impotence of the Army and the apparent subservience of Wilson to Carranza led to even louder political attacks in the American press and Congress. These, in turn, caused Carranza to impose more and more limitations. Senator Albert Fall demanded the immediate mobilization of a large army, and an invasion of Mexico to put an end, once and for all, to border raids. When Wilson's domestic foes and his international antagonist, Carranza, were independently but fully convinced that the President would not widen the conflict by full-scale military action, they pricked him harder: one wanted intervention, while the other wanted him to clear the foreign troops out of Mexico. Carranza never would discuss his own weakness and obvious inability to keep Villa on the Mexican side of the fence, out of the good neighbor's back yard. The basic cause of all this furor was a divided Mexico still in revolt.

The European situation of 1916 explains Wilson's real reluctance to commit himself more deeply in the Mexican affair. He was as touchy about the United States' national honor as Carranza was about Mexico's, but unlike Carranza, Wilson was engaged in an even more important gamble. His critics and Mexico were unaware of its gravity. In April 1916, Germany had started unrestricted submarine warfare; a German U-boat had sunk the unarmed French steamer *Sussex* with presumed loss of two American lives. Wilson had taken this opportunity to write a strong note to Germany; he threatened to break off diplomatic negotiations if such actions did not cease and if Germany did not explain. The road for a declaration of war was open: if Germany rejected the Wilson note, the United States would probably come into the European conflagration by joining the Allies against the Central Powers. Germany was pondering whether to reject the note and undergo Wilsonian wrath while Pershing was trying to break up Villa units in northern Mexico. If the United States was to enter a European war, it would be fatal for Wilson to have all its available force pinned down in the Mexican borderlands; there was little of military or other value for a thousand miles south. To win a war in Mexico always means capturing the Core or its outlets to the world. There was also the November Presidential election to worry about. So Wilson's mind was only partially occupied with what to do about Mexico, a minor element in a large world of difficulties.

His influential advisers were split as to the proper course for him to follow. The trusted Colonel Edward M. House pointed out to him that the inability of the United States to maintain a few thousand troops in Mexico, admittedly a reduced and negligible world power, would probably have a strong influence on Germany's answer to the *Sussex* note. If the United States was shown to be powerless there, the Germans could well risk its entrance into the war and hope for a quick victory before American mobilization could make it a decisive factor. On the other hand, the Secretaries of State and War, Lansing and Baker, equally sensitive to the possibility that the European powder keg was likely to blow up any minute, argued that the President would be justly censured if he did not pull out of Mexico while he could, with honor unimpaired; he could not irrevocably commit all the land forces to this minor theater. The United States had no really vital issue in Mexico, and there was the very real chance that all the energies and army it could muster would be needed suddenly, and at any moment, in Europe. They pointed out that in the ticklish Mexican mine-field an unexpected incident might occur which would make it impossible for Pershing's command to leave without impairing the national honor. No decision was reached. Then on April 12 such an incident did occur to involve the national honor of both Mexico and the United States.

Teetering on the Edge. On April 12, 1916 happened one of those trivial but destiny-fraught episodes that make historical predictions so fruitless. There is every reason to believe that Wilson could and would have quietly evacuated his forces from Mexico and somehow placated his domestic foes, but his hand was suddenly forced. He was presented with an immediate danger of war with Mexico; the possibilities were even greater that Germany would take full advantage of that situation. The Mexican incident itself was commonplace.

Because his airplanes were grounded, Pershing had sent a scouting column 180 miles inside Mexico. At the southern Chihuahuan town of Parral a detachment of the column had stopped to buy supplies. The unit was suddenly fired upon by a civilian mob of patriotic and Villista Mexicans; after unsuccessfully trying to restrain it, the Carranza military garrison then joined the rioting, which drove the foreigners back to their reinforcements, eight miles away. In the running skirmish 40 Mexicans had been killed, as had two American troopers. Nationalistic outcries inevitably followed from each nation.

After this unanticipated and lamentably fatal engagement, Wilson had to abandon all hope of withdrawing Pershing's troops quietly and immediately, or perhaps at all. To have done so would have meant a national, political, and personal calamity. If Wilson followed Carranza's imperious demand to withdraw all American troops immediately and unconditionally, Mexico and the Mexicans would lose all respect for the United States, and that might lead them into really rash actions on the assumption that the "Colossus" could not fight. It can and will. More appalling was the domestic prospect. Congress, including Democrats, would disown Wilson if no action were taken to redress the death of American soldiers at the hands of Mexican civilians; the American public would melt away from Wilson just when delicate negotiations in Europe demanded unity and the November polls were in sight. Carranza, on his part, could do no less than order the Americans out. It was a very loaded situation. The least miscue would bring war, disastrous to both nations.

To the Mexican's demand, Wilson countered with a suggestion that Obregón (Carranza's Secretary of War) and an American military man confer. The conference was held at El Paso, Texas, April 30. A secret arrangement was made for gradual withdrawal of American forces. When Carranza rejected that, the conference ended. He wanted immediate withdrawal, with no talk of return.

The American military officials believed that the reason for the lack of success at the El Paso conference and the continued border raids by Villa lay in real American military weakness. The regular

United States Army had no available reserves; it could not patrol the border adequately; recruiting had fallen below expectations. Mexicans saw these things; a few hotheads began to talk openly of invading the United States, arming the Southern Negroes, and dictating the peace terms from the White House. The old 1845 patterns suddenly revived. Experienced Mexican soldiers, like Obregón, shuddered at such jingoistic talk, but that it existed at all was a serious matter. Extremists in the United States and Mexico could push the nations into war.

Wilson called up National Guard units of Texas, New Mexico, and Arizona for patrol duty. He placed an arms embargo (which even included food and horses) on Carranza. But Carranza, still convinced that Wilson was in no position to intervene, bought arms from Japan, and paid for them by robbing Mexican banks—"forced loans."

The month of June 1916 was a critical one in Mexican-American relations. The Democratic Party platform appeared, with a plank against intervention. The German crisis moved toward the boiling point. Villa stepped up his border atrocities in number and magnitude. An alarming incident took place on the 19th in which an American sailor was killed and two naval officers were taken from a boat (flying the American flag) by Carranza's men at Mazatlán, on the west coast. Anti-American sentiment in Mexico was at fever pitch.

The peak came on June 21, 1916. Carranza had hedged Pershing's operations, and had warned Wilson that if American soldiers moved any direction but north, they would be fired on. A small scouting unit moved eastward, was warned, and continued. Mexican Government troops opened fire at Carrizal, killing 12 American soldiers and capturing 23. The storms over the Santa Ysabel massacre and the Columbus raid could not compare to the American public violence against Mexico (and Wilson) now. The President had to act, quickly and correctly.

Wilson immediately demanded the release of the prisoners. He mobilized the whole National Guard and formally incorporated it into the regular army. Though he had put the country on a war footing, he would not declare war. Germany was still more critical than Mexico. Wilson prepared a speech that would have stated that war with Mexico would unjustly punish the Mexican people, whose powerless and possibly unconstitutional *de facto* Carrancista government was really to blame. He would not "intervene," nor did he want war.* He merely wanted the power to clear the northern states of Mexico of all armed bands by force. Fortunately the speech was never given. Carranza might have had to declare hostilities; he couldn't have backed down.

On June 30 Carranza released the Carrizal prisoners. The American President in the meantime had learned that the United States commander may have been partly to blame for the clash at Carrizal. Wilson clearly did not want war with Mexico if there was any possible way to avoid it. His problem was still to protect the border and yet, for possible dispatch to Europe, to get Pershing's troops out with the least damage to prestige. He still had an election to win.

The New London Meetings. An opportunity to ease the crisis soon came. Carranza apparently felt that matters had approached much too near the flash-point. He sent an unusually courteous note (for him) on July 4 asking whether the United States would prefer direct negotiation or Latin-American mediation to settle the conflict. Lansing, acting for Wilson, preferred direct negotiation; he had previously gotten into difficulties through Latin-American mediation. Lansing arranged for Carranza to make the formal proposal for settling the trouble. The agenda for a mixed Mexican-American Commission was worked out, in a renewed climate of friction.

The only question Carranza would discuss was unconditional withdrawal of the American troops. The United States wanted to make the recalling of troops conditional on the signing of a broader arrangement to end the troubled border conditions that had originally given rise to the Pershing expedition. Difficulties over the agenda extended through the whole proceedings. The Commission first met at New London, Connecticut on September 6, 1916. Luis Cabrera was the Mexican representative; he showed himself a master of obstructionist tactics. He would talk of nothing but immediate withdrawal of troops. The Commission wrangled interminably in secret but finally agreed on a formula for the withdrawal of the intrusive American soldiers; Carranza rejected it. Just as the Constitutional Convention at Queretaro was finishing its task of providing Mexico with a new Revolutionary charter, the Commission broke up in an

---

* Wilson had a personal definition of "intervention" that implied establishment of a protectorate: "re-arrangement and control of Mexico's internal affairs," which he was against. He did not consider sending United States troops as "intervention," or sending forces against Mexico as "war," so long as he felt moral right was on his side.

atmosphere of acrimony on January 15, 1917. Its meetings had carried Wilson through the last stages of his political campaign.

Wilson was reëlected while it appeared that he was getting the Mexican problem settled. At the termination of the New London meetings his advisers suggested that even though Carranza had repudiated Cabrera's agreements concerning the withdrawal of American forces still in Mexico, that these troops be pulled out. They suggested, too, that diplomatic intercourse with Mexico be resumed. The lull created by the New London conferences had also permitted Carranza to set his political house in order and to prepare a presidential campaign of his own. Like the Five Power Conference, the meetings of the Commission were essentially a cover device, productive of propaganda useful chiefly in the domestic realms of both nations.

February 5, 1917 was a notable day in Mexico. To commemorate the promulgation of the Constitution of 1857 by the victorious Liberals it had traditionally been celebrated as "Constitution Day." Reinforcing this sentiment, Carranza chose February 5 to issue the Constitution of Querétar, sixty years later. On that same day, too, the last of the United States punitive expeditionary forces quietly left Mexico.

Their mission was not accomplished. Despite resumption soon of formal diplomatic relations with Mexico, the border remained a security threat. Disgustedly American soldiers, perhaps 40,000, patrolled their side of the line and occasionally chased raiders into Mexico. Fletcher soon came to Mexico City, with orders "to sit on the lid" as the new Ambassador.

Following the prescriptions of the new Constitution, elections were held in Mexico on March 11. Carranza emerged victorious and was inaugurated May 1, ending a constitutional interregnum that had existed since the death of Madero. Constitutionalism and a government publicly committed to reforms had at last emerged. Still hotly debated is whether such a result was helped or hindered by President Wilson's efforts to influence Mexican domestic affairs by direct meddling, manipulation of American public opinion, economic sanctions, arms embargoes, and even armed force.

4. WIDER WORLD STRUGGLES, 1917–1918

The stubborn, proud Mexican had seemingly outwaited and outmaneuvered the stubborn, proud American President. Carranza had won an unbroken series of diplomatic successes through indirect insults, carefully calculated obstructionism, hedged disdain, international law pettifogging, and other familiar tactics by which small states attempt to check and harass the more powerful. One of the chief reasons for this remarkable Mexican record was President Wilson's determination not to use overwhelming force in Mexico; but even more compelling had been, and continued to be, the widening European perplexities. Just as in the early days of the weak American republic, when it used European distresses to full national advantage, so in the twentieth century the Mexican republic exploited to the fullest its several opportunities while the United States was distracted elsewhere. It was to prolong this locally popular course as long as it could. Mexico had a lot of old scores to pay off.

Mexico, Germany, and the United States. The Mexicans never felt quite as disturbed about Imperial Germany as did much of the rest of the world. For that nation, unlike Great Britain, France, Spain, and the United States, had never put its troops on Mexican soil, nor overtly tried to control Mexican destinies. Germany had not committed unfriendly acts in the past; although (in line with the rest of Europe) it had supported Huerta's position, the Kaiser was equally willing now to support Carranza. Germany's recognition of his regime gave the Mexican president a possible counterweight against pressures from the "Colossus of the North."

The Germans saw in Mexico a possible base of espionage and even diversionary activity against an increasingly hostile United States. If Mexico could be persuaded to close her ports to the Allies, the action would cut them off from necessary matériel, especially oil, without which no modern war can be fought. Possibly following orders from their home government, a number of Germans in Mexico enlisted in Carranza's army; General Maximilien Kloss became his chief of artillery. The mutual advantages of Mexican-German friendship seemed manifest.

The United States viewed these developments with growing alarm. Daily Secret Service reports to the State Department indicated that German espionage activities and introduction of saboteurs into the United States via Mexico were constantly occurring. But without conclusive proof that Mexico was conniving in these activities, little could be done. Then a dramatic episode changed the whole face of matters.

The Zimmermann Note. The German Foreign Minister, Zimmermann, sent a note to Carranza, the text of which was intercepted by the British in February 1917. In it Germany offered Carranza an alliance. In return for Mexican aid, Germany promised that territories which Mexico had lost to the United States in 1848 and 1853 would be returned in a peace settlement after the war. Zimmermann urged Carranza to make peace between Germany and Japan, and to bring the latter into the alliance. Carranza rejected these propositions; he knew that faraway Germany, blocked from America primarily by the British, could be of small help in a Mexican war against the United States. But Mexican pride was restored. It was a Power. As a diplomatic move, the Zimmermann note failed in Mexico, but as a propaganda device there, it was a resounding success. Then it boomeranged.

In March 1917, a year after the Pershing expedition, President Wilson was again hovering between a declaration of war on Germany or maintenance of neutrality. After Germany had reopened unrestricted submarine warfare (on the assumption that the United States would not enter the struggle), tensions had mounted, but the critical decision for the United States was yet in the balance. At this psychologically important moment the British released the Zimmermann note, a master stroke of propaganda warfare designed to bring the power of the United States unreservedly to the side of the Allies. It accomplished its purpose.

President Wilson was astounded and angry. The wave of anger and fear that swept through the Administration was an accurate reflection of emotions in Congress and in the country. On April 6, 1917 the United States declared war on Germany. Many complex considerations entered into the fateful decision, but release of the Zimmermann note to Carranza was a climax. The German effort to woo the Mexicans had rebounded in unanticipated fashion indeed.

The United States and Mexico, 1917–1919. The entrance of the United States into the first World War affected its relations with Mexico. Wilson was so preoccupied with the major questions of conducting the crusade for democracy on a grand scale that almost never did he personally notice what was going on in the neighboring southern republic. His general attitudes toward Mexico, good for the duration of European hostilities, were known by his subordinates: no use of force under any circumstances or provocation. Threats, yes; force, no. This stand was based on coincidence of principle and a situation in which it would be suicidal to be involved in the quicksands of Mexico.

The mushrooming wartime bureaucracy meant that innumerable alphabetical agencies were dabbling in Mexico for various reasons. No one department controlled Mexican policy; each had its own. The conduct of diplomatic relations fell back into well-worn grooves as lesser and lesser subordinates penned the notes. These are almost indistinguishable in form and wording from the Republican Taft period. After Carranza had given Ambassador Fletcher assurances that American properties, especially oil holdings, would be protected, he was recognized in full *de jure* on August 31, 1917.

The United States clashed with Germany in Mexico. It was a minor operation, fought with two weapons. One was counterespionage, which was highly successful, and the other, propaganda, which was not. Frank R. McCoy organized the former, whose records are still restricted, while George Creel's Committee on Public Information carried on the effort to win Mexican opinion to a favorable view of the Allies and the United States. In the still heated revolutionary atmosphere of Carranza's Mexico no true patriot there could openly praise the country whose troops still vigilantly patrolled the border and occasionally crossed it in hot pursuit of Mexicans.

During the war the chief problems between the United States and Mexico were not political, but economic. When Mexican raw materials, essential to victory, were for some reason not flowing into the United States, it brought loud cries for action and threats; these did little good. Oil companies who felt they were being squeezed were especially vocal. Local guerrillas attacked them, and the Mexican government had, in spite of Carranza's private promises to Fletcher, started to control their operations. Under cover of aiding the war effort the petroleum producers tried to get intervention. They claimed that restrictive Mexican legislation was hampering their output. The State Department took a generally cold view of their claims, but Secretary of the Navy Daniels espoused their cause; Bernard Baruch opposed it.

There was some merit in the position the companies took: If Carranza continued his course toward nationalizing oil holdings, oil would be cut off from the Allies. As a neutral, Mexico (as owner) would be required to embargo the export of petroleum as contraband of war. That consideration was behind the strong tone of successive notes sent by the State Department during this period, though it was never openly stated to the Mexicans. In August 1917, Carranza had assured Fletcher that the government would not nationalize the oil industry, but a series of domestic moves indicated that he was not going to keep his promise. The United States threatened to intervene.

The issue came to a head when in July 1918 a strong Mexican petroleum law was re-enacted. The American petroleum companies bombarded the State Department with demands for action and threats to shut down operations. They claimed that they could not make a profit and still comply with the Mexican legislation. At best they wanted intervention in Tampico to make their property safe, and at worst, a reduction of Mexican taxes. They got neither.

On August 9 a White House Conference considered the whole matter of Mexican oil. Daniels presented the case of the oil companies; the Fuel Administrator, John R. Garfield, and Bernard Baruch of the War Industries Board took the opposing view, that the producers were taking undue advantage of the war to get unwarranted concessions from Mexico. President Wilson, in one of the rare times he entered the arena in this phase of Mexican affairs, took a firm tone and ended the steaming controversy: the United States would not use force against a weak nation like Mexico—that would be too much like the Germans in Belgium. If Mexican oil supplies could not be obtained without the use of force, then the United States would have to do without. The oil companies then had no recourse but to manipulate the Mexican judicial system to obtain redress over the alleged confiscatory taxation and *ex-post-facto* nature of the Carranza petroleum laws and codes. Their efforts are discussed later.

A less publicized controversy between the United States and Mexico centered around henequen, sisal hemp. Carranza wanted grains and machinery from the United States for the rehabilitation of Mexico; both of these were in short supply in the northern republic. The United States Food Administration was willing to comply if Carranza would first reduce his export controls and prices on henequen, needed for binding twine, ships' cables, and numerous war-inspired economic and military activities. When Carranza used his familiar tactics of obstruction, delay, and domestic blasts against the United States, he got his machines; the United States never did get the concessions the Food Administration had demanded on henequen.

During World War I, then, Mexico had been a security threat.

Though neutral it had been a troublesome irritant within the suddenly extended scope of United States international problems. Tranquillity in Mexico was necessary; almost any peaceful price was paid Carranza to keep him quiet. Wartime censorship, confusion, and greater excitement over the drama of Europe had kept the Mexican policy muffled and screened from American view. The end of the war in November 1918 brought those conditions to a close. The defeat of Germany, which helped establish the unquestioned hegemony of the United States in the Western Hemisphere, seemingly ended any possibility that Europe could threaten or interpose in Mexico as a counterweight to the United States there.

10. Interwar Epilogues

Contrary to the comfortable assumption harbored by most Americans during World War I, things had not been going at all well in Mexico. They were again to get worse before they improved. A country in revolution is not easy to live in or with. In the turbulent atmosphere which followed the European armistice, Mexico and the United States completed another round of acrimony in which crises again nearly precipitated armed intervention and war. While much of the world was talking about peace, and certainly hoping for it, domestic developments in Mexico and the United States bred a steady deterioration of good relations between them. The small amount of mutual good will again drained away quickly.

1. "PEACE?"

The national presidential elections in the United States again brought Mexican troubles. Wilson's handling of Huerta and the Northern chieftains became a prime campaign issue in a bitter political contest. No American leader tried to smooth things over. The Democratic President was in Paris, attempting to clamp the League of Nations on reluctant European statesmen and the world, and with him had gone much of the State Department. Ambassador Fletcher was recalled to Washington, there to handle Mexican affairs. The complicated and often secret European issues were not very useful to those who had smarted under Wilson's hand. The Mexican ones, used in 1916, were familiar and understandable to bitter critics anxious for any means to block Democratic plans. In the 1918 elections the Republicans captured the United States Senate, and almost immediately set out to harass the Administration, mainly in the hope of recapturing the presidency in 1920. Mexico was a major issue.

Wilson's Mexican policy and the Republic of Mexico were in for a thorough factional mauling. Resolutions in the Senate were introduced to purchase Lower California, to review all Mexican affairs, and to investigate claims against Mexico arising from damages to Americans during the Revolution. Senator Fall, fishing for materials useful in the forthcoming presidential campaign, headed a committee that held highly publicized hearings all over the country and played directly to the gallery; in purportedly investigating the Democratic conduct of Mexican affairs he called more than a hundred unfriendly witnesses who spewed hearsay and slander, and divulged bits of dubious information and scandal about the Democrats and Mexico in a wholly sensational fashion. As it became clearer to the public that Mexico was still not a stable, peaceful republic, renewed clamor for intervention "to restore order" again arose.

Carranza's hold on his nation was slipping. In Mexican eyes his domestic policies had not matched his superlative international performance. Counterrevolutions were brewing to dislodge him. Disorders fed the jaundiced American mood that Mexico was slipping back into anarchy; conversely, United States factional demands for intervention swelled the ranks of would-be revolutionaries in Mexico. Each Mexican splinter faction could hope to capitalize on the spreading disorder and perhaps ride to power on it. In Texas, New York, and elsewhere in the United States, little revolutionary *juntas* of Mexicans conspired; Carranza's protests to the State Department about their activities were ignored, partly from sheer overburden of work.

In the Mexican Republic itself old faces reappeared, old names rekindled memories. In Oaxaca Félix Díaz, Huerta's quondam co-conspirator and unsuccessful rival, headed a revolt against Carranza that smoldered and spread. Pancho Villa, once called "Sir Galahad" by Secretary Bryan, named himself provisional president of Mexico and began to raid anew. Talk of possible United States punitive action grew; the attacks on foreigners increased at the hands of irresponsible Mexican factions eager for loot, or to discredit Carranza and precipitate a crisis whose outcome might favor them.

The climax came when in October 1919 one such revolutionary band captured the United States Consul, William O. Jenkins, at Puebla. The State Department protested, but Carranza either could not or would not do anything to secure his release; finally Jenkins had to ransom himself. No sooner was he free, however, than the

Carranza government itself in November imprisoned him on unspecified charges and rather flimsy evidence of collusion in the original abduction. The true facts are still debated.

Sudden talk of war between the nations filled the papers in both countries. It was not an unlikely possibility, since such a war would presumably strengthen the shaky domestic position of each governing party, both under critical fire and for other reasons in danger of losing political support. Jenkins, a controversial figure and strongly anti-Carranza, did little to aid a peaceful arrangement.

The crisis and tense situation was inadvertently complicated by President Wilson. He had returned from Europe and had tried to go over the head of a balky Congress to bring the issue of the League of Nations and America's participation in it directly to the American people. Disillusioned by fierce attacks on him in the Senate, and exhausted by the strain of war and peace, Wilson had collapsed and was secluded in the White House. He was unapproachable. No one knew what was going on. Rumors were floating about that the President was dead, and that Mrs. Wilson and various Wilson cronies were really running the country in the President's name. The Senate, stronghold of Republican foes of Wilson, found the Jenkins crisis a useful device to blacken the efforts of Wilson in the international field.

In November 1919 Senator Fall introduced a resolution which demanded that the United States break off diplomatic relations with Mexico, preparatory to war. Secretary of State Lansing, according to his diary (viewed by Dr. Lowry), had been playing around with the idea that a war with Mexico might not be wholly unfruitful for Wilson and the Democrats: it would unite the badly split United States, put down unrest in the ranks of labor, and stop socialist agitations that seemed to threaten "free enterprise." But in the face of the Republican resolution, Lansing went before the Senate Foreign Relations Committee and urged delay. He said that the President was not fully informed on the Mexican situation and that he needed time to study the matter.

This gave the Republicans precisely the opening they had been looking for. A Senatorial delegation was named to talk to the President about Mexico; its real purpose was to discover whether he was alive, and capable of performing his duties as chief executive of the nation. Senator Fall's resolution was pigeonholed until he and Senator Hitchcock reported to their colleagues. On December 5, 1919 they visited Wilson. He was alive, conscious, and fully abreast of the situation; in a long memorandum to Wilson, Lansing had amassed evidence that oil companies and others with equally suspect motives were behind the drive for intervention and war. While the Senators were in the President's bedroom Lansing dramatically sent the news that Carranza had released Consul Jenkins.* The visit to Wilson had ended the immediate crisis and had temporarily deflated Fall's major issues.

Events in Mexico continued to be troublesome, but did not develop into international crises. Carranza's now almost professional anti-United States posture was not enough to save him from domestic difficulties. A *coup*, headed by Obregón, unseated him. This was the last successful military uprising in Mexico. It closed the epic Revolution and opened a new era of developments, national and international, which paralleled and interacted with the "return to normalcy" of the United States under the Republican Restoration of 1920.

People and Problems. Obregón's *coup* in May 1920 seemed to complete a cycle. When Carranza was fatally machine-gunned in a mud hut on his flight from Mexico (carrying much of the Treasury with him), the parallel was almost too deadly. Woodrow Wilson was still in the White House; his almost instant moral reaction to Huerta's accession to power on the dead body of Madero had provided one of the most complicated chapters in the history of Mexican-American relations. But in this latter instance, Woodrow Wilson was older, more sorrowful, and a much sicker man than in 1913. Moreover, by the time that a provisional president, de la Huerta, had presided over the Constitutional election of Obregón to the presidency of Mexico, Wilson's own Democratic Party had gone down in defeat at the polls. Just as Taft had left him the problem of Huerta as an inauguration present, so Wilson presented Warren G. Harding with the puzzle of what to do about Obregón and Mexico.

2. THE NORTHERN DYNASTY

The task of consolidating the Revolution and setting up the proper political equipment fell to the Northern Dynasty, headed by Alvaro Obregón. His court was composed of an interlocking directorate of

---

* He was later held again, but finally cleared and freed in December 1920. He unsuccessfully sued the Mexican government for his ransom money.

military men, intellectuals, labor leaders, and agrarians. From 1920 through 1933 these leaders hacked away at the roots of Mexican difficulties; slowly and painfully they wrestled with the undramatic chores of reconstruction and rehabilitation. By historical accident national leadership for the Revolution had come primarily from the North; this circumstance goes far to explain the peculiar cast, the emphasis, and the goals of their programs. The general tone of the golden twenties everywhere in the world provided the atmosphere in which they toiled.

The North, it may be remembered, was the chief Mexican heir of the Spanish Bourbon traditions. Until the Madero Revolution of 1910, no Northerner, or group of Northerners, had directed Mexican destinies. With the success of Venustiano Carranza over the opposing factions in 1916, Northern hegemony was provisionally established. Obregón was assisted in his displacement of the "First Chief" by a great many people, the most notable of whom were Luis G. Morones, a labor leader of the Core, and northern henchmen of Obregón, Plutarco Elías Calles and Adolfo de la Huerta. By Obregón's victory in 1920 the Northern dynasty was firmly seated. In almost apostolic succession the ruling power was transmitted by a line of leaders who chose their own successors: de la Huerta (1920), Obregón (1920–1924), Calles (1924–1928); Obregón (1928), and Calles' puppets (1928–1933).

Neo-Bourbons. Strikingly alike in many respects were the means and ends of the Bourbon Dynasty and their remote offspring, this Northern Oligarchy. The Bourbon Renaissance of the late eighteenth century was paralleled by a Mexican Renaissance which burst forth in the 1920's and astounded the world by its performances in many spheres.

Like their Spanish prototypes, the Northern clique were benevolent despots—everything for the people, little by the people. The sanction for their absolutism was not Divine Right but the Constitution of 1917 and their demonstrated ability to mobilize and direct the political and military power generated by the masses of Mexicans who had fought the Revolution under their leadership. With the earlier Bourbons, they shared innumerable features. The principal ones were their insistent drives for material improvements; their reliance on a talented middle-class bureaucracy recently elevated to consideration; their determination to build a yeoman agricultural society; their sponsorship of cultural reforms in aesthetics and education; and a manifest anticlericalism which broadened to include attacks on corporate activities of all sorts.

So near in outlook and methods, so distant in time and immediate backgrounds, these two ruling groups who transformed Mexico differed from each other in fundamental ways and purposes. The Bourbons had been interested in bettering Mexico for dynastic reasons, oriented toward a wholly European situation. The Northern Oligarchy was strongly Mexican and its being was integrated around a program of "Mexico for the Mexicans."

The Problems and Structure of Revolutionary Power. To carry it out, they had to achieve and hold political power. It was threatened by three interwoven circumstances. The outside world, specifically the United States, was generally unsympathetic, even unfriendly, to the aims of the Revolution. It was viewed narrowly as an unscrupulous attempt to redefine and limit property and contractual rights in a way that not only threatened particular American vested interests in oil, mining, and agriculture, but which clashed head-on with an economic internationalism characteristic of the Western world since the sixteenth century. The Revolution was put on the defensive in its attempts to get general recognition of these new departures by the community of nations. The Northern Oligarchy was also specifically faced with the possibility that overt intervention by the United States as agent to enforce international law might take place. Such action could adversely affect them; after all, Wilson had ultimately deposed Huerta.

Perhaps even more dangerous, since the American people were generally apathetic toward any international adventures in the 1920's, was the constant probability that threatened foreign interests would react by aiding the domestic foes of the Revolution and the Oligarchy. The elements around which a general counterrevolution could form had by no means been eliminated during the epic years of civil strife. Though reduced somewhat in size and power, the old antirevolutionary factions—the Church, the large landholders, the established large merchant families, the Porfirian industrialists, and the regional political machines of the West and parts of the South— could, when combined, exert considerable influence and pressure, especially if they were aided from abroad. Others might join. Disappointed revolutionaries were constantly drifting to their ranks. A new class of landlords and industrialists, formed from opportunistic revolutionary leaders, whose political ardor had cooled after they had obtained a sizable personal stake, might now support an anti-revolutionary struggle.

Even within the "revolutionary family" of immaculately conceived leaders there were honest but bitter differences of opinion over the direction and pace which the Revolution should take after 1920. With claims to revolutionary virtue quite as valid as those of the Northern Oligarchy such opponents could threaten their power structure by invoking the same slogans and could well set up a schismatic line of succession. Since the ideology of the Revolution was self-contradictory, vague, and all-inclusive, various revolutionary pretenders to power might well come either from the extremists—radical fringes, representing the Zapata-Villa traditions—or from the moderate-conservative sectors, symbolized by Madero himself.

So long as he lived, Obregón himself was able to handle most of the necessary juggling to retain power. Through force of personality and innate talents polished by successful politico-revolutionary activity he was the unquestioned leader of the group. His death by assassination in 1928 left a dangerous vacuum which the Oligarchy filled by an ingenious device, the creation of the single political party. Within its walls, the revolutionary family feuds and conflicts could be reconciled and quietly accommodated without creating perilous breaches through which counterrevolutionary elements could pour in to capture power and reverse the gains so painfully achieved. Thus though in outlook and programs the Northern Dynasty paralleled the Bourbons along many lines, its general political procedures and structure of power were also comparable to the Porfirian period.

The Northern Oligarchy had, however, to work within a narrower political range than its forebears. To be caught selling out the ideals of the Revolution by truckling to foreign pressures and economic demands meant political, perhaps even literal, death. Only by clever dialectical and political footwork could any revolutionary government walk the narrow line between the international compromises necessary to obtain funds to carry on rehabilitation and thus fulfill promises of the Revolution and yet maintain the now expected national attitudes of intransigence. Carranza had set a high standard for the latter. He, however, was dealing with a Wilson and a United States preoccupied elsewhere, whereas the Oligarchy dealt with Republicans whose eyes were fixed primarily on Mexico.

Obregón's famous "silver cannonballs"—bribes—bowled over most of the overt opposition.* One of his chief talents was an instinct that discriminated between political blackmail and real threat. Though following the Díaz pattern of "a minimum of terror, a maximum of benevolence," Obregón was not too tender-minded to "spill a little bad blood to save the good." When force was needed Obregón used it. The transition and consolidation period is thus strewn with political assassinations, condoned if not ordered by this latter-day *caudillo*. Obregón's empty sleeve reminded Mexicans he had given an arm to the Revolution, just as Santa Anna's wooden leg had been a political wand nearly a century before.

Each presidential campaign was preceded by a purge and followed by an unsuccessful military revolt. These weeded out the disloyal by death or exile. Díaz had kept, so far as possible, a static equilibrium, while the Northern group maintained a dynamic one by replacing the disloyal, unfit, and aged. This narrowing of the ruling clique at the top, while recruiting and promoting loyal subordinates, differed from the Porfirian tendency to keep new blood from entering the old arteries. By a sort of revolutionary social Darwinism only the fittest survived in the twenties to form the closed circle that controlled the Northern Dynasty's edifice of power.

The construction and operation of the system of power is absolutely essential to the understanding of subsequent political developments in Mexico. Just as Mexico is complex, so are its political mechanisms. The simplest explanation of what the Northern Dynasty did is to say that its members retained the guerrilla military organizations of the epic Revolution and clothed them with political titles and offices.

The key military figure remained the regional or state chieftain; his title was usually changed to governor or zone commander. His prestige, derived from successful revolutionary combat and leadership, could still call forth his own personal following of guerrillas and mobilize his subchieftains and their men. The followers were the "underdogs"—peasants, petroleum workers, Indians, miners—whose loyalties belonged to their immediate spokesmen, the political subchiefs. From the latter group came the municipal authorities, in control of the *patrias chicas*. They and their state leader, plus a few urban but provincial intellectuals, were the usual elements of the

---

* To him was attributed the saying, "No Mexican general can withstand a cannonball of 50,000 pesos."

state political machines. The president had only to deal with the regional and state *caciques*, his lieutenants or proconsuls.

Thus in Carranza's descriptive title, the president was "First Chief." Even more accurate was the label Calles pinned on himself: *Jefe Máximo*—Chief of Chiefs. The president and the regional bosses were all military men, on active or inactive duty. The post of Secretary of War became the critical one under any administration; it was in his office that the levers were pulled to obtain the desired end-product, where breakdowns in the circuits were analyzed and corrective measures applied. Impulses transmitted from this central tower broke through the thin resistance of "Federalism" or "municipal autonomy" as they pulsed down increasingly ramified local networks.

While he lived, Obregón was the chief mechanic, assisted by Calles. They were the top echelon, through a process of elimination. In 1924 de la Huerta's presidential ambitions had been too strong for him to resist; before the power system had been fully constructed, he had led a revolt that by a dangerously narrow margin had just missed uncrowning Obregón and his picked successor, Calles. De la Huerta was captured and packed off to California, where he taught voice for a living. In 1928 the other member of the lesser trinity, Morones, fell from grace. He bucked the machine, which had orders to put Obregón back in the presidency. Morones' political eclipse meant the disintegration of the labor movement; to then, his administration-backed Confederation * had enjoyed a monopoly, but now without it the Confederation lost its power and appeal. The forces of labor began to dissolve into smaller and smaller units, which expended their resources and time fighting each other, leaving labor without official or unofficial voice in shaping national policies.

Succession to Calles in 1928 posed a dynastic problem. One of the oldest slogans of the Revolution, dating back beyond it to Díaz' original cry of 1872—"No re-election"—seemed to bar Obregón from resuming the presidential chair. It turned out, through an exegesis of the revolutionary credo, that "Re-election" meant only "consecutive terms"; Obregón could, after the Calles incumbency, be elected again—that was not "re-election," technically defined. As in Porfirian times, the Constitution was changed.

The presidential term was also lengthened to six years. Obregón handily won the election and successfully quelled the expected re-

* Confederación Regional de Obreros Mexicanos (C.R.O.M.).

volt. But before he could be inaugurated, he was shot by a fanatical young Catholic cartoonist.

The Single Party State. Obregón's unanticipated death posed an even more difficult and ticklish situation for his heir-apparent, Calles. It had looked as if the system of alternating control between these two *caudillos* would keep peace and order far into the foreseeable future. But suddenly in 1928 half the equation had been erased. The doctrine of "no re-election" had already been stretched to the limit; Calles simply could not succeed himself as president and serve a second consecutive term without inviting personal and national disaster. Politico-military uprisings would again bleed the nation white.

After calling the major revolutionary chieftains—the governors and zone commanders—to Mexico City and warning them not to get overambitious, Calles in 1929 extricated himself and the dynasty by a useful political contrivance that is still working. It gives a paradoxical cast to Mexican political life. At one and the same time Mexico is a tightly controlled, single-party state, yet it is also one of the most democratic of Latin-American countries. An almost self-perpetuating élite prearranges elections and national legislation; simultaneously Mexico preserves a full roster of civil liberties—free speech, free press, free assembly. Only the right to successful revolution is limited in fact.

One key to that paradox is that the Northern Dynasty under Calles perfected and operated a system which encourages stability and decisive action in emergencies. For the most part it allows the regular political system to function without overt use of force, or even undue pressures. A battery of centralized controls can be manipulated discreetly but effectively. One set is normally already inherent in the office of president. Calles added others derived from the important invention of the single revolutionary party.

Calles' problem in 1929 was to divorce the Mexican executive from the actual exercise of his enormous Constitutional political power. The *Jefe Máximo* wanted real control reserved for himself and the surviving lesser members of the Northern dynasty, while preserving nominal democracy. To do this, he bound the regional and state political machines into a separate, formal, political organization. In turn its heads controlled the constitutionally prescribed organs of government—Executive, Judiciary, Legislature. Thus the "official party"—*Partido Nacional Revolucionario*—came into being. It was an unofficial cartel for directing official action.

Despite its superficial likeness to Communist or Fascist counterparts, the P.N.R. and its subsequent descendants to the present came as pragmatic responses to a particular Mexican political crisis. So long as Calles remained the *Jefe Máximo*, down to 1935, political decisions were made almost exclusively by the Party, guided by his hold on its key executive committee. Presidents from 1928 through 1934 had responsibility without power; Calles had power without responsibility.

The previous informal relationships that only Obregón could manipulate were thus institutionalized. Each of the state political machines gave up its local name and took on that of the P.N.R. in return for a share in national patronage and policy-making; they jointly agreed to give their support to a single slate of national candidates, selected by the party's executive committee. The bureaucracy and the president's cabinet, as well as the offices of deputy and senator in the national Congress, thus were composed solely of party members; since at that time the Legislature named the Judiciary, it automatically became a cog in the Callista party machine. From his private residence the *Jefe Máximo* bossed the whole network through his direction of this political holding company. He controlled the presidency by naming three consecutive puppets; when they tried to deviate from Calles' orders and build up independent strength he summarily dismissed them.

The Service State. Since each of the local revolutionary political machines is made up of a combination of its military chiefs, together with representatives of the intellectuals, and of the "popular classes," the local boss can control them only so long as benefits of some sort flow in his direction for division among his supporters. The president can remain at the head of the organization only so long as he properly performs his duties as head of the revolutionary family. Thus, in Frank Tannenbaum's striking phrase, there is "peace by revolution." The president and national administration must heed demands from the grass roots to fulfill promises of the Constitution of 1917 in terms of local needs or all those .30–.30's come out of the thatches. This tempers the apparent despotism of the president; he must use his powers for the collectivity.

Under the Northern dynasty that meant providing the favored areas with irrigation works, roads, schools, agricultural credit, and the permission to seek higher wages, parcels of land, health services, and the whole host of items needed to minimize local discontents.

Stopping the flow of these favors to a particular chief is tantamount to a vote of "no confidence": he had the choice of becoming orthodox once again or of taking his chances and trying to lead his people, his *gente,* into an opposition camp which might offer them a better deal. The stoppage of national patronage may signalize a grass-roots rebellion, such as that headed by Cárdenas, that sweeps all before it.

Rehabilitation or Reform? Two major circumstances kept the Northern dynasty from perpetuating themselves forever in power by operating the system which they were principally responsible for establishing in modern workable form. One was their own outlook. The other was Mexico's chronic poverty.

They had expressed a normal sentimental interest in Indians, the *ejido* programs, and other basic matters of high concern to the masses of the Core and South. But as Northerners, Obregón and Calles were fundamentally *ranchero-* and hacienda-minded. They were cool to Hapsburg or Russian collectivism. Obregón, in exchange for political backing, was willing to confirm the confiscations and land-grabs made during and just after the epic Revolution by Zapatistas, and to encourage those of his chiefs who felt moved to engage in agrarianism, but he was never four-square behind a full-scale program of land reform; nor was Calles. Ideologically they were for minimum, not maximum, land reforms. The Zapata agrarian program had never been an integral part of the Northern demands; redemption of the Indian meant to Northerners the placating of a few Yaquis rather than a full-blown Indianist program of benefit almost exclusively to the South.

Both, too, were cognizant that food, not land, is a real and immediate prime mover. Mexico was just barely feeding itself. Revolutionary fervor rises with the price of maize. To break up a going rural plant for possible future benefits was to exchange a known risk for an unknown and remote advantage. Without food, Mexicans would immediately rise to change the government.

The problem of money, which complicates all matters, was especially pressing on the Northern dynasty. Productive enterprises were in foreign hands—mines, petroleum, railroads, banks. Any move toward them immediately brought forth vigorous protests and muttered threats of international and domestic countermoves. Land was relatively unproductive so far as public revenues were concerned; large holdings were mortgaged to the hilt and small ones were worthless for tax purposes—to tax the heirs of the Revolution would be far from a wise policy. So how was the Revolution to continue revolving?

The answer was, of course, that it did not. Token payments and promises for the future, plus a modicum of welfare as a manifest of good faith, were about all that the Northern leaders could furnish. Mexican credit abroad was nil until it cleared up its international obligations. To clear those up would again pledge the very revenues needed to maintain a domestic stability, which in turn depended on fulfilling at least part of the Utopian promises of the Constitution of 1917. Balanced on the knife-edge of insolvency—political and economic—the Northern clique managed to juggle and talk their way out of the dilemmas posed by the alternatives of rehabilitation or reform until the Great Depression choked off even the small sums at their disposal for reforms and stepped up demands for revolutionary action, now.

Church and State: An Ancient Problem. Through these turbulent and fecund years from the Armistice of 1918 to the resounding crash that ushered in the Depression, anticlericalism was a useful device for the Northern dynasty to prove their revolutionary virtue, deflect attention from economic difficulties, and bind the "revolutionary family" into a unit. Possibly what anti-Semitism was to Germany in the twenties and thirties, anticlericalism was to Mexico.

The myth of the Church's wealth and power was kept alive, partly because of its own obscurantist and suicidal policy in Mexico. Like Morones, the Church overestimated its popular hold; like him, it was defeated and chastised. For three years after 1926 the Church was on strike; after orders to deport alien priests and register those in the Republic, the Church chose defiance and overt rebellion. No sacraments were performed—baptisms, marriages, Masses—in the hopes that the revolutionary national government would retreat from its advanced anticlerical positions. The rancors, especially of the West, against the Core revived. Political and economic regionalism took a religious cover: *Cristeros*—whose battle cry was "Long live Christ the King" (*El Cristo Rey*)—attacked Federal troops and school teachers and left hair-raising atrocities in their wake. The strike and the rebellion failed in 1929, though embers smoldered on.

Education, as well as the civil constitution of the clergy, was at stake. Article 3 of the 1917 Constitution had marked out primary education as the special preserve of the Revolution and had ordered that "untrammeled" secular knowledge be imparted. This meant a tug of war between Church and State for the mind of the child, the future Mexican citizen. With stakes that high, educational disputes formed a main issue of the anticlerical crusade and the egregious errors of ill-prepared agents of the State became magnified in importance. Catholic voices from the United States did little to calm the furor.

Under the driving energy of a great line of educational pioneers, the Mexican Rural School came into being under the Northern dynasty. It was an attempt to bring "modernity" and "culture" to the countrysides. An "action" unit, the rural school imparted the rudiments of literacy, socialism, and utilitarian crafts to rural adults and children alike. Qualified by nothing but their enthusiasm and willingness to serve, hundreds of city-bred youngsters trooped off into the hinterlands as educational "missionaries." Before they learned that fervor alone does not change Mexico, they reactivated the deep hostility between countrymen and urbanites. The Revolution got a new crop of martyrs.

All these undercurrents and exciting developments made a heady place of Mexico in the twenties, an era of expatriates. Clothed with "social significance" second only to Russia, Revolutionary Mexico drew liberal and radical pilgrims from all over the hemisphere to act as its unpaid publicity agents. Though many of them now have been disillusioned by the obstinate tendency of Mexicans to depart from the blueprints they helped Mexicans draw, they were then touched with the sense of mission that permeated all strata in Mexico during those effervescent years.

The sense of Revolutionary mission, so explicitly stated at the Constitutional Convention of Queretaro, broadened to include the aesthetic and intellectual spheres. As in the matter of the Church, the Northern dynasty found here an open field for sponsored individual action that endangered no national economic or political interest and which was essential for national integration. Painters and writers were given full rein. The State provided them as much cash as the small Treasury could afford after doling out the indispensable "silver cannonballs" to meet Army payrolls, and extracting sums for the most pressing obligations. The painters and intellectuals could raise but few military divisions in crisis, but their influence was out of proportion to their infinitesimal numbers. Many still live and impart their views.

Self-consciously painters like Diego Rivera, José Clemente Orozco, and David Siqueiros rejected foreign influences. Combining a long native tradition of murals with their own experiments and talents, they splashed the message of the Revolution in billboard-like productions to found a wholly unique American art style. The message was Marxian, the technique Mexican.

The analogous development of the "Novel of the Revolution" was equally sensational and significant. Authors like Mariano Azuela, Martín Luis Guzmán, and Gregorio López y Fuentes combined French naturalism with Mexican *genre* traditions of picaresque prose. Their episodic, formless, semi-autobiographical novels permanently captured the bubbling but dreadful atmosphere of the epic period. Too, they probed the social sores of Mexico and called aloud for cures. At the time, these productions staked out a new field; they have now become almost as standardized as American westerns or detective stories. The verve and vitality of other writers flooded all educational and scholarly activity. A sort of renewed Golden Age, reminiscent of the middle years of the Porfirian period, regained for Mexico its cherished and rightful place in the hemispheric world of the intellect and letters. The sum total of these multifarious, often discordant, activities has been variously labeled the "Mexican Renaissance" and the "Constructive Revolution."

The net effect of the period, from a domestic standpoint, was to give Mexico a new, workable, tightly controlled political system, to provide the land with the first rosy blush of economic prosperity, and to add cultural imperatives to the earlier political, social, and economic credos of the Revolution. It was a pioneering, pragmatic period which further defined the Revolution's goals and brought forth some instruments by which they might ultimately be reached.

3. NORMALCY AND THE OLIGARCHY

"Normalcy" had set in. The Republican Restoration was a fact. Charles Evans Hughes took over the Department of State. Mexico's ancient enemy, Senator Fall, became Secretary of Interior. In place of the clear-cut, emotional issue of whether or not to recognize a "bad" dictator, the problems with which Mexico and the United States wrestled for a decade were uninspiring conflicts over modes of law and its application. Mexico stayed out of the headlines, for the most part. Aggression during the period was almost purely verbal; no lives of interest to Americans were lost. Few ideals and scanty high politics dramatized the knotty legal snarls. Obregón had a background that Americans could understand far better than Huerta's; Obregón was an Alger hero, whereas Huerta, the earlier target, was a well-known drunk and professional killer.

A controlling element in the diplomatic field was that prospects of renewed world conflicts seemed exceedingly remote. General apathy toward international affairs was a common response the world over to the revived cults of nationalism and materialism. Crusades for peace and for social betterment were the order of the day. Neither in the United States nor in Mexico could any real sentiment be worked up for a war. Threats to national security seemed to be internal rather than external, and were identified in the public mind with imported radicalisms. So long as there was hope of continuing prosperity, even these were not a major menace. Despite their quite different backgrounds and domestic mandates, the Republican Restoration in the United States and the Northern Oligarchy in Mexico were not too far removed in basic outlooks. Calles and Coolidge could understand each other, in the same sense that Díaz and Taft earlier, Cárdenas and F. D. Roosevelt later, could have a real meeting of minds.

A number of matters were at stake between the neighboring republics. First of all was recognition for the new Obregón government. Obregón needed it badly, for the same reasons that Carranza had. Obregón needed arms to put down possible counterstrokes; he needed money, friendship. There was always the possibility that recent history would repeat itself and the United States would allow war supplies to filter into the hands of his enemies just as Wilson's "neutrality" had supplied the early anti-Huerta Constitutionalists. Obregón had to get recognition, but he also had to remain the Mexican Revolutionary Chief.

The United States withheld recognition until it could get "clarification" on a number of outstanding items. Some of these were ancient, others the product of the epic Revolution. The older matters were Mexico's default on the public debt, railroad bonds, and American citizens' claims against Mexico since 1868, the last time the board had been swept clean.

In the course of the stormy Revolution, the lives and properties of foreigners had been lost and damaged; in accordance with the usages of international law which makes a state responsible for safeguarding them, they and their heirs wanted recompense. Foreigners had been special targets of marauding bands during the epic Revolution, and the victims were now presenting a bill to the Mexican nation. But even after the wave of destruction had passed, American concerns had around a third of a billion dollars invested in mines and petroleum; this they hoped to preserve from Mexican government control or outright nationalization, part of the "Mexico-for-Mexicans" program.

The most critical international issue posed by the Revolution was the matter of private property, domestic or foreign-owned, under Articles 27 and 123. They forthrightly annulled the titles to public lands acquired after 1876, on the theory that the Díaz government had fraudulently given away the nation's patrimony. In American eyes the declaration was a clear *ex-post-facto* one that conflicted with the protection of property rights guaranteed in Article 14 of the same Constitution. Further, Article 27 enunciated the doctrine, common in Iberian lands, in some American states, and in Mexico until Díaz' time, that all subsoil properties belong to the nation. A grant of oil land, or even its purchase, did not entitle the owner to more than the right to use the surface; to dig minerals or extract oil, permission from their owner, the Mexican nation, was necessary.

The two Articles redefined private property by placing on it limitations not recognized in Anglo-American common law: "Social utility" and "national benefit" rather than timeless, contractual principles were enunciated. "Anti-social" use could lead to expropriation —nationalization for the benefit of all Mexicans. Most of the oil, mineral, and agricultural holdings of Americans and other foreigners had been obtained between 1876 and 1917. Therefore they were concerned about the application of these newly evolved doctrines. The Revolution had changed the old *científico* rules.

In the stormy days of 1917 and later, President Carranza had solemnly assured Ambassador Fletcher (in private) that existing American properties would not be subject to action under Article 27. Carranza had not kept those promises; he had demanded that the Americans apply for drilling permits and had begun to tax them. The companies had paid no attention to requests and orders to obtain permits; under Anglo-American and international law they "owned" the land which they had bought, and its subsoil riches as well. Mexican law said they did not, but the government was not yet enforcing that law.

Even before Obregón's election, his agents had come to Washington to ask recognition for de la Huerta. This was withheld, and no recognition was extended to Obregón. Like Carranza, Obregón privately assured the State Department that no action would be taken against American properties, but with the all-too-recent experience with Carranza still in their minds, American officials wanted such a guarantee in the form of an iron-clad treaty. Obregón had promised that Article 27 would not be applied retroactively—that lands and properties acquired before the Constitution of 1917 would not be nationalized. He refused to sign openly a treaty giving the Americans a special privilege. To have done so was tantamount to ending his Mexican political career.

The Doctrine of "Positive Acts." But to ease the growing domestic and international tension, he arranged for the Mexican Supreme Court, which was sitting on a number of oil cases, to enunciate in 1921 the doctrine of "positive acts." The Court declared, in handing down a judgment on September 26 in favor of the Texas Oil Company, that if owners of oil lands had actually erected drilling equipment or otherwise had performed some "positive acts," before the Constitution of 1917 had gone into effect, their holdings were secure. Such lands were exempted from the requirement of getting government permits to drill; and their property rights were sacrosanct under Article 14. For all intents and purposes they "owned" the land and its oil. New oil leases and lands would come under national control; old ones would not.

This Court decision did not placate the State Department. Under Mexican practice, a single decision of the Supreme Court does not form a precedent; five such judgments, without an intervening dissent, are necessary to make the doctrine applicable to future cases. Hughes wanted a specific treaty that would shelter American companies at the present and in the future from any operation of Article 27; they were to operate under the old, internationally standard rules.

For Obregón to acquiesce would have been clearly to uproot some of the major gains that the Revolution thought it had made. It would have built a legal fence around almost the only lucrative enterprise in Mexico, one marked "Mexicans Keep Out." He went as far as he could. By May 1922 the Supreme Court had handed down the necessary decisions to create a binding precedent; even if the composition of the Court changed in future years, the companies which could show that they had performed "positive acts" presumably were safe. Hughes still wanted a firm commitment in treaty form, not subject to judicial whim, and binding on all future Mexican governments.

Hughes increased the pressures, but when it became manifest that Obregón could not and would not sign the desired treaty, the State Department became slightly conciliatory and shifted its line. Threatened at home, Obregón suggested that the countries talk over the matters at issue. Hughes accepted the bid. Two Commissioners from each nation were named to discuss jointly the whole matter of foreign holdings and to report their findings to their respective governments. The United States implemented the Obregón suggestion in April 1923.

The press in both countries thought that such mutual action was long overdue. In Mexico *El Universal* advised its readers and the government "to give proof of its patriotism and show exceptional courage by recognizing that there is justice and equity in foreign claims and that a solution does not oppose national sovereignty and principles." The *New York Times* editorially advised an "honorable solution." These preliminaries led to what are known as the "Bucareli Conferences," named for their meeting place, No. 85 Bucareli, in Mexico City.

The Bucareli Conferences. From May to August 1923 the two Americans and two Mexicans quietly sketched in points of agreement and disagreement in an effort to reach some compromises. Mexicans have consistently taken the view that the Bucareli Conferences were held under duress; the United States had not yet recognized Obregón, and the outcome of the talks would determine their policy in that regard; consequently anything said or promised there was valueless, and binding only on Obregón as an individual, not on the Mexican nation. The United States has maintained that the Mexicans had officially initiated the proceedings and that subsequent Mexican administrations were bound to honor the agreements reached. Neither side has a clear case.

After exploring their opponents' debating and bargaining positions, the Commissioners did settle some matters. Each side sacrificed something. That is the purpose of conferences of this kind. The Americans were willing to retreat from their position that cash, not bonds, should be paid for expropriated American hacienda lands; in turn the Mexicans promised to limit the size of the areas which would be taken from them to form *ejidos*. Mexicans and Americans alike thought it wise to call a general claims commission, of mixed membership, to review and adjudicate miscellaneous claims which had been piling up against both the United States and Mexico since 1868; they further decided to separate these old matters from the new and to set up a special commission to evaluate damages arising solely from the Revolution. On the main problem, too, there was a meeting of minds.

The Mexican Commissioners announced that they could sign no formal treaty regarding Article 27 but that Mexico would unobtrusively continue to follow the policy of "positive acts." Owners who had legitimately acquired oil lands after 1876 and before 1917 were to have them in perpetuity and need not make application for special drilling licenses. This was a gentleman's agreement, technically known as the "Extra-Official Pact." The Commissioners reported their actions and agreements to the parent governments. The "Extra-Official Pact" seemed binding, so the State Department recognized Obregón. On August 31, 1923 there was considerable rejoicing in both countries when a simultaneous statement was released from Mexico City and Washington restoring fully the badly bruised diplomatic relationships between the two neighbors.

The consequences were favorable for Obregón. Within a short time Adolfo de la Huerta launched his revolt from Jalisco, partly on the grounds that Obregón had sold Mexican sovereignty for Washington gold. The uprising nearly unseated Obregón. He was saved from defeat primarily by prompt aid from the United States, in the form of arms and actual military coöperation: seventeen United States planes bombed the de la Huerta revolutionaries in Jalisco for him. Thus the Northern dynasty was established and its continuity preserved in 1924.

Claims. The claims commissions started looking over a mountain of materials in 1924. Mexico took this opportunity to clean the international slate by also inviting France, Great Britain, Germany, Italy, and Spain to come and settle general and mutual outstanding claims. For various reasons none of these Claims Commissions were wholly successful. The least effective was the mixed commission of Mexicans and Americans. Technicians tried to establish the facts and their values but they were bathed in such constant publicity that old sores were reopened. The adjudication of a citizen's routine claim became a matter of national honor overnight.

The Mexican–United States General Claims Commission received a great number of petitions. Citizens of the United States placed in the Commission's hands 2781 of them with a face claim value for Mexican-caused damages worth $513,694,267.17, while Mexicans filed 838 counterclaims that added up to $245,158,395.32. When the effort to settle matters by the mixed commission method was finally abandoned in 1934, only a few cases had been touched: 50 American claims had been disallowed, 89 granted; 4 Mexican ones were dismissed, and 5 granted. Where less emotional factors were involved, the Commissions did better. Europeans managed to settle most of their mutual claims. The speculative and inflated nature of all foreign claims against Mexico is indicated by the fact that, in the cash settlements arrived at, the actual sums awarded to Europeans averaged less than 3 per cent (2.64 per cent) of the face value placed on their injuries.

Even more rancorous and unsatisfactory was the Commission that tried to assess damages due Americans from the Revolution. Here Mexican sentiments and American emotions ran rampant. Each touchy case revitalized old feelings. The peak of the difficulties came when the Mexican Commissioners refused to countenance any award to the heirs of the American engineers massacred by Villa at Santa Ysabel; the United States government entered a claim of $1,225,000 for them. The Mexicans declared that Villa at that time was a private bandit whose unfortunate activities were of no concern or responsibility to the Mexican government. Nearly every case raised the question of whether its perpetrator was a true "revolutionary" or a "bandit." Engaged in constant debate, the Special Commission on Revolutionary Claims never did make any awards on the cases which crowded its docket. Later, and quietly, these damages and claims were settled in orthodox diplomatic channels.

In April 1934 the whole unsuccessful attempt to settle claims by this international arbitration was dropped, in favor of direct bilateral negotiations between the Mexican and American governments. Eventually a formula was worked out: the United States agreed that each individual claim need not be heard and evaluated, but that it would accept a lump sum settlement which in turn the United States would proportion to its nationals for general and for revolutionary claims. The sum, payable in installments, was 2.64 per cent of the total face value of United States claims. That was the ratio of actual judgments to claims that the European settlements had established.

Calles and the United States. While the various claims commissions were wrangling, from 1924 onward, Calles had become president of Mexico. In December 1925 a new petroleum code was introduced into the Mexican Congress. The legislation limited the possession of oil properties acquired before 1917 to a period of fifty years; this was, in Calles' view, the first step toward eventual nationalization of the whole industry. The action contradicted promises of "perpetual ownership" extended by Obregón. The expected flurry of United States' notes and their answers passed between Washington and Mexico over the question of whether the "Extra-Official Pact" was binding on Calles or not. The press, especially the Hearst press, grew heated; a number of oil interests tried to drum up enough sentiment for intervention and perhaps even war in Mexico. Again battleships might hover ominously off Tampico and Veracruz. But the smell of Teapot Dome was too strong.

The conflict during 1925 and 1926 had worsened to the point that President Coolidge informed Congress about the grave and deteriorating Mexican situation. Mexican sources say that by unknown means Calles obtained copies of secret letters between Secretary of State Frank B. Kellogg and Ambassador Sheffield in Mexico City. These purportedly revealed that the two officials were purposely trying to provoke some Mexican act that could be used as a pretext for American intervention. Calles sent copies of these letters directly to President Coolidge, together with an ultimatum: if the United States continued its aggressive, provocative attitudes Calles would make public the Kellogg letters. The world would then see the "Colossus" in action. Coolidge was conciliatory.

On September 22, 1927 Sheffield was withdrawn from the Embassy in Mexico. A week later, on September 30, the two presidents had a friendly chat when the first direct long-distance telephone connections between the capitals was inaugurated. Since autumn 1927 there is no real indication that the United States, officially or unofficially, has seriously considered armed intervention in Mexico. To ease the immediate difficulties, Coolidge named Dwight Morrow as the new Ambassador to Mexico.

The Morrow Mission. Calvin Coolidge's appointment of his Amherst classmate, Dwight Morrow, as Ambassador to Mexico marked a real turning point in relations between the two countries. The Mexican press, unaware that the State Department had decided to shift its attitudes, construed the naming of this partner in the firm of J. P. Morgan as a return to Dollar Diplomacy. They announced that "after Morrow come the Marines."

But unlike many of his ambassadorial predecessors, Morrow made the important decision to like Mexico and to respect the Mexicans. He briefed himself as thoroughly as possible on the Mexican situation. No career diplomat, he tried out a new brand of diplomacy, the informal approach. He avoided all protocol. Shortly after his arrival he had the sign changed on the Embassy to read "United States Embassy" rather than "American Embassy," a small but important matter to Mexicans who justifiably resented the arrogant appropriation of a continental adjective by their large northern neighbor.

Early in November 1927 Morrow and Calles sat down to breakfasts of ham and eggs to discuss face to face how the outstanding issues between the United States and Mexico could be solved. These discussions continued while the two men, accompanied by Will Rogers, made a long inspection tour of newly planned irrigation works in northern Mexico. Rogers' homely reports in the American papers emphasized that Mexicans were people, not pawns, a fact that an increasing number of tourists were beginning to learn for themselves. Morrow purchased a home in Cuernavaca, built by native masons and furnished completely with Mexican products, over which Morrow and his wife were publicly enthusiastic. For the benefit of the town, Morrow commissioned Diego Rivera to paint murals extolling the virtues of the Revolution on the walls of the City Hall of Cuernavaca. At Morrow's invitation Charles Lindbergh, then a national hero, visited Mexico. By this and other means Morrow assiduously and sincerely cultivated the friendship of Mexicans and especially of Calles. It paid huge diplomatic dividends.

It came as no surprise to Morrow that the Supreme Court of Mexico on November 17, 1927 issued a ruling in favor of an American oil company and at the same time reiterated the doctrine of "positive acts" to perpetuity. In December Calles recommended to Congress that the offending articles in the petroleum code limiting holdings to fifty years be amended to conform with the court decision. To make sure that there would be no unconscious errors, a new code was drawn up and issued on March 27, 1928. In the critical sections it followed the exact wording of the Mexican commissioners' statements of the "Extra-Official Pact" at the Bucareli Conference of 1923.

A press release from the State Department of the United States on March 28 put an official period marker to conflict. The announcement said that "these steps, voluntarily taken by the Mexican government, would appear to bring to a practical conclusion discussions which began ten years ago with reference to the effect of the Mexican Constitution and laws upon foreign oil companies." Henceforth questions concerning American oil holdings in Mexico were to be settled through Mexican administrative departments and the Mexican courts. This settlement lasted until 1938. Then the position of Roosevelt and Hull reaffirmed the doctrine that the United States government was giving oil companies no further backing.

The United States government had succeeded in getting the Mexicans to acknowledge that all policies involving international interests could not be changed merely at the whim of the executive, and that obligations of presidential predecessors were binding on successors. On its part the Mexican government, while renouncing retroactive action, had established the important principle that direct ownership of subsoil deposits was vested in the nation; it was making a special, but clear exception to this for the United States. It had hedged on the old concept that all concessions made by Díaz to oil companies and others were untouchable; only those on which specified "positive acts" had been performed before May 1, 1917 were even remotely sacrosanct. The Mexican government had refused to put its concession to the American viewpoint in the form of a treaty. The main achievement of Morrow was to make the Extra-Official Pact binding on all administrations that followed Obregón's.

For the remainder of Morrow's stay in Mexico he continued to be a popular and useful Ambassador. Partly through his good but unofficial offices the deplorable civil war between the *Cristeros* and the central government was terminated by a series of compromises, and he acted (on invitation) to mediate Church-State difficulties. Between 1927 and 1934 the frictions between Mexico and the United States dwindled to rather routine controversies which could be handled in diplomatic channels, without spectacular crises. The passage of time healed some of the open wounds which the Revolution had caused on both sides of the Border.

The Morrow Mission marks an important step in the "retreat from imperialism," a process completed under the Good Neighbor Policy. Thus by 1934 many of the legacies of the epic Revolution had become history. On the domestic and the international sides the years under the Northern Dynasty had been a fruitful epilogue. A termination of political instability, a few steps toward constructive measures, and an apparent liquidation of the outstanding foreign problems made it a period of "tidying-up." It was a prelude to growth.

* * *

World-wide depression and its inevitable reflection in domestic unrest changed the complexion of the governments both in the United States and in Mexico. Solutions adequate for the 1920's became inappropriate for the new situations as national tempers altered and shifts in political regimes brought with them the necessity for new, unprecedented adjustments. These new outlines were established by Lázaro Cárdenas and Franklin D. Roosevelt.

Tides of change were running strongly all over the world in 1933–1934. Three years of ineffectual tinkering by orthodox means in all countries and internationally had failed to improve world conditions created or exposed by widespread economic collapses. The Depression had occurred. The social and political response to emergency had been a concerted drift either to the Right, as in Nazi Germany, or a swing to the Left, as with the New Deal in the United States and the trends in Mexico. The Revolution was revived.

11. The Cárdenas Upheaval

In very general terms, the political swings in Mexico and in the United States display much the same rhythms. At any given time both respond to many of the same forces in the Western world which mold and limit national economic, political, and cultural behavior. The era of Grant, Cleveland, and Taft, for instance, was paralleled in the southern republic by the several developmental stages of the Porfirian regime. The reformist trends of Theodore Roosevelt and Wilson were independently reflected in the Madero and then the epic Mexican Revolution. In like ways, the Republican Restoration and the Northern Oligarchy represented comparable attitudes and activities.

The parallel phenomena did not cease there. In Mexico the rebirth and resurgence of the Revolution under Lázaro Cárdenas, its cooling off and consolidation during World War II by Manuel Avila Camacho, and its slow, calculated extension to unprecedented material heights under Miguel Alemán, find their analogues above the border. The first New Dealism of Franklin D. Roosevelt, its conversion and immersion in the war effort, and the Fair Deal of Harry Truman seem to be but enlarged, more complicated, versions of main Mexican trends in the epochal years from 1933 through 1952. Both the objectives and the means employed to gain them are still vital and controversial issues; but changes did occur.

1. LÁZARO CÁRDENAS AND TRANSITION

Early in 1933 it was clear that the election of a president in 1934 would be an important event in Mexico. There was no question but that the officially endorsed candidate of the P.N.R. would win. Political agitation, therefore, centered on interfactional maneuvering between the Left Wing who wished the Revolution to bound forward in violent fashion and the Right Wing who wished a continuation of the direction and tempo so painfully established since 1920 under the Northern Dynasty. The issue was further confused by an important speech by Plutarco Elías Calles, the *Jéfe Máximo*, on May 30, 1933.

He pointed out that the Mexican Revolution had failed in most of its important objectives. Through corruption, circumstance, and ignorance, the men charged with providing a better life for Mexicans had seen their proposals deferred and defeated. With the example of Russia (which had just successfully completed a Five Year Plan) in mind, Calles stated that the hour had arrived to formulate a detailed program of social action in Mexico to be completed during the next six-year presidential term, 1934–1940.

This Mexican Six Year Plan was to be based on reason, statistics, and the lessons of experience. He suggested that its basis be an agrarian program founded on small properties to be purchased by the peasantry. The formulation of the plan was turned over to President Rodríguez and his cabinet; immediately the ideological splits in revolutionary ranks were revealed. When Rodríguez was unable to get his cabinet to agree, he and Calles worked out a rough draft to be presented to the P.N.R. at the convention which would also choose a presidential candidate.

In December 1933 the P.N.R. met to endorse the preordained candidate, General Lázaro Cárdenas, and to provide his presidential platform: the Six Year Plan. Instead of a docile meeting which rubber-stamped the Rodríguez-Calles proposals, the party convention unexpectedly turned into a contest in recrimination between the Left and Right within the Revolutionary family. After the first gusts of passion had been spent, the inevitable closing of ranks occurred. The conflict made important changes in the party's platform, but perhaps more important, brought Lázaro Cárdenas to the fore as the prospective president of Mexico, 1934–1940. While not completely unknown to his compatriots, the general at that time was still a dark horse, picked by party leaders as a machine candidate to prolong the Oligarchy's hold.

Candidate Cárdenas. Cárdenas' previous record was that of a young and able Revolutionary. Born May 21, 1895 in the village of Jiquilpan, Michoacan, Lázaro was one of eight children bred and raised in modest but comfortable and respectable circumstances; the mestizo family from which he sprang had traditionally been weavers, but Cárdenas' father owned the local billiard-hall. Schooled locally, Lázaro at the tender age of eleven had enrolled in Reyes' militia (1905), and on completion of six grades was apprenticed to the local tax collector as his clerk and town jailer; a fervent Maderista, the collector and friends set up a small newspaper which Lázaro printed. During the exciting days of Díaz' downfall, little happened in this remote area, so the young man stayed at his press until Madero was assassinated.

Cárdenas joined a band of Zapatistas to fight Huerta and was made paymaster and captain, but Federals soon scattered the force and Cárdenas again returned to village life; harried by the Usurper's officials, Cárdenas made a daring escape and joined an Obregón unit, shifted for awhile to Villa, and by March 1915 had ended up under Carranza and Calles. Under the eye of the latter, Cárdenas rose to the rank of general for field performances against Villa and Yaqui Indians and mopping up Zapatistas in Michoacan and Jalisco. As a reward for his services and loyalty when Obregón and Calles, de la Huerta and Morones overthrew Carranza, Cárdenas was promoted to brigadier general at the age of twenty-five and named provisional governor of Michoacan under de la Huerta's presidency. His military reputation was good.

Subsequent years saw his rise as a zone commander, governor of Michoacan, and (as protégé of Calles) he was named president of the newly formed P.N.R. in 1929. Within the Revolutionary family of military veterans Cárdenas had the reputation of being honest, able, anticlerical, and politically astute; he had picked the right side in all the complicated maneuverings since 1913. In him the P.N.R. seemingly had the ideal candidate who could conciliate all factions on a moderate reform program; few thought that he would be an independent master when he was cast in the role of the party's agent to carry out the newly formulated Six Year Plan.

Rather than a blueprint, the Six Year Plan was a sales prospectus. Like the Constitution of 1917, it was a patchwork of compromise, contradictions, and Utopian affirmations. As Cárdenas' mandate from the party, it was an imprecise set of directives that provided neither central planning nor machinery for enforcement. Where Calles had hoped for statistics and reason, there were only rhetoric and politics. Each Mexican section and economic interest had inserted projects dear to its heart without reference to Mexico's ability to pay or the general importance of the works demanded. The trivial and the important were mixed, without assigning any priorities to them. As an administrative guide, the Six Year Plan was a hopeless jumble of orders that reflected the divergent interests within the party. But as a campaign platform, it was full of superb promises which served notice that the Official Party was again subscribing to reform. It was Cárdenas' job as "official" candidate (thus bound to win) to carry the message to the people and then as president to select from the Plan a course appropriate to the changing situation.

Summing up his positive program, Cárdenas stated that he thought the agrarian movement, the coöperative movement, and the educational movement would be the strongest fulcra of the new Mexican government. The future of Mexico lay in replacing a hacienda economy by collective landholdings, in eradicating Church influence by substituting modern schooling, and in exchanging rapacious capitalist industry with workers' coöperatives, backed but not owned by the state. He specifically repudiated the Soviet Russian system with its emphasis on direct state control.

Cárdenas' basic idea was to preserve certain destructive tendencies of the Mexican Revolution to clear the way for new institutions. He was eager to rid the nation of individual and corporative exploitation, and to substitute for them self-run groups of farmers and workers. Exploitation by the state as an employer, or the substitution of foreign capitalism by a native version, fell outside his mass-oriented program. New coöperative ventures would replace the historical institutions. The national state would back organized groups in the destructive phase and also would help but would not control their plans for reconstruction. That was the message which Lázaro Cárdenas carried to most of Mexico in 1934 before he was inaugurated as president. His philosophy was neither wholly socialist nor communist. It represented a set of humanitarian, nationalist attitudes rather than an integrated philosophy whose full implications he clearly understood.

Cárdenas' political campaign departed from the normal pattern.

He took his interpretation of the Six Year Plan in person to the farthest reaches of the hinterlands where no presidential candidate had appeared in generations. While campaigning in the name of the party, he was also building a powerful new personal political machine, based on mass support. He visited nearly every *patria chica* within every state in a grueling 16,000-mile jaunt. On election day, July 1, 1934, he was in Durango and even after the returns were in, continued his village-to-village and bush-to-bush trek. Official counting gave him the expected overwhelming majority.

On his unprecedented journey Cárdenas repeated again and again the slogan "Workers of Mexico, unite!" He settled local labor disputes and attempted to fuse scattered labor groups into one local unit; he promised lands to the peasantry and urged them to be prepared to defend themselves against the encroachments of landlords and other capitalists. Indians were promised schools and justice and exhorted to join the rest of the proletariat in eliminating those state governments which were not defending them from domestic and foreign exploitation.

President or Puppet? When he was inaugurated in December 1934, Lázaro Cárdenas was the first president since Díaz who had not come from the North. This fact was obscured by more important ones. Interested observers waited to see how much of the campaign speeches could be translated into reality and how Cárdenas and Calles would handle the formidable problems posed by a Mexico increasingly eroded by Depression. With the army solidly behind Generals Cárdenas and Calles there was no attempt to upset the election by resort to arms.

As might be expected under the circumstances, Calles picked Cárdenas' first cabinet. One of the most controversial of these figures was Tomas Garrido Canabal, given the strategic post of Agriculture. He was a violent anticlerical governor whose followers wore red shirts; they had almost eliminated the Catholic Church from their state of Tabasco, his private kingdom. The Red Shirts organization was transferred from the provinces to Mexico City and its numbers strengthened. Other less colorful cabinet members began, under Cárdenas leadership, to announce plans for reforming education and labor. Among his first official acts, Cárdenas gave up the gaudy presidential residence in Chapultepec Castle. He also began closing down the gambling casinos and brothels in which prominent Callistas had invested their profits from bribery and industrial activities.

When, in a wave of strikes early in 1935, President Cárdenas supported the workers, it became clear that a test of power between the *Jéfe Máximo* and the new president was in the making. Cárdenas was to be no puppet president. The culminating crisis came in June 1935. Calles, in a speech attacking the "marathon of radicalism," tactlessly but pointedly made reference to one of his earlier synthetic presidents who had gone too far and had been forced to resign. A number of members of the Mexican Congress openly trooped to Calles' house as a symbol of support of him.

The next day, however, both houses of Congress publicly declared their approval of Cárdenas' policies after Cárdenas had dismissed the Calles-dominated cabinet and began to concentrate his own army contingents in Mexico City. Canabal's place in the cabinet was taken by the last old *caudillo*, Saturnino Cedillo, a tough boss of San Luis Potosí who also had powerful support in the national army. Backed up by his own private army and air force, he had resisted the anticlericalism of Calles; to Cedillo is attributed the saying that he did not know whether God existed or not, but if he did, he wanted Him on Cedillo's side.

Cárdenas turned Calles' long-time anticlericalism against him. When the choice came, the Church reluctantly supported Cárdenas as the lesser of two evils; he seemed to offer more hope for toleration and a *modus vivendi* than did Canabal and Calles. With the army, much of the Church, Congress, and new labor organizations behind him, Cárdenas isolated Calles, who announced his retirement from public life on June 17, 1935. To be sure of continuing moderate Church support, it was necessary to take positive action against its archenemy, Canabal. This Cárdenas did in the following months by forcing him into South American exile. When Cedillo threatened to become a focus for a conservative "counterrevolution," he was provoked into premature revolt and killed in 1939. These exciting events were paralleled by Cárdenas' reorganization of power, a fundamental change that connected the Mexican masses to their government.

2. ORGANIZATION AND REORGANIZATION

As one phase of the offensive against Calles and the Northern Dynasty, Cárdenas effected a permanent change in the old "official party." He ended bifurcated control of politics by bringing party apparatus under the direct eye of the president, while at the same time altering its inner structure and outward purposes. It works now much as Cárdenas planned.

To clear the way for alterations, Cárdenas placed Emilio Portes Gil at the head of the P.N.R., with orders to purge it of Callista elements. Gil had been one of the "puppet presidents" so unceremoniously dumped by Calles, and was happy to serve. But when Gil then attempted to build up his own position for a possible comeback, Cárdenas politely returned him to his old political principality of Tamaulipas, where Gil is still a power, though currently Ambassador to India.

There was in 1936 no central political control over the agrarians or labor. Cárdenas created such controls, preparatory to a total revamping of the party. To mobilize, concentrate, and make them both subject to central direction, he sponsored the formation of two parapolitical confederations; into these fitted the smaller units being created by his agrarian and labor reforms. Cárdenas brought both organized peasantry and organized labor into the open political arena to win a class war that he felt Mexicans were engaged in. His government definitely was on the side of the masses against the classes.

The Organized Agrarians. Cárdenas sponsored the National Peasant Confederation—*Confederación Nacional de Campesinos* (C.N.C.). Existing peasant leagues and the newly created *ejido* holders banded themselves into state confederations; these in turn were affiliated to the National, controlled in Mexico City. Some local leagues were denied membership in the C.N.C. because they were deemed to be merely tools of local political *caciques* rather than truly imbued with Revolutionary fervor and ideology. To become acceptable, a number of the agrarian leagues took the opportunity to purge themselves of backsliding revolutionaries and to select new leadership, dependent on Cárdenas. Those who did not join the Confederation got few benefits. The C.N.C. also was a rural militia; from its membership came a Rural Reserve, armed, drilled, and under orders of the state zone commander, also a Cárdenas appointee. Agrarians were thus in a position to help each other defend their newly acquired lands; they also provided the president with a helpful counterpoise and aid to the regular army.

Vicente Lombardo Toledano and Organized Labor. The analogous labor grouping was the Mexican Workers' Confederation—*Confederación de Trabajadores Mexicanos*, C.T.M.—officially created on February 21, 1936. Since Morones' debacle in 1928, organized labor had

had little coherence; it had lost direct voice in politics when dropped from official favor under the Northern Dynasty. Cárdenas from the outset not only approved labor's demands, but threw government support behind the formation of a new labor movement that brought Vicente Lombardo Toledano, still one of the stormy petrels of Mexico, to national fame and power.

Of Italian extraction (through an immigrant family that came to Mexico in Benito Juárez' days), Vicent Lombardo Toledano was born in Teziutlán, Puebla, on July 16, 1894. After his family moved to Mexico City in 1909, Toledano became dissatisfied with the teaching he received in the National Preparatory School. With other militant youths he formed a little band called the "Seven Sages," who soaked themselves in Russian literature, first Tolstoi and Dostoevski, then Engels and Marx. When an official "Popular University" was founded in 1917 to illuminate the masses, the "Seven Sages" helped staff it. Toledano became its secretary, and from this vantage point entered politics; he became governor, then deputy, then senator for Puebla, but split his time by teaching labor law. After much reading in Lenin's works, Toledano decided to give up his brilliant academic career and throw in his lot with organized labor. He claims never to have joined any Communist Party, but as he has held high posts in numerous Communist-sponsored and -dominated organizations this claim is usually considered a hairline technicality.

Toledano served his apprenticeship as an intellectual labor leader in Morones' C.R.O.M. until 1932, when he broke with the older leader on tactical and ideological grounds. By capturing some of the old C.R.O.M. unions and forming new ones, Toledano created in 1933 a Marxian confederation of workers and agrarians. In the fight for power between Cárdenas and Calles, Toledano's confederation joined with other small Marxian and Communist-dominated unions, chiefly electricians and miners, to form a united front; they aided Cárdenas and he aided them. On their report that Morones and Calles were flirting with the Axis for material aid to support a *coup*, Cárdenas exiled both to the United States.

From the small political coalition of labor organizations aiding Cárdenas came the larger, formalized C.T.M. in February 1936. Politically its leadership, under Toledano, demanded that the Six Year Plan be put into effect; tactically the first task was to organize Mexican labor and bring it into the fold. Official support was thrown to this project. By the end of its first year the C.T.M. claimed to represent 1200 organizations, some 200,000 militant workers. Like the peasants, they were drilled as a para-military unit, but not armed.

Cárdenas then expanded the old "official" machine into a Mexican version of a "Popular Front," a political grouping much in vogue at the time. Popular Front experiments were one of the democratic world's attempts to meet the needs of the Depression yet avoid outright social revolutions. Into one political bundle were grouped Communists, home-grown Leftists, Liberals, and even an occasional Conservative group; as a political team they coöperated by prearrangement to carry out national economic and social programs in which they were all interested. Chile, France, and other countries were trying this device in governments by coalition. In Mexico, where no defined parties really existed, the "Popular Front" was indirect and based on changed membership within the old single Revolutionary party. Peasant organizations and labor unions who had qualified as "revolutionary" by combating exploitation were invited in 1936 to join the party. To the nucleus of regional military-political machines were thus added congeries of little organizations grouped under the C.N.C. and C.T.M. which embraced the militant masses. The newly admitted units shared the common political benefits of the P.N.R., contributed to its coffers, and broke the monopoly that military chieftains had maintained since Carranza's day. The Communists sought admission, but the party's high command refused to admit them as such.

Partido Revolucionario Mexicano. Once the various elements—organized labor and agrarians—were ready for kneading, Cárdenas created a new official party. Its manifest function remained the same —to win elections by united support of a single slate of revolutionaries. On the heels of the oil expropriations in March 1938, when Mexican nationalism reached a peak, the P.R.N. was convoked to commit suicide; the enlarged Mexican Revolutionary Party—*Partido Revolucionario Mexicano*, P.R.M.—took its place.

Cárdenas divided the power elements of Mexico into four sectors: military, labor, agrarians, and popular (unorganized little urban groups). Each electoral district in the Republic contained all of them, so the basis of the new party was functional-geographical. An individual belonged to a revolutionary organization which in turn was affiliated with one of the three main national organizations— the Army, the C.T.M., or the C.N.C. Delegates to party conventions, to pick the slates and formulate the programs, were selected by and represented a geographical unit of the sector. Each sector held its own convention before they met as a body and party.

When each sector had prepared its slate, a run-off primary was held; the candidates of each sector campaigned vigorously, then after the party primary election, the successful aspirant became the "official" candidate; the other two sectors agreed to support him alone against the candidates of other parties. The "Popular" sector's role was vague.

In any one electoral district the labor candidate, if he had won the primary against local Army and agrarian rivals, could count on their followers' votes in the national election. Since the C.T.M. represented more than 95 per cent of labor's voting strength, chances were that he would win. Thus each town, state, and region had a political cartel to elect the candidate who had won the pre-election party contest there.

In such fashion, Mexico was democratized, yet kept revolutionary. The key spot in the operation of the system was (and is) the honesty of intra-party primary elections; for tactical purposes and to keep proper balance among the sectors, the high command of the party must occasionally nullify a local cell's primary results and "impose" a candidate or declare that although the agrarian won, the local party unit must support the laborer. Under President Camacho one significant change was made in the system: the military sector was suppressed, to take the Army out of politics and to "professionalize" it. In its place, however, the "popular" sector was organized hierarchically to parallel the agrarians and the laborers by the formation (in 1942) of the National Confederation of Popular Organizations, *Confederación Nacional de Organizaciones Populares*, C.N.O.P.; the backbone of this group are the bureaucrats.

Now in control of the government on his own, and with the backing of these new and organized elements in the revitalized official party, Cárdenas turned to fulfilling in concrete fashion some of the old, postponed promises of the Revolution. It was an intense, shocking, but probably necessary upheaval. It continued until an emptying Treasury and clouds of war in 1939 slowed it down.

3. THE REFORM SURGE

Of the many promises made by the Revolution in the Constitution of 1917 and the Six Year Plan, Cárdenas stressed those concerning education, agrarian reform, labor, and economic nationalism. The developments of any one interlocked with the others, by their own nature and by their interconnection in Cárdenas' mind.

Thousands of new teachers were again sent out as educational missionaries and propagandists of the Six Year Plan. They formed a large labor union whose approximately 97,000 members were affiliated with the C.T.M. Because of its strategic place between the people and the government, the Secretariat of Education became a political plum; during the Cárdenas years it was almost completely captured by Stalinist Communists and fellow travelers. Teachers entering rural areas considered themselves apostles, of Marx and of Mexicanism. Like those of the 1920's, many were martyred. Cárdenas firmly believed that the school should replace the Church as the political and cultural center of every community, large or small.

A large part of the agrarian program was also educational, though its prime emphasis was placed on reversing the Northern Oligarchy's insistence on private property and small peasant holdings in favor of collectivized communities to be created from hacienda lands. With disastrous short-run results on the rural economy, Cárdenas plunged headlong into a program of redistributing Mexico's land. During his tenure a little over 44,000,000 acres passed into the hands of the peasantry, more than twice as much as had been distributed up to his time by all the revolutionary governments. Much, if not most, of this area was carved out of property previously owned by private individuals, who were recompensed by worthless bonds. The new collectivized *ejidos* immediately added strength to the Confederation of agrarians, to which each almost automatically belonged. These strengthened the revamped P.R.M. by increasing its peasant base.

More important in the long run, Cárdenas shifted and enlarged the earlier scope of agrarian programs. The *ejidos* had earlier been conceived as transitional and supplementary grants of land to accustom and indoctrinate Indians and peasants in the concepts of capitalism and private property. Once indoctrinated, they would, it was believed by the Northern Dynasty, become yeomen and purchase more land under government-sponsored credit programs. This had not worked out in fact.

Cárdenas' idea was to "decapitalize" Mexico's land by nationalizing it and then dividing it equitably among the worthy landless. Peon families were to use their *ejido* parcels for personal and national benefit. The portions which each group received would be its *ejido,* the basis of its economic and social life. Rather than private holdings, the *ejidos* collectively would, in the Cárdenas view, form a system of communal units that would fulfill functions and take the role which outmoded and rapacious private haciendas had traditionally taken in Mexican life. *Ejidos* not only would provide subsistence crops for themselves and the nation, but would raise its commercially important agricultural products as well.

For peasant benefit Cárdenas expropriated great portions of the most highly developed rural sections of Mexico, and made co-operative *ejidos* from the haciendas there. Among others these included the rich cotton zones of La Laguna, henequen areas of Yucatan, wheat- and sugar-producing enterprises in various parts of the Republic, and coffee lands of the South. Their former owners retained small plots around their residences; under an elastic interpretation of expropriation, Cárdenas included in the stripping process all the necessary processing and transportation equipment that *hacendados* had built up to prepare raw materials for market. This wave of expropriation on a grand scale in the heart of agricultural areas snapped the spine of the hacienda as the major institution of rural Mexico, though it by no means extinguished all private holdings, as the table on page 291 shows.

As expropriable areas dwindled, the focus of agrarianism shifted. Technical and managerial problems rather than militant redistribution became its keynote. The need to maintain lands and provide their new possessors with credit, guidance, and administrative machinery and skills became a government responsibility. To care for the innumerable economic and social woes of the *ejidatarios,* Cárdenas set up a number of *ad hoc* devices toward the end of his term; it was the task of his successors to give them permanence and make them efficient.

The Cárdenas attack on the industrial and economic systems of Mexico was equally as spectacular and direct. Again the weapon was expropriation. On November 23, 1936 a law covering expropriations—a Nationalization Law—filled in the broad constitutional sanction to regain "Mexico for the Mexicans," specifically for the Mexicans of the popular class.

The process of extinguishing private ownership and turning it over to workers became almost a standardized procedure. Radical unions were formed; they demanded that their employers sign a contract embodying the full set of benefits set forth in Article 123

—high minimum wages, short work week, social welfare benefits—
and often known to be beyond the capacity of the concern to pay;
upon the refusal of an employer to sign away his control and property rights in the form of such a collective contract, the union struck.
To settle the matter, the government intervened in the strike and
expropriated the disputed enterprise, which was then turned over
to the striking workers to operate as a coöperative; the owner received valueless bonds in recompense. Many small concerns, a few
large ones, and a sprinkling of middle-sized businesses owned by
Mexicans fell under this sweep, but primarily it was foreign concerns at which the measures were aimed.

Railroads and oil represented key factors in the economy. To Cárdenas it seemed impossible to have a nationally operated economy if
both were alien-owned and controlled. The most dramatic instances
of expropriation came in these fields. Because of its international implications, the oil developments are detailed later, but almost as
significant for the domestic economy was Cárdenas' wresting the
direction of Mexican transportation from foreign hands.

In the late nineteenth century, American and British capital had
built the rails in Mexico but by 1909 Limantour had acquired stock
control of two-thirds of them for the Porfirian government. Foreign
bondholders, British and American, had from the beginning of the
Revolution continuously clamored for the resumption of payment
on their securities; they hinted at intervention. To transform these
semi-private obligations into national obligations, and thus deprive
foreign creditors of the opportunity of interfering in the management
of the system and their governments from intervening directly,
Cárdenas in June 1937 nationalized most of the railroads. He consolidated their outstanding debts with the general obligations of the
Mexican government. The expropriation affected only the National
Railways of Mexico, those which Limantour had helped consolidate;
minor lines were untouched at the time.

On May 1, 1938 bickering between government officials charged
with administering the nationalized lines and the railroad unions was
resolved by Cárdenas. He turned the administration of the nationalized lines over to a committee of seven officials of the railroad
unions. Under the best of circumstances, they had inherited a di-
lapidated and shaky system, one that had been wrecked by the
Revolution and not maintained since then. To add to the difficulties,
a rash of interunion struggles almost immediately arose over the

positions on the seven-man management committee. The unprecedented relationship of one portion of Mexican labor "employing" another for the benefit of the nation confused all parties. But it was deemed better than foreign control.

"Mexico for the Mexicans," a slogan that had threaded through the Revolution from its earliest days, took on real meaning as the Cárdenas regime narrowed the circles within which economic enterprises dependent on foreign capital for operation or for management were able to move. Both his critics and adulators agree that Cárdenas was a simple man whose few contacts with foreign businessmen had confirmed his youthful prejudices against them. He and most of his followers had swallowed whole the seductive line continuously dangled before them that the total responsibility for Mexico's economic ills derived from a conspiracy among foreign capitalists. "Wall Street," "the interests," and "imperialists," were on the diabolical roster in the folklore of the Revolution.

Labor leaders, dominated by a generation of younger intellectuals who had been brought up on Marx and sometimes had made the pilgrimage to Moscow, did little to dissuade him from these comforting views. Although his economic nationalism had as its emotional base the belief that Mexico should remain an essentially agricultural nation, Cárdenas' most sensational affirmations of "Mexico for the Mexicans" came in the industrial field. The greatest of these was the famed expropriation of foreign-owned oil companies on March 18, 1938. This is a date which Mexicans now hail as the final winning of their economic independence; it ranks with September 16, 1810, date of political independence from Spain. Even if Cárdenas had not pushed forward to new boundaries the manifold reforms in politics, education, land, and labor, this one expropriation act of his would have assured him immortality in Mexican annals.

Within his lifetime Lázaro Cárdenas has literally become a folk hero. Already forgotten are the many and serious contemporary criticisms of his administration—the corruption and venality of his family and friends, the inexcusable excesses of overzealous radicals, the almost indiscriminate wrecking of enterprises, and the condoned political assassinations. Cárdenas' weaknesses as an administrator are transmuted into proof of his virtues as a man. Interminably he traveled the country, dragging with him most of the important policy-making officials to whom he was unwilling to delegate real authority. Hour after hour they would sit in village plazas while delegations of peasants speechified in almost unintelligible Spanish as a prelude to requests for minor village improvements, solemnly noted down by ranking Cabinet ministers. Oft quoted but still relevant is the probably apocryphal story which made the rounds in Mexico at the time; Anita Brenner has preserved it for posterity in her *The Wind that Swept Mexico*. It epitomizes Cárdenas' outlook.

According to this tale, once while Cárdenas was dispatching business in the capital his private secretary laid a list of urgent matters and a telegram on his desk. The list said: *Bank reserves dangerously low.* "Tell the Treasurer," said Cárdenas. *Agricultural production failing.* "Tell the Minister of Agriculture." *Railways bankrupt.* "Tell the Minister of Communications." *Serious message from Washington.* "Tell Foreign Affairs." Then he opened the telegram which read "My corn dried, my burro died, my sow was stolen, my baby is sick. Signed, Pedro Juan, village of Huitzlipituzco."

"Order the presidential train at once," said Cárdenas. "I am leaving for Huitzlipituzco." *

4. OIL

Few topics are as emotionally and legally snarled as the political problems arising from oil. They plagued the Cárdenas years. Their general complexity derives from certain basic geographical and economic considerations. Petroleum and its 1200 by-products make possible the modern world. Industry, transportation, and daily life draw heavily on it as an essential and irreplaceable commodity. It is an indispensable strategic item.

Oil in significant quantities is found in only four main areas in the world. They are all actual or potential international sore spots. One, in the North Polar regions, has basins of oil yet undeveloped and unpublicized. Another row of petroleum basins curves along Sumatra, Borneo, New Guinea, and Java; this chain is considered a minor petroleum area. The two major source areas are the Mediterranean–Middle East, and the Western Hemisphere. The deposits of Russia, Rumania, Iraq, Egypt, and Iran are constantly in the headlines because of their central importance in world affairs. They furnish Europe with only 25 per cent of its oil at the present.

* Anita Brenner and George Leighton, *The Wind that Swept Mexico: The History of the Mexican Revolution, 1910–1942* (New York: Harper, 1943), p. 85. By permission.

About 75 per cent of the world supply is being drawn from the American areas. Starting with the American Gulf Coasts, swinging southeast through Mexico to Venezuela and Colombia, lie rich oil basins. In 1943 a little over 52 per cent of the world's proved reserves, somewhere around 27,000,000,000 barrels of oil, lay in the Americas. Mexico was then credited with 1.5 per cent of them. Later figures, not in agreement, show substantially the same picture.

Though oil was known by the Aztecs, its first commercial production in Mexico came at the turn of the twentieth century. An Englishman, Lord Cowdray, and two Americans, Edward L. Doheny and Charles A. Canfield, controlled 98 per cent of the Mexican output. In 1910 this was only about 13 million barrels of oil a year. Oil was not a real problem to Díaz. Though this was large by contemporary standards, the world's growing need for more and more petroleum was hastened by World War I and the popularization of the automobile as a daily and common possession rather than a luxurious symbol of the leisure classes. By 1921, foreign producers in Mexico were pumping and exporting 193 million barrels of oil; this was more than a quarter of the world's output at the time, and supplied most of the United States' needs. The boom in Texas was then just getting under way, and the Middle East had not been tapped.

Petroleum and the political problems surrounding it are identified with the Revolution; while the oil industry in Mexico and the United States was coming of age, so was the Revolution. The founding of mines and the creation of railroads by foreign hands had disturbed some of the Mexicans under Díaz, but by 1910 these enterprises seemed stable and politically harmless when compared to the activities of the promoters and owners of this new petroleum giant in the Mexican midst.

For reasons already dealt with, the attempt of the Revolution to make good its claims against the oil properties held by foreigners in Mexico had been deflected and compromised. The "Extra-Official Pact" had been scuttled by the Revolution, but then reaffirmed by the Morrow-Calles concord in 1928. Under it American oil companies could not look forward to expanding their activities in Mexico, but on the other hand, properties on which they had performed "positive acts" before 1917 were tacitly theirs for intensive development to perpetuity. They had, in exchange, implicitly agreed that subsoil deposits were national, not privately owned, possessions. It was against this tangled legal and emotionally charged background that the oil controversy in Mexico was resumed in 1934 when Lázaro Cárdenas displaced the Northern Dynasty which had arranged this earlier mutually beneficial *modus vivendi*.

Throughout the oil drama political and emotional considerations rather than legalistic formula dominated the situation. President Cárdenas' attitudes toward foreign businessmen were widely known, as was his avowed purpose to help Mexican labor gain what he thought ought to be its just position and proper role. His view was that class interests bound employers tightly together, but that Mexican workers were not so organized; it was the government's duty to help them combine to end the exploitation of one class by another.

It is essential to remember at the outset that the disputes, which in 1938 culminated in expropriation, did not concern petroleum lands and their legal status as such. That had all been settled. The manifest issues revolved entirely around labor relationships—whether the foreign companies could or would conform to conditions set forth in Article 123. This was demanded by Mexican labor and backed by the Mexican government. Also it is well to bear in mind that the oil expropriation was but one of a whole series of collateral militant actions being taken simultaneously by the labor-dominated, highly nationalistic Cárdenas administration. Their total program aimed at regaining "Mexico for the Mexicans." As the most outstanding popular Mexican symbol of international rapacity, the American and British petroleum companies were natural targets of the resurgent Revolution.

About 13,000 Mexican workers were employed in the oil industry. They were scattered among 21 small unions, each of which had a separate contract with its employers. The work contracts varied widely from union to union, and from employer to employer. The companies themselves were not overly prosperous; the Depression had cut into their business. The main employing group consisted of 15 major producing companies and three shipping enterprises, all affiliates of larger oil corporations owned by British and Americans. A few small independent producers and refiners did not belong to the inner circles; they were not touched by the expropriation. From the peak production of 1921, the large producers (which for sake of simplicity we can call "the companies") had dwindled to an output in 1935 of 40 million barrels of oil, 19 million of which were net exports, one-tenth of the peak in the twenties. (See Appendix I,

Table 13.) Even without a hostile government and the demands of a newly aroused labor, they were locally in a somewhat parlous economic state, though their parent corporations were by no means on the edge of insolvency.

In 1935 the president had his secretary of labor aid the labor organizers to consolidate the 21 little Mexican unions into a single powerful National Petroleum Workers Syndicate. They pooled their strength and bargaining power. In turn this Syndicate in 1936 joined the militant and expanding C.T.M. For the first time in its history the Mexican labor force in the petroleum fields when facing their foreign employers had full government support, plus the weight of other organized labor behind it. The organizational phase was but a prelude to a series of showdowns that climaxed in expropriation.

Cárdenas, busy consolidating his own political position, made no major moves against the companies in his first years as president. His outlook, though, was indicated by his refusal to grant further oil concessions or to renew those on lands not clearly covered by the doctrine of "positive acts." In an early period of experimentation, he sponsored the creation of a national Mexican oil industry, by forming a small and impotent government-owned producing company, Petroleos Mexicanos (Pemex), to drill on public lands. It produced almost nothing.

Labor's Demands. Small organizational strikes in 1934 and 1935 rose in number during 1936. In November of that year the National Syndicate demanded a standard, industry-wide collective contract from the companies. They declared that it should conform to the labor code of 1931 (based on the stipulations found in Article 123 of the Mexican Constitution). The companies were to raise wages, and provide a number of what are now termed "fringe benefits": eight-hour day, double pay for overtime, strike pay, adequate and sanitary housing, schools for workers and their children, and paid vacations. The Syndicate wanted a closed shop, and the enforced inclusion of white-collar office forces within union ranks.

In the hectic and troubled atmosphere, English and American companies formed a common front to bargain with newly organized labor. They were willing to bargain collectively, grant an industry-wide contract, and dicker about fringe benefits. But they objected strenuously to the proposed wage increases, which they termed excessive; they were adamant against union insistence on including what in Mexican labor jargon are "confidential employees"—office staff—under the control of the radical Petroleum Syndicate. They claimed that this was an unwarranted infringement on the rights of management. They knew that with their secretaries and bookkeepers as union members, the Syndicate and the C.T.M. could hamper their every move and be regularly supplied with highly confidential materials to feed a propaganda bonfire. Traditional rights of management were at stake.

When the Syndicate issued a strike call in November, President Cárdenas intervened to stop it. He ordered a six months' "cooling off" period, a sort of armed truce during which management and labor could confer peacefully to iron out their difficulties. The employer-worker conferences talked away the six months without a meeting of minds. Acrimony increased rather than decreased. The companies stated, undoubtedly correctly, that most of the 250 items on the agenda had been placed there by the Syndicate for propaganda purposes; it was filled with far more exaggerated demands for social benefits than *bona fide* issues which could be compromised. When employers refused to concede, the atmosphere became heated. By the end of the truce, May 27, 1937, only 21 of the 250 issues had been mutually agreed upon. The Syndicate demanded that the companies sign the collective agreement, or face a strike. The companies refused.

Strike or "Conflict"? The next day the Syndicate called a general strike in the oil fields, and asked the Mexican public and organized labor to stand behind them in their attempt to raise their standards of living by forcing the companies to sign the worker-proposed collective contract. The public did not respond very sympathetically. Under normal circumstances the strike would have failed, and the workers would have come to the best terms they could after chastising the companies by a work stoppage. But by a quirk of Mexican law, the Syndicate retrieved its deteriorating position.

On June 9, 1937 the Syndicate claimed that their walkout was not a strike but an "economic conflict." Over the vigorous protests of the companies, who said it was a private matter between them and the union, the government recognized the workers' claim. The government machinery began to whir.

The Labor Code of 1931 makes a distinction between a "strike" and an "economic conflict." The latter is a more generalized situation where the basic elements of an industry have become so unbalanced that normal strikes have no power; theoretically if labor got too arrogant, an employer could claim that a "strike" was really blackmail, and term the contest an "economic conflict." If the Federal government recognizes the plea that a worker-employer struggle is an "economic conflict" the mandate is clear: government must arbitrate, conciliate the factions, make an award that will equalize the economic power between employers and workers, and then make both sides conform to the award and the labor laws. Arbitration is mandatory in "economic conflicts." Government, workers, and employers must settle the issues.

The Federal organ charged with equalizing and "harmonizing" the divergent class interests in this recently christened "economic struggle" was a special labor tribunal, the Federal Board of Arbitration and Conciliation. If employers refused to have the issues arbitrated, they made themselves subject not only to the cost of damages caused by their obstinacy, but also to fines equaling three months' pay for the workers who brought charges. The same penalty applied if the employers refused to abide by the Federal Board's award. Once the erstwhile strike of the Petroleum Syndicate was declared an "economic conflict," the matter passed into legal, official, Federal channels. The strike stopped; legal battles began. The companies faced Cárdenas, not the unions.

5. EXPROPRIATION

The Board and the Commission. The regularly constituted Federal Board of Arbitration and Conciliation did not feel prepared to make an award in a case of this magnitude and complexity without some further knowledge. Therefore, this tribunal created its own special investigating commission to determine the facts about the Mexican oil industry and on the basis of their findings to make recommendations for a final Federal award. Two men from Cárdenas' cabinet and Dr. Jesús Silva Herzog, an able professor, comprised the investigating commission. Dr. Herzog did most of the work.

Through the summer of 1937 he and a staff made an exhaustive but not unbiased survey of the Mexican and American oil industries. When comparisons between the two were made, the Commission's somewhat unorthodox calculations indicated that the same oil companies which in Mexico were making 16 per cent profits were, in the United States, earning but 2 per cent; wages were higher in the United States, profits lower. The Commission stated that without major damage to the Mexican branches of the American and British oil industry, they could apply a great part of their "swollen" profits to wage increases and social benefits. The Commission figured that half of the excess profits should be used for wage increases, around 26,000,000 pesos annually; in addition, the companies should provide social benefits and working conditions in conformance with the Labor Code and Article 123. The Commission rendered its report, a million-word document, on August 3, 1937. More millions of words would be written on Mexican oil.

After studying the matter a short time, the Federal Board of Arbitration made its definitive award on August 18, 1937. The Board followed its Commission's suggestions. The Federal Board ordered the companies to sign the collective contract and to raise wages by 27 per cent, calculated at 26,329,393 pesos. Further, the companies were directed to allow their office help to join the petroleum union. The Board commanded the employers to provide a 40-hour, 5-day work week, pensions, vacations, life insurance, housing or housing allowances, and even to supply employees with work clothes or pay for the laundering of their garments. The August 18 award was an official, Federal judgment and order from the authorized Mexican labor tribunal. The companies ignored it while they opened another legal front.

Court Battles. Under Mexican law, the Supreme Court may issue an order suspending the action of administrative agencies until the constitutionality of their actions is decided. The oil companies applied to the court for such a writ. Their application claimed that they were unable to pay the sums awarded. They argued that the wage increases alone were not the 26.3 million pesos (stated by the Board) but 64.5 million; with the social benefits demanded, the total increase would actually top 100.0 million pesos. They said they could not possibly meet it. The issue was joined.

The clash went beyond a legal question. In asking to have the Federal Board's award nullified, the companies were attempting to retain the control of their properties and the rights of management. They had also made themselves subject to a fine of 100.0 million pesos (three months' pay for workers) by defying the Board's order. Much hung on the Court's judgment. Mexican labor couched the issue in nationalistic, class warfare terms: if the companies were forced to accept the Board's order to provide Mexican labor with higher wages and benefits, the victory of the working class would be enormous; if the companies did not comply, subsequent conflict would clearly be waged between the "exploited Mexican people" and "foreign imperialists."

The Supreme Court was under extreme emotional and popular pressures. If it set aside the pro-labor award of the Board, it was joining the foreigners; if it upheld their original ruling of August 18, the Supreme Court was patriotic. Mass efforts to influence the final decision began to accumulate. Lombardo Toledano made innumerable speeches against the alien concerns. Addressing the C.T.M. on February 24, 1938, President Cárdenas told the assembled workers that many of the economic ills of the nation could be traced directly to foreign oil companies and that they were trying to influence Mexican justice by covert economic means—their sudden large withdrawals of funds from the banking system were only attempts to wreck the fiscal system of Mexico. With more than casual interest most Mexicans awaited the verdict of the Supreme Court.

It came March 1, 1938. The Court ruled that the companies would have to obey the Board; their request for a stay-writ was denied. ¡Viva México! Immediately the Federal Board of Arbitration and Conciliation set a deadline of March 7 for compliance with their disputed August 18 order. The companies began to bargain with the Board and workers; they offered to raise wages by 24 million pesos.

Expropriation. Workers and President Cárdenas were inclined to take the belated but concrete proposal of the oil companies. They had already won a moral victory. Speaking in behalf of the workers, President Cárdenas said the companies' terms were acceptable. The companies had hitched conditions to their offer: the 24 million peso raise would be the maximum and final demand. Cárdenas pledged that this would be so. Then the companies made an understandable but inexcusable blunder.

With memories of the broken promises of Carranza, Obregón, and Calles in mind, they demanded that Cárdenas put his acceptance in writing. They wanted an iron-clad, notarized agreement. Unaccustomed to having his word questioned, Cárdenas considered the request a slur on his personal honor and a grave reflection on the integrity of his administration. To the emotion-laden questions already surrounding the petroleum issue were now added personal and national honor.

While the bartering between the companies, the syndicate, and the president had been going on, the Federal Board had extended the deadline for compliance by a week. On March 15, however, the companies bluntly notified the Board that they could not and would not comply. Part of the reasoning behind this was that probably nothing much would happen; the president had been conciliatory. At best the companies had a good case for diplomatic intervention, by claiming flagrant denial of justice; at worst they expected a temporary receivership, in which the government would take over the industry, pay off the laborer's fine money (if it could find it), and management would emerge at the end with its control unimpaired.

As late as the morning of March 15 Cárdenas had said "no expropriation." He actually had at that time an envoy on the way to Washington to inform authorities there that the Mexican government was going to initiate a temporary receivership of the foreign-owned oil industry. But before the emissary even reached the American capital, Cárdenas, on hearing of the companies' flat refusal to obey the Board's order, decided to nationalize—expropriate—the whole industry. The defiance of the petroleum producers—coming on the heels of their veiled insults to him and his government—pushed the President into this irreversible decision. He could not back down and retain the respect of his countrymen.

Lázaro Cárdenas called his cabinet toegther at six o'clock on March 15 and told them what he was going to do, but he did not notify Ambassador Daniels in the United States Embassy. On the national radio at ten o'clock their president told the Mexican people that he was going to nationalize the foreign-owned oil industry, "in the public interest." He openly admitted that his hasty action was irregular, but stated that normal legal proceedings would unduly prolong a situation which, "for the honor of the nation," had to be decided immediately. As the Weyls have correctly remarked in their eulogistic study of Lázaro Cárdenas, "The decision to expropriate the oil industry was not pre-meditated, nor were its economic consequences pondered. It was the impetuous verdict of one man who felt that the national honor of Mexico was at stake." *

The stunned companies did not really believe this could happen to them. The next day, March 16, they offered to pay in full the disputed 26,000,000 pesos. No response. Contrary to their expectations and that of most of the world, Cárdenas issued the expropria-

*Nathaniel and Sylvia Weyl, *The Reconquest of Mexico: The Years of Lázaro Cárdenas* (London and New York: Oxford, 1939), p. 281.

tion decree on March 18, 1938. The foreigners were out. Mexicans consider this the beginning of their "economic independence" comparable to their political independence on September 16, 1810.

After 1938 the whole internal spirit of Mexico changed. The latent inferiority complex so widespread among Mexicans gave way to satisfaction and pride. Part came from Cárdenas' domestic reforms, but a great deal derived from expropriation. Again Mexico had withstood the giants: the chief Goliath had fallen. Constant threat of punitive action from the United States, such as withdrawing silver purchases, merely consolidated the Mexican people behind Cárdenas. His uncalculated risk in this critical matter had enhanced their already high opinion of his political virility.

12. Nationalism, Internationalism, and Oil

The Mexicans believed that by the expulsion of the hated oil companies in 1938 they could now stand upright and breathe free air. Thus they were tolerant of the scandals and mismanagement of the nationalized oil industry which until 1946 stumbled and shambled and occasionally sprawled. The example and sense of national accomplishment in the face of clear danger not only raised Cárdenas to folk-hero stature, it was perhaps his most lasting legacy to his people. At the time, expropriation threatened to bring economic disaster and diplomatic reprisals in its train. It did set off another complicated chain reaction in the relations between the United States and Mexico. The final outcome was beneficial to both. The controversies and their aftermath extended through the terms of Cárdenas' successors in office, Manuel Avila Camacho and Miguel Alemán Valdés.

1. DOMESTIC RESPONSES

Cárdenas accompanied the expropriation decree with a bitter indictment of foreign oil companies in Mexico. Whether the bill of offenses was true or not seemed irrelevant; nearly every Mexican of the day (and since) thought what President Cárdenas said was gospel. He had said the case involved the "very sovereignty of the nation."

Cárdenas pointed out that the companies had not really invested much capital in the country. By means of rebates, special exemptions, and other privileges wrested from Mexican governments they had built up their industry from swollen profits on current production. A graphically emotional section of the speech summarized the adverse social aspects of the oil industry and its unsavory impact on Mexican life in tales of brutal armed guards and stories of "abuse, outrage, and even murder." Cárdenas stressed the discrimination between foreigner and Mexican in oil areas: comfort for the foreigners, misery for the Mexicans. The foreigners had invested or reinvested in the country none of the wealth they drew out of the Mexican land. They had failed to improve the Republic which was providing them with riches.

The companies, of course, heatedly denied all the Mexican charges leveled at them. They countered with recrimination: the venal, envious Mexicans themselves had been responsible for conditions in the oil areas. A Standard Oil of New Jersey pamphlet implied that since no Mexican was able to do much himself, "The temptation to appropriate what foreign ingenuity, energy, and capital were developing in Mexico proved irresistible. Slowly but surely the Mexican Government reached out its fingers and began to squeeze."

In a last ditch legal fight, the companies appealed the expropriation in Mexican Courts. On December 2, 1939 the Mexican Supreme Court upheld its legality. The companies, however, maintained the position that they had been robbed; the oil Mexico was selling had been illegally confiscated. The Mexican government had acted improperly and was paying no one for the goods, which therefore still belonged to their rightful owners, the companies. Under a barrage of articles and pamphlets issued in the United States, many Americans for the first time became dimly aware that there is a distinction between "expropriation" and "confiscation"; the first is paid for, but the second is not.

In their hard-fought war with Mexico, the companies used not only propaganda weapons but economic sanctions—boycott, blacklists, hidden pressures. They apparently even brought the United States Navy to side with them for awhile. In the "free enterprise" atmosphere in which, despite charges to the contrary, American capitalism has carried on its activities, the government of the United States is almost powerless to control anti-Mexican activities of private American corporations.

When Mexicans attempted to sell oil in Europe, the expropriated companies declared economic war on them. Ineffective but irritating was their habit of slapping liens on Mexican oil cargoes under the pretext that Mexicans were selling "stolen goods." In addition, the oil companies started a direct boycott—no foreign-owned tanker or vehicle would move a drop of Mexican petroleum and Mexico itself had no equipment for the chore. They also engineered a secondary boycott: No American firms would supply Mexico with equipment to run the nationalized industry, and they refused to furnish the tetraethyl essential for making high octane gasoline. Marketing the expropriated oil to obtain foreign exchange was badly hampered. The United States offered no market; it was then glutted.

From an economic point of view, expropriation came at a most inauspicious time for Mexico, for the country's economy was tottering under the twin blows of reform and Depression. The agrarian upheavals had cut food production, and basic food items necessarily came from abroad; to purchase them, foreign exchange was needed. Silver and oil were nearly all that propped up an export trade that, with the fall of world prices and "autarchy" abroad, had dwindled to new lows. Reform, actual and threatened, had touched off a panic-stricken flight of foreign and domestic capital, which further undermined the economic system. To have suspended purchases of silver in reprisal for the expropriation of American oil would have brought the Mexican economy crashing.

It was not clear what would happen to Mexican silver, once American oil had been expropriated. Almost the sole market for Mexican silver was the United States government; under a 1937 agreement it was purchasing quantities of the metal at slightly above world prices, partly to protect American markets in Mexico. Thus at any time then and later during the negotiations over expropriated oil, cancellation by the United States of its purchases of silver would seriously have crippled the Cárdenas regime. The United States' attempt to use that lethal weapon lasted only a few days.

Its restraint was not solely due to altruism, though that may have played a part. Seventy per cent of the silver producers in Mexico were American; they, not the Mexicans, were being penalized, and the Washington silver lobby was as powerful as the oil. Further, if Mexicans had no dollars, they could buy no American goods. And beyond that, silver producers employed Mexican labor, too; if pushed at all, Cárdenas was quite likely to expropriate American mining as well as petroleum enterprises. So the chief weapon—withdrawal of silver purchases from Mexico by the United States government—remained sheathed.

The economics of these matters troubled the average Mexicans not a whit, though they began to arouse certain misgivings abroad. The

Mexicans celebrated their new Economic Independence Day, March 18, 1938, with monster rallies and parades. Speaking to his delirious fellow citizens, President Cárdenas pointed out that the nation would now have to pay for the properties it had expropriated, and announced to the world that "Mexico will honor her foreign debt." Typical was the response of the Mexicans, who began to organize public collections to pay off this sudden new obligation. State governors, high Church officials, patriotic grand dames, peasants, students—all the numberless and picturesque types of Mexicans—pitched in what they had, including money, jewels, even homely domestic objects, chickens, turkeys, and pigs. By August 1938 the collection had grown to about $440,000. This was less than half of 1 per cent of the value the American owners placed on their properties; their loss was even smaller than the British, equally affected by the decree.

When it was obvious that the jewels of fine ladies, pigs of peasants, and the students' mites would not begin to cover the obligations created by oil expropriations, it was requisite to take official action. To calm restive opinion abroad, the Mexican Congress talked about issuing internal Mexican bonds to raise 100,000,000 pesos; even when they halved the figure, there was no possibility of extracting that much money from the Mexican people. Those who had funds would not buy bonds; the others had hardly enough cash to keep themselves and their families alive. It looked like an impasse, inviting intervention.

But once again the clouds of European war and threats to the Americas cast their shadows on diplomatic relations between Mexico and the United States. For reasons of "high policy" Great Britain dared not move against Mexico without permission from the United States; the United States for moral, strategic, and political reasons could do little more than bring the weight of hemispheric and world opinion to its cause in the disputes with Mexico. Some of these background features provided a framework into which can be fitted the complicated international paths opened by the Cárdenas expropriations of 1938.

2. INTERNATIONAL REPERCUSSIONS: GREAT BRITAIN AND MEXICO

Two nations, the United States and Great Britain, faced the same tangled situation in the wake of the Mexican expropriations. Uninhibited by the niceties of a Good Neighbor policy, the British took a European approach to the question. On April 8, 1938 the British Foreign Office acknowledged the general right of expropriation but told Mexico that in this particular instance "public interest" was not even an issue. The note implicitly denied the Constitution of 1917's right to sanction actions which were arbitrary and confiscatory. Because of the rigged nature of the Mexican Courts and Boards that had ruled on the petroleum matters, the English charged a denial of justice to their nationals. Therefore, the Mexican government had transgressed well-founded principles of international law. It was a lesson, not a note. But the Foreign Office demanded the return of *El Águila,* chief British holding company, to its Dutch Shell owners. The Dutch Shell interests (a British corporation, despite its name) valued its expropriated holdings at around $250,-000,000, including the oil still to be pumped and sold. It had enjoyed the "Extra-Official Pact" without accepting its Mexican tenets.

The Mexican reply pointed out that *El Águila* was not even British. It had been organized under the laws of Mexico as a Mexican corporation. In May Great Britain suddenly requested $82,000, an overdue installment which Mexico owed for awards under the General Claims Convention of 1935. Mexico forwarded London a check but enclosed with it a stinging reminder of Britain's own repudiation of *its* war debts. Mexico broke off diplomatic relationships with Great Britain.

Until the second World War, these stiff attitudes continued on each side. Their chief result in 1938 was to shift the focus of controversy. From one which had included Europe it became a bilateral quarrel between the United States and Mexico. European-style diplomacy was no great success at the time.

3. INTERNATIONAL REPERCUSSIONS: TESTING THE GOOD NEIGHBOR

Franklin D. Roosevelt and Cordell Hull had to back up a Good Neighbor policy still on probation among other Latin-Americans. Strong and adverse action against Mexico would have alienated forever the growing but very shaky Latin-American trust in the United States. At the same time it could have opened the Mexican door even wider to eager Axis blandishments.

The American oil companies, too, appealed to their home government for redress. They adduced the same international law arguments as the British, but added that the law of Mexico itself had been transgressed. They claimed that they had been robbed under two codes—international, and Mexican. They wanted justice, and their properties returned; if not that, they wanted cash for all the capital invested, plus the value of oil that lay underground. The United States government was not as quick to respond to the American oil companies as the British had been to their shorn nationals.

Under the protocols that formed the Good Neighbor Policy the United States had in 1933 and 1936 agreed to accept "American International Law" which virtually bars unilateral intervention. Part of the same accepted credo was another corollary of hemispheric democracy: foreigners in an American nation can be treated no worse, but certainly no better, than its own nationals. Mexican holdings in land and business had been expropriated without number. Since Mexico had declared the matter to be an "internal affair"—a squabble between the government and companies over labor—the United States was interdicted from being quite as abrupt and unpleasant as the unsuccessful British. By the Good Neighbor Policy the United States had virtually given up forceful protection of American properties in Latin America. Persuasion was about its only weapon.

The first diplomatic interchanges between the United States and Mexico on these touchy matters were cautious and conciliatory. On March 27, 1938 Secretary of State Hull (without mentioning oil) noted that the Mexican government was within its rights in expropriating property for public utility; he mentioned only that there should be fair recompense: prompt and adequate payment. In a note shortly afterwards, Lázaro Cárdenas told the United States that its friendly attitude had won the esteem of Mexicans and that Mexico would honor its obligations, past and present.

President Roosevelt on April 1 publicly stated that the United States was more interested in claims of its former small farmers in Mexico than those of the large interests. He suggested that the American oil companies should get a settlement, but for only the actual cash sums they had invested, less depreciation; under no circumstances should the underground oil beneath their expropriated lands be counted in the final settlement. From the outset it was quite clear that his administration would never go to war with Mexico over oil. Thus the main dimensions of the problem were staked out.

The State Department, following the President's cue, pushed agrarian claims as a stalking horse for the larger issue of oil settlement. Never was the right of Mexicans to expropriate challenged. In April 1938 the penniless Mexicans promised to pay small amounts on a few other items which were overdue. They were dilatory.

In the summer of 1938, the State Department stepped up the pressure. It listed all the outstanding unpaid American claims against Mexico since 1927 arising from expropriation of American-owned lands; their sum was about $10,000,000. Mexico's response to this request for prompter attention to legitimate debts was to ask for a postponement of the issue. This casual attitude, plus the inability of Mexico to see eye-to-eye with the United States on international law, rubbed some of Secretary Hull's basic emotions the wrong way.

His notes began to take on a stronger tone, and in them he outlined the fundamental position of the United States government. In July he reviewed the whole question of all land expropriations since 1915. He read the Mexicans a moral homily: the taking of other people's property without prompt and adequate payment is not expropriation, it is confiscation, which is immoral. Mere promises to pay in the vague and distant future are not enough to change confiscation into expropriation, which is legal. Hull wrote that the United States itself had a program of social betterment; but in carrying it out, when it became necessary for the government to take private property for slum clearance, roads, and other improvements, Roosevelt's government immediately paid the owners a just price. He raised the issue of whether Mexico had complied with the general rules of expropriation or not. He suggested arbitration of the matter.

Hull's note was obviously a propaganda effort to convince the rest of Latin America that Mexico was not wholly in the right in this instance. Further, he had to damp down any hopes harbored by other Good Neighbors that the way to get United States property cheap was to seize it, issue worthless bonds, and call the process "expropriation." *

Ostensibly Hull was still talking only about agrarian claims. The Mexicans rejected his invitation to a general arbitration of their ex-

---

* During this period there was much talk in the world about secret weapons. A current Mexican joke was that Mexico had a better secret weapon than Hitler: If he sent an army to the Americas, Mexico would expropriate it and use it against Mussolini.

propriation techniques, but they did accept the suggestion to set up a joint commission to settle the real value of the $10,000,000 worth of accumulated agrarian claims. As a manifest of good faith, Mexico made a token payment of $1,000,000 towards whatever eventual indemnity the joint commission would establish. But Mexicans also said that such a commission could not set a precedent for the settlement of oil expropriation claims. Thus in midsummer of 1938 the tricky and explosive problem of agrarian claims was removed from the even more inflammable question of petroleum.

The Richberg Mission and Stalemate. The United States State Department encouraged the expropriated oil companies to make a direct settlement of some sort with Mexico. Under this official prodding the companies sent Donald R. Richberg to Mexico to dicker. He and Cárdenas talked matters over from March 8 to March 22, 1939.

Richberg, speaking for the oil companies, wanted cash. The sum, based on an estimated value of holdings, now ran to $260,000,000; if Mexico could not pay this immediately, Cárdenas should return the properties to their true owners. The Americans again were reviving the hoary old idea that the oil yet in the ground also belonged to them, a position Roosevelt had repudiated a year earlier. The Mexicans stood firm on their contention that the Constitution of 1917 had returned such values to the nation.

Richberg, himself a wily trader, bounced back with another offer. Actually it was a series of intermeshed offers: one was to lease back the expropriated properties to the people from whom they had been taken; they would operate them, and when the fifty-year leases expired, they would quietly depart. Another was to form mixed American-Mexican corporations to exploit the oil; American companies would use the value of their expropriated companies to get stock in the new corporations. At times these two sincere men seemed to be nearing agreement, but Cárdenas always held back, probably wisely.

In April 1940 Hull again reviewed the controversy and proposed arbitration to determine the amount to be paid, and the means of payment. He insisted on fair and prompt payment. In May the Mexicans rejected this invitation to arbitrate a matter which they said was purely a domestic one; arbitration, to them, pertained only to international questions.

So the matter rested until the Cárdenas regime drew to a close in

November 1940. To all intents and purposes the ostensible stalemate between the two governments over the oil question continued.

4. INTERNATIONAL SETTLEMENTS

Roosevelt and the State Department were aware that Mexico was unwillingly, reluctantly, but definitely being drawn into the Axis web. Germany, Italy, and Japan were overeager to obtain Mexican oil; with all other markets shut off, Mexico bartered petroleum for needed manufactured goods from the Axis. Totalitarian political influence had begun to follow the economic; there was a sharp and potentially dangerous rise of Fascist activity in Mexico, especially noticeable in the Hispanidad and Fifth Column movements like the Sinarquistas.

Moreover, so long as Mexico and the United States were at odds with one another, no inter-American system could work smoothly. Other Latin-American nations were inclined to follow Mexico's lead in hemispheric defense and to reflect its attitudes toward the approaching conflict. Finally, the strategic materials that Mexico had furnished in World War I were more than ever needed for the second global struggle; the United States was already enmeshed in it, as an active nonbelligerent, the "arsenal of democracy."

In Mexico, Manuel Avila Camacho's new administration had already showed that it was pursuing a domestic policy of conciliation and compromise to prepare the Mexicans for any contingency. The trend had carried into external relations. Toward the end of Cárdenas' term, Mexico's foreign policy had shifted. To break the forced economic connections with the Axis, preliminary and exploratory discussions had been initiated with the United States. Cárdenas had early and long been an open political foe of totalitarianism; he had backed the Spanish Republicans. He was naturally uneasy about the schizophrenic Mexican situation: his protégés in political speeches were blasting the Axis, yet their government was selling oil to tool up the *Wehrmacht* and to kill those same Republicans.

Sinclair oil interests, for reasons best known to them, decided in 1940 to split the united front which the expropriated enterprises had been maintaining. Perhaps to get a better bargain they made a separate peace with Mexico. The Sinclair Oil Company dispatched as their ambassador Patrick Hurley, an army man who stressed his part-Indian background when talking to Cárdenas. After shrewd haggling on both sides, Sinclair agreed to accept $8,500,000 cash for their properties, a valuation based on their actual investments. They renounced claims to oil still in the ground. By anticipating the inevitable, Sinclair actually got a better cash settlement than did the others. Its action opened the way for a final and general settlement handled through more orthodox diplomatic channels.

Fortunately for all concerned, the United States and Mexico reached an accord before Pearl Harbor. Otherwise it would have looked like a shotgun marriage. After what a State Department Bulletin reports as "months of discussion and negotiation," the two countries in November 1941 signed a General Agreement that swept old issues away at one grand stroke—or so it seemed. Both nations were highly conscious of the second World War; as yet it had not directly involved the Americas, but defense efforts were under way throughout the hemisphere. It was necessary to tidy up the diplomatic side in order to meet the new and ominous threats to the Americas with a united vigor.

Against this background a Mexican-American General Agreement was signed on November 19, 1941. It laid a lot of old ghosts to rest. The ancient problem of agrarian claims was cleared: in a full settlement of all these (including accrued interest) Mexico promised to pay a total of $40,000,000. It had already paid $6,000,000; the remaining $34,000,000 was divided into annual installments of $2,500,000 each. These have been faithfully forwarded; by November 1952 the original $40,000,000 had been whittled to $6,500,000. Thus one of the main debts of the Revolution was on the way to liquidation.

A number of economic matters were worked out, for mutual benefit. A reciprocal trade treaty was authorized, which was drawn up and accepted as a war measure in 1942. The Mexican peso was stabilized and given a constant ratio to the dollar by United States backing. The United States committed itself to purchase quantities of silver, at the world price, directly from the Mexican government.

In return for Mexican concessions, the United States also pledged that long-term, low-interest loans would be made available to Mexico through the Import-Export Bank to help rehabilitate the Mexican economy for war. As always, these loans would *not* be cash handouts; they are simply advance payment by the Bank to American business firms who furnish the materials for which the Mexican government then pays the Bank on the installment plan. Though not directly part of the General Agreement of 1941, suitable arrangements were made at about the same time to refurbish the creaky Mexican military machine.

One of the most important parts of the General Agreement was the announcement of a procedure to clear up difficulties over oil. The two nations stated that a joint board of two experts would evaluate the expropriated properties and recommend terms of payment. The basis would exclude oil still in the ground; the governments set a deadline of five months for completing the chore. The United States appointed Morris L. Cooke as its Commissioner, while Manuel J. Zevada represented the Mexican government.

They accomplished their mission within the given span. On April 17, 1942 they jointly reported that they had valued the expropriated oil properties at $23,995,991.* They recommended that one-third of this sum be paid July 1, 1942 and the remainder in five equal and consecutive annual installments. Despite the contention of the expropriated companies that the basis and evaluation were both illegal and discriminatory, the State Department made it clear to them that they could take the settlements suggested by Cooke and Zevada, or else; the United States government would do no further pushing. With no alternatives, the companies took the awards. For technical rather than political reasons, the Mexican and American governments altered slightly the method and timing of payments; a joint statement by Presidents Roosevelt and Avila Camacho after their famous meeting in Monterrey determined the final arrangements.†

Through Cárdenas' major surgery the problem of foreign-owned petroleum enterprises and their relationship to Mexico and the United States was removed as a possible future source of major discord. The United States' acceptance of the Mexican facts, while pushing that nation toward the realization of its inescapable international responsibility for domestic acts, was beneficial to both. In the long run Cordell Hull had made good his only contention: expropriation requires prompt and adequate payment, and is then

* Breakdown: Standard Oil of New Jersey, $18.3 million; Standard Oil of Southern California, $3.6 million; Sábalo, $0.9 million; Consolidated, $0.6 million; and Seaboard, $0.5 million.

† The final arrangements: The total due as the experts suggested, $23,995,991, plus 3 per cent interest from March 18, 1938 to September 30, 1947 (date of final payment); payments to 1943 included $9,000,000. Balance due $20,137,-700.84 to be liquidated by one payment on September 30, 1943 of $3,796,391.04; and then three equal installments, payable on September 30 of $4,085,327.45. These have been met punctually and the debt has been cleared.

justifiable; dilatory tactics and worthless promises to pay at some future and unspecified time is confiscation and is internationally immoral. At no point in the proceedings did the United States ever question the right of Mexico to exercise its sovereignty, but merely argued that with freedom goes responsibility.

Vestigial Settlements, 1948–1951. One of the less-known facets of expropriation was the exemption of small, independent American and British companies from the decree of March 18, 1938. A number of oil lands and producers remained in foreign hands. The small operating companies have, under the Petroleum Code, been required to sell their output to Pemex or to market it in Mexico under fixed prices. The Government has regulated, not owned, them.

A recent trend has been for Mexico to purchase outright these vestigial holdings. In 1948, for an undisclosed sum, Pemex obtained a 40 per cent stock control in the Gulf Oil Corporation's Mexican holdings; in 1950–1951 Pemex purchased them outright for $2,350,-000 by paying a million dollars down and the remainder in installments. Pemex thus added two Gulf subsidiary companies, Gulf's 1500 barrels per day production, a million-barrel Gulf reserve, ten land concessions, and most of the company's buildings to the nationalized Mexican oil industry. In similar fashion Pemex paid Abraham Z. Phillips $2.5 million in November 1950 for his Mexican holdings. At present (July 1952) there are but two tiny foreign oil properties in Mexico, the British-owned Kermex Oil Fields Company, and the United States-operated Charro Oil Company.

The British Settlement. Clearing the air between the United States and Mexico solved only half the international problem, though nearly all the inter-American one. The Mexican nation, for historic reasons, had fastened on to the American companies as the storm center of emotional diatribes against "foreign imperialism." In a considerably less heated atmosphere, where historic wrongs and rights were not dragged in to muddle and distort the specific issues at hand, the British made their peace with Mexico. They were no more successful than the United States in getting the Mexican government to retreat from the Constitution of 1917, but their companies did possibly receive a proportionately greater recompense than did their American counterparts.

As part of the United Nations' war effort, Roosevelt arranged for resumption of diplomatic relationships between Mexico and Great Britain. During the war itself, little was done about their differences over oil. Through normal diplomatic channels the two governments reached a meeting of minds in the postwar period. On September 18, 1947 the two governments announced a settlement of the 1938 expropriation.

Under its terms, Mexico agreed to pay an established principal sum of $81,250,000 with interest. Interest from 1938 through 1948 alone reached the sum of $23,000,000, while for the duration of the contract, 1948 through 1962, it totaled $26,000,000. The British thus have been receiving annual installments of $8,689,257.75, and will continue to do so until the stipulated fifteen payments are cleared up.

In crass money terms, the historic oil expropriations and their aftermath have cost the Mexican people around $175 million. The United States companies received about $42 million; this counts $24 million principal and $5 million interest involved in the general settlements, plus $8 million previous payment to Sinclair and around $5 million later to independent owners. The major debts have all been cleared away. When Mexico made its final general payment on September 30, 1949, the oil controversy with the United States passed into history.

The total British compensation will amount to $130 million. It will not be fully cleared from the books until 1962. At that time, the Mexican people will have their own oil industry, wholly free and clear of historic debt. They believe this to be one of the major accomplishments of the Revolution, and view attempts to force them into allowing re-entrance of foreign petroleum interests into the Republic with a justifiably skeptical eye.

Thus, one of the touchiest episodes in the recent relationships between Mexico and the United States was finally and successfully concluded. The sacrifice of the somewhat dubious claims of the American oil companies was a relatively small price to pay for assuring the safety of the United States along its southern frontier and winning the friendship and esteem of the Mexican nation, and all of Latin America. The oil expropriation, with its diplomatic interchange, was the toughest economic problem involving the Roosevelt Good Neighbor Policy.

5. THE DOMESTIC POSTSCRIPTS

The story of Mexican oil would be sadly incomplete if only its international aspects were stressed. How the industry fared when Mexicans took it over is a revealing object lesson. A standard contention by the oil firms in their campaign of recrimination against the Mexican government was that, in the hands of nationals, Mexican oil could not be produced; they added that selfish Mexican nationalism was depriving the world of an important commodity. In this international context of economic hostility, the ill-prepared, politically minded Mexicans stepped into the management of the companies. The feeble little national company that Cárdenas had sponsored became the nucleus of a vastly ramified public petroleum institution, Petroleos Mexicanos (Pemex). It is a national monopoly.

Troubles. For almost a decade the Mexican oil industry bore out the gloomy predictions of the expropriated owners. Rather than opening up new areas and efficiently exploiting the old, Pemex was long content to drain in somewhat haphazard manner the four major oil zones already developed by the foreign pioneers. Minor extension had occurred within the zones, but the pattern established by foreigners remained static. The accompanying table indicates the zones and their production. In much the same fashion no additions of note were made to Mexican refining capacity for a decade. But the labor force expanded enormously.

PRODUCTION

(Thousands of 42-gallon bbls.)

Field or Zone	1945	1946	1947
Panuco	5,294	8,652	10,062
Golden Lane	10,062	8,523	7,840
Poza Rica	22,949	26,213	31,951
Isthmus	5,242	5,847	6,431
Total	43,547	49,235	56,284

Source: "Fuel Investigation: Mexican Petroleum," 80th Cong., 2nd Sess., H.R. 2470, Dec. 31, 1948 (Washington: G.P.O., 1949), p. 6.

The Mexican petroleum workers felt that their interests had been the cause of the international commotion, and that the industry was to be run by them for their own benefit. Wages were quadrupled, becoming 50 per cent of production costs. Politically immune, the union members slacked their individual efforts; they combined low individual effort with feather-bedding. Individual productivity plummeted. In 1945 the 17,000 oil workers were producing less oil *per man* than the 13,000 of 1937. With a war to win and a stated policy of conciliation, President Avila Camacho made no major attempt to clarify and redefine the relationship of the oil workers to Pemex or to the nation. That was left to his successor, President Miguel Alemán.

Part of the general difficulty in Pemex was due to obsolete and inadequate equipment, but a larger share of the blame was clearly attributable to corruption, patronage, and other political practices. Production and exports hit an almost all-time low in 1942–1944; only about 35 million barrels of oil were produced, and only 4.6 million of these went abroad as exports. (Appendix I, Table 8.)

The Power Contest. Part of the testing process which every president undergoes came to Alemán when, shortly after his inauguration, the national oil syndicate called an illegal, political strike. Their tactics were not very popular among the Mexican people, long disgusted with the odorous conditions of their national oil industry. Even other working groups were loath to back the oil workers; by using their political glamor as heroes in the "battle against imperialism" and their strategic spot in the economy, the oil unions had jacked their members' average salary to 24 pesos a day, about ten to twelve times the national rate. Everyone could see its effects in the high price of gasoline. Alemán correctly decided that the interests of these 20,000 petroleum workers (less than 0.003 per cent of the economically active population) could be restrained and hedged for the benefit of the whole nation. He disallowed the strike, and began to mobilize army units near the fields.

When the recalcitrant and insolent union officials refused to call off their strike, the president had them imprisoned. The oil unions were not smashed, but their rank and file were told to elect new and more representative leaders, non-Communist. Government auditors went over the syndicates' accounts. After discrediting the imprisoned leaders by publishing the personal and political irregularities that they had committed with union funds, the government released them; they have not been heard from since.

These decisive presidential moves were genuinely popular. They not only showed Alemán's "political virility," but they gave the new director of Pemex, Antonio Bermúdez, an opportunity to establish himself as a true manager, rather than a walking delegate for the national oil union and the official party. Chastened and conciliatory, the new leadership of the national union sat down with Bermúdez in 1946 to work out a joint plan to rehabilitate the sagging industry.

Rehabilitation. Senator Antonio Bermúdez ranks high in the group of "new Mexicans" whom Alemán has placed in responsible posts to carry out his promises of a better life for all Mexicans. A self-made man, he became independently wealthy as an agent for Waterfill whisky. His fellow-townsmen elected him mayor of Ciudad Juárez, a tough, corrupt, and important border center across from El Paso, Texas. Bermúdez gave the place a shaking up, cleaned it thoroughly, and gave it an air of semi-respectability. Alemán brought Bermúdez into national politics by backing him for senator. With machine support he came into that office with Alemán in 1946.

He was immediately given the thankless task of doing to Pemex what he had done for Ciudad Juárez, and of solving its technical problems as well. He takes no pay for these duties. He is a business-man, not a politician, general, or reformer. His mandate has been to put the national oil industry in such shape that it can aid rather than hinder the other economic reforms undertaken by the present administration. He has done it. Much of the fat was trimmed off the working force; wage scales were readjusted, and a reasonable social program for workers was evolved. Bermúdez pointed out to them that oil workers were not dealing now with "foreign imperialists" but with a Mexican, speaking for the rest of the Mexicans. He re-trieved the control of management, which had been a political foot-ball between directors and labor since expropriation.

As its director his handling of the Pemex situation has been so successful that for a short while Bermúdez was even talked about as a successor to Alemán. There is no question that in six years, backed by government power and confidence, he has been able to make a going concern in both an economic and a social sense out of the falter-ing national oil monopoly. Every March 18, the anniversary of the oil expropriation, he reports to the nation what he has accomplished and what lies ahead. These reports show an increasingly favorable picture.

In the battle of ciphers that often goes on between critics and apologists for Mexico's nationalized petroleum industry, two years are selected for comparison, depending on the outlook of the writer. Hostile critics like the year 1922, when under private exploitation Mexico produced nearly a quarter of the world's oil supply; some 182 million barrels were pumped and 180 million exported. Mexicans, faced with such comparisons, point to the year 1932: foreigners pumped only 32 million barrels, and exported 20 million of them.

Table 13 in Appendix I indicates that in 1942 the nationalized industry had made little or no improvement over that, but the most recent summary of Pemex's affairs reveals substantial improvement under Bermúdez' tenure as director. Taken from his report on the fourteenth anniversary of expropriation, March 18, 1952, the salient figures tend to speak for themselves.

SUMMARY OF PEMEX ACTIVITIES, 1946–1951

	Production (bbls.)	New Wells	Refined (bbls.)	Export (crude) (bbls.)	Total Revenues (pesos)
1946	49,239,800		42,300,000	9,700,000	569,965,000
1947	56,289,496	64	46,400,000	13,990,000	759,318,000
1948	58,529,201	83	47,547,000	13,047,000	1,972,122,000
1949	62,097,308	163	50,805,000	14,125,000	1,229,394,000
1950	73,881,478	219	51,980,000	23,564,075	1.619,660,500
1951	78,780,387	268	56,780,000	22,392,622	1,838,594,500

Although the accompanying table provides the major dimensions of Pemex's performance during the Alemán years, certain additional considerations must be noted in arriving at a balance. As a national monopoly, Pemex has several almost incompatible missions to perform. For political reasons, it must pay wages as good as or better than those paid by the expropriated private companies and also it must keep increasing the social benefits of its own workers; more politically loaded is the fact that it must provide an expanding Mexican economy with plentiful, cheap, and quality petroleum products. As noted below, Mexicans have a sponge-like capacity for soaking up all the gasoline and lubricants that Pemex can make, while nascent industry is clamoring for more and more of its natural gas and by-products. So inevitably, pushed by both economic and political factors, Pemex must constantly seek to expand its production and search out new sources of supply. For numerous reasons, this increased production is expected to be self-financed, and the equipment needed is purchasable only abroad, in dollar areas. Pemex therefore exports annually only about as much petroleum as is necessary to earn the dollars it needs for expansion. In short, from a privately owned industry primarily producing for export and processing abroad, the Mexican nationalized industry has been reoriented to domestic needs; this has meant large expenditures for capital equipment, especially refining and distribution apparatus. Bermúdez has paid off an extraordinary developmental program from export profits, and pridefully announced in 1951 that Pemex would continue that bootstrap operation. When viewed in detail, the development of the nationalized Mexican petroleum industry is impressive.

First is the matter of supply and reserves; production figures have already been scanned. Since 1946, 24 new producing fields have been explored, and a mounting percentage of the annual Pemex budget goes toward discovering more. Most of the new areas lie in the northeast and southeast of the Republic, the newest and possibly largest being the "José Colomo" located during 1950 in Tabasco and Tenixtepec, a new area beyond the Poza Rica field, opened in August 1952. Mexicans reckon the potential yield of new wells opened in 1952 as 55,000 barrels daily, plus 6 million cubic feet of natural gas. On December 31, 1946 Pemex had as proved reserves some 1058 million barrels of oil; from 1946 to 1951, it pumped out about 330 million barrels, but during the same period proved new reserves of 696 million barrels, so that in 1951 the total was 1424 million barrels. To these are added some 51,000 million cubic meters of natural gas, equivalent to yet another 363 million barrels of oil, and distillates totaling still another 9 million, so that the reserve stock of hydrocarbons equaled about 1796 million barrels of oil. In his final Congressional Address of September 1, 1952 President Alemán reported oil reserves at 1395 million barrels, apart from gas reserves of astronomical proportions.

The use of natural gas in Mexico as an industrial and cooking fuel dates essentially from 1946. Ten large gas fields have been utilized, their output flowing to industrial centers at Mexico City and Monterrey; some is sold to the United States. As a noteworthy contribution to industrial development and agricultural rehabilitation, Pemex has one of the most modern desulphurizing plants in the world to extract sulphur from gas. It uses the by-products as basic materials for the manufacture of artificial fertilizers and acids. Two more sulphur works are on drawing boards for immediate construction.

The processing and distribution of crude petroleum has justifiably captured major attention and funds. One bottleneck to Mexican advance has been shortage of refining equipment and the fact that many specialized lubricants have to be imported. To remedy the one, Pemex enlarged the existing Azcapotzalco refinery (outside Mexico City) to 50,000 barrels per day (b.p.d.) capacity, while building a

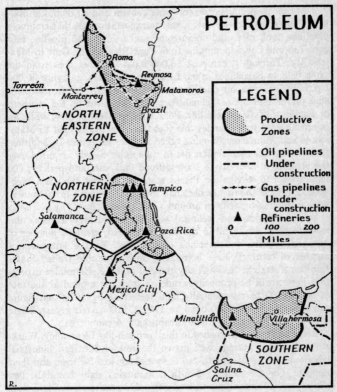

PETROLEUM

Roma
Reynosa
Torreón
Matamoros
Monterrey
Brazil
NORTH EASTERN ZONE

NORTHERN ZONE Tampico

Salamanca
Poza Rica

Mexico City

Minatitlán Villahermosa
SOUTHERN ZONE
Salina Cruz

LEGEND

Productive Zones

Oil pipelines

Under construction

Gas pipelines

Under construction

Refineries

0   100   200
Miles

This map is of 1950. Since then, some gas and oil pipelines under construction have been completed. New oil pipelines have been added at Salamanca.

small new one at Reynosa with 4000 b.p.d. limit; but the darling of the regime is the modern new plant at Salamanca, conceived and constructed by Mexicans, aided by a United States loan (since paid off). It has a 30,000 b.p.d. capacity, and as an integrated unit makes 1100 b.p.d. of special lubricants of the 1900 b.p.d. now needed in Mexico. All told, at the end of 1951, Mexican refining capacity amounted to 223,000 b.p.d.; this is considerably more than the 160,000 b.p.d. acquired at expropriation.

To bring its products to processing centers and to domestic markets, Pemex has had to create a vast transportation net that embraces pipelines, tank cars, and ocean-going tankers. One oil pipeline now runs 250 miles over mountains from Poza Rica on the Gulf to Mexico City. Through it can pass 50,000 b.p.d. Another goes from the same field to Salamanca, almost an equal distance, carrying 30,000 b.p.d. In 1951 an oil duct connected Minatitlán on the northern edge of the Isthmus of Tehuantepec to Salina Cruz on the southern or Pacific side. Gas ducts link Poza Rica to Mexico City, while an interconnected series carries this fuel from the Brazil field to Matamoros and Monterrey, tapping other supplies en route. In addition, there is a smaller but similar net in Campeche. Slowly acquired over the years have been about 2000 railroad tank cars and perhaps 200 tank trucks to service the Pemex stations that dot the main highways. By 1952 the tanker fleet had increased from 12 to 20 vessels, with a carrying capacity of around a million barrels.

On the physical and technical side of the industry, Pemex's immediate plans are to fill in the distribution net, create a number of specialized units, and continue explorations. To the latter end a number of contracts have been made with reputable United States firms on a straight fee basis. By the end of 1952, Bermúdez expects that Pemex will be producing crude oil from the ground at the rate of 90,000,000 barrels annually, and feels that by 1956 that figure can be jumped to 450,000 b.p.d. or 170,000,000 barrels a year. There is no visible reason why these dreams cannot come true.

Labor has not been crushed in this Porfirian-like blossoming. Workers' wages still average well above the rest of Mexican industrial labor, and Pemex has multiplied the social services for them and their families. For the workers' health it maintains eight hospitals, two clinics, and 43 consulting centers. Some 293 teachers provide a wide range of schooling in Pemex's 41 schools. It has also been a heavy contributor to the national campaign for building schools all over the republic, as well as setting up its own technical training centers and maintaining 260 scholarships for workers' children who wish higher education. Housing projects have been completed; others are under way. As 1952 drew to a close, it was clear that the Syndicate was strong, but was also responsible; so was management.

Markets for Pemex's products, especially gasoline, are among the least of its worries. Rather, the problem has been to close the gap between supply and demand. A dynamic triple spiral occurs when output is extended: the more available gas, the more cars, and then more roads; in turn better and longer roads increase vehicle use and hence the need for fueling them. As in the United States, the Mexicans have taken to wheels in the last quarter century, with appropriate changes in social and shopping habits. Mobility, physical as well as social, has come with the Revolution, and more especially since the Northern Dynasty and the days of Cárdenas.

Roads. Since 1925 and chiefly within the last ten years the national government has created about 15,000 miles of new highways. That figure includes the completion of the Mexican portions of the well-known Pan-American Highway from several entry points on the United States limit to the Guatemalan border. Between 1925 and 1948 the National Bureau of Roads spent nearly two billion pesos of direct government subsidy, as well as another billion pesos derived from gasoline taxes to perform its task of creating highway nets in the Core, West, and North. In 1952 some 620.6 million pesos were invested by National, State and local sources in Mexican roadbuilding.

Approximately 8500 miles of the national roads are paved; the remainder are gravel or hard-surface dirt roads. There have been a number of collateral developments: the National government, on a fifty-fifty share basis, has been aiding states in their efforts to develop secondary and tertiary market roads and minor networks. All told, Mexico has about 82,000 miles of highways and roads. At the same time it is emphasizing the building of trunk lines and four-lane super-highways. These fan out from regional and subregional centers to interconnect them with one another and with the United States, permitting a lucrative tourist trade.

Vehicles. In the same era that roads spread out through the Mexican republic, the automobile became an integral part of modern Mexican life. On a world scale, Mexico stands thirteenth in the number of gasoline-powered vehicles. It is outstripped in Latin America by only Argentina and Brazil. In the one decade 1939–1949 Mexico imported about 220,000 vehicles; at the end of 1950 it counted 30,000 busses, 119,000 trucks, and approximately 176,000 passenger cars for a total of over 325,000 vehicles in all, double the 1941 total. (Appendix I, Table 14.)

As farm mechanization proceeds, it too increases the domestic market. Allied have been the demands made for petroleum and its products by the light chemical industry that has come to Mexico during and since World War II. Many of the thermo-powered electric plants, part of the developing industrial system, depend on oil; their number is increasing. The growing tourist trade, which in 1950 saw 373,572 visitors (as compared to 1949's 305,561) in Mexico, many in their own cars, is an added but welcome burden that must be cared for; tourists furnish many needed dollars.

The transition from an industry owned by foreigners, producing raw materials for export, to a national oil industry geared to Mexican needs and hopes, has definitely been made. The national welfare of Mexicans as a whole rather than its stockholders' interests guides Pemex's policies. Profits from its operations are now being reinvested in expansion for Mexican well-being. On the basis of the concrete evidence available one can safely say that after floundering miserably for nearly a decade after expropriation the nationalized Mexican oil industry is far along the road to successful operation by Mexicans themselves.

13. World War II

Mexico could scarcely escape modification by the tremendous currents set in motion throughout the world with the opening of hostilities in Europe during 1939. Its international affairs, as well as its domestic patterns, were increasingly dominated by World War II and the imperious necessity of checking Axis aggression and influences. As indicated in the unfolding record below, Mexico emerged from the troubled war period a stronger nation than it had entered. It changed in many important respects. Many, if not most, of the present tendencies in Mexico stem quite directly from those earth-shaking war years.

Even before Cárdenas turned over his presidential office to his successor the shadows of war had edged to the Mexican area. On the international front, the late Cárdenas regime initiated a shift in policy that drew Mexico nearer to the United States and prepared the way for a sweeping settlement embracing oil, silver, old claims, loans, and a series of lesser matters, as already outlined.

More important, Mexico independently but clearly followed President Franklin D. Roosevelt's lead in preparing the hemisphere for any eventuality. In the same month that Cárdenas' hand-picked successor, Manuel Avila Camacho, was elected 57th president of Mexico, the foreign ministers of the American republics met at Havana (July 1940) to discuss schemes of political and economic coöperation in the crisis. The delegation from the United States announced that half a billion dollars in loans from the Import-Export Bank were earmarked for hemispheric defense, and that in return for materials needed to feed the expanding defense efforts of the United States it would make funds available to Latin America. There was to be a joint effort to combat the dangers of Axis schemes for world domination through military aggression and fifth-column activities. Both Mexico and the United States were in the throes of exciting and crucial domestic political campaigns for the presidency. In defiance of precedent, Franklin Roosevelt was standing for a third term, but so strongly rooted in Mexican sentiments was the Revolutionary principle of "No Re-Election" that even had he been personally inclined to do so, Lázaro Cárdenas was barred from succeeding himself. There is no evidence that he wished a second term.

1. PREPARING FOR THE STORM

From 1938 onward, boomlets for one or another Mexican presidential candidate were launched, but the serious contenders soon narrowed to three. Each represented a fairly important political tendency of the day. One was Francisco J. Múgica. Early a revolutionary (*Obregonista*) he had had a long record of reform activities; he had been head of the reform group which had inserted its radical concepts into the Constitution of 1917. Although never affiliated officially with the Communist Party, Múgica declared that he was no enemy of Communists; he once stated that Article 123 of the Mexican Constitution embodied "the minimum program of Marx." Though he seemed a logical successor to carry on Cárdenas' program of domestic reform, his candidacy was likely to touch off on uncontrollable Right Wing rebellion within the party, or an outright counterrevolution throughout the Republic.

At the opposite extreme from Múgica, yet as widely known, was Juan Andreu Almazán, a wealthy Revolutionary general. Almazán was dynamic and conservative, with strong leanings towards political Catholicism. He could count on powerful political support in the North (especially around Monterrey), the West, and in his home state of Morelos. Schooled politically by the Northern Oligarchy he was believed to be friendly to Big Business and the Americans. More by accident than design he also attracted a number of dissident labor groups outside the C.T.M. and a spectrum of Fascist and neo-Fascist organizations.

The third figure was Administration-backed. With the international situation darkening, the Cárdenas regime did an about-face in international matters, and took correlative steps in the looming political battle for the control of Mexico from 1940 to 1946. Without fanfare, it began to dissociate itself from the Axis and veer toward the United States; at about the same time word filtered into the proper places that President Cárdenas looked with favor on his Secretary of War as a likely successor. This man was a political unknown: Manuel Avila Camacho.

He had been born in Teziutlan, Puebla, April 24, 1897, home town of his friend Lombardo Toledano, and had been brought up in the old *hacendado* tradition. At seventeen Manuel joined the Revolution; he had held a series of administrative posts under Cárdenas as the latter rose in revolutionary ranks. Avila Camacho's chief reputation lay within the Army, where he was known as a conciliator rather than a leader. Without much personal flair or color his appearance had given him the nickname of *El Buchón* (double-chinned). He was chiefly famed for fairness, honesty, and a certain doggedness.

The campaign in 1939–1940 was a bitter and vicious duel, punctuated by violence and threats. Both the Left and the Right in Mexico prepared for the election as though for war. Lombardo Toledano publicly drilled his labor minions while rumors of plots, subplots, and intrigue within intrigue circulated more widely than usual. The Mexican opposition press sardonically dubbed the official candidate "The Unknown Soldier"; his platform had been written by the Party—a second Six Year Plan, similar in its outlook and its eclectic nature to the one foisted on Cárdenas.

Though Avila Camacho made the expected tours, his campaign speeches, studded with revolutionary clichés, were vague and somewhat platitudinous. He viewed his forthcoming presidential job as a consolidation of the gains made by Cárdenas. He would try to conciliate divergent Mexican interests, and govern for all Mexicans rather than for one or another economic group. By announcing that he favored small property in rural areas (rather than the collectivized *ejidos*), he swung considerable moderate support behind him. Variously interpreted but still disquieting to the "revolutionary family" was his reply to a journalist who asked about his attitude on the Catholic Church: *"Soy creyente"* ("I am a believer"), said the presidential aspirant. The doubts Camacho raised during his campaign did not alter the predictability of his election. In July 1940 Manuel Avila Camacho was elected the next president of Mexico, to be inaugurated in December.

In July 1940 the biggest question in Mexican circles was not the recently voiced alarms from the Havana Conference about the Axis but what response Almazán's followers would make to their electoral defeat. Their candidate had publicly promised them that if he were counted out he would take "appropriate action." On election day an

Almazanista group pronounced the whole electoral procedure a fraud and set up a rump Mexican government in the hills of the south, from whence they bombarded the general with calls to head an armed revolt to rectify what they termed the "imposition" of Avila Camacho. Civil war seemed a distinct possibility.

A fairly dangerous conspiracy was woven by the Almazanistas. The general himself claimed that through an interview with Elliott Roosevelt he was led to believe that if he would not make any move until after November 4 (the Third Term election for F. D. R.) and then could demonstrate real strength, he would be given belligerent status; if he dominated enough states, he would be recognized. In another writing he says that F. D. R. discouraged a revolt. Almazanistas in Mexico wearied of their leader's Fabian tactics and endless postponements of the projected revolt which gave Cárdenas time enough to move loyal troops to the potentially troubled spots. By mid-November the Almazanista ardor for an old-fashioned revolt had dropped below the July temperatures. The United States put a definitive end to hopes of a successful rebellion. On November 12, the White House announced that Vice-President Wallace would attend Manuel Avila Camacho's inauguration, December 1, 1940.

Camacho came to the presidency of Mexico in a thoroughly troubled and hostile atmosphere. Large segments of his own official party distrusted him; die-hard Almazanistas still thought of taking the initiative of rebellion into their own hands. The passions aroused by the campaigns were still tearing Mexican society apart, aided and abetted by the two rival networks of local and imported Fascists and Communists. With the example of Calles still in mind, few Mexicans believed Cárdenas' statements that he was divorcing himself from politics and would return quietly to private life. Hope for "national unity," a keynote of the Camacho campaign, seemed ephemeral and illusory.

Avila Camacho surprised both his friends and his critics by capably steering his administration through the early domestic political crises and then asserting real leadership in the more important international tangles created by the coming of the second World War. His original campaign of "national unity and a government for all" took on added importance as Mexico was drawn into the moral and military struggle that was dividing the civilized world. In the face of war, Mexico further democratized itself. Much of the credit goes to *El Buchón*.

At this short distance, and with much of the appropriate documentation still lacking, it is hard to determine how much of the Camacho program of slowing down the Revolution and calming the nation was due to foresight and accurate forecasting of the international climate, how much was due to political expediency, and how much was due to personal temperament. His actions, whatever their motivation, were important. With international skies lowering and with the knowledge that Mexico could not much longer look abroad for customary supplies in quantity, the new president purposely quieted the main agitations in all sectors of society and battened down the hatches for a stormy passage.

2. THE ROAD TO WAR

Though most of Mexican attention was riveted on the new president's handling of domestic matters, impelling forces behind many of them came from outside Mexico. In the United States and in Mexico national decisions were more and more colored by the encroachment of war into the hemisphere. Led by President Roosevelt, the Americas placed their moral, then their material strength as barriers to Axis overseas aggression. While the President of the United States was making his country the "arsenal of democracy," the other American lands, and especially Mexico, were helping stock it. In a fairly unbroken curve Mexico shifted from a passive spectator in 1939 to a partner in the United States' "belligerent neutrality" during 1940 and 1941. As a result Mexico was fully enmeshed as an active belligerent in 1942.

The shift in foreign policy inaugurated by President Cárdenas was carried on and elaborated. In his Pan-American Day speech on April 14, 1941 President Avila Camacho made it clear that Mexico welcomed no "New Order" based on Fascist bayonets. The speeches by officials in his government, especially Ezequiel Padilla, his Foreign Minister, aroused considerable apprehension both in the Right and in the Left that Mexico would be drawn into a conflict.

But despite vocal opposition, President Camacho continued his course. Like the United States, neutral Mexico seized Axis vessels. Trading with Axis powers was restricted. When the so-called Black List was published in Washington on July 17, 1941 there were 1800 persons and firms in the Western Hemisphere who were "deemed to be acting for the benefit of Germany and Italy"—Fifth Columnists. A number of individuals and enterprises in Mexico were included.

The German Ambassador in Mexico immediately sought protection for them. He pointed out that it was a violation of Mexican sovereignty for the United States to decide who could do business in Mexico.

In a tart note, Mexico told the Germans that Mexicans would follow the policy that suited them best; they needed no suggestions from Germany. This strong line was supported by mass meetings and laudatory resolutions by the C.T.M., the National Peasants League, the official party itself, and Congress. On August 22, Mexico broke off economic relations with Germany by canceling its privilege of having a consulate in Mexico and closing Mexican consulates in Germany and in the German-occupied areas. To check possible fifth-column activity, carried on chiefly by Sinarquistas, a Mexican Espionage Law was initiated in September 1941.

Retreat of the Left. Cárdenas' policies had strengthened militant labor in Mexico. Many of its spokesmen were in this period openly Communist or such ardent admirers of Russia that they were willing to follow the Party Line. As relations between Russia, Germany, and the United States changed, so did the Line. At first, when the two variants of totalitarianism were allied, it aimed at weakening the position of Great Britain and the United States. All stops were pulled to discredit these "imperialists." Echoes of the Line resounded in Mexico as Camacho's hostility to the Axis and coöperation with the United States increased.

Late in May 1941 Vicente Lombardo Toledano published a propagandistic piece entitled "Eleven Questions." He demanded a public accounting of the administration's international policies. Avila Camacho answered that there were no secret treaties with the United States, that Mexicans were carrying forward defense efforts without foreign loans or without stopping the march of their own Revolution, and that the nation did not necessarily have to mix in extra-continental conflicts. He added that the existing United States–Mexican pacts were not formal military alliances. They were regional defense arrangements within the framework of the general inter-American resolutions; they left each nation autonomous and sovereign.

Three weeks after Lombardo Toledano's oblique attack, the Soviet-German Pact was ruptured by the unexpected Nazi offensive against Russia. Thereafter, until the end of the war, the militant Left in Mexico vigorously supported the war effort. Attacks on the United States in the radical Mexican press became muted and finally disappeared; some of the more violent organs, like Narciso Bassols' *Combate,* quietly expired. The official Communist Party paper, *La Voz de Mexico,* changed to the new Party Line—"Win the War," "Open the Second Front!"

As a final confirmation of Mexico's foreign policies, the earlier-mentioned general United States–Mexican settlement (concluded on November 19, 1941) was made public.* It was not quite a final arrangement of all outstanding problems accumulated over the years but it unlocked the doors to such agreements. The main outlines for burying the mutual rancors of the past were agreed upon and the way made open for solid coöperation during and after the war.

This settlement had repercussions beyond the two nations concerned. The other Latin-American nations had been more or less treading water until the Latin-American policy of the United States was clarified by its concrete actions in the Mexican imbroglio. The mutually satisfactory compromises thus had a tonic effect not only on the bilateral affairs of Mexico and the United States but on the whole network of inter-American relations. Fortunately this clearing of underbrush and creating firebreaks antedated Pearl Harbor by nearly a month.

On December 8, immediately after the Pearl Harbor attack on the United States, Mexico broke off relations with Japan. The Mexican government impounded Japanese and Axis funds, but did not declare war. Cárdenas was called from private life and named military commander of the vulnerable Pacific Zone. President Avila Camacho sent messages to his state governors concerning Mexico's posture in the conflict which might reach Mexican shores. In his New Year's Day message of 1942 over national radio hookups, the president reaffirmed Mexico's role: Mexican contributions would lie almost exclusively in Mexican factories and fields; the battle which Mexico was to fight was that of increased production. Mexico, too, was to be an arsenal of democracy. It was this policy that brought Mexico directly into the war.

Mexico Enters the War. Even after Pearl Harbor and the Russian flip-flop there was a general apathy towards the war and the international situation in Mexico. Hot interest was displayed only in urban centers and, even there, only among organized groups. The administration continued its strong anti-Axis activities. President Avila Camacho dispatched Minister Padilla to the United States

* See above, pages 248–249.

where he became one of the leading members of the Latin-American team coöperating with the State Department and Roosevelt to strengthen hemispheric defense. On April 17, 1942 Padilla violently condemned the Axis in a New York speech. That he was voicing official administration sentiment was confirmed by Camacho's Pan-American Day address on April 14, 1942. In it the president said "independence is too important to think that others will defend it in our name." Although Mexico had broken off most relations with the Axis, the nation still had not declared war. But Mexico was on the brink.

May 1942 was a critical month in Mexican foreign relations. Under stepped-up demands, a continuous procession of American and Mexican tankers carried petroleum to the United States, where industrial mobilization was getting up a head of steam. As early as March 1942 German submarines had been stopping these "neutral" Mexican vessels and warning them that serious consequences would ensue if oil shipments continued. In face of these threats, Mexico furnished petroleum to the United States.

Finally, on May 14, 1942, a German submarine torpedoed and sank off the Florida coast a Mexican tanker, the *Potrero de Llano*. Five Mexicans were killed. The public shock in Mexico was great. Scarcely had the news filtered to the far reaches of the Republic when on May 22 another Mexican tanker, the *Faja de Oro*, was similarly attacked and seven Mexicans died.

The vocal reaction to these outrages was great but opinion was mixed as to whether Mexico should enter the war as a belligerent. To assess the feelings in the Mexican capital, the newsweek *Tiempo* (no relation of Luce's *Time*) sponsored a poll, the first of a series. It started inquiring "Should Mexico enter the War?" on May 20, 1942, shortly after the news reached Mexico City that the Mexican tanker had been sunk. When asked, only 40.7 per cent of these urban Mexicans said "yes"; 59.3 per cent said "no." But the breakdown by social and political groups is revealing:

Group	Replies	Yes	No
"Man in the Street"	4,152	21.6%	78.4%
Leftist Organizations	2,144	92.2	7.8
Organized Labor	2,686	31.4	68.6
Government-employed workers	630	67.9	32.1
Bureaucrats	982	36.8	63.2

Mass meetings of protest, spearheaded by Leftist organizations and leaders of militant labor, demanded immediate declarations of war. However, the Mexican government at first contented itself by sending energetic notes of protest to Germany. These brought no tangible results.

On May 25 Camacho convened his Cabinet and called Congress into extraordinary session. State governors and zone commanders were also called to Mexico City. Mass meetings and inflammatory speeches against the German outrages occupied more and more public attention. When Congress met on May 28 they heard Camacho's request for a declaration of war; they also considered his proposal for the suspension of the Constitutional Bill of Rights for the duration.

On May 30, 1942 Mexico declared war on the Axis. The declaration was made retroactive to May 14. To insure internal security, Congress gave President Camacho plenary power to suspend personal guarantees, at his own discretion. This action made Camacho legal dictator of Mexico, with a grant of power unprecedented in modern Mexican annals.

Camacho's Secretary of Interior (*Gobernación*), Miguel Alemán Valdes, was responsible for maintaining internal tranquillity in the nation and stamping out subversive activities. The Congressional suspension of the Bill of Rights gave Alemán and the administration an opportunity to convert the government into an old-fashioned military dictatorship. The team of Avila Camacho and Alemán surprised the cynical by a minimum of politicking. To Alemán was also entrusted the important task of popularizing slogans of "national unity" and putting them into practical effect.

Immediately after May 30, *Tiempo* terminated its first poll and started a second one, in which 17,745 persons were asked "Was the President's action patriotic?" This time the results were markedly different: 81.7 per cent said "Yes" and only 18.3 per cent replied "No." In the capital, at least, the president had the bulk of the people behind his defense of Mexican sovereignty, put in jeopardy by Mexico's aid to the United States.

It came as a shock for most of the Mexican people to find themselves fighting with rather than against the Colossus of the North. This surprise was somewhat tempered and made palatable for the Left, which had been so recently flaying "Yankee imperialism," by the shift in the Moscow line. The Far Left constituted itself a sort of Sixth Column to root out Fifth-Column activities. In most cases labor loyally supported the administration's call for greater production. An uneasy truce was called among the divided labor factions of Mexico and a general labor coalition was formed for the duration.

On June 14, 1942 Mexico signed the United Nations Pact in Washington. This placed Mexico on the side of the democracies, in a full moral, military, and economic sense. For the first time since the conflict with the United States in 1847, a responsible Mexican government had formally and officially declared war.

Mexico's principal role was to be a purveyor of prime strategic materials to the industrial machine of the United States. Conversely, the Mexican nation was to become as self-sufficient as possible to lessen the drain on the short supplies of consumer and heavy goods, more urgently needed elsewhere. To intensify the flow of materials abroad and to shore up and extend the national economy it was imperative to have full coöperation of all the economic elements of Mexican society. Their energy, previously expended in inter-group struggles, was to be channeled into the general effort. In the period of increasing shortages and economic mobilization, the government would step in wherever and whenever necessary.

The administration created a Supreme Defense Council to mobilize Mexico for war. All economic and social interests, from agrarians to industrialists, from labor through the middle class, were represented. These representatives helped formulate mobilization and defense plans. In addition, the normally large Mexican bureaucracy bloomed in the hothouse of war; Mexican equivalents of the dollar-a-year men, as well as labor leaders, found they could coöperate on concrete proposals saturated with patriotism.

Shortages brought rationing and a string of bureaucracies in tow. Civil defense sponsored innumerable national and local organizations to plan and carry out blackouts and other wartime exercises presumably dedicated to self-preservation. As in the United States, much of this hectic defense activity was meaningless, undirected, and downright ridiculous. The main consideration, however, was that a vast majority of the Mexican people stoically accepted their new responsibilities.

Conciliation and Mobilization. An outward symbol of the national unity, which was the hub of Avila Camacho's integrated approach, came at an impressive ceremony held on Mexican Independence Day, September 16, 1942. Traditionally at that time the president waves a Mexican flag from the balcony of the National Palace and repeats the "Grito de Dolores." This ritual is followed by patriotic addresses. In 1942 this ceremony was dedicated to National Conciliation—*Acercamiento Nacional.*

At twelve noon, when the ceremonies began, six ex-presidents of Mexico came out and linked arms with President Camacho to signify that all the old political rancors were healed.* The political tendencies associated with Plutarco Elias Calles on the right hand and with Lázaro Cárdenas on the left were thus symbolically joined to the Camacho administration. Throughout the war these ex-presidents were given important posts in the defense effort. They helped to carry out the ideas of national unity and coöperation stressed in the speeches that day. Mexico was closer to being a single nation than perhaps at any time in its previous troubled history.

3. WAR EFFORTS

Few North Americans realize the total contribution which Mexico made during World War II. Its role was usually undramatic and unpublicized, but on important economic, military, and political fronts Mexico's coöperation was superb and its contributions were substantial. In addition to the Mexicans who contributed to the organized and official efforts, a number—like José Rafael Bejarano, an atomic physicist who worked on The Bomb—pooled their special individual skills in the common cause. Mexico's actions and policies plainly showed to the world that it was fully committed to the side of the wartime United Nations.

This was unmistakably signalized by the meeting of Presidents Roosevelt and Camacho in April 1943. In the midst of other overwhelming responsibilities of war, Roosevelt felt it necessary and proper to discuss personally with the Mexican leader their common problems. More than that, both wanted to dramatize the new importance of the mutually beneficial Good Neighbor Policy.

Avila Camacho and F. D. R. When a preliminary security check indicated that Mexico City was not propitious, arrangements were made for the two Chief Executives to meet in Monterrey. After making an inspection tour of war plants in the southern United States,

---

* From exile in the United States or from retirement came Adolfo de la Huerta, Plutarco Elias Calles, Emilio Portes Gil, Pascual Ortiz Rubio, Abelardo Rodríguez, and Lázaro Cárdenas. Calles has died since, but the others are active in nonpolitical lines.

Roosevelt secretly arrived on April 20. This was the first time in history that a president of the United States had officially entered the Republic of Mexico and only the second time that the chiefs of the two neighboring states had met face to face; a number of things had changed since that first interview, when Díaz talked to Taft at the Border.

Although the ceremonial addresses of the two men in Monterrey followed somewhat conventional lines, the fact that they were made at all stood as a landmark in Mexican-American relations. Roosevelt won Mexican hearts when he stated in Monterrey that "we know that the epoch of exploitation of resources and people by one country for the benefit of one group in another now has definitely passed." The presidents chatted together for an hour before Avila Camacho boarded President Roosevelt's train and accompanied him back to Corpus Christi, Texas. The conversations en route were filled with references to Mexican sovereignty, nonintervention, the Good Neighbor Policy, and self-determination. The dramatic meeting of the two presidents strengthened Camacho's hand in domestic politics and served as a base for augmented interchange of goods and men between the neighboring countries.

Economic Coöperation. On a more concrete plane the discussions by the two men and their staffs centered about ways and means to coöperate more effectively in the common war effort. The groundwork for these had already been ably laid by Ezequiel Padilla and Undersecretary of State Sumner Welles. In those days when "coordination" was a magic word, a Mexican–North American Commission on Economic Coöperation was set up to study and coordinate various aspects and problems requiring the mutual interplay of the two nations. This Commission, made up of two Mexicans and two Americans, studied and reviewed statistics, requested opinions from technicians and industrialists, and after an arduous and thorough analysis made recommendations which outlined the major policies which would be followed for the duration.

Aided by the United States, Mexico was to maintain and intensify its production of necessary prime materials for the fabrication of munitions and other elements of war by the North Americans. To facilitate this production the United States promised to deliver certain pieces of scarce but vital machinery and equipment lacking in Mexico. It was also planned that Mexico should try to maintain and increase the local production of food for its own people; the United

States would send technicians to aid in this effort. Part of the program was based on increasing the industrialization of Mexico to provide needed consumer goods for the Mexican people which the United States could not now furnish. The priorities of prime materials were necessarily set higher on war goods than on consumer goods. On the heels of these agreements, American technicians and experts of varying degrees of competence swarmed into Mexico and began, with the enthusiastic coöperation of their Mexican counterparts, to tinker with all sorts of Mexican social and economic mechanisms.

The Railway Mission. One of the most important of these missions set out to rehabilitate the Mexican railways. In addition to the difficulties inherent in antiquated equipment, insufficient rolling stock, entrenched corruption, and other legacies of the Revolution, the American technical mission found itself in the center of an inter-union struggle for power that knew no quarter or surcease. In February 1944 matters had become so involved that the United States–Mexican railroad commission gave up its work with the statement that, due to the indiscipline of workers, the repeated accidents which destroyed construction faster than it could be created, and the venality of labor leaders, little could be done. Both the Mexican manager of the National Railways, Margarito Ramírez, and the head of the American technical mission, J. Oliver Stevens, resigned in February. After his return to the United States, Mr. Stevens published an article, "How Not to Run a Railway."

Starting in March 1944 a series of drastic reform decrees issued by President Camacho gave the manager of the National Railways extraordinary powers to try to straighten out these matters. By June a sort of armed truce between workers and management was arrived at.

After some of these initial frictions had been reduced, a new Mexican-American team did manage to make important dents in the crucial railroad problem of Mexico, but by no means did they clear it up completely. It persisted as a central theme into the postwar period. However, it was on the foundation laid by this wartime Mexican-American Mission that Alemán's administration, aided by loans from the United States, has been able to restore and extend the rail net of Mexico.

Raw Materials for War. The principal job assigned to Mexico during World War II was to maintain and increase a steady flow of raw materials which the industrial machine of the United States transformed into fighting equipment and other direct aids to successful war. The main items which Mexico provided were minerals, especially highly necessary but prosaic commodities like lead, mercury, and rarer earths needed for special purposes. In 1937 Mexico had produced only about 170 tons of mercury but under the stimulation from the United States Metals Reserve Corporation and allied war agencies its production shot up to 1117 tons in 1942. Since it was not directly a "war metal," gold production in Mexico dropped off during the emergency. It was purposely lowered in priority behind zinc, copper, and especially graphite. Antimony for munitions and arsenic for insecticides were produced and shipped in quantities.

In addition, Mexico contributed to the partnership in other ways. It helped feed and clothe other united nations at a real sacrifice to the Mexican population. Local fibers, as well as the more familiar cotton, coffee, beef, wood, and fish, were poured into the common hopper at a time when nascent Mexican industry and an underfed Mexican people were clamoring for them. One of the Mexican steel mills—Altos Hornos—even took military orders from the United States and fabricated Liberty Ship plates for the U. S. Maritime Commission. These brief statements fail to highlight sufficiently how greatly the countless man-hours of toil by anonymous Mexicans in mines, foundries, fields, and plantations contributed to winning the war. In aggregate their efforts were substantial and critically significant.

Mexico is still a supplier of strategic goods. In 1950 the United States Department of Commerce listed a number of important and essential items which were being supplied from outside the United States for mobilization in the face of the Far Eastern emergency. About a third of the United States needs in antimony and graphite were being met by Mexican producers; 83.4 per cent of the cadmium and nearly 20 per cent of the fibers—henequen and sisal—also came from Mexico. These were all tagged "essential." Semi-necessities included Mexican bananas (11.4 per cent of the United States needs); among the products listed as "needed to supplement United States production" come copper, lead, and zinc. During and since World War II the flow of these and similar critical commodities, including petroleum, has bound the two nations together.

Labor for War. A unique contribution that Mexico made to the economic front was a supply of labor. Mexico offered hands as well as commodities. Through the whole twentieth century there has been a fluctuating amount of Mexican migrant labor in the United States, but an organized effort to fill the manpower needs of the United States by temporary Mexican war workers—*braceros*—appeared early in the war.

As the United States' manpower pool was siphoned off into the armed forces and the booming war industries, Mexican volunteers were brought in to replenish it. It soon became apparent that the peacetime methods of recruiting Mexican labor for the important tasks of harvesting crops and keeping the trains rolling were inapplicable. The two governments thereupon negotiated a series of agreements, the first of which was formally signed on August 4, 1942. Mexican nationals already in the United States, and an unknown number of "wet-backs" who furtively and illegally were conducted across the Border, swelled the total of 200,000 Mexicans openly contracted for during the life of the agreements.

Though alike in many respects, there were actually two distinct and separate official *bracero* programs. One furnished labor for agricultural purposes, the other for nonagricultural. Under both, agreements were signed and complex administrative machinery was set up to handle the recruitment, transportation, grievances, conditions of employment, and repatriation through joint coöperation of Mexican and United States official agencies. Due to inexperience and urgency many abuses and errors were committed at the beginning of the programs but these were gradually minimized. At any one time there were seldom more than 75,000 *braceros* (representing a shade over 2 per cent of the total agricultural force) at work in the United States during the war. Their services were more valuable than their numbers would indicate. The *braceros* formed a sort of tactical and strategic reserve which was shifted from harvest to harvest when labor shortages would have been disastrous to perishable commodities. They worked as far north as Wisconsin, and in general were found to be quite able and competent. The nonagricultural *braceros* were largely concentrated on railway maintenance and operations in the southwestern United States.

Reciprocal Inductions. Somewhat allied with the *bracero* program was another relatively unpublicized Mexican contribution to the actual military effort. In the United States there has been, for at least fifty years, a population of Mexican nationals ("aliens"). Some have permanent residence, others form a floating group which follows the seasonal crops. After the United States entered the war, negotiations with Mexico provided that, on a reciprocal basis, nationals could be inducted into the service of the country in which they were found. The American colony in Mexico was suddenly shocked to find that they were subject to the Mexican draft.

But in exchange, more than a quarter of a million Mexicans resident in the United States entered its armed forces. Of these about 14,000 actually saw combat service. The Mexicans were apparently indistinguishable from the great mass of other American men. Of those who saw active combat duty, about 10 per cent were decorated with Purple Hearts; the number of fatalities reached about 1000. A number of Mexicans distinguished themselves; a few, like Sergeant José Mendoza López (a youth whose parents had come from Oaxaca), merited high award. López received the Congressional Medal, the highest military honor that the United States can bestow.

The Mexican Front. With the Axis winning victories, Mexico took national defense seriously. Lázaro Cárdenas lent his prestige and abilities to the Avila Camacho administration as Secretary of Defense, a high command post created January 23, 1944. A draft law provided a year of compulsory military training; it increased the pool of trained reserves in Mexico to nearly a quarter of a million men. At the same time, the regular military establishment took the first steps toward a long-needed shaking-up.

At the beginning of the war the Mexican Army consisted of 52,000 men, 10,000 of whom were staff and administrative personnel, while the remaining 42,000 were inadequately equipped troops. The Army's function had been the traditional one in Latin-American countries— internal police work—with little real thought given to repelling armed aggressors from outside. Camacho dropped the military section from the official party and disbanded the military bloc in Congress in an attempt to divorce the military from politics—never a realized ideal —soon after he was inaugurated. He had already taken some steps towards professionalizing and regrouping the armed forces even before the war speeded up the necessity for such actions.

Earlier steps taken by President Camacho to reorganize and regroup the Mexican Army were hurried by actual hostilities. The host of political generals were put on a "retired" list when they were unable to fit into the new concepts of technical warfare by mechanized guerrilla units. With shortages always present, the president decided to establish local military industries to assemble airplanes, manufacture small arms, smokeless powder, and ammunition. These factories still operate.

Hemispheric and Continental Defense. In the early months of the war ultimate victory by the democracies was an aspiration but by no means a certain fact. The possibility of actual fighting on American soil was always present. To protect the important bastions of the area north of the Canal Zone, detailed plans of defense were formulated jointly by Mexican military men and those of the United States. Both groups coöperated in the more generalized military planning for defense of the hemisphere, but the special problem presented by Mexican proximity to the United States was recognized in a Mexican–North American Joint Defense Committee. It was set up in February 1942 to coördinate and standardize the actions of the two countries.

A Plan of Integral Defense, which involved linking the activities of the Fourth United States Army and the Mexican Pacific Command, was part of this program. It also provided that Mexicans were to be given advanced training in North American military schools and establishments and that American military personnel were to be indoctrinated in the peculiarities of Mexican military problems. This was in marked contrast to World War I, when two or three divisions were pinned down by the need to patrol the hostile Mexican-American border.

The joint United States–Mexican Commission also handled the military side of Lend-Lease to Mexico. It too formed part of the total effort. An initial credit of $40,000,000 was set up for Mexican use to modernize its military matériel and methods. Under the terms of Lend-Lease, Mexico was given the privilege of subsequently buying at 67 per cent discount any articles it wished to retain. Due to higher priorities elsewhere and the changing pattern of the war, the Mexican Army actually received about $18,000,000 worth of equipment during the war. It decided to keep it all—tanks, radar, planes, and a variegated array of modern devices. By 1949 it had paid off the $6,000,000 price set on this equipment. It is currently dickering to acquire 100 additional planes, to strengthen its air force, a war baby of which Mexico is especially proud.

The Mexican Expeditionary Air Force. One of the most important developments as a result of the war was the creation of a separate, small, but modern Mexican air force. By July 1944 enough ground and flying personnel had been trained to warrant its division into three squadrons, one of which—Squadron 201—carried the Mexican flag into the combat zones of the Pacific. Squadron 201 was made up of 300 volunteers from the Mexican Air Force, the National School of Aviation Mechanics, and technical personnel approved by the Director of Military Industries.

Under authorization of the Mexican–North American Commission of Joint Defense the autonomous unit—Expeditionary Squadron 201 —was formed in July 1944 for dispatch abroad. First its men were sent to the United States for training. After the final stages of flight instruction were completed at Randolph Field the flight personnel received their wings and the unit was given an American and also a Mexican flag on February 23, 1945. Thence Squadron 201 was ordered (in March) to a base near the Philippines, where under the instruction of the Fifth Air Corps its members learned actual battle tactics and took P–47 Thunderbolts on routine flights. In June 1945 Squadron 201 entered action by strafing and bombing Japanese installations on the Philippines. From that time until V–J Day the unit took part in offensive operations against the Philippines and later Formosa. Eight of the group lost their lives.

After the Japanese surrender, General Douglas MacArthur commended the unit highly and pinned United States decorations on two of its members. Special decorations for all the men of Squadron 201 were created in Mexico as part of their hero's welcome when they returned to their native land in November 1945.

Alone among the Spanish-speaking states of Latin America, Mexico actually dispatched fighting forces to aid the United Nations. Brazil was the only other Latin-American country to contribute armed forces to combat zones.

4. THE DIPLOMATIC FRONT AND CHAPULTEPEC, 1945

One obvious consequence of the second World War was to increase Mexico's international prestige. It has carried over into the present. Within the inter-American community its traditional rivals for moral and actual leadership had been Argentina, Brazil, and Chile. Throughout the war, Argentina was the problem child of the inter-American system, an obdurate neutral in the throes of a domestic revolution comparable in part to Mexico's epic struggle, 1910–1917. For a considerable period, Chile, too, was an equivocal and unknown quantity whose foot-dragging in the hemispheric defense program required long and prolix explanations. Brazil responded magnificently in a material way, but its local dictatorship under Getulio Vargas was a constant source of embarrassment. On the international balance sheet Mexico amassed credits by its international coöperation that far outweighed its debits. Both the apogee of Mexican wartime coöperation with the United States and the emergence of a new group of problems which might lead to later coolness came at the Inter-American Conference on Problems of War and Peace, held in Mexico from February 21 to March 8, 1945. Because its sessions were held in Chapultepec Castle its cumbersome title is often shortened to the "Chapultepec Conference." The choice of place was a tribute to Mexico's international hegemony in this Inter-American system during the war.

As can be inferred from its name, the Conference of Ministers was held to discuss the intensification of coöperation among the American states in the final drives of the war effort, as well as international coöperation for peace and security during and after the war. As part of their program the Foreign Ministers and their staffs were to exchange ideas and possible solutions to the pressing economic and social problems, common to the Americas, which the war had either revealed or created.

As early as 1942, with the Dumbarton Oaks meetings and then the Moscow Declaration of November 1, 1943, there had been increasing talk of a postwar international organization. Widespread hopes had been voiced that wartime coöperation would ripen in the postwar period. In the Moscow Declaration—made by the United States, Great Britain, the Soviet Union, and China—a general organization, based on the principle of sovereign equality of all peace-loving states, and open to membership of all such states, large and small, had been promised. The Americans had, in deference to Latin-American pressure and feelings, insisted on the "sovereign equality" of such members—it was unEuropean.

The final shape of such a comprehensive international organization was understandably vague during the war. But as the war drew to a close, discordant discussions of its structure, functions, and nature were repeatedly apparent in the press. It was clear after Yalta that some such organization would be formed. The Chapultepec Conference was a preliminary step, designed to get the inter-American system tightened up, preparatory to the formation of the United Nations organization at San Francisco. The American nations wanted their own house in order before taking on the construction of a global edifice.

The United States delegation from the State Department to the Chapultepec Conference was a new team—badly split and relatively unfamiliar with Latin America. Yet it was to "coördinate" the Inter-American system with the proposed "World System" of United Nations. In the delegation ran strong feelings between the "regionalists" who wished to preserve the main outlines and responsibilities of the traditional inter-American system founded in 1889 and the "globalists" who hoped or expected that it would become a mere administrative appendage of a more embracing system. It was the old Centralist-Federalist dilemma in a new guise and on a global scale. Latin-Americans solidly opposed disbanding the Inter-American System in favor of an untried world one, though they were willing, even eager, to join the latter if it was properly designed.

The outstanding political problem in the inter-American system was the studied exclusion of the Argentine from it by the United States. One of the purposes of the Chapultepec Conference was to welcome Argentina back into the lodge. Its return had been earlier and secretly arranged, partly through Ezequiel Padilla's efforts. As Foreign Minister of the host nation, Padilla was chairman of the Chapultepec Conference. He played a conspicuous part in keeping it running. The United States' large and unwieldy delegation, riven by internal splits, and filled with inexperienced policy-makers, made Chairman Padilla's task a doubly difficult one. His manifestly close ties with the United States groups and their reliance on him to voice their projects in public aroused the suspicion in domestic Mexican political circles that he was "truckling," although his efforts along this line were needed to preserve the superficial appearance of harmony and unity.

The Conference had an auspicious beginning. Great applause greeted Padilla's stirring message of welcome. He called for economic and social advance throughout the Americas, based on a postwar "cycle of abundance." In it Padilla said that the enthusiasms and co-operation generated for war should be transferred to objectives of peace. However, the attitude of zealous friendship for the United States, displayed by most of the Latin-American delegations, was soon somewhat cooled when Assistant Secretary of State William L. Clayton outlined for the Conference the national economic policy which the United States was going to follow in the postwar period.

After affirming vaguely that the United States would aid the Latin-American nations in the difficult transition from war to peace, he urged them to lower their tariff barriers and do away with economic nationalism. Clayton stressed the rosy future of Latin America as an agricultural area and one which would support extractive industries. With some reason, a Latin-American commentator sardonically exclaimed that Clayton had plagiarized and repeated a good speech made by Theodore Roosevelt before 1910.

To the Latin-Americans, Clayton's announcements meant that their new and developing industrial systems were asked to compete with the older, much larger, and markedly more efficient enterprises in the United States. They were also asked to remain "semi-colonial." Clayton won few friends for his country by contrasting "your" with "our" ways of life and economic organization. It was the difficulty over these economic matters that had helped split the United States delegation.

They also arose more generally to plague the whole Conference when it tried to write an "Economic Charter of the Americas." This was to be a rounded plan of postwar economic coöperation. The net result was ambiguity rather than real compromise. The discussion of important social and economic issues which were already beginning to override the political ones was thus dodged and deferred until hostilities in Europe and Asia had actually terminated. One thing on which nearly everyone agreed was that Ezequiel Padilla had increased his personal stature and the international prestige of Mexico by his able direction of this potentially refractory Conference. To the world at large, the Inter-American system had preserved its unity—even Argentina was back. Though it did not settle numerous vital matters, the Chapultepec Conference did help clear the way for the creation of the United Nations.

Mexico's national and international situation during World War I contrasted sharply with World War II. During the earlier struggle, the Revolution in Mexico had been flaming; society was being churned up; there was scarcely a Mexican nation at all, and its various elements had little or no interest in what was going on abroad. Mexico had been a diplomatic sore point and an actual security threat to the Allies.

In contrast, the Mexican war record from 1940 was one of which the nation could be justly proud. Mexico was a friendly and valuable supporter on the economic, political, moral, and military fronts;

as a full-fledged partner it took a leading part among the Latin-American states in the common hemispheric and world efforts. At the same time it was moving down the middle of the road toward democratic ideals voiced in its Revolutionary credo and the Four Freedoms.

14. Revolution and World War II

The second World War and the twilight peace thereafter added a new, complicated chapter to the Revolution. For thirty years the ideals of political and economic nationalism had been developing; the war years saw many of them come to maturity and undergo the tempering of voluntary internationalism. For much of the globe, World War II initiated revolution; in Mexico it confirmed one.

In marked contrast to the devastated areas of Europe and the Far East, Mexico emerged from the second World War stronger in most ways than it had entered. Spiritually, physically, and internationally, the Mexican nation benefited during the war years under the guidance of President Manuel Avila Camacho.

His emphasis on unity and common effort bore fruit. Words became deeds, as programs to meet the new demands of war and the old claims of the Revolution were put into effect. Mexicans' cooperative efforts were necessary in setting up universal military training and civil defense, in combating illiteracy, in improving health conditions, and in the planning and execution of Mexico's war effort. Some of the results of these programs were that death rates were cut, and the populations increased; resultant movements of people formed part of the nationalizing influences at work. All these developments encouraged the individual, local, and regional consciousness of belonging to the national unit. Almost visibly Mexico became a united nation.

In material matters Mexico fared well. The nation's productive forces were consciously concentrated, improved, and enlarged to permit a maximum contribution to the common cause of the free world. Never a theater of war, Mexico did not face the postwar era with its basic elements scattered, crushed, and drained, as did so many areas. As a whole, Mexico's productive plant was substantially increased by new additions to the working force, by new skills, knowledge, and capital equipment. To these were added a sizable influx of dollars that accompanied the coöperative exchange with the United States during World War II. Though the short-run impacts of the conflict troubled the Mexican domestic scene, their long-term implications were favorable, spiritually and materially.

While Mexico was engaged in the important tasks of contributing its share to the united war effort, domestic matters were far from static. Whatever Mexico is doing abroad is always of less concern to its own people than the current status of their Revolution. Almost by definition the government and Revolution must constantly provide them with something more and better than they have just had. Under President Avila Camacho the Revolution reached out to embrace middle-class and many neglected moderate sectors of the population, while it made direct contributions to improve social and political spheres. The Four Freedoms, to which the Mexican nation was presumably making wartime sacrifices, quite easily merged with the historic ideals of the Mexican Revolution.

Yet the enormous pressures generated by war precluded completely normal domestic developments in all lines. Economy and society felt their force and in some instances were reshaped. For Mexico, World War II was a period of chronic shortages of everything but politics and money. The nation's main connection with the outside world and the war was an economic nexus; it was, therefore, in the economic realm that wartime changes were first and most clearly visible.

1. THE ECONOMIC IMPACTS

In the long view, some of the permanent alterations in Mexico resulting from World War II were economic. One of the controlling features of the period from 1940 through 1946 was that foreign trade, in the accepted sense of the term, completely ceased. Mexico shipped goods and performed services, but in return received only money —useful, but not edible. The accompanying table summarizes some of the chief developments and their influences.

It indicates that more Mexicans than ever before were gainfully employed, that they doubled the value of their output, but had no way to spend their money, so that most workers did not get benefits proportionate to their increases in salaries. It also shows that without goods to purchase, there was a scramble for the available ones which

THE IMPACT OF WAR ON THE MEXICAN ECONOMY, 1939–1946

	Gainfully Employed (millions)	National Net Product (000's) Pesos	Cost of Living Index 1929 = 100	Average Minimum Salary (daily: pesos)
1939	5.7	6,139	155	2.12
1940	5.8	6,802	156	
1941	6.0	7,686	162	
1942	6.1	8,928	188	
1943	6.3	10,169	247	
1944	6.4	11,090	310	
1945	6.6	11,978	332	
1946	6.8	12,970	440	2.98
Per cent increase	+11.3	+200	+283	+14

Source: *Tiempo*, No. 271 (July 11, 1947), p. 34, based on official statistics.

pushed prices sky-high. Many of the new riches were trapped by a rising class of Mexican entrepreneurs, black-marketeers, and shareholders in mining corporations controlled from the United States. Inflation always tends to redistribute wealth unfairly.

The inflation implied by the above figures, coupled with almost unprecedented opportunities to acquire great and sudden riches, had social consequences. They might be called the "unsocial revolution," perhaps an inevitable concomitant of war. Bribery, graft, and scandal reached new heights and new depths. A wave of official corruption set in which has just begun to recede perceptibly. Government officials could scarcely live on their tiny fixed salaries in an inflationary period. These old practices diffused outward from official spheres to the very lowest and meanest levels, such as demanding a *mordida* (bribe) for a place in line to register a child in school. They also penetrated the official circle, even to the president's brother, a cabinet minister.

So widespread had become the "fever of riches and easy profits" that President Camacho called special attention to this matter in his message to Congress in September 1943. The fact that the rich were growing richer and displaying ostentatious luxury in the midst of a growing want in Mexico was leading to social unrest. He stressed the fact that these *nouveau riche* apparently did not understand that Mexico was at war and their antics were inappropriate at a time when Mexico's allies were paying for Mexican liberty with their blood. But moral homilies did not stop the undesirable activities.

More important in the long run than the ephemeral slackening of the Mexican moral fiber was the constructive uses to which both government and private funds were put. The Camacho administration used part of its hoard to pay off old obligations and to cushion the effect of shortages by subsidizing food imports (when it could get them) and by stimulating a Mexican industrial revolution through a national development corporation, *Nacional Financiera;* private investors, too, found the industrial field rewarding.

As might well be expected, the impacts of war changed the urbanized and "modern" parts of Mexico far more than the rural. Since before the arrival of the Spaniards and for all history thereafter, rural Mexico had become inured to the direct and indirect consequences of war and recurrent devastation; World War II's inflation, shortages, disappearance of populations, and choked transportation were nothing new. That was the "normal" condition, dating far back. With its primitive technology and almost self-subsistent base, integrated around small local markets, rural Mexico was only moderately affected by the shocks that nearly shattered the more highly-organized parts of Mexican society.

Fiscal Adjustments. Avila Camacho's administration decided it could best use its accumulating wealth to clear up foreign obligations. This device of shipping money abroad had the advantage of freeing the country from the inflationary pressures that would result if it were spent at home.

When Camacho took over the presidency from Cárdenas, the till was almost empty. Depression and the economic consequences of the oil expropriations had reduced Mexican reserves to a low of $20 million. Because of the peculiar wartime Mexican trade patterns—goods out, money but no goods returning—those reserves had risen to $370 million by 1945. With cash in pocket, Mexico could talk business.

The foreign debtors who wanted to retrieve some of their old investments and earnings were numerous. One group were the private investors who had bought Mexican government bonds, issued long ago for official enterprises. To this debt of $2471 million Cárdenas had added another, that of the National Railways; it amounted to

$2704 million. Neither interest nor principal on either had been paid for so long that most holders considered them a lost cause.

After protracted and highly technical negotiations extending over many months, the fiscal officials in the Mexican government managed to get the huge sums scaled down. Investors were willing to write off a large part of the original moneys due them in exchange for smaller, but assured, regular payments. In 1942 the holders of Mexican government bonds agreed to accept guaranteed payment of about $240 million for the face value of $2471 million due them for back interest and principal; in 1946 the railroad bondholders approved a similar arrangement. These settlements, plus the final fiscal arrangements for the expropriated oil and various other Revolutionary damage and expropriation claims, reëstablished the external credit of Mexico. This was a necessary pre-condition of industrialization.

As accumulations of imported goods disappeared, Mexican enterprises—usually aided or initiated by Nacional Financiera—grew up to fill the nation's needs. A great range of businesses, including cement and chemical making, food processing, and light manufacturing, that Mexicans call "industries of transformation" (which transform raw materials into semi-finished or finished goods), were initiated. Their appearance heralded a veritable industrial revolution. In the decade from 1930 through 1940 more people had left industry than had entered it, but under wartime conditions and under the benevolent legislation of the Camacho regime, new enterprises appeared at every hand. This industrial boom gained new momentum after 1944 when precautionary but attractive arrangements were made for foreign investment to be mixed with Mexican capital. This reopened the whole expanding Mexican economy to investment from outside, but safeguarded Mexican national interests.

The first beneficiaries of the World War II programs of industrialization were the long-established industries such as textiles and steel; they expanded and extended to meet the pressing basic needs. As early as 1941, however, the Camacho administration promised tax exemptions and other stimulants to new industries which would benefit the national economy by producing consumer goods that were in short supply.

In the abnormal conditions of war, even the high-cost and inefficient Mexican producers could sell locally and abroad at almost their own prices. Mexican beer appeared in New York and Mexican textiles were shipped to Central America, but even the most optimistic did not expect that this condition would persist past the peace.

For both economic and political reasons the Camacho administration cooled the earlier unquestioning government support of labor and checked some of its increasingly voracious demands. The more debatable features of the nationalization law were withdrawn and expropriation of going concerns came to an end. In the emergency of war, and later, the pressing need for increased production, both industrial and agricultural, vied with social justice and the vision of a workers' state as major determinants of official policy.

Two striking examples of the change in direction of labor policies were the replacement of Vicente Lombardo Toledano as the leader of the powerful Mexican Workers Confederation (which he had helped to found) and the replacement of the workers' administration of the nationalized railways by a government-controlled bureaucracy, the National Railways Administration, under a single director appointed by the president. Cocky, powerful, and selfish, the newly revived labor movement in Mexico, backed so strongly by Cárdenas, was by no means crushed, but under the twin circumstances of Administration insistence on fostering industrial enterprises (which required guarantees that they would not be nationalized) and suspension of Russian-inspired agitation for the duration, much of its previous militancy was damped. Inflation brought rashes of strikes, but these were more clearly economic than political in motivation. The ultimate showdown between business and labor influences on national policies was purposely postponed during the war years.

Agriculture. Avila Camacho inherited the disrupted and seething agricultural situation created by the Cárdenas reforms. From it he was expected to feed Mexico, which was growing at the rate of a million new mouths every two years. Contrary to expectations, he did a good job under the most adverse of circumstances. As in the case of labor and its relation to the overriding demands of the war effort, the course pursued toward militant agrarianism was intimately linked with larger political and economic objectives. A war had to be won.

Four main lines of attack on the basic problem of subsistence made up the programs from 1940 through 1946. One was irrigation, to stabilize the yields from fertile lands already under cultivation but normally subject to drought and flood; a small amount of irrigation also created new patches of arable land in hitherto unexploitable semiarid territory. A second and allied approach was to start a "march to the sea." That meant making the fertile but insalubrious strips in the lowland tropical coast habitable and productive; it entailed linking them to the highland centers of distribution by extending rails and roads. A third line, quite signficant, was to modernize Mexican agrarian technology. A start was made by the establishment of experiment stations, the distribution of plows and tractors, the indoctrination in conservation methods, the use of selected seeds, and the training of agricultural technicians who in turn could educate the Mexican farmers. In this the United States aided directly and greatly. The benefits were lasting.

A fourth was a somewhat miscellaneous grouping. It included the expanded effort to increase agricultural production by fostering a rural climate of greater tranquillity among private holders of property—large and small—and breaking up vicious nests of political and economic parasites who were strangling agricultural production by their control of local sources of credit. Peace and money brought bumper crops, though these had to be supplemented by foreign purchases.

Faced with urgent economic and political problems centered on the land and its use, President Camacho thus emphasized lines that had begun to appear in the closing months of the Cárdenas regime and which were hardened into national and permanent policy under Camacho's successor, Miguel Alemán. The fundamental premise was that, rather than attempt to divide less and less land among more and more people, the main job of the government would be to create new agricultural resources through irrigation, to protect and improve those in existence through application of technology, and to derive maximum benefit for the country and the individual rural family by improvement of methods.

The land reforms undertaken by Cárdenas were not reversed, but they were not extended very far. When Camacho came into office in 1940 there still coexisted a number of unlike landholdings, ranging from a handful of *latifundistas* down to small individual holdings that scarcely supported a household; under the varying concepts of the *ejido* some holders of nationalized land were in possession of small tracts, while others were grouped in communally tilled village lands; the great coöperatives producing plantation or commercial crops, on which the *ejidatarios* were paid day-wages and then shared the profits, still operated. For all intents and purposes, President

Camacho froze this array, and gave up attempts to nationalize all Mexico's land and turn it over to peasants, as Cárdenas had envisaged. Militant agrarianism passed into a technical phase of making the Mexican land feed its people better, whether that land was in the form of *ejidos* or private holdings. Under Camacho the landless were not given much hope for the future except to emigrate to cities and become part of the new working force or to migrate to the United States as wartime *braceros*. A few could look forward to having new *ejidos* on good land created by irrigation or by sanitizing coastal areas. As is seen later, President Alemán kept the basic outlines of the Camacho programs but added an important feature to them by the creation of new agro-industrial provinces.

Cárdenas had succeeded in smashing the *latifundia* as an economic and social force in the rural countrysides. The coexistence of nationalized *ejidos* and permanent medium-sized to small private holdings formed the core of the new land policies. These were better adapted to the complexity of Mexican geography and regional rural psychologies than earlier doctrinaire schemes. There was to be no retrogression to *latifundia,* whose evils were notorious. When the "freeze" of further subdivision of Mexico's land went into effect under Avila Camacho, figures indicated that about 40 per cent of Mexico's rural population had fair to excellent lands to work, either as *ejidatarios* or as small private owners, with a sprinkling of large holders. But better than half had inadequate holdings, *minifundias* whose problems are as serious as those created by *latifundia;* many had no land at all. The accompanying tabulation gives the specific number of these various categories. (See page 291.)

Expediency, temperament, and the overwhelming pressures of World War II closed one period in the long history of Mexican land struggles. To get production of food and war materials, Camacho gave guarantees of "no nationalization" to the remaining private owners, large and small. This markedly reduced the effectiveness of the Sinarquista outcries against the Revolution and brought increased acreages and output. On *ejidos*, local option was established; peons decided whether they wished to have land held and tilled communally or whether it should be subdivided among heads of families so that each could utilize his patrimony as he wished. Credit facilities were stepped up and Camacho-created *ejidos* were larger and on better lands than heretofore. A study made in 1947 showed that the *ejidos* possessed nearly 60 per cent of the total cropland of the re-

LAND TENURE IN MEXICO, 1940

		Holders (Thousands)		Area (Millions of hectares)	
		Number	Per Cent	Number	Per Cent
Ejido Programs					
Eligible, no or inadequate land		400	10.5	...	...
Fairly adequate to good		1,223	32.3	28.9	22.2
Total		1,620	42.8	28.9	22.2
Private Holdings — Size (hectares)					
Landless, peons	0–0	1,000	26.3	...	...
Minifundistas	0–5	900	23.5	...	...
Small holder	5–100	235	6.2	6.0	4.6
Medium	100–5,000	53	1.3	29.1	22.3
Latifundista	over 5,000	3	0.0	66.1	50.9
Total		2,191	57.2	101.2	77.8
Totals		3,811	100.0	130.1	100.0

Summary, 1940

Agriculturalists with land (private or *ejido*)	1,500	40.0
Agriculturalists with inadequate or no land	2,300	60.0

public; the quality of *ejido* lands had been improved. By the end of his term over two million rural Mexicans were supported by *ejidos,* some 465,000 families; by 1950 this had risen to 570,000. When the shift came from land distribution to land and agricultural improvement, Mexico had gone further toward democratization of land than any major Latin-American country.

The net result of the Camacho rural policies was to tranquilize the important rural areas. They responded by covering all but 5 per cent of Mexico's food needs. This was despite the boom in population, urbanization, and emigration of farm labor. The situation which he left his successor was considerably different, and better, than the one inherited by President Camacho. (Appendix I, Table 6.)

2. THE STRUGGLE FOR MODERATION

As the vise of war slowly squeezed Mexico, some of the earlier and larger political issues disappeared; localized power struggles with a strong economic undertone displaced them. Before being discontinued in 1943 the succession of polls carried out by *Tiempo* magazine's Institute of Public Opinion indicated problems and the trends of attitudes on these new issues.

Date Started	Replies	Question	Yes %	No %
May 20, 1942	10,594	Should Mexico enter the war?	40.7	59.3
May 29, 1942	17,745	Was the declaration of war proper?	81.7	18.3
June 1942	7,621	Should the Compulsory Military Service Law (draft) be applied?	68.5	31.5
June 1942	6,884	Should relations with Russia be resumed? (Excluded were replies from known Communists and fellow travelers)	43.4	56.6
November 1942	8,038	Should "Free (Fighting) France" be recognized?	87.5	12.5
January 1943	11,606	Do you believe the activities of the National Union of Sinarquistas are unpatriotic?	79.8	20.2
April 1943	9,856	Should the government control in an effective manner the market and direct the price of food?	90.5	9.5

Even from this imperfect testimony it seems clear that in general Avila Camacho had much of the nation behind him but that the Mexican people were far from unanimous on some important matters. President Camacho was faced constantly with a touchy problem: he had promised that (within the limits of security) Mexican political freedoms would be maintained; this was essential to keep and strengthen the support given him and the war effort by moderate and even conservative Mexicans. But, at the same time, the Revolution had to continue to provide new benefits or he would lose all-important mass support, radical in outlook.

Serious and difficult political problems arose when Camacho permitted moderate, conservative, and even reactionary elements to have some voice in policy and openly to criticize men and measures. The opposition to the Revolution and to the P.R.M., which had been furtive and silent for nearly thirty years, soon broke out into the open and was organized into meaningful groups. As a hangover of the bitter political campaign for the presidency in 1940 the *Partido de Acción Nacional,* which had backed Almazán, attracted considerable overt conservative support. Made up largely of northern industrialists and merchants from various parts of the Republic, it also had important drawing power for a middle class being increasingly pressed by inflationary wartime conditions. More avowedly peasant-based and skirting nearer the subversive edge were the Sinarquistas.

Sinarquismo. Under the single rubric *Sinarquismo* have flourished a number of affiliated subversive and semi-subversive movements with Fascist leanings. Basically they have been much the same. *Sinarquismo*—Sinarchism—is the opposite of anarchism; the word means "with order." Sinarquistas are believers in "order."

The particular "order" involved is a variant of Catholic Socialism. In Mexico it borrowed totalitarian trappings and ideology to revitalize long-standing *Hispanidad* tendencies. *Sinarquismo* appealed especially to peasant groups in the marginal regions of Mexico by stressing the excesses of the Revolution and its failure to better their status; the anticlericalism of the Northern Oligarchy and its modified but virulent continuance under Cárdenas gave the Sinarquista organizers a ready-made force of old *Cristeros.* Though all *Sinarquistas* are rabidly Catholic, the Church consistently denied any official connection with the movement; during the war years there was always the suspicion that the Mexican Catholic hierarchy was using the peasant-based Sinarquista organizations for its own purposes. The organizations were willing and able to disrupt Mexico by fighting a constant counter-Revolution, reminiscent of Huerta's days.

Dating from obscure beginnings in 1937, Sinarquismo was a local subversive movement which the Axis proceeded to foster with care and funds. Fifth Column activities in Mexico were primarily based on strengthening and using the Sinarquistas. Axis agents worked through Franco's Spain and the Spanish Falange, one of the major models for the Mexican Sinarquista organization of peasant "soldiers" and neo-Fascist Mexican conservative leaders. At the outbreak of World War II, the Sinarquistas, claiming a membership of 1,000,000, ran affairs from the Sinarquista capital ("Sinarcópolis") at León, Guanajuato, putative birthplace of the movement. It was primarily against their organizations that the Espionage Law of September 1941 was directed.

The leadership of the movement was conservative, Mexican, and often extremist. Ultra-reactionary leaders stressed their hatred of

Communism, openly disparaged the Reforma and the Revolution, but lauded the glories of Mexico under the Hapsburgs, when Church and State were coördinate arms of Catholicism. The ideology emphasized martyrdom, self-sacrifice, and evolved an elaborate jargon, as well as a set of symbols and militant slogans.

World War II divided and subdivided the Sinarquista movement. One parthenogenesis arose from the fiasco which accompanied the founding of Sinarquista agrarian colonies in the strategically located area of the Peninsula of Southern California. Other splits came over power struggles within the group. A large wing of Sinarquistas preferred to enter Mexican politics directly as a party rather than work underground as saboteurs and Fifth Columnists; even this majority was divided on the question of whether to coöperate with the government's war efforts or to follow obstructionist tactics. The extreme wing and the wing of frustrated colonists remained an underground Fifth Column. Operating in marginal areas, they were not a major threat to internal order or a very effective arm of the Axis. Disturbing and irritating without being really dangerous, they were a standing protest to the Revolution's failures and its doctrinaire dogma. But Avila Camacho and the Revolution permitted them to carry on their intolerant activities, one of the prices democracy must pay to remain democratic.

Communism and the Militant Left. At the other extreme from the retrogressive views of the anti-Revolutionary Sinarquistas have been the spectrum of ideas and groups which would merge the Mexican and Russian Revolutions, whose aims, methods, and outlook have at times been very similar. In the current climate of opinion "Communist" has become a useful smear word, but at times in the Mexican past it has been almost synonymous with "Revolutionary," a "good" label. Though the Communist movement in Mexico has many analogies to Sinarquismo in its extremism, violence, tendency to bifurcate endlessly into smaller and smaller organizations, and its present impotence, the differences are notable and noteworthy.

Radicalisms, home-grown and imported, have long operated in Mexico in the name of the Mexican Revolution. With Russia and Mexico independently struggling for and against the same things for half a century, only careful and tedious unraveling of historic strands makes possible the unequivocal assertions of what is home-grown ideology and what is part of the general Russian conspiracy to subvert world and local order in Mexico. There is a broad, powerful and historically generated current of militant radicalism in Mexico that is non-Communist.

Under Cárdenas, radicals of various hues and obscure allegiances had directed official action. Their points of view had become government policy in a fashion denied less extremist credos, and more especially the seemingly unRevolutionary conservative Mexican outlook. Sinarquistas had only the power they would generate outside the official fold, but any attempt to rid the government of fellow-travelers seemed to be a surrender to their charges that the government was hopelessly Communist. Camacho's "middle-of-the-road" trajectory meant in practice his removal from responsible posts of many figures closely identified with the militant Left. Often they were known Communists, and always the dropping of such men and policies created a loud uproar at home and abroad.

During the war Leftists, both home-grown and controlled from abroad, were on the patriotic and winning side. When Russia aligned with Great Britain, Free France, and the United States against the Axis, international affairs affected domestic attitudes of radicals far more than in the case of the Sinarquistas. War seemed to call for a collaboration with the united nations second only to national unity and hemispheric solidarity. Communists, para-Communists, fellow-travelers, admirers of the Soviets, local Marxists, and other grades of the Left lent their efforts to winning the war and acted as a Sixth Column to expose and castigate the local Fifth Column of Sinarquistas. Their efforts affected both international and Mexican developments.

As part of the wartime drive toward unity among nations opposing the Axis, they early and increasingly urged Mexico to resume relations with Soviet Russia. The country was about evenly divided as to the wisdom of such a course, as many Mexicans of moderate and conservative views believed that nation to be a cradle of evil.

Russia and Mexico. Russian influences, direct and indirect, were strong in Mexico in the period just after World War I and the Communist Revolution in Russia. Mexico had been the first country in the Western Hemisphere to recognize the Soviet Union (1924), partly as a sop to the Left Wing supporters of Obregón. But as the Northern Oligarchy's political control was consolidated and its social philosophy began to change, this official warmth cooled and diplomatic relations were broken off in 1927. They were not renewed until the domestic pressure on Avila Camacho, coupled with urgings from Washington, led to resumption of ties during the war.

Despite official Mexican aloofness, admiration for the Soviet Union and its publicized solutions of problems similar to Mexican ones burned brightly in the hearts of many Mexican Left Wingers. The Mexican Communist Party as such, founded in 1923, was and continues to be a negligible organization. Its major proclivity is for violent and often incomprehensible disputes over the finer points of Marxian doctrine and tactics; consequent secessions of die-hards have split it again and again. The presence of Leon Trotsky in Mexico after 1937 and then his spectacular demise in 1940 reactivated many of these long-standing inter-Marxian feuds between Stalinists and non-Stalinists.*

Overtly or covertly many of the Left in Mexico were Party members or such strong sympathizers that their actual membership in an organized cell was a hairsplitting matter. As was usual in Latin America and elsewhere, Stalinist influence was strong in organized labor, and especially in groups of miners, electricians, petroleum workers, and railway employees. When the U.S.S.R.–Nazi Germany Pact was broken in 1941 the local faithful did the necessary about-face, and in addition to muting their cries against "Yankee Imperialism," they began to demand the resumption of diplomatic relations between Mexico and the U.S.S.R.

Resumption of Mexican-Russian Relations, 1942. In this they were but echoing a line being increasingly put out by Radio Moscow. At the time it was not wholly clear why Russia was so eager to gain a diplomatic foothold in Latin America, where its trade stakes were small and where military potential remains so meager. There was little or no historical precedent for renewed and enlarged contacts. It now seems clear that this urgency was part of a general plan to cut down the influence and power of the United States in any international organization which might emanate from the second World War and a careful cultivating of possible allies at the back door of a potential future enemy.

In any event, both the domestic mouthpieces of Soviet foreign policy in Mexico and representatives in Washington and elsewhere increased the pressure for renewal of relations. Under a deal spon-

---

* For an exciting account, see Leandro A. Sanchez Salazar, *Murder in Mexico: The Assassination of Leon Trotsky* (London, 1950). General Sanchez Salazar was then head of the Secret Service of the Mexican Police, assigned to guard Trotsky and then to apprehend his assailants and murderer.

sored by Franklin D. Roosevelt, the Mexican Minister in Washington worked out details with Maxim Litvinov for this move. On November 19, 1942 diplomatic relations between Russia and Mexico were formally reëstablished. A Mexican Minister was sent to Moscow in December 1942. Later the Ministry was raised to an Embassy.

Russia and Latin America. The importance attached by Russia to Latin-American relations in general and Mexican ones in particular was unmistakably emphasized by sending Constantin Oumanski as its first Ambassador to Mexico. Born in 1902, he had studied in Moscow and had early become an official of the Russian news agency, Tass; from there he was transferred to diplomacy in 1931. In 1938 he had come to the Russian Embassy in Washington and in the following year was named Ambassador; he had returned to Russia to assume the high post of subsecretary of Foreign Relations, from which he was suddenly switched to the Mexican Embassy. He was on the first team, and many believed him to be a more powerful figure than the Russian Ambassador in Washington.

Arriving in June 1943, Oumanski lost no time in building up a suspiciously large Embassy staff and appearing in public on all occasions to impress the views and the importance of the Soviet Union upon the Mexicans. Inevitably the creation of this small piece of Soviet territory in the middle of Mexico City, headed by an active, dynamic, and able proponent of the Communist view, had a stimulating effect on local Marxists and became the target of attack from the moderate and Right Wing sectors of Mexican political society. Vicente Lombardo Toledano seemed "Oumanski's errand boy."

Wild charges of Soviet intrigues began to fill the air and press. Many were true, if testimony by the Chief of Secret Police is to be credited. The only other Soviet Embassy of consequence in Latin America was in Cuba, although other smaller ones were established in Central and South America. Chiefly through Oumanski's efforts, seven Hispanic-American countries entered diplomatic relations and signed commercial pacts with the Soviet Union.

The entrance of Russia in the midst of Mexico increased Avila Camacho's political difficulties as the discordant tendencies of the Left and Right polarized. Old radical Cardenistas, Communists, fellow-travelers, and revolutionaries in the anticlerical traditions of Mexico stepped up their offensive against the Sinarquistas and included with them many middle-of-the-road and conservative members of the Camacho administration.

More or less symbolic of the conservative view, which deplored all that Oumanski and Lombardo Toledano stood for, was the president's brother, Maximino. He seemed to be readying a Huerta-like *coup* to replace his brother in 1946. Death put a final end to speculations about the possibility of a dictatorship of the Right, headed by Maximino, or one of the Left, sponsored by Oumanski. Early in the morning of January 25, 1945 Oumanski was killed in a plane crash at the Mexico City airport; less than three weeks later, on February 17, Maximino Avila Camacho died in Puebla under somewhat mysterious circumstances.

For nearly two years the semi-Fascist and the semi- or real Communist forces in Mexico had carried on an ideological battle where world currents took on Mexican names and symbols. The United States, thanks to deft handling, retained its premier position.

As in the case of the Sinarquists, wartime extremisms of the Left persisted into the postwar world as a minor trend in the Mexican stream. The reduction of their combined threat to the internal peace has been the almost automatic result of removing the social and economic conditions on which extremism has fed rather than a planned campaign to root out old style and new style subversives. They have withered on the vine as agricultural production has fed Mexico better and as particular attention has been devoted to regional and local needs and sensitivities in apportioning the benefits of irrigation, electrification, credit, roads, and other long-wanted items in marginal Mexico.

Both the Sinarquistas and Communists have recently been internally split over ideology and tactics. One rock which rives them is the degree to which their organization should and could coöperate with Alemán's obviously popular rule. Neither is very powerful.

No unofficial foreigner can make an accurate estimate of the actual or potential Communist influence in Mexican unions or of the extent of the Red underground. One cheering thought is that President Alemán and his close associates know more about it than anyone else; as Secretary of Interior during the war years, Alemán was specially charged with internal security; his close coöperation with the United States went far during the war to reduce such real dangers. There is little likelihood that the counter-subversive apparatus in Mexico is any less effective now. In the same vein it may be noted that Alemán's successor to the presidency, Adolfo Ruiz Cortines, similarly occupied the post of Gobernación for five years, encharged

with internal security of the nation and the undramatic de-Communization of the government initiated under Camacho. A few notes
on the current situation appear again below.

3. THE MODERATE REVOLUTION

Hedged on the one side by Mexico's international commitments
to help win the battle of production and on the other by recurrent
domestic economic and political crises, President Avila Camacho
had the inescapable duty of any modern Mexican president to extend as well as consolidate gains of the Revolution to date. Three
salient contributions emerged from a Mexico at war: education was
strengthened, public health and social security were buttressed, and
long overdue electoral reforms brought Mexico several steps nearer
political democracy. Any one of these achievements would have been
notable, but when taken with the new departures in agriculture and
industry, they indicated that the Revolution had not lapsed into a
coma for the duration.

Education. During the Camacho years one of the main efforts was
directed toward taking education out of politics, especially out
of Communist hands. Political fights over the leadership of the teachers' union and the direction of the national university crippled the
early effort to consolidate educational gains, but by the end of the
term both objectives had been essentially reached.

As part of Avila Camacho's campaign for national unity and the
modifying of controversial elements which divided Mexicans, he
sponsored a change in the General Law of Public Education (January 16, 1942) and then the rewording of Article 3 of the Constitution (December 1945). The controversial mandate under which the
Cárdenas school system had developed, that education was to be
"socialistic"—based on Marxian dialectical materialism—was shifted
to stress democracy, nationalism, humanism, and the economic independence of Mexico. A considerable reorganization of curricula and
administration followed. Increasing stress was put on training Mexican teachers and technicians.

So far as figures can be trusted, the Camacho regime, with its augmented funds, did as much as or more than its Revolutionary predecessors. In sheer quantity it outstripped the Cárdenas surge, while
reducing some of the barriers that divided Mexicans from each other.

To meet the chronic and growing need for more schools, in March

1944, the Camacho administration launched a Federal "Program for School Construction," a coöperative effort in which the nation, the states, and private agencies joined their resources and ideas. The outlines of this program were retained and given much broader scope and depth by President Alemán's administration.

In Alemán's annual report on the state of the nation on September 1, 1952, Mexican education is given first place in his summary of social activity of the regime. Here his administration was building on a solid foundation laid by a whole series of earlier Revolutionary presidents. Their combined efforts had sketched out an educational system for elementary grades, successively extended (especially by Calles) to secondary levels, and then to higher education and technical training. Many weaknesses persist amid the great strength thus developed. Both in quantity and quality the Mexican educational effort remains inadequate and unbalanced in favor of urban centers, with particular lack of suitable teacher training and secondary schools.

Nonetheless, Alemán's report on six years of activity is impressive. Budgets of the National Ministry of Education had increased to the point that it spent over a million pesos a day, apart from state and local expenditures, to educate all strata of the Mexican nation. Under a revived and broadened school-building campaign, paralleling the Camacho effort, more than 5000 elementary schools (housing an additional million pupils) had sprung up from 1946 to 1952, at a cost of over 300 million pesos. In 1952 alone, 531 new primary schools were put in operation. From 1946 to 1952, some 10,000 new teachers were recruited, much of the budget which had doubled to 450 million pesos annually in 1952 having been used to better the salaries of teachers. The sad fact, however, remains that despite the Herculean efforts of Cárdenas, Camacho, and Alemán, working through devoted Secretaries of Education, about half the Mexican children eligible for schooling do not receive it because of physical deficiencies in the Mexican educational plant.

As the Revolution began to "institutionalize" under Camacho, renewed emphasis was placed on higher and on technical education. Started in the days of Cárdenas, the National Polytechnical Institute underwent parlous days for awhile during the war, but after a reorganization, became a leading center. With excellent equipment, various and skilled faculties in sciences and engineering, it continues to provide for some 20,000 young Mexicans almost unlimited opportunities to acquire technical training and engage in postgraduate research; Mexican and foreign business firms have endowed it with equipment, personnel, and scholarships to supplement the contributions of the government. The Polytechnical Institute has branched out to supervise and aid state technical schools in nine regions of the Republic in a series of programs that range from adult extension work for semiskilled workers to higher degrees.

Occupying a unique niche in Mexican technical education is the Technological Institute of Monterrey, founded in 1942. Privately endowed and supported in large part by the business community of Monterrey, it is modeled on the Massachusetts Institute of Technology, whose high standards it successfully emulates. The Institute has proved a huge practical success and a local show-piece. To its halls come about 1300 students from all over the Republic (about a third on scholarships), and even from other parts of Latin America. It serves also as an important focal point for aiding Mexican industrialism, not only by turning out capable graduates but through its founding of a reliable, non-profit consultant service to aid Mexican manufacturers improve their processes, solve technical and management problems, discover by-products, reduce production costs, and help where it can. In April 1951 announcement was made that the research institute was affiliated with the Southwest Research Institute of San Antonio, Texas, whose 175-man staff substantially aids the top 75 Mexican consultants of the Monterrey establishment.

The story of the ancient and honorable National Autonomous University of Mexico follows much the same pattern as the tale of the National Polytechnical Institute, except that to hoary traditions dating from 1552 have been joined modernity. Winds of change under the Camacho regime brought rashes of student strikes, reorganizations, and then concerted efforts, once the battle of extremisms dwindled. A new chapter is being written in the University's colorful history by consolidation; its scattered schools and faculties, formerly housed in antiquated buildings in the heart of the metropolis, have been brought together in a spectacular new University City which houses and trains an estimated 25,000 of Mexico's 40,000 university students. Dreamed about in 1940, University City was planned by collaborative efforts of alumni and in 1950 construction was started. It began to function in 1952 and by 1955 it will be complete, with the national government bearing slightly more than half of its estimated cost of 85 million pesos for new buildings; the remainder was furnished by alumni and well-wishers.

Another policy was a contribution to national unity, the war effort, and the Revolution. In August 1944, Camacho and Jaime Torres Bodet, Secretary of Education, launched a crusade against illiteracy —"to end the tyranny of ignorance." The literate half of Mexico was to teach the illiterate half how to read and write: the "each one teach one" campaign. Every Mexican capable of reading and writing was required by law to impart these skills to another who lacked them. By 1946 it was claimed that under the organization so developed a million and a half adult illiterates had been "redeemed." So successful were the early programs that by law in 1947 they became a permanent part of the Mexican educational system. With improved techniques, widely copied by lands as far away as India, the permanent anti-illiteracy campaign annually "alphabetizes" between 500,000 and 600,000 adults. Through teaching Indians to read first in their own tongue, then slowly shifting to Spanish, it has materially affected native groups. Numerous towns, and even a few states, have almost completely obliterated illiteracy and thus proudly hoist a special flag to denote that fact. On the seventh anniversary of the campaign (August 1951) it was reported that the crusade had taught a total of 3,665,548 Mexicans to read and write; there were still some 3,096,537 who lacked these elementary skills. If the latter figures are anywhere near the truth, the illiteracy rate in Mexico has dropped from around 50 per cent in 1940 to 30 per cent or 35 per cent in 1951. After discounts for overoptimism, the total achievement is impressive.

The above examples are, of course, samples of the efforts put forth by Mexicans to educate their fellow countrymen. Omitted are innumerable agencies and institutions engaged in the constant battle against ignorance. Fortunately a recent and readable volume by George F. Kneller provides accurate and extensive coverage on this vital topic. Few would deny one of his main conclusions, that "The education of Mexicans is a matter of sincere and sacred concern to Mexico's national leaders. . . . The Mexican school system is a highly vital human institution, constructed and kept going at great personal sacrifice." *

* *The Education of the Mexican Nation* (New York: Columbia University Press, 1951), p. 228.

Social Security and Health. Among the Four Freedoms—the professed war aims of the United Nations—were Freedom from Want and Freedom from Fear. One clear step that Mexico took during the war to bring these heady abstractions to the local area was establishment of a system of social security. With it went renewed emphasis on public health and welfare.

Although Article 123 of the Constitution of 1917 had called for a law of social security which would guard workers against blows due to sickness, death, unemployment, and accidents, no official action had been taken to fulfill these provisions until Camacho's term. In 1941 the president authorized a technical commission to make the necessary preliminary studies; the commission made inquiries abroad and then adapted the experience of other nations to the peculiarities of Mexico. Experts like Emil Schoenbaum were brought in as advisers, and the much-discussed legislation became effective January 19, 1943.

As well as being an extensive welfare program, the Social Security system was part of Avila Camacho's general, ramified scheme of creating unity—to bring the state, workers, and employers into one coöperative venture for the benefit of all. Under the Mexican system the employer contributed 6 per cent, the worker 3 per cent, and the state 3 per cent of the worker's wage for insurance benefits in the event of sickness, pregnancy, old age, unemployment, or death. A semiautonomous governmental Institute of Social Security administers programs and funds.

Initially both employers and workers were skeptical as to whether the scheme would work, but by the end of the Camacho administration 286,773 workers and 31,427 employers were enrolled. The Institute of Social Security performs numerous specific services—prescriptions, injections, medical consultations, dental and optical services, hospitalization, and other similar aids—for eager solicitants. To care for its growing clientele, the Institute has set up a number of its own clinics, sanitariums, and laboratories. The 1952 report by the President mentioned that the Institute now had over 329 million pesos in reserve. He also outlined a vast welfare program that it was carrying on for its 1,600,000 beneficiaries. The large, new Social Security building in Mexico City is an architectural landmark to the importance that the Camacho program has assumed in today's Mexico. An old Revolutionary promise is being kept.

Other efforts to conserve and improve the health of Mexicans were numerous. Sanitary engineers of the Hydraulic Resources Commission planned and executed programs which provided towns and villages with potable water, and with education in personal hygiene, part of an effort to combat endemic illnesses and epidemics. Mexican doctors and scientists paid special attention to the eradication of malaria, tuberculosis, venereal diseases, leprosy, as well as to research on cancer. The famed Mexican Institute of Health and Tropical Diseases (founded in 1938) continued its important investigative and teaching work on tropical ailments. Despite wartime shortages, new hospitals began to rise in the cities and countrysides. Twenty-one had been completed, thirty-two were in progress, with eighteen more on the drawing boards, when Avila Camacho's term ended.

These are, of course, but samples of how the Revolution in Mexico continued during a major war. It had become constructive, in the best and varied senses of the word. This attitude of conciliation, unity, and tolerance surprisingly enough carried over into the political realm.

Although a product of the official political machine himself, Avila Camacho apparently sincerely felt that Mexico after thirty years of Revolution had arrived at a point where constitutional and political democracy could be tried again. He had the electoral laws redrawn in 1945. He expected that wider and newer segments of the Mexican nation which had re-entered national life during the war would be represented politically by stable national parties to rival the "official" one. The presidential election in 1946 held under his auspices is generally agreed to have been the most peaceful and representative one since Madero was swept into the presidential chair in 1911. This alone was an extraordinary achievement during wartime and the troubled initial postwar year.

Wartime Mexico indeed presented a mixed picture. The rich got richer, the poor poorer, but the middle class grew visibly in size and importance. Legally the government was an absolute though constitutional dictatorship, but seldom had Mexicans known such personal freedom and individual tranquillity; bribes were multiplied in quantity and magnitude, and gunmen were less furtive when guarding their political employers, but some of the most honest elections Mexico had ever witnessed were held under President Avila Camacho.

Both in domestic and in international affairs, 1945 seemed to be a watershed between old and new. While the Chapultepec Conference to discuss war and peace was being arranged, Russia's Oumanski crashed; during its meetings, Maximino Avila Camacho also died. Shortly thereafter, Franklin D. Roosevelt passed away. Mexican political agitation over the presidential elections in 1946 had already begun to distract attention away from the war effort even before VE-Day and VJ-Day. Manuel Avila Camacho's "state of the nation" message to Congress on September 1, 1945 was a message of victory. At the close of hostilities, he divested himself of his emergency powers so discreetly used. His final summary to Congress in September 1946 pointed the nation toward the postwar period.

Many of the main questions of the era remain unsettled. There is no agreement as to whether the enormous changes which occurred under the iron necessity of combating the Depression and Axis were merely an accelerated evolution or real revolution, and whether the successors to Roosevelt and Cárdenas have scuttled or merely transmuted the ideals and plans so warmly espoused and so violently debated in their countries during the middle and late thirties. Above argument is the fact that in Mexico the resurgent Revolution became institutionalized under the firm hand of President Avila Camacho.

15. The Era of Good Feeling, 1946-1952

1. ALEMANISMO

A persistent political phenomenon in Mexico is *futurismo*. It is open speculation about presidential timber in the public press and the premature booming of prospective candidates long before presidential elections are held. Every Mexican president dreads *futurismo;* once it is under way even the routine acts of his officials and possible successors become clothed with future and undue political significance. The premature politicking hampers his personal manipulation of men and measures, which is the essence of Mexican politics. It is not surprising, therefore, that Mexican presidents try to defer *futurismo* as long as possible. But at some point each must take cognizance of it and indicate an heir apparent.

On May 5, 1945 President Camacho tacitly opened political campaigns for his successor in 1946 by a speech at Puebla. He merely said that he did not know whether the next president of Mexico would be a civilian or a military man, a lawyer, doctor, or a general, but that the Constitution had a strong civilian bias. Studying these cryptic utterances with the care they deserved, the metropolitan press and coffee-house gossips were not slow to fill in the names of possible presidential candidates. All agreed that Miguel Alemán Valdés would be a strong contender. He was.

Alemán was no political unknown. Through his presence in previous campaigns, the electorate had learned that he was born in 1902 at Sayula, Veracruz, the son of a famous local revolutionary figure. He took a law degree in Mexico City, and as a protégé of Portes Gil had been an able state governor of Veracruz from 1936 to 1940. Many regions had seen Alemán before; he had been campaign director for Manuel Avila Camacho's 1940 election. As the latter's Secretary of Interior Alemán had been the youngest of the Cabinet members and was publicly credited with being chiefly responsible for the unity and domestic stability that had characterized the wartime regime. Intelligence, tolerance, and optimism, plus an extraordinary political sense, were Alemán's outstanding personal qualities.

If elected, he would be the first civilian president since Madero, and the first who had not actually participated in the epic Revolution. A new political generation, sons and grandsons of revolutionaries, was coming of age in Mexico. For them the Revolution is an accepted fact, though not a burning and vivid personal memory. Alemán had been outstanding among these new young men.

More than a year before the actual presidential election, Alemán's undoubted success was assured. On May 24, 1945 leaders who could deliver the mass votes of the Peasant's Confederation, the bureaucrats, the various workers' associations, and the lower-middle-class organizations met secretly and agreed jointly to back him for the presidency. This informal arrangement became known as the "Pact of the Centrals." Alemán was the sole choice as "pre-candidate" and then as Party nominee of these powerful sectors of the Party.

Public announcement of the Pact of the Centrals was deferred until after President Camacho had approved it and the leaders had called on potential rivals of Alemán. A solemn delegation "in friendly, cordial tones" informed General Miguel Henríquez Guzman and another viable pre-candidate, Javier Rojo Gómez, that the support of the three elements of the official party was unanimously pledged to Alemán. Though his election fourteen months hence was a foregone conclusion, Alemán resigned from the cabinet, and (with the president's blessing) began forming a campaign staff.

Soon the smoothly working official party machinery began busily to hum, directed more toward inner agitations for posts of governorships, deputies, and senators than at the presidency, now tacitly settled. The band wagon was in full view, and almost anyone could climb onto it. On January 18, 1946 the 1967 delegates to the second and final national convention of the P.R.M. convened in Mexico City, ostensibly to choose a presidential nominee and candidates for national and state elective offices.

The first and only item on its actual agenda was to commit hara-kiri, as the P.N.R. had in 1936. The delegates voted to dissolve the old party and as a body to reconstitute a new one. The old party (P.R.M.) had faithfully carried out Cárdenas' policies and had then supported Avila Camacho under its slogan—"for a democracy of workers." The end of an epoch was now signalized by changing the stated aims to "democracy and social justice." The structure and operation of the new party were much the same as the old. The new official party took the name of *Party of the Institutional Revolution*. Its very label suggested that the aggressive and militant phases of the Revolution had closed. The task of Revolutionaries within the party henceforth was to make existing institutions work better. Its Spanish name indicates this: *Partido Revolucionario Institucional*.

This party policy was openly avowed at the organizational meeting by its new head, Dr. Rafael Gamboa, who stated that the P.R.I. accepted absolutely, without any reserve, the democratic system of government. He announced that it would fight against imperialist wars and all forms of aggression against peoples of underdeveloped countries. It was now, he said, a premise of the P.R.I. that the ideals of the Revolution had already crystallized into adequate institutions. The party's chief purpose thenceforth was to fight with all its energy for internal and external economic liberation of Mexico until its "semi-feudal physiognomy disappears." In short, the Revolution had openly shifted to an evolutionary approach; militancy was no longer the prime, almost sole, virtue of the true Revolutionary.

As expected, delegates to the P.R.I. then announced that they had chosen Miguel Alemán to carry them to victory in the presidential race. He promised to be faithful to party ideals and he presented them his platform. Unlike the previous two national party nominating conventions, this one made no pretense of creating a Six Year Plan. The candidate, not the Party, set forth the general and specific objectives which were to be met during the next six-year term, 1946–1952. His "Plan Alemán" reiterated Gamboa's statements by emphasizing the necessity for increased agricultural production, industrialization, continued political conciliation, rejection of foreign ideologies, and a moralization of political life. Little or no mention of "class struggle" found its way into these broad planks. "Harmony" was touted over "militancy" and "class struggle."

Campaigns. The campaigns of Alemán's rivals followed the established Mexican patterns. As pre-candidates, and then as the nominees of their respective parties, they individually toured the Republic to encourage the work of their local organizations. The contest essentially narrowed to Miguel Alemán and Ezequiel Padilla. Neither major candidate resorted to personal slander. Although there were a few incidents and clashes between overzealous partisans of each, these episodes were deplored and really were of small moment. Certainly the whole tone of the campaign was much less tense and touchy than it had been in 1940, when Avila Camacho campaigned against Almazán.

Alemán's campaign was essentially an educational effort because his election was a foreordained conclusion. It was designed to make him and his ideas more widely known. They would guide Mexican destinies for six years. Rather than attempting to popularize and explain a prefabricated Six Year Plan, Alemán, by using a new technique, built up his platform as he went along. In the various main centers of the Republic he held round-table forums. At them the local representatives of business, labor, and other social interests together discussed and outlined the outstanding problems of their areas or industries, and worked out jointly with Alemán plans of how they as a team could, with government support, best implement for themselves and the nation the growing "Plan Alemán."

This new synthesis of *Alemanismo* had first been published in September 1945. It covered nearly every aspect of Mexican life in very general terms. More important than its glowing words was the fact that Alemán, supported by the masses in the Pact of the Centrals, was also able to attract during his campaign the ablest young administrators, intellectuals, and even influential businessmen who had remained outside politics since Madero's day. Alemán's campaign literature was technical and pedagogic, not inflammatory. It stressed hard work, team-play, production, and responsibility—foundations of an optimistic future.

The Election. Election Day, July 7, 1946, dawned rainy and drizzly in most parts of the Republic. Early in the morning, long lines formed in front of the clearly designated, available polls. Mexicans waited patiently for hours in the rain to cast their votes. Foreign and domestic observers agreed that this was the most peaceful election that Mexico had ever had. No bloody incidents marred the voting, and the long lines in front of polls kept double voting to an absolute minimum.

The outcome of the election was heartening to those who believed Mexico was moving steadily down the road of liberal, Western-style democracy. One measure is participation. Some 2,358,520 citizens, an estimated 52 per cent of the total electorate, registered for voting. All told, 2,298,603 ballots were cast (46.4 per cent of the electorate).

Miguel Alemán won the presidency. The minority strength which was displayed and counted was significant, and surprising testimony that the new attitudes and mechanisms had brought results. Between them Alemán and Padilla split 97 per cent of the vote; two militarists, Generals Calderón and Castro, almost equally divided the remaining 3 per cent. On a national basis, Miguel Alemán drew more than three-quarters of the popular vote, the first one held under the Camacho reforms aimed at minimizing old abuses.

SUMMARY OF VOTING, PRESIDENTIAL ELECTION, July 7, 1946

Regional Distribution	Vote			Percentage within Region		
	Alemán	Padilla	Castro and Calderón	Alemán	Padilla	Castro and Calderón
Core	971,407	262,737	35,716	76.3	20.7	2.8
South	286,240	43,002	4,324	85.9	13.0	1.2
West	165,874	42,327	11,414	75.8	19.3	5.2
North	363,904	95,350	16,308	76.1	20.0	3.4
Republic	1,787,425	443,416	67,762	77.8	19.2	3.0
Federal District	126,646	88,826	6,666	51.9	39.9	3.0

What amazed impartial observers was the size of the independent or "nonofficial" balloting. It was nearly a quarter of the total, more than half a million votes. Equally or more significant, opposition parties elected Deputies to Congress, though they obtained no Senators. Among the parliamentary opposition were two millionaires (one a banker), a Sinarquista, and four other non-machine candidates. In a Chamber of 147 members they were scarcely a token force, but indicated that the official party's absolute monopoly of political life had slightly relaxed. That a parliamentary opposition, however tiny, existed at all was eloquent testimony that all the campaign rhetoric about respecting the people's will had some factual basis. If Mexico had not moved far by 1946, it had at least started in the right direction.

As usual, when political figures of importance cast their presidential votes, reporters asked them for statements. A specific and revealing one came from Vicente Lombardo Toledano. He summed up, from personal knowledge, a whole generation of political evolution in Mexico when he said "First the generals got together in conclaves to decide who would be the President. Then the Governors did the same thing. A little later the Labor organizations distributed the posts. Today the actions of citizens say the word." Other observers agreed that the whole 1946 election was one of the fairest ever held.

Unlike the aftermath of the 1940 elections, there was no threat of a post-electoral revolution by disgruntled minorities. Neither Alemán nor his chief opponent, Ezequiel Padilla, denied the rumor that the latter had had a private interview after the voting at which he promised to coöperate with the new regime. A small group of die-hard Padillistas voluntarily exiled themselves for a few weeks and wrote manifestos from Los Angeles and Texas. The episode was more picturesque than important, for the erstwhile revolutionaries quietly re-entered the Republic a little later without difficulties.

The election of Miguel Alemán to the presidency of Mexico in July 1946 did seem to close one epoch in Mexican history and open another. Election and immediate post-election developments indicated that he had wide sectors of political opinion behind him. He was one of the few presidents elected in this century by procedures that even approached the normal democratic ideal. Further, he was a civilian president, with an important tradition to uphold. His civilian predecessors in the presidential office had been Benito Juárez, Sebastian Lerdo de Tejada, and Francisco I. Madero. Each of them heralded major transformations—the Reforma, the Porfirian Peace, the epic political Revolution. Alemán was the harbinger of the Economic Revolution, carried on in the Era of Good Feeling established by Manuel Avila Camacho.

2. INSTITUTIONAL REVOLUTION AND FAIR DEAL

President Harry S. Truman and President Miguel Alemán came to the headship of their respective nations in peculiarly troubled times, domestically and internationally. Contained pressures and new forces generated by World War II necessarily had to be blown off and channeled toward a new "normalcy." The sudden dismantling of the machine that won the war, the relaxation of controls necessary in war but questionable in peace, and the obscure and then steadily menacing position of Soviet Russia and its openly more aggressive designs kept the political and economic pots boiling.

But amid the alarms and excursions of domestic politics that each faced in 1947, the two heads of the neighboring states reaffirmed the "Era of Good Feeling" that wartime collaboration had brought to their countries. An exchange of ceremonial visits, each unprecedented, gave conclusive evidence that officially at least the boundary-sharing nations intended to continue their unruffled relations. Unofficially they were closer in mind than at almost any time in earlier history. No real clouds darkened the horizon.

The Truman Visit. When Truman's presidential plane, the "Sacred Cow," landed at Mexico City's airport at 10 A.M., on March 3, 1947, it marked the first time that a president of the United States had officially visited the Mexican capital.* Both presidents claimed the Truman visit of March 1947 was essentially "nonpolitical," as no major problems between the countries were outstanding. The press speculated that there would be some talk about foreign loans, improving the joint program against hoof-and-mouth disease, and tariffs. The primary purpose of the visit was to strengthen friendship. It did. In preparation for the historic occasion, Mexico City was given a scrubbing—physically and for security. President Alemán polished up his English, and the visit was unmarred by any untoward incidents.

The most significant and important unscheduled episode was spontaneous and favorable. President Truman laid a wreath on the statue of the Niños Heroes, and thereby probably won more Mexican esteem for himself and his countrymen than all the ceremonial dinners could generate. The Niños Heroes were Mexican Army cadets who, in the Mexican-American war, had futilely fought United States troops in a critical battle for Mexico City; rather than surrender, they had been wiped out almost to the last man. The survivors had wrapped themselves in Mexican flags and jumped to their deaths rather than become prisoners. Their stand was as symbolic of courage and patriotism to Mexicans as the Alamo has been to Texans. The simple and sincere tribute which Truman paid to them and their cause removed many lingering doubts about United States "nonintervention," repeatedly avowed in speeches during the visit. The effusive Mexican

* President Truman had visited Mexico in 1939; then a senator, he had been a guest of the Mexican Congress.

cordiality that had been displayed up to that time took on added warmth for the remainder of the stay, which terminated March 6.

The Alemán Visit. President Truman sent the "Sacred Cow" to pick up President Alemán and his party a short time later, on April 29. Rather than making up his party exclusively of diplomats, Alemán chose to include a number of Mexican intellectuals, artists, and musicians; this led a Mexican commentator to say that it was "as though a Greek embassy were going to Rome."

It was the first time in history that a Mexican president had made a visit of state to Washington. To be sure that Mexican hospitality was suitably reciprocated, the United States' capital gave President Alemán what it likes to call "the red carpet treatment." He was given the works: his picture adorned the lampposts, his arrival was broadcast in 25 languages, and he was literally given the keys to the city. After the honors at Washington, he continued the triumphal tour to New York, where Mayor O'Dwyer arranged a ticker-tape welcome and Columbia University conferred an honorary doctorate; he made the tour to West Point, T.V.A. and other main points of interest, and returned to Mexico on May 7.

The high point of the trip, for both nations, was President Alemán's address to a special joint session of the United States Congress. He had stated on arrival that "Politics between Mexico and the United States have nothing to hide or dissimulate." The tenor of his message to Congress was that Mexico was neither a vassal nor an enemy. The current harmony, so evident in every sphere where separate national interests touched or overlapped, could and would continue indefinitely so long as the two neighboring democracies exhibited mutual respect, based on law, "stimulated by coöperation, animated to achieve a just goal—that of living with honor and progressing with independence." Both nations had learned much from experience in dealing with each other, especially that aggression did not pay, in bilateral or world relationships; the task of the United States, Mexico, and the hemisphere was to extend the Good Neighbor policy into social and economic realms as well as the political ones.

"The true meaning of Good Neighborliness is coöperation," said President Alemán. He added that it meant more than documents signed in chancelleries or agreements among chiefs-of-staff. Mexico was now and always willing to join and aid the United States toward the hemispheric ideals of peace and progress, but only as a partner. Alemán's address was a polite, firm, and successful reaffirmation of

Mexican and Latin-American views of the Good Neighbor Policy. The fact that their president had personally and successfully enunciated to the United States Congress so clearly, forcibly, yet unprovocatively the basic feelings of most Mexicans gave Alemán a hold over his people that eased all his subsequent domestic problems.

On his return from Washington the greatest demonstration ever given a Mexican president greeted him. From a half to three-quarters of a million Mexicans jammed the square outside the National Palace to which his automobile slowly made its way through packed streets from the airport. Daniel Cosío Villegas, who had not long before published a controversial essay on the "failures of the Revolution," publicly retracted most of his statements in face of the "miracle" represented by Alemán's address to the American Congress. Of greater import was a group visitation that the living ex-presidents of Mexico made to Alemán on May 14, 1947, to give their collective backing to the new administration. Like the wartime "Acercamiento Nacional" this visit signalized the continuity of the Revolution, the unity of the nation, and the nonpartisan moral and political support of these potent elder statesmen. As a body they could still rally Mexico to rise against a "false" leader, but they supported Alemán. Their public act of faith and approval was one direct result of Alemán's Washington visit. He had made it clear at home and abroad that wartime coöperation on a partnership basis would continue during his regime; Mexico was not a vassal state, but was a partner.

More concrete were some of the specific agreements reached between the two governments during and after the ceremonial visits. A joint statement issued while Alemán was in Washington pledged both governments to further coöperation; the United States promised to help stabilize the Mexican peso and to make loans available through the Export-Import Bank to finance the development projects outlined by the Mexicans. By inference, Mexico agreed to support the major United States' foreign stands. On terminating the economic agreements the two presidents took occasion to "congratulate one another on the high degree of cordiality achieved by the peoples they represent."

Burying the Bygones. Carrying out the symbolic cues thrown to them by their presidents, the governments in each country commemorated the new "Era of Good Feeling" by the mutual restoration of oattle flags captured from one another during the War of

1847. Unlike most unilateral actions taken by the United States, the spontaneous decision to return to Mexico the trophies of war captured during 1847–1848 met with widespread enthusiasm in both countries. The project (long a pet of the American Legion Commander in Mexico, Roscoe B. Gaither) was given powerful Congressional and Senatorial approval. On August 5, 1950 President Truman signed a bill ensuring that all captured flags, insignia, and the like, deposited at Annapolis and West Point, would be returned to the Mexican nation.

Solemn, then gay, ceremonies marked the actual devolution. On September 13, 1950 a full military spectacle was staged in Mexico City. On the spot where the heroic Mexican cadets fell, a young West-Pointer handed a symbolic flag to President Alemán; twelve other cadets from West Point, Annapolis, and Randolph Field handed captured Mexican standards to Mexican cadets, while the crowd yelled "Viva México!" This touched off the patriotic and social fiestas that accompany the celebration of Mexican Independence on September 15–16.

Not to be outdone, the Mexican Congress voted to return American flags in Mexican hands. Thus a century of progress was sealed, with the appropriate words about "bygones are bygones." Wrote Harry Truman to Miguel Alemán, "On our nations have descended greatness and prosperity, and to crown it, friendship, comprehension, respect, and peace." In his turn, Miguel Alemán had, in his first message to his Congress in September 1947, announced "Never have our relations with the North American Union reached the broad cordiality of which the presidential visits were public testimony." It is pleasing to record that after all the mutual recriminations which have passed across the border this new "Era of Good Feeling" seems stable, and based on realities.

Neither nation has been forced to make great sacrifices of its national interests to bring about this healthy condition. In fact, it has been seen long and clearly that one of the principal lessons of World War II should not be forgotten: a chief national interest of each country lies in supporting the main policies of the other. These include bilateral arrangements negotiated directly between them to ease divergent points of view, especially in the economic interplay where differences are sharpest, as well as multilateral arrangements sponsored by the inter-American system and the United Nations, in which both nations take an active part. The willingness to discuss, compromise, and even agree that no agreement can be reached at this time, is a sounder foundation than a sickly unanimity based on ambiguity and vague formulas that suppress rather than air occasional differences.

Later pages spell out in more detail a myriad of joint enterprises that have sprouted and continue to grow in the warm atmosphere of good feeling between the neighbors. In line with the sentiments expressed, nearly all of these have been on a partnership basis, fiscally and administratively. Without fanfare, material improvements and moral strengthening have proceeded on a real coöperative basis. In general, the United States has supplied technical aid and initial sums of money, as loans rather than gifts; Mexican counterparts have shouldered equal responsibilities for planning and execution, while the Mexican government has either shared the original capital investments or seen that repayment was prompt. It cannot be stressed too often that international loans made by the United States to underdeveloped areas like Mexico are paid to *United States* business for equipment and personnel, for which the receiving nation agrees to repay on the installment plan.

From wartime and even earlier experiences, planners in both nations had learned the basic but sometimes forgotten lesson that psychological and social factors, though intangible and not easily quantified, were usually more important in the success of a joint enterprise than the physical ones that can be graphed and calculated. Besides the more grandiose plans worked out in common by the two governments were equally significant ones launched by semiprivate and private organizations and individuals in almost any sphere that can be named. Bonds of mutual benefit interlaced Mexico and the United States more firmly together under the Fair Deal and Institutional Revolution than at any time in their previous history. Healing of old rancors helped free Mexican energies for improving their land, aided but not guided by the ex-bogy, the Colossus of the North.

3. RIPENING DEMOCRACY

One of the important trends in Mexican domestic affairs is the measurable advance toward western-style political democracy which Mexico has made during and after World War II. It would be unwise and unrealistic to claim that many deplorable features of politics *a la Mexicana* have suddenly evaporated. It is equally shortsighted and incorrect to insist that patterns of the roaring twenties and troubled thirties persist unmodified past mid-century.

In general, four main strands can be abstracted to indicate the nature, direction, and significance of recent shifts. First, wartime extremisms have continued to decline and currently are a negligible political factor. Secondly, while remaining basically unchanged, the overt political apparatus of Mexico as a state has been improved. Thirdly, though the "official" party remains the major force in elections, its structure has undergone real modification, partly as a result of its almost undisputed hold, partly by the sincere and driving desire of President Alemán to democratize Mexico. Finally, through the electoral reforms first sketched by Camacho, then improved and extended by Alemán, Mexican elections are increasingly meaningful. These several elements are closely interwoven, but when examined separately reveal many of the present currents on the Mexican political scene.

The Extremists. From Camacho, President Alemán inherited a Mexico in which Sinarquistas on the Right, Communists and fellow-travelers on the Left, were potential problems. By firmness and without overt force, by removing through various positive programs the conditions which sustained each, the Alemán regime has reduced each to a dwindling and vocally subdued collection of splinters. No serious observer rates either one as an actual or potential disturber of public order or a threat to security.

By the end of World War II, the Sinarquistas, whose earlier career has been dealt with above,* were a riven group. In 1945, Sinarquista national leadership changed, and with it came a turn in policy. Openly the main body attempted to constitute itself as a "Third Force," equidistant from the "liberal capitalism" represented by the United States, and "Communism" symbolized by Russia, and to lesser degree, by the Mexican Revolution.

Sinarquistas came out openly as ultra-nationalists to flay excesses of the "official" party. They set up a competitive political party, *Popular Force,* in the hope that they would ultimately gain control of Mexico constitutionally and legally. Concentrating on municipal and state posts, Sinarquistas won a few offices as a first step toward this seizure of the nation and their proposed transformation of Mexico into a modified version of the old Hapsburg regime. The outlines

* See pp. 293–294.

of the forthcoming "order" were displayed in a widely read pamphlet, *Mexico 1960*.

With minor political success came renewed militancy. The fact of having Sinarquista members in state legislatures and even one in the national Congress apparently led the leaders to underrate the precautionary eye which the national government had on them. Sinarquistas overrated their own power. To symbolize their resentment of the Reforma and the Revolution, Sinarquistas in 1948 draped the statue of Benito Juárez (on the Alameda in Mexico City) with a black cloth. For this misdeed the Sinarquista political party (*Fuerza Popular*) lost its officially approved registration and was outlawed. It took no open part in the congressional elections of 1949. When in 1949 President Alemán visited León, the traditional capital of Sinarquismo, local revolutionaries hung up a sign for him to read —"Sinarquismo is dead." This was almost true. In that year only 6000 members had made the annual pilgrimage to that city, an event that once drew ten times that number.

But though much of the old force had left Sinarquism, it did not completely give up the ghost. The national leadership of the main movement was scheduled to change in 1951. An inner squabble for power brought from obscurity many old Sinarquista faces. The winner, who took office on May 20, 1951, was Juan Ignacio Padilla (no relative of Ezequiel Padilla). It was generally assumed that he would revert to the original pattern of Sinarquism; known to be violent in outlook, ruthless in action, and repeatedly quoted as stating that the blood of Sinarquista martyrs and Revolutionary foes was needed to fertilize the movement, he had outlined his stand in a volume significantly titled *Sinarquismo: Counter-Revolution* (1948). Contrary to expectations, Padilla took few of the steps that observers had forecast.

Rather than make a militant Fascist-like organization from the remnants of Sinarquismo, Padilla strove first to unify the movement by inviting back into the fold its strayed leaders and their flocks. He began to dismantle some of the para-military organization by allowing the smallest Sinarquista units—"municipalities" (five to ten families)—more voice in policy-making. As a revived group, Sinarquista slogans and demands took on a new tone of moderation: like other Catholic bodies, they agitated peacefully for even further relaxation of Article 3 in the Constitution (dealing with education) and modification of Articles 24 and 130 which set forth the anti-clerical biases of the Revolution.

An ultimate in the Sinarquista "new look" came when politicking for the presidency of Mexico began to bubble. Padilla at first announced that the organization would support the P.R.I.'s candidates. But then he found that many of his followers remembered that the heir presumptive had been the Secretary of Gobernación who had canceled the Sinarquista party privileges. After shopping around, the Sinarquista organization somewhat reluctantly endorsed the presidential candidate of *Acción Nacional,* a moderately conservative party. In May 1952, even that endorsement was undercut by statements from the Sinarquista high command. In their official paper, *Órden,* began to appear the command, "Register and vote! But vote for whomsoever you want!" Exit Sinarquismo.

In short, Sinarquismo has for the nonce given up its ultramontane extremism and has become a small, peasant-based pressure group, with Catholic leanings. Recently (April 1952), in pondering this curious resolution to what was once a real threat, Padilla said, "Sinarquism of the present time is in many ways better than that of before. It was necessary for it to be a child in order to reach this new stage."

Many explanations can be put forward to account for the reduction in potency of the Sinarquistas during and after the war. Split leadership and internal squabbles rank high. Perhaps equally strong is the fact that the Mexican government had learned that ridicule rather than martyrdom was effective against the early, unauthorized and disturbing demonstrations. Policemen and soldiers were trained to slip into the grim parades and cut the belts of Sinarquista marchers; it was rather hard to look like the wave of the future with one's pants dragging. A variation was to let a live bull loose amid the demonstration; for female Sinarquistas, a few mice freed among them did an equivalent job of scattering the phalanx. Further, the Catholic Church in Mexico, speaking through a semiofficial organ (*Atisbos*), increasingly attacked Sinarquism as being "un-Mexican," a sure sign that the hierarchy had cut whatever connections it may have had when the movement boasted more than a million members. Too, the P.A.N. has tried to disavow any connection with it. Sinarquism, like Communism, has withered on the vine as moderation and visible material benefits envelop the countrysides: Mexicans *are* better governed, better fed, better housed.

Communism. The elements that diminished the Sinarquista hold on Mexican groups have likewise weakened the lure that Communism once held. As the cold war intensified and Mexican conditions generally improved, numbers of the semi-faithful have dropped. The known "official" card carriers total only a little more than 3000, according to published Mexican estimates; if to these were added various shades of Trotskyites, Leninists, and other deviant sects of the cult, perhaps a sum of 5000 to 8000 might be reached. Circulation of the official Communist paper, *Voz de México,* was only 9087 in 1950, even after a recruiting and circulation drive. It reported that only three industrial cells were active then. For 1952 seemingly 10,000 "hard core" Communists would be an outside limit. The "official" Communist Party of Mexico (P.C.M.) could not muster the 30,000 adherents which electoral laws require of a registered party. The "de-Communization" of strategic unions and bureaucracies that Miguel Alemán carried out first as Secretary of Interior for President Camacho, then as president himself, has gone on without hysteria but with marked success. Exit Communism.

Neither the domestic nor the international climate has been propitious for Communism in Mexico. The first power tests facing President Alemán came from Red-tinged unions in the oil fields; his deft handling of them made clear his position. This was reaffirmed when the markedly Communist mining unions staged a dramatic march from the coal-fields of the north to Mexico City in 1951; the regime treated them kindly but did not alter one whit its basic policy of fostering strong, but non-Communist unions.

As bellwether of Mexican Marxists, Vicente Lombardo Toledano tried in 1948 to lure the "progressive" (that is, Marxian) elements into a political party called *Partido Popular.* He called on the C.T.M. to leave the official party (P.R.I.), but little happened. For the presidential elections of 1952, a coalition comprised of the Partido Popular, the Mexican Communist Party, and a splinter group of "deviant" Communists under the name of "The Mexican Workers and Farmers" campaigned for Lombardo Toledano's candidacy for presidency of Mexico, closely parroting the Moscow line. Again no significant political strength of this vocal but impotent minority was evidenced. Lombardo Toledano seems to be a very faded valentine.

The small hold that extremists had on the voting public of Mexico was manifested in the 1949 congressional elections and reaffirmed in the presidential and congressional race of 1952. In 1949 the combined total of Sinarquistas and Marxists was but 1847 out of a vote of over two millions, an infinitesimal percentage. Slightly more, but still insignificant, was *Partido Popular*'s showing. In 1952 the Sinarquista vote was scattered too widely to allow computation, but the Partido Popular and its avowedly Communist affiliates polled only 3 per cent. These bogies, Sinarquism and Communism, worry uninformed foreigners considerably more than they do the Mexicans of today.

The Political Apparatus. As one of his campaign planks, Alemán promised a "moralization" of government and improvement of its efficiency. Though it would take a superman to achieve these ends in a short time, the ugly wave of bribery and nepotism that accompanied wartime government of Mexico has ebbed: scandals are less numerous and flagrant, and normal minor public services can be obtained without paying special fees, though some cronies of the president have reputedly enriched themselves by the expected "honest graft" inherent in contracts. These peccadilloes have not pressed so heavily on the day-to-day activities of the great mass of Mexicans and foreigners as they did a decade ago. Offsetting some of these smirches is the undoubted fact that government is more efficient and cheaper than before; the administrative outlay has taken less and less of the national budget, and hovers at about 5 per cent of public expenditures.

Headlines were made when Alemán revised and improved the Mexican judiciary and its procedures. The number of justices was augmented, to cut down the backlog of unheard cases, but even more significant was a change in the nomination and tenure systems. After Mexico had toyed with both elected and perpetual judges (the one group was unskilled and the other venal), a procedure whereby Supreme Court judges achieved life tenure, while lesser ones served probationary periods of varying length, was installed by Alemán, who acted in this on the advice of the Mexican bar. Court rules, especially those centering around stay-writs (*amparos*), were redrawn by Congress. Though still a serious problem, important steps were thus taken to assure a more equitable and speedy administration of justice, a Reforma-born aspiration espoused by the Revolution.

As in the past (and for the foreseeable future), the Mexican Congress more or less remained the creature of the Executive. It contented itself with making minor changes in projects handed it by cabinet ministers or the president, and its numerous ceremonial appearances. On no occasion did it take the bit in its teeth and defy the president. Perhaps the most notable move that affected Congress was an increase in its size, effective in 1952.

The change stemmed from two important facts. One was that the Mexican population was tabulated in 1950, and the added Mexicans shown by the census called for redistricting and added representation. Article 52 of the Constitution was reworded to provide that there would be one deputy for each 170,000 population, raised from 150,000. Increased was the number of electoral districts and seats to 161 over the 147 of the Camacho and Alemán administrations. It also meant that demographic changes were translated into political terms: Yucatan, San Luis Potosí, and the state óf Mexico each lost one congressional seat, while nine states and the Federal District gained; the latter's representation jumped from twelve to nineteen. The other fact that slightly altered political balances was the addition of a new state to the Mexican union.

Baja California Norte, lying on the peninsula above the 28th parallel, became the 29th state. Suggested in September 1951 by President Alemán, the necessary approval for the transition by other state legislatures and national Congress came by December; the decree establishing its new status became official on January 16, 1952, but it was not until October 1952 that necessary supplementary legislation allowing the entity to elect its own governor and take on the other attributes of statehood received final approval. Thus though it sent two deputies to Congress in the elections of 1952, it as yet had no Senators. From a 1930 population of 48,327 (when it became a separate Territory under Executive control) this upper half of the California peninsula had sprouted to 226,967 by 1950, chiefly because with irrigation its lands yielded bonanza crops for nearby United States markets. There was short-lived talk in 1951 of naming the new sovereignty "Alemán" in honor of the outgoing President, to whom virtual creation of the unit was imputed by his adulators. When Baja California Norte in 1955 sends its two Senators to Mexico City, the national Senate will have 60 members, with an unchanged Chamber of 161, a bicameral legislature of 221.

But despite the fact that main divisions of the Mexican government had been strengthened and enlarged, the Executive continued to dominate the governing of Mexico, perhaps an inevitable fact. Monarchy had founded the tradition, which was rehabilitated and strengthened by thirty years under Díaz and then by the Northern

Dynasty. Rooted custom prescribes that the head of the state take a personal, paternalistic interest in the public and private life of each citizen. That legacy continues. Recently in *Hoy*, a Mexican review, a writer complained that "We have put the Constitution and Revolutionary theories aside in order to strengthen the executive in so unbalanced a way that from the President of the Republic alone we expect all our political norms, as well as our economic and religious ones, even to the point of settling our conjugal difficulties." The president is still the head of the Mexican family, and more specifically the Revolutionary family grouped in the single party. He is both legal head of state and unofficial party chief. Paradoxically, though machine-made candidates, both Presidents Camacho and Alemán took steps to broaden the base of party membership and bring to its ranks the elements of Mexican life overlooked by earlier versions of the "official" party. It now might be a moot question as to which is more powerful, the president as Constitutional head or the president as Party leader, since they continue to reinforce one another by dealing with the same strata. Until an "opposition" president is elected there is no real way of deciding the theoretical point.

The Revamped "Official" Party. The historical evolution of democracy under the auspices of the Mexican Revolution befuddles the unwary. When judged by usual standards, Mexico seems one of the least democratic of states. The same party always wins all the presidential elections; the judiciary and the legislature are made up of party members, and seldom count each other out. Yet analysis should go one step further. Though it is clear that the "official" party nearly always takes all elective offices, the important development has been the democratizing of the party itself.

Since Cárdenas ended a "duarchy" whereby party control and formal government apparatus were run separately, they have become almost inseparable. There has been a trend toward broader representation within party ranks; that means, in effect, that the real government has gradually been representing more and more people as party structure has changed. Expanding the groups from which membership comes democratizes Mexico. While maintaining numerous controls that ensure its necessary stability, Mexico has become one of the freest and most democratic of Latin-American nations, less by formal reform than by changes in the bylaws of party membership. This is a pragmatic rather than doctrinaire approach that seems suited to Mexican needs and background.

From earlier pages it will be recalled that the "official" party was created in 1929 to maintain stability in a political crisis and that under various names it has continued to dominate Mexican elections. That is still the case, but the significant points to be noted are the changed complexion of the party's makeup and its recent orientations. It started out as an exclusive lodge of military *caudillos,* was shaken up and broadened under Cárdenas to bring in mass support of organized peasantry, labor, and the rank and file of the Army. Though President Avila Camacho quietly demilitarized the party by dropping the soldiery, he made important changes in its operation by having the lower middle classes represented. Moreover, the electoral reforms of 1945, by altering the mode of joining political parties, opened their ranks.

Membership was put on an individual rather than a group basis; it was made direct rather than indirect, to cut down "bossism." Previously one belonged to a union or an *ejido* or a "popular organization" that in turn was under one of the Federations or centrals speaking for Agrarians, Labor, or "Popular Organizations," all boss-ridden. Only by enrolling himself in a group that in turn had party affiliations could an individual gain a coveted party-card. Now, if he wants, he can enroll, pay his dues, and vote a straight ticket. It permits him to steer clear of the bosses, whose number has increased, but whose individual power has been whittled away. An enlarged national executive committee and augmented regional directing boards reflect these new interests and additions to party ranks.

Primaries and conventions have been cleaned up to restrict the "imposition" of unpopular, unrepresentative senators and deputies. Alemán is reported to have told aspirants for his favor in nominations, "Talk to the people, not to me." But despite the dismantling process, the president of Mexico can virtually name his own successor. The Revolution will have come of age when the machine peacefully allows power to fall into the hands of a respectable opposition.

Perhaps equally as significant as the successive democratization of the "official party" is its present orientation. In February 1950 the P.R.I. issued a long set of "Principles" to define the outlook and programs of this powerful extraconstitutional machine. It openly invited into its ranks "all citizens who aspire to realize the program of the Mexican Revolution, within the bounds of the Constitution . . . for the benefit of *all* the inhabitants of the nation." It placed itself on record as dedicating itself to middle-class ideals by giving up the earlier concept of the class-struggle and the "democracy of workers and agrarians" of Cárdenas' days. The party is now pledged to remove, so far as possible, the inequalities among all social classes. It aims especially to provide political expression for the middle class and to foster its growth, since, as the platform declares, "the participation of the middle class in the history of Mexico has been a constant and decided help in bringing to realization social benefits of major magnitude."

In scanning the Mexican horizons for signs of democracy, one looks at the groups eligible to enter the single official party. Their weights within its councils, and how they influenced deliberations in the actual procedure by which the P.R.I. named its candidates in 1952 are worth noting. After a quick meeting in October 1951 to rubber-stamp Adolfo Ruiz Cortines as its presidential choice, the party deferred decision on other posts until April 1952. State conventions, following local party primaries, were held, to name candidates for the Senate and Chamber. Though in each state convention Agrarian, Labor, and Popular (middle class) sectors were allowed an equal number of delegates, the national official slate of deputies and senators gave approximately 40 per cent of the P.R.I.'s candidacies to each of the Agrarian and Popular sectors, with Labor getting 20 per cent. That is approximately the weight which the Alemán regime has attached to these segments of Mexican life. Many a Mexican suddenly realized his own age, and that of the Revolution, when the P.R.I. in 1952 backed for posts of deputy the *sons* of Venustiano Carranza, Pancho Villa, and Emiliano Zapata.

Elections and Procedures. The Camacho reforms (mentioned before) were important. Almost since Carranza's day the electoral procedure in Mexico had gone fundamentally unchanged. It facilitated machine control by permitting governmental and party manipulation of registration, voting, and tallying; these were done by municipal officials, usually creatures of the state bosses. In 1946 the technical aspect of suffrage—registration and polling—was separated from the political side, which dealt with definitions of parties and individual eligibility to vote. The Camacho reforms set up criteria for parties, as to numbers and distribution of adherents, to foster large, national, and permanent Mexican political groupings that had defined programs. Alemán, building on this foundation, improved the workings of the mechanism by creating a central Commission of Federal Elections. It is formed by representatives of three major parties, Congress, and the Secretary of Interior (Gobernación). Parties have three members, Congress two, the Executive one, tacitly giving P.R.I. four votes, and the opposition parties two. Seldom have issues been settled by that score, each member tending to be independent rather than partisan.

The Commission became responsible for conducting honest elections. Seeing that an honest registration was made, naming poll supervisors and challengers, and local tally teams, made up of multipartisan representatives to assure an honest count, were part of their responsibilities. As before, Congress remains the electoral college, but its duties in this respect have been largely superseded by the Commission. The latter also was empowered to hear disputes and investigate incidents during campaigns, to assure a fair chance that all registered parties could carry on their pre-electoral activities on an equal basis. The party representatives on the Commission assured their own groups that the registration for the 1952 election was as honest as one could obtain. The final number of registered potential voters was 5,123,655. After scrutiny, the C.F.E. issued 4,924,293 voter's credentials. This number was about 90 per cent of the electorate, each of whom received a "one admission" ticket to the polls. The idea of ballots over bullets grows.

Despite its faults, the Camacho electoral law had worked better than most commentators had predicted. As related, the 1946 presidential election that brought Alemán to the presidency and provided him with his first legislature went off with only a few hitches; lack of polls was the most notable shortcoming. In 1949, Mexican voters had a chance to express some opinion of what they thought of the régime to date when congressional seats and senatorial posts for Alemán's second legislature were at stake. The results were a clear sweep for the P.R.I., though a small "protest" vote went to P.A.N. In a routine, peaceful election, opposition parties lost their precarious hold in the Chamber of Deputies, which became exclusively composed of P.R.I. members.

A spokesman for the P.R.I. said that election tabulations showed that "radical theoreticians of the extreme Left lack any popular roots" and that the conservatives of the P.A.N. had on their side "much money but few people." For the common man, the returns were a vote of confidence for Alemán. It remained for the presidential elections of 1952 to clarify and corroborate these mid-passage signs. Under adequate legal safeguards, parties could campaign and the

		Actual votes cast *	Percentages	
			Eligible voters	Ballots cast
			%	%
Partido Revolucionario Institucional	P.R.I.	1,821,781	31.4	89.2
Partido de Acción Nacional	P.A.N.	178,952	3.1	8.9
Partido Popular	P.P.	38,712	0.7	1.9
Sinarquistas, Communists	P.F.P. } P.C.M. }	1,847	0.0	0.0
Totals		2,041,292	35.2	100.0

* Two electoral districts of San Luis Potosí omitted.

electorate could vote with some assurance that such activity was not wholly futile. The presidential elections of July 6, 1952 were a test not only of the Alemán electoral reforms but of democracy itself in Mexico.

4. NEO-ALEMANISMO: ADOLFO RUIZ CORTINES, 1952–1958

Like the pungent smoke from milpa fires heralding spring rains, the haze of *futurismo* began to drift over Alemán's administration in early 1951. A premature effort within the P.R.I. was made by a number of ex-Cárdenas politicians to veer the party to the Left. By booming for its candidate, General Miguel Henríquez Guzmán, a multimillionaire contractor who had unsuccessfully run for president in 1946 and who was reputed to have Lázaro Cárdenas' backing, they believed that he would revive the militancy of the past. President Alemán demonstrated his control over the official apparatus by quashing the boomlet and indicating that an heir-apparent would be named at an appropriate time.

Foiled in their efforts to capture party leadership, the dissidents bolted and began to organize a rival party, Federation of People's Parties (F.P.P.). As the only avowed candidate for president, Henríquez Guzmán stumped Mexico and his followers undertook a violent campaign that by election day had cost them 22 lives. As party registration day, June 30, 1951, neared, other opposition groups mobilized their forces to meet the requirements of the electoral law, which stipulates that each shall have at least 30,000 members, distributed over two-thirds of the republic.

The P.R.I., as the official and permanent party, topped all others in registered strength. Opposition to it was provided by five smaller ones. In addition to the Federation of People's Parties, the Left was represented by a splinter of southern agrarians who took the name "Party of the Revolution" and by the Partido Popular, formed in 1949. It remained a Marxist-dominated aggregation, to which smaller outright Communist parties, each too small to meet registration requirements, pledged their support. Oldest of the opposition, the Party of National Action (P.A.N.), bid for moderately conservative Mexicans in the West and the North. On the Right a new grouping made its appearance: Mexican Nationalist, a purged and purified lineal descendant of the prewar Gold Shirts. Now under direction of "Revolutionary Catholics," the Nationalists hoped to temper even further the reduced anticlericalism of the régime.

Shortly after his fifth "State of the Nation" message to Congress on September 1, President Alemán put an end to much fruitless speculation and political calculations by designating his choice of successor: his Secretary of Interior, Adolfo Ruiz Cortines. Modest, honest, able, and somewhat colorless, he had followed half a pace behind his chief up the ladder of national politics; as a trusted subordinate he could be counted on to carry to completion many programs dear to the administration. In the middle of October a national convention of the P.R.I. by acclamation ratified the president's selection and formally nominated Ruiz Cortines as its presidential standard-bearer; later the party met to fill its slate for senators and deputies. The party and the candidate were pledged to "continuation of President Alemán's work."

Politicking accelerated during the winter and spring of 1952. Ruiz Cortines also became a nominee of the Mexican Nationalist Party. The Partido Popular selected aging Vicente Lombardo Toledano. The Party of the Revolution prevailed upon old General Cándido Aguilar to head its lists; he made it clear that he did not expect to win the presidency and in fact withdrew from the race just before the election, turning his strength over to Henríquez Guzmán. The P.A.N. tapped Efraín González Luna, an able lawyer-banker from Guadalajara, to carry their message of free enterprise. In commenting on the contestants, the Mexican daily *Excelsior* concluded that in a fair election the P.R.I. would win: its candidate was a civilian widely known as an honorable and moderate person who attracted independents; he was not an unpopular "imposition" candidate even though he had support of the official apparatus; and finally, the opposition was too badly split to stop the P.R.I.'s steam roller. An attempt to form an alliance among the parties of the Left came to naught when none would sacrifice its candidates or program.

Campaigns were lively and vigorous, and followed the standard patterns. The opposition attacked the P.R.I. as a corrupt monopoly and charged that Ruiz Cortines had collaborated with Americans during the 1914 occupation of Veracruz; that old canard was quickly disproved. On the positive side, the P.R.I. poured large sums into the organization of regional round-tables as in 1946 and to this useful technique Ruiz Cortines added a new one to build up a governmental "Plan." He had prepared long and detailed questionnaires which he sent with a covering personal letter asking for suggestions from nearly a thousand outstanding figures in all walks of Mexican life. All these data were culled and shaped into an impressive volume, *Plan Ruiz Cortines,* released on the eve of the election; in 23 chapters and 113 subchapters it summarized the attitudes and promises of the candidate and party on 726 main questions of national policy, ranging from natural resources to tourist trade.

Resolved that Mexico would hold a fair and trouble-free election, President Alemán walked the tightrope between allowing absolutely free campaigning and checking violent excesses. As the climax of elections approached, a spate of public statements by prestigious figures, including ex-presidents and the archbishop, reminded the Mexican people of their growing political maturity and outlawed the idea of a post-electoral armed revolt by disappointed office-seekers. Just to make sure, however, on election eve all army leaves were canceled and more than 80,000 troops and police were stationed at strategic spots for Sunday, July 6. Hushed expectancy rather than dangerous tenseness marked these final preliminaries.

Early Sunday morning, long streams of voters lined up in front of some 14,552 polling places, each guarded by seven soldiers. The electorate was expected to choose a president from among four candidates, 58 senators from a field of 206, and 161 deputies from 567 aspirants for seats in the lower house. The elections were an impressive and truly national event, the culmination of an unfoldng process that had touched all reaches of the republic and embraced its many strata. Both the foreign and local press hailed the orderly and peaceful civic display as another and important milestone on Mexico's rocky road to democracy.

"In the quietest election of her modern history," stated *Time,* "Mexico this week chose Adolfo Ruiz Cortines, 59, as President for the next six years." Noting the unprecedented number of ballots, *Newsweek* reported that Mexicans "cast their votes in practically complete peace and quiet. . . . The size and orderliness of the poll is all to the good." Official results of the Presidential election were given to the public by the Chamber of Deputies sitting as the electoral college. On September 12 they announced that Adolfo Ruiz Cortines had a clear majority of the 3,651,483 ballots cast and therefore would be president of Mexico from December 1, 1952 to November 30, 1958. By candidates and parties the total voting appears in the following table.

SUMMARY OF VOTING, PRESIDENTIAL ELECTION, July 6, 1952

Candidate	Party	Popular Vote	Per Cent
Adolfo Ruiz Cortines	P.R.I.	2,713,419	74.3
Miguel Henríquez Guzmán	F.P.P.	579,745	15.8
Efraín González Luna	P.A.N.	285,555	7.9
Vicente Lombardo Toledano	P.P.	72,482	2.0
Unregistered candidates	———	282	0.0
Totals		3,651,483	100.0

As in 1946, elections to the national legislature gave the "official" P.R.I. a dominant position but provided a token opposition in the Chamber. All 58 Senators, after argument over two, were seated for the P.R.I., a clean sweep. At the opening of Congress on September 1 the election committees, called into meeting earlier, had determined that 149 out of 161 places in the lower house were undisputed; the P.R.I. had 139, raised to 146 when their candidates won 7 of the 12 questionable posts. Together the "non-official" new Deputies numbered 7, one of them from the F.P.P. and two each from Acción Nacional, Nacionalistas, and the Partido Popular.*

It seems clear that political patterns foreshadowed in 1946, and strengthened in 1949, were apparent again in 1952. For the outside world, Mexico had passed this test of its democracy with fair to good marks; when a loyal opposition grows even larger, its skepticism may

* The five remaining disputed places would be decided in December.

shrink even further about full-scale democracy emerging from the chrysalis of the Revolution.

Partisan feelings aroused during the campaigns quickly evaporated as the nation, united as never before, looked forward with pleasurable anticipation to the Ruiz Cortines administration, scheduled to begin December 1, 1952. He comes to the post with an enviable reputation for self-effacement, hard work, and guaranteed results by competent staff-work. Though he has stood constantly in the shadow of Alemán for nearly two decades, it is improbable that president-elect Ruiz Cortines will be a puppet. Another characteristic is his intellectual and personal integrity. With the major lines of Mexico's continuing advancement sketched out by his immediate predecessors, Ruiz Cortines' main task, for which he is well equipped, is to improve further the intricate mechanisms of the "Institutional Revolution" that is already fulfilling so many historic aspirations and promises. Under him, Mexico is more than likely to remain a good friend and partner of the United States and the free world.

16. The Economic Revolution

"The interior panorama of the Republic," President Alemán reported to Congress and Mexico's first television audience, "is one of work and tranquillity. The Administration will reinforce its efforts to carry forward its programs of raising the standards of living of the people, and of developing the collective welfare. . . . We enjoy political independence to direct the destinies of our country and the social conquests that continue the improvement of our people. It has been necessary, though, to add accelerating forces to fortify our economic independence."

As the 58th president to occupy the chief executive's post in modern Mexico, President Alemán thus spoke for himself, his government, and the Institutionalized Revolution when he delivered this annual message to his Congress on September 1, 1950. The importance of this required "State of the Nation" address went beyond the fact that it officially launched television in Latin America and brought his person into numerous Mexican homes and public places; that alone symbolized the innumerable and great changes that have been occurring in the postwar years.

By almost any yardstick that economists can apply, Mexico is better off in mid-twentieth century than at any other point in its long history. The imposing arrays of figures now pouring forth strengthen the inescapable conclusion that an economic revolution of major magnitude has been taking place for a decade and still is in full motion. Only the barest profile of this newest phase of an old Revolution can be sketched. The salient fact is that the upward sweep of production curves, graphs of increased participation, carloadings, and all the other paraphernalia entailed in economic analysis add up to a slowly rising standard of living for the Mexican nation which even inflation and its own increasing numbers have not reversed. Mexicans, as well as Mexico, have benefited materially. With material improvement have come cultural and social gains to the individual and the nation.

1. PROFILES

In its rejection of the Porfirian system, the Revolution shifted the responsibility for the economic as well as the social welfare of the Mexican people to the government, where it has remained and broadened. The economic policies and decisions have taken on political and social overtones. Many practices and operations that, strictly defined, are "un-economic" must be carried forward through official economic action. A nation is more than just an abstract economic system: it is composed of people, whose conflicting hopes and desires can be expressed by votes, and in Mexico, by guns. Social, political, and economic objectives become intertwined, and unless the government takes active steps to increase the well-being of all groups, militancy can rise to a dangerously high pitch. The old Revolution underlies the new.

The chief difficulty facing the Mexican government is that Mexico is not a single economic unit. The varying pressures from its many segments demand antithetical policies. All modern governments face much the same problem, but in Mexico it is more acute because the historical processes earlier described have left atomistic pieces of one and another economic system behind. More than half the nation, the "transitional" social group and the Indians described in the opening pages of this volume, lie outside a money economy; with few wants, little purchasing power, parochial outlook, and limited opportunities, they have played a small role in economic affairs and have had negligible influence on national economic policies. They want expensive benefits, now. They have numbers, slogans, and latent power to make these desires felt in political spheres.

The "modern" sector is in some ways as divided as the dwellers in the *patrias chicas*. Still a mainstay of economic activity in Mexico are "semi-colonial" extractive activities such as mining, whose major traditions date back to Hapsburg times; under Díaz, ownership and direction passed to foreigners, where they remained. Closely connected with this "old" part have been large plantation owners, some of the industrialists auxiliary to mining, large merchants, and the private banking systems of Mexico. Much that the Revolution stands for they reject by appeals to "free enterprise"; these arguments carried more weight before 1910. Since a little more than a third of the national government's revenues derive from this segment, their attitudes cannot always be lightly brushed aside, even though politically and economically speaking they seem to be anachronisms in the Revolutionary climate.

The Revolution itself has spawned other segments of the modern economic unit. In the golden days of the 1920's (under the Northern Oligarchy), a new group of Mexican industrialists came into being; apart from asking for cheap national credit and docile labor, they took on many laissez-faire characteristics of the Porfirian concerns. They preferred to produce for a fairly small, static urban Mexican market. Aligned with them, often as copartners, have been a wide range of "filial" businesses, subsidiaries or branches of foreign concerns that have made numerous types of arrangements to market their products in Mexico. Control, and often financing, technology, and management, have come from abroad. Recently these "filial" concerns have increased in number and have begun to stress production of consumer goods for a widening Mexican market; they assemble Ford cars, bottle Coca-Cola and Canada Dry, and the like.

World War II brought into being the "Newest Group" of industrialists. This group opposes the political and economic concepts on which nearly all others work and has a great deal of emotional backing in Mexico. The "Newest Group" in general is collectively made up of the small, nationalistic manufacturers who stepped in to fill the vacuum left by almost complete cessation of Mexican imports of consumer goods when, after Pearl Harbor, sources of supply dried up in the United States. Most of them furnished their own capital; unlike the "old" group, which often depended completely on foreign private money, or the "new," which often sopped up Mexican savings formerly buried in landholdings, the "Newest Group" relied on themselves for initial sums and technical direction.

Active, aggressive, young, and very Mexican, they have had a different outlook from either of their industrial colleagues. They are primarily concerned with manufacturing consumer goods; many of them look toward Mexican autarchy: the day when Mexico will even manufacture its own machine tools and all the other items needed for a true and matured industrial system. They are convinced that "Mexico for the Mexicans" means a complete shutting out of foreign competition and a lack of concern with export of raw materials; it also means that the "transitional" economy must be wiped out through upgrading all Mexicans into the "modern" sector by providing them with modern techniques, new wants, and purchasing power. As the Centralists of old, the "Newest Group" view Mexico as a single unit; they want economic "Hands Off" notices posted all around this private preserve, the market for their new enterprises. They have endowed all the classical "infant industries" arguments with a Mexican-Spanish accent by demands for high tariffs, import licensing to cut down "unfair competition" by filial foreign concerns, and pressures to have the raw materials shipped abroad by the "old" sector kept at home to feed their swaddling industries. Though they expect the government to intervene in social matters to provide markets and the means by which they can be reached, they too deplore direct government intervention in their own affairs.

To make matters even more complex, the national government is the most important economic institution in the system, both by heritage and through its day-to-day operations as banker, employer, and consumer. The government controls the largest fonts of credit by direct means or by owning majority shares in a network of semi-public fiscal institutions, such as the Banco de Mexico, Social Security Institute, and a festoon of special ones set up to handle import-export trade, credit to small private agriculturalists, and to the *ejidos*. Through semiautonomous agencies already discussed, the government operates the petroleum monopoly and the equally exclusive railway monopoly. It owns military industries that tie it into the rest of the systems. For its vast and growing public works and social projects the national government is an enormous consumer of goods and labor. Its infinitely ramified bureaucracies furnish a significant share of the middle-class incomes. Its almost absolute power over money supply, subsidies, exemptions from taxes, labor legislation, and a swatch of other economic items makes it the single most important economic element in Mexico.

Mexico is thus a mixture of "colonial," "semi-colonial," and "modern" economic sectors. As in the social and geographical sense, in the economic area there are also "many Mexicos."

These several developments and traditions have endowed contemporary Mexico with a peculiar economic system. Neither "Socialistic" nor "free enterprise" it is one that, with constitutional sanction and Revolutionary cachet, guides and acts in selected circumstances and sectors. The government takes leadership as an economic entrepreneur and trustee for the whole, marks out certain spheres for its exclusive control, and exercises indirect favorable or unfavorable pressures on others to make them conform to the national economic policy. Yet it leaves wide open other segments to be filled in and operated autonomously by private capitalism in the historic mode.

In general, the Mexican system comes nearest to what Europeans call a "directed economy." But unlike most such directed economies, the Mexican one does not have a basic plan on which it is working or detailed specifications for the future. The result has been that national economic policies change in accordance with the rise and fall of domestic and international political and economic circumstances. Tugs of war are constantly going on within the country and administration to veer the course one way or another. In general this is perhaps the only possible course, in view of Mexico's past. The disadvantages of this "economic democracy" that reflects changing situations are perhaps less perilous than a fixed "plan" based on needs of the moment and projected infinitely into a yet unpredictable future.

The economic panorama in 1950 was as confused and full of ideological crosscurrents as the political one was in 1810. A main difference, however, is that at mid-twentieth century Mexicans have some achievements on which to base their generally optimistic views. A 1950 report of the government's main development corporation, Nacional Financiera, sketched an inclusive view that even since then has improved. National income in 1950 had risen to a nominal 29,800 million pesos, and when inflation was discounted this marked a real 6.5 per cent advance over 1949. Industrialization was expanding and bringing concrete results as production, quality, and productivity crept upward. Nacional Financiera reported that the 4604 tractors of 1940 had swelled to 30,800 in 1950, and farm units now included cultivators, seeders, and other aids to mechanized agriculture almost unknown a decade ago. Petroleum production for 1950 had risen to better than 72 million barrels, and electrical energy output had placed high in Latin America; production and use of electricity had multiplied since 1946. In the decade from 1940 to 1950, national roads had lengthened from 9000 to 22,000 kilometers, many of them strategic market arteries.

Because it is primarily a fiscal institution, Nacional Financiera stressed advances in that realm. It noted that savings accounts had risen in ten years from 35 to 450 million pesos, while savings in the form of life insurance had developed equally. Face values rose from 47 to 365 millions, with a collateral ascent of paid-in amounts from 27 to 134 million pesos since 1940. Calculating all Mexican savings in 1940 as 100, the index stood at 480 in 1950. Monetary circulation swelled from 1.0 billion to 6.2 billions, from 17.2 per cent to 20.5 per cent of national income, but by 1950, unlike a decade earlier, much of it was in the form of checks. Sight deposits in 1940 were 419 million pesos, but in 1950 they were 3360 million. Savings and liquid assets were being put to use, as the private banking network ramified and grew from 1940. Credit transactions in that year were 478 million pesos, while in 1950 they totaled 5.2 billion; their investments climbed from 495 million pesos to 4.65 billion, while the loans and investments of insurance companies accompanied them by increasing from 95 million in 1940 to 507 million in 1949.

The figures for 1951, drawn from the annual report of the semi-official Banco de Mexico, indicated that 1950 was a normal rather than a special year, since trends already evident had continued. The national product, almost the same as national income, during 1951, had grown 20 per cent over 1950, to a total of 45,500 million pesos. Private banking credit was increased 27 per cent, but as part of a battery of anti-inflationary controls the national money supply had remained almost static. Again there was a rise of real (as opposed to monetary) national income of 6.2 per cent over 1950. Following a "pay-as-we-go" policy on improvements and additions to capital equipment, the government had collected a whopping 4.3 billion pesos in taxes and had ended up not only with a balanced budget, but with a 337 million pesos surplus, 327 million of which was used to retire old debts; a surplus in 1950 of 178 million had similarly redeemed interior bonds and had aided a refinancing of the debt from 6 per cent to 5 per cent. Fiscally, the ship of state and the nation seemed on as even a keel as in Limantour's heydey, but without many of the burdens that the Díaz regime had been forced to take aboard as very dubious cargo.

Like most of the world, Mexico's financial situation has been disturbed by the undertows and waves of inflation. To that has been added technically important but hard-to-explain pressures arising from devaluations of the peso, and the more readily visible difficulties of a rising population. The query naturally and inevitably arises as to what the manifest advances have meant to the individual Mexican and his family, and whether his income is more or less than before this new economic revolution began to move toward a crest. The answers cannot be clear-cut, for lack of proper data and space to array those available, but in very general terms, it can be said that individual incomes, in real terms, have risen, and that the mass of Mexicans have been helped. In short, when allowances and deductions are made for all adverse factors, the nation has advanced.

Samples must suffice to illustrate rather than prove this view. Domestic consumption of foodstuffs was 70 per cent greater in 1950 than in 1939, Cárdenas' day, and the *per capita* index of foodstuff consumption stood at 130 in 1950 (1939 = 100). Mexican economists state that real *per capita* income has risen over 1939 (which many take as a base year). In 1946 it stood at 147 per cent of 1939. It had risen to 161 per cent by 1950.

Independently, the matter can be put in even more precise terms, though minor discrepancies emerge from the often whimsical nature of Mexican statistics. In money terms, total Mexican income jumped from 6.0 billion pesos in 1939 to 30.0 in 1950 and about 36.0 in 1951, a 500–600 per cent boost; devaluations and inflation has made the real increase less startling, from 6.0 to 10.0 billion pesos in 1951. The enlarged sums, however, must be parceled out among more Mexicans, as population has grown, and with it, the working force. In money terms, the individual or *per capita* income was around 316 pesos in 1940, but a decade later it amounted to 1181; real *per capita* shares moved from 309 pesos a year to 363.

Much the same picture appears when an even more significant item is calculated, the *per capita* income of the working force. In real terms it rose from 1040 to 1250 pesos a year in the decade after 1940. In brief, *all* the gains made in the financial field were not eroded away by adverse factors, though the real advance is somewhat less spectacular than a first glance at comparative figures might show. As a whole, Mexico and Mexicans were being better fed and had more material benefits than in any previous economic Golden Age. Yet Utopia was not at hand.

Incomes still show great variation, more or less in accordance with the social and cultural groupings outlined earlier. Figures for 1950 showed that 1.4 per cent of the Mexican economically active population had money incomes of over 1000 pesos a month; 14 per cent ranged between 301 and 1000 pesos, while the rest fell below the 300 peso a month mark. The single largest body, 44 per cent had incomes of from 101 to 300 pesos a month, while nearly an equal group, 40 per cent, had cash earnings of less than 100 pesos monthly. The latter could, with some probability of accuracy, be equated to the nonmonetary segment of the Mexican economy, politically powerful but economically negligible at the moment. One of the hopes of Mexican policy-makers is that this segment can be gradually drawn into the economic circle and thus provide an ever-expanding market for national production.

The forces transforming the Mexican economy have not played evenly over social classes. In comparable fashion, they have affected various sectors of the total economy in diverse ways. "Semicolonial" parts have lost ground to the "modern." Mexicans consider this part of a "de-colonization" process basic to the Revolution —to reduce the hold of foreign-owned extractive enterprises on the economy in favor of complex, nationally controlled processing. The merits of the view are controversial, but the fact remains that changes have taken place.

In 1929 extractive activities like mining and petroleum production, almost exclusively owned by foreigners and geared to markets outside the Republic, accounted for better than a third of the national income. By 1949 these mainstays of the "semi-colonial" segment had dropped to 9 per cent, though their volume and value had risen markedly since the days of Dwight Morrow and Calles. In 1929, agriculture and pastoral items provided more than a quarter of the national income; it was 16 per cent in 1949. In contrast, at the height of the golden twenties, manufacturing in 1929 contributed 12 per cent, but in 1949 this had more than doubled to 28 per cent. The remaining percentages involve exchange of services not materially affected by the trends.

To particularize these shifts, a Mexican investigator made elaborate calculations to compare the national product of 1925 with that of 1947. His results seem self-explanatory, and reinforce the conclusions one can draw from trade patterns, discussed later.

Subject to minor qualifications, it can be said in summary that Mexico has followed the upward economic surge that has characterized the United States since the end of World War II. Locally the Mexican government has continued to foster a guided or directed economy. In it a keynote is official intervention to develop and spur needed activities, while leaving large sectors open to private enterprise. Various combinations of private, semiofficial, and official efforts have merged to bring forth generally favorable results in

RELATIVE CONTRIBUTIONS TO NATIONAL PRODUCT, 1925 VS. 1947
(Millions of pesos)

Economic Activity	1925 Amount	1925 Per Cent	1947 Amount	1947 Per Cent
Agricultural	427	24.0	2,651	18.9
Mineral-Metallurgic	295	16.6	1,145	8.2
Petroleum production	367	20.7	809	5.8
Electric energy	49	2.8	220	1.5
Manufacturing	634	35.4	9,187	65.6
Totals	1,772	100.0	14,012	100.0

Source: Emilio Alanis Patiño, "Las tierras del riego," *Problemas Agrícolas e Industriales de México* II (No. 2, Apr.–June, 1950, Notas), 161. He has recalculated all values in terms of a mythical "gold peso," to equate 1925 with current (1947) purchasing power.

nearly every economic sphere. The incipient wartime industrial endeavor has become a permanent part of modern Mexico, after the first uncritical enthusiasms and adverse criticisms and predictions of failure had passed. Industrialism turned out to be neither the panacea nor the diabolical development that polemics of five years ago proclaimed. It remains a new, permanent, and complex phenomenon with which Mexicans have settled down to live. The most important fact of all, however, is that many more Mexicans are living better than before as benefits percolate directly or indirectly through the evolving system.

2. GOVERNMENT AND ECONOMY

In the welter of currents and crosscurrents generated by an economic boom, the Alemán administration has selected certain principles and institutions as the foundations of its economic programs. They can be briefly summarized.

Diversity and increase of economic activity are goals. That diversity now means ultimately providing the nation with a full-blown, self-contained industrial system of its own. It will include research, manufacturing, transportation, distribution, heavy industry, light industry, and feeders of raw materials to them. It also means providing Mexican industry with its essential local markets by uplifting the economically and socially depressed millions in rural Mexico and in city slums.

It has meant retaining wartime Mexican export markets by devaluation, barter deals in Europe and other parts of Latin America. It includes inventorying and analyzing markets and resources—often by contract to foreign experts like Higgins Industries, the Armour Research Foundation, Ford Bacon & Davis, Inc.—and eager collaboration on techniques with large private Foundations in the United States.

Above all, it has meant maintaining flexible policies which adopt suggestions from any or all the various economic segments, but which reserves the right to widen them from narrow advantage to national benefit. Tariffs are kept high, but yet low enough on some items to encourage imports. The policy prevents local producers from forming cartel-like monopolies, which, with the coöperation of complacent labor, gouge the Mexican public. Import controls and export licenses are rigid in neither number nor terms. They vary with circumstance. Now that Mexico is brimming with dollar reserves from unexpectedly high metal prices, tax receipts from booming manufacturing concerns, and tourist pockets, many of them have been removed entirely; inflow of goods checks inflation.

The government must guard constantly against the threats which inflation poses. A main bulwark against runaway credit expansions is the "pay as we go" policy in regard to the vast public works programs. No major bond issues have been floated for some years; the expanding economy has provided funds for capital improvement from public revenue. The budgets have soared to record heights, and now annually exceed 3 billion pesos. Since 1947 they have been balanced, with respectable surpluses. In the main these have been applied to reduction of old obligations, with the result that from 1946 to 1951 Mexico's public debt was lowered by a total of 4.2 billion pesos, and in June 1952 hovered around 3.3 billions. When they do appear, bonds authorized for special, limited purposes sell at or above par. In line with its policy of restricting money and credit, few new fiat sums are thus pumped into the bloated economy.

National Policy and National Budget. The allocation of sums within the budget indicates the cash value which the administration places on various Revolutionary dogmas. About 43 per cent of public income in 1951 went for irreducible fixed charges and administrative expenses. Nearly a quarter (23.9 per cent) must be

19.

spent for keeping up payments on principal and int
lic debt and international settlements. Nonprodu
tive expenditures have been cut from 238 million ~~~~~ (o.7 per
cent) in 1950 to a modest 194.2 million (6.5 per cent) in 1951.

More than half the national revenues of 1951 poured back into
the country in developmental and social expenditures. For Roads
and Railroads, the Ministry of Communications received the largest
sum, 537.9 million pesos; next came Education, with 355.7 million,
followed by Hydraulic Resources with 326 million; the Army received 275 million. It should be remembered that the allocations from
the national budget are in addition to special bond issues and foreign
loans negotiated for economic and social improvement, and distinct
from moneys loaned or given toward the same ends by the semi-
official Banco de Mexico and Nacional Financiera.

Nacional Financiera. The chief link between the government, its
various bureaus, the investing public, foreign economic interests,
and entrepreneurs, is Nacional Financiera. Its policies and operations are the main "guide" to the "guided" or "directed" new Mexican economy. It is the sole authorized government agent to negotiate foreign loans. In addition to its own management, it has its own
funds, from the sale of capital stock (in which the government owns
51 per cent), returns on stock shares in companies it owns or or-
ganizes, trust certificates, and a number of other fiscal devices to
mobilize and underwrite both risk and development capital.

N.F.'s chief job as a development corporation is to round out the
Mexican industrial economy by fostering, as it sees fit, any legitimate
enterprise which will benefit the whole, with special stress on certain critically needed elements. When Mexico was importing sugar,
it was up to N.F. to finance sugar industries; glass, paper, and a
whole range of consumer items attracted its interest when Mexico
was short of them and of dollars; now that Mexico is better stocked
with both, N.F. has almost exclusively turned to basic items which
are bottlenecks in the basic economy—chemicals, coke works, steel
specialty plants, fishing industries. Its interests are as broad as the
Mexican economy. Appendix I, Table 28, gives details on its operations to 1949. They have increased since then.

Highly flexible and variable are its methods. It may take over
a feeble concern, and by refinancing and expanding it, make it pay.
It may start a whole new concern by bringing together foreign capital, technical patents, and Mexican enterprisers. A favorite approach

ıs to form these "mixed" companies in which foreign private capital, Mexican private capital, and the government (through N.F.) jointly coöperate.

From the ideological point of view, N.F. is committed to "free enterprise." When an N.F.-sponsored concern has been launched and is over the first shoals, N.F. divests itself of its holdings by selling the stock, exchanging it for bonds, or arranging for private third parties to acquire interests in the business.

Though initially created under Cárdenas, Nacional Financiera began to edge toward greater importance during and just after World War II. As an expediter, it was charged with creating or obtaining consumer goods then in extremely short supply, which it did by contributing to the organization and financing of about 172 industrial enterprises. By the end of 1947 it had a hand in 21 iron and steel works, 18 sugar-processing outfits, 14 textile mills, and a long list of lesser companies.

With a change of administration and altered Mexican needs, President Alemán in 1947 strengthened, enlarged, and placed Nacional Financiera in the front row of an allied group of developmental and credit organizations. Its emphasis shifted from sponsorship of light industrial activities to longer-term developmental works and the creation of "key" pieces needed to integrate the burgeoning Mexican industrial plant. In 1946 N.F. had outstanding some 374 million pesos in loans and investments; in 1949 the sum was 968 millions, and in 1950 and again in 1951 the total topped a billion pesos. In the past two years (1950–1951), the preponderant sums poured into transportation and communication, with important grants to electrical generating plants and coal-producers, while fertilizers, iron and steel goods, sugar, and paper producers continued to get important grants. In 1950, 75 million pesos went to purchase agricultural machinery, and N.F. announced that 365 million pesos had fed into key pieces. For 1951, 390 millions went into communication and transport alone, and with housing shortages looming, 150 millions into building material industries. In its nearly eighteen years of handling large sums, no breath of scandal has touched Nacional Financiera, a record of which it is justifiably proud.

Because of its central position as the active agent of an enterprising government, Nacional Financiera has strong influence on economic policy, and acts as a "watchdog" and planning agency to keep various sectors moving harmoniously. It derives much of its

power from the fact that it is the exclusive agency for 1.
foreign loans that bring to Mexico the needed capital for ba.
provements. In this highly competitive field its record for secu. ,
and repaying such grants-in-aid is almost unsurpassed.

3. CAPITAL AND CONTROL

International Loans. A chief vote of confidence in Mexico comes
from inflowing dollars, especially international loans. These are
chiefly parceled out by the United States Export-Import Bank and
the "World Bank"—International Bank for Reconstruction and Development—in which the United States is the principal shareholder.
The sums these institutions authorize are lines of credit to American
suppliers of capital equipment, technical services, and the like. They
must be matched by the petitioning government, which guarantees
to put up as much local money for relieving basic economic needs
as comes from abroad. With overabundant pleas from nearly every
country on the globe, both institutions are justifiably insistent about
scrutinizing the purposes of the loan and the chances of its repayment before making a grant.

International loan statistics are not in absolute accord, but they
are congruent enough to present the essential broad outline. From
December 31, 1940 to January 1, 1951, Mexico, through Nacional
Financiera, had successfully borrowed about $391 million. The
World Bank furnished $50 million, private banks in the United
States $10.5 million; the remainder came from the Import-Export
Bank. To the end of 1950, $159 million of this had been spent, leav-
ing an unexpended balance, yet to be drawn on, of $232 million;
Mexico has repaid $59 million and its current payments on princi-
pal and interest are up to date. With the exception of Brazil, which
has received slightly more from the Export-Import Bank ($345.5
million to Mexico's $308.9), none of the Latin-American countries
has a better record for borrowing and repaying than Mexico. At the
close of June 1952. Import-Export Bank figures indicated that it had
outstanding some $67 million in loans to Mexico, with yet $127 million more authorized but undisbursed.

Three matters should be stressed in connection with these important transactions. These loans are not handouts; they represent
advance payment to American business concerns which the international banks pay and then retrieve on the installment plan from

borrowing governments. Secondly, they are noninflationary for the countries receiving them: solid items like railway cars, bulldozers, and coke-ovens enter the "underdeveloped" area, and thus, because they have to be paid for immediately out of tax revenues, are deflationary—money goes abroad. Thirdly, and most important, such loans are for critical items which, when slipped into place, allow the going economic system to mushroom.

An outstanding example of this process in Mexico is the rehabilitation of the railway net and its extension. Nacional Financiera, the Export-Import Bank, and the autonomous but semiofficial Mexican Railways Administration joined forces to relieve one of the most critical bottlenecks of Mexico's postwar era. The Bank furnished much of the money, while the Mexican government and its agencies furnished the plans and forcefulness to carry them out.

Rehabilitation and extension have gone forward together. New lines have connected Yucatan and the Southwest to main centers of the Core, while in like fashion the Peninsula of Southern California has been put into rail contact with the centers of the North; for the first time in Mexican history one extremity of the land has been linked to the other by these steel bands of union. Equally important, trunk lines have been strengthened by replacing light rails (90-lb.) with heavier track, and the gauges have been standardized. To January 1951 Alemán's regime had thus placed nearly 200,000 tons of rails in place, three times as much as had been laid in the previous twenty-five years. The National Railways has on hand another 250,000 tons to complete the job. In much the same fashion, antiquated and obsolete equipment has been repaired and replaced by purchases from Japan, Europe, and the United States; to relieve Mexico of a dollar drain for freight-car rentals and purchases, a car-building plant (of German design) that will produce 1000 units annually is being constructed by the joint efforts of the National Railways and Nacional Financiera. During 1951 Mexico purchased 70 new Diesel units, 1600 freight cars, and 32 luxury trains for its all-important tourist runs. In June 1952 reports said that France was to swap Diesel equipment for Mexican cotton and that Western Germany had sold Mexico another 38 million pesos' worth of Diesel cars and railroad maintenance machinery.

These improvements are paid for from revenues derived from passengers, freight, international loans, and various deals. Recently the National Railways sold a number of its high value urban holdings on which various Mexico City stations and terminals were placed, and from the profits the corporation is building a modern centralized freight and passenger terminal to speed handling of goods and people. By the end of 1952, President Alemán and his officials will have invested a little over a billion pesos in railroad rehabilitation; half of this comes from Mexican sources, the other half from international loans. Total trackage will have been raised to around 15,000 miles. Both for peace and war, the rail net is in much sounder shape than Stevens found it in 1943. Moreover, in 1952 the rail system became exclusively Mexican, after the purchases of the Mexican Southern Pacific and the Northwestern of Mexico by the government completed the removal from foreign hands of all major lines.

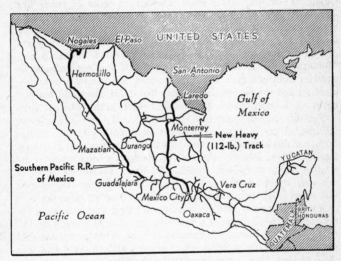

THE MODERN RAILWAY NET
(Courtesy of *Business Week*)

Capital Generation in "Underdeveloped" Mexico. The honest and determined efforts made during the 1940's to reëstablish Mexico's private and public credit and to attack basic problems in a technical rather than a political way, are paying off. The international loans have given the initial impetus to development and improvement programs, which in turn have multiplied domestic and foreign confidence. Mexican sources have, through a variety of channels, underwritten and paid for about 70 per cent of the industrialization and improvement activities since 1940; foreign sources have accounted for less than a third. Few Mexicans realize that, but it is true.

Large sums have been brought back from Mexican hoards abroad. In 1941 Mexicans held $37 million worth of private and government securities in the United States; from January 1943 to September 1948 the amount had grown by another $18.4 million. But now the outward flow of Mexican capital has been reversed; it is repatriated. In addition, the Mexican investing public, large and small, have begun to snap up national government bonds. Recently Alemán's administration issued (for small investors) a series of bonds like United States Defense or War Bonds; these Mexican counterparts double their value in ten years. Even tourists go home with a few of them. More important, the stock certificates of Nacional Financiera and the bonds of the Banco de Mexico find an eager Mexican public. Mobilization of local capital has permitted the semiautonomous agencies to extend their various operations, and has by accomplishment refuted the foreign declarations that Mexicans would not and could not underwrite their government's efforts in the economic field.

Nothing succeeds quite like success. With Mexican industrialism returning 8 per cent to 20 per cent on capital, with low income taxes, a stable and friendly (though watchful) government in charge, foreigners have followed the lead of Mexican private investors by sending flights of dollars, pounds, and francs to Mexico. Some of this was "fright" capital as well as the normal "flight" money that will travel half way around the world to pick up an extra per cent of interest. To many, Mexico seemed safer than France or even the tax-hungry United States as a haven for their hoards. Other sums entered to buy up pesos on a speculative basis, lured by rumors that the peso was going to be revalued upward against the dollar. For these reasons, Mexico was inundated with dollars during 1950. The government estimated in 1951 that as of December 1950 there was approximately $100 millions of speculative capital in Mexico sitting out the cold war and hot Korean crisis.

Foreign Investment Stakes. Information on working dollars rather than these parasitic hoards is rather elusive and unsatisfactory. The general picture is fairly clear. All told there is somewhere between half a billion and a billion dollars' worth of foreign-held stakes in the Mexican economic system. Great Britain has left around $100 million of these, and Canada some $27 million, chiefly in utilities. The remainder is United States' private investment. In 1950 the Banco de Mexico said the total of all foreign holdings was $430 million, divided up as the accompanying little table indicates; but Ambassador Walter Thurston recently told Edgar Snow (for publication in the May 12, 1951 *Saturday Evening Post*) that the present total United States investments were around $800 million.

DIRECT FOREIGN INVESTMENTS IN MEXICO, 1948

	Millions of Dollars	Per Cent
Mining and smelting	103.2	24.1
Public utilities	93.0	21.6
Transport and communication	77.8	18.1
Commerce	43.4	10.0
Manufacturing	90.9	21.1
Not listed	21.7	5.1
Totals	430.0	100.0

Source: Banco de Mexico, in *Noticias*, VI, No. 51 (Dec. 19, 1950), p. 4.

Some trends in these foreign investments are worth noting. One is the gradual shrinkage of directly owned United States enterprises from a high in 1929 to a low in 1943. There has been a slow replacement since then; in 1947 the United States Department of Commerce estimated that direct holdings amounted to some $325 million. With the drop in total stake, the size and importance of the companies have also decreased. In 1943 their average worth was about $420,000 each, held by some 424 owners, who represented 684 different concerns. Since these various tabulations were published, the direct holdings of Americans in Mexico have been further reduced through purchases by the Mexican government; it has bought the little remaining stake in petroleum, and in 1951 similarly added to the National Railways of Mexico the one major United States-held line, the Southern Pacific, for about $20 million.

With the decline of direct investments has gone a shift in the categories in which such dollars lodge. The accompanying tabulation indicates the impact of Revolutionary attempts to decolonize Mexico and the gradual movement from "old" sectors into manufac-

UNITED STATES DIRECT INVESTMENTS IN MEXICO, 1914–1943

| | *Millions of Dollars* | | | | *Percentages* | | | |
	1914	*1929*	*1940*	*1943*	*1914*	*1929*	*1940*	*1943*
Mining and smelting	302	230	168	108	51.4	33.7	46.9	37.6
Utilities and transport	144	164	116	106	24.6	24.0	32.5	36.0
Trade	4	9	7	22	0.6	1.3	1.9	7.8
Petroleum	85	206	42	5	14.4	30.2	11.7	1.7
Agriculture	37	59	10	14	6.3	8.6	2.8	4.8
Others (mixed companies)	5	9	5	12	0.9	1.3	1.4	4.2
Manufacturing	10	6	10	22	1.8	0.9	2.8	7.8
Totals	587	683	358	287	100.0	100.0	100.0	100.0

Source: Committee on Interstate and Foreign Commerce, "Fuel Investigation: Mexican Petroleum," H.R. 2470, 80th Cong. 2nd Sess. (Washington: GPO, 1949), p. 82. Percentages by H. F. C.

turing by American investors and entrepreneurs. It can be noted that between 1940 and 1943 holdings in these more than doubled.

Of even greater political and psychological significance has been the recent tendency for the working dollars to seek indirect investment. That means that instead of holding companies outright, dollars have purchased stock, bonds, or other commercial paper issued by Mexican concerns, or have entered into "mixed" companies in which Mexican capital and American money or other investment are joined to form a Mexican-controlled business. Figures on the ratios of direct to indirect investments are not available, but from scattered reports it seems evident that perhaps two-thirds of American capital investments in Mexico are these indirect ones. In 1946, for instance, the dividends coming into the United States from Mexico were about evenly split between those derived from direct and indirect holdings ($21 million each), while in 1947 the latter had almost doubled, and the direct had stayed about the same. Since that time public news of American-financed enterprises reflects indirect holdings. In these a well-known American manufacturer sets up a Mexican assembly plant or filial subsidiary to produce for the Mexican market, and usually management and part of the ownership is Mexican.

The picture of foreign holdings indicates that the renewed cries of "foreign economic imperialism" are largely a domestic bogy, trotted out on the appropriate political occasions. Mexicans themselves have set the pace for industrialization, own most of the enterprises, and have a large share of control in the remainder. It also indicates, however, that the American business community has given a large vote of confidence in the future of Mexico by sending its money and men there in increasing quantities.

Foreigners, their skills, their money, and their trade and coöperation, are welcome to participate in the Mexican boom so long as they understand that Mexicans are making the rules. Many outsiders are still eager to become pioneers, despite the red tape, corruption, and minor personal irritants. They seem a small price to pay for the extraordinary personal satisfactions and profits obtainable in developing and tapping an increasingly important new market. As modernism and industrialism spread, new Mexican wants are suddenly uncovered. For instance, though the Mexican chemical industry is now well past the swaddling stage, Mexico bought more chemicals—those it cannot make—from the United States in 1950 than any country in the hemisphere except Canada, also industrializing. In 1939 Mexico purchased $7.7 million; in 1950, $60.8. In creating a market for their own output, Mexicans are automatically enlarging one for foreign traders, too.

Dollars from various sources threatened to swamp the Mexican economy. The United States Federal Reserve reported that at the end of 1950 Mexico had a total of $415 million in gold and dollars. As part of the machinery to keep inflation in check, the Mexican Treasury in January 1951 "sterilized" excess foreign money by having it drained off from private banks and impounded to keep it out of circulation and as a basis for more credit. At the same time interest rates on national bonds were lowered and other devices were used to slow the influx. Mexican reserves dropped at the end of 1951 to around $366 million, $208 million of which was held as monetary gold. Purchases of foreign holdings, oil and rail, plus heavy imports of expensive machinery and the deliberate ousting of speculative dollars waiting to gobble up a cheapened peso, brought cash reserves in July 1952 to around $170 million.

After the flurry, President Alemán reported to Congress on September 1, 1952 that national reserves were the same as the previous September and that in the face of extraordinary pressures "the peso has demonstrated its constant firmness." Once again worries centered around too many rather than too few dollars in Mexico as 1952 drew to a close. Mexico could also draw on $22 million in the International Monetary Fund; by treaty with the United States, Mexico had an additional $50 million of unused credits to stabilize the peso if it had begun to waver from the ratio of 8.65 pesos to 1 dollar set by international treaty. The present guardians of the Revolution have revealed themselves as canny and prudent householders, firm builders of the new "Middle Way."

4. INTERNATIONAL PATTERNS

Though foreign trade and balances of payment are complicated and often hopelessly dull topics, their outlines are simple and their meaning great for Mexico. Summarily it can be said that the domeŝtic economic boom extends to foreign economic relations and has colored them. Mexico is a brisk and busy trader in the world mart; the things it buys and sells and the modes of paying for them have changed markedly over earlier arrangements. "Semi-colonialism" has given way more and more to "modernity."

Perhaps four things stand preëminent in a quick survey of Mexican foreign trade. First, Mexico and the United States are firmly wedded together by this nexus. Secondly, the steadily increasing size of Mexico's foreign trade is remarkable. Thirdly, the composition of interchange is notably different from pre-World War II years in terms of commodities sent and received. Finally, a troubled international atmosphere and global postwar economic developments have turned Mexican attention to new devices to maintain and extend its market position; success has marked this effort.

As for the past twenty years, the United States remains Mexico's dominant partner. Only once from 1934 through 1940 did Mexico fail to send from half to three-fourths of its exported goods there or to receive from the United States two-thirds or more of its imports. The war years riveted the relationship, which continues to the present. In 1950 Mexico was the United States' best customer in Latin America, and seldom does it drop below third place; conversely, from 80 per cent to 90 per cent of the goods which Mexico needs flow from the United States.

In 1951, a record year in Mexican trade, a little less than 20 per cent of Mexico's trade was with the 74 countries of Europe, the Near East, and Asia, the remaining four-fifths (both imports and exports) being with its northern neighbor. Canada, Great Britain,

France, and Western Germany all are competitors for runner-up positions after the United States' massive 80 per cent; none has yet managed to secure for itself as much as 5 per cent of the business, most hovering around 3 per cent. The impressive array of other nations who exchange goods with Mexico tends to represent symbolic relationships. A few are suppliers of special items. Few or none account for more than 2 per cent each.

Mexico has taken special interest in trading with the Middle East, both the new state of Israel and the Arab and Moslem world, but apart from selling them coined money (Mexican silver) the effort has small economic significance, whatever its political import may be. With Western Europe on the road to recovery through Marshall Plan and other United States aid, those nations have made a definite effort to gain a foothold in the Mexican market. Mexico welcomed such gestures, which would widen its range of choice in trade circles. Normally Mexico sells more items than it buys in Europe and the rest of the world (outside the United States) and then applies the favorable balances thus obtained against the deficits it normally runs in trading with the United States.

Trade figures reveal both the growing magnitude and some of the major outlines of recent trends. Values are purposely stated in pesos; peso values at different times have ranged from about $.30 to $.11. Mexican trade has grown; it has also begun to show rather consistent "unfavorable" balances—Mexicans buy more goods than they sell. But what cannot be inferred is the generally beneficial effect of these apparently "negative" balances. In the days of the Mexican Northern Oligarchy and even under Cárdenas, commodities like oil and metals were sold abroad for round sums that kept the trade sheet showing a Mexican "profit." But since the firms were foreign-owned, the "profit" later was withdrawn in the form of dividends; these transactions do not show on the *trade* sheets.

Nor do trade balances show the export of intangibles. The single biggest export item Mexico has is pleasure. Memories, scenery, excitement, and hospitality lure tourists whose dollar expenditures within the Republic provide it with fat sums that more than cover the apparent shortages on the trade sheet. To the dollars that tourists freely leave behind in return for goods and services are added a few millions sent to Mexico by another of their exports—*braceros*. Many, if not most, of the migrant laborers from Mexico send a fair share of their earnings home as a nest egg against their return. So the casual reader need not be unduly alarmed at the apparently enormous trade deficits that are now a companion of the augmented Mexican international trade, tabulated in the following columns.

MEXICAN INTERNATIONAL TRADE, 1900–1951

(Thousands of Mexican pesos)

Year	Imports	Exports	Total	Balance	Regime
1900	133,020	158,009	291,029	+ 24,989	Díaz
1910	205,874	293,754	499,628	+ 87,880	Díaz
1915	52,831	251,203	304,034	+ 198,372	Revolution
1920	396,682	855,094	1,251,776	+ 458,412	Obregón
1925	390,996	682,485	1,073,481	+ 291,489	Calles
1930	350,178	458,674	808,852	+ 108,496	Calles
1935	406,136	750,292	1,156,428	+ 344,156	Cárdenas
1940	669,016	960,041	1,629,057	+ 291,025	Cárdenas
1945	1,604,404	1,271,878	1,876,282	− 332,526	Camacho
1946	2,636,787	1,915,261	4,552,048	− 721,526	Camacho
1947	3,230,294	2,150,936	5,381,230	−1,079,358	Alemán
1948	2,951,495	2,661,271	5,612,766	− 290,224	Alemán
1949	3,527,321	3,623,081	7,150,402	+ 95,760	Alemán
1950	4,403,368	4,339,405	8,742,773	− 63,963	Alemán
1951	6,773,000	5,447,000	12,220,000	−1,326,000	Alemán

Trade. The historian's eye tends to correlate "Imports" and "Exports" in the same years with a changing Mexican economy and world crises. From early times and through recent years, Mexico has bought manufactured and luxury items from abroad. This practice continues, but the type of goods has shifted. With wartime austerity in the United States, Mexico purchased as many consumer items as it could get, but began more and more to demand chemicals, industrial machinery, scientific instruments, rail equipment, and similar props of industrialism. Momentarily after the war (1946–1947) there was a buyers' market for all the hard-to-get items that Mexican industry was either not producing or whose then inferior quality could not compete with foreign-made rivals. The hoarded gold bars (import items during war years) were turned into cash, and much of it went to buy Cadillacs, cigarettes, perfumes, and other fripperies, to the point that the Alemán administration slapped on import-export controls as a financial and political gesture.

With plans to expand and change Mexican countrysides and urban places by more soundly based scientific and industrial usages, tariffs and other controls were rigged to favor tractors and earth-moving machinery over nonproductive imports. Assembly plants of foreign companies rose in Mexico; parts, rather than ready-for-the-road automobiles or finished refrigerators, took precedence. Employment of Mexican labor in their assembly became an open purpose. Beginnings of the rehabilitation of Pemex and the railroads necessitated buying of complicated and expensive fabricated products. New Mexican manufacturing concerns demanded imports of steel as a raw material. As the economic boom picked up, these trends continued, and were given special urgency by the Korean crisis. With memories of World War II, when machinery was worth its weight in gold, Mexican purchasers have been stocking up on rails, bulldozers, generators, and the multitude of productive equipment so essential to further growth; the industrial plant has developed far enough to cover most consumer wants in things like shoes, clothing, and household needs, and Mexican goods can now compete on a quality basis with imported. Nearly all import-export controls were relaxed in 1951 for that reason, and because the Treasury shifted its anxieties from worries over its dollar reserves to concern about inflation. Inflow of goods helped stem it. Relaxed controls and Mexican prosperity bade to make 1952 yet another record foreign trade year. In the six months, January–June, Mexicans had imported 3920 million pesos' worth of goods and had exported 2871 million worth, with the heaviest transactions yet to come.

As might be expected, the United States was a chief furnisher of these newer-type imports—machinery and steel being predominant. But France, Great Britain, Canada, the Benelux group, Switzerland, and Western Germany have machinery and precision equipment, chemicals and locomotives, which Mexico is willing to buy. Italy, Spain, and Portugal occasionally make attractive offers to Mexican trade missions which prowl the world on the lookout for favorable deals. Needed railroad tracks were located in Japan, for instance, and Spain agreed to build fishing vessels for the fleet the Mexicans are putting into the water to exploit their offshore maritime riches. Price and quality, service and reputation, have displaced almost monopolistic control of source as market factors; while the United States has by no means lost its long lead, the stirrings of competition have been beneficial to all: the Mexicans get better goods and services and a certain psychological satisfaction in being sought out as buyers, the Atlantic Charter nations are economically benefited, and the United States businessmen are pricked into salutary alertness and politeness by the new developments of "free enterprise."

A corollary to the alteration in imports has been a shift in Mexican exports. Here the displacement of "semi-colonial" items from extractive industries by new agricultural and industrial items is a keynote, the fruits of the economic boom and industrialization. Base metals such as lead and zinc, and precious ones like silver, are still found in the eight leading exports, with crude oil eighth in 1951. Topping the list, however, was cotton, grown largely on new lands created by irrigation; Mexico now ranks next to Egypt as a world supplier of this important item; not far down the list (No. 5) are exports of cotton textiles. Outranking silver almost two to one in value is another war-spawned export crop—coffee; Mexico has climbed to top rank as a world producer, behind Brazil and Colombia. In 1950 Mexico exported 46,000 tons of coffee, worth nearly 334 million pesos; in 1951 this had risen to 51,525 tons, valued at over 402 million pesos.

The patterns of 1951 carried over into 1952, for which data to May are available. Zinc concentrates, for defense, had just edged out cotton as the leading export. Third, however, was a newcomer —tomatoes. Literally the fruits of the intensive rehabilitation of the countrysides have appeared, as melons and winter vegetables have pushed aside some old mainstays like henequen as export items. Minor trends are seen by the fact that Mexico sells some sugar abroad, in place of importing it, and even sold maize for one year (1950).

Industrialized Mexico has added to sales value of standard exports like metals by processing them and exporting them in a semi-finished rather than a raw state. In some instances it has created new metal exports, as in the case of locally produced electrolytic copper. Both coal and iron ore now flow to the United States from the bountiful Mexican supplies uncovered since 1948. Potentially important exports, already shipped in small quantities abroad, are tinned meats and canned fish and shrimps. Mexican industrial items seek out small and often specialized markets; while slipping (as expected) in postwar competition from a high point of 22 per cent of total exports, Mexican industrial items by no means have lost all their buyers. They currently account for around 10 per cent of export trade.

In the postwar scramble for markets, amid the pressures of the Cold War, Mexico has had to adjust its trade to the fact that there are "hard" currency countries and "soft" currency nations, and that those lucky enough to have dollars prefer to trade them for needed goods in the United States. Especially in its dealings with Europe,

Mexico has resorted to a series of semi-barter deals, by which it trades fibers, food, oil, and metals for equipment, machinery, and finished goods. Normally these pacts are arranged for two- or three-year periods, with the understanding that at the close of each year a small dollar interchange will even out discrepancies. In November 1950 a Mexican trade mission returned from Europe with $150 million worth of such deals: Western Germany ($62 million), Great Britain ($20 million), France ($10 million) and smaller ones with the Benelux group. In 1952 France agreed to swap Diesel train equipment for cotton; earlier, Spain sent olive oil and vessels for Mexican chick-peas; sugar to Japan brought back the rails, worth $6.8 million. Thus, in addition to the ECA and Mutual Security Administration programs, which dropped $66 million for direct purchases in Mexico, the revitalization of Europe's economy outside the Iron Curtain has benefited the Mexicans.

A somewhat parallel series of trade negotiations have gone on during postwar years between Mexico and its Latin-American colleagues, though here Mexico steps forward as a supplier of industrial materials and goods. Barters with Central American countries have been put on this basis, but with its ranking friends, Argentina and Brazil, trade pacts have been shaped in the European manner. Details on a proposed trade of Mexican for Brazilian products are obscure and unavailable, but characteristic of the times and places was an interchange between the two Revolutions—Mexican and Peronista. In February 1951 Mexico sent its prize tanker, *Miguel Alemán*, with 35,000 barrels of oil to exchange for Argentine *quebracho*, wheat, wool, greases, and meat. Representatives of the two presidents decorated each with high honors, while trade talks went on amid mutual felicitations. At this writing, nothing further has transpired after this pilot attempt to link the complementary economies of Argentina and Mexico by trade; undoubtedly the recent near-collapse of Argentina's system rather than coolness is responsible for the subsequent doldrums.

It should be evident from even this foreshortened sketch that Mexico's international trade is booming, is changing, and in general is healthy. The items it buys go to strengthen its productive capacity, and most of the items it sells bring returns which invigorate the same Mexican productive plant.

Balances. It should be borne in mind, however, that trade balances are but one of many entries on the international economic balance sheet. Much like totting up a personal checkbook, nations at the close of each year try to balance their international books by adding up all moneys they have received, how much paid. Often a small shipment of gold is sent by the debtors to the creditors to even up the score.

The bookkeeping is quite complex, but for our purposes it suffices to point out that on the international balance of payments register, Mexico's sound economic condition is again evident. After running small deficits (paid up in cash), in 1949 Mexico became the recipient of payments—it had become a creditor, despite its large adverse trade balances. One or two matters need to be singled out for special comment.

One is that a considerable amount of Mexican "outgo" is equivalent to money in the bank. It contributes regularly to various international funds and organizations, as well as meeting its debt and loan payments punctually. In 1950, for example, it made scheduled payments on the British oil debt, on old Revolutionary claims, railroad debts, Export-Import and World Bank loans, as well as one earlier acquired to stabilize its currency, all of which aggregated about $74 million. Despite all these, it showed a favorable balance. On the income side there is an entry under "Errors and Omissions." It would seem to represent United States military expenditures which for security reasons have not been specified; the income had allowed Mexican public revenues to pour into developmental activity and thus both nations have benefited.

A second important feature is the extent to which the American tourist stream has become "Big Business." The expanding band of pleasure-seekers from above the Border has been a key element in Mexico's shift into the favorable balance column. The moneys spent for enjoyment just about equal the value either of the total agricultural production or the output of extractive industries as dollar producers. The growing importance of the tourist as an economic factor can be seen from the accompanying tabulation, which shows that Mexico has been trapping a lion's share of this lucrative and generally beneficial pilgrimage to Latin America in the postwar years.

Aware of the implications, the Alemán regime has fostered the development of tourism by increased advertising and better facilities for visitors. Intensive efforts to improve hotels and their services for all economic strata of visitors have begun to pay dividends. The

RETURNS FROM TOURISM, 1946–1951

Year	Tourist Expenditures (Millions of dollars)		
	All Latin America	Mexico Dollars	Per Cent
1946	164	125	76.5
1947	166	115	69.5
1948	171	116	68.0
1949	182	134	73.5
1950	194	145	74.5
1951		208	

1951 total of 450,000 foreign tourists is expected to grow to 600,000 by the end of 1952 under programs for luring more people to the country and treating them even better. As roads pierce the fascinating countrysides and link the varied cities and hamlets tourism will grow. It is now a billion peso business.

Seldom noted by orthodox economists, who seem hypnotized by tangibles, is the market for Mexican-made goods represented by this peripatetic market. If each tourist bought only $10 worth of Mexican-made goods, their purchases would represent a yearly sales value of nearly 40 million pesos. Perhaps it will be some solace to those who exceed their personal budgets while touring the Republic that they are contributing concretely to their host's sound position in the arena of international payments.

For those who recall the turmoils recorded in earlier pages and who have followed the evolution of modern Mexico this far, the contrast with earlier days is marked. While at the same time it is prosperous, filled with hope and achieving new material heights, the Mexican Revolution is also fulfilling at long last some of the promises repeated for more than a generation that a better life was in store for the people, politically, morally, and economically speaking. With good reason United Nations economists could report (1950), "The principal economic event in Mexico during the period between 1947 and the middle of 1950 was the termination of the inflationary process which had lasted more than ten years. At the same time, the industrial and agricultural development achieved during the ten year period was in large measure consolidated." Let us scan them, and extend them to the end of the Alemán term.

17. The Industrial Revolution

"Mexico has started an industrial revolution destined to go far and to transform the economic and social life of the country," recently wrote Sanford Mosk. He added, "There will be no turning back. The process will go on. In a generation, say, it will have culminated in the sense that the economic and the social structure will differ radically from anything that Mexico has had in the past." *
Developments have already borne out these predictions.

The only useful basic premise from which to discuss the modern Mexican economy is that such industrialism has arrived as a permanent, dynamic, and central feature of national life. It has by far passed the stage of inquiring "should we?" In its train, industrialism has brought numerous problems. Others yet will appear. But the venture has passed the point of no return. In general it can be said that the auguries for successful industrialization are favorable. Potentially Mexico has a wide assortment of resources, natural and human; it has capital and markets; it has a successful and stable democratic government, and it is on good terms with its neighbors in the hemisphere and throughout the world. More important than all these, perhaps, is the driving will to overcome any obstacles that may appear until unqualified success is assured.

Drawbacks and hazards are numerous, but not insurmountable. Mexico's resources are not always of first quality; many are also so badly placed that large capital investments in transportation must be made before they can be utilized. Its capital has been difficult to mobilize and channel into industrial expansion. The internal market expands slowly. Sudden bottlenecks in materials, transport, quality, and quantity of intermediate furnishers, all slow down the total process of industrialization, and throw its different sectors out of

* Sanford Mosk, *Industrial Revolution in Mexico* (Berkeley: University of California Press, 1950), p. 310.

balance. But even after all deductions are made, the prospects for the future are good and the achievements to date are impressive.

To detail these would require much more space than is available here; the interested reader can find thoughtful and authoritative elaborations in Sanford Mosk's recent *Industrial Revolution in Mexico* and in George Wythe's summary of Mexico in a general work devoted to Latin-American industrialization.* Here we must be content with some summary observations.

1. URBAN PHASES

The Basic Elements: Resources. Mexican resources are virtually unknown. They are plentiful and various. Technical surveys recently undertaken by Armour Research Foundation, Higgins Industries, Ford Bacon & Davis, the Banco de Mexico, and numerous Mexican agencies all come out with about the same answer: there are innumerable renewable and nonrenewable items extant which need classification, analysis, and exploitation. Coal is an example; contrary to myths, Mexico has considerable coal and even coke suitable for making steel as well as replacing charcoal as the national fuel. Recent estimates place coal reserves at two billion tons and iron ore (63 per cent or better) at 222 million tons. These are conservative figures.

Power. Mexico is among the best, if not the best, endowed of Latin-American countries so far as fuel sources to generate power are concerned. Its coal fields, oil deposits, water power, and potential atomic energy from fissionable materials lock up more than enough power to drive an industrial machine for ages. Only a little of it thus far has been tapped. In the Republic's five hydraulic zones there is enough water-power potential to produce 7.3 million KW of electricity.† Of this less than 0.9 million KW were being utilized in 1947. By 1950, installed capacity grew to about 1.0 million KW, but that was doubled by 1952. Of 1950's electric power (3.2 billion kilowatt hours a year), 1.1 billion KWH were thermoelectric, 1.6 billion were hydroelectric, and the remainder Diesel-produced. Private and pub-

* George Wythe, *Industry in Latin America* (rev. ed.; New York: Columbia University Press, 1950). Both these volumes take Mexico up to about 1948; therefore their appraisal is less optimistic than the 1948–1952 situation warrants, and conclusions here differ from their views.

† KW hours (KWH) result when time is gained to potential; thus the absolute maximum, by water power, would be 7.3 mill. on KW × 24 hours a day or 175.2 million KWH.

lic agencies are strenuously trying to bring the electrical power facilities in line with pressing industrial and consumer needs.

Speaking in September 1952, President Alemán reported to Congress that in 1947 the FCE's capacity was 23 plants that produced 44,000 KW. These had grown to 215 generating plants and 390,000 KW. Power lines over the same period expanded from 620 to 1527 kilometers. A total of 1912 million pesos had gone to electrify Mexico, apart from the substantial investments made by private enterprise to meet the rising demands for electric power. From 1953 onward, sights are set to produce 8 billion KWH through a network of plants. The private and public systems are tied together, technically and fiscally. Mexico currently stands behind Brazil and Argentina as the third largest power producer (electric) in Latin America.

Uranium. The important progress that Mexicans have made in the discovery and study of fishionable materials is good testimony that there is more to Mexico than oil and *mañana*. Not much is published on these new departures; some of the things printed are not true. It is worth pausing a moment to review some of the main facts.

Mexico has two important factors for the exploitation of this new source of power: Mexican uranium deposits and Mexican scientists. At two points in Chihuahua fairly extensive finds of pitchblende containing radioactive materials have been uncovered, as well as a number of lesser veins in Oaxaca. In 1947 the Mexican government was spending about 10 million pesos for the exploration and development of these resources. In May 1951, the United States suggested that under a Point IV project, Mexico and the United States exchange scientists between Washington and Mexico City to work out a joint scheme for broadening and intensifying search and research. By various decrees and legislation, radioactive materials and research have been nationalized, so that the Mexican government through its own Atomic Energy Commission is keeping a close eye on developments, which are promising.

What does Mexico's uranium mean to it and to the world? In the first place, missing factors dampen down any immediate hope or fear that Mexico will begin turning out atomic bombs. Apart from its stated policy of using its finds for peaceful means, the physical conditions in Mexico make it unlikely that immediate or large-scale exploitation of its fissionable riches for domestic use will be possible. The limiting factors are serious at present.

Contrary to most popular conceptions, there is a fairly large available supply of uranium in the world; intensive search has uncovered a considerable amount. Scarcity is not the problem. The main inhibiting factors in its immediate use for military purposes or as a power source lie in mechanical ingenuity, large-scale atomic piles, and enormous inputs of electrical power and water. The astronomical capital investment needed to make large enough piles to provide significant amounts of radioactive materials are at the moment prohibitive for Mexico. Its tight supply of electrical energy and inadequate water supplies also necessarily put off hopes for large-scale tapping of Mexican uranium and similar resources for at least a generation.

Labor and Technology. Foreigners and Mexicans alike agree that the Mexican workman has exceptional skill and is eminently teachable, but that the technological level at which he now operates is very low. The pool of highly trained, skilled, and semiskilled industrial labor is still small. By extension programs, sponsored especially by the National Polytechnic Institute and its regional branches, this handicap is only partially being overcome. Technical education has come to Mexico. It is much too early to decide in any sort of definitive fashion which is likely to be more affected, the Mexicans or the education. This spreading educational activity has begun to reduce some of the feverish flush of enthusiasm induced by the early rush to industrialism. Mexicans are now realizing that technology is not a collection of gadgets, but a state of mind.

To analyze each step of a process day after day, to improve it and simplify it, is the essence of the technological creed. Research is now being disentangled from chemical analysis; industrial standardization, the absolute requirement for an integrated industrial system, is slowly being disengaged from the idea that it is somehow connected with political control. Process control, not political fiat, is a newly recognized need of Mexican industry. "Made in Mexico" is not enough to win consumers to inferior and unreliable products. To aid technology, Mexico now has available not only the Monterrey Research Institute at Monterrey, but an impressive one that Armour and Company established in Mexico City during 1952.

Capital. Many of the gloomiest predictions about future Mexican industrialization were based on the now exploded premise that there would be insufficient capital to carry on basic developmental work. Admittedly capital is essential to increase the internal markets. Money also must be found to finance factories for turning out the goods. As noted, the upped tax revenues and international loans have more than met the first need; transportation, irrigation, electrification, mechanization of agriculture, and similar massive projects have been benefiting Mexicans and creating markets. Further, these same sources have made it possible for Nacional Financiera to foster the creation and expansion of specific industrial activities whose lack threatened to hamper industrialization; N.F. sponsored the manufacture of sulphuric acids and other chemicals, increased steel and coke capacity, and a similar crucial filling-in of the evolving system. With markets expanding, purchasing-power rising, and generally beneficent legislation, private capital at home and from abroad has suddenly begun to pour into Mexico.

Perhaps one of the main features in financing the industrialization of Mexico is that better than two-thirds of it has been done by local capital. A second and equally important characteristic is that the foreign investments in Mexican industrialism are indirect, and as such are subject to Mexican control, private and governmental. The previous chapter touched on this in general, but it is worth pursuing here again because of its direct bearing on Mexico's potential industrialization.

Regarding the first, the outgoing president of the private bankers association of Mexico reported to his colleagues in April 1951 that collectively they had loaned a little less than 3.8 billion pesos during 1950. He claimed that around 60 per cent had remained in old channels, going to mining, commerce, agriculture, and pastoral activities, but that now 40 per cent had poured into "constructive" industry. The Mexican Treasury Department gave a slightly less roseate view for 1950, but indicated clearly that private banks were now investing in industrial securities—stocks, bonds, and other long-term paper floated by new enterprisers. Of 836 million pesos invested by private banks during 1949, 601 million (73.6 per cent) had flowed to industry; during 1950, 864 million pesos out of a total investment of 1182 million (73 per cent) had been similarly directed into industrial concerns. The year 1951 confirmed the pattern; private credit had expanded 27 per cent above 1950, and from January to June these sources had poured 1537 million pesos into industrial enterprises, while allocating only 358 million to agriculture, 119 million to cattle, and 21 million to mining and other loans. In 1950 Nacional Financiera calculated that between 10 and 15 per cent of Mexico's national income had been reinvested in Mexican industrial activities; since 1943 this amounted to over a billion pesos annually.

One can say that with constantly rising national income, Mexicans themselves invest four times as much in their industrial system as they did in 1940. These statistical shorthand notes add up to a new trend, that of closing some of the ideological and political gaps between the "Old Group" and the "Newest Group" by having the former won partially over to the latter's views. It also means that industrialization, as now carried on, does not carry with it a necessary freight of inflation; though profits are high, they are reinvested in capital equipment by the same Mexicans who receive them. Money supply has remained almost the same for the past two years, while there has been a rising national product and clear evidence of reinvestment activities by all credit agencies. Mexican sources provide the following evidence.

TOTAL PUBLIC AND PRIVATE INVESTMENTS, 1950–1951
(Millions of pesos)

	Productive Fields (Industry, etc.)	Nonproductive Fields
1950	3,751.8	1,660.3
1951	5,165.2	1,729.9
1952 (1 qu.)	5,896.1	1,898.9

Precise quantities on private Mexican investment versus foreign are hard to locate. An important bit of evidence, though, comes from the recent developments in the Federal District. Newly created industrial concerns during 1949 numbered 395, of which only 40 (9.9 per cent) were foreign backed; the foreign companies accounted for around 12 per cent of the capital investment. The remainder, 355 firms, representing about 85 million pesos of Mexican capital, were largely privately financed. In 1950, the new industrial plants launched there were 438 in number, and amounted to an investment of 162.7 million pesos; no data are available on how that amount was divided between local and foreign capital. Nor are financing details clear on the 466 new firms started there in 1951 but we do know a few things about it: foreign investment increased by $13 million, half of which went into manufacturing; 94 per cent of the new foreign investment came from the United States, with 4 per cent from Great Britain and the tiny remainder split among Switzerland, Canada, and France.

As the previous chapter indicated, there is no dearth of foreign money for Mexican economic expansion. It now combines with local capital and Mexican management for mutual benefits. Nearly every major automobile manufacturer now has a Mexican assembly plant, and this includes the chief European concerns like Anglia Ford and the Italian Fiat. The latter is using Mexico as a base for providing all Latin America with Diesel trucks and passenger cars. Sears, Roebuck and Company have successfully launched a chain of their stores which rely exclusively on Mexican personnel and, so far as possible, on Mexican-made items for which they often furnish the specifications and suggest the know-how. Radios and television sets, appliances of all sorts, industrial equipment, such as pumps, pour off assembly lines.

The Results. Mexico has been in the throes of an industrial revolution for about a decade. It has been attempting to bring together or create the main elements of an industrial system. As we have seen, most of the basic requisites now exist. It is fair to ask, what are the tangible results to date? Some matters can be quantified to provide an answer, provisional at best.

In the first place, manufacturing and industrial activity have grown markedly, in quantity and value. The accompanying table illustrates recent attempts to measure these. Though various investigations have taken different years for bases, the broad trend is clear. Mexico is, next to Argentina and Brazil, the most industrialized country of Latin America, and during 1950 outstripped both in rate of expansion and growth of production. Due in large part to industrialized activities, the value of goods and services in Mexico rose from 38,112 million pesos in 1950 to 45,543 million in 1951, according to the Banco de Mexico. The national product is growing, even after discount for inflation has been made—about 30 per cent of the rise was "real" rather than "monetary."

This undoubted advance has been uneven from one sector of manufacturing to another, as Appendix tables show (Table 30). As might be expected, consumer goods have boomed, while some of the older items have showed much slower rises. Critical and important to any evaluation of Mexican industrialism is the situation in heavy industry, especially steel. In 1938, Mexico's annual steel consumption was about 195,000 long tons.

The total ingot production of Mexico was 300,000 long tons in 1949, and about 400,000 in 1951. This is a 110 per cent increase

SELECTED INDICES OF INDUSTRIAL ACTIVITY IN MEXICO

Base Year (100 on Index)	Most Recent Year Compared with Base	All Industry Volume	Industrial Manufacturing Value	Industrial Manufacturing Volume	Source
1929 (100) vs.	1947	161.7	610.2	210.3	A
1929	1948	162.5		217.4	B
1929	1949	179.0			B
1929	1950	192.3			I
1929	1951	205.6			I
1929	1952	207.1			I
1937	1947		331.2	153.0	C
1939	1946	124.3		174.6	B
1939	1947			136.0	B
1939	1950	150+			D
1939	1950	172.3		228.2	A
1941	1949	160.7			E
1943	1949			148.0	F
1946	1952	142	188		H
1947	1940	74			G
1947	1950	118			G
1947	1951	129			G
1949	1950	109		112	C
1949 (100) vs.	1951	118		121	C

Sources: A.—Ministry of Economics; B.—Banco de Mexico; C.—United Nations; D.—U. S. Dept. of Commerce; E.—S. M. Holguín, in *Rev. de Econ* (1950); F.—Nacional Financiera; G.—*Noticias*, VIII, No. 18 (April 29, 1952), p. 8; H.—VI Informe del Pres. Alemán; I.—*Noticias*, VIII, No. 35–36, p. 4, for first quarter 1952.

from 1939. Recent reports indicate that Altos Hornos and other new mills have recovered from their many organizational difficulties and are increasing capacity as fast as the tight equipment situation will allow; the former produces 120,000 tons annually. Under construction in 1952 were new installations to double this amount by 1953; other steel producers have similar plans for expansion.

In his final (1952) summary to Congress, President Alemán spoke at length about iron and steel. He stated that the country had just produced 600,000 tons, and that the new capacity would raise output by 1954 to more than 800,000 tons, but that demands were growing so fast that to cover their needs some 1,500,000 would soon be necessary. He stressed the competitive cost of Mexican steel and the efficiency of its mills, plus the new finds of cokable coal and iron deposits. He expressed his belief that Mexican heavy industry was in good shape to aid further industrialization, as it was integrated into the national system and was growing with it. A recent and important addition to the foundations of industrialization is aluminum. In November 1950 Reynolds Metals Corporation announced plans to build a $20 million plant with an annual capacity of 40 million pounds.

Yet another way to draw a profile of increased industrialization is to note the number of manufacturing establishments responsible for this obviously rising curve of physical output. It grows by 5 per cent a year while population grows at 3 per cent. Many "industrial plants" in Mexico are but small shops, with three or less people.

The foundations on which statistics about the number of plants in Mexico rest are extremely shaky. The Census of 1950 will give a real view, but it has not yet been published. A convenient summary of the available materials, borrowed from Mosk, is illustrative. It can be seen that by expanding wage payments, Mexican industry is partially creating its own market.

AN ILLUSTRATIVE VIEW OF MEXICAN MANUFACTURING

	Number of Establishments	Investment (millions of pesos)	Value of Output (millions of pesos)	Number of Employees	Wages and Salaries (millions of pesos)
Census of 1930	48,850	980	915	318,763	181
Census of 1935	6,916	1,670	1,890	318,041	286
Census of 1940	13,510	3,135	3,115	389,953	568
Questionnaire, 1945	51,128	4,352	5,342	593,970	1,125
Estimates, 1950	53,000?	5,000– 10,000?	8,500?	700,000– 900,000?	?

Sources: 1930–1945, Sanford Mosk, *The Industrial Revolution in Mexico* (University of California Press, 1950), Table 10; note qualifying warnings about unwary use of these figures, *ibid.*, pp. 114–115. 1950 = author's guesses.

The nature of growth is again highlighted by a Federal District "case history" for 1949–1950. It deals only with *additions* made in one year. A tabular view, presented below, shows that Mexican industrialism there, largest of the aggregates, is still at a fairly primitive stage; more than half the new enterprises were dedicated to the necessary but humble tasks of providing for elementary needs —food, shelter, clothing. A substantial segment could be classed as intermediate and auxiliary suppliers to other parts of the industrial system; alongside them blossomed a sizable number of very small firms, each capitalized at less than half a million pesos, to fill an extraordinarily long list of minor needs. New business primarily aimed at leisure and luxury accounted for but a small per cent.

SUMMARY, NEW INDUSTRIAL CONCERNS IN THE FEDERAL DISTRICT, 1949–1950

Type	Plants		Investment (millions of pesos)	
	Number	Per Cent	Amount	Per Cent
Food, shelter, clothing	442	53.0	136.2	53.0
Industrial auxiliaries	144	17.3	61.8	24.0
Leisure and luxury	106	12.4	18.6	7.3
Miscellaneous	141	17.3	40.8	15.7
Totals	833	100.0	257.4	100.0

Source: Appendix I, Table 23.

Finally, it may be briefly noted here that manufactured items play a ponderable role in Mexican export trade. From 1.5 per cent in 1939 they now hover around 10 per cent of Mexican products sold abroad. Even before the Korean crisis, Mexico had managed to retain some of its World War II foreign markets, a matter discussed in the previous chapter

Many of the initial hurdles of industrialism have been cleared. Contrary to expectations, the rise of productive capacity has not completely outstripped increase of Mexican purchasing power, though the latter is still low. At the same time, the quantity, quality, variety, and value of manufactured items have climbed. Before 1947 about 97 per cent of all record players, washing machines, refrigerators, irons, were imported; today 97 per cent are manufactured or assembled locally. Mexican consumers have become more satisfied with improved Mexican-made products. Hardware made abroad— United States, German, Swiss—is one of the few consumer lines in which foreign domination is confidently supreme. Viewing recent sales figures, one American businessman remarked, "We may not be able to sell as many Hershey bars and sports shirts in the future, but we'll sell lots more locomotives, light and power plants, and textile machinery." Industrialism has arrived.

Summary and Prospect. As we have seen, the tempo of social, political, and economic change has been stepped up in the past five years. Many things claimed to be impossible in 1946 have already been done. Yet Mexican industrialism is so new, scattered, and different from anything customarily associated with Mexico before 1940 that all prophecy, favorable or pessimistic, rests on a very slim factual basis. Both the eventual benefits and the perils which many believe will engulf the whole nation if the present enthusiasm remains unbridled are highly subjective. One thing is sure: industrialism will continue. All Mexicans have a vested interest of one sort or another in it.

It is to the credit of the Mexican thinkers that their main argument in favor of industrialism considers the improvement of all social conditions as its ultimate goal. Throughout its history, Mexico has had able, articulate, and dedicated spokesmen who have repeated the familiar and general arguments that the creation of an industrial system is the best and perhaps only route to better standards of living in Mexico and elsewhere. A powerful, recent argument is that Mexico cannot remain agricultural; only 12 per cent of its land is really habitable and is insufficient to support well a large rural population; the only alternative is to industrialize. Mexicans argue that with Mexican resources it is possible to clothe, house, and feed the Mexican people as well as improve their education, health, and leisure activities by converting the old semifeudal economic structure into a modern technological one. They believe that industrialism opens up specialized activities, which in turn increase social mobility and undermine the static, poverty-ridden, and isolated conditions that have been endemic in Mexico since pre-Conquest days.

They argue persuasively that the Revolution was a revolt against poverty. The Revolution, through the Mexican government, is morally committed to drain this swamp of misery which breeds so many social maladies. The facts of the past ten years have gone a long way to buttress these contentions. Mexico has gone further down its new road to industrialism than most observers in the United States had thought possible.

Usually overlooked is that the recurring cries of "industrialization" which echo in modern Mexico embrace the improvement and mechanization of rural areas as well as the construction of urban factories and the increased output of steel. Industrialism is meant to enclose each. Both the government and leading economic thinkers of all ideological stripes agree that its countrysides must form a major Mexican domestic market. Rural workers in turn must feed and supply raw materials to an expanding industrial machine which is more and more to be made up of nonagricultural people congregated in towns and cities. Therefore, to the older humanitarian interest in helping the *campesino* for his own sake are now added these newer and more compelling economic incentives. The progress being made in rural Mexico is unlikely to cease or even slow appreciably, spurred as it is both from the rural and the urban sides. Industrialism and modern agrarianism are merely two aspects of the same thing, a better life for *all* Mexicans.

Political and economic romantics in Mexico and abroad have claimed that emphasis on major transformations makes impossible a happy rural peasantry, and that Mexico should remain a land of small villages. Unfortunately both history and the times are against such a thesis, which rests on the untested assumption that Mexican "folk" are somehow endowed with more virtues than urbanites. Where available, modern Rorschach and other tests indicate rural minds are generally more tension-ridden, whatever their economic circumstances, than their city counterparts. Happiness is not a function of habitat.

2. RURAL PHASES

Carrying on the policies adumbrated by his predecessor, Miguel Alemán's inaugural address stressed the necessity of increased agricultural production in Mexico. He stated that "we can succeed in getting a great agricultural production by applying to the exploitation of land the force of our labor, the resources of technology, and a policy which equally guarantees the *ejido*, small private farms, and small livestock interests . . . [and by] imposing tranquillity on the countryside by all legal means." The Alemán agrarian program proposed a vast irrigation project to stabilize old and create new good land, a strengthened colonization enterprise, and a vigorous credit policy to be carried on through official and semiofficial institutions.

The use of irrigation and drainage works to create and improve agricultural lands is not a new concept in Mexico. Though even colonial and early republican leaders had talked about it, very little was done officially to incorporate hydraulic works as a part of the Revolutionary agrarian reform until 1925. In January 1926 President

Calles created a special Irrigation Commission under the Ministry of Agriculture. Until Cárdenas' time the Commission had accomplished very little. Like so much else in Mexico in that period, its budgets were tiny, and its grand plans were deferred and deflected by political pulls—dams arose where politicians were, not where they were urgently needed. Some of its technical work was slipshod. Cárdenas scarcely had the time or resources to push a full-scale irrigation program, but he did have the Commission sketch out general lines for one. When Avila Camacho came into office the net result of about fourteen years' previous national official action on irrigation had created only about 150,000 hectares of irrigated lands.

Though pinched by war shortages of personnel and equipment, President Camacho fostered the work of the Irrigation Commission. During his term, it added an impressive quantity to the previous total—a little over 686,000 hectares. This quadrupling was a real acceleration. In December 1946 official figures gave Mexico a total of 816,224 hectares of irrigated land.

Goals. Alemán set as the goal of his administration to improve or create about 1,000,000 additional hectares of this superb crop land. He promised to spend about 1.5 billion pesos in the effort. A new Irrigation Code was drawn up to make the best possible use of existing resources. The old Irrigation Commission was raised to the status of a Ministry. Adolfo Orive Alba, a well-trained enthusiast, was put in charge of carrying out the presidential mandates. Alemán has backed his promises with cash. Since November 1944, Mexico has borrowed a total of $381 million from the Export-Import Bank and the World Bank; next to communication and transport, irrigation has benefited most from these loans, to the tune of $32.5 million. The remainder came from Mexican sources. Summarizing achievements of his six years in office, President Alemán told Congress on September 1, 1952, "The investment in irrigation . . . rose to 2,103 million pesos." During 1952, investments in irrigation amounted to 26 pesos per inhabitant, claimed to be the highest such figure in the world. These sums represent the combined efforts of the Federal budget, state and local contributions for coöperative projects under the Ministry, revenues from water rents, and other minor trickles.

Results of the Irrigation Programs, 1946–1952. Summing up the achievements is not simple. The objectives of the irrigation programs are several and diverse. Each project is tailored to the specific need of a given area or a regional problem. Some of the huge dams and canals, under construction or completed, aim primarily to control floods; others trap elusive, irregular moisture and store it for watering previously arid territory or parceling out water during dry spells; a number of works have as their main purpose the generation of hydroelectric power, with irrigation of arable lands as a secondary one. The hydraulics program is a coördinated attack on basic ills.

Some of the hydraulic projects are massive, long-term improvements whose continuing benefits will not appear for a number of years. Others have been so recently completed that their full impact has not yet been reflected in statistics or even in reports. In 1950 alone, the Ministry reported the termination of some 12 large-scale works, progressing work on 25 others, and the initiation of seven new ones. These are apart from innumerable special projects and small irrigation works. Alemán's additions bring the total amount of irrigated land in Mexico to 1,216,437 hectares (as of January 1, 1951), and the total arable land in Mexico to about 15 million hectares (37 million acres). Speed-up was scheduled for the final months of the terms to reach the Alemán goals. The work goes on around the clock. Newly irrigated land produces a third of Mexican crops, measured by value. The Ministry of Hydraulic Resources points out that the lives and properties saved by the works during recent floods are an incalculable benefit. In the almost unbroken series of serious droughts that have beset Mexico in the recent five years, the 28 completed major dams (even operating at only 30 per cent of their storage capacity of 13,417 million cubic meters of water) have made it possible to cultivate 400,000 hectares that otherwise would have been unproductive.

Mexican officials feel that even if they were allowed only one normal season of rainfall to demonstrate the full utility of their investments in hydraulic works the outcome would be sensational. They are also fond of pointing out that from 1946 to 1952 Mexico has irrigated more land than the United States has in the past twenty-five years including the whole New Deal period.

Part of the recent irrigation effort aims as much at aiding industry as it does at improving rural prospects. Collateral with the creation and preservation of soil resources has been an electrification program. During January through March 1951, for instance, the Federal Electric Commission, which works closely with the Ministry of Hydraulic Resources, inaugurated power plants which produce 200,000 KW. Both Mexican and United States technicians agree that the electrical power requirements of Monterrey and its affiliated industrial and agricultural clusters will be met by the huge generators to be installed at the great international Falcón Dam, jointly being constructed by the two countries on the Rio Grande. As an interesting side light on the international aspects of Mexico's hydraulic programs has come a recent request to the Ministry of Hydraulic Resources from Venezuela: it wants Mexicans to plan and carry out for Venezuela comprehensive water programs similar in scope and objects to the ones Mexico has already so successfully executed.

New Departures: Tepalcatepec and Papaloapan. Literally and figuratively the Ministry of Hydraulic Resources has broken new ground on its two pet projects. One is under the Commission of Tepalcatepec and the other, the Commission of Papaloapan. They are new versions of old colonization schemes. Their significance has led to a more detailed scrutiny below; here are the highlights.

Created on August 1, 1947, the Tepalcatepec project has been headed by ex-President Lázaro Cárdenas. The TVA-like plan has been directed toward improving the material, economic, and social life in the drainage basin of the Tepalcatepec River and its tributaries. It runs from western Michoacan to the Pacific. This area, potentially rich but vastly underpopulated, lies athwart the western edge of the Core and embraces a great deal of the West. The basic plan calls first for minor irrigation works, railroad and road connections to new market centers, and then a network of large-scale works. Together these will add a whole new electrically equipped, agricultural province to Mexico, one in which people from overcrowded areas can be resettled. The first stage, scheduled for completion by 1952, will have created about 36,000 hectares of irrigated land; no terminal date has been placed on the second phase which will increase the cultivable land by another 130,000 hectares. To September 1951 some 32,180 of the projected 36,000 had come under cultivation, and the dams currently provide 50,000 KW of electricity from these plants. The land thus created grows every description of crops, produced by small owners living in modern rural communities fully equipped with material and social conveniences and necessities. To date the Commission has spent about 50 million pesos. Its work already has benefited a number of extant small communities, but its chief contributions are yet to come.

The Commission of the Papaloapan, created in 1947, is similar to that of the Tepalcatepec but on a much grander scale. It is in charge of the largest irrigation and resettlement project in Latin America, one of the largest in the world. Its plans envisage more than mere irrigation and drainage of a large area. It is a colossal and integrated socio-geographical scheme to reshape and rearrange 27,000 square miles of useless Mexican area into one whose balanced agrarian-industrial economy will provide the material benefits of civilization without its major drawbacks. It is reported that Miguel Alemán, on his retirement from the presidency in 1952, will assume personal charge of the Papaloapan Project, as Cárdenas has for Tepalcatepec.

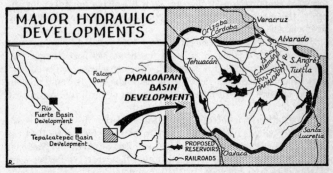

The Agricultural Revolution. Though some of the most outstanding recent efforts of Mexicans to solve problems posed by land have gone toward creating new soil and human resources, equal or more attention has been devoted to conserving and improving elements which already exist. These departures concern such prosaic matters as soil conservation, increased use of fertilizers (being produced since 1944 by the nascent industrial machine), mechanization, introduction of substitute food crops to raise the caloric intake while lessening strains on the land, and carrying forward basic agricultural research that has resulted in higher-yield seeds adapted specifically to Mexican conditions. Much of the new florescence emerged directly from wartime coöperation with the United States. Then (as now) it was to the interest of both nations to raise the quality and quantity of Mexican agricultural output. Only the briefest mention of the innumerable day-to-day improvements that have gone on since 1946 can here be made. Cumulatively and collectively they represent the most important revolution Mexico has undergone, the agricultural revolution. It has taken the ceilings off expansion of the nation.

While promising better things for the future, it has fed more Mexicans better than at nearly any time for which we have data (as earlier pointed out).*

A case history, the unlovely subject of fertilizers, illustrates some of the new departures of the agricultural revolution. The use of artificial fertilizers is a recent and salutary development in rural Mexico. To 1942 the amounts used were negligible. For one thing, the soils of Mexico were almost unstudied; there was no way of telling what would restore or increase their life-giving qualities; for another, too many other large distractions kept attention from being fixed on such a simple matter.

But since 1942—and especially after 1947—soil studies have appeared and propaganda in favor of fertilizers has been stepped up. One study indicated that if 215,000 hectares of selected irrigated land were properly fertilized, yields would be prodigious; it would take an annual massive dose of nearly 200,000 tons of fertilizers to do that one job.

The prospects for increased fertilization of the Mexican lands are good to excellent. All fertilizers had to be imported up to 1944, so their distribution was very limited. Under auspices of Nacional Financiera a small plant was inaugurated that year; two other even smaller ones later joined it. In 1949 their total production was about 22,000 metric tons, to which was added an imported tonnage of around 10,000. Through the use of a $10 million Export-Import loan, Nacional Financiera completed the largest fertilizer plant in Latin America; it was officially opened by President Alemán on May 22, 1951.

This enterprise illustrates vividly the intertwining of industrial and agricultural procedures. The plant is at Cuautitlán, about 20 miles outside Mexico City; it processes ammonium sulphate from natural gas pumped through new pipelines from Pemex's Poza Rica oil and gas field 175 miles away. Its output, scheduled for 66,000 tons annually, was quickly reached. In fiscal 1952, Mexico was producing 93,000 metric tons of fertilizers, doubling the 1951 output and covering about 90 per cent of the current market. The Cuautitlán plant is already expanding to cover the small deficit and to make available even more life-giving substances to aid food production.

Technology. The old problem of primitive agricultural technology is not unique to Mexico or even to most of Latin America, where

* See above, pp. 69–72.

similar conditions prevail. Much of the world is in the same state. Hunger pangs *must* be relieved before the higher and nobler ideals of democracy and international amity even have a chance of fulfillment. In the Mexican case two related aspects have been singled out as the most serious causes of chronic shortages of food: primitive agricultural techniques and the traditionally poor crops associated with them. They have combined with other maladjustments to keep Mexican agricultural technology at a low, inefficient level.

The amount of time an agriculturist must spend in Mexico to work an acre of ground and the results of a month's work are revealing and appalling figures. In the fecund areas of the Bajío, Jalisco, and Guanajuato, agriculturists invest from 111 to 126 hours a month to grow one acre of maize; in a month a farmer produces about 20 bushels; this is based on a yield of 13 bushels per acre, which is well above the usual Mexican average of less than 10. In Iowa it would take him about 16½ hours of work each month to till the same area and he would produce 567 bushels of corn; in Georgia, where agricultural conditions are scarcely optimum, he would spend 37.7 hours and get 56 bushels for a month's work; the United States average is an expenditure of 27.3 hours and a return of 207 bushels per man per month. Similar divergences can be enumerated for wheat, rice, cotton, and sugar. The highest yields in Mexico, measured in bushels of maize per man per acre per month are found in northern Mexican areas where mechanization has progressed most. The top figure, 196, came from Cajeme (Sonora). The low averages from all but these favored Mexican spots reveal the magnitude of the problem of modernizing the agricultural plant to feed an expanding nation.

Notwithstanding the apparent barriers, Mexican administrators have attacked this enormous and critical problem, with aid from the United States. In 1940 the average investment in mechanized equipment for Mexican land parcels was around $8, with the total national investment only in the order of 105 million pesos. From 1940 through 1945, Manuel Avila Camacho managed to obtain another 130 million pesos' worth of tractors and similar machinery. Half way in Alemán's term (1948) yet another 238 million pesos had already been spent to add some 14,712 new tractors to the countryside. Contrary to pessimistic forecasts, peasant farmers proved teachable. The bottlenecks in further improvements and mechanization lie in the scarcity and price of equipment, and in the nature of the Mexican land problem.

Much of the Mexican area is not capable of mechanization. Staples like maize, beans, and many other crops are grown on very small scattered plots. To bring up the efficiency of these small holdings, attention has increasingly turned to substitution of high-yield hybrid corn varieties for traditional seed. Mexico's average in 1940 was somewhere around 9 to 10 bushels an acre, placing that country 79th on a world-scale of maize raisers. The tendency of the Mexican farmer to feed his government false production figures was partially responsible, but the fact remained that for all his work, the peasant got little back from the land. Acting on suggestions from Henry Wallace, President Camacho in 1944 set up a corn-breeding program that was aided by scientists from the Rockefeller Foundation.

These preliminary and pioneering moves were broadened and strengthened by President Alemán's creation of the Mexican Maize Commission in October 1946. The Commission was given the broad mandate of finding ways to cut Mexico's foodstuff deficits. Taking the available high-yield seeds already developed, the Commission began a self-hoisting operation. It applied the multiplier principle by parceling out 30 tons of high-yield seed to selected farmers under contract and purchasing back at high prices half their crop, to be redistributed on a similar basis to them and others. The first year (1946) the farm contractors sowed and reaped 2500 hectares of the new maize; for its second year, the Maize Commission had enough to plant 250,000 hectares. By geometric proportions the new hybrids have been driving out the old, low-yield maize plants. It is hoped that within less than a decade the old seed will be as anachronistic and obsolete as it would be in Iowa. Currently, around 40 per cent of the maize crop comes from the new varieties.

It was found, of course, that no one hybrid was suitable for the whole Mexican republic. Each area, every *patria chica*, is likely to need a specific one. Continued research has gone on to fill in these specifications. In March 1951 a variety suitable for most places in the Core was publicly announced. To signalize President Alemán's insistent demands for better seeds and the unstinted aid given them, the scientists called the breed *Presan* (*Pres*ident Alem*án*). It has experimentally produced ten tons of maize per acre, 200,000 lbs., as compared with the Mexican average of 560 lbs. per acre in 1940. To especially depressed areas, such as the Otomí villages, some 300 tons of this wonder grain was dispatched. Even less fabulous hybrids are now able to increase traditional yields by two- or three-fold.

This partially accounts for the amazing fact that in 1950 Mexico exported maize after feeding its enlarged population.

Success of the Maize Commission's techniques has stimulated similar semiprivate efforts to breed better Mexican cotton. Several United States producers and state agricultural schools, as well as the United States Department of Agriculture, teamed up with Mexican cotton producers and the national government in a concerted attack on upping production and productivity of Mexican agricultural workers. In 1951 National Commissions modeled on the Maize Commission were formed and were carrying on comparable activities for coffee, olives, and sugar. Rockefeller scientists and Mexicans were still actively following up earlier successes in maize and were making genetic studies of rust-resisting wheat, and proper varieties of beans, legumes, rice, peppers, and forage for diverse Mexican conditions.

Yet even casual travelers are impressed when they see that the ancient digging stick and the colonial wooden plow—a sharpened tree trunk patiently forced into the reluctant earth by bullock power—are still characteristic features of the Mexican rural landscape. Tractors, threshers, and all the wonderful gadgetry available to modern agriculturists are still an exceptional and remarkable intrusion in much of rural Mexico. Although it would be more than misleading to overstress the strides taken to overcome these basic conditions, that they are appearing at all, in conjunction with high yield food plants, is noteworthy.

It was found early, of course, that up-grading of rural technology was but one part of a larger series of problems. Lack of credit and communications were equal, if not more serious, hazards. Alemán has pumped money into far reaches of the republic to aid both the *ejidos* and the small farmers. Previously, many of them had little incentive to produce because speculative parasites had year after year preempted their crops by extension of credit on exorbitant terms. Increase of rural credits to *ejidos* from 131 million pesos in 1946 to 357 million in 1951 has been an important factor. From December 1946 to September 1952, the Alemán régime had pumped, via official agencies, a total of 2190 million pesos of agricultural credit into *ejidos* and small private holdings, a partial explanation of increased production over those years.

More dramatic is what happens when market roads are placed in a hitherto isolated Mexican nook. A case history is Nayarit. The small state of Nayarit has traditionally been the one center of the

West where Indian populations have persisted. During the middle nineteenth century it was the scene of caste wars like those of Yucatan. When these burned themselves out, the Indians of Nayarit settled down to raising maize for their own use and producing tobacco for the national market. In 1945 there were about 15 kilometers of roads in the area and the annual maize production was in the neighborhood of 30,000 tons, all for local consumption.

Between 1946 and 1950, some 510 kilometers of new market roads (100 of which are fully paved) were completed. Land under cultivation grew 25 per cent greater; crop output multiplied about 600 per cent. Corn production alone jumped to between 150,000 and 178,000 tons a year, of which 90,000 goes to Mexico City. About 20 million pesos' worth of tobacco a year is grown. A study of the erstwhile peasants of this area indicated that most of them are far from poor now. They spend an average of 15 pesos a day to meet the needs of their families; above this sum, a few save around 10,000 pesos annually. As one result they have become small capitalists in their own right. They are buying trucks and tractors; before 1945, only 15 tractors were tabulated for the area, but in 1950 there were around 450. It is on cases like these that optimism in Mexico thrives.

Although individual case histories could be multiplied, it seems wiser to pose the more general question of results on a national scale and their meaning to the individual Mexican family.

Short-Run Results. Some short-run improvements are unquestionable. The cultivated area, now the largest in recent history, amounted in 1952 to about 24 million acres (9.5 million hectares), an increase of about a million acres over 1951. That is still less than one acre of cultivated land per person (0.8). It can be raised higher, but probably cannot be doubled.

More planted acreage, and the combined impact of improvements dealt with above, have raised agricultural production within the last few years. The alarming trends noted from 1935 onward are reversed. Mexico is improving rapidly, not deteriorating. In 1946 the total agricultural production added up to 5.17 million metric tons, while in 1949 it was 5.77 million, with marked increases in subsistence items. As a result, *per capita* shares were largest in recent Mexican history. A million more tons of foodstuffs were grown in 1950 than were produced five years earlier. In 1951–1952, the production exceeded 1950–1951 by almost 20 per cent. Statistics are on the side of the optimists, though in the battle of ciphers each side employs agricultural and land figures which at best are far from real precision because of errors in reporting and other distracting elements.

The upward jump in output and value of food crops has been paralleled in commercial items. In 1946, for instance, the land produced 396,000 bales of cotton, while in 1952 the output was 2,000,-000. Much of this was grown by Cárdenas-created collectivized *ejidos* which benefited from high local prices in the Core and a very favorable world market. Though the fetish of autarchy—auto-production of food—still reigns in Mexico, a number of agricultural economists and policy-makers there are pointing out that it is better for Mexico to grow cotton, which can be sold abroad for dollars, and then use a part of those dollars to purchase wheat that can be grown more cheaply elsewhere; given the small portion of valuable land in Mexico, they say, it should be put to the economically best purposes—local and national.

Concurrent with augmented volume has been an upward trend in the absolute and relative value of the agricultural output. Both the dollar and the peso have radically changed their positions in terms of purchasing power and to each other, so meaningful comparisons are hard to draw. The value of the gross agricultural output in 1940 was 0.5 billion pesos; in 1946 it rose to 2.5 billion pesos. In 1951, President Alemán stated its total value for 1950 as 5.1 billion pesos and for 1951 as 5.7 billion. At the pegged 1946 exchange rate of 4.85, that year's product was worth about 517 million dollars; under the 8.65 devalued peso, the figure was equivalent to about 670 million dollars. Abstruse calculations by Emilio Patiño in 1950 showed that in general the agriculturist is getting more for his products; since 1939 the real returns on maize had increased by 15 per cent, rice 38 per cent, coffee 75 per cent, cotton 31 per cent, but the producer's returns on sugar cane and wheat had hardly risen at all since 1938. The confusing welter of numbers means that rural areas have been booming, too.

Improvement and Demography. The improvement of the agricultural plant and the slow advance toward increasing its efficiency have had important demographic consequences. Without serious loss to national producing capacity, *braceros* have come to the United States; their absence from Mexican fields did not cut production. Within Mexico there has been a substantial shift from field to city. In 1930 about 72 per cent of the gainfully occupied population was in agriculture; in 1952 less than 60 per cent were so engaged. Thanks to slowly rising efficiency, less and less people can produce more and more foods and commercial crops.

If figures show anything at all, they indicate that peons are being upgraded both in rural areas and as they drift to cities. The ambitious *campesino* can thus go to town, and the higher production of his former fellows will feed him. As rural incomes rise, he will begin soon to pay more for their products. Presumably the cityward trek will continue until conditions—economic and social—between urban areas and countrysides reach an equilibrium. Under the twin drives of industrialism and technical agrarianism, some of the wide gaps between city and country are slowly being bridged, not by "ruralizing" the nation but by "urbanizing" it. No one expects the final balance to be achieved overnight. It is a slow, painful, expensive process in terms of money and human lives.

In making judgments about Mexican progress, it is more important to measure how far Mexicans have already *come* than to carp about how far they have yet to *go*. And they have come far in rural Mexico under President Miguel Alemán. He has built solidly on the foundations laid by Presidents Cárdenas and Avila Camacho. Alemán turns a going concern over to his successor, who is pledged to continue these basic and successful programs.

3. PROSPECTS AND POLICY: PAPALOAPAN AND THE FUTURE

The major new departure which President Alemán added to policies he inherited is the idea of rehabilitating vast waste areas by drainage and irrigation. The Tepalcatepec Project is one example. It is overshadowed by the analogous but greater scheme for the Papaloapan area, touched on above. So successful have these two new departures been that in 1951 a third project, to transform the basin of the Rio Fuerte, was created. A fourth one, about which only a little is now known, was officially announced in September 1952; it covers the Grijalva River systems which wander through Chiapas and Tabasco before debouching into the Gulf of Mexico. These socio-hydraulic works will play an important part in the Mexican future, and will undoubtedly influence similar projects throughout the hemisphere. They are worth scrutinizing a little more closely. The work of the Papaloapan Commission can serve as a revealing example.

The area involved is the potentially fertile drainage basin of the Papaloapan River and its large tributaries. These course through the states of Puebla, Oaxaca, and Veracruz. The Papaloapan Project is shaped like a huge square, overlapping state lines; it stretches from Mount Orizaba southward almost to the Isthmus of Tehuantepec and from Tehuacan and Oaxaca City to the Gulf Coast, an area about the size of Belgium or Costa Rica. The territory has great potentialities. It lies between the new oil fields of the South and the industrial centers of the Core. The completion of the Papaloapan Project in the indefinite future will tie the South and the Core together just as the Tepalcatepec Project binds the West to the Core. More important, it joins agrarianism and industrialism into a harmonious whole.

The territory was in 1947 occupied mainly by independent Indian groups and mezti-Indios whose economic and social status has been at a mudsill level. Annually the large rivers of the Basin running to the Gulf overflow their banks; floods have prevented any intensive and planned exploitation of the especially rich coastal lands. Malaria, yellow fever, and other tropical diseases have also minimized the social and economic progress of the present 1,250,000 inhabitants. These diseases have almost been extinguished by a concerted medical attack.

Basically the idea of the Papaloapan Commission is to establish at the center of the region (where the Isthmus Railroad crosses the Papaloapan River) a pre-planned city, Ciudad Alemán, to act as the social, administrative, and economic hub of the zone. This has been done. From it radiates outward a network of roads, canals, and airways to lesser but comparable urban groupings, each in turn surrounded by agricultural and industrial villages. These all grow subsistence and industrial crops—vegetables, maize, sugar cane, cotton, high-grade bananas, pineapples, and the like—and support light manufactures now being established in and around the edges of the zone. An aluminum works and a paper factory got under way in 1952. Both the factories and the new inhabitants benefit from the hydroelectric power created by four huge dams; only partially completed, they now (1952) provide 100,000 KW. Reported discoveries of iron and coal during 1951–1952 at the western limits and beyond open up the possibility that heavy industry can be added to light when the whole area becomes sufficiently developed.

One special feature of the Papaloapan Project is magnitude. Four major headwater dams will be constructed for flood control, irrigation, and generation of electrical energy. The largest of these is the Alemán Dam * on which work was started in 1949. It will be two and a half times larger than any previous dam in Mexico and will be perhaps the biggest in Latin America. Its estimated cost is 150 million pesos. Its reservoir will hold over 6 billion cubic meters of water and cover an area of 46,000 hectares. Alemán Dam alone will irrigate a new area of 170,000 hectares. It compares in size with Bonneville Dam in the United States. Primarily for flood control, but also to provide cheap and easy water communication, the course of the Papaloapan River is being changed and straightened, a prodigious feat in itself. Since much of the Papaloapan area lies in a zone of sufficient or overabundant rain, drainage rather than irrigation occupies first attention.

More interesting in many ways than the sheer magnitude of the enterprise is its concept of harmonious and balanced development. Both in plan and execution, scientists and social scientists, engineers and officials, inhabitants of the area and foreigners, have worked closely together to avoid the many pitfalls which can so easily beset a vast attempt to remodel Nature and society. The scheme is designed less as a showpiece than as a functional mechanism whose ramifications are incalculable.

The first stage of the Commission's work has been concentrated on the central area around the new Ciudad Alemán (not far from Tuxtepec, Oaxaca). Much effort is being expended in pushing roads through virgin areas which have from pre-Columbian days separated small communities from one another. It was estimated that in 1946 about 95 per cent of the inhabitants of this first District of the Project lacked any form of adequate transport or communication. One trunk-line road connects Ciudad Alemán with the main road between Veracruz and Córdoba. Another, a three-lane highway, parallels the Papaloapan River and connects riparian communities with Ciudad Alemán as well as with highways along the Gulf Coast. Many of the subsidiary roads have already been put in. The center of the project, Ciudad Alemán, has been pre-fabricated to hold 300,000 people; 12,000 charter residents are there already. Between 75 per cent and 80 per cent of the work on Alemán Dam and about 50

---

* Named for General Miguel Alemán, father of the current president of the Republic. While doing archaeology nearby in 1951, I had opportunity to see work in progress. It was officially opened in November 1952.

per cent of the work of straightening out the Papaloapan River has already been completed. The local agricultural experiment stations report success with at least fifteen varieties of selected hybrid maize, deemed especially suitable for the area. University of Mexico sociologists and economists have begun issuing summary reports of their findings and general prospects. Nearly every one of these is soberly optimistic.

Detailed, specific reports of the actual progress to date have reduced domestic and foreign skepticism that the Papaloapan Project was only *proyectismo*. It is already becoming one of the great works in Mexico and Latin America. Of equal significance, the now unquestionable success of the Papaloapan Project provides a concrete example of how grandiose dreams can be blended with the "philosophy of small things" so devoutly praised by Frank Tannenbaum recently as a necessary element for the happiness of Mexicans.* Within the broad framework, individual communities lead self-respecting lives. Opened to them is a new opportunity to rejoin national life and to share in the material benefits that technology can bring. For those who may be worried about the soul of the Indian, it may be remarked that groups of Chinantecs in the area profess themselves more pleased with the practice they have now developed of spotting likely milpa sites from commercial airplanes than trudging over mountains.

Prospect. The longer-run implications of recent policies seem obvious. They have served to unify as well as diversify the Mexican economic scene and social panorama. The transference of population from low-grade skills in the countrysides to higher-paying jobs in nascent industry has not been the only augury of the future. Equally as important has been a large-scale, long-term attempt to interweave the two aspects of the industrial revolution, urban and rural, and to bring them into some definite relation to each other.

The current Mexican policies are designed to let some important agricultural provinces remain as such, but to bring to them the material benefits long denied all but dwellers in the largest places— pure water, schools, electric lights, libraries, health centers, and the like. In addition, some of the new localities are becoming deregionalized and decentralized; they are mixed and balanced—such as in the Papaloapan zones—between light industries and local agricultural producers of subsistence and commercial items. At yet other points

---

* Frank Tannenbaum, *Mexico: The Struggle for Peace and Bread* (New York: Alfred A. Knopf, 1950), pp. 242–245.

older industrial clusters and urban centers are expanding, while new ones are coming into being. A new Mexico is visibly forming, and some generalizations based on the older ones do not now hold true.

Concerted and continuous efforts to tie these varied groups together by transport nets, credit structures, educational systems, health programs, and other devices are being successfully made. The consequence is the appearance of a new, interdependent pattern in which strong sentiments attached to the *patria chica* and weaker ones that have produced the regions are more and more being submerged in favor of a tempered economic and political nationalism. Interdependence rather than regional independence will grow.

In summary, it is clear that Mexico has embarked on yet a new phase of an old Revolution. Arguments over its particular goals often seem as heated as discussions of the political phases were in 1917. Standing clear of the polemic, however, is the conclusion that the "industrial revolution" has merged two distinct recent tendencies: urban industrialism, which was rejuvenated during and after World War II, and "technical agrarianism," that similarly marked a new departure in the almost age-old land question. General increases and improvements in credit, transportation, irrigation, marketing, political mechanisms, finances, and national morale, so noticeable during the past decade, have bound countrysides and towns together. Both share the immediate blessings thus created. The reciprocal effect of urban developments on rural life, and country betterment on city-bound interests, is a fact of prime magnitude. Mexico can be neither wholly "rural" nor completely "urban." It must be both.

18. Mexico and the United States

In the "Era of Good Feeling" which has marked relationships between the United States and Mexico since 1940, economic rather than political matters have been in the forefront. The flow of capital, goods, ideas, and men from the northern republic to the southern has been an important element in the economic and industrial revolution taking place in Mexico. However, that interchange has raised some new problems between the two countries. None of these is serious. As President Alemán reported to his Congress on September 1, 1951, "Our relations with the United States have developed on a plane of mutual understanding."

1. PARTNERSHIP AND PROBLEMS

In most international economic affairs, the United States has remained the dominant focus of Mexican attention. The overwhelming power of the United States in the present world and the proximity of Mexico to it have been fundamental conditioning factors. In trade and monetary matters the actions of the United States are decisive in influencing Mexican domestic trends. One of the current Mexican policies is to lessen that complete dependence by national legislation and by reaching abroad for markets and suppliers, but the basic arrangements remain essentially unaltered.

Another and equally important feature of the decade (especially the past five years) is broadening the areas where mutual interests have led to coöperative efforts on a partnership basis. The joint international irrigation work on the Rio Grande at Falcón Dam is a typical sample. The coöperative effort to stamp out Mexican hoof-and-mouth disease which threatened vast cattle holdings in the American Southwest is another.

Akin to these has been growing integration and mutual dependence.

Mexican migrant labor has not only proved its worth, but is now almost a prerequisite for many agricultural enterprises in the United States. The widening stream of American tourists to Mexico is the main supplier of dollars that permit it to balance its international books.

The sum is that Mexico and the United States are interacting more vigorously, more extensively, and more intensely than at any earlier time. But unlike some previous epochs, contacts are friendly, cordial, and largely routine. Infrequently problems arise as small ripples on a generally serene surface. Thus the empirical approach, which at one time or another has employed nearly every gambit and policy—from outright imperialism to studied disdain of the Mexicans—was not wholly in vain. A distillation from experience has firmly established the working conclusion (accepted by both countries): the only viable long-term basis for living together is partnership, based on mutual esteem and reciprocal confidence.

Contacts between the republics, "international relations," have multiplied. Probably more Americans know Mexico than any other foreign land. Across countless conference tables, in numerous joint enterprises, and in informal, popular interchanges among businessmen, students, and just plain citizens, Mexicans meet United States citizens. The deep reservoir of good will that has been thus accumulated displaces many of the hidden resentments which formerly poked above the surface to founder the unwary. Deep and extensive, this good will is less self-conscious and forced than some of the wartime "unity" impressed on other Latin-American countries by parades of movie stars and floods of ill-prepared articles and books dedicated to "hemispheric solidarity." The courting, marriage, and honeymoon stages of relationship with Mexico are long past. The United States and its southern neighbor have settled down to a ripe, mature, solid *entente* that does not require public love-making to reassure the participants and the world that all is well. In the truest sense they are partners.

The clearest proof is that now they can amicably agree to disagree, yet maintain emotional equilibrium. The current problems are not critically serious, though they are important and involved. The two main ones center on trade and the Border.

Current Problems. Foreign commerce of Mexico is bound to the United States. Despite its magnitude the growing trade has no firm international treaty structure to regulate or guide it. Each country takes a friendly but obstinate view of what a suitable basis for a mutual trade treaty should be. So far neither has retreated, nor, unless declared war presses heavily on political patterns, is it likely to.

Mexico voices the now standard Latin-American complaint that the United States' drive for "free trade"—lowering of all barriers to international commerce—is merely a device to increase its markets at the expense of local Mexican industry that has developed since the war. Further, if the Korean crisis suddenly ended and the United States began "dumping" to rid itself of surplus goods (as it did in the twenties), such competition would completely flatten the Latin-American agricultural as well as industrial economies. Therefore, matters are at a stalemate. This anomalous situation is recent. Like many other facets of Mexican-American relations, the contemporary situation takes World War II as the point of departure.

The Trade Treaty of 1942. On December 23, 1942, the United States and Mexico signed a reciprocal trade treaty which became effective January 30, 1943. It was a wartime agreement that lowered specific duties on a long list of manufactured items entering Mexico from the United States, and gave Mexican oil, metals, and other raw materials needed for the defense effort similar privileged treatment above the Border. During the war years, there were few manufactured goods available for Mexico; afterwards its raw materials were a glut on the market. During World War II, Mexico's manufactures began to sprout to cover consumer items. But there was a great backlog of unfilled wants which, on the termination of hostilities, Mexicans proceeded to fill by purchases in the United States. The inflation in both countries had altered the price levels on which the 1942 treaty rested. In both countries economic policies shifted after the war.

The consequences were predictable. The first thing that happened was the rapid draining of Mexican foreign exchange. Dollars that had accumulated during the war flew to the United States for luxuries and frivolous items. Several times during 1945 and 1946 the Mexican government worried about its dwindling reserves, and sought to stem the tide by getting the 1942 Treaty changed. Low tariffs were encouraging dollars to drain northward. Added to the decline in foreign exchange, there was considerable domestic pressure from the "Newest Group" of war-born industrialists to get protection for their infant industries.

The marked unbalanced trade of 1947 led the two governments to agree to a provisional change in the reciprocal treaty. In July 1947,

Mexico was allowed to prohibit completely the entrance of a great number of United States-manufactured items covered by the 1942 accord. In November, Mexico placed high tariffs (*ad valorem* rather than specific rates) on about 5000 items *not* covered by the 1942 document. As the drain on reserves and agitation for more protection continued, it became clear to the United States in December 1947 that Mexico was going to raise duties unilaterally even on items *covered* by the reciprocal pact. Rather than cause a breach in American-Mexican friendship, the State Department gave permission for the Mexicans to raise certain duties and to figure them on an *ad valorem* basis rather than holding them to the specific fixed tariffs earlier provided. Mexico agreed to negotiate about items it had placed on the prohibited list, not already covered by any treaty.

For months after April 1948, when negotiations got under way to revise the wartime document in light of the postwar world, representatives of the two nations talked. They could reach no agreement. The Mexicans wanted protection via tariff; the United States wanted "free trade." These were friendly talks, but it became manifestly impossible for the strongly held but divergent views to be ironed out. Therefore, by mutual consent, Mexico and the United States decided to terminate the old wartime treaty. This was announced to the press on June 23, 1950. The treaty died at midnight, December 31, 1950.

The Current Situation. The termination of the 1942 Reciprocal Treaty left the United States and Mexico without a formal treaty basis of trade relations. Mexico is currently but voluntarily granted a "most-favored-nation" status. If the United States lowers duties on any item for any other country (but Cuba), Mexico automatically benefits; it gets as low a tariff as "the most favored nation." This arrangement cushioned a good number of the shocks which might have ensued when United States duties were suddenly doubled on Mexican oil, lead, toys, leather goods, and the like. This status as "most-favored-nation" is an informal rather than a formal agreement; the United States could unilaterally withdraw it, but for many reasons has not. Probably it should not, either.

GATT. There is a United States international economic policy that is not widely publicized. The United States makes no more direct bilateral treaties with nations which have not joined it in a huge multilateral conclave of countries by signing a United States-sponsored General Agreement on Trade and Tariffs. The object of the organization, GATT, is to remove barriers to international trade by mutual consent and joint concessions. Within the GATT organization is being worked out what the Mexicans always refer to as the "Plan Clayton"—the views expressed many times by Assistant Secretary of State Will Clayton, especially at the Chapultepec Conference.*

Little nations like Mexico, which are industrializing, refuse to commit themselves to lowered tariffs without correlative guarantees against the "dumping" which they remember from the twenties and thirties. The GATT documents say nothing about that. Mexico has, therefore, refused to join the GATT group. The likelihood that a new bilateral trade treaty with the United States will be signed in the near future is very small.

At the moment, Mexico is getting a free ride. Every time the United States makes a concession to a GATT member, Mexico gets it anyway, because of the "most-favored-nation" status. So why join? The United States must think very seriously about the political and international implications of threatening to withdraw the privileges it is voluntarily extending to Mexico. But the definite termination of economic treaties with the United States has allowed the Alemán government to operate a "flexible" trade policy based on quotas and licenses in accordance with the rapidly changing Mexican economic system. Since the government is no longer completely dependent on sums derived from foreign commerce to carry on its activities, it can and does follow this "flexible" line to protect dollar reserves, to preserve infant industries, to increase or decrease inflation, and to implement a series of other economic and commercial ends. It opens and shuts the import valves as the situation demands. It could be characterized as a tempered economic nationalism.

Braceros. In its drives to replace imported consumer items by local manufactures and to integrate Mexico into a single economic unit, the Mexican government has also come into conflict with the United States over the matter of migrant Mexican labor. This problem, too, stems largely from World War II, although there is a long previous history which we need not recount in full.

The difficulties are threefold. Rather than exporting people, Mexico wants to keep them at home; annual agricultural needs in the United States require the services of some 200,000 or more Mexicans a year. Secondly, Mexicans in the United States have traditionally been subject to various sorts of exploitation and discrimination; the

* See above, pp. 280–281.

Mexican government, when persuaded to allow some people to migrate, wants closely regulated civil and economics rights guarantees that the *braceros* will be honestly contracted for and safeguarded during their stay in the United States under supervision of official United States agencies. Finally, despite all official actions and regulations set up jointly to protect legally defined *braceros,* a mass of furtive "wet-backs" trade hopeless peonage in Mexico for only slightly bettered conditions in the United States where, as renegades, they are subject to unscrupulous handling and generate deplorable social problems. But, though fugitives, they are Mexican nationals and their government seeks to protect them.

Mexican officials feel that the manpower pool from which *braceros* are drawn could better be employed on the new irrigated lands being created in the North. Some should join the working force in the industrial centers coming to life all over Mexico. Further, Mexican concern for the civil treatment of its nationals in the United States is now as touchy as was the earlier United States' sensitivity to its citizens' property rights in Mexico. Organized labor in Mexico and the United States have (for different reasons) consistently opposed the *bracero* exodus and its clandestine cousin, the wet-back migration. In the Imperial Valley of California, for instance, the farms employ about 14,000 workers—5000 Americans, 5000 legally contracted Mexican *braceros,* and 4000 wet-backs; the last-mentioned keep wage levels low for all. The problem of the "wet-backs" is less amenable to rapid solution than the allied matter of *braceros* for whom international bargaining recently achieved some accord.

Much in the fashion of talks about trade treaties, negotiations between Mexico and the United States over migrant labor have been inconclusive. After extending and then withdrawing the wartime agreements, the Alemán government sat down with the United States late in 1950 in an attempt to resolve some of the thorny issues. Friendly but obstinate bickering went on at this mixed commission— 13 Mexicans, 12 Americans—through January 1951. The conferences hoped to evolve a formula whereby *braceros* would continue to aid American farmers under contracts that assured migrant Mexicans of fair wages, good treatment, and freedom from discrimination. As though not fully aware of the difference in governmental systems, Mexicans wanted a "responsible" United States government agency to supervise these matters, with power to intervene and punish American citizens and localities which fell below the high standards of civil and economic rights stipulated; it is somewhat difficult to explain that despite political speeches to the contrary, there are numerous segments of American life into which a national bureaucracy cannot enter and dominate as it wills. Though no definitive treaty emerged, the draft of one included a "black list" of places to which Mexicans refused to send their nationals, mainly in Texas and other places of the American South.

In its slow progress through the United States Senate the proposed treaty was loaded with crippling amendments and touched off a number of uncomplimentary remarks about the Mexicans. At the same time, zealous Mexican journalists were filling newspapers with lurid tales of mistreatment of Mexicans in the United States, especially *braceros* in California. As a consequence, Alemán announced that after July 15, 1951 no more *braceros* would be permitted to migrate. The mixed commission continued its quiet work. At the beginning of August 1951 it brought forth a workable compromise, a temporary accord, to last until a more definitive arrangement could be made. Nearly all the civil and social guarantees demanded by Mexicans, who were to be employed exclusively as farm (not pastoral) labor, were included. Mexico made it clear that a final treaty would be contingent on the United States' taking some effective steps to implement the guarantees thus provided and also doing something concrete to end the "wet-back" migration by enforcing statutes already on the books. The temporary agreement was scheduled to lapse in February, then the date was pushed forward to May 1952.

Obviously no one knows the total number of wet-backs. Gladwin Hill in the *New York Times* claimed as high as half a million Mexicans a year are willing to exchange Mexican exploitation for almost the same thing in the United States. The flow of peons perpetuates some of the worst social and economic conditions in the United States and is an explosive international issue involving Mexicans whose highly nationalistic country now is willing to press for their civil rights. The plight of the wet-backs—bamboozled by unscrupulous Mexican contractors, robbed, beaten, and outside the law of either nation—has become a literary theme comparable to the sad state of the Indian in the 1920's and 1930's.

The United States did take some action. It began repatriating illegally entered Mexicans, and in March 1952 Congress passed legislation on the subject. Fines of $2000 and five-year jail terms were penalties for anyone who recruited, transported, concealed, or "harbored" wet-backs; some of the sting was removed by exempting "employment," which is not considered "harboring." With 1952 an election year in both countries, the respective governments evidently hoped to keep the inflammable *bracero*–wet-back questions from becoming entangled in domestic political campaigns. When the temporary agreement expired in May, its provisions were quietly renewed until the end of the year. Each side made and got minor concessions: United States citizens were permitted to appeal their inclusion on the "black list," while Mexico obtained a better system of record-keeping and changed methods of payment to *braceros* by individual contractors. Its current status is recapitulated in President Alemán's "State of the Nation" message of September 1, 1952. He reported that the accord reached in August 1951 improved the 1949 arrangements, and through 1952 "contracting for our workers has been going on with improved results without hurting [our] national economy." In fact, however, the issues are likely to be argued for some time to come. The temporary agreements will be subjected to political mauling before a stable solution, if any, can be reached. The only final answer is, of course, to equalize Mexican and American conditions. When migrant labor can find as much or more opportunity at home, it will not go abroad. Until that condition appears under the drives of rural electrification, school systems, creation of farmland by irrigation, and raised rural standards, the wet-backs will continue to fill the vacuum created by labor shortages along the northern side of the boundary. It is not a simple problem, nor one which will be solved quickly.

Thus the matter rests. When it again comes to view, it is well to remember that the basic issues are somewhat complicated and highly emotional. Further, viewed in perspective, minor frictions over migrant labor are irritating rather than dangerous; any settlement will set off loud outcries. Counterbalancing these should be placed the resolution of many difficulties in the postwar relationships between Mexico and the United States and the number of unpretentious schemes in which they are joint partners. One of the most heartening tales is the victory won over hoof-and-mouth disease (*fiebre aftosa*), which could have endangered the hard-won amity built up during World War II.

Early in 1947 news got out that in southern Mexico there had started an epizootic of *aftosa*, hoof-and-mouth disease. It affects cattle in a highly unattractive way; the udders, mouths, and hooves become infected with blister-like sores. The few animals which live are henceforth useless. The disease also affects human beings. The Mexican outbreak threatened to wipe out food and leather supplies, as well as the rural motive power that these animals represented. Because numerous Mexican cattle are sold and slaughtered in the United States, the disease seriously endangered that country's billion-dollar cattle industry. Mexican cattle were quarantined. Presidents Truman and Alemán, with their respective agricultural officials, swung into immediate action against *aftosa*. The United States lent experts and money to help the Mexicans contain the disease to restricted zones.

The first approach to the problem (January to November 1947) was to kill the infected cattle and pay their owners a just compensation, around $400 a head. But the "sanitary rifle" was politically and economically loaded. Sinarquista leaders organized peasant resistance, and Mexican farmers responded to their fiery antigovernment, anti-American appeals. To carry on the extermination campaign would have lit the fires of an agrarian revolt that might have unseated the government. Mexican officials persuaded the United States to try a new vaccination technique. To that time serums against hoof-and-mouth disease had been few, expensive, and unreliable, therefore limited. But the Joint American-Mexican Aftosa Commission set up laboratories, and within a very short time appropriate and effective inoculations were in mass production. Under the revised scheme, cattle in suspect zones were each given four shots; the amount of serum needed was prodigious.

The *aftosa* story has a happy ending. After five years of existence, the Joint Commission was formally dissolved on March 12, 1952, with the statement, "Hoof-and-mouth disease has disappeared from the country." All told, laboratories set up in Mexico had produced more than 52.5 million doses of vaccine, with which better than 17 million animals had been treated. Argentine and Brazilian technicians had helped develop it; the original 100,000 dosages had been quickly provided by Great Britain, Chile, the Low Countries, as well as by Argentina and Brazil. Throughout the grueling and dangerous campaigns practical international coöperation had been magnificent.

"On September 1, 1947 I informed this National Representation of the appearance in our country of *fiebre aftosa*," President Alemán reported to his Congress on September 1, 1952. "Today . . . we are pleased to announce . . . that the campaign against hoof-and-mouth disease has terminated, and this day Mexico is declared

officially rid of that epizootic." With the eradication of *fiebre aftosa*
an accomplished fact, the quarantine against entrance of Mexican
cattle into the United States was lifted.

The effort cost the United States a total of around $160 million.
When an audit was made of Mexican-American expenditures, the
small sum of around $6000 was all that could not be accounted for.
The Alemán government had been absolutely ruthless with any attempted politicking or corruption in this important *aftosa* campaign.
Among the by-products of the episode was the stimulation of meat-
packing plants in Mexico (to use cattle not allowed to cross the
Border); a new technique and materials to fight this dreaded outbreak—Mexicans went to Venezuela to help that country fight a
similar campaign; and a considerable mutual respect built up between the 7559 Mexican and American technicians, joint allies against
disease and ignorance. The *aftosa* crusade is but a dramatic illustra-
tion of the solid body of technical coöperation between the United
States and Mexico that has gone on for more than a decade.

Perhaps more important in some ways are the unofficial programs
carried on by organizations in the United States to help the Mexicans
help themselves. The Foundations—Rockefeller, Guggenheim, and
others—have contributed greatly, especially in research. Without fanfare, religious and semireligious groups have toiled quietly among
the lowly in Mexico to improve their lot. The Y.M.C.A., the Society
of Friends, and the Wyclif Translators are but a few of those who
have ventured afield to teach rural groups the rudiments of sanitation, literacy, and aids to everyday living. Individuals are legion who
have lent their talents and time to forward studies and to execute
programs for improvement of Mexican conditions.

There is a countercurrent of Mexicans who come to the United
States, not as *braceros* or wet-backs, but as students. The largest
Latin-American group are Mexicans, outranked in number only by
Canadians, Chinese, and Germans. During 1951–1952 a total of 1185
were recorded as students of a wide range of curricula. The largest
single body of Mexicans enrolled for religious instruction (430), but
budding engineers (170), doctors (56), businessmen (100), agriculturists (53), and scientists (58) were well represented. Many
pursued liberal arts (119) and social sciences (53), while Mexican
concern with the fine arts was carried on by 30 university students.

At almost every level and in nearly every sphere it could be
demonstrated that the relations between the United States and Mex-

ico were basically serene. After the roller-coaster-like twists and drops of previous days and years, both parties were justifiably complacent about the Era of Good Feeling. In a troubled world, this was a haven of tranquillity.

2. POSTWAR HEMISPHERIC ORDER

With the United States and Mexico in agreement on fundamentals, and openly pledged to discuss amicably their other differences of opinion, the inter-American system has continued to work smoothly, and embarrassing incidents between the United States and its southern neighbors in the United Nations have been minimized. Neither all the old nor the increasing new problems arising between Mexico and the United States were sponged completely from the slate. But it was clear after May 1947 that the wartime collaboration had more than an opportunistic base. It has continued to the present.

The Inter-American System in the Postwar World. Scarcely had the mushroom-shaped smoke from Hiroshima cleared away when a chill of disillusionment, if not fear, again began to penetrate the hemisphere. With one aggressor and its satellites crushed at enormous sacrifices, Soviet shadows began to darken the world. Subversion from within rather than direct attack from without seemed a greater threat. Within the hemisphere, the renewed equivocal and self-centered actions of Argentina caused some apprehension. Wartime shortages remained peacetime difficulties in many Latin-American nations; high prices and rationing in the United States barred Latin-Americans from acquiring needed materials; just when their exported goods, which had helped win the war, were a glut on the United States' market. To tidy up a number of these matters a Conference of Ministers of the various American Republics was called at Rio de Janeiro in August 1947.

The Rio Conference aimed mainly at converting the temporary wartime inter-American system into a permanent, flexible organization to quash military aggression from within or from outside the American herisphere's state system. Latin-American nations were not fully satisfied with the mechanisms set up by the untried United Nations, and therefore decided to maintain, within its framework, their historic regional arrangements. At their insistence Article 51 of the United Nations Charter had allowed such regional action to be taken. The details of this "inherent right of individual or collective self-defense" were filled in at the Rio Conference, thus linking the United Nations to the Inter-American system.

It is of the greatest importance to note that this pioneering effort laid the groundwork and served as a model for the Atlantic Charter and the North Atlantic Treaty Organization. By getting the United States Senate to ratify the Rio Treaty, Senators Connally and Vandenberg more than half won the battle that came a year later when the United States promised to aid Western European nations which (under Winston Churchill's prod) began to form a North Atlantic "regional system for individual and collective self-defense," somewhat on the unconscious model of the New World state system, though with its own peculiar European backgrounds.

Writes Alberto Lleras, then Director-General of the Pan-American Union, "The Inter-American Treaty of Reciprocal Assistance, as the agreement of Rio de Janeiro is officially called, is probably the most serious and decisive step which has been taken in the relations of the states of our hemisphere." It provided that when threatened, this regional section of the United Nations could and would act to meet aggression from outside the hemisphere. It set up a number of devices and degrees of collective action within the hemisphere to settle disputes peaceably. More important, it gave the Inter-American system sanction and power to act as a whole group against a state or states which might rupture the peace of the Americas by threatening the territorial integrity or political independence of any one of the members. As a new departure in the state documents of the Americas, the delegates signed in the name of their peoples, rather than as representatives of governments.

The signers are automatically bound to aid the victim against the aggressor, once it is agreed that aggression has occurred. Action is determined by joint consultation. Armed force is but one of several possible sanctions in regulating and stopping actual or potential conflict. In short, the New World, including the United States, professed themselves willing to bind themselves into a protective network which can almost instantly flash into some sort of anticipatory or remedial action when the security so dearly won in World War II is placed in jeopardy.

As president of the Mexican delegation at Rio, Jaime Torres Bodet, the only cabinet member who had served both under Avila Camacho and under Alemán, added luster to Mexico's ability to present forceful yet conciliatory views. A brilliant littérateur then with six novels, three volumes of poetry, and fifteen foreign decorations to his credit, Torres Bodet had entered the Mexican diplomatic service in 1929, and was switched to the Ministry of Education under Avila Camacho. When the Rio Conference was deadlocked between the United States' view that only a treaty of political-military arrangements should be made and the Latin-American position that economic matters should first be threshed out, the Mexicans produced a formula to bring the Conference out of the doldrums. They suggested a separate meeting to be held on the topic of economic coöperation.

Though this Conference of Ministers at Rio had been called specifically and almost exclusively to prepare and ratify reciprocal and joint assistance in political and military matters, the conferees expressed its other sentiments in fifteen additional resolutions. The chief of these concerned economic and social matters, especially the strengthening of economic coöperation to ease the postwar strains. The Mexican suggestion deferred further discussion of these problems until the more comprehensive Inter-American meeting, a plenary session rather than just a limited Conference of Ministers, which was held at Bogotá in 1948. President Truman flew down for the closing moments of the sessions in Rio, where he outshone even the late Eva Perón, also present. He promised the Latin-Americans that he had not forgotten their difficulties. They had hoped for a little firmer commitment but that was the best they could obtain.

The Organization of American States: Bogotá, 1948. At Bogotá, Colombia, from March 30 through May 2, 1948, one historic epoch of Pan-Americanism closed and another opened. Amid exciting surroundings—a sudden outpouring of confused masses that carried on Colombia's first revolution in nearly fifty years—the old organizations were reviewed, streamlined, and regrouped into the present Organization of American States. It would go beyond the scope of the present work to outline these alterations in any detail, especially since the essentials have recently been put in readable form by Arthur Whitaker.* The Ninth International Conference of American States was a full-scale meeting, in the series which was first initiated in Washington in 1889 and held at five-year intervals since, except when interrupted by war or other major difficulty.

The Conference was to round out the work of Rio, which it did.

* "Development of American Regionalism: The Organization of American States," Carnegie Endowment for International Peace, *International Conciliation*, No. 469 (March 1951).

The Bogotá Meeting produced two agreements of basic importance: the OAS Charter—"Constitution of the Americas"—and an American Treaty of Pacific Settlement—"Pact of Bogotá." In September 1950, Mexico was the only member of the system which had signed and ratified all three documents—Rio Treaty of Mutual Assistance, and these two. Taken together, the three pacts form the perimeters of international affairs within the New World.

The Rio and the Bogotá meetings consolidated rather than innovated. Most of the items signed and resolved had been on the books one way or another for nearly half a century. The new Charter provided for meetings of the plenary body of American states at five-year intervals; meetings of foreign ministers are to be held whenever necessary. The day-to-day work of the OAS is carried on by an OAS Council which is charged with carrying out the provisions of the Rio Treaty and other tasks assigned to it. It also supervises subsidiary coördinating organs, three Inter-American Councils: Economic and Social, Jurists, and Cultural. The old Pan-American Union lingers on as the secretariat of the main OAS Council and a host of other organizations. Their number has been variously estimated at from 33 to 73. Each is now under one of the three Inter-American specialized Councils, which are trying to reduce their number and duplication.

Again the Mexicans, under Jaime Torres Bodet, took notable leadership in the formulation of the Charter and lesser works completed at Bogotá. More or less accustomed to proper actions in crises, the Mexican delegation, when the riots in Bogotá broke out, lined up in military manner, unfurled a Mexican flag, and strode out into the street; both sides of the Bogotá revolution cheered them as they marched to the Mexican Embassy. Those Mexicans who weren't in the assembly hall remained unmoved at their hotels, where they organized a series of literary and musical salons among the immured.

In more serious matters, the Mexicans stressed their thesis that hemispheric peace rested on raised standards of living. These in turn had as a foundation the ability to obtain capital goods and long-term, cheap credit for developmental work. The Mexicans also had an important hand in formulating a "New World Declaration of the Rights of Man," still subject of much controversy.

Along with other Latin-American delegations the Mexican one was at first visibly disappointed that there would be no Marshall Plan for Latin America. The Marshall Plan was devised to rehabilitate a developed European economy weakened by war; the problem of

Latin America was to build such an economy from the ground up. Consistently Mexico sided with the other Latin-American nations which wanted an end put to colonial holdings—like British Honduras —in the Western Hemisphere. To provide the curious with a record of its posture on each of the incredibly prolix social, economic, and political questions that arose at Bogotá, the Mexican Ministry of Foreign Relations issued a fat volume.*

Few things are duller or more significant in the long run than this endless sitting around conference tables, spinning millions of words to cushion brute force and to foster coöperation. The Bogotá Conference marks a maturing of the Americas. Since Bogotá, the OAS Council has met regularly to keep an eye on hemispheric matters. Each of the subsidiary Councils and other bodies have convened from time to time for meetings that range from agriculture to zinc production. The complicated machinery really works.

Fourth Conference of Ministers, Washington, March 26–April 6, 1951. Of all these meetings perhaps the most significant was a called gathering of American Foreign Ministers in Washington. The first since World War II, it considered common actions to be taken after the Korean crisis had run for almost a year.

Three topics seemed urgently to require discussion: military coöperation, internal security against resurgent Communism, and emergency economic coöperation, to divide equally the sacrifices made necessary by the efforts to stop aggressive action in Korea. The United States wanted moral and material help from the Latin-Americans. As in World War II, they assigned themselves the task of providing an augmented flow of strategic materials. The United States delegation could offer longer-term contracts than in World War II, to prevent local dislocations when stockpiling and mobilization needs terminated. They offered to make loans available for the output of needed goods and commodities.

After the preliminaries, in which President Truman and Secretary of State Dean Acheson sketched the United States' policies, the Ministers jointly issued a "Declaration of Washington." It reaffirmed hemispheric unity—"spiritual and material"—in the present emergency or any future one; it stated that in order to restore and maintain peace, it was essential to support the United Nations' actions in the Far East.

* *Mexico en la IX Conferencia Internacional Americana,* Dpto. de Información para el Extranjero (Mexico, 1948).

As final results, the Conference produced some thirty resolutions, which covered a vast military, economic, and political program to check international Communism in the Americas and in the world. Rather than set up a "hemispheric army," each nation promised to strengthen its own forces and make available what surplus troops it could to the United Nations to carry out the "United for Peace" policy. Fortunately all the machinery that had helped win World War II had not rusted. Rather it was strengthened, so that in general the Western Hemisphere is currently better prepared to face world and regional crises than it was in 1941. In 1952 President Alemán felt moved to reassure the Mexican Congress and people that his government had made no secret agreements, but stood on "our position of solidarity in democracy and our free and firm resolve to defend the [American] Continent against any sort of foreign aggression."

3. WORLD ORDER

During the 1945 Chapultepec Conference, Mexico introduced a resolution calling for an international organization along modified lines sketched earlier by the Great Powers at the Dumbarton Oaks meetings (1942). Mexico wanted the role of the General Assembly spelled out more completely; it called for an extended World Court, and a special organization to foster intellectual and moral coöperation. Like other Latin-American states, it demanded preservation of the Inter-American System within any such world political body.

At the founding of the United Nations and the writing of its charter in San Francisco (April 25–June 26, 1945), Mexico was one of the fourteen nations on the Executive Committee. Its ideas about international matters appeared in 28 proposals, some 20 of which were written into the final Charter. Mexico, like other underdeveloped nations, was a strong proponent of an Economic and Social Council. Mexico also expressed clearly the small state's view of the Security Council. Mexican proposals encharged the Permanent Members with keeping a real peace if by the veto they were to be given so much power. More or less as a reward for its war services and its aid in getting the United Nations under way, Mexico was given one of the original nonpermanent seats on the Security Council. Here it acted as a representative of small countries in general and Latin America in particular.

This was in marked contrast to its position in the League of Nations. There Woodrow Wilson would not even permit Mexico to be a member. On nearly every one of the important councils and committees which the world organization began immediately to breed, Mexico has a post, sometimes a chairmanship. Summing up its 1952 activities in the United Nations, President Alemán noted that Mexico had completed another cycle of active and uninterrupted participation on all principal organs, and Mexicans have now sat on the Security Council, the Council of Fiduciary Administrations (Mandates), the Economic and Social Council, and have headed the General Assembly.

Of all these United Nations activities perhaps the one nearest to the Mexicans' heart is UNESCO—United Nations Educational, Scientific and Cultural Organization. Its doings are often unpredictable, as its job is to do good, everywhere. It writes declarations of the Rights of Man, of Woman, and represents the underprivileged. UNESCO proposes the rehabilitation of the Amazon and of downtrodden peoples and areas wherever found. Beneath its froth, it performs many needed and admirable tasks in the intangible field of culture under the able chairmanship of Mexico's Jaime Torres Bodet. Fed up with bickerings and lack of coherence among members of the Council, he once turned in his resignation; he was persuaded to stay. In November 1952 he finally resigned when UNESCO's budget was cut.

Among UNESCO's major concerns is education. In this field, Mexico has much that it can give the world from its own Revolutionary experience. In recognition of this fact, when UNESCO decided to implement a resolution it had passed in 1948 at Mexico City, it created in Mexico the first of six projected Regional Fundamental Educational Centers.

The beautiful little city of Patzcuaro was selected as the official center for the experiment. The aim of the Center is to instruct teachers and to prepare appropriate pedagogic material for all underdeveloped Latin-American areas. Rural teachers, welfare and other qualified social workers, are brought together on fellowships to pool their experiences and interchange the techniques which have proved effective in raising the intellectual and economic standards of rural populations in their particular part of Latin America. Beyond receiving advanced training in such methods, they coöperate in writing the teaching materials needed for this necessary and specialized problem.

In the first year of operation fifty teachers, five from each of ten countries, will attend.* The fellowships from UNESCO pay their living expenses and $100 a month. Designated as Director of this pilot effort is Lucas Ortíz Benítez, a Mexican educator who has had a long experience with the Mexican rural school, the literacy compaign, and similar problems. The Alemán government and other Mexicans have joined international organizations to back the effort. Mexico promised to provide an adequate plant, vehicles, and an annual subsidy, currently a million pesos, for operating expenses. Ex-President Lázaro Cárdenas donated grounds and a charming hacienda, Eréndira, to house the enterprise. The Organization of American States has made the Regional Center of Fundamental Education a grant of $40 million, and UNESCO has given it $15 million.

If it goes well, the idea (said Torres Bodet) will be extended to Africa, the Far East, the Near East, and Oceania, to complete the network of such regional centers. With great éclat, the Latin-American Regional Center was inaugurated on May 10, 1951 by President Alemán, Jaime Torres Bodet, and a great assembly of educational and diplomatic dignitaries. It is the first step toward providing the 12,000 teaching specialists needed to make some dent on the world's 1200 million illiterates. It will be surprising indeed if Mexican ideas do not now circle the globe. The Center at Patzcuaro promises to become a showplace of the New World as well as a beacon in the educational universe.

Partly as a tribute to Mexico's unflagging interest in United Nations affairs and its sincere efforts to foster international coöperation and peace, its representative, Luis Padilla Nervo, was elected president of the Sixth General Assembly. In his inaugural address on November 6, 1951 he sketched out the world's hopes for a just and lasting peace based on liberty and international equality. Padilla Nervo is well versed in United Nations lore, as he served at the constituent assembly in San Francisco, and was Mexico's representative on the Security Council. Mexico was among the first members to establish a permanent delegation to the United Nations, of which Padilla Nervo has been head.† The Mexican delegation, carrying out Alemán's foreign policies, has consistently urged the liquidation of

* Bolivia, Peru, Ecuador, Honduras, Costa Rica, El Salvador, Panama, Haiti, Guatemala, and Mexico. Each government designates its own candidates.

† On leaving his post, he was less optimistic than earlier. He is to be Minister of Foreign Affairs after Dec. 1, 1952.

World War II by signing of peace treaties, and continues to voice the Mexican and small-nation thesis that the large powers who have the veto also have the moral responsibility of creating peace by reaching agreement among themselves. Understandably, Mexico has from the outset been against Franco and the admission of Spain. It has actively carried on committee work in the councils and organizations under United Nations, and has a member, Isidro Fabela, on the International Court of Justice.

Many facets of Mexico's relations with the United Nations have here been reluctantly omitted for lack of space. In very general terms it can be said that in fields where enthusiasm, intelligence, and moral rectitude rather than where economic or military power determine the outcome, Mexico is among the top leaders. It is far from a parochially inclined nation. Now that its own house is in good order, it feels the urge to spread the lessons of the Revolution on a global scale and it is successfully doing it. Mexico is a good friend for the United States to have in the United Nations.

That the studied and carefully cultivated friendship between the United States and Mexico has not been entirely in vain was revealed clearly not long ago, and also offers testimony on Mexico's current outlook. Speaking for Mexico, rather than as a mouthpiece for the United States, the Mexican delegate at a meeting of the Economic and Social Conference of the United Nations (held in Santiago, Chile in March 1951), countered Russian-inspired charges there that the economic difficulties of Latin America were due to "imperialist re-armament by the United States." Ten years ago few people would have thought it possible that a responsible Mexican official announcing his government's policy would dare to defend the United States against Russia.

Representatives of the United States and of Mexico now meet at a bewildering variety of points almost unknown in Woodrow Wilson's day. They sit side by side on commissions, boards, and committees in the United Nations and in the parallel apparatus set up by the Organization of American States. They increasingly join for formal and informal bilateral talks in an incredible array of government bureaus in both capitals. In a sense there are literally hundreds of United States–Mexican policies quietly ticking away in pleasantly humdrum fashion.

A constant problem in United States foreign policy is to fit this sprawling multilateral network of commitments into its general foreign policy. At the same time it must keep its particular bilateral policy toward any one Latin-American country, like Mexico, from straying outside the narrowed bounds set by both. To complicate matters, the Latin-American nations face the United States as juridical equals at plenary conferences of the Organization of American States (held at intervals of five years) but as "small powers"—subordinates and lesser figures—in the United Nations, to which they all also belong. In our troubled times, such minor technical difficulties shrink to zero in significance beside the fact that immediately south of the border a sturdy democracy is growing, a helpful ally and partner in any foreseeable crisis. It seems truly to be an American "Middle-Way."

4. RETROSPECT AND PROSPECT

Since neolithic wanderers traversed the present boundaries of the United States, and settled in the Valley of Mexico, peoples, ideas, and practices have been crossing and recrossing the territory now shared by the United States of Mexico and the United States of North America. Through an immeasurably long aboriginal period, a comparable colonial era, and then as separate and independent nations, interplay between the two has been constant and significant. As the years have worn on, the intensity of interpenetration has risen. There is small likelihood that it will decrease.

The twentieth century has been a troubled one. Relations between the United States and Mexico were long uneasy because of reigning attitudes in both lands. These suppressed anxieties, resentments, and fallacious views of national self-interests required twenty years or more of rubbing and the hammer-blows of Revolution to smooth and polish into the current cordiality.

The Good Neighbor Policy was a start toward readjustment, but domestically and internationally World War II vividly illustrated how much constructive force could be liberated by conciliation, compromise, and coöperation under wise leadership. That self-evident conclusion was only tentative at the opening of the postwar world, but events since have confirmed it. Despite their blunders, errors, and pin-point irritations, both the Institutionalized Mexican Revolution and the Fair Deal have made a notable record of success in the field of relations between the United States and Mexico. The future looks bright if the gains to date are not inexcusably squandered by regression on either side to earlier and unsuccessful attitudes and shortsighted actions.

That Mexico and the United States are likely to continue the partnership which has proved beneficial to each was indicated on December 1, 1952. Representing President-elect Dwight D. Eisenhower at the peaceful inauguration of Adolfo Ruiz Cortines was Vice-President-elect Richard M. Nixon. His presence was unmistakable proof of moral approval by the new Republican regime in the United States for the new Mexican one. Before this special mission from the United States and those of 56 other nations and to assembled Mexican dignitaries, Adolfo Ruiz Cortines pledged Mexico's continued support of democracies in world affairs and moderation in domestic matters. He promised reductions in costs of living and a balanced emphasis on rural and industrial developments—the continued Institutional Revolution.

A salient feature of recent developments in Mexico is a clear demonstration that beneficial social and economic change *can* be brought about in so-called "underdeveloped" areas while preserving and increasing political and economic democracy as defined in the New World. Mexican *kulaks* are now driving Fords and hope soon to buy Buicks or Nashes, made in Mexico. Can Communism match this?

Epilogue: A Decade of Developments, 1952-1962

Early in 1963 Mexico was different in many ways from what it appeared at the close of 1952 when Adolfo Ruiz Cortines donned the presidential sash. It is also fundamentally much the same. In general Mexicans find it is a better place for them to live and work. Large problems remain unsolved, but most seem soluble. At the risk of superficiality and over-generalization, let us note some of the significant trends and some of the changes over the past decade.

1. CONSTANTS AND VARIABLES

PEOPLE

The people of Mexico remain its major resource. Continuing demographic trends still pose serious problems.

In 1950 the Seventh National Census showed a total of 25.8 million Mexicans; the preliminary figures of the Eighth raised this total to 34.2 million. Annually nearly a million new Mexicans appear, still almost exclusively through natural increase.

Thus against this key figure all sorts of developments must be measured: merely to maintain a relative *status quo,* a given development must increase annually by at least 3.5 per cent., before further progress can be made. This would apply to a wide spectrum of economic and social matters such as gross national product and the elements which form it, new jobs, teachers, schools, among other things.

Fortunately one problem, subject of much polemic a decade ago, has nearly disappeared. Mexico's agricultural production is keeping pace with population growth, even slightly exceeding it. The earlier generalization (p. 72) is valid for 1963: Mother Mexico *is* feeding her children.

The parallel demographic trend toward urbanization also persists nearly unabated. In 1940, about 4.0 per cent. of the population lived in cities of 100,000 and over; in 1959 this proportion had more than doubled. Even more significant are other 1959 population data: 43 per cent. of the Mexicans, more than 11 millions, dwelt in urbanized communities; about 28 per cent., in rural pueblos; and the remainder huddled in remote small clusters of only a few families. Politics and planning, with an eye to votes and needs, necessarily have followed such population shifts. The *campesino* is no longer predominant. More and more he is moving from smaller to larger urban centers.

A matter of special interest is the rapid breakup of many Indian groups, as evidenced by the decreasing number of individuals who retain knowledge of ancient native tongues. Between 1940 and 1950 those who could communicate only in such languages (monolinguals) and those who were bilingual (a native language and Spanish) dropped from about 15 per cent. of the total population to a little over 11 per cent. The decline has continued, as the preliminary figures for the 1960 census make clear. It becomes ever more difficult to isolate and identify an "Indian" in modern Mexico.

Part of the demographic revolution is, of course, the changing structure of classes and subclasses. Widely used has been the previous table showing the situation in 1940 (p. 86). A parallel recent investigation, summarizing scattered data, shows significant rises in the upper levels, and a marked decline toward the bottom of the pyramid. The table on p. 410 synthesizes present conclusions. It is a significant matter that in two decades the upper and middle classes have nearly tripled, and the "popular" class has declined in relative numbers and influence.

REGIONALISM AND SECTIONALISM

A strong trend in present-day Mexico is the waning of regionalism and sectionalism, once major elements and still powerful. Various nationalizing activities, many purposeful, have by no means obliterated the "personalities" of the several Mexican regions and subregions, but they have transmuted them into interesting variations of a more unified and homogeneous single national pattern. When the analysis which appears in Chapter 6 was initially made, four main divisions emerged. For 1960 there are five. The Metropolis, consti-

MEXICO'S CHANGING CLASS STRUCTURES, 1895–1960
Percentages of Total Population

Class & Sub-classes	1895	1940	1950	1960
UPPER				
Leisure	0.4	0.4	0.5	1.5
Semi-leisure	1.1	2.5	1.5	5.0
Sub-total	1.5	2.9	2.0	6.5
MIDDLE				
Stable	6.1	6.1	8.0	17.0
Marginal	1.7	6.5	17.0	16.5
Sub-total	7.8	12.6	25.0	33.5
TRANSITIONAL	—	6.5	20.0	20.0
POPULAR	90.7	78.0	53.0	40.0

Source: Cline, *Mexico, 1940–1960*, Table 30 (p. 124), adapted; see *ibid.*, Tables 22–29.

tuted by Mexico City and the Distrito Federal, must now be treated apart; it has as much population as the South's several subregions combined.

Basic to the political and economic unification of Mexico has been further development of its transportation and communications systems. Several railway plans that were merely projects in 1952 have been completed in 1963. Rails, now amounting to about 14,700 miles, carry a steadily increasing volume of freight and passengers, largely through improvement of physical equipment and modernized practices. Still far from perfect, the railroads link all parts of the Republic. Recent Mexican planners estimate that a minimum of 600 million dollars (about 8,000 million pesos) should be invested between 1960 and 1970 to provide adequate railroad services.

An earlier national goal to complete trunk highways has now been fully achieved. These now even include some traverse routes, running east and west, linking the previous north-south routes. The main trend now is steady development of secondary and tertiary networks to bring smaller communities and areas into the general transportation system. Since 1940 the total mileage of Mexican roads has been increased fourfold, from 10,000 kilometers to about 40,000 in 1961.

Correlative, of course, has been the increased use of automobiles and trucks, whose number have also risen about four times from the 168,000 recorded for 1941. More nearly true now is the slightly exaggerated statement made by this author in 1953, that "Mexican *kulaks* are now driving Fords and hope soon to buy Buicks or Nashes, made in Mexico." (p. 407)

One of the more obvious phenomena of recent years is the rapid rise of air transportation. Civil aviation has boomed. There are two major national airlines, Campañia de Aviación and Aeronaves de México and at least 20 secondary or feeder routes operated by Mexican nationals. The network fans out from the central hub of Mexico City to more than 50 Mexican cities and towns having their own airports and connects with the various continental and global systems.

Radio, television, and the telephone systems have also broken down previous isolation and regionalisms. All have grown in spectacular fashion.

The cumulative effect of internal migrations of people moving from isolated ranchos to towns, from towns to cities, and many to the Metropolis, plus the enlarged and relatively comprehensive transportation systems, and the movement of ideas and modes through communications media, has been to strengthen nationalism at the cost of militant regionalism. Local accent in Spanish yet identifies the *jarocho* from Veracruz or the *tapatío* of Jalisco, but now he is as likely to be heard in Monterrey as in his own *patria chica*.

One special feature that has promoted Mexican unification and basic homogeneity is the creation of large new socio-economic provinces through "hydraulic works." The developments of the Tepalcaltepec and Papaloapan Projects were presented in earlier pages as beginnings of what might prove to be important directed social change. They have been quite successful. To these original large projects have been added similar programs in the basins of the Rio Fuerte and Yaqui, the Valley of Mexico, and the Southern Grijalva-Usumacinta drainage systems.

Through 1958 about 6.3 million acres of land have been reclaimed through all such programs. The large dams, producing electrical energy, stimulating new communities and mixed agro-industrial economies which have been supplied with essential roads, schools, and the other apparatus of modern living, all add up to a major epic of achievement. The Mexican program, in magnitude and in complexity, can scarcely be matched in the world today.

The Mexicans have found a way to cope with some of the seemingly immutable features of a limited and often hostile physical base, chiefly because they decided to do so themselves. Common pride in these visible achievements is part of Mexican nationalism.

2. THE INSTITUTIONAL REVOLUTION, 1952–1962

In December 1952, Adolfo Ruiz Cortines succeeded Miguel Alemán as President of Mexico, one civilian succeeding another. Fortunately this historian's crystal ball was not completely clouded when he wrote in July 1952, "Though he has stood constantly in the shadow of Alemán for nearly two decades, it is improbable that president-elect Ruiz Cortines will be a puppet . . . [his] main task, for which he is well equipped, is to improve further the intricate mechanisms of the 'Institutional Revolution' that is already fulfilling so many historic aspirations and promises." (p. 332)

In his final State of the Union Message to Congress on September 1, 1958, Ruiz Cortines summed up his philosophy of government, as well as some notable gains recorded over his six year term. He indicated that he had tried to set new standards of harmony, unity, and hard work among various Mexican groups and factions. He stated that while many of his efforts had been dedicated to implementing policies he had inherited from his predecessors, he was leaving an enriched legacy to his successors. His earlier reputation for honesty was enhanced when among his early acts he fired a number of the more notorious grafters and enforced a standard of bureaucratic morality seldom seen in any government, and especially in Mexico. Skillfully avoiding capture by the more predatory elements who had supported Alemán, he also managed to elude the attempts constantly made by the more radical elements of the Left to ensnare him.

Apart from doubling the electorate by enfranchising women, Ruiz Cortines made few dramatic moves in domestic or foreign affairs. But somehow constructive programs quietly blossomed, the "official party" was enlarged to include nearly every interest group, and a society of affluence began to emerge. How much is due to the man, how much due to the times, is debatable. During Ruiz Cortines' term a new generation of Mexicans came of age, one for whom the tales of the militant Revolution and the heady days of Lázaro Cárdenas are but stories told by their fathers.

Quite clearly, however, the shift from revolution to evolution quickened in the Ruiz Cortines years. Administration, including beginnings of long-needed national planning, tended to outweigh politics as a central feature. Moderate in all matters, Ruiz Cortines apparently gave most Mexicans exactly the sort of government they wanted. He left office fully as popular, but much better known, than when he entered. As always, there was a buzz of excitement when various names came up as his possible successor.

Various considerations coincided to bring Adolfo López Mateos to the fore. He had the approval of three Great Electors: the ex-presidents Cárdenas, Alemán, and Ruiz Cortines. He had made a good record as Secretary of Labor, and he was a young man. Much in the pattern that had been set long before him, his electoral campaigns were educational, with something to offer each group. In July 1958 some 6.8 million Mexicans, men and women, cast their vote for him, sweeping him into the Presidency. His inaugural address of December 1, 1958 was a pledge to maintain freedom and harmony among Mexicans, and to guide the nation through a period of "impetuous growth and transformation."

Picked primarily as a "team-man" rather than a strong and vigorous leader in his own right, López Mateos has attempted to keep Mexican growth balanced, in Mexican hands, and expanding. Many Mexicans have felt that he has been too moderate, that changed times called for a Mexican version of the New Frontier, bubbling with vigor and action. Unlike Ruiz Cortines, he has had to face a revived Right in the re-emergence of Alemán as a political force, and a revitalized Left, with the return of Lázaro Cárdenas. Mexico's future is again the subject of debate.

The rise of Fidel Castro in Cuba, with the avowed policy of fomenting "people's revolutions" throughout Latin America, has complicated the domestic scene in Mexico, intertwining local and international issues. Despite various purposeful incidents to test the stability of the Mexican governmental structure, no responsible observer feels that Mexico has been or is seriously endangered. But already predictions are being made that in 1964 the next president is likely to be a forceful figure. Perhaps even the chain of civilian presidents which started with Alemán in 1946 could be broken. The oxygen of "futurismo" is currently making political hearts beat faster but the anticipated winner of this greatest of national lotteries is not evident in March 1963.

If nothing else, the elections of 1958 showed the relative bankruptcy of political opposition to the "official party," the P.R.I. The oldest and best organized of opposition parties, the P.A.N., riven internally on ideological matters, waged an almost irresponsible campaign and managed to garner only 9.5 per cent. of the total vote and six seats in the Congress. Little extremist groups polled an infinitesimal number of votes. All this seemed to show a tendency long established and still increasing: that the P.R.I. itself remains so elastic that intramural jockeying by its sectors and their own internal diverse interest groups now replaces inter-party competition. None of these sectors has strength enough of its own to break away and become the nucleus of a competitive "official" party. The risk of losses in such an attempt is outweighed by gains from staying within the fold. Hence it would appear that Mexico will probably retain for a few years its peculiar one-party democracy.

None of the extremists groups of the late 1940's seem to have viable programs or much real strength beyond lungpower. Sinarquismo died as an important movement, and P.A.N. found that its own cause was hurt rather than abetted by absorbing some Sinarquista remnants. The Communists similarly have almost no meaningful foothold or leverage in today's Mexico, even swelled by the local Fidelistas.

For Mexicans, Communism has always been suspect as a later, foreign competitor of their own Revolution, with little novel or important to add to the latter's somewhat chaotic but homegrown doctrines. As the P.R.I. is the sole meaningful party, dedicated to running Mexico for Mexicans, the normal communist tactic of allying with a national party and supporting opportunistic politicians within it for later favors does not work in Mexico.

A real blow was dealt Mexican communists and their sympathizers by the so-called Cuban crisis of October 1962, when as a result of the confrontation of the United States and the U.S.S.R. Fidel Castro was unmasked as a pitiful puppet. His revolution had obviously been captured lock, stock, and barrel by an apparatus directed from the Kremlin. Both the popular and official Mexican position is summed up in the recurring phrase that "Mexico neither imports nor exports revolutions." Communists retain a certain nuisance value in Mexico but pose little or no significant threat to overthrow or capture the government.

Two other constants in the political realm warrant brief mention. From establishment of the Republic, church-state relationships have been troubled. The Revolution has always had a strong anti-clerical component, notably evident in the 1920's and again under Lázaro

Cárdenas. Manuel Avila Camacho, Miguel Alemán, and Adolfo Ruiz Cortines developed a quiet *modus vivendi*. López Mateos has not officially altered this, but there are inescapable signs of possible change. Church establishments, including schools, have increased, almost automatically rekindling latent anti-clerical doctrines of the classic Revolution. Within the present administration these sentiments are particularly strong, although not voiced as official policy. In 1963, popular preoccupation with church-state relationships still does not exist, but minor portents indicate that perhaps another round of militant testing and struggle, so familiar to the historian of Mexico, is imminent.

Militarism has also been a constant on the Mexican scene since Independence. Stemming in large part from Mexico's participation in the Second World War, its army and other defense forces have been increasingly professionalized, and have gradually withdrawn as a group from overt participation in the political process. The fading of militarism is one of the more remarkable phenomena of the Institutional Revolution. A recent student, Professor Lieuwen, in an examination of arms and politics in Latin America as a whole, felt that the Mexican example was noteworthy enough for a whole chapter; he concluded "militarism has been dead for over a generation. . . . Mexico has unquestionably solved its problems of militarism." * Perhaps a more prudent statement would be "latent for a generation."

Streets of Mexican towns and cities are remarkably free of men in uniform. Most of the portly colonels and generals of the late 1930's and early 1940's have long been on the retired list or have passed away. The new breed of officers are generally thoughtful and able technicians who quietly maintain order. There is little or no evidence of the military's plotting to advance its position by direct or indirect political means. Although the sums for defense have doubled since 1940, the annual budget still devotes twice as much to education as to defense. There are more teachers than soldiers in Mexico.

It would seem that Professor Lieuwen is correct. Yet the student of Latin America, and particularly Mexico, is or should be aware that the military as a group has a strong veto power, usually expressed privately. Things in Mexico have been running well, under strong and able leadership for nearly three decades. So long as they continue along that path, militarism will remain latent.

* Edwin Lieuwen, *Arms and Politics in Latin America* (New York: Council on Foreign Relations, 1960), pp. 101–21, 168–70.

3. THE ECONOMIC REVOLUTION

To an earlier statement, that "an economic revolution of major magnitude has been taking place for a decade and still is in full motion" (p. 333), can now be added one additional decade. Economic forces first generated during World War II have exerted increasingly powerful and complex pressures. The net result has kept the Mexican economy expanding. Its rate of development has seemingly outrun population growth, hence shows positive advances.

The boom has conferred real as well as relative benefits on the people as a whole, despite the fact that raised national incomes and other benefits are by no means equitably distributed. From a general economic level that was scarcely above subsistence some 25 years ago, Mexico generally has been moving rather steadily toward a society of limited affluence. There is still some distance to go, but the burgeoning of the economy has opened unprecedented opportunities. Several general and technical studies of Mexican economic matters stress two features of the current boom: size and balance. Reams of statistics attest to the former.

The single most impressive figure is the steadily rising sum of goods and services, the gross national product. In monetary terms it rose from about 58 thousand mega-pesos in 1952 to over 122 thousand mega-pesos in 1959. More important is the "real" growth, after allowances have been made for inflation and related factors; here we find that over the same period the rise has been from 45 to 63.4 thousand mega-pesos. The general average real growth rate over those years is 2.3 per cent. per year. Perhaps more indicative of current rates is the average annual increase of 5.2 per cent. for the five years 1955–1959. One elaborate calculation shows that individual shares of real gross national product rose from a yearly average of 1,720 pesos in 1955 to 1,900 in 1959. In the latter years the individual's personal gain was 18 per cent. more than in 1950. This helps explain general satisfaction with the Institutional Revolution's policies.

Statistics, to have meaning, should be translated into living standards. They have risen. Since 1950 the share of the worker, as a member of the economically active population, climbed from 4,500 pesos a year to 9,900 in 1959. Rising prices for food, shoes, and many other items gnawed away at these apparent gains, but it was found that in 1959 the average household (made up of economically active and inactive persons) earning about 820 pesos a month, was about 13 per cent. better off than in 1950 when the same unit earned 380 pesos per month. We have already seen the effect of generally spreading and increased affluence on the social structure of Mexico (above, p. 410). Another way of stating the same idea is that rising standards are diminishing the groups living in abject poverty and increasing the groups enjoying or aspiring to better material life than in 1950, itself above the low plateau of 1940.

The benefits do not spread evenly through the social and economic system. One study suggested that about half of the national income returned to less than a quarter of the economically active population, the remainder being shared by a rather large body. The most numerous, agriculturalists and laborers, were at the bottom of this scale. Thus ferment among them is predictable.

The second feature of the Mexican economy, balance, is noteworthy. Unlike a number of other Latin American economies, the Mexican has not developed by dangerous dependence on a single, readily exploitable export resource or crop, such as petroleum in Venezuela, copper in Chile, or cattle and wheat in Argentina. Economic advance in Mexico has proceeded simultaneously on nearly all fronts, and at about the same rate. Generally successful has been the consistent attempt to keep the agricultural sector expanding as manufacturing and commercial activities have grown in size and output. In the following table we can scan the gross national product and discern the various elements and their relatively even contributions to it.

An interesting and detailed study of the Mexican economy by a group of German investigators noted the expansion and balance of the Mexican system. They concluded that, "All in all, it appears that Mexico is on the right track. Consequently it can, in a few years, bring Mexico into the ranks of the 'developed' countries." * This is even more true now than when written in 1957.

As Mexico nears modernity and full development, the system inevitably becomes more interdependent with world political and economic trends. The Mexican business cycle tends to follow that of the United States, with which it interacts most vigorously, as well as to reflect activities of and within the European Common Market. The spiral of growth is contingent on some external developments beyond Mexico's control. Even those factors within Mexico itself are neither as simple nor as tractable as they were when the economic complex

* W. Lichey, *Mexiko: Ein Weg zur wirtschaftlichen Entwicklung* . . . (Hamburg: Verlag Weltarchiv, [1958]), p. 127.

MEXICAN GROSS NATIONAL PRODUCT, 1959, BY SECTORS
(Amounts in millions of mega-pesos)

Activity	Amount	Per cent
PRIMARY ACTIVITIES		
Agriculture (& related)	27.9	22.9
SECONDARY ACTIVITIES		
Mining	2.9	2.4
Petroleum	4.5	3.7
Manufacturing	28.5	23.4
Sub-total	35.9	29.5
TERTIARY ACTIVITIES		
Construction	6.1	5.0
Commerce	24.8	20.3
Transportation	6.0	4.9
Sub-total	36.9	30.2
VARIOUS SERVICES	21.3	17.4
Totals	122.0	100.0

Source: Cline, *Mexico* (1962), Table 64 (p. 260).

was less developed and less matured. The boom requires a constant influx of capital, widened markets, increased job opportunities, higher productivity, and a score or more of other variables that demand unceasing vigilance on the part of Mexican leaders and workers. That Mexico's economic spiral has continued nearly unchecked for nearly a quarter of a century is a remarkable phenomenon. The system is basically sound and is currently operating well.

GOVERNMENT AND THE ECONOMY

The peculiarities of the Mexican economic system recorded for 1952 (p. 336) have passed the experimental stage and remain at the heart of Mexico's forward thrust in economic matters. The unique Mexican blend of statism, free enterprise, socialism, and the "guided economy" concept has been a subject of recurring interest to international economists. They cannot explain fully why it works, but agree that it does.

The German study mentioned above is but one example. Yet another writer considered the Mexican system functional, neither fully capitalistic nor socialistic, and labelled the Mexican approach a

"Third system." * Whatever it is called, it is largely home-grown.

In general the so-called "New Group" program outlined under Alemán and given status by the "Law for the Development of New and Necessary Industries" in February 1946 still in modified form underlies the present situation. To carry out what the late Sanford Mosk noted as "business intervention in government rather than government intervention in business" the "Law of Attributes of the Executive Branch in Economic Matters" (revised in 1950) applies. Broad mandates are given the state to regulate production, distribution, and consumption of goods and services, to coordinate and balance the total economy and to stimulate its growth.

One key concept is the balanced economy, noted above, wherein equal attention is paid to various sectors, especially agriculture and industrialism. Another is a series of co-partnerships between government and the economy, with certain spheres marked out for relatively exclusive development by private capital, others almost exclusively preserved for direct government responsibility, and yet others in which responsibility shifts from the public to the private sector, or vice-versa. In short, instead of a static structure comparable to the Western European or United States, the Mexican one is shifting and flexible. It is too complex to summarize briefly.

Direct government intervention is supposed to be limited to cases where the general welfare and public interest are clearly concerned. The latter are usually developmental problems, reinforcing and creating segments of what economists call the infra-structure: transportation and communications, production of electrical energy, irrigation and similar public works. For historic reasons, the government also enters into certain basic industrial activities, such as petroleum. But iron and steel remain private enterprises, as do other extractive activities such as coal and metal mining.

Open for development by private hands is a large segment of the economy, especially in the commercial and manufacturing fields. In some instances the needed capital comes from completely private sources; in others the government aids either in obtaining or even furnishing initial investment, gradually withdrawing its support as a needed industry gains economic strength.

Near the hub of a network of official, semi-official, and private organizations that guide Mexico's economy remains Nacional Finan-

---

* George N. Sarames, "Third system in Latin America: Mexico," *Interamerican Economic Affairs*, v.5:4 (Spring, 1952), 59–72.

ciera. Its role and importance as a co-ordinating and developmental agency has steadily expanded. Table 28 (Appendix) shows its investments in 1949 were measured in thousands of pesos; in 1960 they must be expressed in millions. Without entering into further detail, the total investment of Nacional Financiera since 1941 through June 1960, tabulated here, gives some idea of the general scope and magnitude of its operations.

INVESTMENTS BY NACIONAL FINANCIERA, 1941–1960 (JUNE 1)

(Amounts in millions of mega-million pesos)

Type Investment	Amount	Per cent
INFRA STRUCTURE. Electric power; transport; communications	5.8	52.0
BASIC INDUSTRIES. Oil; iron; steel; cement	2.0	18.0
MANUFACTURING INDUSTRIES	2.3	20.3
OTHER ACTIVITIES	1.0	9.7
Totals	11.1	100.0

Source: Cline, *Mexico,* Table 58 (adapted).

At the 25th anniversary celebration of Nacional Financiera on July 2, 1959, President López Mateos indicated that in addition to its present activities, the institution should give special attention to two major problems: stimulating greater employment, and developing higher real incomes for the rural population. He also called upon it to help the private sector plan coordinated efforts to get maximum benefit from Mexico's relatively scant resources, and to mobilize funds in the hands of medium and small investors. To these ends he authorized Nacional Financiera to increase its working capital from 200 to 500 million pesos. He reiterated the basic policy, that "the State many times assumes the role of a pioneer. Nacional Financiera has been the prime instrument in the execution of this policy, with the object of accelerating economic development . . . in coordinating efforts at breaking the circle of our traditional limitations."

AGRARIANISM AND AGRICULTURE

Somewhat to the dismay of foreign and domestic observers who still view Mexico in simplistic terms of the Lázaro Cárdenas era, the concept of balance and harmony developed for Mexican social and economic progress extends to rural areas. The *ejido* system, once programmed to replace individual land ownership, co-exists with another private system of small, medium, and rather large-sized agricultural enterprises. Both systems have expanded. The government is seemingly committed to let neither swallow the other, and to enforce legislation protecting the legitimate interests of each.

A continuing problem in Mexico is to achieve some stable equilibrium between agrarianism and agricultural reform, two quite different matters. The one, agrarianism, is essentially political and social. Dividing the land among the landless who want and can utilize it, fulfills an old Revolutionary dream and promise. Agricultural reform, on the other hand, seeks to use Mexico's rather limited resources most effectively so that the rural sector becomes both a widened consumer market and a steady supplier of crops needed to feed a booming industrial system and an expanding population. Agricultural reform tends therefore to be economic and technical.

In the wake of the Cárdenas agrarianism of the 1930's came economic chaos. Nor did the creation of several thousand semi-collectivized *ejidos* bring many of the predicted social and political benefits. Hence in the ensuing years, under Alemán and Ruiz Cortines, the pendulum swung far in the other direction, toward agricultural reform. Prerequisite were basic government decisions to increase the amount of tillable land, to foster incentives of private owners by guarantees against expropriation, and to develop new crops for the domestic and international markets with government aid and support.

Agricultural reform has, in general, been spectacularly successful. Both subsistence crops and exportable money crops appreciated sufficiently in quantity and value to cover national needs for food and foreign exchange. A wide range of raw materials for industry appeared, stimulated by current emphasis on cutting down the necessity for purchasing abroad items that can be produced in Mexico. Wool and rubber are two such targets for the immediate future. The steady pressure to create new areas through hydraulic works and to improve present ones by technical means—fertilizers, high yield seed, pest control, and similar available methods, has not slackened. Nor has the development of apparatus to furnish credit, marketing facilities, and related functions. There are numerous pending problems, but experience over two decades, and especially in the last ten years, indicates that agricultural reform is working, generally to the benefit of the total economy and social structure.

But after lying fallow during the same period, forces favoring revived agrarianism re-emerged toward the close of the Ruiz Cortines term. Presently they are quite active. Their hand was strengthened by a fusion of national and international issues posed by Castro's Cuba and its policies. Fidelismo in Mexico calls for a return to Revolutionary virtue and a resumption of Cárdenas' policies of direct action on behalf of the "people," meaning those favoring such action. The reappearance of General Cárdenas himself as a political figure in Mexico and as a hero in Havana, fanned the re-ignited zeal of Mexican agrarians.

Loudest of the newly organized groups is the Central Campesino Independiente (CCI), but of similar extremest persuasion is the Movimiento de Liberación Nacional (MLN). Their reiterated cries of being "true Mexican agrarians" must be judged against the fact that they are also the most vocal pro-Fidel Castro partisans and resort to the direct action tactics he is attempting to foment throughout Latin America. The CCI and the MLN have announced that they will put up a candidate for President of Mexico in next year's elections. It probably would be a national, as well as a personal tragedy, if they persuaded Lázaro Cárdenas to accept that candidacy. It is doubtful that the radical agrarians' power to garner headlines is equalled by their ability to deliver votes. But, like all radical movements, they do stir the conscience and recall the hopes of yesteryear.

During his first two years of office, President López Mateos and his advisers had to take into account this revived agrarianism. In 21 months he redistributed as much land as had his two predecessors combined. He has also tried to clear up some of the more venal practices about which *ejidatarios* complained. On occasion, he has been forced to employ Federal troops to prevent reoccurence of the so-called "parachutist" tactics that were nearly routine in the late 1930's.

The tactics are the same but government responses are now different. Then a group of landless would suddenly drop in and squat on a piece of private property, simultaneously petitioning for it to be declared an *ejido*, a request Cárdenas officials seldom denied. Now, however, the government is expected to protect such private rural holdings against invasion by radical agrarians. A number of invasions have been deliberately staged to make the regime appear anti-Revolutionary, and its agrarianism hypocritical. At the moment these actions are irritating rather than dangerous to the general stability of the Mexican government, but they do point up the dilemma that it now continuously faces.

Early in January 1963, newspapers carried reports about a new policy announced by President López Mateos. His statements promised a seven-point plan that would complete the distribution of big tracts of land, *latifundias,* before he left office in 1964. The first point was that all *latifundias* would be distributed to landless peasants, that surveyors were already at work identifying the plots to be given. The new *ejidatarios* are to be taught modern cultivation techniques. Various grants of land given to private owners in the past will be reviewed, and those failing to meet legal requirements will be revoked. Petitions for land will be endorsed by state governors. It was also stated that small and communal agricultural properties will continue to have official support, that they will not be disturbed.

As these lines are written in March 1963, it is obviously premature to assess the repercussions of this announced proposal, or of the continued efforts of radical agrarians. Undoubtedly the almost inherent conflicts between Mexican agrarianism and agricultural reform efforts of the past decade will become sharper in the next months preceding the 1964 Presidential election. The outcome of the test of strength will have an important bearing on Mexico's future in the next few years.

THE INDUSTRIAL REVOLUTION

The steady growth of Mexico's industrial plant is a fact. Its productive units have shown marked advances in quantity, quality and kinds of products. Mexicans have by no means achieved total industrial self-sufficiency for the nation, but there are now few goods they need which are not also produced (or assembled) by them. Manufacturing outstrips agriculture in its contribution to the total effort. (See table, p. 418.)

The rise of industrialism may be measured in various ways. Here we use an index of physical volume, developed by Mexican economists, which takes 1945 as the base year, or 100. Unfortunately detailed figures after 1958 are not readily available, but partial data indicate that the main trends are continuing.

In manufacturing, iron and steel outstrip other activities, by substantial margins. A main development in that field has been consolidation of companies. Ownership of them has passed to Mexican hands through individual Mexican purchases of foreign-owned stock. The nationalized pertroleum industry having weathered its early difficulties and completed an elaborate program of plant expansion is moving into the important petro-chemical field.

PHYSICAL VOLUME OF INDUSTRIAL PRODUCTION
1950 v. 1958

Class of Industry	1950	1958
General (all sectors)	122.7	192.1
Mining	92.4	97.3
Petroleum	153.5	326.1
Electrical energy	144.2	296.5
Construction	154.2	255.4
Manufacturing	121.4	187.1

Source: Cline, *Mexico,* Table 68 (p. 282), adapted.

A significant move was made when the Mexican government nationalized the electrical power industry. Rather than expropriate, as was habitual some years ago, the Mexican government eliminated foreign companies in April 1960 when it bought holdings outright from the controlling American and Foreign Power Company. In September 1960 it similarly obtained by purchase 90 per cent. of Mexican Light (a Canadian company). The purpose of these transactions was to permit Mexican official planners to accelerate expansion of power production.

A relative soft spot in the industrial complex is the mining industry, still largely in foreign hands. It has been plagued by fiscal and technical difficulties. At this writing, mining's future remains uncertain, despite private and official efforts to hurdle some serious obstacles.

As a result of the generally healthy and booming industrial revolution, there has been a parallel expansion in the commercial and financial fields. We shall not attempt details here.

Another and significant consequence has been the growth of public revenues. As for many years past, Mexican tax revenues draw from various sources, nearly all based on domestic activities rather than taxes on international trade. Returns in 1960 from individual and corporate income taxes and those on industry and trade account for better than 55 per cent. of federal revenues, a little over 10 thousand mega-pesos. These healthy sums permit the national government to carry forward the social objectives of the Revolution to a degree denied many earlier Mexican administrations.

Quoting recently released figures from the Bank of Mexico, *Time* (March 15, 1963) noted the continued surge of the economy. For 1962 recorded were the following per cent. rises over 1961: gross national product, 4.2; manufacturing output, 5.2; total investment,

6; merchandise exports, 12.1. Thus nourished, *Time* reported, "Mexico is fast developing a middle class." The same news magazine stated, "In many ways, the Mexican economy appears as hardy as a flowering desert cactus, a bright contrast to its hemisphere neighbors."

4. THE INTERNATIONAL SCENE

Polarization of the world because of Cold War is the backdrop against which Mexico's international activities over the past decade must be seen. As a small power, contiguous to the United States, a leading member of the Organization of American States, and a respected member of the United Nations, such activities have been numerous, and generally along policy lines already long visible.

INTERNATIONAL ECONOMICS

As might be expected of a developing nation, Mexico's international interests have been heavily weighted on the economic side. Here, with minor variations, earlier patterns are followed. The United States remains Mexico's principal trading partner, but recent Mexican efforts to lessen this dependence have brought more than 92 nations into trade relationships. In 1958, for instance, about 79 per cent. of Mexico's total trade was with North America; it sold about 11 per cent. of its goods to Europe, which supplied about 18 per cent. of its needs. Trade with Latin American colleagues was negligible as were exchanges with Asia, Africa, and Oceania. There is almost no trade with the Soviet Union.

The composition of trade items has been altering as the economy has become more sophisticated. Capital rather than consumer items are purchased abroad, while the traditional pattern of selling merely oil, minerals, and plantation products has changed. Only about half of current Mexican exports are raw materials, a third special agricultural products, and the remainder are semi-processed and manufactured items. Thus both imports and exports show a marked diversification, a reflex to the evolving complexity of Mexican social and economic life.

A long term trend has been reversed, in that rather than exporting more than it bought, Mexico in recent years has become a debtor. It buys more than it sells. The difference, or slack, however, is made up by "invisible exports." Returns from Mexico's major industry, tourism, makes it possible to balance its international books. Income from tourism (which includes transactions made mostly by tourists in the border towns on the United States frontier), has been running about 600 million dollars per year for the period since 1956. A minor addition to the stream of dollars entering Mexico is the total of remittances from Mexican *braceros* working in the United States, amounting to about 35 million dollars annually.

MEXICO AND GUATEMALA

Many of the troubles Mexico experienced facing the United States at the north are reversed when it looks southward to its small neighbor, Guatemala. Guatemalans feel strongly that Mexico in the nineteenth century absorbed part of Guatemala's territory. A series of Guatemalan governments, ranging from harsh homegrown to Communist-infiltrated dictatorships, have not always met full approval of Mexican authorities and press. Perhaps the most persistent and troublesome issues between these Latin American neighbors is one that had also been a moot point between the United States and Mexico: extent of territorial waters, i.e., how far off-shore the sovereignty of the nation extends.

Less than a month after President López Mateos was inaugurated this matter caused a real crisis in Mexican-Guatemalan relations. On December 28, 1958 planes of the Guatemalan air force killed three Mexicans, wounded 16, and destroyed two of five Mexican fishing vessels which Guatemalans claimed were "pirates" within national waters. Mexico denied the "piracy" charge and suggested adjudication by the International Court. When Guatemala refused, Mexico broke off diplomatic relations on January 23, 1959.

Details of subsequent negotiations can be omitted. It suffices to say that both parties accepted the good offices of Chile and Brazil to resolve the matter. On September 15, 1959 an accord was reached and published simultaneously in the Guatemalan and Mexican capitals, smoothing over the immediate episode. Seemingly this re-established harmony, but some of the deeper-lying differences of view remain, submerged for the moment. There is probably more potential tension at Mexico's Southern border than at its Northern.

MEXICO AND CUBA

The most important international development affecting Mexico and Latin America has been the rise in Cuba of the revolutionary government that took power on New Year's Day 1959. Here we cannot rehearse the background and activities of that regime, headed by Premier Fidel Castro, except to note how it has affected Mexican matters, directly and indirectly.

It was from Mexico that in November 1956 the July 26th Movement, a boatload of exiles under Castro, sailed to Cuba to overthrow dictator Batista. From the outset Mexico took the attitude that Castro would re-enact the Mexican Revolution for the benefit of the people of Cuba. Various excesses committed by this junior national revolutionary group could and should be excused, especially by senior Revolutionaries, who a generation earlier had trod the same path. Although in popular and official circles enthusiasm for the bearded Cubans waned as events more and more clearly unmasked the regime as a Communist apparatus, directed from abroad, Mexico has retained diplomatic relations with Cuba. It is one of five Latin American countries holding these ties.

Why? Explanations are not simple, but boil down to long-established Mexican foreign policies and domestic Mexican politics. Mexican foreign relations have as a fixed principle an almost pathological concern for "non-intervention"; withdrawal of recognition or breaking off relations to influence local events is construed as "intervention." Whether the Mexican government approves or disapproves of Castro and his antics is irrelevant, in its view. There has also been the deep-seated feeling, perhaps expectation, that (like Huerta) Castro was a passing figure in a great cause, that the "true" Cuban Revolution would unseat him and go on to correct long-standing social, economic, and political evils, as did the Mexican. Until the "eyeball to eyeball" confrontation of Washington and Moscow over Soviet military equipment in Cuba, many Mexicans could shrug off the Communist label for Cuba as merely repetition of similar charges hurled at them and their leaders earlier in their Revolution.

Despite this official stance, it cannot be said that the Mexican government has encouraged or very directly aided the recent Cuban movement and regime. On the contrary, it has tended more and more to be coolly correct, sympathizing with the Cuban people, but pointedly attempting to disassociate them from their present government. To date, the Cubans on their side have not directly threatened the few specific Mexican interests on the island nor have they resorted to the name-calling, the attempted assassinations, the direct (and abortive) military invasions which have caused other Latin American nations to break ties with them. Cuba itself has created no bilateral crisis sufficient for Mexico to withdraw its Ambassador.

Also inhibiting Mexican actions on Cuba is the identification of this international issue with local controversy over the proper course of the Mexican Revolution. The radical Left, which has castigated the Institutional Revolution as a return to Científico days, not only has sympathized with Castro but has attempted to inject his views into local politics. Student organizations, labor groups, agrarians, and of course, Communist-front and infiltrated organizations do the Fidelista work. We noted the case of the agrarians, above. They call for closer ties between the two Revolutions, and for more militant policies by Mexico's government. Sharp rebukes of Cuban actions would jeopardize delicate political balances in Mexico itself, still nominally dedicated to the Revolution.

The Mexican radical elements within the Revolution, within the official party (P.R.I.), even within the government, have a long and respectable pedigree. The more moderate, even conservative Revolutionary leaders, must move cautiously to neutralize or counteract the generally pro-Fidelista sentiments. In their position of power and responsibility, they see the dangers of precipitating an overt local crisis that could do the image of the harmonious Revolutionary family more harm than good, at the same time shattering Mexico's hard-won reputation for freedom of speech and political action. They stand pat on the repeated phrase, "Mexico does not export or import Revolution."

It can be seen that Mexican relations with Cuba, scarcely mentioned in the 1953 version of this work, ten years later have become a matter of vital concern to Mexico. In the showdown over Cuba between the United States and Russia in October 1962, Mexico voted with the United States. What future course Mexico will choose to steer is not fully clear.

MEXICO AND THE UNITED STATES

The Era of Good Feeling reported earlier in these pages has settled down to a way of life for Mexico and the United States, so far as direct dealings with each other are concerned. This bilateral relationship must be sharply distinguished from Mexico's positions in international organizations where the two countries share membership.

No real issues—political, economic, social—currently disturb what amount to routine diplomatic relations. No emotionally-laden episodes have excited public reaction on either side of the border for many years, despite differences of views on water use, *bracero* treatment, and the everpresent Chamizal.

Ritual visits between Presidents to the neighboring nation go on unbroken in their regularity. There is no Mexican President since Avila Camacho who has not paid a state visit to the United States on its invitation, and none in the United States since Franklin Roosevelt who has not made a similar pilgrimage to Mexico. On the most recent of these, President and Mrs. John F. Kennedy were given an outpouring of welcome which one Mexican said was unmatched since Madero rode down the same storied streets in 1911. Prior to this visit there had been muttered threats by the Left to turn the occasion into an embarrassing one for the Mexican host government and a slap at the United States. Nothing happened to mar the occasion, which both Presidents and their ladies obviously enjoyed.

From these face-to-face meetings at the summit come renewed assurances that cooperation and harmony will continue. Discussions range a wide spectrum of plans for cooperative actions of mutual interest and benefit: hydroelectric projects on the Rio Grande (Rio Bravo) del Norte, campaigns for public health, narcotics controls, and other non-controversial but quite important matters.

One of the matters discussed by Presidents López Mateos and Kennedy was the lingering and embarrassing problem of the Chamizal. Negotiations to settle that old matter were stepped up, but in March 1963 President Kennedy could merely announce, "We are close, I would hope, to an agreement." Stating that the prognosis was good, he indicated that his administration was quite anxious to erase a black mark "where we refused to accept an arbitration claim 40 years ago." It was then (March 1963) thought to be merely a matter of weeks before final accord could be reached.

These symbolic encounters of the heads of the two states also signify the constant interplay between their officials, and even more important, their peoples. Except to add that the pattern now has aged another decade and become even more fixed, there is really little to add to the report of the situation in 1952. "At almost every level and in nearly every sphere it could be demonstrated that relations between the United States and Mexico were basically serene. . . . In a troubled world this was a haven of tranquillity." (pp. 396–397).

MEXICO AND REGIONAL ORDER

Many of the views which Mexico later expressed on the Cuban issue were voiced at the Tenth Conference of the Organization of American States, held in Caracas, March 1954. There the prime issue was a strong resolution introduced by the United States condemning extension of Communism into the Western Hemisphere, and specifically aimed at solving the problems then posed by Guatemala, ruled by a Communist-dominated government since overthrown.

Mexico felt in 1954 that although it might deplore the Guatemalan choice of government, national self-determination was being threatened by the resolution. Mexico believed that even verbal intervention by the collectivity of American States against one of its members was repugnant. The Mexican delegate finally did sign the condemnation of Communism after he and others worked successfully to alter the wording of the draft presented by John Foster Dulles to conform with Mexico's hypersensitivity to intervention.

From 1954 through 1959, few actions on the part of the O.A.S. evoked much Mexican response. No meetings of consequence took place. Scheduled for 1959, then 1961, then indefinitely postponed, the Eleventh Conference has not yet been held. Problems of the Caribbean, notably Cuba and its divisive effect and tactics, have underlain such postponements. In the meanwhile a series of lesser meetings have taken place, notably the Sixth and Seventh Consultations among Foreign Ministers (Costa Rica, 1960) to discuss Caribbean matters.

The late dictator Rafael Trujillo and his regime in the Dominican Republic were the subject of the Sixth. The body voted to place sanctions on that unhappy land, but Mexico (aided by Venezuela) rather quietly killed a move by the United States to have a special committee of the O.A.S. hold and supervise free elections once the dictatorship had been tumbled. "Obvious intervention!"

The Seventh Consultation was even more stormy. It dealt with Castro's Cuba. The United States delegation had come primed and prepared to demonstrate that Cuba was Communist; the Cubans were there to forestall any punitive action its Latin American colleagues might agree to take. For Mexico, Manuel Tello rehearsed the Mexican view that revolutions pass through phases, and that the Cuban people should be left alone to work out their own destinies, without meddling from the O.A.S., in which Cuba had a legal place. The final resolutions retained many of the "hard-line" approaches wished by the United States, but skillfully avoided naming Cuba specifically, as a result of immovable views by Uruguay, Brazil, Colombia, and Mexico. In line with Mexico policies toward Cuba, Sr. Tello issued a supplementary statement to the "Declaration of Costa Rica" that the resolution "in no form constitutes a condemnation or a threat against Cuba, whose aspirations for economic improvement have the strongest sympathy of the government and people of Mexico." This statement, explained his President López Mateos, was based on the established views of Mexico against intervention and for self-determination.

When the chips were down, however, Mexico lined up with the other members of the Organization of American States (except Cuba) when the Council of that Organization met in solemn session in October 1962 to discuss the revelations made by the President of the United States that Soviet missile bases on Cuba threatened the security of the United States and of the Western Hemisphere. Mexico signed the strongly worded resolution condemning the U.S.S.R. and Cuba and gave moral support to the United States for measures it might have to take to remove the threat.

Mexico legitimately wishes to show that it is a sovereign nation, a partner but not a lackey or satellite of the United States. It does so in international organizations. Many of the general patterns of behavior followed by Mexico in the O.A.S. are transferred to the larger arena of the United Nations. Space prevents giving details.

5. RETROSPECT AND PROSPECT

During the 1950's most of the trends which had developed in Mexico from about 1940 continued. The nation grew in all ways, moving perceptibly toward urbanization and modernity. Mexico had already made long strides toward solving many of the problems that the Alliance for Progress was set up to help members of the Latin American community tackle. Mexico had done this in spite of limited resources and as heavy a chain of history as any of its hemispheric colleagues.

On the basis of this record of demonstrated achievement, there seems in 1963 no strong likelihood that national efforts will slacken. They are likely to continue. We should expect to see Mexico embellish its image as a moderately governed, western-style democracy whose citizens will more and more share economic benefits and more clearly and directly govern themselves. What many underdeveloped nations aspire to be, Mexico has become. It is a good model.

Appendix I.   Facts about Mexico

Note: Certain tables printed in the 1953/61 edition of *The United States and Mexico* have been deleted, but the original numeration of tables has been retained.

1. TOTAL POPULATION; REGIONS, AREAS, AND DENSITIES, 1950

Region and States	Political Capital	Elevation of Capital (feet)	Area of Unit (sq. mi.)	Population 1950	Density 1950 (per sq. mi.)
CORE			*127,576*	*13,426,886*	*105.3*
Aguascalientes	Aguascalientes	6,260	2,498	187,036	71.4
Federal District	Mexico City	7,349	572	2,942,594	5,240.0
Guanajuato	Guanajuato	6,837	11,802	1,317,629	111.5
Hidalgo	Pachuca	8,025	8,056	840,760	104.1
Mexico	Toluca	8,661	8,266	1,383,640	157.5
Michoacan	Morelia	6,188	23,196	1,412,830	61.4
Morelos	Cuernavaca	5,059	1,916	268,863	139.8
Puebla	Puebla	7,093	13,122	1,595,920	122.1
Queretaro	Queretaro	6,119	4,431	282,608	63.7
San Luis Potosí	San Luis Potosí	6,158	24,411	855,336	35.1
Tlaxcala	Tlaxcala	7,388	1,554	282,495	182.1
Veracruz	Jalapa	4,682	27,752	2,057,175	74.4
SOUTH			*153,716*	*4,273,149*	*27.9*
Campeche	Campeche	16	19,667	121,361	6.2
Chiapas	Tuxtla Gutierrez	1,738	28,724	895,782	31.7
Guerrero	Chilpancingo	4,462	24,881	917,719	36.8
Oaxaca	Oaxaca City	5,069	36,365	1,444,929	39.8
Quintana Roo	Chetumal	10	19,435	26,996	1.4
Tabasco	San Juan Bautista	32	9,780	351,106	36.8
Yucatan	Merida	29	14,864	515,256	34.7
WEST			*71,712*	*2,813,927*	*38.4*
Colima	Colima	1,653	2,009	112,490	56.0
Jalisco	Guadalajara	5,092	31,144	1,744,700	56.1
Nayarit	Tepic	3,002	10,442	292,343	28.1
Zacatecas	Zacatecas	8,189	28,117	664,394	23.6
NORTH			*407,168*	*5,050,256*	*12.4*
Baja Calif., Norte	Ensenada	3	27,800	224,333	7.7
Baja Calif., Sur	La Paz	42	27,819	58,764	1.9
Coahuila	Saltillo	5,246	58,052	715,720	12.3
Chihuahua	Chihuahua	4,632	94,806	841,077	8.2
Durango	Durango	6,315	47,679	629,502	13.2

1. TOTAL POPULATION; REGIONS, AREAS, AND DENSITIES, 1950 (*Continued*)

Region and States	Political Capital	Elevation of Capital (feet)	Area of Unit (sq. mi.)	Population 1950	Density 1950 (per sq. mi.)
Nuevo Leon	Monterrey	1,765	25,130	743,297	28.6
Sinaloa	Culiacan	275	22,576	618,439	27.4
Sonora	Hermosillo	777	70,465	503,095	7.2
Tamaulipas	Cd. Victoria	1,102	30,726	716,029	24.3
FEDERAL ISLANDS			2,115	...	...
REPUBLIC OF MEXICO	Mexico City	7,349	760,172	25,564,218	35.0

RECAPITULATION

	Area		Population		Density
	Sq. Mi.	*Per Cent*	*People*	*Per Cent*	
Core	127,576	16.8	13,426,886	52.6	105.3
South	153,716	20.3	4,273,149	16.8	27.9
West	71,712	9.5	2,813,927	10.8	38.4
North	407,168	53.4	5,050,256	19.8	12.4

Sources: *Statesman's Yearbook; Anuario Estadístico, 1943–1945;* Nathan L. Whetten, *Rural Mexico* (1948), Table 4.

2. RANKING CITIES OF MEXICO, 1950
(Over 100,000 population)

City	State	Population	Region
1. Mexico City	Federal District	2,233,709	Core
2. Monterrey	Nuevo Leon	339,634	North
3. Guadalajara	Jalisco	337,000	West
4. Puebla	Puebla	229,976	Core
5. San Luis Potosí	S.L.P.	156,324	Core
6. Mérida	Yucatan	155,899	South
7. Culiacan	Sinaloa	144,550	North
8. Mexicali	B. California, N.	141,189	North
9. León	Guanajuato	140,000	Core
10. Torreón	Coahuila	132,101	North
11. Cd. Juárez	Chihuahua	128,782	North
12. Veracruz	Veracruz	123,368	Core
13. Matamoros	Tamaulipas	118,215	North
14. Aguascalientes	Aguascalientes	117,409	Core
15. Toluca	Mexico	115,422	Core
16. Chihuahua	Chihuahua	110,779	North
17. Morelia	Michoacan	103,516	Core

Source: *Statesman's Yearbook, 1951.* See also Table 5.

3. SUMMARY VIEW OF COMPARABLE CONDITIONS IN THE REGIONS

	National Average or Total	Core	South	West	North
Millions of people, 1940	19.7	10.3	3.4	2.3	3.6
1946	22.7	11.7	3.9	2.7	4.4
1950	25.6	13.4	4.3	2.8	5.1
Economically active (millions of people), 1940	5.6	3.1	1.0	0.7	1.1
1946	6.8	3.5	1.1	0.8	1.3
Per cent of total regional population (economically active), 1940	30.0%	30.2%	29.5%	30.0%	29.3%
1946	29.8	29.4	28.9	30.0	29.4
Density (inhabitants/sq. km.), 1940	9.9	31.1	8.5	12.2	3.5
1946	11.5	35.5	9.7	14.4	4.2
Urbanized (living in communities over 10,000) [000's of people]	4,308.2	2,673.7	248.6	424.0	961.8
Per cent of regional population	21.9%	26.0%	7.3%	19.3%	26.7%
Thousands of persons over 5 years old who still speak Indian languages (only Indian; Indian-Spanish), 1940	2,480.9	1,208.0	1,198.0	6.0	65.0
Per cent of total persons in region	12.5%	10.7%	32.4%	0.0%	1.8%
Thousands of persons over 10 years old unable to read or write, 1940	7,198.8	3,945.4	1,619.7	763.6	870.1
Per cent of such persons in region	51.4%	54.4%	68.3%	46.5%	32.3%
Thousands of persons engaged in agriculture	3,830.5	1,892.8	810.7	469.0	658.3
Per cent of economically active population, 1940	65.9%	60.8%	82.0%	67.9%	62.1%
Thousands of *ejidatarios*	1,601.4	902.1	259.4	169.1	269.9
Per cent of agricultural population	41.8%	47.4%	32.4%	36.0%	40.9%
Thousands of persons in industry, 1940	639.3	399.2	63.8	74.7	101.6
Per cent of regional economically active population, 1940	11.0%	12.9%	6.4%	10.7%	10.2%
Average minimum urban wage (pesos/day), 1940	$1.90	$1.72	$2.29	$2.22	$2.84
Average minimum rural wage (pesos/day), 1940	$1.65	$1.44	$2.06	$1.88	$2.32
Index, 1940 urban wages [1934 = 100]	165.2	136.3	149.1	225.6	184.3
Index, 1940 rural wages [1934 = 100]	151.4	128.5	139.5	192.6	159.9

4. REGIONAL SHARES, 1940–1945

Date of Data		Total National Items (100%)	Percentage of These in			
			Core	South	West	North
	Total area (000's sq. km.)	1,964.6	16.8%	20.3%	9.5%	53.4%
1900	Total population	13,607,272	53.9	17.2	13.5	11.3
1940	Total population	19,653,552	52.5	17.5	11.5	18.5
1946	Total population	22,752,700	51.9	17.1	11.4	19.6
1950	Total population	25,564,218	52.6	16.8	10.8	19.8
1940	Economically active population	5,858,116	53.1	16.9	11.6	19.8
1946	Economically active population	6,777,100	52.5	16.6	11.8	19.1
1940	Croplands (000's hectares)	14,874.0	32.2	23.7	15.0	22.2
1945	Lands cultivated in 54 principal crops	6,412.7	44.9	15.3	15.1	24.7
1945	Value of crops (millions of pesos)	2,101.1	37.6	17.3	11.9	33.2
1940	Landholdings					
	1000–5000 hectares	6,883	17.5	16.2	8.5	58.8
	Over 10,000 hectares	1,472	9.0	18.0	8.0	65.0
1940	Persons living in communities of over 10,000 ("urbanites")	4,308,240	62.2	5.7	9.8	22.4
1940	Persons over 5 years old who speak only Indian languages	1,237,018	46.1	52.6	0.0	1.7
1940	Persons over 5 years old who speak Indian *and* Spanish	1,253,891	51.3	44.3	0.4	3.6
1940	Persons over 10 years old who can neither read nor write	7,198,756	54.8	22.5	10.7	12.0
1945	Electrical energy consumed (millions of kvh)	2,435.1	73.6	2.0	4.5	19.9
1945	Developed telephone lines (kilometers)	1,410.4	74.3	1.4	6.0	18.3
1945	Railway lines (000's kms)	22,953.7	35.1	11.3	9.4	44.2
1945	Automobiles	113,317	59.1	2.9	5.6	32.4
1945	Busses	12,407	54.2	6.1	7.4	32.3
1945	Trucks	59,814	48.7	4.9	6.8	39.6

5. POPULATED PLACES IN MEXICO, 1940

Type	Size	Number	Population	
			Number	Per Cent
CITIES	over 10,000	97	4,308,240	21.9
Large	over 50,000	13	2,674,792	13.6
Medium	25,000–50,000	18	624,920	3.2
Small	10,000–25,000	66	1,008,528	5.1
TOWNS	2,500–10,000	603	2,588,429	13.2
Large	5,000–10,000	165	1,101,781	5.6
Small	2,500– 5,000	438	1,486,648	7.6
VILLAGES	100– 2,500	28,809	10,753,036	54.7
Large	1,000– 2,500	1,988	2,976,016	15.1
Small	100– 1,000	26,821	7,777,020	29.6
HAMLETS	11– 100	48,779	1,837,886	9.4
Large	50– 100	13,623	972,830	5.0
Small	11– 50	35,156	865,056	4.4
ISOLATED	less than 10	26,897	165,961	0.8
Totals		105,185	19,653,552	100.0

Source: Whetten, *Rural Mexico*, Table 8, adapted. See above, Table 2, for 1950 cities.

6. LANDS, 1915–1947

| | AREAS (millions of hectares) | | | PERCENTAGES | | |
| | Total Republic[a] | Ejidos | | Total Republic[a] | Ejidos | |
		1915–44[a]	1947[b]		1915–44[a]	1947[b]
CROPLANDS	15.0	7.9	11.7	7.6	26.3	30.2
Irrigated or humid		1.3	2.0		4.4	5.5
Seasonal		6.6	7.0		21.9	17.8
Unreliable		...	2.7		...	6.9
NONAGRICULTURAL LANDS	181.5	22.1	27.6	92.4	73.7	59.8
Woodlands	38.6	5.3	8.7	19.7	17.7	22.1
Pastures	58.0	13.1	14.0	29.6	43.6	35.6
Unproductive	8.8	...	3.1	4.5	...	7.9
All others	76.1	3.7	1.8	38.6	12.4	4.4
Totals	196.5	30.0	39.3	100.0	100.0	100.0

Source: [a] Whetten, *Rural Mexico*, pp. 137, 576, 589 (adapted); [b] Study by General Cándido Aguilar (adapted).

7. INDIAN SPEECH GROUPS IN MEXICO, 1940

Size of Language Group	Number of Languages	Number of Persons	Languages (in order of size)
500,000 or more	0	0	None
250,000–500,000	1	360,000	Nahuatl
100,000–250,000	3	343,666	Mixteco; Zapoteco; Maya
50,000–100,000	3	202,389	Otomí; Totonac; Mazatec
25,000– 50,000	5	176,149	Tzotzil; Tzendal; Mazahua; Mixe; Huastec
10,000– 25,000	5	85,653	Chinantec; Tarascan; Chol; Tlapanec; Tarahumara
5,000– 10,000	6	47,296	Chatino; Amusgo; Mayo; Zoque; Popluca; Chontal
1,000– 5,000	2	5,822	Cuicateco; Tepehua
100– 1,000	3	1,225	Huichol; Yaqui; Matlazinca
Less than 100	7	20,789	

8. CULTURAL DIVISIONS, 1940
(Thousands of people)

	LANGUAGE DIVISIONS					
	Only Native		Native and Spanish		Only Spanish	Total
						Number	Per Cent

	Only Native		Native and Spanish		Only Spanish	Number	Per Cent
THE INDIAN WORLD *							
(Maize-eaters)							
Barefoot, miserable	1,115	75.0%	753	51.6%		1,868	63.5
Huaraches, native dress	210	14.1	242	16.7		452	15.3
Huaraches, no costume	107	7.2	251	17.1		358	12.1
Shoes, native dress	55	3.7	53	3.6		108	3.6
Shoes, no costume	...	...	159	10.9		159	5.5
Total	1,487	100.0%	1,458	100.0%		2,945	100.0
THE TRANSITIONAL WORLD *							
(Maize-eaters)							
Barefoot, miserable					3,365	3,365	46.4
Huaraches, native dress					1,051	1,051	14.5
Huaraches, no costume					2,769	2,769	38.1
Shoes, native dress					83	83	1.0
Total					7,268	7,268	100.0
THE MODERN WORLD †							
(Wheat-eaters; modern dress)							
Proletariat; squalor					750	750	7.9
Petite bourgeoisie; marginal					7,131	7,131	75.6
Comfortably equipped					1,500	1,500	15.9
Lavishly equipped					60	60	0.6
Total					9,441	9,441	100.0

Sources: * Gilberto Loyo, "Esquema demográfico de México," Segundo Congreso Mexicano de Ciencias Sociales (1946), *Memoria*, III, 673–796. (Adapted.)

† Estimates by H. F. C., guided by Loyo, and Lucio Mendieta y Nuñez, "Presente social del país," in *Seis Años de Actividad Nacional* [1940–1946] (Mexico, 1946), pp. 167–186.

9. DEVELOPMENT OF MEXICAN EDUCATION, 1892–1950

	Budgets (millions of pesos)	Schools (thousands)	Pupils (millions)	Illiteracy (millions)	Per Cent
1892	3.3	?	?	?	
1900	6.8	?	?	7.3	74.2
1907	10.6	11.9	0.8		
1910	?	?	?	7.5	69.7
1921	?	?	?	6.9	66.2
1925	38.1	13.2	1.0		
1930	54.6	19.5	1.7	6.9	59.3
1935	60.2	20.5	1.8		
1940	106.3	23.4	2.2	7.2	51.6
1945	230.4	22.0	2.7		
1950 (estimates)	400.0	? 24.0	3.0	? 6.0	? 45.0

12. MEXICAN ELECTIONS, 1917–1952

		Votes
1917	Venustiano Carranza	797,305
	Pablo González	11,615
	Alvaro Obregón	4,008
1920	Alvaro Obregón	1,131,751
	Alfredo Robles Domínguez	47,442
1924	Plutarco Elías Calles	1,340,634
	Angel Flores	250,599
1929	Pascual Ortiz Rubio	1,948,848
	José Vasconcelos	110,979
	Pedro V. Rodríguez Triana	23,279
1934	Lázaro Cárdenas	2,225,000
	Antonio I. Villareal	24,395
	Adalberto Tejada	16,037
	Hernan Laborde	539
1940	Manuel Avila Camacho	2,176,641
	Juan Andreu Almazán	151,101
	Rafael Sánchez Tapía	9,840
1946	Miguel Alemán	1,786,901
	Ezequiel Padilla	443,357
	J. Agustín Castro	28,537
	Carlos I. Calderón	1,181
1952	Adolfo Ruiz Cortines	2,713,419
	Miguel Henríquez Guzmán	579,745
	Efraín González Luna	285,555
	Vicente Lombardo Toledano	72482

Source: *Tiempo, núm.* 533 (July 18, 1952), p. 4, *et passim.*

13. PRODUCTION, EXPORTS, AND IMPORTS OF PETROLEUM, 1921–1947

[In thousands of barrels of 42 gallons each]

Year	Production	Exports	Imports	Net Exports
1921	193,398	172,268	489	171,779
1922	182,278	180,866	300	180,566
1923	149,585	135,607	2,142	133,465
1924	139,678	129,700	5,732	123,968
1925	115,515	96,517	3,749	92,768
1926	90,421	80,722	1,322	79,400
1927	64,121	48,421	6,384	42,037
1928	50,151	33,262	2,018	31,244
1929	44,688	26,602	2,846	23,756
1930	39,530	26,835	2,744	24,091
1931	33,039	22,491	2,329	20,162
1932	32,805	22,580	1,994	20,586
1933	34,001	19,717	1,453	18,264
1934	38,172	22,694	1,488	21,206
1935	40,241	20,573	1,484	19,089
1936	41,028	23,215	1,503	21,712
1937	46,907	23,065	2,348	20,717
1938	38,506	13,885	1,670	12,215
1939	42,898	17,997	1,382	16,615
1940	44,036	20,012	2,162	17,850
1941	42,196	15,812	2,148	13,664
1942	34,815	6,265	1,572	4,693
1943	35,163	5,732	1,856	3,876
1944	38,203	4,998	2,060	2,938
1945	43,547	8,369	2,429	5,940
1946	49,235	9,405	3,380	6,025
1947	56,284	14,826	4,641	10,185

Source: Banco de Mexico, Annual Report for 1947, in Committee on Interstate and Foreign Commerce, "Fuel Investigation: Mexican Petroleum," 80th Cong., 2nd Sess., HR 2470 (Washington: GPO, 1949), p. 8.

14. GROWTH OF VEHICLES, 1941–1950

Year	Total Vehicles	Automobiles	Busses	Trucks
1941	168,156	106,327	11,257	50,572
1942	178,041	113,427	11,145	53,469
1943	177,817	112,041	10,996	54,780
1944	181,304	111,947	12,064	57,293
1945	185,538	113,317	12,407	59,814
1946	205,494	120,906	12,915	71,673
1947	235,057	134,079	14,790	86,188
1948	266,885	150,251	16,872	99,762
1949	283,070	158,251	20,057	104,762
1950	325,575	176,251	30,062	119,262

Source: *Noticias*, VII, No. 25 (June 19, 1951), p. 4.

15. GROSS NATIONAL INCOME, 1939-1950

	Nominal National Income			Real National Income	
Year	Amount (000's pesos)	Per Cent Increase	Dollar Equivalent *	Amount (000's pesos)	Per Cent Increase
1939ᵃ	6,000	...	1,260	6,000	...
1940ᵃ	6,200	3.3	1,278	6,050	0.8
1941ᵃ	6,900	11.2	1,420	6,300	4.1
1942ᵃ	8,300	20.2	1,710	6,900	9.5
1943ᵃ	10,000	20.5	2,060	7,200	4.3
1944ᵃ	13,400	34.0	2,760	7,500	4.1
1945ᵃ	16,000	18.5	3,300	8,050	7.3
1946ᵃ	19,200	20.0	3,970	8,400	4.4
1947ᵃ	20,900	1.7	4,320	8,600	2.4
1948ᵃ	22,800	9.1	4,690 *	8,800	2.3
1949ᵇ	25,600	12.7	3,610	9,000	2.2
1950ᶜ	29,800	16.4	3,450	9,250	2.8

* Calculated here at 4.85 pesos per dollar to July 1949; 8.65 thereafter.

Sources: ᵃ A. C. Flores, "Desarrollo Económica de México," *Problemas Agrícolas e Industriales de México*, II (No. 1, Jan.–Mar. 1950), 43, Table 17 (based on Banco de Mexico's unpublished figures).

ᵇ *Noticias*, VI (No. 39, September 26, 1950), 3, reproducing U.N. figures.

ᶜ *Noticias*, VII (No. 13, March 27, 1951), 3, based on International Monetary Fund Bulletin, March 16, 1951.

16. NATIONAL INCOME AND GROSS INVESTMENTS, 1940–1948

	National Income (millions pesos)	Gross Investments (millions pesos)	Per Cent	Gross Investments Equivalent (millions U. S. dollars)	Adjusted to 1940 (millions pesos)
1940	6,200	685	11.0	141	685
1941	6,900	851	8.1	175	798
1942	8,300	976	11.8	201	829
1943	10,500	1,114	10.8	230	784
1944	13,400	1,472	10.9	303	845
1945	16,000	1,942	12.1	400	1,002
1946	19,200	2,734	14.2	564	1,225
1947	20,900	2,802	13.4	579	1,185
1948	22,800	3,330	14.5	583	1,299

Source: Antonio Carrillo Flores (Head of Nacional Financiera), "El desarrollo economico de Mexico," *Problemas Agrícolas e Industriales de México*, II (No. 1, Jan.–Mar. 1950), Table 1, p. 11.

28. FINANCIAL ASSISTANCE EXTENDED BY NACIONAL FINANCIERA

(As of December 31, 1949)

(Thousands of pesos)

Enterprises and Activity	Total Assistance	Credits Extended	Securities Purchased
Ferrocarriles Nacionales de Mexico, Railway	187,215	187,215	....
Comision Federal de Electricidad, Electric Power	169,101	169,101	....
Altos Hornos de Mexico, S. A., Iron and Steel	83,930	14,688	69,242
Nueva Cia. Electrica Chapala, S. A., Electric Power	71,700	4,997	66,703
Central Sanalona, S. A., Sugar	50,717	9,782	40,935
Cia. Mexicana de Luz y Fuerza Motriz, S. A., Electric Power	40,740	40,740	....
Cia. Azucarera del Rio Guayelejo, S. A., Sugar	39,077	33,692	5,385
Guanos y Fertilizantes de Mexico, S. A., Fertilizer	39,068	34,176	4,892
Cia. Industrial de Atenquique, S. A., Paper	32,163	20,627	11,536
Ingenio Independencia, S. A., Sugar	32,108	32,108	....
Petroleos Mexicanos, Petroleum	30,130	30,130	....
La Consolidada, S. A., Steel Products	14,252	14,252	....
Industria Electrica de Mexico, S. A., Electrical Goods	9,308	6,250	3,058
Ayotla Textil, S. A., Cotton Goods	8,709	8,709	....
Establecimiento Publico Ingenio del Mante, Sugar	7,454	....	7,454
Cementos Guadelajara, S. A., Cement	7,320	683	6,637
Carbonifera Unida de Palau, S. A., Coal and Coke	5,091	4,491	600
Telefonos de Mexico, S. A., Telephone	5,025	....	5,025
Cobre de Mexico, S. A., Electrolytic Copper	4,697	1,695	3,002
Others	130,878	42,354	88,524
Totals	968,683	655,690	312,993

Source: *Chicago Journol of Commerce*, XXXI, No. 63 (Dec. 29, 1950), part 2, p. 6.

29. OUTPUT OF MAJOR MANUFACTURING INDUSTRIES IN MEXICO

Industry	Unit	Quantity 1948	Quantity 1949	Value (in pesos) 1949
Cotton yarn and cloth	Kg.	53,371,487	45,036,915	717,408,897
Sugar	...	551,621,459	506,593,534	386,489,379
Iron and steel	Metric ton	997,570	993,925	317,874,327
Beer	Liter	336,041,288	344,175,803	307,327,635
Flour	Kg.	390,793,965	408,518,714	271,175,969
Soap	....	86,122,964	97,700,840	217,220,964
Vegetable oils	....	163,938,720	191,376,316	205,839,399
Cigars, cigarettes	....	....	....	188,961,132
Rubber manufacturers	....	....	....	186,042,186
Wool yarn and cloth	Kg.	3,811,126	4,223,339	141,683,133
Paper	....	73,286,494	74,708,309	125,025,737
Cement	Ton	836,830	1,224,211	121,867,716
Rayon yarn and cloth	Kg.	3,014,752	3,575,377	103,055,606
Glass	....	....	....	64,625,620
Dry goods	...	....	....	39,966,767
Preserved foods	Kg.	28,803,497	22,279,276	36,629,713
Matches	....	....	....	40,253,606
Shoes	Pairs	2,313,586	2,391,405	39,328,311
Alcohol	Liter	30,455,415	29,135,166	24,526,206

Source: *Chicago Journal of Commerce*, XXXI, No. 63 (Dec. 29, 1950), part 2, p. 6.

30. INDUSTRIALISM: INDICES OF PHYSICAL VOLUME

(1929 = 100)

Year	General Index	Mining—Metals			Crude Oil	Refined	Electric Energy	Textiles	Beer and Cigarettes	Light Manufacturing		Total
		Total	Gold Silver	Industrial						Clothing Recreation	Diverse	
1939	119.95	76.97	80.77	74.30	96.00	181.07	151.42	127.05	191.92	136.05	120.55	144.37
1940	119.61	75.03	86.76	66.85	98.55	162.17	154.39	135.98	209.97	121.58	136.71	153.66
1941	124.94	76.27	81.49	72.63	96.35	176.67	154.11	149.85	213.66	126.00	152.53	163.72
1942	131.75	86.75	86.36	87.02	77.92	172.43	160.36	162.71	246.76	122.49	169.17	180.15
1943	137.54	87.43	82.68	90.75	78.69	186.47	167.33	164.53	287.46	91.33	185.95	189.88
1944	141.39	77.92	69.57	87.74	85.50	197.27	168.05	167.11	344.85	98.88	191.45	207.41
1945	150.69	79.24	59.98	92.67	97.46	214.66	187.49	162.69	356.78	110.34	237.56	219.10
1946	155.30	59.80	44.36	70.56	110.19	237.81	202.73	160.64	421.02	112.10	261.28	239.61
1947	161.70	78.03	57.31	92.49	125.97	273.74	219.85	147.40	341.99	97.08	258.03	210.25
1948	162.49	71.03	53.56	83.22	130.94	265.64	242.49	153.32	357.31	109.85	250.23	217.40

Source: Banco de Mexico, *Problemas Agrícolas e Industriales de México*, II (No. 1, Jan.–Mar. 1950), 22, Table 14.

Appendix II. Suggested Reading

Mexico has produced and attracted innumerable writers. As befits the complicated land in which the first New World printing press was established, its varied aspects have heaped up a continuous and mounting bibliography which may be characterized as vast, sprawling, and bewildering—the most written-about of the Latin-American lands. The following notes are primarily directed to the general reader restricted to English language works; they are, therefore, highly selective, limited, and somewhat impressionistic suggestions.

The best way to learn about Mexico is to go there. Numerous guides ease the trip and contain a wealth of lore not readily available elsewhere. Kept scrupulously up-to-date is the 25-cent pamphlet of the Pan-American Union, Travel Division, *Motoring to Mexico* (13th ed., 1951), "a compilation of information on highways and facilities for the motorist" with a selected list of suggested readings. Its dozen or so enumerated guide-books have peculiarly individual merits. The nearest to a "standard" one is Philip Terry, *Guide to Mexico* (Chestnut Hill, Mass.; rev. 1947), overwhelming in detail. Lighter in tone are Anita Brenner, *Your Mexican Holiday* (New York: Putnam; rev. 1947); Ralph Hancock, *The Magic Land: Mexico* (New York: Coward-McCann, 1948); and MacKinley Helm, *Journeying through Mexico* (Boston: Little, Brown, 1948). The first volume of Earl P. Hanson, ed., *New World Guides to the Latin American Republics* (New York: Duell, Sloan, 1950), has a chapter on Mexico. Pemex and the National Commission for Tourism (Mexico City) issue numerous publications in English to aid the traveler. The Pan-American Highway system is represented by Cecil and Fred Carnes, *You Must Go to Mexico* (Chicago: Ziff-Davis, 1947), and Roger Stephens, *Down that Pan American Highway* (New York: R. Stephens, 1948).

1. GENERAL WORKS

In the steady stream of books and articles on Mexico, interpretive syntheses appear regularly, and nearly as regularly become outdated. Among the recent crop of general summary works worth reading are

Herbert Cerwin, *These Are the Mexicans* (New York: Harcourt, Brace, 1947); Frank Tannenbaum, *Mexico, the Struggle for Peace and Bread* (New York: Knopf, 1950); and a new edition of Lesley Byrd Simpson, *Many Mexicos* (New York: Putnam, 1941; rev. 1952), a lively and readable account recommended above the others. Standard college texts on Latin-American history include one or two chapters devoted to Mexico that serve as introduction; the most recent and important of these summaries is in Harry Bernstein, *Modern and Contemporary Latin America* (Chicago: Lippincott, 1952), pp. 3–158, which brings the story through the early Alemán years and appends invaluable further reading suggestions. Concisely presented is much basic information in the Pan-American Union pamphlet *Mexico*. At the close of these notes are mentioned some publications which can help the reader find further leads.

2. CHIEFLY HISTORICAL

Henry Bamford Parkes, *A History of Mexico* (Boston: Houghton Mifflin; rev. 1950), is now about the only single-volume history in English aimed at the non-specialist; outmoded in parts and slanted from the left, it nonetheless is a popular and exciting account down to Avila Camacho, with a usable bibliography for the general student. There is a wide gap between Parkes and the detailed, multi-volume works of nineteenth-century historians, chief of whom (in English) is H. H. Bancroft. His *Works,* 39 stately tomes, include *The Native Races* (5 vols., 1883–1888), *The History of Mexico* (6 vols., 1883–1888), *The Northern States of Mexico and Texas* (2 vols., 1887–1889); in 1909 he published a fore-shortened version of these in his single volume *History of Mexico*. There is a miserable English translation of Justo Sierra, ed., classic *Mexico: Its Social Evolution* (1900–1902), a temperate synthesis of many phases of Mexican life through to the twentieth century. A helpful historical baseline is provided by the several essays in A. P. Whitaker, ed., *Mexico Today* (Annals of the American Academy of Political Science, 1940). Certain "thread" treatments also include a sweeping panorama, such as the final chapters of Lloyd Mecham, *Church and State in Latin America* (Chapel Hill, N. C.: University of North Carolina Press, 1934), a scholarly, semi-legal approach; more heated, and avowedly polemic is the Catholic view adumbrated in Joseph H. Schlarman, *Mexico, Land of Volcanoes* (Milwaukee: Bruce, 1950).

Writings on pre-Conquest Mexico are voluminous. By the time findings of specialists filter into general works they have become obsolete, but standard introductory volumes include for the Maya, S. G. Morley, *The Ancient Maya* (California: Stanford University Press, 1946); Ralph Roys, *The Indian Background of Colonial Yucatan* (Washington, D.C., 1943); and Frans Blom, *The Conquest of Yucatan* (Boston: Houghton Mifflin,

1936). The highland groups are sketched in John Eric Thompson, *Mexico before Cortes* (New York: Scribner, 1933); and in G. C. Vaillant, *The Aztecs of Mexico* (New York: Doubleday, 1941; rev. Penguin ed., 1950).

The epics of conquest and exploration have stimulated authors for nearly half a millennium. W. H. Prescott, *History of the Conquest of Mexico* (2 vols., 1843), remains standard and classic; R. B. Merriman, *Rise of the Spanish Empire* (4 vols., 1918–1934), stresses the European contexts, while Cortés' own letters and Bernal Diaz' *True History* provide exciting, if often inaccurate eye-witness views. General works on the Spanish Empire, which had a main focus at Mexico, devote much space to narratives and institutions; recommended for their copious notes, reliability, and sweep are Bailey Diffie, *Latin-American Civilization: Colonial Period* (Harrisburg, Pa.: Stackpole Sons, 1945), and C. H. Haring, *The Spanish Empire in America* (Oxford, 1946; rev. 1952), each of which opens the door to much further reading. J. A. Crow, *The Epic of Latin America* (New York: Doubleday, 1946) is a semi-popular treatment weighted on the colonial side. Much standard literature is also touched on in Lesley Byrd Simpson, *The Encomienda in New Spain* (Berkeley: University of California Press, 1929; rev. 1950). The colonial period in Mexico probably accounts for better than half the writings on that land, so advanced exploration can be made via the "Further Study" section below.

Many social trends of the colonial period are encompassed in the Mexican portion of H. I. Priestley's *The Coming of the White Man, 1492–1848* (New York: Macmillan, 1929); considerably broader than its title indicates is George Kubler's *Mexican Architecture in the Sixteenth Century* (2 vols.; Yale University Press, 1948), as it deals with the social contexts affecting building crafts and arts. Numerous monographs in the University of California's *Ibero-Americana* series deal with economic history of colonial times.

Biographies form a large part of the literature on colonial Mexico. Chronologically the volumes on Cortés by F. A. MacNutt (1909) and by H. R. Wagner (1938) are followed by A. S. Aiton, *Antonio de Mendoza, First Viceroy of New Spain* (1927), leaving aside for a moment the numerous portraits of individual explorers limned in works like J. L. Mecham, *Francisco de Ibarra* (1927) and the numerous writings on the Borderlands by H. E. Bolton and his students. In Spanish there are innumerable biographies of colonial figures of varying stature, for which the best finding list appears in the bibliographies of general works.

The Bourbon Renaissance fuses into Independence so far as works in English are concerned, with a heavy emphasis on biography. A basic work, opening wide the gates to further readings, is William Spence Robertson's recent study of Iturbide and his times, *Iturbide of Mexico* (Duke, 1952); of nearly equal value bibliographically is John Rydjord,

Foreign Interest in the Independence of New Spain (Duke, 1935). William Forrest Sprague, *Vicente Guerrero* (Chicago: R. R. Donnelley & Sons Company, 1939), deals with an early patriot. The age of Santa Anna is introduced by Wilfrid Hardy Callcott in his *Church and State in Mexico, 1822–1857* (1926) and his *Santa Anna* (Norman: University of Oklahoma Press, 1936). There is a highly ramified and extensive literature on diplomatic relations concerning Texas and then the war with the United States; old standards are G. L. Rives, *The United States and Mexico, 1821–1848* (1913); J. H. Smith, *The Annexation of Texas* (1911), and his *The War with Mexico* (2 vols., 1919), E. C. Barker, *Mexico and Texas* (1928), and J. F. Rippy's *Joel R. Poinsett* (Duke, 1935); and his *The Rivalry of the United States and Great Britain over Latin America* (1929). O. Morton, *Terán and Texas: a Chapter in Texas-Mexican Relations* (Austin, Texas: State Historical Association 1948), is more recent, while C. E. Castañeda, ed., *The Mexican Side of the Texas Revolution* (1928), fulfills its title's promise. Richard A. Johnson, *The Mexican Revolution of Ayutla, 1854–1855* (Rock Island, Ill.: Augustana College Library, 1939), closes the age of Santa Anna, side lights on which can be found in Rufus Kay Wyllys, *The French in Sonora (1850–1854)* (Berkeley: University of California Press, 1932). Travel accounts of this period are invaluable, the most notable of which is probably Mme. Calderon de la Barca, *Life in Mexico* (1843); vistas on these important aids are helpfully opened by C. H. Gardiner's annotated listings, "Foreign travelers' accounts of Mexico, 1810–1910," *The Americas*, VIII (January 1952) 321–351.

A volume that sweeps through the period after 1857 is Wilfrid Hardy Callcott's scholarly continuation of earlier interests in his *Liberalism in Mexico, 1857–1929* (Stanford University Press, 1931), but for the most part the latter half of the nineteenth century is approached biographically. The Reforma and Intervention are covered by such volumes as Ralph Roeder's overwritten but solid *Juárez and His Mexico* (2 vols.; New York: Viking, 1947), and U. R. Burke's even more unsatisfactory *Life of Benito Juárez* (1894). Standard treatments of the phantom throne are E. C. Corti, *Maximilian and Charlotte of Mexico* (2 vols., 1928); Daniel Dawson, *The Mexican Adventure* (London, 1935); H. M. Hyde, *Mexican Empire* (London: Macmillan, 1946); and José Luis Blasio, *Maximilian, Emperor of Mexico; Memoirs of his Private Secretary* (trans.; Yale University Press, 1934). Rescued from near oblivion has been *The Life of Sebastian Lerdo de Tejada, 1823–1889* (Austin: University of Texas Press, 1951), by Frank A. Knapp, Jr.

The Díaz period is but little explored. Inaccurate in part and biased in the whole is Carleton Beals, *Porfirio Díaz, Dictator of Mexico* (Philadelphia: Lippincott, 1932), nearest to a "standard" life of the Hero of the Americas who was the subject of several eulogistic works during his lifetime. C. A. Conant, *The Banking System of Mexico* (1910), is largely technical but gives economic data on the period 1896–1909, as does W. F. McCaleb, *The Public Finances of Mexico* (1922), which treats a longer span. Acute judgments on Díaz are found in C. L. Jones, *Mexico and Its Reconstruction* (1921), which edges through the epic Revolution. J. K. Turner's *Barbarous Mexico* (1911), is an I.W.W.-slanted and highly colored indictment of the Díaz regime. Evolution of Mexican land tenure is described by G. M. McBride, *The Land Systems of Mexico* (1923), centering on the nineteenth century, often with major errors concerning colonial matters. The overthrow of Díaz is recounted in a new volume, Charles Cumberland, *Mexican Revolution: Genesis under Madero* (New Brunswick: Rutgers University Press, 1952), received too late for use in this volume. Its findings confirm the treatment here.

Books on the Revolution are legion, yet no scholarly synthesis has yet appeared. Purporting to be the only history in English is Anita Brenner and George Leighton, *The Wind that Swept Mexico: the History of the Mexican Revolution, 1910–1942* (New York: Harper, 1943), a short, emotional text with superb photographs. As viewed from the liberal Left, the Revolution is summarized and interpreted to their publication dates by Ernest Gruening, *Mexico and Its Heritage* (1928), and by Frank Tannenbaum, *The Mexican Agrarian Revolution* (1929), and his *Peace by Revolution* (Columbia University Press, 1933). Heroes of the Revolution are well represented in Spanish but in English there is only a handful of biographies of generally unsatisfactory nature; examples are Edgcumb Pinchon's separate and novelesque treatments of Pancho Villa (London, 1933) and his *Zapata the Unconquerable* (New York: Doubleday, 1941); the Hearst reporter who rode with Zapata gives an exciting account in Harry H. Dunn, *The Crimson Jester: Zapata of Mexico* (New York: McBride, 1934), while John Reed, in *Insurgent Mexico* (1913), catches important vignettes of northern chieftains with whom he lived. Some of the excitement and data of the epic Revolution are retained in E. I. Bell, *The Political Shame of Mexico* (1914); Rosa King, *Tempest over Mexico* (Boston: Little, Brown, 1935); and E. W. Baerlin, *Mexico, the Land of Unrest* (1914). Highly technical is E. W. Kemmerer, *Inflation and Revolution, Mexico's Experience of 1912–1917* (Princeton University Press, 1940). E. J. Dillon, *President Obregon, a world reformer* (London, 1923), sets a pattern of hagiography followed by the biographers of Cárdenas, the only other president to acquire an English "life"; there are a pair of these, Nathaniel and Sylvia Weyl, *The Reconquest of Mexico, the Years of Lázaro Cárdenas* (Oxford, 1939), by a professed ex-Communist; more recent is a view by an American linguistic missionary who often advised him, William Cameron Townsend, *Lázaro Cárdenas, Mexican Democrat* (Ann Arbor, Mich., 1952). With but few exceptions, the history of recent years appears in the interpretative syntheses mentioned in Section 1 or in topical works dealt with below, as the broadening Revolution encompasses all Mexican life.

3. CHIEFLY SOCIAL AND CULTURAL

Rural sociology, Indians, and education have tended to dominate much of the writing which might be classed as "social." Books by McBride and Tannenbaum, mentioned above, are dated but helpful introductory pieces on agrarian matters to which should be added Eyler N. Simpson, *The Ejido, Mexico's Way Out* (University of North Carolina Press, 1937), which with a semi-collectivist bias takes matters through failures to 1934; prodigiously fat in data, thin in analysis is Nathan L. Whetten, *Rural Mexico* (University of Chicago Press, 1948), a truly indispensable volume. The pessimistic view of Mexico's future because of its eroding resources adumbrated in William Vogt, *Road to Survival* (New York: Sloane, 1947), chapter 7 has been spelled out in more detail by another conservationist in Tom Gill, *Land Hunger in Mexico* (Pack Foundation, Washington, D.C., 1951). Often cited but of relatively small value is Helen Phipps, *Some Aspects of the Agrarian Question in Mexico* (1925).

Living Indians and rural communities have attracted much attention from professional investigators. A summary introduction to the major items dealing specifically with Indian groups appears in Ralph Beals, Robert Redfield, and Sol Tax, "Anthropological Research Problems with Reference to the Contemporary Peoples of Mexico and Guatemala," *American Anthropologist*, n.s. XLV (January–March 1943), 1–21; these data are updated and discussed in papers of the Viking Fund Seminar edited by Sol Tax, *Heritage of Conquest: The Ethnology of Middle America* (Glencoe, Ill.: Free Press, 1952). More than two dozen Mexican communities have been studied by various persons following the footsteps of Robert Redfield's *Tepoztlan* (Chicago, 1930); closing a cycle in such investigations is the superb job performed by Oscar Lewis in his *Life in a Mexican Village: Tepoztlan Restudied* (Urbana, Illinois, 1951). A long critique of these studies, with complete listing of them and selected allied works on regionalism in Mexico, is provided by my "Mexican Community Studies," *Hispanic American Historical Review*, XXXII (May 1952), 212–242. A vast store of lore has been compressed in Frances Toor, *A Treasury of Mexican Folkways* (New York: Crown Publishers, 1947). Important for crafts is the recent *Made in Mexico: The Story of a Country's Arts and Crafts* (New York: Knopf, 1952) by Patricia F. Ross.

Mexican preoccupation with education has fostered an extensive bibliography, summed up neatly and ably in George F. Kneller, *The Education of the Mexican Nation* (New York: Columbia University Press, 1951), which synthesizes matters to about 1948. Earlier phases and special topics are represented in George I. Sánchez, *Mexico: a Revolution by Education* (New York: Viking, 1936), and his *The Development of Higher Education in Mexico* (Columbia University Press, 1944); George C. Booth, *Mexico's School-Made Society* (Stanford University Press, 1941); and for the nineteenth century, Irma Wilson, *Mexico, a Century of Educational Thought* (New York: Hispanic Institute in the United States, 1941). John Tate Lanning's *Academic Culture in the Spanish Colonies* (1940) tells a lot about colonial Mexican culture, as do *Don Carlos de Sigüenza y Góngora* (1929) and *Books of the Brave* (Harvard University Press, 1949) by Irving Leonard. Heavily loaded on the colonial side, too, is the standard survey of *belles-lettres* by Carlos Gonzalez Peña, *History of Mexican Literature* (University Press in Dallas; trans., 1943). A successful and unique attempt at an intellectual survey since 1910 is Patrick Romanell, *Making of the Mexican Mind* (University of Nebraska Press, 1952).

The general reader should savor Mexico through novels in translation and laid in Mexico by competent craftsmen. Among the former a sample swatch includes Mariano Azuela, *Marcela* (trans. of *Mala Yerba;* New York: Farrar & Rinehart, 1932), and his classic *The Underdogs* (trans. of *Los de Abajo;* New York, 1929), as well as Gregorio Lopez y Fuentes, *They that Reap* (London: Harrap, 1937), and his *El Indio* (in English; New York, Norton, 1940); Mauricio Magdaleno, *Sunburst* (New York: Viking, 1944); Miguel A. Meléndez, *Nayar*, and above all, Martín L. Guzmán, *The Eagle and the Serpent* (New York: Knopf, 1930). The nineteenth century provides a really funny masterpiece, E. Lizardi, *The Itching Parrot*. Informal and novelized views of Mexico with the unmistakable stamp of authenticity would embrace Dane Chandos (pseud.), *The Village in the Sun* (New York: Putnam, 1945) and the later *The House in the Sun;* Gertrude Diamant, *The Days of Ofelia* (Boston: Houghton Mifflin, 1942); Alvin and Darley Gordon, *Our Son Pablo* (New York: McGraw-Hill, 1946); MacKinley Helm, *A Matter of Love* (New York: Harpers, 1946); Josephina Niggli, *Mexican Village* (Chapel Hill: University of North Carolina Press, 1945); B. L. Traven, *The Bridge in the Jungle* (New York: Knopf, 1938); Alice Tisdale Hobart, *The Peacock Sheds His Tail* (Indianapolis: Bobbs-Merrill, 1945); and D. H. Lawrence, *Mornings in Mexico* (1927).

Folk art and the "Revolutionary school" are treated in Anita Brenner, *Idols behind Altars* (1929), to which can be added a number of small monographs on particular figures by Frances Toor. L. E. Schmeckebier, *Modern Mexican Art* (University of Minnesota Press, 1939), and Mac-Kinley Helm, *Modern Mexican Painters* (New York: Harpers, 1941), form a useful pair. One of the better known painters has been sympathetically limned in Bertram D. Wolfe, *Diego Rivera, His Life and Times* (New York: Knopf, 1939), while biographer and subject teamed to produce D. Rivera and B. Wolfe, *Portrait of Mexico* (New York: Covici, 1937). Pál Kelemen has done a number of helpful bits to link archaeology and art, especially in his *Battlefield of the Gods* (London: Allen and Unwin, 1937).

4. CHIEFLY ECONOMIC

To its date of publication a vast array of economic materials is found in the Mexican section of *The Economic Literature of Latin America* (2 vols., 1935–1936), II, which is considerably broader than its title implies. Relatively recent developments (to around 1948) are touched on in the chapter on Mexico in George Wythe, *Industry in Latin America* (Columbia University Press; rev. 1950), and in the now standard Sanford Mosk, *Industrial Revolution in Mexico* (University of California Press, 1950). Much interesting material is supplied in short papers issued by the University of Texas, Institute of Latin American Studies, *Basic Industries in Texas and Northern Mexico* (1950). The Pan-American Union, *Foreign Commerce of Mexico, 1939–1949* (1951), is a short statistical summary with some discussion. *Inter-American Economic Affairs*, a quarterly, often contains relevant articles on Mexico.

Mexican labor is miserably or incompletely represented in Spanish or English. J. W. Brown, *Modern Mexico and its Problems* (London, 1927), and M. R. Clark, *Organized Labor in Mexico* (Chapel Hill: University of North Carolina Press, 1934), are outdated but cover early phases of the Revolution. Some of the recent problems are dealt with in W. E. Moore, *Industrialization and Labor* (Ithaca: Cornell University Press, 1951).

Mexican economists are technically well advanced and support a number of journals. Of special note are *Trimestre económico* and the invaluable (and expensive) *Problemas industriales a Agrícolas Mexicanos*, a quarterly. Of special concern, too, is the illuminating description of the Papaloapan in José Attolini, *Economía de la cuenca del Papaloapan* (2 vols.; Mexico City, 1949–1950). The most recently released compilation of official statistics is the Sec. de Economía, *Anuario estadístico de los Estados Unidos Mexicanos, 1943–1945* (1950). Not only for economic but for other allied information, the summaries published by each administration are helpful if one can separate the chaff of propaganda; recent are Cárdenas' *Seis años de gobierno al servicio de México, 1934–1940* (1940), and the overpowering Avila Camacho, *Seis años de actividad nacional, 1940–1946* (1946). The Alemán volume has yet to make its appearance, but annual messages provide much data.

The United States Department of Commerce, The Pan-American Union, and various United Nations agencies provide a flow of information and statistics. Footnotes to Appendix I provide references to some of these. In addition, two United Nations publications have a wealth of useful data: *Recent Events and Trends in Mexico* (1951: ECN. 12/217/Add. 8) and *Foreign Investments in Selected Latin American Countries: Mexico* (1950: ECN. 12/166/Add 8) Received too late for use in this volume are several essays by Mexicans in *El Desarrollo Económico de México* (Mexico City: Escuela Nacional, U.N.A.M., 1952), part of their continuing series, *Investigacion Económica*.

5. INTERNATIONAL

Mexico's relations with the world are not well represented in English. Troubles with creditors are outlined in E. Turlington, *Mexico and Her Foreign Creditors* (Columbia University Press, 1930), and detailed in A. H. Feller, *The Mexican Claims Commissions, 1923–1934* (New York: Macmillan, 1935), while the omnipresent boundary troubles are listed by Gordon Ireland, *Boundaries, Possessions, and Conflicts in Central and North America and the Caribbean* (Harvard University Press, 1941). The European aspects of the Maximilian adventure have been listed under "Chiefly History."

For specific United States–Mexico interplay, a helpful introduction is S. F. Bemis, *The Latin American Policy of the United States* (New York: Harcourt; rev. 1952), supplemented by J. Fred Rippy, *The United States and Mexico* (New York: Appleton-Century-Crofts; rev. 1931) and J. M. Callahan, *American Foreign Policy in Mexican Relations* (New York: Macmillan, 1932), neither of which is broadly based on multi-archival research. Special topics of interest are treated in F. S. Dunn, *The Diplomatic Protection of Americans in Mexico* (Columbia University Press, 1933); Stuart A. MacCorkle, *American Policy of Recognition towards Mexico* (Baltimore, 1933); R. D. Gregg, *The Influence of Border Troubles on Relations between the United States and Mexico, 1876–1910* (Baltimore: Johns Hopkins, 1937); and W. C. Gordon, *The Expropriation of Foreign-Owned Property in Mexico* (Washington, D. C.: Public Affairs Press, 1941).

The diplomacy of the Revolution is touched on by most volumes dealing with Woodrow Wilson and American presidents since his time, and specifically in C. W. Hackett's short and unsatisfactory *The Mexican Revolution and the United States, 1910–1926* (1926). Interesting but misleading, too, are memoirs of American ambassadors to Mexico, notably Henry Lane Wilson, *Diplomatic Episodes in Mexico, Belgium and Chile* (Garden City: Doubleday, Page and Co., 1927), and Josephus Daniels, *Shirt-Sleeve Diplomat* (Chapel Hill: University of North Carolina Press, 1947); to the latter should be added the few extra crumbs in Daniels' letters, collected and edited by Carroll Kilpatrick, *Roosevelt and Daniels: a Friendship in Politics* (Chapel Hill: University of North Carolina Press, 1952). The *Memoirs* (2 vols.; New York: Macmillan, 1948) of Cordell

Hull throw some feeble light on the expropriation of oil and other Mexican matters, as do various volumes of Sumner Welles. A small monograph with interesting material on a special World War II problem is Robert C. Jones, *Mexican War Workers in the United States . . . 1942–1944* (Washington, D. C.: Pan-American Union, Division of Labor and Social Information, 1945).

6. FURTHER STUDY AND KEEPING UP

The numerous titles listed above are but a small fraction of available materials. Two helpful guides will fill in many lacunae: Robin A. Humphreys, *Latin America, a Selective Guide to Publications in English* (London and New York: Royal Institute of International Affairs, 1949), which lists only books, but unrolls systematically 900 of them, including standard aids to general students, and R. F. Behrendt, *Modern Latin America in Social Science Literature* (Albuquerque, 1949), which includes articles as well as books. Many paths are cleared by the Mexican section of C. K. Jones, *A Bibliography of Latin American Bibliographies*, (1922; rev., 1942). Readers of Spanish should also see A. Millares Carlo and J. I. Mantecón, *Ensayo de una Bibliografía de Bibliografías Mexicanas* (Mexico, 1943). Annita M. Ker, *Mexican Government Publications, a Guide . . . 1821–1936* (Washington, D. C., 1940), is a handy tool. *The Americas* and the *Hispanic American Historical Review* contain many articles on Mexico, and book reviews cover a wide swath; Ruth L. Butler's *Guide to the Hispanic American Historical Review, 1918–1945* (Durham, N. C.: Duke, 1950) is a great time-saver. Annual volumes of the *Handbook of Latin American Studies* (1936), now prepared by the Hispanic Foundation of the Library of Congress aided by specialists in a broad spectrum of fields, makes available much recent bibliographical output.

Keeping up-to-date is difficult enough for those who handle Spanish, and is even more arduous for non-linguists. Beyond the standard *New York Times* and *Washington Post* coverage a helpful entry is *Noticias, a Weekly Digest of Hemisphere Reports*, an eight-page digest of English-speaking journals and periodicals that carry any news of Latin America. Much current information is contained in the *Mexican-American Review*, weighted on the economic-political side; for the returned tourist or the casually interested is *Mexican Life: Mexico's Monthly Review*. Among the innumerable Spanish language periodicals I have preferred the weeklies *Hoy* and *Tiempo* for a steady diet. The Banco Nacional de Mexico's *Examen de la Situación Económica de México* has appeared monthly since 1884 and highlights current activities throughout Mexico. Many inquiries are ably cared for by addressing the Pan-American Union, Washington, D. C., or the Hispanic Foundation, Library of Congress.

Appendix III.   A Bibliographical Supplement, 1953-1962

The following summary supplements the materials prepared for the 1953 version of *The United States and Mexico*. In general it contains titles that have appeared in the past decade, or those which should have been included earlier. It is the merest sampling of the spate of materials which annually appear from and about Mexico, recording some works which may be helpful to the general reader or student.

The titles have been grouped in a loose classification which makes no pretense of being comprehensive. The bibliographical works listed first should (with those already mentioned in the original essay) provide the reader with a start toward further materials of his interest. The basic point of departure is still the *Handbook of Latin American Studies*, a continuing cooperative enterprise now reaching to 25 annual volumes covering the social sciences and humanities. Abbreviations used are as follows:

BNCE	Mexico. Banco Nacional de Comercio Exterior.
DGE	Mexico. Dirección General de Estadística.
SDE	Mexico. Secretaría de Economía.
SRE	Mexico. Secretaría de Relaciones Exteriores.
UNAM	Mexico. Universidad Nacional Autónoma de México.
U.P.	University Press
USBFC	U.S. Bureau of Foreign Commerce.
WTIS	World Trade Information Service (USBFC)

BIBLIOGRAPHY

GENERAL
   Some highly selected general items and noteworthy subject bibliographies.

González y González, Luis, and others. *Fuentes de la historia contemporánea de Mexico.* Colegio de Mexico. 3 v. Mexico. 1961–1962.

Massive and indispensable listing of main sources of Mexican history, 1872–1940 by a team of Colegio de México investigators. A basic work.

Potash, Robert A. "Historiography of Mexico since 1821." *Hispanic American Historical Review,* xl (Aug. 1960), 383–424.

Comprehensive evaluative summary of books and articles produced in and about Mexican national history, broadly defined.

Ramos, Roberto. *Bibliografía de la Revolucion Mexicana.* 3 v. rev. ed. 1958–1960.

Vols. 1 and 2 are reprints of the 1931 and 1940 versions. Vol. 3 covers items from 1940 to 1960, greatly expanding previous coverage. Basic point of departure for further study.

SPECIAL TOPICS

Bayitch, S. A. *Guide to Inter-American Legal Studies: a Selective Bibliography of Works in English.* Coral Gables, Fla., Univ. of Miami Law Library, 1957.

The major Mexican items are listed.

Bernal, Ignacio. *Bibliografía de arqueología y etnografía.* Mexico, Instituto Nacional de Antropología e Historia, 1962.

Nearly comprehensive, this notable work contains nearly 14,000 entries.

Chase, Gilbert. *A guide to the music of Latin America.* Washington, Division of Music, Pan American Union, 1963.

Revision and extension of the 1945 volume, this bibliography adds 1,084 items to the original 2,700. A chapter on Mexico is preceded by evaluation of most significant works.

Comas, Juan. *Bibliografía selectiva de las culturas indígenas de América.* Mexico, Pan American Institute of Geography and History, 1953. (Publ. 166.)

Covers main literature in all languages; Mexican areas have excellent coverage.

Cumberland, Charles C. *The United States-Mexican border: a selective guide to the literature of the region.* Supplement to *Rural Sociology,* v. 25 (June) 1960.

Essays and bibliographies, including books, manuscripts, articles, on numerous phases of border matters.

Marino Flores, Anselmo. *Bibliografía lingüística de la república mexicana.* Mexico, Inst. Indigenista Interamericano, 1957.

Wauchope, Robert. *Ten years of Middle American archaeology: annotated bibliography and news summary, 1948–1957.* Reprint, Middle American Research Institute. New Orleans, Tulane University, *Publication* 28, 1961.

Consolidation of items contributed to Vols. 14–21 of the *Handbook of Latin American Studies*.

GENERAL WORKS ON MEXICO

Beals, Ralph L., and Humphrey, Norman D. *No Frontier to Learning; the Mexican Student in the United States.* Minneapolis, Minnesota U.P., 1957.

Cline, Howard F. *Mexico: Revolution to Evolution, 1940–1960.* Royal Institute of International Affairs. London, Oxford U.P., 1962.
Re-issue scheduled for 1963. General work, covering numerous phases, with emphasis on developments 1950–1960. Tabular material especially useful. Complements the present volume.

Considine, John J. *New Horizons in Latin America.* N.Y., 1958.
A temperate Catholic view, with useful chapter on Mexico. Much data on Church matters.

Edmondson, Munro S. *A Triangulation on the Culture of Mexico.* New Orleans, Tulane University, Middle American Research Inst., 1957. (Publication 17, pp. 201–40.)

Hanke, Lewis. *Mexico and the Caribbean. Modern Latin America: Continent in Ferment.* Vol. I. Princeton, 1959.
Pp. 68–95 present a summary comment on Mexico, with selected readings (some translated Mexican materials), pp. 169–183, with bibliography, pp. 185–86.

Johnson, William Walker, and others. *Mexico.* N.Y., Life World Library, 1961.
Mixed graphic and text; general introduction to Mexico, by editors of *Life.* Many factual errors in detail are compensated by outstanding photographs and general excellence.

Martínez, José Luis, comp. and ed. *El ensayo mexicano moderno.* Fondo de Cultura Economico. 2 v. Mexico, 1958. (*Letras Mexicanas,* 39, 40).
Anthology of Mexican essays touching nearly every topic of interest in the past 75 years: Mexicanism, philosophy, art, anthropology, race mixture; excludes political essays.

Mexico: realización y esperanza. Mexico, 1952.
Essays by Mexicans covering various social economic, political, and related topics, the semi-official report of the Alemán administration on accomplishments.

Mexico en el Mundo de Hoy. Mexico, 1952.
Companion piece to *Mexico: realización y esperanza,* with essays by non-Mexicans on various aspects of the Alemán régime, including a eulogistic biography of the President (1946–52).

Mexico: 50 años de Revolución. 2 v. Mexico, 1961.

The first vol. deals with economic and related subjects; vol. 2 is "Vida Social." Basically the semi-official summary of achievements during the Ruíz Cortines years, following patterns of similar works issued by earlier regimes.

Mexico 1960: Facts, Figures. Trends. BNCE. Mexico, 1960.

Most recent edition of continuing general source-book prepared for foreigners, covering history, economic, social, and political matters. Planned to be issued every two years.

Paz, Octavio. *The Labyrinth of Solitude. Life and Thought in Mexico.* Trans. by Lysander Kemp. N.Y., 1961.

Nine essays (first published in 1950) by a serious and talented Mexican, assessing Mexico's past, examining the nature of the Mexican; required reading.

Ramos, Samuel. *Profile of Man and Culture in Mexico.* Trans. by Peter G. Earle. Austin, University of Texas U.P., 1962.

Work of a major Mexican *pensador*, whose essays sketching Mexico's *ethos* (first published 1934) are also required reading, unmatched in any language.

Simpson, Lesley Byrd. *Many Mexicos.* 3rd. ed. Berkeley and Los Angeles, University of California Press, 1952. Reprinted, 1959.

Readable, popular summary, first published in 1941 and up-dated twice, this hardy perennial is now available in handsome paper back (reprinting 1952 version).

Tannenbaum, Frank. *Mexico: the Struggle for Peace and Bread.* N.Y., 1950.

A general survey, with nostalgic appeal for return to Cárdenas' policies.

HISTORY

Still missing is a single volume professional history of Mexico in English for the student and general reader. However, numerous excellent works on various important periods have appeared in the past decade. Of these, the massive and notable series on *Historia Moderna de México*, produced by Daniel Cosío Villegas and associates, is an epoch-making achievement. For further readings see bibliographies by González y González (1961–62), Humphreys (1958), Potash (1960), and Ramos (1958–60), noted above.

ANCIENT MEXICO

Especially significant in the past decade has been advance in knowledge about preconquest Mexico and various general volumes synthesizing these new data. The classic works of Vaillant and Morley on Aztec and Maya are now outdated. The technical literature, as well as general works, are listed in bibliographies noted above: Bernal (1962), Comas (1953), and Wauchope (1961).

Coe, Michael D. Mexico. *Ancient peoples and places.* N.Y., 1962.
  Summary of recent archeological findings and hypotheses with illustrations and maps.
Cook de Leonard, Carmen, ed. *Esplendor del México antiguo.* Mexico, Centro de Investigaciones Antropológicas de México, 1959, q. v.
  Uneven essays by many hands; magnificent illustrations. Useful bibliographies.
Peterson, F. *Ancient Mexico.* London, 1960.
  A semi-popular summary, with fine illustrations.

COLONIAL PERIOD

There has been a general decline in major historiography of the colonial, independence, and early national periods, with few outstanding works over the decade. The work by Gibson below has important bibliography for the general reader and student.

Chevalier, Francois. *La formation des grandes domaines au Mexique. Terre et societe aux xvie-xviie siècles.* Paris, 1952.
  A major contribution. The translation into Spanish has many illustrations not in the French original.
Foster, George M. *Culture and Conquest: America's Spanish Heritage.* N.Y., Wenner-Gren Foundation, 1960. (Viking Fund Publications in Anthropology, 27.)
Gibson, Charles. *The Colonial Period in Latin American History.* American Hist. Ass., Service Center for Teachers of History, 1958.
  Summary of recent interpretations by a leading historian.
Leonard, Irving. *Baroque times in Old Mexico, seventeenth century persons, places, and practices.* Ann Arbor, University of Michigan Press, 1959.

INDEPENDENCE AND NATIONAL PERIODS

For the pre-Revolutionary national period, the era following Intervention now forms the main focus of investigation, leaving a noticeable gap for the Independence, Reform, and Intervention years. Notable is the fact that much of the important history is being written by professionally trained and capable Mexican writers, due in large part to the impetus given by the Colegio de México.

Cosío Villegas, Daniel, ed. *Historia moderna de México*. Mexico, 1955–1963. 6 v.

A major historiographical achievement, tracing Mexican developments 1872–1910. A continuing project, with several volumes yet to come.

Pletcher, David M. *Rails, Mines and Progress: Seven American Promoters in Mexico*. Ithaca, Cornell U.P., 1958.

Covers the period 1867–1911; case studies. Documented, but no bibliography.

Reyes Heroles, Jesús. *El Liberalismo mexicano*. Mexico. 1957–58. 2 v.

Acute study of nineteenth century political ideology, indicating influence of European doctrines on Mexican minds; shows the eclectism and changing nature of lines. Basic work.

Scholes, Walter V. *Mexican Politics during the Juárez Regime, 1855–1872*. Columbia, Mo., 1957. (Univ. of Missouri Studies, 30.)

Sierra, Catalina. *El nacimiento de México*. UNAM. Mexico. 1960.

First rate analysis of Mexico in 1821, in transition from colonial to national life: geographic, social, demographic analysis against brilliant historical sketch.

Tischendorf, Alfred. *Great Britain and Mexico in the era of Porfirio Díaz*. Durham, N.C., Duke U.P., 1961.

A study of British investment and enterprise, loss of English economic hegemony 1876–1911. Documented.

MEXICAN REVOLUTION

The Revolution is still one of the main topics of polemic, popular, and an increasing number of scholarly works. The mass materials is listed in the González and Ramos (esp. v. 3) bibliographies noted under "General Bibliographies." Notable features are the increasing interest of Soviet historians, Mexican attempts at objective evaluations, and the large body of United States investigators working on various phases of the Revolution.

Al'perovich, Moisei S. and Boris T. Rudenko. *Meksikanskaia revoliutsiia, 1910–1917. gg. i politika S.Sh.A.* [The Mexican Revolution, 1910–1917 and the policy of the U.S.A.] Moscow, 1958.

Detailed Soviet study of Mexican Revolution, symptomatic of recent rising Russian interest in the Mexican movement. Disagrees violently with Cline's interpretations. Large bibliography, of well known non-Russian materials.

Blaisdell, Lowell L. *The Desert Revolution. Baja California, 1911*. Madison, University of Wisconsin Press, 1962.

Detailed examination of Flores Magón's attempt to revolutionize Mexico, removing the aura of filibustering and separatism from these episodes in Lower California.

Cassola, Gustavo. *Historia gráfica de la Revolución Mexicana, 1900–1960.* 4 v. Mexico, 1960.

Magnificent pictorial coverage of Mexican developments, extending the original 1921 coverage to include recent events.

Clendenen, Clarence C. *The United States and Pancho Villa: a study in unconventional diplomacy.* Ithaca, Cornell U.P., 1961.

Dulles, John W. F. *Yesterday in Mexico; a chronicle of the Revolution, 1919–1936.* Austin, Texas U.P., 1961.

Day-today reconstruction; uncritical; magnificently illustrated. Full bibliography.

González Ramírez, Manuel. *La revolución social de México. I. Las ideas. La violencia.* Fondo de Cultura Económica. Mexico, 1960.

Initial volume of a proposed scholarly history, probably first serious such effort by Mexican hands, of the Revolution. Interpretative; based on documentary and printed sources.

Mancisidor, José. *Historia de la Revolución Mexicana.* Mexico, 1958.

Synthesis in Marxian terms, (Mexican version). Stresses groups and economic elements over usual hagiographical approach.

Morales Jiménez, Alberto. *Hombres de la Revolución Mexicana: 50 semblanzas biográficas.* Mexico, 1960.

Quirk, Robert E. *The Mexican Revolution, 1914–1915; the Convention of Aguascalientes.* Bloomington, Indiana U.P., 1960.

Ross, Stanley R. *Francisco I. Madero: Apostle of Mexican Democracy.* N.Y., Columbia U.P., 1955.

Vera Estañol, Jorge. *La Revolución Mexicana: orígenes y resultados.* Mexico. 1957.

Ex-Porfirian, ex-Huerta Cabinet Minister's critique; thoughtful and substantial, this work raises problems not easily dismissed, and is an antidote to much thoughtless writing about the glories of the Revolution.

SOCIAL MATTERS

Continuous concern with social effects (and shortcomings) of the Revolution produces an enormous literature, some of it with enduring value. We still lack summaries of many important phases. Apart from the specialized sections of the *Handbook of Latin American Studies,* there is no single bibliographical source that reflects the rising output of works on social matters.

GENERAL

Alba, Victor. *Las Ideas sociales contemporáneas en México.* Mexico, Fondo de Cultura económica, 1960.

Labor-slanted intellectual history since 1910.

Bermúdez, María Elvira. *La Vida familiar del mexicano*. Mexico, 1955.
Reconstruction of family life from literary works from colonial to recent times. A pioneering effort.

DEMOGRAPHY

Durán Ochoa, Julio. *Población*. Fondo de Cultura Económica. Mexico, 1955. (*Estructura económica y social de México*, 5).
Major summary, with comparative data, trends, changes. Important bibliography.

Espinosa Olvera, René. "Los Recursos humanos en el desarrollo económico de México," *Investigación económica*, xvi (1956), 335–49.

Flores de la Peña, Horacio. "Crecimiento demográfico, desarrollo agrícola, y desarrollo económico," *Investigación económica*, xiv (1954), 519–36.

Glinstra-Bleeker, R. J. P. van. "Algunos aspectos de la emigración y la inmigración," *Investigación económica*, xiii (1953), 27–40.
Indicates immigration and emigration are negligible demographic factors.

Moreno, Daniel. *Los Factores demográficos en la planeación económica*. Mexico, Cámara Nacional de la Industria de la Transformación, Comisión de la Planeación Económica, 1958.

United Nations., Dept. de Asuntos Sociales, Divis. de Población. *La Población de la América Central y México en el período* 1950 a 1980. N.Y., 1958.
Data on 1950 base, projected to 1980, with graphs.

Rodríguez Mata, Emilio. "Evolución de la población de México y de algunas entidades típicas," *Investigación económica*, xiv (1954), 385–96.
Interesting study of selected regions and their changes under recent trends.

EDUCATION AND COMMUNICATION

Alisky, Marvin. "Early Mexican Broadcasting," *Hispanic American Historical Review*, xxxiv (Nov. 1954), 513–26.

Alisky, Marvin. "Growth of Newspapers in Mexico's Provinces," *Journalism Quarterly*, xxxvii (Winter 1960) [unpaginated].

Castaño, Luis. *El Régimen legal de la prensa en México*. Mexico, 1958.
Discusses freedom of the press; important legislation in appendices.

Cosío Villegas, Daniel. "The Press and Responsible Freedom in Mexico." In Angel del Río, ed., *Responsible Freedom in the Americas*. Garden City, N.Y., 1955, pp. 272–90.

Johnston, Marjorie C. *Education in Mexico*. Washington, U.S. Dept. of Health, Education, and Welfare, Office of Education, [1956]. (U.S. Office of Ed., Bulletin 1956, No. 1.)
The bibliography is especially important.

Navarrete, Ifigenia M. de. "El Financiamiento de la educación pública en México," Mexico, UNAM, 1959. (Suplementos del Seminario de Problemas Cientifícos y Filosoficos, 2nd ser., No. 15.) Reprinted from *Investigación económica,* xviii (1958), 21–55.

Outlines educational needs and estimated costs to overcome them.

CASE HISTORIES AND COMMUNITY STUDIES

Bailey, Helen M. *Santa Cruz of the Etla hills.* Gainesville, University of Florida Press, 1958.

Leslie, Charles M. *Now we are civilized: a study of the world view of the Zapotec Indians of Mitla, Oaxaca.* Detroit, Wayne State Press, 1960.

Lewis, Oscar. *Five Families: Mexican Case Studies in the Culture of Poverty.* N.Y., 1959.

A day in the life of five different social and cultural strata, four in Mexico City and including a newly arrived middle-class household. Dramatic non-fiction.

Lewis, Oscar. *The Children of Sánchez Autobiography of a Mexican Family.* N.Y., 1961.

The self-portrait of one of the Five Families (1959), revealing much about lower-class Mexico City. Novelesque presentation of sociological data.

Lewis, Oscar. *Life in a Mexican Village: Tepoztlán Restudied.* Urbana, Illinois U.P., 1951.

A basic study, reappraising Redfield's earlier idealized findings on a modern Aztec community.

Madsen, William. *The Virgin's Children. Life in an Aztec village today.* Austin, University of Texas Press, 1960.

Soustelle, Georgette. *Tequila: un village nahuatl du Mexique oriental.* Institut d'Ethnologie. Université de Paris. Paris. 1958 *(Travaux et Memoires,* lxii).

Young, Frank W. and Ruth C. Young, "Social integration and change in 24 Mexican villages." University of Chicago, *Economic Development and Cultural Change,* 8:4, Part 1 (July 1960), pp. 366–77.

Changes imposed by industrialization and national attempts to standardize communities to tap their labor and resources, to integrate them into the larger systems.

INDIANS

Native contributions to Mexican culture and nationality and Indian problems are especially significant. Many of the titles listed in other parts are relevant, but specifically the following works deal nearly exclusively with Indians. Further reading will be found under "History: Ancient Mexico," "Social: Case Histories." Important bibliographies include Comas

(1953), and Marino Flores (1957). The volume by Eric Wolf, noted below, also has extensive bibliography.

Aguirre Beltrán, Gonzalo. *Problemas de la población indígena de la Cuenca de Tepalcatepec.* Mexico, Instituto Indigenista Nacional, 1952. (Memoria, 3.)

    Demographic and cultural survey of the area, preceding the Tepalcatepec Commission Project in west central Mexico.

Comas, Juan. "Indígenas de México," *Revista Población,* i (Aug. 1953), 36–44.

    Analysis of 1940 Census returns re natives.

Densidad de la población de habla indígena en la República Mexicana (por entidades federativas y municipios, conforme al Censo de 1940). Instituto Nacional Indigenista. Mexico, 1950. Introd. by Manuel Germán Parra. (*Memorias,* 1, No. 1.)

    Analysis of 1940 data, with good maps; provides municipal data.

Mariano Flores, Anselmo, "Indígenas de México; algunas consideraciones demográficas," *America indígena,* xvi (Jan. 1956), 41–48.

    Synthesis of Census data of 1950, compared with 1940, on Mexican Indians.

Villoro, Luis. *Los Grandes momentos del indigenismo en México.* México, 1950.

    History of the attitudes toward Indians at different epoche of Mexican history.

Wagley, Charles, and Marvin Harris. "The Indians of Mexico," *Minorities in the New World.* N.Y., 1958, pp. 48–86.

Wolf, Eric R. *Sons of the Shaking Earth.* Chicago U.P., 1959.

    Personalized synthesis of native Indian history from earliest times to the present. The bibliography is replete on anthropological items, deficient in history. A very helpful introductory survey.

CULTURAL MATTERS

There is a vast corpus of writings on the humanistic aspects of Mexico and Mexican creative efforts. In the United States various specialized reviews such as *Hispania* contain book reviews, articles, and bibliographies to aid in keeping up-to-date. Especially recommended in the field of music is the bibliographical work noted above by Chase (1963). Again, the *Handbook of Latin American Studies* devotes several annual sections to art, literature, music, and philosophy.

Brushwood, John S., and José Rojas Garcidueñas. *Breve historia de la novela mexicana.* Mexico, 1959. (*Manuales Studium,* 9).

Brief but authoritative survey, including contemporary writers not treated elsewhere. Bibliography should be supplemented by Charles V. Aubrun's *Lettres hispano-américaines* (Paris, 1954).

Crawford, W. Rex. *A Century of Latin American Thought*. Cambridge, Mass., Harvard U.P., Rev. ed. 1961.

Ch. 9 sketches the Mexicans. No real revision since the 1945 edition, but a few bibliographical additions.

Fernández, Justino. *Arte mexicano de sus origenes a nuestros dias*. Mexico, 1958.

Outstanding synthesis, well-illustrated, showing Mexican art through the ages, by a leading historian of art.

"The eye of Mexico," *Evergreen Review*, vii (1959), pp. 22–213.

Translations of young and important Mexican writers.

Paz, Octavio, comp. *An anthology of Mexican poetry*. Trans. by Samuel Beckett. Bloomington, Indiana U.P., 1958.

Important selection by one of Mexico's (and Latin America's) outstanding writers. The Introduction by Paz is a summary of literary trends and history.

ECONOMIC MATTERS

The predominantly economic nature of Mexico's recent and contemporary problems spawns annually a torrent of materials, often in article form, of short-lived utility in a rapidly changing situation. Interesting is the attention paid by non-Mexican economists, international agencies, as well as by a large group of official and non-official groups in Mexico itself. No single bibliography spans all these materials.

Alanís Patiño, Emilio. "La Riqueza nacional," *Investigación económica*, xv (1955), 53–81.

National incomes and products to 1945, converted to 1955 values.

"Basic Data on the Economy of Mexico" WTIS, pt. 1, Economic Reports, No. 59–5 [prepared by Katherine E. Rice. Jan. 1959]. USBFC. Washington, 1960.

Diagnóstico económico regional, 1958. SDE and Inst. Mexicano de Investigaciones Económicas. Mexico, 1959.

Basic studies of national and regional developments, with recommendations; excellent statistics, maps, and charts.

The Economic Development of Mexico during a Quarter of a Century. Nacional Financiera. Mexico, 1959.

"*Economic Developments in Mexico*" [annually, 1954–8, prepared by Katherine E. Rice]. USBFC, WTIS, Nos. 55–78, 56–24, 57–41, 58–36 Washington, 1955–9.

Summaries of main trends, with supporting statistical data.

Investment in Mexico: Conditions and Outlook for United States Investors.
USBFC, American Republics Division. Washington, [1956].
Considerably broader than title implies: summary economic analysis with important appendices.

Jaffe, Abram J. *People, Jobs and Economic Development; a Case History of Puerto Rico supplemented by Recent Mexican Experiences.* Glencoe, Ill., Columbia Univ., Bureau of Applied Soc. Research, 1959.
More pessimistic about Mexico than other economists, basing conclusions on rather thin information.

Lichey, W. *Mexiko: Ein Weg zur wirtschaftlichen Entwicklung zwischen staatlicher Lenkung und privater Initiative: auf der Grundlage der Forschungergebnisse von R. v. Gersdorff, C. Kapferer, I. Schaafhausen.* (Schriften des Hamburgischen Welt-Wirtschafts-Archivs, No. 8. Sonderreihe; Entwicklungsgebiete.) Hamburg, Verlag Weltarchiv, [1958].
A co-operative monograph, bringing data to about 1957. A very sound optimistic summary based on much data; important tabular statistical data; bibliography published separately.

Martín Echeverría, Leonardo. "La Leyenda dorada sobre la riqueza de México," *Investigación económica,* xiv, 231–87.
Historical survey of the concept of unlimited Mexican resources.

Navarrete R[omero], Alfredo, jr. "Los Programas revolucionarios y el futuro progreso económico de México," PRI, *Cuadernos de orientación política,* i/3 (Mar. 1956), 17–25.
Indicates that prosperity is not necessarily anti-Revolutionary.

Sarames, George N. "Third system in Latin America: Mexico," *Interamerican Economic Affairs,* v.5:4 (Spring 1952), 59–72.

Teichert, Pedro C. M. *Economic Policy Revolution and Industrialization in Latin America.* Univ. of Mississippi, Bureau of Business Research, 1959. Ch. 12.

COMMUNICATIONS AND TRANSPORT

"Civil Aviation in Mexico." USBFC, WTIS, pt. 4, Economic Reports, No. 57–2. Washington, Jan. 1957.

"Highways of Mexico." USBFC WTIS, pt. 4. Economic Reports, No. 57–2. Washington, Sept. 1956.

Villafuerte, Carlos. *Ferrocarriles.* Mexico, Fondo de Cultura Economica, 1959. (Estructura económica y social de México, 7.)

FISCAL AFFAIRS

Aguilar, G. F. *Los Presupuestos mexicanos desde los tiempos de la colonia hasta nuestro días.* Mexico, 1947.

Espinosa de los Reyes, Jorge. "La Distribución del ingreso nacional." In

UNAM, Escuela Nacional de Economía. *Problemas del desarrollo económico mexicano: cursos de invierno 1957*. Mexico, 1958, pp. 161–224.

Navarrete R[omero], Alfredo, jr. "Financiamiento del desarrollo económico de México." In UNAM, Escuela de Economía. *Problemas del desarrollo económico mexicano: cursos de invierno 1957*. Mexico, 1958, pp. 135–39.

Policy statements by a then high official of N.F.

Taxation in Mexico. Harvard Univ., Int. Program in Taxation. [Primarily the work of Henry J. Gumpel . . . and Hugo B. Margáin. . . .] Boston, 1957. (World Tax Series.)

Basic and comprehensive coverage, with much history.

Urquidi, Víctor L. "El Impuesto sobre la renta en el desarrollo económico de México," *Trimestre económico*, xxiii (Oct.-Dec. 1956), 424–37.

Discussion of income taxes—personal and corporate.

POWER

Bermúdez, Antonio J. *Doce años al servicio de la industria petrolera mexicana, 1947–1958*. Mexico, 1960.

Account by its Director (1947–58) of developments and final success of PEMEX.

Lara Beautell, Cristóbal. *La Industria de energía eléctrica*. Mexico, Fondo de Cultura Económica, 1953. (Estructura económica y social de México, 3.)

Summary of data to beginning of the Ruíz Cortines term, before all industry nationalized.

Powell, J. Richard. *The Mexican Petroleum Industry, 1938–1950*. Berkeley and Los Angeles, Univ. of Calif., Bureau of Business and Econ. Research, 1956.

Standard to point before industry recovered.

LABOR

El Empleo de personal técnico en la industria de transformación. Banco de México, Dept. de Investigaciones Industriales. Mexico, 1959.

Problems of skilled, semi-skilled labor.

Navarrete R[omero], Alfredo, jr. "Productividad, ocupación y desocupación en México; 1940–1965," *Trimestre económico*, xxiii (Oct.-Dec. 1956), 415–23.

Rivera Marín, Guadalupe. *El Mercado de trabajo: relaciones obrero-patronales*. Mexico, Fondo de Cultura Económica, 1955. (Estructura económica y social de México, 4.)

Economic rather than historical analysis. Important regional differentials noted.

Salazar, Rosendo. *Historia de la CTM*. Mexico, 1956.

> Like other works by author is patchy, but important. One of the few histories of unions. There is no satisfactory history of the important Mexican labor movement.

LAND

Land is an emotional issue, as well as an economic, social, and political topic. Significant in the recent literature is the high level of Mexican technical analyses of the complex problems. Most of the volumes listed below have ample bibliographies, filling the gap caused by lack of a single comprehensive guide to the unbelievably scattered and enormous literature on land.

Fernández y Fernández, Ramón. *Política agrícola*. Mexico, 1961.

> Summary treatment, including discussion of problems of agrarian reform.

Flores, Edmundo. *Tratado de economia agrícola*. Mexico-Buenos Aires, Fondo de Cultura Económico, 1961.

> A basic treatise, linking Mexican with Latin American trends and problems; very recent (1959–60) data, and excellent technical bibliography.

González Santos, Armando. *La Agricultura: estructura y utilización de los recursos*. Mexico, Fondo de Cultura Económica, 1957. (Estructura económica y social de México, 6.)

> Fundamental study and summary of complex problems. Technical rather than political or polemic.

Palomo Valencia, Florencio, comp. *Historia del ejido actual*. Mexico, 1959.

> Collection of documents concerning present ejidos.

Senior, Clarence. *Land Reform and Democracy*. Gainesville, Florida U.P., 1958.

> Chiefly a study of La Laguna and the ejido program in general to c. 1950, sympathetic but critical.

Silva Herzog, Jesús. *El Agrarianismo mexicano y la reforma agraria, exposición y crítica*. Mexico, Fondo de Cultura Economica, 1959.

> An anthology, with interpersed, generally critical commentary.

Yáñez Pérez, Luis, assisted by Edmundo Moyo Porras. *Mecanización de la agricultura mexicana*. Mexico, Inst. Mex. de Investigaciones Económicas, 1957.

> Elaborate technical analysis of Mexican agricultural problems c. 1950; a basic treatment.

POLITICS

Government, politics, and administration loom large in Mexican life, but in general are inadequately described and analyzed objectively in the extant writings. The major descriptive efforts come from North American writers; the Mexican writings tend to be impressionistic and highly subjective about political matters as contrasted with a high professionalism in economics. Apart from polemics the bibliography is small, but there is no handy summary of it beyond that contained in the general works cited. An exception is the Bayitch bibliography on legal matters.

Goodspeed, Stephen S. "El Papel del jefe del ejecutivo en México," *Problemas industriales e agrícolas de México*, vii (Jan.-Mar. 1955), 13–208.
  Spanish translation of a doctoral dissertation; biographies of Revolutionary Presidents.

Johnson, John J. *Political Change in Latin America; the Emergence of the Middle Sectors*. Stanford U.P., 1958. (Studies in History, Economics and Political Science, 15.)
  Important general analysis, with ch. 7 specifically on Mexico. Extended bibliography.

Scott, Robert E. *Mexican Government in Transition*. Urbana, Illinois U.P., 1959.
  Important functional analysis. Identifies "interest" groups and their interaction, noting decline of absolute presidential power.

Tucker, William P. *The Mexican Government Today*. Minneapolis, Minnesota U.P., 1957.
  Descriptive compilation, with an extensive bibliog. Essentially a reference work.

RECENT POLITICS AND POLITICIANS

Barrales V., José, ed. *El Pensamiento político del Liceniado Adolfo López Mateos*. Mexico, 1958.
  Campaign and related pronouncements.

González Luna, Efráin. *Humanismo político*. Mexico, 1955.
  Statements by leader of the PAN.

María y Campos, Armando de. *Un ciudadano. Como es y como piensa Adolfo López Mateos*. 2d. ed. Mexico, 1958.
  Political biography, with liberal excerpts from campaign speeches.

Padgett, Leon V. 'Mexico's One Party System; a Re-evaluation,' *American Political Science Review*, li (Dec. 1957), 995–1008.

Taylor, Philip B. "The Mexican Elections of 1958: Affirmation of Authoritarism?" *Western Political Science Quarterly*, xiii (Sept. 1960), 722–44.

LAWS AND ADMINISTRATION

Bremauntz, Alberto. *Por una justicia al servicio del Pueblo*. Mexico, 1955.
Recent trends in judiciary.

Burgoa, Ignacio. *Las garantías individuales*. 2nd ed. Mexico, 1954.

Cabrera A., Lucio. 'History of the Mexican Judiciary.' In David S. Stern,
ed., *Mexico: a Symposium on Law and Government*. Coral Gables,
Fla., Miami U.P., 1958, pp. 22–31. (Univ. of Miami School of Law,
Interamerican Legal Studies, 3.) Summary sketch in a monographic
volume devoted to Mexican problems.

García Valencia, Antonio. *Las Relaciones humanas en la administración
pública mexicana*. Mexico, 1958.
Pioneering historical and sociological study of administrative and
bureaucratic groups. Chapter 8 deals with recent Mexico.

Pérez Palma, Rafael. *Memorias de un juez de pueblo*. Mexico, 1961.
Delightfully written memoirs of a local judge, giving intimate views of
government and politics at the local level.

Tena Ramírez, Felipe. *Derecho constitucional mexicano*. 3rd ed. Mexico,
1955.

Tena Ramírez, Felipe, comp. *Leyes fundamentales de México, 1808–1957*.
Mexico, 1957.

Velasco, Gustavo R. 'The Rule of Law in Mexico.' *In* Stern, ed., *Mexico:
a Symposium on Law and Government*, pp. 9–12.
Summary of concept of jurisprudence by a Mexican authority.

MILITARISM

Alba, Victor. *El militarismo*. UNAM. Mexico, 1959. (Instituto de Investigaciones Sociales).
Important statement on problems of militarism and its relationship
to other aspects of society; Mexican data.

Lieuwen, Edwin. *Arms and Politics in Latin America*. N.Y., Council on Foreign Relations, 1960.
A recent pioneering summary; Mexico is cited as a model, pp. 101–21.

McAlister, Lyle N. "The Military and Government." *Hispanic American
Historical Review*, xl (Nov. 1960), 582–590.
Review article, discussing Lieuwen; provides extensive bibliography
and context for viewing militarism in Mexico (or elsewhere).

Ross, Stanley R. 'Some Obstrvations on Military Coups in the Caribbean.'
In A. Curtis Wilgus, ed., *The Caribbean: Its Political Problems*.
Gainesville, Univ. of Florida, School of Inter-American Affairs, 1956,
pp. 110–28. (Series One, 6.) Notes wane of Mexican militarism.

COMMUNISM

Alba, Victor. *Esquema histórico del comunismo en Iberoamérica*. 3rd. ed. Mexico, 1960.
First published in 1954. This work has useful bibliography, with considerable data on Mexico.

Alexander, Robert. *Communism in Latin America*. New Brunswick, N.J., Rutgers U.P., 1957.
Standard introductory coverage.

Allen, Robert L. *Soviet Influence in Latin America: the Role of Economic Relations*. Washington, Public Affairs Press, 1959.
Finds little Mexican-Soviet exchanges. Mexico especially cool.

García Treviño. Rodrigo. *La Ingerencia rusa en México*. Mexico, 1959.
Former leader of CTM and presently head of Grupo de Socialistas Mexicanos sketches important aspects of the Communist party in Mexico. Important documents are included.

Washington, S. Walter. "Mexican Resistance to Communism," *Foreign Affairs*, xxxvi (Apr. 1958), 504–15.

INTERNATIONAL AFFAIRS

Like literature on domestic politics, the writings on Mexican international affairs are singularly unsatisfactory. There are few or no bibliographies, documentary collections, or summary monographs and histories, especially for the period since 1910. These strictures apply both to bi-lateral and multi-lateral relations, political, economic, social, and cultural. For Border matters we have the recent bibliography by Cumberland (1960).

Cosío Villegas, Daniel. *Change in Latin America: the Mexican and Cuban Revolutions*. Lincoln, University of Nebraska, 1961.
Important lectures by an outstanding Mexican on the changing nature of the Mexican Revolution; comparisons with other recent movements in Latin America, and implications for international affairs.

La Política international de México, 1952–1956. SRE. Mexico, 1957. (*Serie Problemas Nacionales y Internacionales*, 32.)

Las Relaciones internacionales de México, 1935–1956 a través de los mensajes presidenciales. Mexico, 1957. SRE. (Archivo histórico-diplomático, 2 ser, no. 9.)

Sepúlveda, César. "Historia y problemas de los límites de México," *Historia Mexicana*, viii (1958), 1–34, 145–74.
Synthesis of diplomatic and other aspects of setting boundaries with the United States and with Guatemala, extensive bibliography.

MEXICO-UNITED STATES RELATIONS
Cronon, E. David. *Josephus Daniels in Mexico*. Madison, Wisconsin U.P., 1960.
> U.S. ambassador during Cárdenas régime; much new and important diplomatic data on U.S.-Mexican relations.

Fabela, Isidro. *Buena y mala vecindad*. Mexico, 1958.
> Various articles by a respected former diplomat, praising U.S. relations 1934–53, but critical of present policies, as being a "bad neighbor."

Galarza, Ernesto. "Trabajadores mexicanos en tierra extraña," *Problemas agrícolas e industriales de México,* x (Jan.-June 1958), 1–84.
> Summary of bracero matters, with illustrations and U.S.-Mexican treaty texts.

"Trade of the United States with Latin America: Years 1956–8 and Half-Years January 1958-June 1959." USBFC. WTIS, Statistical Reports, No. 59–35.

WORLD AND REGIONAL ORDER
Castañeda, Jorge. *Mexico and the United Nations*. Prepared for El Colegio de México and the Carnegie Endowment for International Peace. N.Y., 1958. (National Studies on International Organization.)
> Eng. trans. of *México y el orden internacional*. Colegio de México, [1956]. Nationalistic view of Mexico's foreign affairs, especially of its multilateral relations.

Padilla Nervo. Luis. *Discursos y declaraciones sobre política internacional, 1948–1958*. Mexico, 1958.
> Speeches and policy pronouncements by Mexico's delegate to the U.N.

INDEX

(A separate index for the epilogue follows.)

INDEX TO THE EPILOGUE

HOWARD F. CLINE was born in Detroit in 1915 and was educated at Harvard. He taught history there, at Yale, and at Northwestern before becoming the director of the Hispanic Foundation of the Library of Congress in 1952. He has served as a representative of the United States Government and as an advisor to the U.S. delegation at numerous conferences on Latin American and Western Hemisphere affairs. He is also the author of *Mexico: From Revolution to Evolution* and the editor, with others, of *William Hickling Prescott, A Memorial.*